REFERENCE GUIDE

TO THE ARCHAEOLOGY

OF WEST MAUI

REFERENCE GUIDE TO THE ARCHAEOLOGY OF WEST MAUI

compiled by AMI MĀLIE MULLIGAN

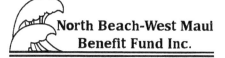

North Beach-West Maui
Benefit Fund Inc.

Lahaina, Maui, Hawai'i

30 29 28 27 26 25   6 5 4 3 2 1

ISBN 978-1-9524-6109-5 (pbk : alk. paper)

Published by the North Beach-West Maui Benefit Fund, Inc.

P O Box 11329

Lahaina, Hawai'i 96761

Distributed by University of Hawai'i Press

2840 Kolowalu Street

Honolulu, HI 96822-1888

Every effort has been made to trace copyright holders
and to obtain their permission for the use of copyright material.
The publisher apologizes for any errors or omissions and
would be grateful if notified of any corrections that
should be incorporated in future reprints or editions of this book.

This book is printed on acid-free paper and
meets the guidelines for permanence and durability
of the Council on Library Resources.

Print-ready files provided by North Beach-West Maui Benefit Fund, Inc.

CONTENTS

FOREWORD

This book is another project of the HK West Maui Community Fund in partnership with the University of Hawai'i at Mānoa's College of Social Sciences to provide a reference bibliography of archaeological research in West Maui.

For a long time, as noted by Haunani-Kay Trask in *From a Native Daughter: Colonialism and Sovereignty in Hawai'i*, "Anthropology and archaeology [were] not publicly debated or even acknowledged by its practitioners in the university or the museum or the field, and certainly not in the contract firm." This has changed as Native Hawaiians have engaged the discipline of archaeology over the last few decades. One longstanding limitation has been the (in)accessibility of the products of archaeology and the power differentials that inaccessibility reproduces.

The aim of this volume is to assist Kānaka Maoli and other community members by making accessible the known archaeological study of West Maui to assist in holding the discipline and profession of archaeology to account and to bring the research of the "contract firms" to the public.

The HK West Maui Community Fund expresses its profound gratitude to the North Beach–West Maui Benefit Fund for agreeing to publish this important work for a general public audience. Both organizations hope this project will continue to deepen interest in the study and understanding of West Maui and its peoples, and contribute to the further reform and development of archaeology in Hawai'i.

Lance D. Collins
Wainalu, Honokōwai

INTRODUCTION

with *Brian Richardson*

Nearly four decades ago, the unexpected disinterment of Kanaka Maoli burial sites at Honokahua forced people to reckon with the question of who matters in Hawai'i. In the late 1980s, construction of beachfront luxury hotel the Ritz-Carlton Kapalua unearthed hundreds of iwi (bones) and moepū (funerary objects) in the sand dunes of Honokahua. Though this site was a known burial site—it was previously on the Hawai'i State historic register in the late 1970s and later removed—the scale had been grossly underestimated. Until recently, iwi throughout Hawai'i have been largely ignored, beyond the few that have been taken to museums for storage and study. It was easier to assume that, except when placed in cemeteries, bones were unimportant—partly because the bones could get in the way of development, and partly because there was no documentation acceptable to the state and federal governments that would allow people to assert any rights over them. There were no Western-style cemeteries, and so, practically, there were no bones to worry about.

At Honokahua, the concerns of competing interests surfaced throughout the process. While the developers were concerned with meeting construction deadlines and profit margins, and the hotel designers were concerned with creating an aesthetic and functional experience for future tourists, many Kānaka Maoli, and particularly those in West Maui, were concerned over the treatment of the iwi kūpuna (ancestral remains), and various government entities were concerned about what course of action would appease all parties concerned. There was no precedent on a statewide level for how to treat these remains. Instead, it was a process of trial and error alongside impatience, outrage, and activism that resulted in changes necessary to acknowledge Kanaka Maoli burials as critical sites for preservation. At roughly the same time, in 1990, the federal government would pass the Native American Graves Protection and Repatriation Act (NAGPRA).

Over conversations and contestations between government entities, the archaeological firm handling the excavations, the Kanaka Maoli–led activist group Hui Alaloa o Mākena, the broader Kanaka Maoli community, and the developers, statewide procedures, protections, and regulations emerged for burial sites that would prevent the events at Honokahua from happening again. The conflict had been expensive and heated. For instance, in late 1989, the Kapalua Land Company requested $7 million from the government to help pay for reinterment and the costs to move the planned hotel further inland.

The contestations served as a foundation for legislation intended to safeguard Kanaka Maoli rights while allowing construction and development of land in Hawai'i. Though the Hawai'i Revised Statutes Chapter 6E were not amended in the 1989 legislative session, five burial councils were created under the purview of the newly formed State Historic Preservation Office, a section of the Department of Land and Natural Resources (DLNR), which would provide guidance to the state on matters pertaining to burials older than fifty years. The burial council consisted of a majority of members from the Kanaka Maoli community as well as large landowners and developers. This was a significant development in providing the Kanaka Maoli legal avenues for their voices to be heard in matters relating to the treatment of their kūpuna. The following year, the state legislature passed Act 306, which amended the state historic preservation law that, among other changes, established permanent burial councils for Hawai'i, Moloka'i, Maui/Lāna'i, O'ahu, and Kaua'i/Ni'ihau, criteria for how to preserve Native Hawaiian burial sites, determine a process for the treatment of inadvertently discovered human skeletal remains, and requiring the development and promulgation of administrative rules to carry out the newly passed laws. The administrative rules require professional archaeological research and the supervision of construction sites, which generates documentation. These activities mitigate or eliminate the inadvertent discovery of human remains, which is an important outcome of the rules. In effect, the archaeological procedures function in a way that mirrors the role churches often play in protecting documented cemeteries.

One implication of these new regulations is that documenting burial sites has become much more important and much more expansive. In the decades since the adoption of these laws governing iwi and moepū, there have been hundreds of official reports written by archaeological firms to help fulfill administrative requirements. The nature of these reports vary—most are concerned with either planning or reporting the results of archaeological site monitoring, while others are historical or architectural in nature, helping to determine which sites are priorities for preservation. The reports generally consist of several elements, including site-specific historical research, previous archaeological work performed, planning for archaeological work to be done on the current site along with documenting the subsequent results, and recommendations of the archaeologist on how to proceed with the project. Since these reports contain a wealth of detail, they provide an excellent resource for information about what was done and what was found in specific locations, as well as historical events to provide context and a bibliography of works the researchers consulted in their analyses.

Kānaka Maoli have lived and died on these islands for centuries. Stories tell of their arrival from the East and of the countless generations of people who have arisen from and returned to the ʻāina. In a society that is so closely tied to the land, the bodies of ancestors figure highly in Hawaiian sense of place. Conflicts over bodies, and eventually bones, have occurred as far back as can be remembered. Bodies are desecrated, they are protected, they are divided between the chiefs, and some parts are returned to foreign ships full of panicked sailors. There is a social history to bodies, and more importantly there are deep existential aspects to iwi—especially the iwi of the ancestors.

Stepping back from particular projects, one issue with these archaeological reports is that they share no single repository. The primary source for the documents are the following:

- State Historic Preservation Division (SHPD) offices in Kapolei, Oʻahu and in Wailuku, Maui—https://shpd.hawaii.gov/hicris/ (Search > Library)
- University of Hawaiʻi at Mānoa, Hamilton Library, Hawaiian and Pacific collection—https://manoa.hawaii.edu/library/

Other archives that might be useful for research are:

- The Bishop Museum—http://data.bishopmuseum.org/HAS2/index.php
- Hawaiian Mission Children's Society Archive at the Hawaiian Mission Houses—https://hmha.missionhouses.org

For the researcher, it can be difficult to create a general picture of what has been found, and by implication, of where and how Kānaka Maoli lived and buried their ancestors in the islands.

The current reference work is a compilation of the archaeological reports that pertain specifically to West Maui, as well as a compilation of the works on Hawai'i that were cited by the researchers. In the document lists, an attempt has been made to standardized and update place names to contemporary usage. When searching for the original material in the online databases, earlier variations of the names might be more effective.

The reports included in the bibliography are presented in five different ways:

- Author, alphabetical
- Date of creation, chronological
- Company name, alphabetical
- Ahupua'a, alphabetical, Aholo to Waiokama
- TMK (tax map keys, as they occur in the title), which have been standardized to (2) W-X-YY:ZZZ, where the "(2)" indicates Maui County. Where parcel information is not provided, the larger-scale designations are still included.

Finally, the last section provides a bibliography of works that are cited in the reports, including maps, monographs, and articles. Works include those written by David Malo, Samuel Maniākalani Kamakau, Mary Kawena Pukui, and E. S. Handy. Elspeth Sterling's *Sites of Maui* also dominates the bibliographic entries. C. S. Silva and Helen Wong-Smith also contributed to archaeological reports using Hawaiian sources in their reports' sections on an area's history.

The bibliography is intended to be a resource that will allow people a starting point for their research. There is much still that can be learned about the history of these sites. Though these reports provide a considerable amount of information, the historical sections can become a bit repetitive. Certain published secondary sources, often in English translation, are recurring and provide an important foundation for understanding the history of a place.

The bibliographic research here is only recently being built upon with primary sources—sources from the time and place it was created—and sources written in Hawaiian. More recent reports have added considerable historical information to their sections that focus on the history of the sites they are researching. In Hawai'i, where place-based history is central, it is critical that reports be composed with as much information as possible, in part to help make better decisions on preservation and development in the future.

The current monograph is an attempt to move the conversations forward by allowing researchers to see what has already been done.

FURTHER READING

Ayau, Edward Halealoha. "Honokahua Nani Ē: Returning to Who We Are." In *Social Change in West Maui*, Bianca K. Isaki and Lance D. Collins, eds., pp. 238–271. Lahaina, HI: North Beach-West Maui Benefit Fund, 2019.

Hanada, Tomone K. T. "The Honokahua Burial Site Controversy." In *Social Change in West Maui*, Bianca K. Isaki and Lance D. Collins, eds., pp. 188–237. Lahaina, HI: North Beach-West Maui Benefit Fund, 2019.

REPORTS

PUBLICATIONS BY AUTHOR

[A]

Ah Sam, Jessica A., Solomon H. Kailihiwa III, and Paul L. Cleghorn. *Archaeological Inventory Study and Cultural Impact Assessment for the Comfort Station Replacement During the Lahaina Pier Improvement Project, Lahaina, Maui [TMK (2) 4-6-01:001]*. Kailua, HI: Pacific Legacy, Inc., 2004.

Ahlo, Hamilton M. and Maurice E. Morgenstein. *Archaeological Test Excavations Near the Mouth of Kahoma Stream, Lahaina, Maui*. Honolulu, HI: Hawai'i Marine Research, 1979.

Aki Sinoto Consulting. *Archaeological Monitoring During the Renovation of the Lahaina Center Parking Structure, Lahaina, Maui*. Honolulu, HI: Aki Sinoto Consulting, 1995.

Aki Sinoto Consulting. *Archaeological Monitoring Plan for Utility Trenching at the Lahaina Shopping Center, Paunau, Lahaina, Maui*. Honolulu, HI: Aki Sinoto Consulting, 1996.

Andricci, Nicole and Michael F. Dega. *AAAAA Rent-A-Space Extension Project Honokōwai, Māhinahina 4 Ahupua'a Lahaina (Kā'anapali) District, Maui Island Hawaii [TMK (2) 4-4-01:026]*. Honolulu, HI: Scientific Consultant Services, Inc., 2015.

Andricci, Nicole and Michael F. Dega. *An Archaeological Assessment for the Lahaina Square Redevelopment Project, Lahaina, Waine'e Ahupua'a, District of Lahaina, Island of Maui, Hawai'i*. Honolulu, HI: Scientific Consultant Services, Inc., 2017. [SHPD ID: 2019LI80016]

Andricci, Nicole and Michael F. Dega. *An Archaeological Monitoring Plan for a Residential Parcel 33 at 572 Waine'e Street, Waine'e Ahupua'a, Lahaina District, Maui Island, Hawai'i [TMK (2) 4-6-12:033]*. Honolulu, HI: Scientific Consultant Services, Inc., 2016.

Andricci, Nicole and Michael F. Dega. *Archaeological Assessment of a 15.7 Acre Section of Undeveloped Land and a Proposed Road Extension, Kuʻia Ahupuaʻa, Lahaina District, Island of Maui, Hawaiʻi [TMK (2) 4-6-018:003 por.].* Honolulu, HI: Scientific Consultant Services, Inc., 2015.

Athens, J. Stephen. *Archaeological Monitoring Plan, Trenching at Taco Bell, Lahaina, Kāʻanapali Ahupuaʻa, Lahaina District, Maui [TMK (2) 4-5-07:034].* Honolulu, HI: International Archaeological Research Institute, Inc., 1999.

Athens, J. Stephen. *Archaeological Reconnaissance at Honokahua Well B, Lahaina District, West Maui,* 1985.

[B]

Barrera, William Jr. *Honoapiʻilani Highway, Maui: Archaeological Reconnaissance.* Honolulu, HI: Chiniago, Inc., 1988.

Barrera, William Jr. *North Beach, Maui: Archaeological Reconnaissance.* Honolulu, HI: Chiniago, Inc., 1986. [SHPD ID: 2019LI81288]

Bassford, B. A. and Michael F. Dega. *Burial Site Component of an Archaeological Data Recovery and Preservation Plan for Site 50-50-08-8284 at Camp Olowalu in Olowalu, Olowalu Ahupuaʻa, Lahaina District, Maui Island, Hawaiʻi [TMK (2) 4-8-03:084 por.].* Honolulu, HI: Scientific Consultant Services, Inc., 2015. [No location available]

Buffum, Amy and Michael F. Dega. *An Archaeological Monitoring Report for Construction work at Honokōwai, Māhinahina Ahupuaʻa, Kāʻanapali District, Maui Island, Hawaii.* Honolulu, HI: Scientific Consultant Services, Inc., 2002.

Bulgrin, Lon E. and Robert B. Rechtman. *An Archaeological Assessment Survey of TMK (2) 4-4-08:016 Hanakaʻōʻō Ahupuaʻa, Lahaina District, Island of Maui.* Rechtman Consulting, LLC, 2005.

Burgett, Berdena and Robert L. Spear. *An Archaeological Inventory Survey of an 8.8 Acre Parcel in the Land of Kainehi, Lahaina District, Paunau Ahupuaʻa, Island of Maui.* Honolulu, HI: Aki Sinoto Consulting, 1994.

[C]

Calis, Irene. *Archaeological Monitoring Report: Parking Lot Drainage System Installation, Panaʻewa Ahupuaʻa, Lahaina District, Island of Maui, Hawaiʻi.* Honolulu, HI: Scientific Consultant Services, Inc., 2002. [SHPD ID: 2019LI80642]

Chaffee, D. and C. Monahan. *A Monitoring Plan for 3.054 Acres of Partially Developed Land in Honokōwai, Māhinahina 4 Ahupuaʻa, Lahaina District, Maui Island, Hawaiʻi.* Honolulu, HI: Scientific Consultant Services, Inc., 2005.

Chaffee, David B. and Michael F. Dega. *An Archaeological Monitoring Plan Covering Three Parcels at the Hyatt Regency Maui Resort Kāʻanapali, Hanakaʻōʻō Ahupuaʻa, Lahaina District, Maui Island, Hawaiʻi [TMK (2) 4-4-13:005, 008, 004].* Honolulu, HI: Scientific Consultant Services, Inc., 2014.

Chaffee, David B. and Michael F. Dega. *An Archaeological Monitoring Plan for Approximately 12,365 Foot sq. Property Located on Waineʻe Street in Lahaina, Ahupuaʻa of Panaʻewa, Lahaina District, Maui Island, Hawaiʻi [TMK (2) 4-6-09:024].* Honolulu, HI: Scientific Consultant Services, Inc., 2005. [SHPD ID: 2019LI81580]

Chaffee, David B. and Michael F. Dega. *An Archaeological Monitoring Plan for Kāʻanapali Beach Hotel Beach Front, Restaurant/Canoe Hale, Hanakaʻōʻō Ahupuaʻa, Lahaina District, Island of Maui, Hawaiʻi.* Honolulu, HI: Scientific Consultant Services, Inc., 2014.

Chaffee, David B. and Michael F. Dega. *An Archaeological Monitoring Plan for Subdivision Construction of a 450-Acre Parcel of Land, Ahupuaʻa of Ukumehame, Lahaina District, Island of Maui, Hawaiʻi [TMK (2) 4-8-02:09].* Honolulu, HI: Scientific Consultant Services, Inc., 2003.

Chaffee, David B. and Michael F. Dega. *An Archaeological Monitoring Plan for the Maui Countywide Wastewater Pump Station Renovations, Phase II Project at Multiple Locations, Hanakaʻōʻō Ahupuaʻa and Mākila Ahupuaʻa, Lahaina District, Maui Island, Hawaiʻi [TMK: (2) 4-4-013:003, por. and 4-6-028:054].* Honolulu, HI: Scientific Consultant Services, Inc., 2014.

Chaffee, David B. and Michael F. Dega. *An Archaeological Monitoring Plan for the West Maui Recycled Water Expansion Project (Phase 2), Honokōwai Ahupuaʻa, Lahaina District, Maui Island, Hawaiʻi [TMK (2) 4-4-002:018 por].* Honolulu, HI: Scientific Consultant Services, Inc., 2013.

Chaffee, David B. and Robert L. Spear. *An Archaeological Monitoring Plan for Construction Activities on a 13,237 Square Foot Parcel in ʻAlaeloa Ahupuaʻa, Lahaina District, Maui Island, Hawaii.* Honolulu, HI: Scientific Consultant Services, Inc., 2001.

Chapman, P. S. and P. V. Kirch. *Archaeological Excavations at Seven Sites, Southeast Maui, Hawaiian Islands.* Honolulu, HI: Department of Anthropology, Bernice P. Bishop Museum, 1979. [UH Call Number: DU624.A1 B47 no.79-1]

Chapman, Phillips, Brandt and Associates. *Lahaina Banyan Courtyard Preliminary Development and Restoration Plans,* 1972. [SHPD ID: 2019LI81398]

Ching, Francis K. W. *Archaeological Assessment of the Property on Which the Proposed Marriott Kāʻanapali Hotel is to be Built, Kāʻanapali, Maui Island.* Lāwaʻi, HI: Archaeological Research Center Hawaiʻi, 1979. [SHPD ID: 2019LI81267]

Chong Jin and Michael F. Dega. *Archaeological Assessment for the Launiupoko Water System Line Extension to Waineʻe Project, Pūehuehu Nui and Pāhoa Ahupuaʻa, Lahaina District, Island of Maui, Hawaiʻi [TMK: (2) 4-6-013: portion of 022; 4-7-002: portion of 004; 4-7-003: portion of 031].* Honolulu, HI: Scientific Consultant Services, Inc., 2022. [SHPD ID: 2022LI00556]

Chong Jin and Michael F. Dega. *Archaeological Monitoring Report for the Kapalua Sinkhole Remediation and Native Plant Restoration Project, Nāpili 2-3 Ahupuaʻa, Lahaina District, Island of Maui [TMK: (2) 4-2-04:025 and (2) 4-2-04:059].* Honolulu, HI: Scientific Consultant Services, Inc., 2021. [SHPD ID: 2022LI00634]

Chong Jin, Garcia Alondra and Michael F. Dega. *Archaeological Monitoring Plan for 7,804 sq. ft. Parcel at 432 Ilikahi Street, Paunau Ahupuaʻa, Lahaina District, Island of Maui, Hawaiʻi [TMK: (2) 4-6-06:056 por.].* Honolulu, HI: Scientific Consultant Services, Inc., 2021. [SHPD ID: 2021LI00125]

Chun, Allison and Michael F. Dega. *Addendum Archaeological Assessment Report on 0.13 Acres of Partially Developed land in Honokōwai, Māhinahina 4 Ahupuaʻa, Maui Island, Hawaiʻi.* Honolulu, HI: Scientific Consultant Services, Inc., 2005. [SHPD ID: 2019LI81043]

Clark, Matthew R. and Robert B. Rechtman. *An Archaeological Inventory Survey of 333 Acres for the Proposed Expansion of the Kaheawa Wind Farm (TMK: 2-4-8:001: por. 001).* Rechtman Consulting, LLC, 2008. [SHPD ID: 2019LI81628]

Cleghorn, Paul L. *A Progress Report upon Completion of Fieldwork at the Seamen's Hospital, Lahaina, Maui (Phase 1).* Honolulu, HI: Department of Anthropology, Bernice P. Bishop Museum, 1975. [UH Call Number: DU629.L3 C54 1975]

Cleghorn, Paul L. *Phase 1 Archaeological Research at the Seamen's Hospital (Site D5-10), Lahaina, Maui.* Honolulu, HI: Department of Anthropology, Bernice P. Bishop Museum, 1975. [UH Call Number: DU629.L3 C544 1975]

Cliver, Blaine E., *Architectural Restorationalist. Architecturally speaking... The Baldwin House,* Lahaina, Maui, 1966. [SHPD ID: 2019LI81038]

Collins, Sara L. *Archaeological Monitoring Plan for Ground-Altering Activities During the Grading and Excavations for Construction Associated with the Mokuʻula/Mokuhinia Ecosystem Restoration Project, Phase I, Lahaina, Island of Maui.* Honolulu, HI: Pacific Consulting Services, Inc., 2007. [SHPD ID: 2019LI01493]

Collins, Sara L., Dennis Gosser, and Stephan D. Clark. *Archaeological Assessment of a Single Developed Parcel [TMK (2) 4-6-10:006] Lahaina, Island of Maui.* Honolulu, HI: Pacific Consulting Services, Inc., 2006. [No location available]

Community Planning, Inc. *Lahaina Historical Restoration and Preservation.* Community Planning Inc., 1961. [UH Call Number: DU629.L3 M3]

Connolly, Robert D. III. *Phase I Archaeological Survey of Kahoma Stream Flood-Control-Project Area, Lahaina, Maui.* Honolulu, HI: Department of Anthropology, Bernice P. Bishop Museum, 1974.

Conte, Patty J. *Archaeological Assessment Report for TMK (2) 4-3-03:043 Mailepai Ahupuaʻa, Lahaina District, Island of Maui.* Makawao, HI: CRM Solutions Hawaiʻi, Inc., 2005. [SHPD ID: 2019LI81298]

Conte, Patty J. *Archaeological Inventory Survey of the Stoops Property TMK (2) 4-1-01:018, Honolua Ahupuaʻa, Kāʻanapali District, Maui, Hawaiʻi.* Makawao, HI: CRM Solutions Hawaiʻi, Inc., 2006. [SHPD ID: 2019LI81424]

Conte, Patty J. *Archaeological Monitoring Plan for Construction Within TMK (2) 4-5-14:013 Por. 8A, Lahaina District, Wahikuli Ahupuaʻa, Island of Maui.* Makawao, HI: CRM Solutions Hawaiʻi, Inc., 2005. [SHPD ID: 2019LI81348]

Conte, Patty J. *Archaeological Monitoring Plan for On and Off-Site Construction Related to Pending and Future Improvements, Puunoa Ahupuaʻa, Lahaina District, Island of Maui.* Makawao, HI: CRM Solutions Hawaiʻi, Inc., 2008. [SHPD ID: 2019LI80599]

Conte, Patty J. *Archaeological Monitoring Plan for On and Off-Site Construction Related to the Proposed Amano Demo/Reconstruction, TMK (2) 4-5-12:008 Wahikuli Ahupuaʻa, Lahaina District, Island of Maui.* Makawao, HI: CRM Solutions Hawaiʻi, Inc., 2005. [SHPD ID: 2019LI81347]

Conte, Patty J. *Archaeological Monitoring Plan for On and Off-Site Construction Related to the Proposed Kent Property Demo/Reconstruction, TMK (2) 4-5-12:010 Moaliʻi Ahupuaʻa, Lahaina District, Island of Maui.* Makawao, HI: CRM Solutions Hawaiʻi, Inc., 2007. [SHPD ID: 2019LI81346]

Conte, Patty J. *Archaeological Monitoring Plan for On and Off-Site Construction Within and Related to TMK (2) 4-1-01:018, Honolua Ahupuaʻa, Kāʻanapali District, Maui, Hawaiʻi.* Makawao, HI: CRM Solutions Hawaiʻi, Inc., 2006. [SHPD ID: 2019LI81424]

Conte, Patty J. *Archaeological Monitoring Plan for On and Off-Site Construction Within and Related to TMK (2) 4-5-13:006 Lahaina District, Pana'ewa Ahupua'a, Island of Maui.* Makawao, HI: CRM Solutions Hawai'i, Inc., 2006. [SHPD ID: 2019LI81349]

Conte, Patty J. *Archaeological Monitoring Plan for On and Off-Site Construction Within and Related to TMK (2) 4-5-14:073 Lahaina District, Wahikuli Ahupua'a, Island of Maui.* Makawao, HI: CRM Solutions Hawai'i, Inc., 2006. [SHPD ID: 2019LI81354]

Conte, Patty J. *Archaeological Monitoring Report for Construction, Lahaina District, Wahikuli Ahupua'a, Island of Maui.* Makawao, HI: CRM Solutions Hawai'i, Inc., 2005. [SHPD ID: 2019LI81345]

Conte, Patty J. *Archaeological Monitoring Report for Off-Site Construction (Maile-pai Hui Land Lots 51-C-4-A, B & C) Lahaina District, Mailepai Ahupua'a, Island of Maui.* Makawao, HI: CRM Solutions Hawai'i, Inc., 2007. [SHPD ID: 2019LI81324]

Conte, Patty J. *Archaeological Monitoring Report for On and Off-Site Construction Within and Related to TMK (2) 4-5-14:073 Lahaina District, Wahikuli Ahupua'a, Island of Maui.* Makawao, HI: CRM Solutions Hawai'i, Inc., 2007. [SHPD ID: 2019LI81356]

Conte, Patty J. *Archaeological Monitoring Report Within and Related to a Parcel on Front Street, Pana'ewa Ahupua'a, Lahaina District, Maui Island, TMK (2) 4-5-13:006.* Makawao, HI: CRM Solutions Hawai'i, Inc., 2007. [No location available]

Conte, Patty J. *Archaeological Preservation Plan for the Portion of Site #50-50-01-1756 Within TMK (2) 4-1-01:018 Honolua Ahupua'a, Kā'anapali District, Maui, Hawai'i.* Makawao, HI: CRM Solutions Hawai'i, Inc., 2007. [SHPD ID: 2019LI81428]

Conte, Patty J. *Assessment of a Lot for Proposed Residential Construction, Kahana Ahupua'a, Lahaina District, Maui, Hawai'i.* Makawao, HI: CRM Solutions Hawai'i, Inc., 2004. [SHPD ID: 2019LI81300]

Cordle, Shayna and Michael F. Dega. *An Archaeological Monitoring Plan for 1.835 Acres in Napili, Napili 2-3 Ahupua'a, Lahaina District, Maui Island, Hawai'i.* Honolulu, HI: Scientific Consultant Services, Inc., 2008. ID: 2019LI81066]

Cordle, Shayna and Michael F. Dega. *An Archaeological Monitoring Report on Approximately 0.448-Acres for the Maui Marriott Vacation Club, Hana-ka'ō'ō Ahupua'a, Lahaina District, Island of Maui, Hawai'i [TMK (2) 4-4-*

13:001]. Honolulu, HI: Scientific Consultant Services, Inc., 2007. [SHPD ID: 2019LI80029]

Cordle, Shayna, Cathleen A. Dagher, and Michael F. Dega. *An Archaeological Monitoring Report for Work on County Roadway (WTP T2008/0014) For the Lahaina Store Water Meter Replacement Project, Lahaina, Kuʻia Ahupuaʻa, Lahaina District, Island of Maui, Hawaiʻi [TMK: (2) 4-6-09:007]*, 2009. Honolulu, HI: Scientific Consultant Services, Inc. [SHPD ID: 2019LI81563]

Cordle, Shayna, Jennifer Hunt, and Michael F. Dega. *An Archaeological Monitoring Report for a 12,365 Ft Sq. Property, Waineʻe St., Lahaina, Panaʻewa Ahupuaʻa, Lahaina District, Island of Maui, Hawaiʻi [TMK (2) 4-6-09:244]*. Honolulu, HI: Scientific Consultant Services, Inc., 2007. [SHPD ID: 2019LI81566]

[D]

Dagan, Colleen P. M. and Hallett H. Hammatt. *Archaeological Preservation Plan for SIHP 50-50-01-5672C and 50-50-01-5673H*. Wailuku, HI: Cultural Surveys Hawaiʻi, Inc., 2008. [SHPD ID: 2019LI81026]

Dagher, Cathleen A. *Request for Information Pertaining to the Ukumehame Subdivision and the Impacts to Preserved Site 50-50-08-4438 Ukumehame Ahupuaʻa, Lahaina District, Island of Maui*, 2009. [SHPD ID: 2019LI81644]

Dagher, Cathleen A. and Michael F. Dega. *An Archaeological Assessment of the Kāʻanapali Beach Hotel Beach Front Restaurant/Canoe Hale, Hanakaʻōʻō Ahupuaʻa, Lahaina District, Island of Maui, Hawaiʻi [TMK: (2) 4-4-08:003]*. Honolulu, HI: Scientific Consultant Services, Inc., 2014. [SHPD ID: 2019LI81259]

Dagher, Cathleen A. and Michael F. Dega. *An Archaeological Monitoring Plan for Olowalu Lot 24, Olowalu Ahupuaʻa, Lahaina District, Island of Maui, Hawaiʻi [TMK: (2) 4-8-03:107]*. Honolulu, HI: Scientific Consultant Services, Inc., 2019. [SHPD ID: 2019LI05336]

Dagher, Cathleen A. and Michael F. Dega. *An Archaeological Monitoring Plan for the Napili Culvert Replacement Project, Nāpili 4 and 5 Ahupuaʻa, Lahaina (Kāʻanapali) District, Island of Maui, Hawaiʻi*. Honolulu, HI: Scientific Consultant Services, Inc., 2015. [SHPD ID: 2019LI81056]

Dagher, Cathleen A. and Michael F. Dega. *An Archaeological Monitoring Plan for the Nāpili No. 3 WWPS Force Main Replacement, Lower Honoapiʻilani Road Right-of-Way, Kahana Ahupuaʻa, Lahaina (Kāʻanapali) District Island of Maui, Hawaiʻi. [TMK (2) 4-2-05:999 and 4-3-10:999]*. Honolulu, HI: Scientific Consultant Services, Inc., 2020. [SHPD ID: 2021LI00158]

Dagher, Cathleen A. and Michael F. Dega. *An Archaeological Monitoring Plan for the Nāpili No. 4 WWPS Force Main Replacement, Lower Honoapiʻilani Road Right-of-Way, Honokeana and ʻAlaeloa Ahupuaʻa, Lahaina, (Kāʻanapali) District, Island of Maui, Hawaiʻi.* Honolulu, HI: Scientific Consultant Services, Inc., 2020. [SHPD ID: 2021LI00158]

Dagher, Cathleen A. and Michael F. Dega. *An Archaeological Monitoring Plan for the Napili No. 5 & 6 WWPS Force Main Replacement Honokahua Ahupuaʻa, Lahaina (Kāʻanapali) District, Island of Maui, Hawaiʻi [TMK (2) 4-2-04: portion of 48 (Lot 3-A-1 of Kapalua Makai Subdivision No. 4) and TMK (2) 4-2-04: portion of 59 (Lot A-1-A-2 of Kapalua Development (Large-Lot) Subdivision)].* Honolulu, HI: Scientific Consultant Services, Inc., 2015. [SHPD ID: 2019LI81016]

Dagher, Cathleen A. and Michael F. Dega. *An Archaeological Monitoring Plan for the Poseley Residence, Olowalu Ahupuaʻa, Lahaina District, Island of Maui, Hawaiʻi [TMK: (2) 4-8-03:047 and portions of 001 and 084 (Easement G)].* Honolulu, HI: Scientific Consultant Services, Inc., 2015. [SHPD ID: 2019LI81660]

Dagher, Cathleen A. and Michael F. Dega. *An Archaeological Monitoring Plan for the Proposed Kapalua Coastal Trail Corridor Located in Kapalua and Honokōhau and Nāpili 2&3 Ahupuaʻa Lahaina District, Island of Maui, Hawaiʻi [TMK: (2) 4-2-Various].* Honolulu, HI: Scientific Consultant Services, Inc., 2007. [SHPD ID: 2019LI81421]

Dagher, Cathleen A. and Michael F. Dega. *An Archaeological Monitoring Plan for the Proposed Kapalua Coastal Trail Located in the Areas of Nāpili, Kapalua, Honokahua, and Honolua, Ahupuaʻa of Nāpili 2 & 3, Honokahua, and Honolua, Lahaina district, Island of Maui, Hawaiʻi.* Honolulu, HI: Scientific Consultant Services, Inc., 2008. [SHPD ID: 2019LI81410]

Dagher, Cathleen A. and Michael F. Dega. *A Preservation Plan for Multiple Archaeological Sites Located in the Kapalua Coastal Trail Corridor in the areas of Nāpili, Kapalua, Honokahua, and Honolua, Ahupuaʻa of Nāpili 2 & 3, Honokahua, and Honolua, Lahaina District, Island of Maui, Hawaiʻi.* Scientific Consultant Services, Inc.: Honolulu, HI, 2008. [SHPD ID: 2019LI79694]

Dagher, Cathleen A. and Michael F. Dega. *A Preservation Plan for the "Brick Palace" (A Component of State Site 50-50-03-3001) Within the Proposed Lahaina Harbor Complete Streets Project Area, Lahaina, Paunau Ahupuaʻa, Lahaina District, Island of Maui, Hawaiʻi [TMK (2) 4-6-01:004].* Honolulu, HI: Scientific Consultant Services, Inc., 2017. [SHPD ID: 2019LI81386]

Dagher, Cathleen A. and Michael F. Dega. *Archaeological Field Inspection Results and Recommendations for the Proposed Maui Police Department Communications*

Facility at Lahainaluna Water Treatment Site, Pana'ewa Ahupua'a, Lahaina District, Maui Island, Hawai'i [TMK: (2) 4-6-18:012 por.]. Honolulu, HI: Scientific Consultant Services, Inc., 2016. [SHPD ID: 2019LI81527]

Dagher, Cathleen A. and Michael F. Dega. *Archaeological Field Inspection Results and Recommendations for the Proposed Maui Police Department Communications Facility at Māhinahina Water Treatment Plant, Māhinahina Ahupua'a, Lahaina District, Maui Island, Hawai'i.* Honolulu, HI: Scientific Consultant Services, Inc., 2016. [SHPD ID: 2019LI81036]

Dagher, Cathleen A. and Michael F. Dega. *Archaeological Inventory Survey for the Proposed West Maui Water Source Development Project Māhinahina Well (State Well No. 6-5638-004) (West Maui Well No. 1) and the Kahana Well (State Well No. 6-5738-002) (West Maui Well No. 2), Honokōwai, Māhinahina, and Māhinahina 1, 2, 3 Ahupua'a, Lahaina (Kā'anapali) District, Island of Maui, Hawai'i [TMK: (2) 4-3-01:017, (2) 4-3-01:084; (2) 4-4-02:014, 015, and 018; and (2) 4-4-004:009, 011, 017, and 019].* Honolulu, HI: Scientific Consultant Services, Inc., 2022. [SHPD ID: 2022LI00356]

Dagher, Cathleen A. and Michael F. Dega. *Archaeological Monitoring Plan for 790 Front Street Waterline (WTP T2017-00280) Lahaina, Paunau Ahupua'a, Lahaina District, Island of Maui, Hawai'i [TMK: (2) 4-6-09:999].* Honolulu, HI: Scientific Consultant Services, Inc., 2020. [SHPD ID: 2022LI00633]

Dagher, Cathleen A. and Michael F. Dega. *Archaeological Monitoring Plan for the Maui Sands Sea Wall Repair Project, Mo'omuku 'ili, Honokōwai Ahupua'a, Lahaina (Kā'anapali) District, Island of Maui, Hawai'i.* Honolulu, HI: Scientific Consultant Services, Inc., 2018. [No location available]

Dagher, Cathleen A. and Michael F. Dega. *Revised Preservation Plan for Site 50-50-08-4438, Ukumehame Ahupua'a, Lahaina District, Island of Maui, Hawai'i [TMK (2) 4-8-002:066; formerly (2) 4-9-002:009 por.].* Honolulu, HI: Scientific Consultant Services, Inc., 2010. [SHPD ID: 2019LI81625]

Davis, Bertell D. *Archaeological Surface Survey, Honokōwai Gulch, Kā'anapali, Maui Island.* Lāwa'i, HI: Archaeological Research Center Hawai'i, 1977. [SHPD ID: 2019LI81277]

Davis, Bertell D. *Preliminary Report, Mala Wharf Burials, Phase 1, Mala, Lahaina, Maui Island.* Lāwa'i, HI: Archaeological Research Center Hawai'i, 1977. [No location available]

Dega, Michael F. *An Addendum Archaeological Inventory Survey in Ukumehame Ahupua'a, Lahaina District, Island of Maui, Hawai'i [TMK (2) 4-9-02:008 por.].* Honolulu, HI: Scientific Consultant Services, Inc., 2006. [SHPD ID: 2019LI81645]

Dega, Michael F. *An Archaeological Inventory Survey Plan for Kāʻanapali Beach Hotel Beach Front Restaurant/Canoe Hale, Hanakaʻōʻō Ahupuaʻa, Lahaina District, Island of Maui, Hawaiʻi [TMK: (2) 4-4-008:003 por.].* Honolulu, HI: Scientific Consultant Services, Inc., 2013. [SHPD ID: 2019LI80674]

Dega, Michael F. *An Archaeological Monitoring Plan for Construction Work at Honokōwai, Māhinahina Ahupuaʻa, Kāʻanapali District, Maui Island, Hawaiʻi.* Honolulu, HI: Scientific Consultant Services, Inc., 2000. [SHPD ID: 2019LI81247]

Dega, Michael F. *An Archaeological Monitoring Plan for Improvements at D. T. Fleming Beach Park for the County of Maui, Department of Parks and Recreation, Honokahua Ahupuaʻa [sic], Lahaina District, Island of Maui, Hawaiʻi.* Honolulu, HI: Scientific Consultant Services, Inc., 2015. [SHPD ID: 2019LI81042]

Dega, Michael F. *An Archaeological Monitoring Plan for Improvements at Honokōwai Beach Park for the County of Maui, Department of Parks and Recreation, Honokōwai Ahupuaʻa, Lahaina District, Island of Maui, Hawaiʻi [TMK (2) 4-4-01:046 por. & 047 por].* Honolulu, HI: Scientific Consultant Services, Inc., 2015. [SHPD ID: 2019LI81042]

Dega, Michael F. *An Archaeological Monitoring Plan for the Ulupono Center Project, Lahaina, Panaʻewa Ahupuaʻa, Lahaina District, Hawaiʻi, TMK (2) 4-5-10:054.* Honolulu, HI: Scientific Consultant Services Inc., 2017. [SHPD ID: 2019LI80597]

Dega, Michael F. *An Archaeological Monitoring Plan for the West Maui Recycled Water Expansion Project (Phase 2), Honokōwai Ahupuaʻa, Lahaina District, Maui Island, Hawaiʻi.* Honolulu, HI: Scientific Consultant Services, Inc., 2015. [SHPD ID: 2019LI81246]

Dega, Michael F. *A Preservation Plan for Multiple Archaeological Sites on Portions of a 570.3 Acre Property in the Launiupoko (Large Lot, Phase V) Subdivision No. 2, Launiupoko Ahupuaʻa, Lahaina District (Formerly Kāʻanapali), Island of Maui [TMK (2) 4-7-01:02].* Honolulu, HI: Scientific Consultant Services, Inc., 2006. [SHPD ID: 2019LI81606]

Dega, Michael F. *Archaeological Inventory Survey of a 3-Acre Parcel in Kahana-Kai, Kahana Ahupuaʻa, Kāʻanapali District, Island of Maui, Hawaiʻi.* Honolulu, HI: Scientific Consultant Services, Inc., 2001. [SHPD ID: 2019LI81327]

Dega, Michael F. *Archaeological Inventory Survey of the Punakea Loop Corridor in Launiupoko and Polanui Ahupuaʻa, Lahaina District (formerly Kāʻanapali), island of Maui, Hawaiʻi [TMK: (2) 4-8-01:002 por. & 4-7-01:029 por.].* Honolulu, HI: Scientific Consultant Services, Inc., 2008. [SHPD ID: 2019LI81597]

Dega, Michael F. *Archaeological Monitoring Plan for Limited Construction Work in Lahaina, Kuʻia Ahupuaʻa, Lahaina District, Island of Maui, Hawaiʻi.* Honolulu, HI: Scientific Consultant Services, Inc., 2003. [SHPD ID: 2019LI80641]

Dega, Michael F. *Archaeological Monitoring Plan for the Front Street Waterline Replacement Project, Panaʻewa Ahupuaʻa, Lahaina District, Island of Maui, Hawaiʻi [TMK (2) 4-5-04, 05, and 08].* Honolulu, HI: Scientific Consultant Services, Inc., 2002. [SHPD ID: 2019LI80631]

Dega, Michael F. *Archaeological Monitoring Plan for the Installation of a Septic System, Maui County Parks, Launiupoko Ahupuaʻa, Lahaina District, Maui Island, Hawaiʻi [TMK: (2) 4-7-01:17].* Honolulu, HI: Scientific Consultant Services, Inc., 2005. [SHPD ID: 2019LI81619]

Dega, Michael F. *Archaeological Monitoring Plan for the Maui Marriott Vacation Club, in the Ahupuaʻa of Hanakaʻōʻō, Lahaina District, Island of Maui, Hawaiʻi [TMK: (2) 4-4-13:001].* Honolulu, HI: Scientific Consultant Services, Inc., 2005. [SHPD ID: 2019LI80663]

Dega, Michael F. and David B. Chaffee. *An Archaeological Monitoring Plan for a Private Residence Demolition in Lahaina, Moaliʻi Ahupuaʻa, Lahaina District, Maui Island, Hawaiʻi [TMK (2) 4-6-02:003].* Honolulu, HI: Scientific Consultant Services, Inc., 2006. [SHPD ID: 2019LI81394]

Dega, Michael F. and David B. Chaffee. *Archaeological Monitoring Plan for Construction at the Lahaina Shores, Moaliʻi Ahupuaʻa, Lahaina District, Maui Island, Hawaiʻi.* Honolulu, HI: Scientific Consultant Services, Inc., 2004. [SHPD ID: 2019LI81373]

Dega, Michael F. and David B. Chaffee. *Archaeological Monitoring Plan for Construction Work on Approximately 25.3 Acres in Kapalua, Napili 2-3 Ahupuaʻa, Lahaina District, Maui Island, Hawaiʻi.* Honolulu, HI: Scientific Consultant Services, Inc., 2004. [SHPD ID: 2019LI81041]

Dega, Michael F. and Mary Sullivan. *Archaeological Monitoring Plan for Construction at the Lahaina Store, Lahaina, Kuʻia Ahupuaʻa, Lahaina District, Island of Maui, Hawaiʻi [TMK: (2) 4-6-09:007 & 062].* Honolulu, HI: Scientific Consultant Services, Inc., 2002. [SHPD ID: 2019LI81578]

Desilets, Michael and Patrick O'Day. *Preservation Plan for Proposed Fenceline Corridor for the West Maui Forest Reserve, Kuʻia, Mākila, Pāhoa, Halakaʻa, Polaiki, Launiupoko, and Olowalu Ahupuaʻa, Lahaina District, Maui Island, Hawaiʻi.* Kailua, HI: Garcia & Associates, 2016. [SHPD ID: 2019LI81528]

Devereux, Thomas K., Ian A. Masterson, Melody Heidel, Victoria Creed, Leilani Pyle, and Hallett H. Hammatt. *Archaeological Inventory Survey and Subsurface Testing of a 440 Acre Parcel, Ahupuaʻa of Ukumehame, Lahaina District, Island of Maui.* Wailuku, HI: Cultural Surveys Hawaiʻi, Inc., 1999. [SHPD ID: 2019LI81639]

Devereux, Thomas K., William H. Folk, and Hallett H. Hammatt. *Archaeological Survey of the Lands Comprising Project District 2 at Kapalua, Honokahua, and Nāpili 2 & 3 Ahupuaʻa Lahaina District of Maui.* Wailuku, HI: Cultural Surveys Hawaiʻi, Inc., 2001. [SHPD ID: 2019LI81007]

Dobyns, Susan and Jane Allen-Wheeler. *Archaeological Monitoring at the Site of the Kāʻanapali Aliʻi Condominium, Island of Maui.* Honolulu, HI: Department of Anthropology, Bernice P. Bishop Museum, 1982. [SHPD ID: 2019LI80673]

Dockall, John E. and Hallett H. Hammatt. *An Archaeological Inventory Survey for a Proposed Town Center and Residential Village, Nāpili Ahupuaʻa, Lahaina District.* Wailuku, HI: Cultural Surveys Hawaiʻi, Inc., 2005. [SHPD ID: 2019LI81011]

Dockall, John E., Tanya L. Lee-Greig, and Hallett H. Hammatt. *An Archaeological Assessment of a Proposed Road Corridor for Maui Preparatory Academy, Alaeloa Ahupuaʻa, Lahaina District, Maui Island.* Wailuku, HI: Cultural Surveys Hawaiʻi, Inc., 2005. [SHPD ID: 2019LI81052]

Donham, Theresa K. *Addendum Report: Additional Subsurface Testing of Area III, Subsurface Archaeological Testing, Revised Ritz-Carlton Kapalua Hotel Project Site, Areas I, II, and III, Land of Honokahua, Lahaina District, Island of Maui.* Hilo, HI: Paul H. Rosendahl, Ph.D., Inc., 1989. [SHPD ID: 2019LI81414]

Donham, Theresa K. *Archaeological Monitoring Plan for American Disabilities Act Improvements at the Lahaina Public Library, Paunau, Lahaina District, Maui, TMK: (2) 4-6-01:007 & 010.* Kīhei, HI: Akahele Archaeology, 2004. [SHPD ID: 2019LI81381]

Donham, Theresa K. *Archaeological Monitoring Plan for Construction of a Pool & Spa at the Hurlock Property, Moaliʻi, Lahaina District, Maui, TMK: (2) 4-5-13:004.* Kīhei, HI: Akahele Archaeology, 2003. [SHPD ID: 2019LI81351]

Donham, Theresa K. *Archaeological Monitoring Plan for the Remodeling of a Dwelling at the Phleger Property, Halaka'a, Lahaina District, Maui TMK: (2) 4-6-05:014.* Kīhei, HI: Akahele Archaeology, 2004. [SHPD ID: 2019LI81558]

Donham, Theresa K. *Archaeological Monitoring Report for American Disabilities Act Improvements at the Lahaina Public Library, Paunau, Lahaina District, Maui, TMK: (2) 4-6-01:007 & 010.* Kīhei, HI: Akahele Archaeology, 2005. [SHPD ID: 2019LI81403]

Donham, Theresa K. *Archaeological Survey Test Excavations Kapalua Hotel Development Site 2-H, Kapalua Bay Resort, Land of Honokahua, Lahaina, Island of Maui.* Hilo, HI: Paul H. Rosendahl, Ph.D., Inc., 1986. [2019LI80998]

Donham, Theresa K. *Field Inspection of a Proposed Culvert Location, USDA-SCS Lahaina Watershed Project, Pola Nui, Lahaina District, Maui [TMK (2) 4-7-01:018].* Wailuku, HI: State Historic Preservation Division, Maui Section, 1991. [SHPD ID: 2019LI81607]

Donham, Theresa K. *Interim Report: Kapalua Mitigation Program Data Recovery Excavations at the Honokahua Burial Site, Land of Honokahua, Lahaina District, Island of Maui.* Hilo, HI: Paul H. Rosendahl, Ph.D., Inc., 1989. [SHPD ID: 2019LI81417]

Duensing, Dawn E. and Michael W. Foley. *Lahaina Design Guidelines, Lahaina Town, Maui, Hawai'i,* 2003. [SHPD ID: 2019LI81377]

[F]

Ferguson, Lee, Arne Carlson, and Berdena Burgett. *Subsurface Archaeological Testing, Revised Ritz-Carlton Kapalua Hotel Project Site, Areas I, II and III.* Hilo, HI: Paul H. Rosendahl, Ph.D., Inc., 1989. [SHPD ID: 2019LI81006]

Folio, Katie M. and Hallett H. Hammatt. *An Archaeological Monitoring Plan for Proposed Improvements at the Feast of Lele, Waiokama Ahupua'a, Lahaina District, Island of Maui TMK: (2) 4-6-002:007 (por.).* Wailuku, HI: Cultural Surveys Hawai'i, Inc., 2014. [SHPD ID: 2019LI81372]

Folio, Katie M. and Hallett H. Hammatt. *Archaeological Monitoring Plan for the Special Use Permit Application for the Napili Point 1 AOAO (SMX 2015/0465) and Napili Point II (SMX 2015/0472) Project, Honokeana Ahupua'a, Lahaina District, Island of Maui, Napili Point I.* Wailuku, HI: Cultural Surveys Hawai'i, Inc., 2016. [SHPD ID: 2019LI81068]

Folio, Katie M. and Hallett H. Hammatt. *Archaeological Monitoring Report for the Special Use Permit Application for the Napili Point I (SMX 2015/0465) and*

Napili Point II (SMX 2015/0472) Project, Honokeana Ahupuaʻa, Lahaina District, Island of Maui, Napili Point I TMK: (2) 4-3-002:021 (por.), Napili Point II. Wailuku, HI: Cultural Surveys Hawaiʻi, Inc., 2016. [SHPD ID: 2019LI81068]

Folk, William. *Letter to Noel Kennett Re: End of Fieldwork of Archaeological Monitoring at Mala Wharf for an Electrical Line.* Wailuku, HI: Cultural Surveys Hawaiʻi, Inc., 1993. [SHPD ID: 2019LI80619]

Fox, Robert M. *Site Survey & Inventory, Hale Paʻi o Lahainaluna.* Honolulu, HI: AIA, 1977. [SHPD ID: 2019LI81590]

Fredericksen et al. *An Archaeological Inventory Survey of a 9.976 Acre parcel in the Kahana/Mailepai/Alaeloa District, Lahaina District, Maui, Hawaiʻi.* Pukalani, HI: Xamanek Researches, 1990. [SHPD ID: 2019LI81060]

Fredericksen, Demaris. *Monitoring Report for the Sheraton-Maui Redevelopment Project, Hanakaʻōʻō Ahupuaʻa, Lahaina District, Maui Island.* Pukalani, HI: Xamanek Researches, 1998. [SHPD ID: 2019LI81263]

Fredericksen, Demaris L. *Monitoring Report for the Sheraton-Maui Redevelopment Project Hanakaʻōʻō Ahupuaʻa, Lahaina District, Maui Island [TMK: (2) 4-4-08:005].* Pukalani, HI: Xamanek Researches, 1998. [SHPD ID: 2019LI81263]

Fredericksen, Demaris L. and Erik M. Fredericksen. *An Archaeological Inventory Survey of a portion of land in Nāpili 2-3 Ahupuaʻa, Lahaina District, Island of Maui [TMK: (2) 4-2-07: Parcels 007 and 008].* Pukalani, HI: Xamanek Researches, 2003. [SHPD ID: 2019LI81044]

Fredericksen, Demaris L. and Erik M. Fredericksen. *An Archaeological Inventory Survey of the Proposed Sandwich Isles Communications, Inc. Fiber Optics Landing Location near the Lahaina Post Office, Wahikuli Ahupuaʻa, Lahaina District, Island of Maui (TMK: 4-5-21:015).* Pukalani, HI: Xamanek Researches, 2003. [SHPD ID: 2019LI81336]

Fredericksen, Demaris L. and Erik M. Fredericksen. *Archaeological Inventory Survey for Kahana-Kai Subdivision, Kahana Ahupuaʻa, Lahaina [Kāʻanapali] District, Maui Island.* Pukalani, HI: Xamanek Researches, 1995. [SHPD ID: 2019LI81330]

Fredericksen, Demaris L. and Erik M. Fredericksen. *Archaeological Inventory Survey of a 24-Acre Parcel, Kapalua Lot 19, Located in Napili 2-3 Ahupuaʻa, Lahaina District, Maui Island [TMK: (2) 4-2-04: por. 024].* Pukalani, HI: Xamanek Researches, 2000. [SHPD ID: 2019LI81025]

Fredericksen, Demaris L. and Erik M. Fredericksen. *Archaeological Inventory Survey of Makai Portion (Phase 1) of Olowalu Development Parcel, Olowalu*

Ahupuaʻa, Lahaina District, Maui Island [TMK: (2) 4-8-03: por. 05]. Pukalani, HI: Xamanek Researches, 2000. [SHPD ID: 2019LI81638]

Fredericksen, Demaris L. and Erik M. Fredericksen. *Archaeological Inventory Survey (Phase 1) in the ʻIli of Pakala, Puako Ahupuaʻa, Lahaina District, Maui Island [TMK: (2) 4-6-07:007].* Xamanek Researches: Pukalani, HI, 1999. [SHPD ID: 2019LI81547]

Fredericksen, Demaris L. and Walter M. Fredericksen. *Archaeological Monitoring Plan for the Sheraton-Maui Redevelopment Project, Ahupuaʻa of Hanakaʻōʻō, Lahaina District, Maui Island.* Pukalani, HI: Xamanek Researches, 1995. [SHPD ID: 2019LI80672]

Fredericksen, Demaris L., Walter M. Fredericksen, and Erik M. Fredericksen. *Archaeological Inventory Survey of a 9.976 Acre Parcel in the Kahana/Mailepai/Akeloa Lands, Lahaina District, Maui, Hawaiʻi.* Pukalani, HI: Xamanek Researches, 1990. [SHPD ID: 2019LI81060]

Fredericksen, Erik M. *An Archaeological Assessment for the Proposed Maui Preparatory Academy, Alaeloa Ahupuaʻa, Lahaina District, Island of Maui [TMK (2) 4-3-01: 01 por.].* Pukalani, HI: Xamanek Researches, 2004. [SHPD ID: 2019LI81053]

Fredericksen, Erik M. *An Archaeological Assessment Survey of a c. 5 Acre Portion of Land for the Proposed Temporary Off-Site Parking Project, Hanakaʻōʻō/Honokōwai Ahupuaʻa, Lahaina District, Maui Island [TMK: (2) 4-4-002: 003].* Pukalani, HI: Xamanek Researches, 2007. [No location available]

Fredericksen, Erik M. *An Archaeological Monitoring Plan for a Detector Check Upgrade Project for the Lahaina Square Shopping Center, Waineʻe Ahupuaʻa, Lahaina District, Maui.* Pukalani, HI: Xamanek Researches, 2008. [SHPD ID: 2019LI80611]

Fredericksen, Erik M. *An Archaeological Monitoring Plan for an Inventory Survey Concurrent with Construction Activities on a Parcel of Land in Puako Ahupuaʻa, Lahaina District, Lahaina, Maui [TMK: (2) 4-6-08:48 and 53].* Pukalani, HI: Xamanek Researches, 2003. [SHPD ID: 2019LI81569]

Fredericksen, Erik M. *An Archaeological Monitoring Plan for a Parcel of Land in Napili, Mailepai Ahupuaʻa, Lahaina District, Napili, Maui, TMK: (2) 4-3-15:014.* Pukalani, HI: Xamanek Researches, 2004. [SHPD ID: 2019LI81293]

Fredericksen, Erik M. *An Archaeological Monitoring Plan for a Portion of Land in Alaeloa Ahupuaʻa, Lahaina District, Maui TMK: (2) 4-5-014:032.* Pukalani, HI: Xamanek Researches, 2005. [SHPD ID: 2019LI81355]

Fredericksen, Erik M. *An Archaeological Monitoring Plan for the Dickenson Street Power Pole Replacement Project, Paunau Ahupuaʻa, Lahaina District, Island of Maui.* Pukalani, HI: Xamanek Researches, 2004. [SHPD ID: 2019LI81570]

Fredericksen, Erik M. *An Archaeological Monitoring Plan for the Emerald Plaza II Project, Land of Moaliʻi, Lahaina District, Island of Maui, TMK: (2) 4-5-10:052.* Pukalani, HI: Xamanek Researches, 2019. [No location available]

Fredericksen, Erik M. *An Archaeological Monitoring Plan for the Kaahanui Place Electrical Improvements Project, Land of Puunoa, Lahaina District, Maui Island [TMK: (2) 4-5-04 por.].* Pukalani, HI: Xamanek Researches, 2009. [No location available]

Fredericksen, Erik M. *An Archaeological Monitoring Plan for the Proposed Kāʻanapali Loop Road Project, Hanakaʻōʻō Ahupuaʻa, Lahaina District, Island of Maui.* Pukalani, HI: Xamanek Researches, 2004. [SHPD ID: 2019LI81268]

Fredericksen, Erik M. *An Archaeological Monitoring Plan for the Proposed Lower Honoapiʻilani Highway Improvements Phase IV Project (Hoʻohui Road to Napilihau Street) in Kahana, Mailepai, and Alaeloa Ahupuaʻa, Napili, Lahaina District, Maui [F. A. P. No. STP 3080 (8)].* Pukalani, HI: Xamanek Researches, 2005. [SHPD ID: 2019LI81299]

Fredericksen, Erik M. *An Archaeological Monitoring Plan for the West Side Resource Center in Lahaina, Waineʻe Ahupuaʻa, Lahaina District, Maui Island [TMK: 4-6-15: por. of 1 and 4-6-18: por. of 2).* Pukalani, HI: Xamanek Researches, 2002. [SHPD ID: 2019LI81534]

Fredericksen, Erik M. *An Archaeological Monitoring Report for a Parcel of Land in Puako Ahupuaʻa, Lahaina District, Maui [TMK: (2) 4-6-008:022].* Pukalani, HI: Xamanek Researches, 2005. [SHPD ID: 2019LI81565]

Fredericksen, Erik M. *An Archaeological Monitoring Report for Offsite Parking for the Lot 3 Temporary Parking Project, Kāʻanapali, Hanakaʻōʻō Ahupuaʻa Lahaina District, Island of Maui.* Pukalani, HI: Xamanek Researches, 2006. [SHPD ID: 2019LI80660]

Fredericksen, Erik M. *An Archaeological Monitoring Report for the West Side Resource Center in Lahaina, Waineʻe Ahupuaʻa, Lahaina District, Maui Island [TMK: (2) 4-6-15: por. of 1 and TMK: (2) 4-6-18: por. of 2].* Pukalani, HI: Xamanek Researches, 2004. [SHPD ID: 2019LI81535]

Fredericksen, Erik M. *A Preliminary Report Summarizing Results of Field Research for an Archaeological Inventory Survey to Satisfy Requirements of SHPD at [TMK:*

(2) 4-2-04:por. 024] located in Honokahua Ahupuaʻa, Lahaina District, Island of Maui, Hawaiʻi. Pukalani, HI: Xamanek Researches, 2003.

Fredericksen, Erik M. *A Preservation Plan for the Sites Contained within Kāʻanapali Coffee Estates Subdivision (aka Pioneer Farms Subdivision 1) Project Area, Hanakaʻōʻō Ahupuaʻa, Lahaina District, Island of Maui.* Pukalani, HI: Xamanek Researches, 2005. [SHPD ID: 2019LI81274]

Fredericksen, Erik M. *Archaeological Assessment Report for a Portion of Land in Puako Ahupuaʻa, Lahaina District, Lahaina, Maui [TMK: (2) 4-6-08:053].* Pukalani, HI: Xamanek Researches, 2004. [SHPD ID: 2019LI81545]

Fredericksen, Erik M. *Archaeological Inventory Survey for the Proposed Lahaina Cannery Fuel Station Project, Land of Moaliʻi, Lahaina District, Island of Maui [TMK: (2) 4-5-11: 004 Por.].* Pukalani, HI: Xamanek Researches, 2023. [SHPD ID: 2023LI00137]

Fredericksen, Erik M. *Archaeological Monitoring Plan for a Parcel of Land in the ʻIli of Pakala, Puako Ahupuaʻa, Lahaina District, Island of Maui [TMK: (2) 4-6-07:003].* Xamanek Researches: Pukalani, HI, 1998. [SHPD ID: 2019LI81549]

Fredericksen, Erik M. *Archaeological Monitoring Plan for a Water Lateral and Sewer Lateral Installation Project for a Parcel of Land in Lahaina, Moaliʻi Ahupuaʻa, Lahaina District, Maui.* Pukalani, HI: Xamanek Researches, 2003. [SHPD ID: 2019LI81270]

Fredericksen, Erik M. *Archaeological Monitoring Plan for Improvements at 815 Front Street, Paunau Ahupuaʻa, Lahaina District, Maui.* Pukalani, HI: Xamanek Researches, 2001. [SHPD ID: 2019LI80644]

Fredericksen, Erik M. *Archaeological Monitoring Plan for Lot 29 (Site 29) Honokahua and Napili 2-3 Ahupuaʻa, Lahaina District, Maui, Hawaiʻi.* Pukalani, HI: Xamanek Researches, 1999. [SHPD ID: 2019LI81028]

Fredericksen, Erik M. *Archaeological Monitoring Plan for Sewer Lateral Installation Project at 460 Alio Street, Land of Nalehu, Mākila Ahupuaʻa, Lahaina District, Maui [TMK (2) 4-6-06:031].* Pukalani, HI: Xamanek Researches, 2003. [SHPD ID: 2019LI81270]

Fredericksen, Erik M. *Archaeological Monitoring Plan for the King Kamehameha III Elementary School Building B, Building D, and PT 201 Restroom Renovation Project, Puako Ahupuaʻa, Lahaina District, Maui [TMK: (2) 4-6-02:013 & 014].* Pukalani, HI: Xamanek Researches, 2001. [SHPD ID: 2019LI81392]

Fredericksen, Erik M. *Archaeological Monitoring Plan for the Proposed Plantation Inn Improvements Project (GPC 2002/43), Panaʻewa Ahupuaʻa, Lahaina District,*

Maui [TMK: (2) 4-6-009: 036, 037 and 044]. Pukalani, HI: Xamanek Researches, 2002. [SHPD ID: 2019LI81579]

Fredericksen, Erik M. *Archaeological Monitoring Plan for the Sabia Building Development and Improvement Project at 816A Front Street, Paunau Ahupua'a, Lahaina District, Maui.* Pukalani, HI: Xamanek Researches, 2000. [SHPD ID: 2019LI80617]

Fredericksen, Erik M. *Archaeological Monitoring Plan for the Wharf Street Accessibility Improvements at Lahaina Harbor—Electrical Underground Work Project, Puako Ahupua'a, Lahaina District, Maui [TMK: (2) 4-6-01 and 4-6-01: Portion of Parcel 1].* Pukalani, HI: Xamanek Researches, 2002. [SHPD ID: 2019LI81402]

Fredericksen, Erik M. *Archaeological Monitoring Plan on a 1.3 Acre of Land on the Olowalu Makai Project Area, Olowalu Ahupua'a, Lahaina District, Maui [TMK: (2) 4-9-03:044].* Pukalani, HI: Xamanek Researches, 2001. [SHPD ID: 2019LI81635]

Fredericksen, Erik M. *Archaeological Monitoring Report for a 1.3 Acre of Land on the Olowalu Makai Project Area, Olowalu Ahupua'a, Lahaina District, Maui (TMK 2-4-8-03:44).* Pukalani, HI: Xamanek Researches, 2003. [SHPD ID: 2019LI81637]

Fredericksen, Erik M. *Archaeological Monitoring Report for a Portion of Land in Moali'i Ahupua'a, Lahaina District, Maui.* Pukalani, HI: Xamanek Researches, 2004. [SHPD ID: 2019LI81269]

Fredericksen, Erik M. *Archaeological Monitoring Report for the Coconut Grove Development (Site 29), Honokahua and Napili 2-3 Ahupua'a Lahiana District, Island of Maui.* Pukalani, HI: Xamanek Researches, 2001. [SHPD ID: 2019LI17106]

Fredericksen, Erik M. *Archaeological Monitoring Report for the Proposed Plantation Inn Improvements Project (GPC2002/43) Pana'ewa Ahupua'a, Lahaina District, Maui, TMK: (2) 4-6-09:036, 037, and 044.* Pukalani, HI: Xamanek Researches, 2003. [SHPD ID: 2019LI81574]

Fredericksen, Erik M. *Archaeological Monitoring Report for the Verizon Hawaii, Inc. Equipment Installation project at TMK: (2) 4-2-04:021 Ritz-Carlton, Kapalua, Honokahua Ahupua'a, Lahaina District, Maui, Hawai'i.* Pukalani, HI: Xamanek Researches, 2001. [SHPD ID: 2019LI81014, 2019LI81029]

Fredericksen, Erik M. *Archaeological Monitoring Report on the Pioneer Inn Swimming Pool Construction Project.* Pukalani, HI: Xamanek Researches, 1997. [SHPD ID: 2019LI81383]

Fredericksen, Erik M. *Archaeological Reconnaissance Report for the County of Maui Honokōhau Water System Improvements Project, Lahaina District, Maui Island.* Pukalani, HI: Xamanek Researches, 1998. [SHPD ID: 2019LI80994]

Fredericksen, Erik M. *Preservation Plan for Possible Burial Features Contained Within Sites 50-50-01-5139, 5142, 5157 and 5158 Located on the Kapalua Mauka Project area, Honokahua and Napili 2 & 3 Ahupuaʻa, Lahaina District, Island of Maui.* Pukalani, HI: Xamanek Researches, 2003. [SHPD ID: 2019LI81407]

Fredericksen, Erik M. and Demaris Fredericksen. *Archaeological Inventory Survey for the Proposed Honokōhau Water System Improvement Project, Honokōhau Ahupuaʻa, Kāʻanapali District, Maui Island. DRAFT.* Pukalani, HI: Xamanek Researches, 1999. [SHPD ID: 2019LI80995]

Fredericksen, Erik M. and Demaris Fredericksen. *Archaeological Inventory Survey Report for Portion of Land in Puako Ahupuaʻa, Lahaina District, Lahaina, Maui, [TMK: (2) 4-6-08:53 and 48].* Pukalani, HI: Xamanek Researches, 2002. [SHPD ID: 2019LI81571]

Fredericksen, Erik M. and Demaris L. Fredericksen. *Additional Archaeological Inventory Survey Level Work for Site 50-50-03-4797, Lower Honoapiʻilani Road Improvements Project Corridor; Alaeloa, Mailepai and Kahana Ahupuaʻa, Lahaina District, Maui Island [TMK (2) 4-3-15].* Pukalani, HI: Xamanek Researches, 2001. [SHPD ID: 2021LI00221]

Fredericksen, Erik M. and Demaris L. Fredericksen. *An Archaeological Inventory Survey of Honoapiʻilani Highway Corridor from Alaelae Point to Honolua Bay, Honolua and Honokahua Ahupuaʻa, Lahaina District, Maui Island.* Pukalani, HI: Xamanek Researches, 2000. [SHPD ID: 2019LI81045]

Fredericksen, Erik M. and Demaris L. Fredericksen. *An Archaeological Inventory Survey of the Lahaina Watershed Flood Control Project Area, Lands of Polanui, Paha, Pueuehunui, Lahaina District, Maui Island [TMK: 4-6-13:016, 18, 26; TMK 4-7-01, 02].* Pukalani, HI: Xamanek Researches, 2003. [SHPD ID: 2019LI81442]

Fredericksen, Erik M. and Demaris L. Fredericksen. *An Archaeological Inventory Survey (Phase 2) of a New Alignment for the Honokōhau Waterline Project, Honokōhau, Ahupuaʻa, Kāʻanapali District, Island of Maui.* Pukalani, HI: Xamanek Researches, 2002. [SHPD ID: 2019LI81426]

Fredericksen, Erik M. and Demaris L. Fredericksen. *Archaeological Inventory Survey for the Proposed Golf Academy Project Kapalua, Maui, Hawaiʻi, TMK 4-2-04: por. 24.* Pukalani, HI: Xamanek Researches, 1998. [SHPD ID: 2019LI81012]

Fredericksen, Erik M. and Demaris L. Fredericksen. *Archaeological Inventory Survey of 475 Acres in Kapalua District 2 Project Area, Located in Napili and Honokahua Ahupuaʻa, Lahaina District, Maui Island, TMK: (2) 4-2-01: por. 1.* Pukalani, HI: Xamanek Researches, 2002. [SHPD ID: 2021LI00311]

Fredericksen, Erik M. and Demaris L. Fredericksen. *Archaeological Inventory Survey of the Lower Honoapiʻilani Road Improvements Project Corridor (TMK 4-3-03; 4-3-05; 4-3-10; 4-3-15) Lahaina District, Maui Island.* Pukalani, HI: Xamanek Researches, 1999. [SHPD ID: 2021LI00220]

Fredericksen, Erik M. and J. J. Frey. *An Archaeological Monitoring Report for the Kāʻanapali Shores Roadway Improvements Project, Honokōwai Ahupuaʻa, Lahaina District, Maui.* Pukalani, HI: Xamanek Researches, 2008. [SHPD ID: 2019LI81243]

Fredericksen, Erik M. and J. J. Frey. *Burial Site Component of an Archaeological Data Recovery Plan for Inadvertently Discovered Human Skeletal Remains, Site 50-50-03-08973, Located in Previously Imported Sand Fill During Utilities Installation for the Lahaina Cannery Fuel Station Project, Ahupuaʻa of Moaliʻi, Lahaina District, Island of Maui [TMK: (2) 4-5-11:004 por.].* Pukalani, HI: Xamanek Researches, 2023. [SHPD ID: 2023LI00074]

Fredericksen, Erik M. and Jennifer J. Frey. *An Archaeological Inventory Survey of a Portion of Land in Mailepai Ahupuaʻa, Lahaina District, Maui Island.* Pukalani, HI: Xamanek Researches, 2008. [SHPD ID: 2019LI81302]

Fredericksen, Erik M. and Jennifer L. Frey. *An Archaeological Monitoring Report for the Kāʻanapali Shores Roadway Improvements Project, Honokōwai Ahupuaʻa, Lahaina District, Maui [TMK: (2) 4-4-001:097, and TMK: (2) 4-4-001 (Right of Way)].* Pukalani, HI: Xamanek Researches, 2008. [SHPD ID: 2019LI81243]

Fredericksen, Erik M. and Jennifer J. Frey. *An Archaeological Monitoring Report for the King Kamehameha III Elementary School Parking Lot Improvements Project, Puako Ahupuaʻa, Lahaina District [TMK (2) 4-6-002:13].* Pukalani, HI: Xamanek Researches, 2008. [SHPD ID: 2019LI81374]

Fredericksen, Erik M., Demaris Fredericksen, and W. M. Fredericksen. *An Archaeological Inventory Survey at Honokōwai Beach Park, Honokōwai Ahupuaʻa, Lahaina District, Maui Island.* Pukalani, HI: Xamanek Researches, 1994. [No location available]

Fredericksen, Erik M., Demaris L. Fredericksen, and Walter M. Fredericksen. *An Archaeological Inventory Survey of a 12.2 Acre Parcel. Honokahua and Napili 2-3 Ahupuaʻa, Lahaina District Maui Island.* Pukalani, HI: Xamanek Researches, 1994. [SHPD ID: 2019LI81030]

Fredericksen, Erik M., Walter M. Fredericksen, and Demaris L. Fredericksen. *Additional Archaeological Inventory Survey Subsurface testing at Kapalua Bay Hotel [TMK (2) 4-2-04:26], Honokahua and Napili 2-3 Ahupuaʻa, Lahaina District, Maui Island.* Pukalani, HI: Xamanek Researches, 1996. [SHPD ID: 2019LI81024]

Fredericksen, Walter M. *An Historic and Traditional Land Use Study Utilizing Oral History Interviews for Assessing Cultural Impacts, for the Kapalua Project 2 and Expanded Project 2, Kapalua, Maui, Hawaiʻi.* Pukalani, HI: Xamanek Researches, 2001. [No location available]

Fredericksen, Walter M. *Archaeological Monitoring Report for the Remodeling Project of the Lahaina Yacht Club, 835 Front Street, Paunau Ahupuaʻa, Lahaina District, Island of Maui.* Pukalani, HI: Xamanek Researches, 2002. [SHPD ID: 2019LI80645]

Fredericksen, Walter M. and Demaris Fredericksen. *Archaeological Monitoring Report for The Kai Ala Subdivision, Ahupuaʻa of Hanakaoʻo, Lahaina District, Island of Maui.* Pukalani, HI: Xamanek Researches, 1996. [SHPD ID: 2019LI81251]

Fredericksen, Walter M. and Demaris L. Fredericksen. *An Archaeological Inventory Survey on a Parcel of Land Located in the Ahupuaʻa of Paunau, Lahaina District, Island of Maui TMK (2) 4-6-09:012.* Pukalani, HI: Xamanek Researches, 1993. [SHPD ID: 2022LI00237]

Fredericksen, Walter M. and Demaris L. Fredericksen. *Archaeological Data Recovery Report on the Plantation Inn Site, Lahaina, Maui, Hawaiʻi.* Pukalani, HI: Xamanek Researches, 1990. [SHPD ID: 2019LI81589; UH Call Number: DU629.L3 F738 1990a]

Fredericksen, Walter M. and Demaris L. Fredericksen. *Archaeological Data Recovery Report on the Plantation Inn Site, Lahaina, Maui, Hawaiʻi.* Pukalani, HI: Xamanek Researches, 1993. [SHPD ID: 2019LI81589]

Fredericksen, Walter M. and Demaris L. Fredericksen. *Report on the Archaeological Excavation Conducted at Hale Paʻi Site, 1981-1982.* Pukalani, HI: Xamanek Researches, 1988. [SHPD ID: 2019LI81532]

Fredericksen, Walter M. and Demaris L. Fredericksen. *Report on the Archaeological Excavation of the "Brick Palace" of King Kamehameha I at Lahaina, Maui, Hawaiʻi, 1965.* [SHPD ID: 2019LI81384; UH Call Number: DU629.L3 F74]

Fredericksen, Walter M. Jr. and Demaris L. Fredericksen. *Report on the Excavation of the Outbuildings Adjacent to the Baldwin House, Undertaken for the*

Lahaina Restoration Foundation, Lahaina, Maui, Hawai'i. Pukalani, HI: Xamanek Researches, 1978. [SHPD ID: 2019LI81568]

Fredericksen, Walter M., Demaris Fredericksen, and Erik M. Fredericksen. *Report on the Archaeological Inventory Survey at Historic Site #15, Lahaina Maui, Hawai'i.* Pukalani, HI: Xamanek Researches, 1988. [SHPD ID: 2019LI81406]

Fredericksen, Walter M., Demaris L. Fredericksen, and Erik M. Fredericksen. *An Archaeological Inventory Survey of a Parcel of Land Adjacent to Malu-Ulu-o-Lele Park, Lahaina, Maui, Hawai'i.* Pukalani, HI: Xamanek Researches, 1989. [SHPD ID: 2019LI81548]

Fredericksen, Walter M., Demaris L. Fredericksen, and Erik M. Fredericksen. *An Archaeological Inventory Survey of the Plantation Inn Site, Lahaina, Maui, Hawai'i.* Pukalani, HI: Xamanek Researches, 1989. [SHPD ID: 2019LI81588]

Fredericksen, Walter M., Demaris L. Fredericksen, and Erik M. Fredericksen. *Archaeological Data Recovery Report on the AUS Site, Lahaina, Maui, Hawai'i.* Pukalani, HI: Xamanek Researches, 1989. [SHPD ID: 2019LI81562]

Fredericksen, Walter M., Demaris L. Fredericksen, and Erik M. Fredericksen. *The AUS Site: H. S. #50-03-1797 A Preliminary Archaeological Inventory Survey Report.* Pukalani, HI: Xamanek Researches, 1989. [No location available]

Frey, Jennifer J. and Erik M. Fredericksen. *An Archaeological Monitoring Report for the King Kamehameha III Elementary School Campus Exterior Awning and Gutter Project, DOE Job No. P01090-06, Puako Ahupua'a, Lahaina District [TMK: (2) 4-6-02:013, and (2) 4-6-02:014].* Pukalani, HI: Xamanek Researches, 2009. [SHPD ID: 2019LI81561]

Frey, Jennifer J., Josephine M. Yucha, and Hallett H. Hammatt. *Archaeological Monitoring Report for the Valley Isle Resort Renovation Project, Kahana Ahupua'a, Lahaina District, Maui Island, TMK: (2) 4-3-10:004.* Wailuku, HI: Cultural Surveys Hawai'i, Inc., 2021. [SHPD ID: 2022LI00135]

Frey, Jennifer J., Josephine M. Yucha, and Hallett H. Hammatt. *Archaeological Monitoring Report for the Westin Maui Resort & Spa Master Plan Improvements Project, Parking Garage, Lobby, and Porte Cochere Driveway, Hanaka'ō'ō Ahupua'a, Lahaina District, Island of Maui, TMK (2) 4-4-008:019.* Wailuku, HI: Cultural Surveys Hawai'i, Inc., 2019. [SHPD ID: 2019LI80683]

Frey, Jennifer J., Ryan Luskin, Angela L. Yates, and Hallett H. Hammatt. *Archaeological Monitoring Report for the Hololani Resort Condominiums Shoreline Protection Project, Kahana Ahupua'a, Lahaina District, Maui Island.* Wailuku, HI: Cultural Surveys Hawai'i, Inc., 2019. [SHPD ID: 2019LI81312]

Frost, Lockwood H. *A Report and Recommendations on the Restoration and Preservation of Hale Aloha, Lahaina, Maui,* 1973. [No location available]

[G]

Gallo and Michael F. Dega. *Archaeological Assessment for a New Farm Dwelling for Mākila Ranches, Lot 4, Polanui Ahupuaʻa, Lahaina District, Island of Maui, Hawaiʻi [TMK: (2) 4-7-14:004 por.].* Honolulu, HI: Scientific Consultant Services, Inc., 2021. [SHPD ID: 2022LI00382]

Goodwin, Conrad and Spencer Leinewebber. *Archaeological Inventory Survey Report, Pioneer Mil Company, Ltd. Sugar Enterprise Lands, Site No. 50-50-03-4420, Villages of Leialiʻi Project, Lahaina, Maui Hawaiʻi.* Honolulu, HI: International Archaeological Research Institute, Inc., 1997. [SHPD ID: 2019LI81363]

Graves, Donna and Susan Goodfellow. *Archaeological Inventory Survey, Launiupoko Golf Course, Land of Launiupoko, Lahaina District, Island of Maui.* Hilo, HI: Paul H. Rosendahl, Ph.D., Inc., 1991. [SHPD ID: 2019LI81595, 2019LI81610]

Griffin, Bion P. and George W. Lovelace, eds. *Survey and Salvage—Honoapiʻilani Highway: The Archaeology of Kāʻanapali from Honokōwai to ʻAlaeloa Ahupuaʻa.* Lāwaʻi, HI: Archaeological Research Center Hawaiʻi, Inc., 1977. [UH Call Number: DU628.M3 A7 1977]

Guerriero, Diane and Jeffrey Pantaleo. *Archaeological Inventory Survey Report of a 0.361 Acre Coastal Parcel, Waineʻe Ahupuaʻa, Lahaina District, Island of Maui.* Wailuku, HI: Archaeological Services Hawaii, LLC, 2005. [SHPD ID: 2019LI81560]

Guerriero, Diane, Lisa Rotunno-Hazuka, and Jeffrey Pantaleo. *Archaeological Assessment for the Royal Lahaina Resort Redevelopment Hanakaʻōʻō Ahupuaʻa, Lahaina District, Island of Maui.* Wailuku, HI: Archaeological Services Hawaii, LLC, 2005. [SHPD ID: 2019LI81261]

Guerriero, Diane, Lisa J. Rotunno-Hazuka, and Jeffrey Pantaleo. *Archaeological Assessment Report of a 0.428 Acre Parcel of Land at TMK 4-5-07:004 Kuholilea Ahupuaʻa, Lahaina District, Island of Maui.* Wailuku, HI: Archaeological Services Hawaii, LLC, 2005. [SHPD ID: 2019LI80606]

Guerriero, Diane A., Charvet-Pond, and S. Goodfellow. *Archaeological Monitoring and Data Recovery, Kapalua Ritz-Carlton Hotel Site, Land of Honokahua, Lahaina District, Island of Maui [TMK: (2) 4-2-01:004, 005, por. 012, 013, por. 018, 034].* Hilo, HI: Paul H. Rosendahl, Ph.D., Inc., 1993. [No location available]

[H]

Hammatt, Hallett H. *An Archaeological Field Inspection of the Lahaina Bypass Highway, Phase 1A, Keawe Street Extension to Lahainaluna Road, and Current Condition of SIHP Number -2484.* Wailuku, HI: Cultural Surveys Hawai'i, Inc., 2007. [SHPD ID: 2019LI81366]

Hammatt, Hallett H. *Archaeological Investigation and Monitoring, Mala Wharf Boat-Launch Ramp Area, Lahaina, Maui Island.* Lāwa'i, HI: Archaeological Research Center Hawai'i, Inc., 1978. [SHPD ID: 2019LI81387; UH Call Number: GN486 .H35]

Hammatt, Hallett H. *Archaeological Preservation Plan for 10 Sites Within for 440 Acre Parcel, Ahupua'a of Ukumehame, Lahaina District, Island of Maui.* Wailuku, HI: Cultural Surveys Hawai'i, Inc., 2000. [SHPD ID: 2019LI81626]

Hammatt, Hallett H. *Archaeological Reconnaissance at the Proposed Hyatt Regency Site, Hanaka'ō'ō, Kā'anapali, Maui Island, Tax Map Key; 4-4-06:31 Lot 60, ARCH 14-129.* Lāwa'i, HI: Archaeological Research Center Hawai'i, 1978. [SHPD ID: 2019LI81264; UH Call Number: GN486 .H35]

Hammatt, Hallett H. *Lahaina (Front Street) Archaeological Test Excavations, TMK 4-5-3:012, Island of Maui.* Wailuku, HI: Cultural Surveys Hawai'i, Inc., 2003. [SHPD ID: 2019LI80649]

Hammatt, Hallett H. *Restoration Plan for Pole 69 (Original Location) at Ukumehame Gulch, Ma'alaea to Lahaina Third 69 KV Transmission Line.* Wailuku, HI: Cultural Surveys Hawai'i, Inc., 1996. [SHPD ID: 2019LI81632]

Hammatt, Hallett H. and David W. Shideler. *Draft Proposal for an Archaeological Mitigation Plan at the Lahaina Courthouse, Lahaina, Lahaina District, Maui Island, Hawai'i.* Wailuku, HI: Cultural Surveys Hawai'i, Inc., 1999. [SHPD ID: 2019LI81400]

Hammatt, Hallett H. and David W. Shideler. *Preservation Plan for Four Sites (50-50-01-5234, A Water Exploration Tunnel; -5235, A Petroglyph; -5425, A Historic Trail, and -5426, A Pre-Contact Habitation Site) Located Within a 400-Acre Parcel at Honolua Ahupua'a.* Wailuku, HI: Cultural Surveys Hawai'i, Inc., 2003. [SHPD ID: 2019LI81003]

Hammatt, Hallett H. and David W. Shideler. *Written Findings of Archaeological Monitoring at the Lahaina Courthouse, Lahaina, Lahaina District, Maui Island, Hawai'i.* Wailuku, HI: Cultural Surveys Hawai'i, Inc., 1998. [SHPD ID: 2019LI81401]

Hammatt, Hallett H. and Rodney Chiogioji. *Archaeological Monitoring Plan for a ½-Acre parcel in Napili 2-3 Ahupuaʻa, Lahaina District, Island of Maui.* Wailuku, HI: Cultural Surveys Hawaiʻi, Inc., 2002. [SHPD ID: 2019LI81063]

Hammatt, Hallett H., David W. Shideler, and Tony Bush. *Archaeological Inventory Survey of an Approximately 400-Acre Parcel at Honolua Ahupuaʻa Lahaina District of Maui.* Wailuku, HI: Cultural Surveys Hawaiʻi, Inc., 2003. [SHPD ID: 2019LI80993]

Hart, Christopher. *Final Report of the Preparation for Exhibit of King Kamehameha I's "Brick Palace" at Lahaina, Maui, Hawaiʻi.* Maui Historic Commission, 1970.

Haun, A. E. *Subsurface Archaeological Reconnaissance Survey, Lahaina Cannery Makai and Mauka Parcels, Land of Moaliʻi, Lahaina District, Island of Maui,* 1988. [SHPD ID: 2019LI80612]

Haun, Alan E. *Archaeological Assessment, Lands of Polanui, Polaiki, and Launiupoko, Lahaina District, Island of Maui.* Kailua-Kona, HI: Haun and Associates, 2002. [SHPD ID: 2019LI81608]

Haun, Alan E. *Archaeological Assessment TMK (2) 4-7-02:005 Land of Pāhoa, Lahaina District, Island of Maui.* Kailua-Kona, HI: Haun and Associates, 2001. [SHPD ID: 2019LI81616]

Haun, Alan E. *Archaeological Inventory Survey Kauaʻula Development Parcel, Lands of Pūehuehu Iki, Pāhoa, and Pola Nui, Lahaina District, Island of Maui.* Kailua-Kona, HI: Haun and Associates, 1999. [No location available]

Haun, Alan E. *Archaeological Site Documentation, Site 5401, Lands of Polanui and Pāhoa, Lahaina District, Island of Maui (TMK: 4-8-01:002, 4-7-01:001).* Kailua-Kona, HI: Haun and Associates, 2004. [SHPD ID: 2019LI81622]

Haun, Alan E. and Dave Henry. *Archaeological Inventory Survey, Proposed 124-Acre Mākila Subdivision, Lands of Launiupoko, Polanui and Pūehuehu Nui, Lahaina District, Island of Maui (TMK: 4-7-01: por. 1 and TMK: 4-7-04: Por. 4).* Kailua-Kona, HI: Haun and Associates, 2001. [SHPD ID: 2019LI81623]

Haun, Alan E. and Dave Henry. *Archaeological Inventory Survey, TMK 4-6-7:010 ʻIli of Pakala, Land of Puako District, Island of Maui.* Kailua-Kona, HI: Haun and Associates, 2001. [SHPD ID: 2019LI81555]

Haun, Alan E. and Dave Henry. *Final Archaeological Monitoring Plan, TMK (2) 4-5-13:016, Wahikuli Ahupuaʻa, Lahaina District, Island of Maui.* Kailua-Kona, HI: Haun and Associates, 2014. [SHPD ID: 2019LI81350]

Haun, Alan E. and Dave Henry with Maria E. K. Orr. *Archaeological Inventory Survey Portion of TMK 4-7-01:002, Land of Launiupoko, Lahaina District, Island of Maui.* Kailua-Kona, HI: Haun and Associates, 2001. [SHPD ID: 2019LI81599]

Haun, Alan E. and Jack D. Henry. *Archaeological Data Recovery Plan Sites 4141 and 4143, Land of Honolua, Lahaina District, Island of Maui,* 2002. [SHPD ID: 2019LI81010]

Haun, Alan E. and Jack D. Henry. *Archaeological Site Preservation Plan Kauʻaula Development Parcel, Lands of Pūehuehu Iki, Pāhoa, and Polanui Ahupuaʻa, Lahaina District, Island of Maui [TMK (2) 4-7-02:04, 05, & 07, (2) 4-7-03:por. 01].* Kailua-Kona, HI: Haun and Associates, 2003. [SHPD ID: 2019LI81618]

Haun, Alan E. and Jack D. Henry. *Archaeological Site Preservation Plan, Kauaʻula Development Parcel, Lands of Pūehuehu Iki, Pāhoa, and Polo Nui, Lahaina District, Island of Maui [TMK: (2) 4-7-03:001].* Kailua-Kona, HI: Haun and Associates, 2000. [SHPD ID: 2019LI81613]

Havel, BreAnna and Michael F. Dega. *An Archaeological Assessment Report on 0.11 Acres of a Partially Developed Land in Honokōwai Ahupuaʻa, Lahaina District, Maui Island, Hawaiʻi [TMK 4-4-01:106].* Honolulu, HI: Scientific Consultant Services, Inc., 2005. [SHPD ID: 2019LI81285]

Havel, BreAnna and Michael F. Dega. *Archaeological Monitoring Plan for the Maui Islander Project, Lahaina, Paunau Ahupuaʻa District, Maui Island, Hawaiʻi [TMK: 4-6-011:008].* Honolulu, HI: Scientific Consultant Services, Inc., 2005. [SHPD ID: 2019LI81582]

Heidel, Melody, William H. Folk, and Hallett H. Hammatt. *An Archaeological Inventory Survey for Waiola Church, Ahupuaʻa of Waineʻe, Lahaina District, Island of Maui.* Wailuku, HI: Cultural Surveys Hawaiʻi, Inc., 1994. [SHPD ID: 2019LI81552]

Hill, Robert, Tanya Lee-Greig, and Hallett H. Hammatt. *An Archaeological Inventory Survey Report and Mitigation Plan for the Hawaiʻi State Department of Education Cesspool Conversion Project at the Lahainaluna High School, Panaʻewa Ahupuaʻa, Lahaina District, Maui Island, TMK (2) 4-6-18:005, 007, 012.* Wailuku, HI: Cultural Surveys Hawaiʻi, Inc., 2008. [No location available]

Hill, Robert R., Joseph Arnold, and Hallett H. Hammatt. *Archaeological Monitoring Report for a Dust Barrier Relocation at North Kāʻanapali, Honokōwai Ahupuaʻa, Lahaina District, Island of Maui. TMK (2) 4-4-014:004 (por.)* Wailuku, HI: Cultural Surveys Hawaiʻi, Inc., 2006. [SHPD ID: 2019LI80658]

Hill, Robert R., Joseph Arnold, and Hallett H. Hammatt. *Archaeological Monitoring Report for Shoreline Improvements at Lot 3, North Kāʻanapali, Honokōwai Ahupuaʻa, Lahaina District, Maui Island [TMK (2) 4-4-014:005 (por.)].* Wailuku, HI: Cultural Surveys Hawaiʻi, Inc., 2008. [SHPD ID: 2019LI80653]

Hill, Robert R., Tanya L. Lee-Greig, and Hallett H. Hammatt. *Preservation Plan for a Fishing Koʻa, SIHP 50-50-03-6275, North Kāʻanapali, Lot 3, Honokōwai Ahupuaʻa, Maui Island [TMK (2) 4-4-014:005 por.].* Wailuku, HI: Cultural Surveys Hawaiʻi, Inc., 2008. [SHPD ID: 2019LI80654]

Hill, Robert R., Tanya L. Lee-Greig, and Hallett H. Hammatt. *Archaeological Monitoring Report for Dust Barrier Construction at Lot 3, North Kāʻanapali, Honokōwai Ahupuaʻa, Lahaina District, Island of Maui [TMK (2) 4-4-014:005 (por.)].* Wailuku, HI: Cultural Surveys Hawaiʻi, Inc., 2008. [SHPD ID: 2019LI80655]

Hill, Robert R., Tanya Lee-Greig, and Hallett H. Hammatt. *Archaeological Monitoring Report for Shoreline Improvements at Lot 1, North Kāʻanapali, Honokōwai Ahupuaʻa, Lahaina District, Maui Island TMK: (2) 4-4-014:003 (por.).* Wailuku, HI: Cultural Surveys Hawaiʻi, Inc., 2008. [SHPD ID: 2019LI80657]

Hill, Robert R., Thomas K. Devereux, and Hallett H. Hammatt. *An Archaeological Assessment of a 9.650 Acre Parcel, ʻAlaeloa Ahupuaʻa, Lahaina District, Maui Island, for the West Maui Village Project.* Wailuku, HI: Cultural Surveys Hawaiʻi, Inc., 2006. [SHPD ID: 2019LI81037]

Hoerman, Rachel and Michael F. Dega. *An Archaeological Monitoring Plan for the Pavilion Restaurant Renovation at the Hyatt Regency Maui Resort and Spa, Kāʻanapali, Hanakaʻōʻō Ahupuaʻa, Lahaina District, Maui Island, Hawaiʻi.* Honolulu, HI: Scientific Consultant Services, Inc., 2007. [SHPD ID: 2019LI80666, 2019LI80665]

Hommon, Robert J. *An Archaeological Reconnaissance Survey of an Area Near Waineʻe Village, West Maui.* Hawaiʻi: Science Management, Inc., 1982. [SHPD ID: 2019LI81389; UH Call Number: DU629.W346 H66 1982]

Hommon, Robert J. *An Archaeological Reconnaissance Survey of the North Beach Mauka and South Beach Beach Mauka Areas, Hanakaʻōʻō, West Maui.* Hawaiʻi: Science Management, Inc., 1982. [No location available]

Hommon, Robert J. *Report on a Walk Through Survey of the Kahoma Stream Flood Control Project Area.* Honolulu, HI: Department of Anthropology, Bernice P. Bishop Museum, 1973.

Hommon, Robert J. and Hamilton M. Ahlo, Jr. *An Archaeological Reconnaissance Survey of the Site of a Proposed Airstrip at Māhinahina, West Maui.* Science Management, Inc., 1982. [SHPD ID: 2019LI81050; UH Call Number: DU629. M345 H66 1982]

Hunt, Jennifer, Lauren Morawski, and Michael F. Dega. *An Archaeological Monitoring Report for the Installation of New Sewer Lines and Force Mains and the Replacement of Waterlines for the County of Maui at Shaw, Front, and Dickenson Streets and Honoapiʻilani Highway in Lahaina AND The Installation of Underground Electrical Lines, Panels, and Meters at Armory Park/Kamehameha Iki Park on Front Street in Lahaina for Maui Parks and Recreation Division, Various Ahupuaʻa, Lahaina District, Island of Maui, Hawaiʻi [TMK (2) 4-6002:003, 005, 006, 007, 010, 012, 015, 016, and 027].* Honolulu, HI: Scientific Consultant Services, Inc., 2011. [SHPD ID: 2019LI81393]

[J]

Jensen, Peter A. and Jenny O'Claray. *Supplemental Archaeological Survey, Lahaina Master Planned Project Offsite Sewer, Water Improvements, and Cane Haul Road.* Hilo, HI: Paul H. Rosendahl, Ph.D., Inc., 1991. [SHPD ID: 2019LI81419]

Jensen, Peter M. *Archaeological Inventory Survey Honoapiʻilani Highway Realignment Project Lahaina Bypass Section—Modified Corridor Alignment, Lands of Honokōwai, Hanakaʻōʻō, Wahikuli, Panaʻewa, Kuʻia, Halakaʻa, Pūehuehu Nui, Pāhoa, Polanui, and Launiupoko, Lahaina District, Island of Maui.* Hilo, HI: Paul H. Rosendahl, Ph.D., Inc., 1991. [SHPD ID: 2019LI81242]

Jensen, Peter M. *Archaeological Inventory Survey Lahaina Bypass Highway New Connector Roads Project Area, Ahupuaʻa of Hanakaʻōʻō and Paunau, Lahaina District, Island of Maui.* Hilo, HI: Paul H. Rosendahl, Ph.D., Inc., 1994. [SHPD ID: 2019LI81611]

Jensen, Peter M. *Archaeological Inventory Survey Lahaina Master Planned Project Site: Land of Wahikuli, Lahaina District, Island of Maui.* Hilo, HI: Paul H. Rosendahl, Ph.D., Inc., 1989. [SHPD ID: 2019LI80636]

Jensen, Peter M. *Archaeological Inventory Survey South Beach Mauka Development Site, Ahupuaʻa of Hanakaʻōʻō, Lahaina District, Island of Maui.* Hilo, HI: Paul H. Rosendahl, Ph.D., Inc., 1990. [SHPD ID: 2019LI81262; UH Call Number: DU628.M3 J46 1990]

Jensen, Peter M. *Letter Report: Additional Field Survey Lahaina Bypass Section, Modified Corridor Alignment, Honoapiʻilani Highway Realignment Project, Lands of Pāhoa and Polanui, Lahaina District, Island of Maui [TMK: (2) 4-7-01, 02].* Hilo, HI: Paul H. Rosendahl, Ph.D., Inc., 1992. [SHPD ID: 2019LI81609]

Jensen, Peter M. and G. Mehalchick. *Archaeological Inventory Survey North Beach Mauka (Kāʻanapali) Site, Ahupuaʻa of Hanakaʻōʻō, Lahaina District, Island of Maui.* Hilo, HI: Paul H. Rosendahl, Ph.D., Inc., 1993. [UH Call Number: DU628.M3 J46 1989]

Jensen, Peter M. and Gemma Mahalchick. *Archaeological Inventory Survey, The Puʻukoliʻi Village Project Area, Ahupuaʻa of Hanakaʻōʻō, Lahaina District, Island of Maui.* Hilo, HI: Paul H. Rosendahl, Ph.D., Inc., 1992. [SHPD ID: 2019LI81252]

Joerger, Pauline King and Michael W. Kaschko. *A Cultural Historical Overview of the Kahoma Stream Flood Control Project, Lahaina, Maui and Maʻalaea Small Boat Harbor Project, Maʻalaea, Maui.* Honolulu, HI: Hawaiʻi Marine Research, Inc., 1979. [SHPD ID: 2019LI80298; UH Call Number: DU629.L3 J63]

John Carl Warnecke and Associates. *Lahaina Small Boat Harbor Study.* San Francisco, CA: John Carl Warnecke and Associates, Architects and Planning Consultants, 1965. [SHPD ID: 2019LI81397]

Johnston-OʻNeill, Emily and Michael F. Dega. *Archaeological Monitoring Plan for the Exterior Staircase Addition to the Convent Building at the Sacred Hearts Roman Catholic Property at 712 Waineʻe Street, Paunau Ahupuaʻa, Lahaina District, Island of Maui TMK: (2) 4-6-10:001 (por.).* Honolulu, HI: Scientific Consultant Services, Inc., 2007. [SHPD ID: 2019LI81541]

[K]

Kaschko, Michael W. *Archaeological Survey of the Honolua Development Area, Maui.* Department of Anthropology, Honolulu, HI: Bernice P. Bishop Museum, 1973. [SHPD ID: 2019LI81019]

Kaschko, Michael W. *Archaeological Walk-Through Survey of Specified Areas in the Wailuku Flood Prevention Project and the Honolua Watershed, Maui.* Honolulu, HI: Department of Anthropology, Bernice P. Bishop Museum, 1974. [SHPD ID: 2019LI81443]

Kawachi, Carol. *Archaeological Monitoring Plan for Phase 1 of the Proposed Lahaina Watershed Flood Control Project Including Conservation District Use Application MA-3204 Board Permit, Polanui Ahupuaʻa, Lahaina District, Maui, Island TMK: (2) 4-8-01: por. 002, 018, 2005.* [SHPD ID: 2019LI81601]

Keau, Charles. *Archaeological Reconnaissance (Surface Survey) for Hanakaʻōʻō (Hahakea) Beach Park. Includes cover letter: An Archaeological Reconnaissance of*

Hahakea Beach Park, Hanakaʻōʻō, Maui. TMK: 4-4-06:33 by Earl Neller. State Historic Preservation Office, March 1982. [SHPD ID: 2019LI81272; UH Call Number: DU629.H364 K43 1981]

Kehajit, Chonnikarn and Michael F. Dega. *Archaeological Assessment for shoreline mitigation at the Hyatt Regency Maui Resort, Hanakaʻōʻō Ahupuaʻa, Lahaina District, Island of Maui, Hawaiʻi.* Honolulu, HI: Scientific Consultant Services, Inc., 2018. [No location available]

Kehajit, Chonnikarn and Michael F. Dega. *Archaeological Monitoring Plan for 1191 Front Street Replacement of an Existing Water Supply Project, Lahaina, Wahikuli Ahupuaʻa, Lahaina District, Island of Maui, Hawaiʻi.* Honolulu, HI: Scientific Consultant Services, Inc., 2018. [SHPD ID: 2022LI00191]

Kennedy, Joseph. *Archaeological Inventory Survey and Subsurface Testing Report for a Property Located at TMK: 4-3-03:108 and 110, ʻAlaeloa Ahupuaʻa, Lahaina District, on the Island of Maui,* 1992. [SHPD ID: 2022LI00219]

Kennedy, Joseph. *Archaeological Inventory Survey and Subsurface Testing Report for TMK: (2) 4-3-01:031, Located at Kahana Ahupuaʻa, Island of Maui,* Revised May 1992, 1992. [SHPD ID: 2019LI81051]

Kennedy, Joseph. *Archaeological Inventory Survey of Kahana, Maui.* Haleʻiwa, HI: Archaeological Consultants of Hawaii, 1985. [No location available]

Kennedy, Joseph. *Archaeological Inventory Survey of TMK (2) 4-3-02:068 & 069, Located at Napili, Island of Maui.* Haleʻiwa, HI: Archaeological Consultants of Hawaii, 1990. [SHPD ID: 2019LI81061]

Kennedy, Joseph. *Archaeological Inventory Survey Report for TMK (2) 4-3-01:31, located at Kahana, Island of Maui.* Haleʻiwa, HI: Archaeological Consultants of Hawaii, 1991. [SHPD ID: 2019LI81069]

Kennedy, Joseph. *Archaeological Inventory Survey Report for TMK: (2) 4-3-01:031; Located at Kahana, Island of Maui.* 1990. [SHPD ID: 2019LI81054]

Kennedy, Joseph. *Archaeological Investigations at Kahana, Maui,* 1986. [No location available]

Kennedy, Joseph. *Archaeological Report Concerning Subsurface Testing at TMK: (2) 4-6-08:012, Lahaina Maui.* Haleʻiwa, HI: Archaeological Consultants of Hawaii, 1989. [SHPD ID: 2019LI81544]

Kennedy, Joseph. *Archaeological Walk Through Examination of Quarry Site located Mauka of Honoapiʻilani Highway near Lipoa Point, Honolua, Maui.* Haleʻiwa, HI: Archaeological Consultants of Hawaii, 1988. [SHPD ID: 2019LI81425]

Kennedy, Joseph. *Archaeological Walk Through Reconnaissance of (2)4-3-01:001 Napili Fire Station, TMK (2) 4-3-01:001 (por.)*, 1989. [SHPD ID: 2019LI81054]

Kennedy, Joseph. *Field Inspection: Stone Building at Kahana,* Maui, 1986. [SHPD ID: 2019LI81332]

Kennedy, Joseph. *Hawea Point Residential Project: Archaeological Review, Survey, and Assessments.* Haleʻiwa, HI: Archaeological Consultants of Hawaii, 1990. [SHPD ID: 2019LI81416]

Kennedy, Joseph and Tim Denham. *Archaeological Inventory Survey and Subsurface Testing Report for TMK(2) 4-3-01:031, located at Kahana Ahupuaʻa, Maui.* Haleʻiwa, HI: Archaeological Consultants of Hawaii, 1992.

Kirch, Patrick V. *Archaeological Excavations at Site D13-1, Hawea Point, Maui, Hawaiian Islands.* Honolulu, HI: Department of Anthropology, Bernice P. Bishop Museum, 1973. [SHPD ID: 2019LI81021; UH Call Number: DU629. H393 K57 1973]

Kirch, Patrick V. *Archaeological Survey of the Honolua Development Area, Maui.* Honolulu, HI: Department of Anthropology, Bernice P. Bishop Museum, 1973. [SHPD ID: 2019LI81019; UH Call Number: DU629.K374 K57 1973]

Kirkendall, Melissa, Kimberly M. Mooney, Elizabeth L. Kahahane, and Paul L. Cleghorn. *Archaeological Monitoring Plan for the Lahaina Pier Improvement Project, Waineʻe Ahupuaʻa, Lahaina District, Island of Maui [TMK: (2) 4-6-01:001].* Kailua, HI: Pacific Legacy, Inc., 2010. [No location available]

Klieger, Paul Christiaan and Lonnie Somer. *Emergency Mitigation at Maluʻulu o Lele Park, Lahaina, Maui, Hawaiʻi, Site of Mokuʻula, Residence of King Kamehameha III (Site 50-50-03-2967; TMK (2) 4-6-7 Parcel 002: BPBM 50-MA-D5-12).* Honolulu, HI: Department of Anthropology, Bernice P. Bishop Museum, 1989. [SHPD ID: 2019LI81550]

Klieger, Paul Christiaan and Susan A. Lebo. *Archaeological Inventory Survey of Waiōlaʻi and Waiokila Catchments, Kahakuloa, West Maui, Hawaiʻi.* Honolulu, HI: Department of Anthropology, Bernice P. Bishop Museum, 1995. [No location available]

Knecht, Daniel P. and Timothy M. Rieth. *Archaeological Monitoring Plan for the Lahainaluna High School New Classroom Building Project, Panaʻewa Ahupuaʻa, Lahaina District, Maui.* Honolulu, HI: International Archaeology, LLC. [No location available]

Komori, Eric K. *Archaeological Investigations at Kahana Gulch, Lahaina District, Maui.* Honolulu, HI: Department of Anthropology, Bernice P. Bishop Museum, 1983. [SHPD ID: 2019LI81070; UH Call Number: DU629.K343 K66 1983]

Kurashina, Hiro and Aki Sinoto. *Archaeological Reconnaissance of the Proposed Shopping Center at Lahaina, Maui, Hawaiʻi, TMK: (2) 4-5-02:009.* Honolulu, HI: Department of Anthropology, Bernice P. Bishop Museum, 1984. [SHPD ID: 2019LI80648; UH Call Number: DU629.L3 K87 1984]

[L]

Ladd, Edmund J. *Archaeological Survey Report,* 1980. [No location available]

Lash, Erik and Michael F. Dega. *An Archaeological Monitoring Plan for the Proposed Lahaina Harbor Complete Streets Project on Approximately 3.11 Acres (1.26 Hectares) in Lahaina, Paunau Ahupuaʻa, Lahaina District, Island of Maui, Hawaiʻi [TMK (2) 4-6-001:001, 004, 007, 009, 010, 012, and Adjacent Roadways].* Honolulu, HI: Scientific Consultant Services, Inc., 2017. [SHPD ID: 2019LI81388]

Launiupoko Associates, LLC. *Archaeological Preservation Plan, Mahanalua Nui Subdivision.* Launiupoko Associates, 1998. [SHPD ID: 2019LI81602]

Lee and Michael F. Dega. *An Archaeological Assessment for a New Wastewater System at the Olowalu Plantation Manager's House in Olowalu, Olowalu Ahupuaʻa, Lahaina District, Island of Maui, Hawaiʻi [TMK: (2) 4-8-03:005 por.].* Honolulu, HI: Scientific Consultant Services, Inc., 2021. [SHPD ID: 2021LI00436]

Lee-Greig, Tanya, Constance OʻHare, Hallett H. Hammatt, Robert R. Hill, and Colleen Dagan. *Archaeological Data Recovery and Additional Testing at Land Commission Award 310: Pikaneleʻs Kuleana at Pakala, Pakala Ahupuaʻa, Lahaina District, Maui Island.* Wailuku, HI: Cultural Surveys Hawaiʻi, Inc., 2010. [SHPD ID: 2019LI81573]

Lee-Greig, Tanya, Robert Hill, and Hallett H. Hammatt. *An Archaeological Inventory Survey Report for the Lahaina Bypass Modified Alignment from Kahoma Stream to the Keawe Street Extension, Kelawea, Paeohi, and Wahikuli Ahupuaʻa, Lahaina District, Maui Island TMK (2) 4-5-021, 010, 015, and 031: Multiple Parcels.* Wailuku, HI: Cultural Surveys Hawaiʻi, Inc., 2008. [SHPD ID: 2019LI81368]

Lee-Greig, Tanya L. *Archaeological Monitoring Plan for the Traffic Signal Improvements at Pāpalaua Street/Waineʻe Street Intersection, Federal Aid Project No. STP-3020 (001) Aki and Uhao Ahupuaʻa (Paunau Modern Ahupuaʻa), Lahaina Moku* and Modern Tax District, Mokupuni of Maui [TMK: (2) 4-5-002:999 ROW, 4-5-006:999 ROW, 4-5-006:004, and 4-5-006:015]. Honolulu, HI: Aina Archaeology, 2023. [SHPD ID: 2023LI00149].

Lee-Greig, Tanya L. and Hallett H. Hammatt. *Addendum to An Archaeological Treatment Plan for no Adverse Effect the Honoapi'ilani Highway Realignment—Lahaina Bypass Section, Phase 1A, Keawe Street Extension to Lahainaluna Road, Pana'ewa Ahupua'a, Lahaina District, Maui Island, TMK (2) 4-5-031: 999 por., (2) 4-5-015:010 por., and (2) 4-5-021:022 por.* Wailuku, HI: Cultural Surveys Hawai'i, Inc., 2007. [SHPD ID: 2019LI81365, 2019LI81340]

Lee-Greig, Tanya L. and Hallett H. Hammatt. *An Archaeological Inventory Level Documentation for an Inadvertent Historic Property Discovery Identified During Pre-Construction Walk Through for the Lahaina Bypass Phase IA, Project: State Inventory of Historic properties 50-50-03-6277 (Lee-Greig et al. 2008).* Wailuku, HI: Cultural Surveys Hawai'i, Inc., 2009. [No location available]

Lee-Greig, Tanya L. and Hallett H. Hammatt. *An Archaeological Monitoring Plan for Whalers Village Renovation and Expansion Project, Hanaka'ō'ō Ahupua'a, Lahaina District, Maui Island.* Wailuku, HI: Cultural Surveys Hawai'i, Inc., 2014. [SHPD ID: 2019LI80675]

Lee-Greig, Tanya L. and Hallett H. Hammatt. *Archaeological Assessment for the Proposed Westin Maui Resort & Spa Master Plan Improvements, Hanaka'ō'ō Ahupua'a, Lahaina District, Island of Maui, TMK (2) 4-4-008:019.* Wailuku, HI: Cultural Surveys Hawai'i, Inc., 2014. [SHPD ID: 2019LI80684]

Lee-Greig, Tanya L. and Hallett H. Hammatt. *Archaeological Inventory Survey Plan for Honoapi'ilani Highway Realignment Phase IA, Future Keawe Street Extension to Lahainaluna Road: Ikena Avenue Alignment with Modified Extension Kelawea, Paeohi, and Wahikuli Ahupua'a, Lahaina District, Maui Island TMK (2) 4-5-021, 010, 015, and 031: Multiple Parcels.* Wailuku, HI: Cultural Surveys Hawai'i, Inc., 2008. [SHPD ID: 2019LI81341]

Lee-Greig, Tanya L. and Hallett H. Hammatt. *Archaeological Inventory Survey Plan for the Proposed Mokuhinia Ecosystem Restoration Project Waiokama and Lower Waine'e Ahupua'a, Lahaina District, Maui Island.* Wailuku, HI: Cultural Surveys Hawai'i, Inc., 2014. [SHPD ID: 2019LI81554]

Lee-Greig, Tanya L. and Hallett H. Hammatt. *Archaeological Monitoring Plan for the Honoapi'ilani Highway Safety Improvements at Kā'anapali Parkway and Halelo Street Hanaka'ō'ō Ahupua'a, Lahaina District, Maui Island [TMK (2) 4-4-006:999 por; 4-4-009:036 por.).* Wailuku, HI: Cultural Surveys Hawai'i, Inc., 2014. [SHPD ID: 2019LI81271]

Lee-Greig, Tanya L. and Hallett H. Hammatt. *Archaeological Monitoring Plan for the Lahaina Bypass Modified Alignment from Kahoma Stream to the Keawe Street Extension, Kelawea, Paeohi, and Wahikuli Ahupuaʻa, Lahaina District, Maui Island.* Wailuku, HI: Cultural Surveys Hawaiʻi, Inc., 2009. [SHPD ID: 2019LI81369]

Lee-Greig, Tanya L. and Hallett H. Hammatt. *Archaeological Monitoring Plan for the Puʻunēnē School and Lahainaluna High School Hawaiʻi Inter-Island DOE Cesspool Project, Island of Maui TMK (2) 4-6-018 and (2) 3-8-006.* Wailuku, HI: Cultural Surveys Hawaiʻi, Inc., 2007. [SHPD ID: 2019LI81526]

Lee-Greig, Tanya L. and Hallett H. Hammatt. *Preservation Plan for Thirty-Three Historic Properties Located in and Adjacent to the Kapalua Mauka Project Area, Honokahua, Nāpili 2 & 3, and Nāpili 4-5 Ahupuaʻa, Lahaina District, Maui Island.* Wailuku, HI: Cultural Surveys Hawaiʻi, Inc., 2005. [SHPD ID: 2019LI80997]

Lee-Greig, Tanya L., Robert Hill, and Hallett H. Hammatt. *An Archaeological Survey Report for the Realignment of a Section of the Honoapiʻilani Highway, Phase IA, Kelawea, Paeohi, and Wahikuli Ahupuaʻa, Lahaina District, Maui Island TMK (2) 4-5-021, 010, 015, and 031: Multiple Parcels.* Wailuku, HI: Cultural Surveys Hawaiʻi, Inc., 2008. [SHPD ID: 2019LI81361]

Liston, Jolie. *Archaeological Monitoring of Trenching Activities at Taco Bell, Lahaina, Maui.* Honolulu, HI: International Archaeological Research Institute, Inc., 1999. [SHPD ID: 2019LI80605]

Lum, Francis. *Amendment to Testing at Kahana Desilting Basin, Holoua [Honolua?] Watershed, Lahaina District, Maui, Hawaiʻi, Francis Lum, Soil Conservation Service.* Soil Conservation Service, 1983. [SHPD ID: 2019LI81058]

Lyman, Kepa and Michael F. Dega. *Addendum—Archaeological Monitoring Plan for Lahaina Wastewater Pump Station No. 1 Improvements Honokōwai Ahupuaʻa, Lahaina District, Maui Island, Hawaiʻi [TMK (2) 4-4-002:33 and portions of 29 & 39].* Honolulu, HI: Scientific Consultant Services, Inc., 2018. [No location available]

Lyman, Kepa and Michael F. Dega. *Archaeological Monitoring Plan for the Hanakaʻōʻō Beach Park Parking Improvements, Hanakaʻōʻō Ahupuaʻa, Lahaina (Kāʻanapali) District, Island of Maui.* Honolulu, HI: Scientific Consultant Services, Inc., 2020. [SHPD ID: 2021LI00062]

[M]

Madeus, Jonas K. and Hallett H. Hammatt. *An Archaeological Monitoring Plan for the Proposed Hololani Resort Condominiums Shoreline Protection Project in*

Kahananui Ahupuaʻa, Lahaina District, Maui Island TMK: (2) 4-3-010:009 por. Wailuku, HI: Cultural Surveys Hawaiʻi, Inc., 2014. [SHPD ID: 2019LI81312]

Madeus, Jonas K. et al. *Archaeological Inventory Survey for the Villages of Leia-liʻi, Phase 1-B Subdivision and Related Improvements Project, Wahikuli Ahupuaʻa, Lahaina District, Maui Island, TMKs: (2) 4-5-021:010 por., 014 por., 020, and 021 por.; (2) 4-5-36:109, 110, and 112; and Honoapiʻilani Highway Right-of-Way.* Wailuku, HI: Cultural Surveys Hawaiʻi, Inc., 2022. [SHPD ID: 2022LI00589]

Madeus, Jonas K., Josephine M. Yucha, and Hallett H. Hammatt. *Archaeological Monitoring Report for Improvements at Feast of Lele, Waiokama Ahupuaʻa, Lahaina District, Maui Island, TMK (2) 4-6-002:007 (por.).* Wailuku, HI: Cultural Surveys Hawaiʻi, Inc., 2018. [No location available]

Madeus, Jonas K., Tanya L. Lee-Greig, and Hallett H. Hammatt. *Archaeological Assessment of an 80-Acre Parcel in Kapalua, Honolua Ahupuaʻa, Lahaina District, Maui Island.* Wailuku, HI: Cultural Surveys Hawaiʻi, Inc., 2005. [SHPD ID: 2019LI80999]

Madeus, Jonas K., Tanya Lee-Greig, and Hallett H. Hammatt. *An Archaeological Monitoring Report for the Lahaina Bypass Modified Alignment from the Lahainaluna Road Intersection to the Keawe Street Extension Kelawea, Paeohi, and Wahikuli Ahupuaʻa, Lahaina District, Maui Island TMK (2) 4-5-021, 010, 015, and 031: Multiple Parcels.* Wailuku, HI: Cultural Surveys Hawaiʻi, Inc., 2010. [SHPD ID: 2019LI81338]

Magnuson, Carol M. *Supplemental Archaeological Survey of Turbine Pad Alignments, Kaheawa Pastures, Upland Ukumehame Ahupuaʻa, Maui.* Honolulu, HI: International Archaeological Research Institute, Inc., 2003. [SHPD ID: 2019LI81630]

Major, Maurice. *Ridgetops and Gulch Bottoms: An Archaeological Inventory Survey of Waiōlaʻi and Waiokila Catchments, Kahakuloa, West Maui, Hawaiʻi. TMK (2) 3-1-01:003.* Honolulu, HI: Department of Anthropology, Bernice P. Bishop Museum, 1996. [SHPD ID: 2019LI80145]

Major, Maurice and P. Christiaan Klieger. *Historical Background and Archaeological Testing at Pikaneleʻs Kuleana in Lahaina, Maui: An Inventory Survey Report of LCA 310.3 (Royal Patent 1729.2, TMK (2) 4-6-07:013).* Honolulu, HI: Department of Anthropology, Bernice P. Bishop Museum, 1995. [SHPD ID: 2019LI81546; UH Call Number: DU629.L3 M36 1996]

Major, Maurice, P. Christiaan Klieger, and Susan A. Lebo. *Historical Background and Archaeological Testing at Pikaneleʻs Kuleana in Lahaina, Maui: An Inventory Survey Report of LCA 310.3 (Royal Patent 1729.2, TMK (2) 4-6-07:013.* Honolulu,

HI: Department of Anthropology, Bernice P. Bishop Museum, 1996. [SHPD ID: 2019LI81546]

Mason Architects, Inc. *Reconnaissance Level Survey, Honokōwai Reservoir for the West Maui Recycled Water and Kāʻanapali Resort R-1 Water Distribution Expansion Project. TMK (2) 4-4-02:019.* Honolulu, HI: Mason Architects, Inc., 2022. [SHPD ID: 2023LI00017]

Masterson, Ian and Hallett H. Hammatt. *An Addendum Report for the New Alignment Section between Points 14D, 15, and 16 along the Proposed Maʻalaea-Lahaina Third 69 kV Transmission Line, Maui.* Wailuku, HI: Cultural Surveys Hawaiʻi, Inc., 1995. [SHPD ID: 2019LI81633]

Masterson, Ian and Hallett H. Hammatt. *Report on the Completed Reconstruction of Walls at Hikiʻi Heiau Ukumehame Ahupuaʻa, Island of Maui.* Wailuku, HI: Cultural Surveys Hawaiʻi, Inc., 1999. [SHPD ID: 2019LI81631]

McCurdy, Todd D. and Hallett H. Hammatt. *Addendum Report for Archaeological Inventory Survey Documentation of Inadvertent Finds Identified during the Honoapiʻilani Highway Realignment (Lahaina Bypass) Phase 1B-1, Paunau Ahupuaʻa to Polanui Ahupuaʻa, Lahaina District, Maui Island TMK (2) 4-6-014:001, 002: (2) 4-6-018:002, 003; (2) 4-8-001:002 and (2) 4-8-003:001.* Wailuku, HI: Cultural Surveys Hawaiʻi, Inc., 2010. [SHPD ID: 2019LI81537]

McCurdy, Todd D. and Hallett H. Hammatt. *An Archaeological Monitoring Plan for the Honoapiʻilani Highway Realignment (Lahaina Bypass), Phase 1B-1, Paunau Ahupuaʻa to Polanui Ahupuaʻa, Lahaina District, Maui Island TMK: (2) 4-6-014:001-002, 4-6-018:002-003, 4-7-001:002 and 4-7-003:001.* Wailuku, HI: Cultural Surveys Hawaiʻi, Inc., 2010. [SHPD ID: 2019LI81539]

McCurdy, Todd D. and Hallett H. Hammatt. *Archaeological Inventory Survey Documentation of Inadvertent Finds Identified during the Honoapiʻilani Highway Realignment (Lahaina Bypass) Phase 1B-1, Paunau Ahupuaʻa to Polanui Ahupuaʻa, Lahaina District, Maui Island TMK: (2) 4-6-014:001, 002; (2) 4-6-018:002, 003; (2) 4-8-001:002 and (2) 4-7-003:001.* Wailuku, HI: Cultural Surveys Hawaiʻi, Inc., 2009. [SHPD ID: 2019LI81536]

McCurdy, Todd D. and Hallett H. Hammatt. *Archaeological Literature Review and Field Inspection for Honoapiʻilani Highway Realignment (Lahaina Bypass), Phase 1B-1, Paunau Ahupuaʻa to Polanui Ahupuaʻa, Lahaina District, Maui Island TMK (2) 4-6-014:001-002, 4-6-018:002-003, 4-8-001:002 and 4-7-003:001.* Wailuku, HI: Cultural Surveys Hawaiʻi, Inc., 2008. [SHPD ID: 2019LI81538]

McGerty, Leann and Robert L. Spear. *A Cultural Impact Assessment for a Portion of the Mauian Hotel Property, Nāpili Ahupuaʻa, Lahaina District, Maui Island,*

Hawai'i. Honolulu, HI: Scientific Consultant Services, Inc., 2007. [SHPD ID: 2019LI81065]

McGerty, Leann and Robert L. Spear. *A Cultural Impact Assessment for Maui Marriott Ocean Club, Situated in the Ahupua'a of Hanaka'ō'ō, Lahaina District, Island of Maui, Hawai'i.* Honolulu, HI: Scientific Consultant Services, Inc., 2002. [SHPD ID: 2019LI80664]

McGerty, Leann and Robert L. Spear. *A Cultural Impact Assessment of Approximately 0.8 Acres of Land in Olowalu Ahupua'a, Wailuku District, Maui, Hawai'i [TMK (2) 4-9-003:45A].* Honolulu, HI: Scientific Consultant Services, Inc., 2006. [SHPD ID: 2019LI81636]

McGerty, Leann and Robert L. Spear. *A Cultural Impact Assessment of Wastewater Pump Station No. 1 in Honokōwai Ahupua'a, Kā'anapali, Lahaina District, Maui Island, Hawai'i [TMK: (2) 4-4-02:003, (2) 4-4-02:029].* Honolulu, HI: Scientific Consultant Services, Inc., 2010. [SHPD ID: 2019LI81254]

McGerty, Leann and Robert L. Spear. *A Cultural Impact Assessment on a Piece of Property Located in Kā'anapali, Hanaka'ō'ō Ahupua'a, Lahaina District, Maui Island, Hawai'i [TMK: (2) 4-4-06:056].* Scientific Consultant Services, Inc.: Honolulu, HI, 2003. [SHPD ID: 2019LI81266]

McGerty, Leann and Robert L. Spear. *An Archaeological Inventory Survey at the Maui Marriott Ocean Club, in the Ahupua'a of Hanaka'ō'ō, Lahaina District, Island of Maui, Hawai'i.* Honolulu, HI: Scientific Consultant Services, Inc., 2002. [SHPD ID: 2019LI80107]

McGerty, Leann and Robert L. Spear. *An Inventory Survey of a 3.3 Acre Parcel in Māhinahina 4 Ahupua'a, Lahaina District, Island of Maui, Hawai'i [TMK (2) 4-3-06:003],* 1996. [SHPD ID: 2019LI81305]

McGerty, Leann and Robert L. Spear. *Cultural Impact Assessment on Two Parcels Incorporating the Royal Lahaina Hotel in Kā'anapali, Hanaka'ō'ō Ahupua'a, Lahaina District, Maui Island, Hawai'i.* Honolulu, HI: Scientific Consultant Services, Inc., 2005. [SHPD ID: 2019LI80678]

McGerty, Leanne and Robert L. Spear. *Cultural Impact Assessment of a Parcel of Land in Lahaina Town, Alio Ahupua'a, Lahaina District, Maui Island, Hawai'i.* Honolulu, HI: Scientific Consultant Services, Inc., 2007. [SHPD ID: 2019LI81360]

Medeiros, Colleen and Hallett H. Hammatt. *Archaeological Monitoring Report for the Kā'anapali North Beach Development Area, Lot 3, Site Excavation,*

Honokōwai Ahupuaʻa, Lahaina District, Maui Island. Wailuku, HI: Cultural Surveys Hawaiʻi, Inc., 2017. [SHPD ID: 2019LI80652]

Medrano, Stephanie and Michael F. Dega. *An Archaeological Assessment for a 1.02-Acre Project Area in Lahaina, Kuʻia Ahupuaʻa, Lahaina District, Island of Maui, Hawaiʻi [TMK: (2) 4-6-009:036, 038, & 044].* Honolulu, HI: Scientific Consultant Services, Inc., 2013. [SHPD ID: 2019LI81581]

Monahan, Christopher M. *An Archaeological Assessment Report on 17.746 Acres of Land (Lahaina Business Park, Phase II) on an Undeveloped Lot in Lahaina, Moaliʻi Ahupuaʻa, Lahaina District, Maui Island, Hawaiʻi [TMK: (2) 4-5-10:007].* Honolulu, HI: Scientific Consultant Services, Inc., 2003. [SHPD ID: 2019LI80604]

Monahan, Christopher M. *An Archaeological Assessment Report on 3.054 Acres of Partially Developed Land in Honokōwai, Māhinahina 4 Ahupuaʻa, Lahaina District, Maui Island, Hawaiʻi [TMK (2) 4-3-06:002 and 069].* Honolulu, HI: Scientific Consultant Services, Inc., 2003. [SHPD ID: 2019LI81314, 2019LI81304]

Monahan, Christopher M. *An Archaeological Inventory Survey Report on Three Contiguous Parcels Measuring Approximately 25.3 Acres in Kapalua, Napili 2-3 Ahupuaʻa, Lahaina District, Maui Island, Hawaiʻi.* Honolulu, HI: Scientific Consultant Services, Inc., 2005. [SHPD ID: 2019LI81018]

Monahan, Christopher M., Lauren Morawski, and Michael F. Dega. *Archaeological Monitoring Plan for Pool Installation at TMK (2) 4-5-04:037 Lahilahi Street, Kuʻia Ahupuaʻa, Lahaina District, Island of Maui.* Honolulu, HI: Scientific Consultant Services, Inc., 2003. [No location available]

Mooney, Kimberly M. and Paul L. Cleghorn. *Archaeological Monitoring Report for the Lahaina Small Boat Harbor Comfort Station Improvements, Lahaina, Maui.* Kailua, HI: Pacific Legacy, Inc., 2007. [SHPD ID: 2019LI81379]

Mooney, Kimberly M., Paul L. Cleghorn, and Elizabeth L. Kahahane. *Archaeological Inventory Survey for the Lahaina Pier Improvement Project Waineʻe Ahupuaʻa, Lahaina District, Island of Maui.* Kailua, HI: Pacific Legacy, Inc., 2008. [SHPD ID: 2019LI81382]

Moore, James R. and Joseph Kennedy. *An Archaeological Inventory Survey with Subsurface Testing Report for Portions of the Proposed Kahana Ridge Subdivision Located at TMK: (2) 4-3-05:016 & 018, in Kahana Ahupuaʻa, Lahaina District, Island of Maui.* Haleʻiwa, HI: Archaeological Consultants of Hawaii, 1994. [SHPD ID: 2019LI81329]

Moore, Kenneth R. *Archaeological Survey of Honolua Valley, Maui.* Honolulu, HI: Department of Anthropology, Bernice P. Bishop Museum, 1974. [SHPD ID: 2019LI81436; UH Call Number: DU629.H69 M66 1974]

Morawski, Lauren and Michael F. Dega. *Archaeological Inventory Survey of a 7.65 Acre Property at Lot 10-H Ahupuaʻa of Hanakaʻōʻō, Lahaina District, Island of Maui, Hawaiʻi [TMK: (2) 4-4-06:056].* Honolulu, HI: Scientific Consultant Services, Inc., 2003. [SHPD ID: 2019LI81273]

Morawski, Lauren and Michael F. Dega. *Archaeological Inventory Survey Report of an Approximate 10-Acre Parcel in Kapalua in the Ahupuaʻa of Honokahua, Lahaina District (Formerly Kāʻanapali), Island of Maui, Hawaiʻi.* Honolulu, HI: Scientific Consultant Services, Inc., 2004. [SHPD ID: 2019LI81017]

Morawski, Lauren, Adam Johnson, Tomasi Patolo, and Michael F. Dega. *An Archaeological Inventory Survey of 520 Acres in the Launiupoko (Large Lot) Subdivision No. 1, Launiupoko Ahupuaʻa, Lahaina District (formerly Kāʻanapali), Island of Maui, Hawaiʻi [TMK (2) 4-7-01:002 por.].* Honolulu, HI: Scientific Consultant Services, Inc., 2008. [SHPD ID: 2019LI81603]

Mulrooney et al. *Archaeological Inventory Survey Report for the Kahana Solar Project in Ahupuaʻa of Kahana and Māhinahina 1-3, Moku of Kāʻanapali (Lahaina Modern Tax District), Island of Maui [TMK: (2) 4-3-01:017 por.; (2) 4-3-01:082 por.; (2) 4-3-01:084 por.].* Kailua, HI: Pacific Legacy, Inc., 2022

Munekiyo & Hiraga, Inc. *Historic Resources Inventory Submittal, Makaʻoiʻoi Demolition.* Wailuku, HI: Munekiyo & Hiraga, Inc., 2003. [SHPD ID: 2019LI81049]

Munekiyo & Hiraga, Inc. *Makaʻoiʻoi (Honolua Plantation Managers Residence, Pineapple Hill Restaurant), Historical Report.* Wailuku, HI: Munekiyo & Hiraga, Inc., 2003. [SHPD ID: 2019LI81022]

Munekiyo, Michael T. *Redevelopment of ABC Store at 726 Front Street, Application for Historic District Approval.* Wailuku, HI: Michael T. Munekiyo Consulting, Inc., 1993. [SHPD ID: 2019LI81540]

[N]

Nagata, Ralston H. *CDUA-MA-5/12/82-1407, Land Clearing and Planting of Commercially Valuable Tree Species at Kahakuloa, Wailuku, Maui. Memorandum to: Roger Evans, Planning Office from DLNR, Division of State Parks,* 1983. [No location available]

Nagata, Ralston H. and Martha Yent. *CDUA: MA-1436, Taro Planting at Kahakuloa Valley, Wailuku, Maui. Memorandum to Mr. Roger Evans, Planning Office from DLNR, Division of State Parks,* 1982. [UH Call Number: DU629. K344 N34 1982]

Neller, Earl. *An Archaeological Reconnaissance Along the Coast at Ukumehame, Maui,* 1982. [SHPD ID: 2019LI81640; UH Call Number: DU629.U38 N45 1982]

Neller, Earl. *An Archaeological Reconnaissance of Hahakea Beach Park, Hanaka'ō'ō, Maui.* Honolulu, HI: State of Hawai'i Preservation Office, 1982. [SHPD ID: 2019LI81272; UH Call Number: DU629.H364 N45 1982]

[O]

O'Claray, Jenny. *Additional Field Work for Drainage 11 Kapalua Plantation Estates Project Area, Lands of Honokahua, Honolua, Napili 2-2 Lahaina District, Island of Maui.* Hilo, HI: Paul H. Rosendahl, Ph.D., Inc., 1991. [SHPD ID: 2019LI81415]

O'Day, Patrick and David Byerly. *Archaeological Inventory Survey of Proposed Fenceline Corridor for the West Maui Forest Reserve, Ku'ia, Mākila, Pāhoa, Halaka'a, Polaiki, Launiupoko, and Olowalu Ahupua'a, Lahaina District, Maui Island, Hawai'i.* Kailua, HI: Garcia & Associates, 2015. [SHPD ID: 2019LI81533]

O'Hare, Constance, Thomas K. Devereux, William H. Folk, and Hallett H. Hammatt. *Preservation Plan for Specific Sites in the Land Comprising Project District 2 at Kapalua, Honokahua and Nāpili 2 & 3 Ahupua'a Lahaina District of Maui.* Wailuku, HI: Cultural Surveys Hawai'i, Inc., 2003. [SHPD ID: 2019LI81002]

Oceanit. *Final Sampling Analysis Plan: Field Sampling and Quality Assurance Plans for the Mokuhinia Pond Site Investigation, Lahaina, Maui, Hawai'i.* Honolulu, HI: Oceanit, 2009. [SHPD ID: 2019LI81553]

Ogg, Randy and Michael F. Dega. *An Archaeological Assessment of Lahaina Wastewater Pump Station No. 1 Improvements, Honokōwai Ahupua'a, Lahaina District, Maui Island, Hawai'i [TMK: (2) 4-4-02:003 & (2) 4-4-02:029].* Honolulu, HI: Scientific Consultant Services, Inc., 2007. [SHPD ID: 2019LI81279]

Olowalu Elua Associates, LLC. *Archaeological Mitigation and Preservation Plan, Makai Portion (Phase 1), Olowalu Ahupua'a, Lahaina District, Maui Island.* Olowalu, HI: Olowalu Elua Associates, LLC, 2001.

Olowalu Elua Associates, LLC. *Archaeological Preservation Plan, Mauka Portion (Phase 2), Olowalu Ahupua'a, Lahaina District, Maui Island.* Olowalu, HI: Olowalu Elua Associates, LLC, 2002. [SHPD ID: 2019LI00099]

Olowalu Elua Associates, LLC. *Monitoring Plan for Sites 50-50-08-4820 and 50-50-08-4821; Olowalu Ahupuaʻa, Lahaina District; Island of Maui [TMK (2) 4-8-003: portion of 10].* Olowalu, HI: Olowalu Elua Associates, LLC, 2002. [No location available]

Olson, Larry G. *Appendix II—A Geoarchaeological Report of Site 225, Māhinahina Gulch, Maui, Hawaiʻi.* Lāwaʻi, HI: Archaeological Research Center Hawaiʻi, 1977. [No location available]

[P]

Pacheco, Robert. *A Cultural Impact Assessment for the Proposed Kāʻanapali Beach Restoration Project, Hanakaʻōʻō Ahupuaʻa, Lahaina District, Island of Maui, Hawaiʻi TMK (2) 4-4-008:001, 002, 003, 004, 005, 019, 022; 4-4-013:001, 002, 006, 007, 008.* Honolulu, HI: International Archaeology, LLC, 2006. [SHPD ID: 2019LI80681]

Pacheco, Robert. *An Archaeological Literature Review for the Proposed Kāʻanapali Beach Restoration Project, Hanakaʻōʻō Ahupuaʻa, Lahaina District, Island of Maui, Hawaiʻi TMK (2) 4-4-008:001, 002, 003, 004, 005, 019, 022; 4-4-013:001, 002, 006, 007, 008.* Honolulu, HI: International Archaeology, LLC, 2015. [SHPD ID: 2019LI81260]

Pantaleo, Jeffrey. *Archaeological Inventory Report of a 1.65-Acre Parcel of Land Pūehuehue Iki Ahupuaʻa, Lahaina District, Island of Maui TMK (2) 4-7-04:001.* Wailuku, HI: Archaeological Services Hawaii, LLC, 2006. [SHPD ID: 2019LI81615]

Pantaleo, Jeffrey. *Archaeological Monitoring Plan Phase 2 of the Proposed Lahaina Watershed Flood Control Project, Polanui and Pāhoa Ahupuaʻa, Lahaina District, Maui Island [TMK (2) 4-8-001:por. 02; 4-7-02:por. 4, 5, 7],* 1991. [No location available]

Pantaleo, Jeffrey. *Archaeological Survey of the Proposed Lahainaluna Reservoir and Treatment Facility, Lahaina, Maui.* Honolulu, HI: Public Archaeology Section, Applied Research Group, Bernice P. Bishop Museum, 1991. [SHPD ID: 2019LI81530]

Pantaleo, Jeffrey and Paul Titchenal. *An Archaeological Inventory Survey Report for the Pulelehua Community Project TMK (2) 4-3-01:031 Por. Māhinahina 1, 2, 3, Māhinahina 4, and Kahana Ahupuaʻa, Lahaina and Kāʻanapali Districts, Island of Maui.* Wailuku, HI: Archaeological Services Hawaii, LLC, 2004. [SHPD ID: 2019LI81072]

Paraso, C. Kanani and Michael F. Dega. *An Archaeological Assessment of three parcels at the Hyatt Regency Maui Resort, Kāʻanapali, Hanakaʻōʻō Ahupuaʻa, Lahaina District, Maui Island, Hawaiʻi [TMK (2) 4-4-013:004, 005, 008];* Honolulu, HI: Scientific Consultant Services, Inc., 2006. [SHPD ID: 2019LI80041]

Paraso, C. Kanani and Michael F. Dega. *An Archaeological Inventory Survey of 633 Acres in the Launiupoko (Large Lot) Subdivision Nos. 3, 4, and 7, Launiupoko and Polanui Ahupuaʻa, Lahaina District (formerly Kāʻanapali), Island of Maui, Hawaiʻi [TMK (2) 4-8-01:2 por.].* Honolulu, HI: Scientific Consultant Services, Inc., 2006. [SHPD ID: 2019LI81600]

Perzinski, David. *Archaeological Field Inspection for the West Maui Recycled Water Expansion Project, Phase 2 County Job No. WW12-13, Lahaina, Maui, Hawaiʻi.* Honolulu, HI: Scientific Consultant Services, Inc., 2013. [No location available]

Perzinski, David and Michael F. Dega. *An Archaeological Assessment of a Seawall/ Revetment Structure in Honokōwai.* Honolulu, HI: Scientific Consultant Services, Inc., 2013. [SHPD ID: 2019LI81283]

Perzinski, David and Michael F. Dega. *An Archaeological Inventory Survey of Three Contiguous Parcels of Land Totaling 0.417 Acres in Waineʻe Ahupuaʻa, Lahaina District, Maui Island, Hawaiʻi.* Honolulu, HI: Scientific Consultant Services, Inc., 2011. [SHPD ID: 2019LI81543]

Perzinski, David and Michael F. Dega. *An Archaeological Inventory Survey Report for a Bridge Replacement in Honolua, Honolua Ahupuaʻa, Lahaina District, Maui Island.* Honolulu, HI: Scientific Consultant Services, Inc., 2010. [SHPD ID: 2019LI81430]

Perzinski, David and Michael F. Dega. *An Archaeological Monitoring Report for the Installation of Subsurface Utilities in Nāpili, Kapalua, Honokahua Ahupuaʻa, Lahaina District, Island of Maui, Hawaiʻi.* Honolulu, HI: Scientific Consultant Services, Inc., 2015. [SHPD ID: 2019LI81034]

Perzinski, David and Michael F. Dega. *An Archaeological Monitoring Report of the Construction at the Maui Marriott Vacation Club, Hanakaʻōʻō Ahupuaʻa, Lahaina District, Island of Maui, Hawaiʻi.* Honolulu, HI: Scientific Consultant Services, Inc., 2009. [No location available]

Perzinski, David and Michael F. Dega. *Archaeological Assessment for the West Maui Well No. 2 Exploratory, DWS Job No. 11-06, Kahana Ahupuaʻa, Lahaina (Kāʻanapali) District, Maui, Hawaiʻi.* Honolulu, HI: Scientific Consultant Services, Inc., 2014. [SHPD ID: 2019LI81057]

Perzinski, David and Michael F. Dega. *Archaeological Monitoring Report for Lahaina No. 3 Force Main Replacement Project Wahikuli and Hanaka'ō'ō Ahupua'a, Lahaina District, Island of Maui, Hawai'i [TMK (2) 4-4-013].* Honolulu, HI: Scientific Consultant Services, Inc., 2014. [SHPD ID: 2019LI80661]

Pestana, Elizabeth and Michael F. Dega. *Archaeological Inventory Survey of a 5.18 Acre Parcel in Kahana, Kahana Ahupua'a, Kā'anapali District, Island of Maui, Hawai'i [TMK: (2)-4-3-15:069].* Honolulu, HI: Scientific Consultant Services, Inc., 2018. [SHPD ID: 2019LI81301]

Peterson, Charles E. *Notes on the Lahaina Court and Custom House, Lahaina, Maui, Hawai'i, Built 1859,* 1966. [SHPD ID: 2019LI81376]

Pickett, Jenny L. and Michael F. Dega. *An Archaeological Assessment for 16.8 Acres in Lahaina, Mākila Ahupua'a, Lahaina District, Maui Island, Hawai'i [TMK (2) 4-5-10:005 & 006 por.].* Honolulu, HI: Scientific Consultant Services, Inc., 2005. [SHPD ID: 2019LI80600]

Pickett, Jenny L. and Michael F. Dega. *An Archaeological Inventory Survey of 583 Acres at Lipoa Point, Honolua Ahupua'a, Lahaina (Formerly Kā'anapali) District, Maui Island, Hawai'i.* Honolulu, HI: Scientific Consultant Services, Inc., 2006. [SHPD ID: 2019LI81431]

Pietrusewsky, Michael and Michele T. Douglas. *An Analysis of Additional Historic Human Skeletal Remains from the Kahoma Stream Flood Control Project, 1989, Lahaina, Maui.* Honolulu, HI: University of Hawai'i at Mānoa, 1990. [SHPD ID: DU629.L3 P54 1990]

Pietrusewsky, Michael, Michele T. Douglas, and Rona Ikehara. *An Osteological Study of Human Remains from the Kahoma Stream Flood Control Project, Lahaina, Maui.* Honolulu, HI: University of Hawai'i at Mānoa, 1989. [UH Call Number: DU629.K76 P54 1989]

Pietrusewsky, Michael, Michele T. Douglas, Patricia A. Kalima, and Rona M. Ikehara. *Human Skeletal and Dental Remains from the Honokahua Burial Site, Land of Honokahua, Lahaina District, Island of Maui, Hawai'i.* Hilo, HI: Paul H. Rosendahl, Ph.D., Inc., 1991. [Call Number, DU629.H67 H86 1991a]

Pyle, Dorothy. "The Intriguing Seamen's Hospital." *The Hawaiian Journal of History,* vol. 8, 1974, pp. 121–135. [UH Call Number: DU620 .H44]

[R]

Rechtman, Robert B. *Archaeological Monitoring Plan Associated with the Demolition of the Pioneer Mill, TMK (2) 4-5-09:007, Pana'ewa Ahupua'a, Lahaina*

District, Island of Maui. Rechtman Consulting, LLC, 2005. [SHPD ID: 2019LI80603]

Rechtman, Robert B. *Archaeological Monitoring Plan for the Subdivision and Development for the Subdivision and Development of TMK: (2) 4-4-08:016.* Rechtman Consulting, LLC, 2006. [SHPD ID: 2019LI80679]

Rechtman, Robert B. *Archaeological Monitoring Report Associated with the Demolition of the Pioneer Mill, Pana'ewa Ahupua'a, Lahaina District, Island of Maui.* Rechtman Consulting, LLC, 2006. [SHPD ID: 2019LI80602]

Rechtman, Robert B. and Ashton K. Dircks Ah Sam. *An Archaeological Inventory Survey for the Kaheawa Wind Power (KWP) Phase 2 Project Area [TMK: (2) 3-6-001:por. 14 & (2) 4-8-01: Por. 001].* Rechtman Consulting, LLC, 2009. [SHPD ID: 2019LI80301]

Riford, Mary F. and Paul L. Cleghorn. *Documentary Assessment of Archaeological Potential of Ten Prospective Power Plant Sites on Maui.* Honolulu, HI: Public Archaeology Section, Bernice P. Bishop Museum, 1989. [SHPD ID: 2022LI00168]

Rogers, Donnell J. and Paul H. Rosendahl. *Archaeological Survey and Recording Iliilikea and Maiu Heiau on the North Coast of Maui, Land of Honokōhau, Lahaina District, Island of Maui.* Hilo, HI: Paul H. Rosendahl, Ph.D., Inc., 1992. [SHPD ID: 2019LI81440]

Rogers, Scott. *An Archaeological Monitoring Plan for the Kā'anapali—Hyatt Force Main Replacements, Kā'anapali Resort Complex, Hanaka'ō'ō, Honokōwai Ahupua'a, Lahaina District, Island of Maui.* Pukalani, HI: Xamanek Researches, 2007. [SHPD ID: 2019LI80682]

Rosendahl, Margaret L. K. *Archaeological Field Inspection, Sheraton Maui Master Plan Project Area, Lands of Honokōwai and Hanaka'ō'ō, Lahaina District, Island of Maui.* Hilo, HI: Paul H. Rosendahl, Ph.D., Inc., 1986. [No location available]

Rosendahl, Margaret L. K. *Subsurface Archaeological Reconnaissance Survey, North Beach Development Site, Ahupua'a of Hanaka'ō'ō, Lahaina Eistrict, Island of Maui.* Hilo, HI: Paul H. Rosendahl, Ph.D., Inc., 1987. [SHPD ID: 2019LI81244]

Rosendahl, Paul H. *Additional Inventory Survey for Drainage Easement 11 Kapalua Plantation Estates Project Area, Lands of Honokahua, Honolua, and Napili 2-3, Lahaina District, Island of Maui.* Hilo, HI: Paul H. Rosendahl, Ph.D., Inc., 1991. [SHPD ID: 2019LI80996]

Rosendahl, Paul H. *A Plan for Archaeological Monitoring of Shoreline Construction, Kā'anapali North Beach Development Site, Ahupua'a of Hanaka'ō'ō, Lahaina*

District, Island of Maui. Hilo, HI: Paul H. Rosendahl, Ph.D., Inc., 1987. [SHPD ID: 2019LI80659]

Rosendahl, Paul H. *Archaeological Field Inspection Hawea Point Residence Site; Hawea Point, Lands of Napili 2 & 3 Lahaina District, Island of Maui.* Hilo, HI: Paul H. Rosendahl, Ph.D., Inc., 1988. [SHPD ID: 2019LI81001]

Rosendahl, Paul H. *Archaeological Monitoring Plan, Mala Village Subdivision, Land of Puʻunoa, Lahaina District, Island of Maui [TMK: (2) 4-5-04:008, 009, 059, 060, 061, 062].* Hilo, HI: Paul H. Rosendahl, Ph.D., Inc., 2002. [SHPD ID: 2019LI80615]

Rosendahl, Paul H. *Archaeological Reconnaissance Survey, The Cottages Project Area Kapalua Development Site 2-A, Lands of Honokahua and Napili 2 & 3, Lahaina District, Island of Maui.* Hilo, HI: Paul H. Rosendahl, Ph.D., Inc., 1988. [SHPD ID: 2019LI81009]

Rosendahl, Paul H. *Archaeological Treatment Plan for No Adverse Effect, Lahaina Bypass Highway Project, Lands of Honokōwai, Hanakaʻōʻō, Wahikuli, Panaʻewa, Kuʻia, Halakaʻa, Pūehuehu Nui, Pāhoa, Polanui, and Launiupoko, Lahaina District, Island of Maui.* Hilo, HI: Paul H. Rosendahl, Ph.D., Inc., 1994. [SHPD ID: 2019LI81439]

Rosendahl, Paul H. *Phase I Monitoring Plan: Archaeological Mitigation Program, Ritz-Carlton Hotel Project Site, Land of Honokahua, Lahaina District, Island of Maui. PHRI Memo 857-070390.* Hilo, HI: Paul H. Rosendahl, Ph.D., Inc., 1990. [No location available]

Rosendahl, Paul H. *PHRI Status Reports on Honokahua.* Hilo, HI: Paul H. Rosendahl, Ph.D., Inc., 1987. [SHPD ID: 2019LI81004]

Rosendahl, Paul H. *Subsurface Reconnaissance Testing, Kapalua Place Project Area, Kapalua Development Site 2-A, Lands of Honokahua and Napili 2 & 3, Lahaina District, Island of Maui.* Hilo, HI: Paul H. Rosendahl, Ph.D., Inc., 1988. [SHPD ID: 2019LI81000]

Rotunno-Hazuka, Lisa J. *Archaeological Assessment for the Proposed Well Site in Launiupoko, Lahaina, Maui TMK 4-7-02:001 Lot B.* Wailuku, HI: Archaeological Services Hawaii, LLC, 1997. [SHPD ID: 2019LI81617]

Rotunno-Hazuka, Lisa J. and Jeffrey Pantaleo, M.A. *Archaeological Preservation and Monitoring Plan for Site 50-50-03-4096 Feature 1 Located on a Residential Lot, TMK (2) 4-7-01:001 Pūehuehue Iki Ahupuaʻa, Lahaina District: Island of Maui.* Wailuku, HI: Archaeological Services Hawaii, LLC, 2006. [SHPD ID: 2019LI81591]

Rotunno-Hazuka, Lisa J. and Jeffrey Pantaleo. *Archaeological Monitoring Plan for All Ground Disturbing Activities Associated with the Construction of the Waine'e Self Storage Facility located at TMK: (2) 4-5-07:004 Kuholilea Ahupua'a, Lahaina District, Island of Maui.* Wailuku, HI: Archaeological Services Hawaii, LLC, 2006. [SHPD ID: 2019LI80607]

Rotunno-Hazuka, Lisa J. and Jeffrey Pantaleo. *Archaeological Monitoring Plan for All Improvements at the McFarland Residence TMK: (2) 4-5-13:003, Moali'i Ahupua'a Lahaina District, Island of Maui.* Wailuku, HI: Archaeological Ser-vices Hawaii, LLC, 2006. [SHPD ID: 2019LI81352]

Rotunno-Hazuka, Lisa J. and Jeffrey Pantaleo. *Archaeological Monitoring Plan for All Improvements Related to the Proposed Construction of an Ohana and Garage at the Stiebinger Residence, Kau'aula Ahupua'a, Lahaina District, Island of Maui TMK (2) 4-6-06:005.* Wailuku, HI: Archaeological Services Hawaii, LLC, 2005. [SHPD ID: 2019LI81405]

Rotunno-Hazuka, Lisa J. and Jeffrey Pantaleo. *Archaeological Monitoring Plan for All Improvements Related to the Redevelopment of the Royal Lahaina Resort, Hana-ka'ō'ō Ahupua'a; Lahaina District, Island of Maui, TMK:4-4-08:007& 013.* Wailuku, HI: Archaeological Services Hawaii, LLC, 2007. [SHPD ID: 2019LI80677]

Rotunno-Hazuka, Lisa J. and Jeffrey Pantaleo. *Archaeological Monitoring Plan for a Waterline Installation at TMK: (2) 4-5-01:045 Old Lahaina Center, Papalua Street, Pana'ewa Ahupua'a, Lahaina District, Island of Maui.* Wailuku, HI: Archaeological Services Hawaii, LLC, 2002. [SHPD ID: 2019LI80638]

Rotunno-Hazuka, Lisa J. and Jeffrey Pantaleo. *Archaeological Monitoring Plan for Pool Installation at TMK (2) 4-5-04:037 Lahilahi Street, Ku'ia Ahupua'a, Lahaina District, Island of Maui.* Wailuku, HI: Archaeological Services Hawaii, LLC, 2002. [SHPD ID: 2019LI80627]

Rotunno-Hazuka, Lisa J. and Jeffrey Pantaleo. *Archaeological Monitoring Plan for the Construction of an Accessory Dwelling at the Meston Residence at TMK (2) 4-6-07:030 Paunau Ahupua'a, Lahaina District, Island of Maui.* Wailuku, HI: Archaeological Services Hawaii, LLC, 2004. [SHPD ID: 2019LI81551]

Rotunno-Hazuka, Lisa J. and Jeffrey Pantaleo. *Archaeological Monitoring Plan for the Construction of a Swimming Pool and Associated Utilities at the Allan Residence, Lahaina Ahupua'a, Lahaina District, Island of Maui.* Wailuku, HI: Archaeological Services Hawai'i, LLC, 2004. [SHPD ID: 2019LI80623]

Rotunno-Hazuka, Lisa J. and Jeffrey Pantaleo. *Archaeological Monitoring Plan for the Demolition of an Existing Single Family Residence & Pool Cover and Construction of a New Single Family Residence at TMK: (2) 4-5-04:048 Pu'unoa*

Ahupuaʻa, Lahaina District, Island of Maui. Wailuku, HI: Archaeological Services Hawaii, LLC, 2004. [SHPD ID: 2019LI80625]

Rotunno-Hazuka, Lisa J. and Jeffrey Pantaleo. *Archaeological Monitoring Plan for the Demolition of an Existing Single Family Residence and Construction of a new Single Family Residence at TMK (2) 4-5-04:004, Puʻunoa Ahupuaʻa, Lahaina District, Island of Maui.* Wailuku, HI: Archaeological Services Hawaii, LLC, 2004. [SHPD ID: 2019LI80621]

Rotunno-Hazuka, Lisa J. and Jeffrey Pantaleo. *Archaeological Monitoring Plan for the Installation of a Grease Interceptor at TMK: (2) 4-5-02:009 Kelawea Ahupuaʻa, Lahaina District, Island of Maui.* Wailuku, HI: Archaeological Services Hawaii, LLC, 2007. [SHPD ID: 2019LI80646]

Rotunno-Hazuka, Lisa J. and Jeffrey Pantaleo. *Archaeological Monitoring Plan for the Renovation and Revitalization of the Napili Kai Resort, Napili Ahupuaʻa, Lahaina District, Island of Maui.* Wailuku, HI: Archaeological Services Hawaii, LLC, 2005. [SHPD ID: 2019LI81067]

Rotunno-Hazuka, Lisa J. and Jeffrey Pantaleo. *Archaeological Monitoring Plan for the Renovations to the Lahaina-Kaiser Clinic, Panaʻewa Ahupuaʻa, Lahaina District, Island of Maui.* Wailuku, HI: Archaeological Services Hawaii, LLC, 2003. [SHPD ID: 2019LI80608]

Rotunno-Hazuka, Lisa J. and Jeffrey Pantaleo. *Final Archaeological Monitoring Plan for Demolition and New Construction along Front Street, Paunau Ahupuaʻa, Lahaina District, Kula Moku, Island of Maui.* Wailuku, HI: Archaeological Services Hawaii, LLC, 2018. [SHPD ID: 2019LI80633]

Rotunno-Hazuka, Lisa J. and Jeffrey Pantaleo. *Final Archaeological Monitoring Plan for the Installation of a New Water Service and Relocated Power Pole Along Kalena Street Kelawea Ahupuaʻa, Lahaina District, Island of Maui.* Wailuku, HI: Archaeological Services Hawaii, LLC, 2015. [No location available]

Rotunno-Hazuka, Lisa J. and Jeffrey Pantaleo. *Final Archaeological Monitoring Report for All Ground Disturbing Activities Associated with the Development of a Residential Structure Located at TMK (2) 4-05-04:048 Puʻunoa Ahupuaʻa, Lahaina District, Island of Maui.* Wailuku, HI: Archaeological Services Hawaii, LLC, 2008. [SHPD ID: 2019LI80614]

Rotunno-Hazuka, Lisa J. and Jeffrey Pantaleo. *Final Archaeological Monitoring Report for All Ground Disturbing Activities Associated with the Development of a Residential Structure Located at TMK (2) 4-5-04:004, Puʻunoa Ahupuaʻa, Lahaina District, Island of Maui.* Wailuku, HI: Archaeological Services Hawaii, LLC, 2008. [SHPD ID: 2019LI80622]

Rotunno-Hazuka, Lisa J., Mia Watson, and Jeffrey Pantaleo. *Archaeological Monitoring Plan for the Improvements to a Commercial Restaurant Facility at TMK: (2) 4-5-07:034, Kāʻanapali Ahupuaʻa, Lahaina District, Island of Maui.* Wailuku, HI: Archaeological Services Hawaii, LLC, 2010. [SHPD ID: 2019LI80610]

Rotunno-Hazuka, Lisa J., Mia Watson, and Jeffrey Pantaleo. *Archaeological Monitoring Plan for the Repair and Installation of Underground Conduit at Front & Wharf Street, Lahaina and Waineʻe Ahupuaʻa, Lahaina District, Island of Maui.* Wailuku, HI: Archaeological Services Hawaii, LLC, 2008. [SHPD ID: 2019LI81385]

[S]

Scientific Consultant Services, Inc. *An Archaeological Inventory Survey for Six Proposed Solar Voltaic Cell Sites Located in the Ahupuaʻa of Honokahua, Honokeana, and Honokōwai, Lahaina (Kāʻanapali) District, Island of Maui, Hawaiʻi.* Honolulu, HI: Scientific Consultant Services, Inc., 2012. [SHPD ID: 2019LI81005]

Sea Engineering, Inc. *Final Environmental Assessment for Permanent Shore Protection of the Hololani Resort Condominiums Kahananui, Lahaina, Maui.* Honolulu, HI: Sea Engineering, Inc., 2013. [No location available]

Shefcheck, Donna M. and Michael F. Dega. *A Preservation Plan for Site 50-50-08-5968 and Site 50-50-08-5969 in Ukumehame Ahupuaʻa, Lahaina District, Island of Maui, Hawaiʻi [TMK: (2) 4-8-02:008 por.].* Honolulu, HI: Scientific Consultant Services, Inc., 2006. [SHPD ID: 2019LI81643]

Shefcheck, Donna M. and Michael F. Dega. *An Archaeological Inventory Survey of 122.84 Acres in the Launiupoko (Large Lot) Subdivision 6 Launiupoko and Polanui Ahupuaʻa, Lahaina District, Maui, Hawaiʻi [TMK (2) 4-7-01:029 por.].* Honolulu, HI: Scientific Consultant Services, Inc., 2008. [SHPD ID: 2019LI81593]

Shefcheck, Donna M. and Michael F. Dega. *An Archaeological Inventory Survey of 123.31 Acres in the Launiupoko (Large Lot) Subdivision 6 Launiupoko and Polanui Ahupuaʻa, Lahaina District (formerly Kāʻanapali) Island of Maui, Hawaiʻi TMK (2) 4-8-01:002 por.).* Honolulu, HI: Scientific Consultant Services, Inc., 2007. [SHPD ID: 2019LI81596]

Shefcheck, Donna M. and Michael F. Dega. *An Archaeological Monitoring Plan for Lahaina Wastewater Pump Station No. 1 Improvements, Honokōwai Ahupuaʻa, Lahaina District Maui Island, Hawaiʻi [TMK (2) 4-4-02:033 and portions of 29 and 39]*. Honolulu, HI: Scientific Consultant Services, Inc., 2008. [SHPD ID: 2019LI81253]

Shefcheck, Donna M. and Michael F. Dega. *An Archaeological Monitoring Plan for the Puunoa Subdivision No. 2, Lahaina, Pu'uiki Ahupua'a, Lahaina District, Island of Maui, Hawai'i*. Honolulu, HI: Scientific Consultant Services, Inc., 2008. [SHPD ID: 2019LI80647]

Shefcheck, Donna M. and Michael F. Dega. *An Archaeological Monitoring Report for the Maui Islander Project, Lahaina, Paunau Ahupua'a, Lahaina District, Maui Island, Hawai'i [TMK: (2) 4-6-011:008]*. Honolulu, HI: Scientific Consultant Services, Inc., 2008. [SHPD ID: 2019LI81576]

Shefcheck, Donna M. and Michael F. Dega. *Site Report for a Previously Unrecorded Heiau in Launiupoko Ahupua'a, Lahaina District, Island of Maui, Hawai'i*. Honolulu, HI: Scientific Consultant Services, Inc., 2006. [SHPD ID: 2019LI81592]

Silva, C. L. *Appendix A: Preliminary Historical Documentary Research, in Archaeological Survey Test Excavations, Kapalua Hotel Development Site 2-H, Kapalua Bay Resort, Land of Honokahua, Lahaina District, Island of Maui. PHRI Report 224-052286*, 1986. [No location available]

Sinoto, Aki. *An Archaeological Assessment of the Native Plant Conservatory Project, Ukumehame Firing Range, Ukumehame, Lahaina, Maui TMK (2) 4-8-2:047*. Honolulu, HI: Aki Sinoto Consulting, 1997. [SHPD ID: 2019LI81624]

Sinoto, Aki. *An Archaeological Reconnaissance of the Mala Wharf Boat Launch Ramp Area, Lahaina, Maui*. Honolulu, HI: Department of Anthropology, Bernice P. Bishop Museum, 1975. [SHPD ID: 2019LI80624; UH Call Number: DU629.M353 S56 1975]

Sinoto, Aki. *Field Examination of Six Sites in the Honolua Watershed, Maui*. Honolulu, HI: Department of Anthropology, Bernice P. Bishop Museum, 1975. [SHPD ID: 2019LI81435; UH Call Number: DU629.H69 S56 1975]

Sinoto, Aki. *Proposed Kai Ala Subdivision, Kā'anapali, Maui*. Honolulu, HI: Bernice P. Bishop Museum, 1990. [SHPD ID: 2019LI81265]

Sinoto, Aki and Jeffrey Pantaleo. *Archaeological Inventory Survey of the Proposed Site for the New Lahaina Kingdom Hall Puunoa, Paunau Ahupua'a, Lahaina District, Maui Island TMK (2) 4-4-04:042 & 044)*. Wailuku, HI: Archaeological Services Hawaii, LLC, 2003. [SHPD ID: 2019LI80616]

Sinoto, Aki and Jeffrey Pantaleo. *Archaeological Inventory Survey of TMK (2) 4-4-01:002, 11, and 12 (Revised Final 9-92)*. Honolulu, HI: Aki Sinoto Consulting, 1991. [No location available]

Six, Janet L. *A Final Archaeological Assessment Report for Maui County Work on County Roadway (WTP T20160044) and grading and grubbing (GT20160132) Proposed Sunset Terrace Lot Beautification Project, Honokōwai Ahupuaʻa, Lahaina District Maui Island, TMK (2) 4-4-02:029 and 034 (por.).* Pāhoa, HI: Sixth Sense Archaeological Consultants, LLC, 2018. [SHPD ID: 2019LI81282]

Six, Janet L. *Archaeological Monitoring Plan for Deck and Bar Repairs for: Leilani's on the Beach, Whalers Village Shopping Center, Building J 2435 Kāʻanapali Parkway, Hanakaʻōʻō Ahupuaʻa, Lahaina District, Maui Island.* Pāhoa, HI: Sixth Sense Archaeological Consultants, LLC, 2011. [SHPD ID: 2019LI80676]

Six, Janet L. *Final Archaeological Monitoring Plan for Maui County Work on County Roadway (WTP T20160044) and Grading and Grubbing (GT2016132) Proposed Sunset Terrace Lot Beautification Project Honokōwai Ahupuaʻa, Lahaina Project Honokōwai Ahupuaʻa, Lahaina District, Maui Island, Hawaiʻi.* Pāhoa, HI: Sixth Sense Archaeological Consultants, LLC, 2018. [SHPD ID: 2019LI81282]

Six, Janet L. *Final Archaeological Monitoring Plan for Special Management Area Application (SMX2017/0098) for the Proposed Kahana Beach Resort DCDA Upgrade, Kahana Ahupuaʻa, Lahaina District, Island of Maui.* Pāhoa, HI: Sixth Sense Archaeological Consultants, LLC, 2018. [SHPD ID: 2019LI81303]

Six, Janet L. *Final Archaeological Monitoring Plan for Work on County Roadway Permit Application (WTP T2017-0055) Installation Communication Utilities, West Maui Village, Kohi & Napilihau St., Napili, ʻAlaeloa Ahupuaʻa, Kāʻanapali District, Island of Maui.* Pāhoa, HI: Sixth Sense Archaeological Consultants, LLC, 2018. [SHPD ID: 2019LI81317]

Smith, Helen Wong. *Historical Documentary Research in Archaeological Inventory Survey, Lahaina Master Planned Project Site, Land of Wahikuli, Lahaina District, Island of Maui.* Hilo, HI: Paul H. Rosendahl, Ph.D., Inc., 1989. [No location available]

Spear, Robert L. *Field Inspection of a Sea Wall on the Brayton Property, 303 Front Street, Aholo/Kauʻaula Ahupuaʻa, Lahaina District, Island of Maui, Hawaiʻi TMK: 4-6-3-05 (Seaward).* Honolulu, HI: Scientific Consultant Services, Inc., 2007. [SHPD ID: 2019LI81559]

Spencer Mason Architects. *Historic Site Survey for Lahainaluna Road and Waineʻe Street Widening Projects.* Honolulu, HI: Spencer Mason Architects, 1988. [SHPD ID: 2019LI81432]

Spencer Mason Architects. *Historic Structures Report: Old Lahaina Courthouse.* Honolulu, HI: Spencer Mason Architects, 1996. [SHPD ID: 2019LI81378]

Spencer Mason Architects. *Various Historic Site Survey for Lahainaluna Road and Waine'e Street Widening Projects.* Honolulu, HI: Spencer Mason Architects, 1988. [SHPD ID: 2019LI81432]

Spriggs, Matthew. *Trip Report: Makaluapuna Point, Honokahua, Lahaina District, Maui,* 1989. [SHPD ID: 2019LI81413; UH Call Number: DU629.M356 S67 1989]

Stankov, Pavel and Michael F. Dega. *Archaeological Monitoring Plan for the Renovations and Landscaping at the Stakelbeck Property at Olowalu Ahupua'a, Lahaina District, Island of Maui, Hawai'i [TMK (2) 4-8-03:002 por.].* Honolulu, HI: Scientific Consultant Services, Inc., 2021. [SHPD ID: 2021LI00103]

[T]

Tome, Guerin and Michael F. Dega. *An Archaeological Inventory Survey for the Proposed Kapalua Coastal Trail Located in the Areas of Kapalua and Honokāhau, Honokahua and Nāpili 2 & 3.* Honolulu, HI: Scientific Consultant Services, Inc., 2007. [SHPD ID: 2019LI81433]

Tome, Guerin and Michael F. Dega. *An Archaeological Monitoring Plan for the Proposed Kapalua Coastal Trail Located in the areas of Nāpili, Kapalua, Honokahua, and Honolua, Ahupua'a of Nāpili 2&3, Honokahua, and Honolua, Lahaina District, Island of Maui, Hawai'i.* Honolulu, HI: Scientific Consultant Services, Inc., 2008. [SHPD ID: 2019LI81410]

Tome, Guerin, Irene Calis, and Michael F. Dega. *An Archaeological Inventory Survey in Honolua, Honolua Ahupua'a, Lahaina District, Island of Maui, Hawai'i [TMK: (2) 4-1-01:005].* Honolulu, HI: Scientific Consultant Services, Inc., 2002. [SHPD ID: 2019LI81423]

Tomonari-Tuggle, M. J. *An Archaeological Reconnaissance Survey for 27 Wind Turbines in the Ukumehame Uplands, Island of Maui.* Honolulu, HI: International Archaeological Research Institute, Inc., 2003. [SHPD ID: 2019LI81627]

Tomonari-Tuggle, M. J. and Coral Rasmussen. *Preservation Plan for Site 50-50-09-5232, An Upland Heiau in Ukumehame Ahupua'a, Island of Maui TMK 4-8-01:1.* Honolulu, HI: International Archaeological Research Institute, Inc., 2005. [SHPD ID: 2019LI81629]

Tomonari-Tuggle, M. J. and H. D. Tuggle. *Archaeological Survey of Two Demonstration Trails of the Hawai'i Statewide Trail and Access System.* Honolulu, HI: International Archaeological Research Institute, Inc., 1991. [SHPD ID: 2019LI79001; UH Call Number: DU628.M3 T66 1991]

Tourtellotte, Perry A. *Archaeological Inspection Report for Rainbow Ranch*, 1988. [SHPD ID: 2019LI81059]

Tulchin, Jon and Hallett H. Hammatt. *Archaeological Assessment of a 0.2-Acre Parcel and Waterline, Māhinahina 4 Ahupuaʻa, Lahaina District, Island of Maui.* Wailuku, HI: Cultural Surveys Hawaiʻi, Inc., 2003. [SHPD ID: 2019LI81315]

[W]

Walker, Alan T. and Paul H. Rosendahl. *Testing of Cultural Remains Associated with the Kahana Desilting Basin, Honolua Watershed, Land of Kahana, Lahaina District, County of Maui, Hawaiʻi.* Hilo, HI: Paul H. Rosendahl, Ph.D., Inc., 1985. [SHPD ID: 2019LI81071; UH Call Number: DU629.K343 W35 1985]

Walton, Beth. *A Preliminary Report on an Archaeological Survey of the Portion of Piilani Highway from Stake 195+00 to Stake 250+00*, 1972. [SHPD ID: 2019LI79374]

Wasson, Eugene C. IV and Michael F. Dega. *An Archaeological Monitoring Report for the Lahaina No. 4. Force Main Replacement Project, in Lahaina, Wahikuli Ahupuaʻa, Lahaina District, Island of Maui, Hawaiʻi.* Honolulu, HI: Scientific Consultant Services, Inc., 2016. [SHPD ID: 2019LI80628]

Watanabe, Farley. *Archaeological Site Investigation Kahoma Stream Flood Control Project TMK (2) 4-5-15:008.* Honolulu, HI: Army Corps of Engineers, 1987. [SHPD ID: 2019LI81342]

Webb, Erika L. *Inventory Survey of Honolua Plantation Shop Buildings Located at the Kapalua Central Resort, TMK (2) 4-2-4:024.* Honolulu, HI: Mason Architects, Inc., 2005. [SHPD ID: 2019LI81047]

Weisler, M. *Field Inspection of Hanakaʻōʻō Construction Site, Maui.* Honolulu, HI: Department of Anthropology, Bernice P. Bishop Museum, 1983. [No location available]

Wiley, Tiffany E. and Michael F. Dega. *Addendum to an Archaeological Monitoring Plan for the Poseley Residence, Olowalu Ahupuaʻa, Lahaina District, Island of Maui, Hawaiʻi [TMK (2) 4-8-003:047, and portions of 001 and 084 (Easement G)].* Honolulu, HI: Scientific Consultant Services, Inc., 2017. [No location available]

Willman, Michael R., Robert R. Hill, Tanya L. Lee-Greig, and Hallett H. Hammatt. *Archaeological Monitoring Report for Sand Replenishment at Lots 1, 2, and 3, North Kāʻanapali, Honokōwai Ahupuaʻa, Lahaina District, Island of Maui [TMK (2) 4-4-014: 03, 04, 05 (por.)].* Wailuku, HI: Cultural Surveys Hawaiʻi, Inc., 2009. [SHPD ID: 2019LI80656]

Willman, Michael R., Tanya Lee-Greig, and Hallett H. Hammatt. *Addendum to Archaeological Monitoring Plan for the Puʻunēnē School and Lahainaluna High School Hawaiʻi Inter-Island DOE Cesspool Project, Island of Maui TMK (2) 4-6-18 and (2) 3-8-06.* Wailuku, HI: Cultural Surveys Hawaiʻi, Inc., 2008. [SHPD ID: 2019LI81524]

Windley, Larry. *Recommended Action Plan for the Preservation/Restoration of the Hale Paʻahao Prison Site, Lahaina.* Lahaina, HI: Lahaina Restoration Foundation, 1967. [SHPD ID: 2019LI81257]

Wong, Charmaine and Michael F. Dega. *An Archaeological Assessment for the West Maui Hospital and Medical Center, Hanakaʻōʻō Ahupuaʻa, Lahaina (Kāʻanapali) district, Maui Island, Hawaiʻi [TMK: (2) 4-4-02:052].* Honolulu, HI: Scientific Consultant Services, Inc., 2014. [SHPD ID: 2019LI81245]

Wong, Charmaine and Michael F. Dega. *An Archaeological Assessment for the West Maui Hospital and Medical Center, Hanakaʻōʻō Ahupuaʻa, Lahaina (Kāʻanapali) District, Maui Island, Hawaiʻi, TMK: (2) 4-4-02:052.* Honolulu, HI: Scientific Consultant Services, Inc., 2008. [No location available]

[Y]

Yates and Hallett H. Hammatt. *Archaeological Monitoring Plan for the Kāʻanapali 2020 Master Plan, Kāʻanapali Coffee Farms Subdivision Phase II Project, Hanakaʻōʻō and Honokōwai Ahupuaʻa, Lahaina District, Maui Island, TMK (2) 4-4-02:002.* Wailuku, HI: Cultural Surveys Hawaiʻi, Inc., 2020. [SHPD ID: 2021LI00326, 2022LI00365]

Yeomans, Sarah K. *Archaeological Monitoring Plan Parking Lot Drainage System Installation, Panaʻewa Ahupuaʻa, Lahaina District, Island of Maui, Hawaiʻi.* Honolulu, HI: Scientific Consultant Services, Inc., 2019. [SHPD ID: 2019LI80640]

Yucha, Josephine M. and Hallett H. Hammatt. *Archaeological Monitoring Plan for the Lahaina Intermediate School Campus Fire Alarm Replacement Project, Panaʻewa and Kuʻia Ahupuaʻa, Lahaina District, Maui Island TMK (2) 4-6-18:013 por.* Wailuku, HI: Cultural Surveys Hawaiʻi, Inc., 2019. [No location available]

Yucha, Josephine M. and Hallett H. Hammatt. *Archaeological Monitoring Plan for the Puʻukoliʻi Village Mauka Project, Hanakaʻōʻō Ahupuaʻa, Lahaina District, Maui Island, TMKs: (2) 4-4-02:002, 048, and 053 por., (2) 4-4-06:070, 086 and 087 por., and (2) 4-4-15:034 through 072. 24:026 (por.).* Wailuku, HI: Cultural Surveys Hawaiʻi, Inc., 2023. [SHPD ID: 2023LI00111]

Yucha, Josephine M. and Hallett H. Hammatt. *Archaeological Monitoring Plan for the Sheraton Maui Resort & Spa Sewer Improvements Project, Hanaka'ō'ō Ahupua'a, Lahaina District, Maui Island, TMKs: (2) 4-4-08:005 and 011 (pors).* Wailuku, HI: Cultural Surveys Hawai'i, Inc., 2018. [SHPD ID: 2019LI80670]

Yucha, Josephine M. and Hallett H. Hammatt. *Archaeological Monitoring Plan for the Valley Isle Resort Renovation Project, Kahana Ahupua'a, Lahaina District, Maui Island, TMK: (2) 4-3-10:004.* Wailuku, HI: Cultural Surveys Hawai'i, Inc., 2020. [SHPD ID: 2021LI00211]

Yucha, Josephine M. and Hallett H. Hammatt. *Archaeological Monitoring Plan for the Villages of Leiali'i, Village 1-B Subdivision and Related Improvements Project, Wahikuli Ahupua'a, Lahaina District, Maui Island, TMKs: (2) 4-5-021:010 por., 014 por., 015 por., 020, and 021 por.; (2) 4-5-36:109, 110, and 112; and Honoapi'ilani Highway Right-of-Way.* Wailuku, HI: Cultural Surveys Hawai'i, Inc., 2022. [SHPD ID: 2023LI00106]

Yucha, Josephine M. and Hallett H. Hammatt. *Archaeological Monitoring Report for the Sheraton Maui Sewer Improvements Project, Hanaka'ō'ō Ahupua'a, Lahaina District, Maui Island, TMKs: (2) 4-4-008:005 and 011 (pors.).* Wailuku, HI: Cultural Surveys Hawai'i, Inc., 2018. [SHPD ID: 2019LI81258]

Yucha, Josephine M. et al. *Archaeological Inventory Survey for the Pu'ukoli'i Village Mauka Project, Hanaka'ō'ō Ahupua'a, Lahaina District, Maui Island, TMKs: (2) 4-4-02:002, 048, and 053 por., (2) 4-4-06:070, 086 and 087 por., and (2) 4-4-15:034 through 072.* Wailuku, HI: Cultural Surveys Hawai'i, Inc., 2022. [SHPD ID: 2023LI00110]

Yucha, Josephine M., Jennifer Frey, and Hallett H. Hammatt. *Burial Site Component of an Archaeological Data Recovery Plan for SIHP # 50-50-03-8842 at the Westin Maui Resort & Spa Improvements Project, Phase III, Hanaka'ō'ō Ahupua'a, Lahaina District, Maui, TMK: (2) 4-4-08:019.* Wailuku, HI: Cultural Surveys Hawai'i, Inc., 2021. [SHPD ID: 2021LI00104]

Yucha, Trevor M. and Hallett H. Hammatt. *Archaeological Monitoring Plan for the Westin Maui Resort & Spa Master Plan Improvements, Hanaka'ō'ō Ahupua'a, Lahaina District, Island of Maui, TMK (2) 4-4-08:019.* Wailuku, HI: Cultural Surveys Hawai'i, Inc., 2018. [SHPD ID: 2019LI80683]

PUBLICATIONS BY YEAR

1961

Community Planning, Inc. *Lahaina Historical Restoration and Preservation.* Community Planning Inc., 1961. [UH Call Number: DU629.L3 M3]

1965

Fredericksen, Walter M. and Demaris L. Fredericksen. *Report on the Archaeological Excavation of the "Brick Palace" of King Kamehameha I at Lahaina, Maui, Hawai'i,* 1965. [SHPD ID: 2019LI81384; UH Call Number: DU629.L3 F74]

John Carl Warnecke and Associates. *Lahaina Small Boat Harbor Study.* San Francisco, CA: John Carl Warnecke and Associates, Architects and Planning Consultants, 1965. [SHPD ID: 2019LI81397]

1966

Cliver, Blaine E., *Architectural Restorationalist. Architecturally speaking... The Baldwin House,* Lahaina, Maui, 1966. [SHPD ID: 2019LI81038]

Peterson, Charles E. *Notes on the Lahaina Court and Custom House, Lahaina, Maui, Hawai'i, Built 1859,* 1966. [SHPD ID: 2019LI81376]

1967

Windley, Larry. *Recommended Action Plan for the Preservation/Restoration of the Hale Pa'ahao Prison Site, Lahaina.* Lahaina, HI: Lahaina Restoration Foundation, 1967. [SHPD ID: 2019LI81257]

1970

Hart, Christopher. *Final Report of the Preparation for Exhibit of King Kamehameha I's "Brick Palace" at Lahaina, Maui, Hawai'i.* Maui Historic Commission, 1970.

1972

Chapman, Phillips, Brandt and Associates. *Lahaina Banyan Courtyard Preliminary Development and Restoration Plans,* 1972. [SHPD ID: 2019LI81398]

Walton, Beth. *A Preliminary Report on an Archaeological Survey of the Portion of Piilani Highway from Stake 195+00 to Stake 250+00,* 1972. [SHPD ID: 2019LI79374]

1973

Frost, Lockwood H. *A Report and Recommendations on the Restoration and Preservation of Hale Aloha, Lahaina, Maui,* 1973. [No location available]

Hommon, Robert J. *Report on a Walk Through Survey of the Kahoma Stream Flood Control Project Area.* Honolulu, HI: Department of Anthropology, Bernice P. Bishop Museum, 1973.

Kaschko, Michael W. *Archaeological Survey of the Honolua Development Area, Maui.* Department of Anthropology, Honolulu, HI: Bernice P. Bishop Museum, 1973. [SHPD ID: 2019LI81019]

Kirch, Patrick V. *Archaeological Excavations at Site D13-1, Hawea Point, Maui, Hawaiian Islands.* Honolulu, HI: Department of Anthropology, Bernice P. Bishop Museum, 1973. [SHPD ID: 2019LI81021; UH Call Number: DU629. H393 K57 1973]

Kirch, Patrick V. *Archaeological Survey of the Honolua Development Area, Maui.* Honolulu, HI: Department of Anthropology, Bernice P. Bishop Museum, 1973. [SHPD ID: 2019LI81019; UH Call Number: DU629.K374 K57 1973]

1974

Connolly, Robert D. III. *Phase I Archaeological Survey of Kahoma Stream Flood-Control-Project Area, Lahaina, Maui.* Honolulu, HI: Department of Anthropology, Bernice P. Bishop Museum, 1974.

Kaschko, Michael W. *Archaeological Walk-Through Survey of Specified Areas in the Wailuku Flood Prevention Project and the Honolua Watershed, Maui.* Honolulu, HI: Department of Anthropology, Bernice P. Bishop Museum, 1974. [SHPD ID: 2019LI81443]

Moore, Kenneth R. *Archaeological Survey of Honolua Valley, Maui.* Honolulu, HI: Department of Anthropology, Bernice P. Bishop Museum, 1974. [SHPD ID: 2019LI81436; UH Call Number: DU629.H69 M66 1974]

Pyle, Dorothy. "The Intriguing Seamen's Hospital." *The Hawaiian Journal of History,* vol. 8, 1974, pp. 121–135. [UH Call Number: DU620 .H44]

1975

Cleghorn, Paul L. *A Progress Report upon Completion of Fieldwork at the Seamen's Hospital, Lahaina, Maui (Phase 1).* Honolulu, HI: Department of Anthropology, Bernice P. Bishop Museum, 1975. [UH Call Number: DU629.L3 C54 1975]

Cleghorn, Paul L. *Phase 1 Archaeological Research at the Seamen's Hospital (Site D5-10), Lahaina, Maui.* Honolulu, HI: Department of Anthropology, Bernice P. Bishop Museum, 1975. [UH Call Number: DU629.L3 C544 1975]

Sinoto, Aki. *An Archaeological Reconnaissance of the Mala Wharf Boat Launch Ramp Area, Lahaina, Maui.* Honolulu, HI: Department of Anthropology, Bernice P. Bishop Museum, 1975. [SHPD ID: 2019LI80624; UH Call Number: DU629.M353 S56 1975]

Sinoto, Aki. *Field Examination of Six Sites in the Honolua Watershed, Maui.* Honolulu, HI: Department of Anthropology, Bernice P. Bishop Museum, 1975. [SHPD ID: 2019LI81435; UH Call Number: DU629.H69 S56 1975]

1977

Davis, Bertell D. *Archaeological Surface Survey, Honokōwai Gulch, Kāʻanapali, Maui Island.* Lāwaʻi, HI: Archaeological Research Center Hawaiʻi, 1977. [SHPD ID: 2019LI81277]

Davis, Bertell D. *Preliminary Report, Mala Wharf Burials, Phase 1, Mala, Lahaina, Maui Island.* Lāwaʻi, HI: Archaeological Research Center Hawaiʻi, 1977. [No location available]

Fox, Robert M. *Site Survey & Inventory, Hale Paʻi o Lahainaluna.* Honolulu, HI: AIA, 1977. [SHPD ID: 2019LI81590]

Griffin, Bion P. and George W. Lovelace, eds. *Survey and Salvage—Honoapiʻilani Highway: The Archaeology of Kāʻanapali from Honokōwai to ʻAlaeloa Ahupuaʻa.* Lāwaʻi, HI: Archaeological Research Center Hawaiʻi, Inc., 1977. [UH Call Number: DU628.M3 A7 1977]

Olson, Larry G. *Appendix II—A Geoarchaeological Report of Site 225, Māhinahina Gulch, Maui, Hawaiʻi.* Lāwaʻi, HI: Archaeological Research Center Hawaiʻi, 1977. [No location available]

1978

Fredericksen, Walter M. Jr. and Demaris L. Fredericksen. *Report on the Excavation of the Outbuildings Adjacent to the Baldwin House, Undertaken for the Lahaina Restoration Foundation, Lahaina, Maui, Hawai'i.* Pukalani, HI: Xamanek Researches, 1978. [SHPD ID: 2019LI81568]

Hammatt, Hallett H. *Archaeological Investigation and Monitoring, Mala Wharf Boat-Launch Ramp Area, Lahaina, Maui Island.* Lāwa'i, HI: Archaeological Research Center Hawai'i, Inc., 1978. [SHPD ID: 2019LI81387; UH Call Number: GN486 .H35]

Hammatt, Hallett H. *Archaeological Reconnaissance at the Proposed Hyatt Regency Site, Hanaka'ō'ō, Kā'anapali, Maui Island, Tax Map Key; 4-4-06:31 Lot 60, ARCH 14-129.* Lāwa'i, HI: Archaeological Research Center Hawai'i, 1978. [SHPD ID: 2019LI81264; UH Call Number: GN486 .H35]

1979

Ahlo, Hamilton M. and Maurice E. Morgenstein. *Archaeological Test Excavations Near the Mouth of Kahoma Stream, Lahaina, Maui.* Honolulu, HI: Hawai'i Marine Research, 1979.

Chapman, P. S. and P. V. Kirch. *Archaeological Excavations at Seven Sites, Southeast Maui, Hawaiian Islands.* Honolulu, HI: Department of Anthropology, Bernice P. Bishop Museum, 1979. [UH Call Number: DU624.A1 B47 no.79-1]

Ching, Francis K. W. *Archaeological Assessment of the Property on Which the Proposed Marriott Kā'anapali Hotel is to be Built, Kā'anapali, Maui Island.* Lāwa'i, HI: Archaeological Research Center Hawai'i, 1979. [SHPD ID: 2019LI81267]

Joerger, Pauline King and Michael W. Kaschko. *A Cultural Historical Overview of the Kahoma Stream Flood Control Project, Lahaina, Maui and Ma'alaea Small Boat Harbor Project, Ma'alaea, Maui.* Honolulu, HI: Hawai'i Marine Research, Inc., 1979. [SHPD ID: 2019LI80298; UH Call Number: DU629.L3 J63]

1980

Ladd, Edmund J. *Archaeological Survey Report,* 1980. [No location available]

1982

Dobyns, Susan and Jane Allen-Wheeler. *Archaeological Monitoring at the Site of the Kāʻanapali Aliʻi Condominium, Island of Maui.* Honolulu, HI: Department of Anthropology, Bernice P. Bishop Museum, 1982. [SHPD ID: 2019LI80673]

Hommon, Robert J. *An Archaeological Reconnaissance Survey of an Area Near Waineʻe Village, West Maui.* Hawaiʻi: Science Management, Inc., 1982. [SHPD ID: 2019LI81389; UH Call Number: DU629.W346 H66 1982]

Hommon, Robert J. *An Archaeological Reconnaissance Survey of the North Beach Mauka and South Beach Beach Mauka Areas, Hanakaʻōʻō, West Maui.* Hawaiʻi: Science Management, Inc., 1982. [No location available]

Hommon, Robert J. and Hamilton M. Ahlo, Jr. *An Archaeological Reconnaissance Survey of the Site of a Proposed Airstrip at Māhinahina, West Maui.* Science Management, Inc., 1982. [SHPD ID: 2019LI81050; UH Call Number: DU629. M345 H66 1982]

Keau, Charles. *Archaeological Reconnaissance (Surface Survey) for Hanakaʻōʻō (Hahakea) Beach Park. Includes cover letter: An Archaeological Reconnaissance of Hahakea Beach Park, Hanakaʻōʻō, Maui. TMK: 4-4-06:33 by Earl Neller.* State Historic Preservation Office, March 1982. [SHPD ID: 2019LI81272; UH Call Number: DU629.H364 K43 1981]

Nagata, Ralston H. and Martha Yent. *CDUA: MA-1436, Taro Planting at Kahakuloa Valley, Wailuku, Maui. Memorandum to Mr. Roger Evans, Planning Office from DLNR, Division of State Parks,* 1982. [UH Call Number: DU629. K344 N34 1982]

Neller, Earl. *An Archaeological Reconnaissance Along the Coast at Ukumehame, Maui,* 1982. [SHPD ID: 2019LI81640; UH Call Number: DU629.U38 N45 1982]

Neller, Earl. *An Archaeological Reconnaissance of Hahakea Beach Park, Hanakaʻōʻō, Maui.* Honolulu, HI: State of Hawaiʻi Preservation Office, 1982. [SHPD ID: 2019LI81272; UH Call Number: DU629.H364 N45 1982]

1983

Komori, Eric K. *Archaeological Investigations at Kahana Gulch, Lahaina District, Maui.* Honolulu, HI: Department of Anthropology, Bernice P. Bishop Museum, 1983. [SHPD ID: 2019LI81070; UH Call Number: DU629.K343 K66 1983]

Lum, Francis. *Amendment to Testing at Kahana Desilting Basin, Holoua [Honolua?] Watershed, Lahaina District, Maui, Hawai'i, Francis Lum, Soil Conservation Service.* Soil Conservation Service, 1983. [SHPD ID: 2019LI81058]

Nagata, Ralston H. *CDUA-MA-5/12/82-1407, Land Clearing and Planting of Commercially Valuable Tree Species at Kahakuloa, Wailuku, Maui. Memorandum to: Roger Evans, Planning Office from DLNR, Division of State Parks,* 1983. [No location available]

Weisler, M. *Field Inspection of Hanaka'ō'ō Construction Site, Maui.* Honolulu, HI: Department of Anthropology, Bernice P. Bishop Museum, 1983. [No location available]

1984

Kurashina, Hiro and Aki Sinoto. *Archaeological Reconnaissance of the Proposed Shopping Center at Lahaina, Maui, Hawai'i, TMK: (2) 4-5-02:009.* Honolulu, HI: Department of Anthropology, Bernice P. Bishop Museum, 1984. [SHPD ID: 2019LI80648; UH Call Number: DU629.L3 K87 1984]

1985

Athens, J. Stephen. *Archaeological Reconnaissance at Honokahua Well B, Lahaina District, West Maui,* 1985.

Kennedy, Joseph. *Archaeological Inventory Survey of Kahana, Maui.* Hale'iwa, HI: Archaeological Consultants of Hawaii, 1985. [No location available]

Walker, Alan T. and Paul H. Rosendahl. *Testing of Cultural Remains Associated with the Kahana Desilting Basin, Honolua Watershed, Land of Kahana, Lahaina District, County of Maui, Hawai'i.* Hilo, HI: Paul H. Rosendahl, Ph.D., Inc., 1985. [SHPD ID: 2019LI81071; UH Call Number: DU629.K343 W35 1985]

1986

Barrera, William Jr. *North Beach, Maui: Archaeological Reconnaissance.* Honolulu, HI: Chiniago, Inc., 1986. [SHPD ID: 2019LI81288]

Donham, Theresa K. *Archaeological Survey Test Excavations Kapalua Hotel Development Site 2-H, Kapalua Bay Resort, Land of Honokahua, Lahaina, Island of Maui.* Hilo, HI: Paul H. Rosendahl, Ph.D., Inc., 1986. [2019LI80998]

Kennedy, Joseph. *Archaeological Investigations at Kahana, Maui,* 1986. [No location available]

Kennedy, Joseph. *Field Inspection: Stone Building at Kahana,* Maui, 1986. [SHPD ID: 2019LI81332]

Rosendahl, Margaret L. K. *Archaeological Field Inspection, Sheraton Maui Master Plan Project Area, Lands of Honokōwai and Hanakaʻōʻō, Lahaina District, Island of Maui.* Hilo, HI: Paul H. Rosendahl, Ph.D., Inc., 1986. [No location available]

Silva, C. L. *Appendix A: Preliminary Historical Documentary Research, in Archaeological Survey Test Excavations, Kapalua Hotel Development Site 2-H, Kapalua Bay Resort, Land of Honokahua, Lahaina District, Island of Maui. PHRI Report 224-052286,* 1986. [No location available]

1987

Rosendahl, Margaret L. K. *Subsurface Archaeological Reconnaissance Survey, North Beach Development Site, Ahupuaʻa of Hanakaʻōʻō, Lahaina Eistrict, Island of Maui.* Hilo, HI: Paul H. Rosendahl, Ph.D., Inc., 1987. [SHPD ID: 2019LI81244]

Rosendahl, Paul H. *A Plan for Archaeological Monitoring of Shoreline Construction, Kāʻanapali North Beach Development Site, Ahupuaʻa of Hanakaʻōʻō, Lahaina District, Island of Maui.* Hilo, HI: Paul H. Rosendahl, Ph.D., Inc., 1987. [SHPD ID: 2019LI80659]

Rosendahl, Paul H. *PHRI Status Reports on Honokahua.* Hilo, HI: Paul H. Rosendahl, Ph.D., Inc., 1987. [SHPD ID: 2019LI81004]

Watanabe, Farley. *Archaeological Site Investigation Kahoma Stream Flood Control Project TMK (2) 4-5-15:008.* Honolulu, HI: Army Corps of Engineers, 1987. [SHPD ID: 2019LI81342]

1988

Barrera, William Jr. *Honoapiʻilani Highway, Maui: Archaeological Reconnaissance.* Honolulu, HI: Chiniago, Inc., 1988.

Fredericksen, Walter M. and Demaris L. Fredericksen. *Report on the Archaeological Excavation Conducted at Hale Paʻi Site, 1981–1982.* Pukalani, HI: Xamanek Researches, 1988. [SHPD ID: 2019LI81532]

Fredericksen, Walter M., Demaris Fredericksen, and Erik M. Fredericksen. *Report on the Archaeological Inventory Survey at Historic Site #15, Lahaina Maui, Hawai'i.* Pukalani, HI: Xamanek Researches, 1988. [SHPD ID: 2019LI81406]

Haun, A. E. *Subsurface Archaeological Reconnaissance Survey, Lahaina Cannery Makai and Mauka Parcels, Land of Moali'i, Lahaina District, Island of Maui,* 1988. [SHPD ID: 2019LI80612]

Kennedy, Joseph. *Archaeological Walk Through Examination of Quarry Site located Mauka of Honoapi'ilani Highway near Lipoa Point, Honolua, Maui.* Hale'iwa, HI: Archaeological Consultants of Hawaii, 1988. [SHPD ID: 2019LI81425]

Rosendahl, Paul H. *Archaeological Field Inspection Hawea Point Residence Site; Hawea Point, Lands of Napili 2 & 3 Lahaina District, Island of Maui.* Hilo, HI: Paul H. Rosendahl, Ph.D., Inc., 1988. [SHPD ID: 2019LI81001]

Rosendahl, Paul H. *Archaeological Reconnaissance Survey, The Cottages Project Area Kapalua Development Site 2-A, Lands of Honokahua and Napili 2 & 3, Lahaina District, Island of Maui.* Hilo, HI: Paul H. Rosendahl, Ph.D., Inc., 1988. [SHPD ID: 2019LI81009]

Rosendahl, Paul H. *Subsurface Reconnaissance Testing, Kapalua Place Project Area, Kapalua Development Site 2-A, Lands of Honokahua and Napili 2 & 3, Lahaina District, Island of Maui.* Hilo, HI: Paul H. Rosendahl, Ph.D., Inc., 1988. [SHPD ID: 2019LI81000]

Spencer Mason Architects. *Historic Site Survey for Lahainaluna Road and Waine'e Street Widening Projects.* Honolulu, HI: Spencer Mason Architects, 1988. [SHPD ID: 2019LI81432]

Spencer Mason Architects. *Various Historic Site Survey for Lahainaluna Road and Waine'e Street Widening Projects.* Honolulu, HI: Spencer Mason Architects, 1988. [SHPD ID: 2019LI81432]

Tourtellotte, Perry A. *Archaeological Inspection Report for Rainbow Ranch,* 1988. [SHPD ID: 2019LI81059]

1989

Donham, Theresa K. *Addendum Report: Additional Subsurface Testing of Area III, Subsurface Archaeological Testing, Revised Ritz-Carlton Kapalua Hotel Project Site, Areas I, II, and III, Land of Honokahua, Lahaina District, Island of Maui.* Hilo, HI: Paul H. Rosendahl, Ph.D., Inc., 1989. [SHPD ID: 2019LI81414]

Donham, Theresa K. *Interim Report: Kapalua Mitigation Program Data Recovery Excavations at the Honokahua Burial Site, Land of Honokahua, Lahaina District, Island of Maui.* Hilo, HI: Paul H. Rosendahl, Ph.D., Inc., 1989. [SHPD ID: 2019LI81417]

Ferguson, Lee, Arne Carlson, and Berdena Burgett. *Subsurface Archaeological Testing, Revised Ritz-Carlton Kapalua Hotel Project Site, Areas I, II and III.* Hilo, HI: Paul H. Rosendahl, Ph.D., Inc., 1989. [SHPD ID: 2019LI81006]

Fredericksen, Walter M., Demaris L. Fredericksen, and Erik M. Fredericksen. *An Archaeological Inventory Survey of a Parcel of Land Adjacent to Malu-Ulu-o-Lele Park, Lahaina, Maui, Hawai'i.* Pukalani, HI: Xamanek Researches, 1989. [SHPD ID: 2019LI81548]

Fredericksen, Walter M., Demaris L. Fredericksen, and Erik M. Fredericksen. *An Archaeological Inventory Survey of the Plantation Inn Site, Lahaina, Maui, Hawai'i.* Pukalani, HI: Xamanek Researches, 1989. [SHPD ID: 2019LI81588]

Fredericksen, Walter M., Demaris L. Fredericksen, and Erik M. Fredericksen. *Archaeological Data Recovery Report on the AUS Site, Lahaina, Maui, Hawai'i.* Pukalani, HI: Xamanek Researches, 1989. [SHPD ID: 2019LI81562]

Fredericksen, Walter M., Demaris L. Fredericksen, and Erik M. Fredericksen. *The AUS Site: H. S. #50-03-1797 A Preliminary Archaeological Inventory Survey Report.* Pukalani, HI: Xamanek Researches, 1989. [No location available]

Jensen, Peter M. *Archaeological Inventory Survey Lahaina Master Planned Project Site: Land of Wahikuli, Lahaina District, Island of Maui.* Hilo, HI: Paul H. Rosendahl, Ph.D., Inc., 1989. [SHPD ID: 2019LI80636]

Kennedy, Joseph. *Archaeological Report Concerning Subsurface Testing at TMK: (2) 4-6-08:012, Lahaina Maui.* Hale'iwa, HI: Archaeological Consultants of Hawaii, 1989. [SHPD ID: 2019LI81544]

Kennedy, Joseph. *Archaeological Walk Through Reconnaissance of (2)4-3-01:001 Napili Fire Station, TMK (2) 4-3-01:001 (por.),* 1989. [SHPD ID: 2019LI81054]

Klieger, Paul Christiaan and Lonnie Somer. *Emergency Mitigation at Malu'ulu o Lele Park, Lahaina, Maui, Hawai'i, Site of Moku'ula, Residence of King Kamehameha III (Site 50-50-03-2967; TMK (2) 4-6-7 Parcel 002: BPBM 50-MA-D5-12).* Honolulu, HI: Department of Anthropology, Bernice P. Bishop Museum, 1989. [SHPD ID: 2019LI81550]

Pietrusewsky, Michael, Michele T. Douglas, and Rona Ikehara. *An Osteological Study of Human Remains from the Kahoma Stream Flood Control Project,*

Lahaina, Maui. Honolulu, HI: University of Hawai'i at Mānoa, 1989. [UH Call Number: DU629.K76 P54 1989]

Riford, Mary F. and Paul L. *Cleghorn. Documentary Assessment of Archaeological Potential of Ten Prospective Power Plant Sites on Maui.* Honolulu, HI: Public Archaeology Section, Bernice P. Bishop Museum, 1989. [SHPD ID: 2022LI00168]

Smith, Helen Wong. *Historical Documentary Research in Archaeological Inventory Survey, Lahaina Master Planned Project Site, Land of Wahikuli, Lahaina District, Island of Maui.* Hilo, HI: Paul H. Rosendahl, Ph.D., Inc., 1989. [No location available]

Spriggs, Matthew. *Trip Report: Makaluapuna Point, Honokahua, Lahaina District, Maui,* 1989. [SHPD ID: 2019LI81413; UH Call Number: DU629.M356 S67 1989]

1990

Fredericksen et al. *An Archaeological Inventory Survey of a 9.976 Acre parcel in the Kahana/Mailepai/Alaeloa District, Lahaina District, Maui, Hawai'i.* Pukalani, HI: Xamanek Researches, 1990. [SHPD ID: 2019LI81060]

Fredericksen, Demaris L., Walter M. Fredericksen, and Erik M. Fredericksen. *Archaeological Inventory Survey of a 9.976 Acre Parcel in the Kahana/Mailepai/Akeloa Lands, Lahaina District, Maui, Hawai'i.* Pukalani, HI: Xamanek Researches, 1990. [SHPD ID: 2019LI81060]

Fredericksen, Walter M. and Demaris L. Fredericksen. *Archaeological Data Recovery Report on the Plantation Inn Site, Lahaina, Maui, Hawai'i.* Pukalani, HI: Xamanek Researches, 1990. [SHPD ID: 2019LI81589; UH Call Number: DU629.L3 F738 1990a]

Jensen, Peter M. *Archaeological Inventory Survey South Beach Mauka Development Site, Ahupua'a of Hanaka'ō'ō, Lahaina District, Island of Maui.* Hilo, HI: Paul H. Rosendahl, Ph.D., Inc., 1990. [SHPD ID: 2019LI81262; UH Call Number: DU628.M3 J46 1990]

Kennedy, Joseph. *Archaeological Inventory Survey of TMK (2) 4-3-02:068 & 069, Located at Napili, Island of Maui.* Hale'iwa, HI: Archaeological Consultants of Hawaii, 1990. [SHPD ID: 2019LI81061]

Kennedy, Joseph. *Archaeological Inventory Survey Report for TMK: (2) 4-3-01:031; Located at Kahana, Island of Maui.* 1990. [SHPD ID: 2019LI81054]

Kennedy, Joseph. *Hawea Point Residential Project: Archaeological Review, Survey, and Assessments*. Haleʻiwa, HI: Archaeological Consultants of Hawaii, 1990. [SHPD ID: 2019LI81416]

Pietrusewsky, Michael and Michele T. Douglas. *An Analysis of Additional Historic Human Skeletal Remains from the Kahoma Stream Flood Control Project, 1989, Lahaina, Maui*. Honolulu, HI: University of Hawaiʻi at Mānoa, 1990. [SHPD ID: DU629.L3 P54 1990]

Rosendahl, Paul H. *Phase I Monitoring Plan: Archaeological Mitigation Program, Ritz-Carlton Hotel Project Site, Land of Honokahua, Lahaina District, Island of Maui. PHRI Memo 857-070390*. Hilo, HI: Paul H. Rosendahl, Ph.D., Inc., 1990. [No location available]

Sinoto, Aki. *Proposed Kai Ala Subdivision, Kāʻanapali, Maui*. Honolulu, HI: Bernice P. Bishop Museum, 1990. [SHPD ID: 2019LI81265]

1991

Donham, Theresa K. *Field Inspection of a Proposed Culvert Location, USDA-SCS Lahaina Watershed Project, Pola Nui, Lahaina District, Maui [TMK: (2) 4-7-01:018]*. Wailuku, HI: State Historic Preservation Division, Maui Section, 1991. [SHPD ID: 2019LI81607]

Graves, Donna and Susan Goodfellow. *Archaeological Inventory Survey, Launiupoko Golf Course, Land of Launiupoko, Lahaina District, Island of Maui*. Hilo, HI: Paul H. Rosendahl, Ph.D., Inc., 1991. [SHPD ID: 2019LI81595, 2019LI81610]

Jensen, Peter A. and Jenny O'Claray. *Supplemental Archaeological Survey, Lahaina Master Planned Project Offsite Sewer, Water Improvements, and Cane Haul Road*. Hilo, HI: Paul H. Rosendahl, Ph.D., Inc., 1991. [SHPD ID: 2019LI81419]

Jensen, Peter M. *Archaeological Inventory Survey Honoapiʻilani Highway Realignment Project Lahaina Bypass Section—Modified Corridor Alignment, Lands of Honokōwai, Hanakaʻōʻō, Wahikuli, Panaʻewa, Kuʻia, Halakaʻa, Pūehuehu Nui, Pāhoa, Polanui, and Launiupoko, Lahaina District, Island of Maui*. Hilo, HI: Paul H. Rosendahl, Ph.D., Inc., 1991. [SHPD ID: 2019LI81242]

Kennedy, Joseph. *Archaeological Inventory Survey Report for TMK (2) 4-3-01:31, located at Kahana, Island of Maui*. Haleʻiwa, HI: Archaeological Consultants of Hawaii, 1991. [SHPD ID: 2019LI81069]

O'Claray, Jenny. *Additional Field Work for Drainage 11 Kapalua Plantation Estates Project Area, Lands of Honokahua, Honolua, Napili 2-2 Lahaina District, Island of Maui.* Hilo, HI: Paul H. Rosendahl, Ph.D., Inc., 1991. [SHPD ID: 2019LI81415]

Pantaleo, Jeffrey. *Archaeological Monitoring Plan Phase 2 of the Proposed Lahaina Watershed Flood Control Project, Polanui and Pāhoa Ahupua'a, Lahaina District, Maui Island [TMK (2) 4-8-001:por. 02; 4-7-02:por. 4, 5, 7],* 1991. [No location available]

Pantaleo, Jeffrey. *Archaeological Survey of the Proposed Lahainaluna Reservoir and Treatment Facility, Lahaina, Maui.* Honolulu, HI: Public Archaeology Section, Applied Research Group, Bernice P. Bishop Museum, 1991. [SHPD ID: 2019LI81530]

Pietrusewsky, Michael, Michele T. Douglas, Patricia A. Kalima, and Rona M. Ikehara. *Human Skeletal and Dental Remains from the Honokahua Burial Site, Land of Honokahua, Lahaina District, Island of Maui, Hawai'i.* Hilo, HI: Paul H. Rosendahl, Ph.D., Inc., 1991. [Call Number, DU629.H67 H86 1991a]

Rosendahl, Paul H. *Additional Inventory Survey for Drainage Easement 11 Kapalua Plantation Estates Project Area, Lands of Honokahua, Honolua, and Napili 2-3, Lahaina District, Island of Maui.* Hilo, HI: Paul H. Rosendahl, Ph.D., Inc., 1991. [SHPD ID: 2019LI80996]

Sinoto, Aki and Jeffrey Pantaleo. *Archaeological Inventory Survey of TMK (2) 4-4-01:002, 11, and 12 (Revised Final 9-92).* Honolulu, HI: Aki Sinoto Consulting, 1991. [No location available]

Tomonari-Tuggle, M. J. and H. D. Tuggle. *Archaeological Survey of Two Demonstration Trails of the Hawai'i Statewide Trail and Access System.* Honolulu, HI: International Archaeological Research Institute, Inc., 1991. [SHPD ID: 2019LI79001; UH Call Number: DU628.M3 T66 1991]

1992

Jensen, Peter M. *Letter Report: Additional Field Survey Lahaina Bypass Section, Modified Corridor Alignment, Honoapi'ilani Highway Realignment Project, Lands of Pāhoa and Polanui, Lahaina District, Island of Maui [TMK: (2) 4-7-01, 02].* Hilo, HI: Paul H. Rosendahl, Ph.D., Inc., 1992. [SHPD ID: 2019LI81609]

Jensen, Peter M. and Gemma Mahalchick. *Archaeological Inventory Survey, The Pu'ukoli'i Village Project Area, Ahupua'a of Hanaka'ō'ō, Lahaina District, Island of Maui.* Hilo, HI: Paul H. Rosendahl, Ph.D., Inc., 1992. [SHPD ID: 2019LI81252]

Kennedy, Joseph. *Archaeological Inventory Survey and Subsurface Testing Report for a Property Located at TMK: 4-3-03:108 and 110, ʻAlaeloa Ahupuaʻa, Lahaina District, on the Island of Maui,* 1992. [SHPD ID: 2022LI00219]

Kennedy, Joseph. *Archaeological Inventory Survey and Subsurface Testing Report for TMK: (2) 4-3-01:031, Located at Kahana Ahupuaʻa, Island of Maui,* Revised May 1992, 1992. [SHPD ID: 2019LI81051]

Kennedy, Joseph and Tim Denham. *Archaeological Inventory Survey and Subsurface Testing Report for TMK(2) 4-3-01:031, located at Kahana Ahupuaʻa, Maui.* Haleʻiwa, HI: Archaeological Consultants of Hawaii, 1992.

Rogers, Donnell J. and Paul H. Rosendahl. *Archaeological Survey and Recording Iliilikea and Maiu Heiau on the North Coast of Maui, Land of Honokōhau, Lahaina District, Island of Maui.* Hilo, HI: Paul H. Rosendahl, Ph.D., Inc., 1992. [SHPD ID: 2019LI81440]

1993

Folk, William. *Letter to Noel Kennett Re: End of Fieldwork of Archaeological Monitoring at Mala Wharf for an Electrical Line.* Wailuku, HI: Cultural Surveys Hawaiʻi, Inc., 1993. [SHPD ID: 2019LI80619]

Fredericksen, Walter M. and Demaris L. Fredericksen. *An Archaeological Inventory Survey on a Parcel of Land Located in the Ahupuaʻa of Paunau, Lahaina District, Island of Maui TMK (2) 4-6-09:012.* Pukalani, HI: Xamanek Researches, 1993. [SHPD ID: 2022LI00237]

Fredericksen, Walter M. and Demaris L. Fredericksen. *Archaeological Data Recovery Report on the Plantation Inn Site, Lahaina, Maui, Hawaiʻi.* Pukalani, HI: Xamanek Researches, 1993. [SHPD ID: 2019LI81589]

Guerriero, Diane A., Charvet-Pond, and S. Goodfellow. *Archaeological Monitoring and Data Recovery, Kapalua Ritz-Carlton Hotel Site, Land of Honokahua, Lahaina District, Island of Maui [TMK: (2) 4-2-01:004, 005, por. 012, 013, por. 018, 034].* Hilo, HI: Paul H. Rosendahl, Ph.D., Inc., 1993. [No location available]

Jensen, Peter M. and G. Mehalchick. *Archaeological Inventory Survey North Beach Mauka (Kāʻanapali) Site, Ahupuaʻa of Hanakaʻōʻō, Lahaina District, Island of Maui.* Hilo, HI: Paul H. Rosendahl, Ph.D., Inc., 1993. [UH Call Number: DU628.M3 J46 1989]

Munekiyo, Michael T. *Redevelopment of ABC Store at 726 Front Street, Application for Historic District Approval.* Wailuku, HI: Michael T. Munekiyo Consulting, Inc., 1993. [SHPD ID: 2019LI81540]

1994

Burgett, Berdena and Robert L. Spear. *An Archaeological Inventory Survey of an 8.8 Acre Parcel in the Land of Kainehi, Lahaina District, Paunau Ahupuaʻa, Island of Maui.* Honolulu, HI: Aki Sinoto Consulting, 1994.

Fredericksen, Erik M., Demaris Fredericksen, and W. M. Fredericksen. *An Archaeological Inventory Survey at Honokōwai Beach Park, Honokōwai Ahupuaʻa, Lahaina District, Maui Island.* Pukalani, HI: Xamanek Researches, 1994. [No location available]

Fredericksen, Erik M., Demaris L. Fredericksen, and Walter M. Fredericksen. *An Archaeological Inventory Survey of a 12.2 Acre Parcel. Honokahua and Napili 2-3 Ahupuaʻa, Lahaina District Maui Island.* Pukalani, HI: Xamanek Researches, 1994. [SHPD ID: 2019LI81030]

Heidel, Melody, William H. Folk, and Hallett H. Hammatt. *An Archaeological Inventory Survey for Waiola Church, Ahupuaʻa of Waineʻe, Lahaina District, Island of Maui.* Wailuku, HI: Cultural Surveys Hawaiʻi, Inc., 1994. [SHPD ID: 2019LI81552]

Jensen, Peter M. *Archaeological Inventory Survey Lahaina Bypass Highway New Connector Roads Project Area, Ahupuaʻa of Hanakaʻōʻō and Paunau, Lahaina District, Island of Maui.* Hilo, HI: Paul H. Rosendahl, Ph.D., Inc., 1994. [SHPD ID: 2019LI81611]

Moore, James R. and Joseph Kennedy. *An Archaeological Inventory Survey with Subsurface Testing Report for Portions of the Proposed Kahana Ridge Subdivision Located at TMK: (2) 4-3-05:016 & 018, in Kahana Ahupuaʻa, Lahaina District, Island of Maui.* Haleʻiwa, HI: Archaeological Consultants of Hawaii, 1994. [SHPD ID: 2019LI81329]

Rosendahl, Paul H. *Archaeological Treatment Plan for No Adverse Effect, Lahaina Bypass Highway Project, Lands of Honokōwai, Hanakaʻōʻō, Wahikuli, Panaʻewa, Kuʻia, Halakaʻa, Pūehuehu Nui, Pāhoa, Polanui, and Launiupoko, Lahaina District, Island of Maui.* Hilo, HI: Paul H. Rosendahl, Ph.D., Inc., 1994. [SHPD ID: 2019LI81439]

1995

Aki Sinoto Consulting. *Archaeological Monitoring During the Renovation of the Lahaina Center Parking Structure, Lahaina, Maui.* Honolulu, HI: Aki Sinoto Consulting, 1995.

Fredericksen, Demaris L. and Erik M. Fredericksen. *Archaeological Inventory Survey for Kahana-Kai Subdivision, Kahana Ahupuaʻa, Lahaina [Kāʻanapali] District, Maui Island.* Pukalani, HI: Xamanek Researches, 1995. [SHPD ID: 2019LI81330]

Fredericksen, Demaris L. and Walter M. Fredericksen. *Archaeological Monitoring Plan for the Sheraton-Maui Redevelopment Project, Ahupuaʻa of Hanakaʻōʻō, Lahaina District, Maui Island.* Pukalani, HI: Xamanek Researches, 1995. [SHPD ID: 2019LI80672]

Klieger, Paul Christiaan and Susan A. Lebo. *Archaeological Inventory Survey of Waiōlaʻi and Waiokila Catchments, Kahakuloa, West Maui, Hawaiʻi.* Honolulu, HI: Department of Anthropology, Bernice P. Bishop Museum, 1995. [No location available]

Masterson, Ian and Hallett H. Hammatt. *An Addendum Report for the New Alignment Section between Points 14D, 15, and 16 along the Proposed Maʻalaea-Lahaina Third 69 kV Transmission Line, Maui.* Wailuku, HI: Cultural Surveys Hawaiʻi, Inc., 1995. [SHPD ID: 2019LI81633]

1996

Aki Sinoto Consulting. *Archaeological Monitoring Plan for Utility Trenching at the Lahaina Shopping Center, Paunau, Lahaina, Maui.* Honolulu, HI: Aki Sinoto Consulting, 1996.

Fredericksen, Erik M., Walter M. Fredericksen, and Demaris L. Fredericksen. *Additional Archaeological Inventory Survey Subsurface testing at Kapalua Bay Hotel [TMK (2) 4-2-04:26], Honokahua and Napili 2-3 Ahupuaʻa, Lahaina District, Maui Island.* Pukalani, HI: Xamanek Researches, 1996. [SHPD ID: 2019LI81024]

Fredericksen, Walter M. and Demaris Fredericksen. *Archaeological Monitoring Report for The Kai Ala Subdivision, Ahupuaʻa of Hanakaoʻo, Lahaina District, Island of Maui.* Pukalani, HI: Xamanek Researches, 1996. [SHPD ID: 2019LI81251]

Hammatt, Hallett H. *Restoration Plan for Pole 69 (Original Location) at Ukumehame Gulch, Maʻalaea to Lahaina Third 69 KV Transmission Line.* Wailuku, HI: Cultural Surveys Hawaiʻi, Inc., 1996. [SHPD ID: 2019LI81632]

Major, Maurice. *Ridgetops and Gulch Bottoms: An Archaeological Inventory Survey of Waiōlaʻi and Waiokila Catchments, Kahakuloa, West Maui, Hawaiʻi. TMK*

(2) 3-1-01:003. Honolulu, HI: Department of Anthropology, Bernice P. Bishop Museum, 1996. [SHPD ID: 2019LI80145]

Major, Maurice, P. Christiaan Klieger, and Susan A. Lebo. *Historical Background and Archaeological Testing at Pikanele's Kuleana in Lahaina, Maui: An Inventory Survey Report of LCA 310.3 (Royal Patent 1729.2, TMK (2) 4-6-07:013.* Honolulu, HI: Department of Anthropology, Bernice P. Bishop Museum, 1996. [SHPD ID: 2019LI81546]

McGerty, Leann and Robert L. Spear. *An Inventory Survey of a 3.3 Acre Parcel in Māhinahina 4 Ahupua'a, Lahaina District, Island of Maui, Hawai'i [TMK (2) 4-3-06:003],* 1996. [SHPD ID: 2019LI81305]

Spencer Mason Architects. *Historic Structures Report: Old Lahaina Courthouse.* Honolulu, HI: Spencer Mason Architects, 1996. [SHPD ID: 2019LI81378]

1997

Fredericksen, Erik M. *Archaeological Monitoring Report on the Pioneer Inn Swimming Pool Construction Project.* Pukalani, HI: Xamanek Researches, 1997. [SHPD ID: 2019LI81383]

Goodwin, Conrad and Spencer Leinewebber. *Archaeological Inventory Survey Report, Pioneer Mil Company, Ltd. Sugar Enterprise Lands, Site No. 50-50-03-4420, Villages of Leiali'i Project, Lahaina, Maui Hawai'i.* Honolulu, HI: International Archaeological Research Institute, Inc., 1997. [SHPD ID: 2019LI81363]

Rotunno-Hazuka, Lisa J. *Archaeological Assessment for the Proposed Well Site in Launiupoko, Lahaina, Maui TMK 4-7-02:001 Lot B.* Wailuku, HI: Archaeological Services Hawaii, LLC, 1997. [SHPD ID: 2019LI81617]

Sinoto, Aki. *An Archaeological Assessment of the Native Plant Conservatory Project, Ukumehame Firing Range, Ukumehame, Lahaina, Maui TMK (2) 4-8-2:047.* Honolulu, HI: Aki Sinoto Consulting, 1997. [SHPD ID: 2019LI81624]

1998

Fredericksen, Demaris. *Monitoring Report for the Sheraton-Maui Redevelopment Project, Hanaka'ō'ō Ahupua'a, Lahaina District, Maui Island.* Pukalani, HI: Xamanek Researches, 1998. [SHPD ID: 2019LI81263]

Fredericksen, Demaris L. *Monitoring Report for the Sheraton-Maui Redevelopment Project Hanaka'ō'ō Ahupua'a, Lahaina District, Maui Island [TMK: (2) 4-4-08:005].* Pukalani, HI: Xamanek Researches, 1998. [SHPD ID: 2019LI81263]

Fredericksen, Erik M. *Archaeological Monitoring Plan for a Parcel of Land in the 'Ili of Pakala, Puako Ahupua'a, Lahaina District, Island of Maui [TMK: (2) 4-6-07:003].* Xamanek Researches: Pukalani, HI, 1998. [SHPD ID: 2019LI81549]

Fredericksen, Erik M. *Archaeological Reconnaissance Report for the County of Maui Honokōhau Water System Improvements Project, Lahaina District, Maui Island.* Pukalani, HI: Xamanek Researches, 1998. [SHPD ID: 2019LI80994]

Fredericksen, Erik M. and Demaris L. Fredericksen. *Archaeological Inventory Survey for the Proposed Golf Academy Project Kapalua, Maui, Hawai'i, TMK 4-2-04: por. 24.* Pukalani, HI: Xamanek Researches, 1998. [SHPD ID: 2019LI81012]

Hammatt, Hallett H. and David W. Shideler. *Written Findings of Archaeological Monitoring at the Lahaina Courthouse, Lahaina, Lahaina District, Maui Island, Hawai'i.* Wailuku, HI: Cultural Surveys Hawai'i, Inc., 1998. [SHPD ID: 2019LI81401]

Launiupoko Associates, LLC. *Archaeological Preservation Plan, Mahanalua Nui Subdivision.* Launiupoko Associates, 1998. [SHPD ID: 2019LI81602]

1999

Athens, J. Stephen. *Archaeological Monitoring Plan, Trenching at Taco Bell, Lahaina, Kā'anapali Ahupua'a, Lahaina District, Maui [TMK (2) 4-5-07:034].* Honolulu, HI: International Archaeological Research Institute, Inc., 1999.

Devereux, Thomas K., Ian A. Masterson, Melody Heidel, Victoria Creed, Leilani Pyle, and Hallett H. Hammatt. *Archaeological Inventory Survey and Subsurface Testing of a 440 Acre Parcel, Ahupua'a of Ukumehame, Lahaina District, Island of Maui.* Wailuku, HI: Cultural Surveys Hawai'i, Inc., 1999. [SHPD ID: 2019LI81639]

Fredericksen, Demaris L. and Erik M. Fredericksen. *Archaeological Inventory Survey (Phase 1) in the 'Ili of Pakala, Puako Ahupua'a, Lahaina District, Maui Island [TMK: (2) 4-6-07:007].* Xamanek Researches: Pukalani, HI, 1999. [SHPD ID: 2019LI81547]

Fredericksen, Erik M. *Archaeological Monitoring Plan for Lot 29 (Site 29) Honokahua and Napili 2-3 Ahupua'a, Lahaina District, Maui, Hawai'i.* Pukalani, HI: Xamanek Researches, 1999. [SHPD ID: 2019LI81028]

Fredericksen, Erik M. and Demaris Fredericksen. *Archaeological Inventory Survey for the Proposed Honokōhau Water System Improvement Project, Honokōhau*

Ahupuaʻa, Kāʻanapali District, Maui Island. DRAFT. Pukalani, HI: Xamanek Researches, 1999. [SHPD ID: 2019LI80995]

Fredericksen, Erik M. and Demaris L. Fredericksen. *Archaeological Inventory Survey of the Lower Honoapiʻilani Road Improvements Project Corridor (TMK 4-3-03; 4-3-05; 4-3-10; 4-3-15) Lahaina District, Maui Island.* Pukalani, HI: Xamanek Researches, 1999. [SHPD ID: 2021LI00220]

Hammatt, Hallett H. and David W. Shideler. *Draft Proposal for an Archaeological Mitigation Plan at the Lahaina Courthouse, Lahaina, Lahaina District, Maui Island, Hawaiʻi.* Wailuku, HI: Cultural Surveys Hawaiʻi, Inc., 1999. [SHPD ID: 2019LI81400]

Haun, Alan E. *Archaeological Inventory Survey Kauaʻula Development Parcel, Lands of Pūehuehu Iki, Pāhoa, and Pola Nui, Lahaina District, Island of Maui.* Kailua-Kona, HI: Haun and Associates, 1999. [No location available]

Liston, Jolie. *Archaeological Monitoring of Trenching Activities at Taco Bell, Lahaina, Maui.* Honolulu, HI: International Archaeological Research Institute, Inc., 1999. [SHPD ID: 2019LI80605]

Masterson, Ian and Hallett H. Hammatt. *Report on the Completed Reconstruction of Walls at Hikiʻi Heiau Ukumehame Ahupuaʻa, Island of Maui.* Wailuku, HI: Cultural Surveys Hawaiʻi, Inc., 1999. [SHPD ID: 2019LI81631]

2000

Dega, Michael F. *An Archaeological Monitoring plan for Construction Work at Honokōwai, Māhinahina Ahupuaʻa, Kāʻanapali District, Maui Island, Hawaiʻi.* Honolulu, HI: Scientific Consultant Services, Inc., 2000. [SHPD ID: 2019LI81247]

Fredericksen, Demaris L. and Erik M. Fredericksen. *Archaeological Inventory Survey of a 24-Acre Parcel, Kapalua Lot 19, Located in Napili 2-3 Ahupuaʻa, Lahaina District, Maui Island [TMK: (2) 4-2-04: por. 024].* Pukalani, HI: Xamanek Researches, 2000. [SHPD ID: 2019LI81025]

Fredericksen, Demaris L. and Erik M. Fredericksen. *Archaeological Inventory Survey of Makai Portion (Phase 1) of Olowalu Development Parcel, Olowalu Ahupuaʻa, Lahaina District, Maui Island [TMK: (2) 4-8-03: por. 05].* Pukalani, HI: Xamanek Researches, 2000. [SHPD ID: 2019LI81638]

Fredericksen, Erik M. *Archaeological Monitoring Plan for the Sabia Building Development and Improvement Project at 816A Front Street, Paunau Ahupuaʻa,*

Lahaina District, Maui. Pukalani, HI: Xamanek Researches, 2000. [SHPD ID: 2019LI80617]

Fredericksen, Erik M. and Demaris L. Fredericksen. *An Archaeological Inventory Survey of Honoapiʻilani Highway Corridor from Alaelae Point to Honolua Bay, Honolua and Honokahua Ahupuaʻa, Lahaina District, Maui Island.* Pukalani, HI: Xamanek Researches, 2000. [SHPD ID: 2019LI81045]

Hammatt, Hallett H. *Archaeological Preservation Plan for 10 Sites Within for 440 Acre Parcel, Ahupuaʻa of Ukumehame, Lahaina District, Island of Maui.* Wailuku, HI: Cultural Surveys Hawaiʻi, Inc., 2000. [SHPD ID: 2019LI81626]

Haun, Alan E. and Jack D. Henry. *Archaeological Site Preservation Plan, Kauaʻula Development Parcel, Lands of Pūehuehu Iki, Pāhoa, and Polo Nui, Lahaina District, Island of Maui [TMK: (2) 4-7-03:001].* Kailua-Kona, HI: Haun and Associates, 2000. [SHPD ID: 2019LI81613]

2001

Chaffee, David B. and Robert L. Spear. *An Archaeological Monitoring Plan for Construction Activities on a 13,237 Square Foot Parcel in ʻAlaeloa Ahupuaʻa, Lahaina District, Maui Island, Hawaii.* Honolulu, HI: Scientific Consultant Services, Inc., 2001.

Dega, Michael F. *Archaeological Inventory Survey of a 3-Acre Parcel in Kahana-Kai, Kahana Ahupuaʻa, Kāʻanapali District, Island of Maui, Hawaiʻi.* Honolulu, HI: Scientific Consultant Services, Inc., 2001. [SHPD ID: 2019LI81327]

Devereux, Thomas K., William H. Folk, and Hallett H. Hammatt. *Archaeological Survey of the Lands Comprising Project District 2 at Kapalua, Honokahua, and Nāpili 2 & 3 Ahupuaʻa Lahaina District of Maui.* Wailuku, HI: Cultural Surveys Hawaiʻi, Inc., 2001. [SHPD ID: 2019LI81007]

Fredericksen, Erik M. *Archaeological Monitoring Plan for Improvements at 815 Front Street, Paunau Ahupuaʻa, Lahaina District, Maui.* Pukalani, HI: Xamanek Researches, 2001. [SHPD ID: 2019LI80644]

Fredericksen, Erik M. *Archaeological Monitoring Plan for the King Kamehameha III Elementary School Building B, Building D, and PT 201 Restroom Renovation Project, Puako Ahupuaʻa, Lahaina District, Maui [TMK: (2) 4-6-02:013 & 014].* Pukalani, HI: Xamanek Researches, 2001. [SHPD ID: 2019LI81392]

Fredericksen, Erik M. *Archaeological Monitoring Plan on a 1.3 Acre of Land on the Olowalu Makai Project Area, Olowalu Ahupuaʻa, Lahaina District, Maui*

[TMK: (2) 4-9-03:044]. Pukalani, HI: Xamanek Researches, 2001. [SHPD ID: 2019LI81635]

Fredericksen, Erik M. *Archaeological Monitoring Report for the Coconut Grove Development (Site 29), Honokahua and Napili 2-3 Ahupuaʻa Lahiana District, Island of Maui.* Pukalani, HI: Xamanek Researches, 2001. [SHPD ID: 2019LI17106]

Fredericksen, Erik M. *Archaeological Monitoring Report for the Verizon Hawaii, Inc. Equipment Installation project at TMK: (2) 4-2-04:021 Ritz-Carlton, Kapalua, Honokahua Ahupuaʻa, Lahaina District, Maui, Hawaiʻi.* Pukalani, HI: Xamanek Researches, 2001. [SHPD ID: 2019LI81014, 2019LI81029]

Fredericksen, Erik M. and Demaris L. Fredericksen. *Additional Archaeological Inventory Survey Level Work for Site 50-50-03-4797, Lower Honoapiʻilani Road Improvements Project Corridor; Alaeloa, Mailepai and Kahana Ahupuaʻa, Lahaina District, Maui Island [TMK (2) 4-3-15].* Pukalani, HI: Xamanek Researches, 2001. [SHPD ID: 2021LI00221]

Fredericksen, Walter M. *An Historic and Traditional Land Use Study Utilizing Oral History Interviews for Assessing Cultural Impacts, for the Kapalua Project 2 and Expanded Project 2, Kapalua, Maui, Hawaiʻi.* Pukalani, HI: Xamanek Researches, 2001. [No location available]

Haun, Alan E. *Archaeological Assessment TMK (2) 4-7-02:005 Land of Pāhoa, Lahaina District, Island of Maui.* Kailua-Kona, HI: Haun and Associates, 2001. [SHPD ID: 2019LI81616]

Haun, Alan E. and Dave Henry with Maria E. K. Orr. *Archaeological Inventory Survey Portion of TMK 4-7-01:002, Land of Launiupoko, Lahaina District, Island of Maui.* Kailua-Kona, HI: Haun and Associates, 2001. [SHPD ID: 2019LI81599]

Haun, Alan E. and Dave Henry. *Archaeological Inventory Survey, Proposed 124-Acre Mākila Subdivision, Lands of Launiupoko, Polanui and Pūehuehu Nui, Lahaina District, Island of Maui [TMK: 4-7-01: por. 1 and TMK 4-7-04: Por. 4].* Kailua-Kona, HI: Haun and Associates, 2001. [SHPD ID: 2019LI81623]

Haun, Alan E. and Dave Henry. *Archaeological Inventory Survey, TMK 4-6-7:010 ʻIli of Pakala, Land of Puako District, Island of Maui.* Kailua-Kona, HI: Haun and Associates, 2001. [SHPD ID: 2019LI81555]

Olowalu Elua Associates, LLC. *Archaeological Mitigation and Preservation Plan, Makai Portion (Phase 1), Olowalu Ahupuaʻa, Lahaina District, Maui Island.* Olowalu, HI: Olowalu Elua Associates, LLC, 2001.

2002

Buffum, Amy and Michael F. Dega. *An Archaeological Monitoring Report for Construction work at Honokōwai, Māhinahina Ahupua'a, Kā'anapali District, Maui Island, Hawaii.* Honolulu, HI: Scientific Consultant Services, Inc., 2002.

Calis, Irene. *Archaeological Monitoring Report: Parking Lot Drainage System Installation, Pana'ewa Ahupua'a, Lahaina District, Island of Maui, Hawai'i.* Honolulu, HI: Scientific Consultant Services, Inc., 2002. [SHPD ID: 2019LI80642]

Dega, Michael F. *Archaeological Monitoring Plan for the Front Street Waterline Replacement Project, Pana'ewa Ahupua'a, Lahaina District, Island of Maui, Hawai'i [TMK (2) 4-5-04, 05, and 08].* Honolulu, HI: Scientific Consultant Services, Inc., 2002. [SHPD ID: 2019LI80631]

Dega, Michael F. and Mary Sullivan. *Archaeological Monitoring Plan for Construction at the Lahaina Store, Lahaina, Ku'ia Ahupua'a, Lahaina District, Island of Maui, Hawai'i [TMK: (2) 4-6-09:007 & 062].* Honolulu, HI: Scientific Consultant Services, Inc., 2002. [SHPD ID: 2019LI81578]

Fredericksen, Erik M. *An Archaeological Monitoring Plan for the West Side Resource Center in Lahaina, Waine'e Ahupua'a, Lahaina District, Maui Island [TMK: 4-6-15: por. of 1 and 4-6-18: por. of 2].* Pukalani, HI: Xamanek Researches, 2002. [SHPD ID: 2019LI81534]

Fredericksen, Erik M. *Archaeological Monitoring Plan for the Proposed Plantation Inn Improvements Project (GPC 2002/43), Pana'ewa Ahupua'a, Lahaina District, Maui [TMK: (2) 4-6-009: 036, 037 and 044].* Pukalani, HI: Xamanek Researches, 2002. [SHPD ID: 2019LI81579]

Fredericksen, Erik M. *Archaeological Monitoring Plan for the Wharf Street Accessibility Improvements at Lahaina Harbor—Electrical Underground Work Project, Puako Ahupua'a, Lahaina District, Maui [TMK: (2) 4-6-01 and 4-6-01: Portion of Parcel 1].* Pukalani, HI: Xamanek Researches, 2002. [SHPD ID: 2019LI81402]

Fredericksen, Erik M. and Demaris Fredericksen. *Archaeological Inventory Survey Report for Portion of Land in Puako Ahupua'a, Lahaina District, Lahaina, Maui, [TMK: (2) 4-6-08:53 and 48].* Pukalani, HI: Xamanek Researches, 2002. [SHPD ID: 2019LI81571]

Fredericksen, Erik M. and Demaris L. Fredericksen. *An Archaeological Inventory Survey (Phase 2) of a New Alignment for the Honokōhau Waterline Project, Honokōhau, Ahupua'a, Kā'anapali District, Island of Maui.* Pukalani, HI: Xamanek Researches, 2002. [SHPD ID: 2019LI81426]

Fredericksen, Erik M. and Demaris L. Fredericksen. *Archaeological Inventory Survey of 475 Acres in Kapalua District 2 Project Area, Located in Napili and Honokahua Ahupuaʻa, Lahaina District, Maui Island, TMK: (2) 4-2-01: por. 1.* Pukalani, HI: Xamanek Researches, 2002. [SHPD ID: 2021LI00311]

Fredericksen, Walter M. *Archaeological Monitoring Report for the Remodeling Project of the Lahaina Yacht Club, 835 Front Street, Paunau Ahupuaʻa, Lahaina District, Island of Maui.* Pukalani, HI: Xamanek Researches, 2002. [SHPD ID: 2019LI80645]

Hammatt, Hallett H. and Rodney Chiogioji. *Archaeological Monitoring Plan for a ½-Acre parcel in Napili 2-3 Ahupuaʻa, Lahaina District, Island of Maui.* Wailuku, HI: Cultural Surveys Hawaiʻi, Inc., 2002. [SHPD ID: 2019LI81063]

Haun, Alan E. *Archaeological Assessment, Lands of Polanui, Polaiki, and Launiupoko, Lahaina District, Island of Maui.* Kailua-Kona, HI: Haun and Associates, 2002. [SHPD ID: 2019LI81608]

Haun, Alan E. and Jack D. Henry. *Archaeological Data Recovery Plan Sites 4141 and 4143, Land of Honolua, Lahaina District, Island of Maui,* 2002. [SHPD ID: 2019LI81010]

McGerty, Leann and Robert L. Spear. *A Cultural Impact Assessment for Maui Marriott Ocean Club, Situated in the Ahupuaʻa of Hanakaʻōʻō, Lahaina District, Island of Maui, Hawaiʻi.* Honolulu, HI: Scientific Consultant Services, Inc., 2002. [SHPD ID: 2019LI80664]

McGerty, Leann and Robert L. Spear. *An Archaeological Inventory Survey at the Maui Marriott Ocean Club, in the Ahupuaʻa of Hanakaʻōʻō, Lahaina District, Island of Maui, Hawaiʻi.* Honolulu, HI: Scientific Consultant Services, Inc., 2002. [SHPD ID: 2019LI80107]

Olowalu Elua Associates, LLC. *Archaeological Preservation Plan, Mauka Portion (Phase 2), Olowalu Ahupuaʻa, Lahaina District, Maui Island.* Olowalu, HI: Olowalu Elua Associates, LLC, 2002. [SHPD ID: 2019LI00099]

Olowalu Elua Associates, LLC. *Monitoring Plan for Sites 50-50-08-4820 and 50-50-08-4821; Olowalu Ahupuaʻa, Lahaina District; Island of Maui [TMK (2) 4-8-003: portion of 10].* Olowalu, HI: Olowalu Elua Associates, LLC, 2002. [No location available]

Rosendahl, Paul H. *Archaeological Monitoring Plan, Mala Village Subdivision, Land of Puʻunoa, Lahaina District, Island of Maui [TMK: (2) 4-5-04:008, 009, 059, 060, 061, 062].* Hilo, HI: Paul H. Rosendahl, Ph.D., Inc., 2002. [SHPD ID: 2019LI80615]

Rotunno-Hazuka, Lisa J. and Jeffrey Pantaleo. *Archaeological Monitoring Plan for a Waterline Installation at TMK: (2) 4-5-01:045 Old Lahaina Center, Papalua Street, Pana'ewa Ahupua'a, Lahaina District, Island of Maui.* Wailuku, HI: Archaeological Services Hawaii, LLC, 2002. [SHPD ID: 2019LI80638]

Rotunno-Hazuka, Lisa J. and Jeffrey Pantaleo. *Archaeological Monitoring Plan for Pool Installation at TMK (2) 4-5-04:037 Lahilahi Street, Ku'ia Ahupua'a, Lahaina District, Island of Maui.* Wailuku, HI: Archaeological Services Hawaii, LLC, 2002. [SHPD ID: 2019LI80627]

Tome, Guerin, Irene Calis, and Michael F. Dega. *An Archaeological Inventory Survey in Honolua, Honolua Ahupua'a, Lahaina District, Island of Maui, Hawai'i [TMK: (2) 4-1-01:005].* Honolulu, HI: Scientific Consultant Services, Inc., 2002. [SHPD ID: 2019LI81423]

2003

Chaffee, David B. and Michael F. Dega. *An Archaeological Monitoring Plan for Subdivision Construction of a 450-Acre Parcel of Land, Ahupua'a of Ukumehame, Lahaina District, Island of Maui, Hawai'i [TMK (2) 4-8-02:09].* Honolulu, HI: Scientific Consultant Services, Inc., 2003.

Dega, Michael F. *Archaeological Monitoring Plan for Limited Construction Work in Lahaina, Ku'ia Ahupua'a, Lahaina District, Island of Maui, Hawai'i.* Honolulu, HI: Scientific Consultant Services, Inc., 2003. [SHPD ID: 2019LI80641]

Donham, Theresa K. *Archaeological Monitoring Plan for Construction of a Pool & Spa at the Hurlock Property, Moali'i, Lahaina District, Maui, TMK: (2) 4-5-13:004.* Kihei, HI: Akahele Archaeology, 2003. [SHPD ID: 2019LI81351]

Duensing, Dawn E. and Michael W. Foley. *Lahaina Design Guidelines, Lahaina Town, Maui, Hawai'i,* 2003. [SHPD ID: 2019LI81377]

Fredericksen, Demaris L. and Erik M. Fredericksen. *An Archaeological Inventory Survey of a portion of land in Napili 2-3 Ahupua'a, Lahaina District, Island of Maui [TMK: (2) 4-2-07: Parcels 007 and 008].* Pukalani, HI: Xamanek Researches, 2003. [SHPD ID: 2019LI81044]

Fredericksen, Demaris L. and Erik M. Fredericksen. *An Archaeological Inventory Survey of the Proposed Sandwich Isles Communications, Inc. Fiber Optics Landing Location near the Lahaina Post Office, Wahikuli Ahupua'a, Lahaina District, Island of Maui (TMK: 4-5-21:015).* Pukalani, HI: Xamanek Researches, 2003. [SHPD ID: 2019LI81336]

Fredericksen, Erik M. *An Archaeological Monitoring Plan for an Inventory Survey Concurrent with Construction Activities on a Parcel of Land in Puako Ahupua'a, Lahaina District, Lahaina, Maui [TMK: (2) 4-6-08:48 and 53].* Pukalani, HI: Xamanek Researches, 2003. [SHPD ID: 2019LI81569]

Fredericksen, Erik M. *A Preliminary Report Summarizing Results of Field Research for an Archaeological Inventory Survey to Satisfy Requirements of SHPD at [TMK: (2) 4-2-04:por. 024] located in Honokahua Ahupua'a, Lahaina District, Island of Maui, Hawai'i.* Pukalani, HI: Xamanek Researches, 2003.

Fredericksen, Erik M. *Archaeological Monitoring Plan for a Water Lateral and Sewer Lateral Installation Project for a Parcel of Land in Lahaina, Moali'i Ahupua'a, Lahaina District, Maui.* Pukalani, HI: Xamanek Researches, 2003. [SHPD ID: 2019LI81270]

Fredericksen, Erik M. *Archaeological Monitoring Plan for Sewer Lateral Installation Project at 460 Alio Street, Land of Nalehu, Mākila Ahupua'a, Lahaina District, Maui [TMK (2) 4-6-06:031].* Pukalani, HI: Xamanek Researches, 2003. [SHPD ID: 2019LI81270]

Fredericksen, Erik M. *Archaeological Monitoring Report for a 1.3 Acre of Land on the Olowalu Makai Project Area, Olowalu Ahupua'a, Lahaina District, Maui (TMK 2-4-8-03:44).* Pukalani, HI: Xamanek Researches, 2003. [SHPD ID: 2019LI81637]

Fredericksen, Erik M. *Archaeological Monitoring Report for the Proposed Plantation Inn Improvements Project (GPC2002/43) Pana'ewa Ahupua'a, Lahaina District, Maui [TMK: (2) 4-6-09:036, 037, and 044].* Pukalani, HI: Xamanek Researches, 2003. [SHPD ID: 2019LI81574]

Fredericksen, Erik M. *Preservation Plan for Possible Burial Features Contained Within Sites 50-50-01-5139, 5142, 5157 and 5158 Located on the Kapalua Mauka Project area, Honokahua and Napili 2 & 3 Ahupua'a, Lahaina District, Island of Maui.* Pukalani, HI: Xamanek Researches, 2003. [SHPD ID: 2019LI81407]

Fredericksen, Erik M. and Demaris L. Fredericksen. *An Archaeological Inventory Survey of the Lahaina Watershed Flood Control Project Area, Lands of Polanui, Paha, Pueuehunui, Lahaina District, Maui Island (TMK: 4-6-13:016, 18, 26; TMK 4-7-01, 02).* Pukalani, HI: Xamanek Researches, 2003. [SHPD ID: 2019LI81442]

Hammatt, Hallett H. *Lahaina (Front Street) Archaeological Test Excavations, TMK 4-5-3:012, Island of Maui.* Wailuku, HI: Cultural Surveys Hawai'i, Inc., 2003. [SHPD ID: 2019LI80649]

Hammatt, Hallett H. and David W. Shideler. *Preservation Plan for Four Sites (50-50-01-5234, A Water Exploration Tunnel; -5235, A Petroglyph; -5425, A Historic Trail, and -5426, A Pre-Contact Habitation Site) Located Within a 400-Acre Parcel at Honolua Ahupua'a.* Wailuku, HI: Cultural Surveys Hawai'i, Inc., 2003. [SHPD ID: 2019LI81003]

Hammatt, Hallett H., David W. Shideler, and Tony Bush. *Archaeological Inventory Survey of an Approximately 400-Acre Parcel at Honolua Ahupua'a Lahaina District of Maui.* Wailuku, HI: Cultural Surveys Hawai'i, Inc., 2003. [SHPD ID: 2019LI80993]

Haun, Alan E. and Jack D. Henry. *Archaeological Site Preservation Plan Kau'aula Development Parcel, Lands of Pūehuehu Iki, Pāhoa, and Polanui Ahupua'a, Lahaina District, Island of Maui [TMK (2) 4-7-02:04, 05, & 07, (2) 4-7-03:por. 01].* Kailua-Kona, HI: Haun and Associates, 2003. [SHPD ID: 2019LI81618]

Magnuson, Carol M. *Supplemental Archaeological Survey of Turbine Pad Alignments, Kaheawa Pastures, Upland Ukumehame Ahupua'a, Maui.* Honolulu, HI: International Archaeological Research Institute, Inc., 2003. [SHPD ID: 2019LI81630]

McGerty, Leann and Robert L. Spear. *A Cultural Impact Assessment on a Piece of Property Located in Kā'anapali, Hanaka'ō'ō Ahupua'a, Lahaina District, Maui Island, Hawai'i [TMK: (2) 4-4-06:056].* Scientific Consultant Services, Inc.: Honolulu, HI, 2003. [SHPD ID: 2019LI81266]

Monahan, Christopher M. *An Archaeological Assessment Report on 17.746 Acres of Land (Lahaina Business Park, Phase II) on an Undeveloped Lot in Lahaina, Moali'i Ahupua'a, Lahaina District, Maui Island, Hawai'i [TMK: (2) 4-5-10:007].* Honolulu, HI: Scientific Consultant Services, Inc., 2003. [SHPD ID: 2019LI80604]

Monahan, Christopher M. *An Archaeological Assessment Report on 3.054 Acres of Partially Developed Land in Honokōwai, Māhinahina 4 Ahupua'a, Lahaina District, Maui Island, Hawai'i [TMK (2) 4-3-06:002 and 069].* Honolulu, HI: Scientific Consultant Services, Inc., 2003. [SHPD ID: 2019LI81314, 2019LI81304]

Monahan, Christopher M., Lauren Morawski, and Michael F. Dega. *Archaeological Monitoring Plan for Pool Installation at TMK (2) 4-5-04:037 Lahilahi Street, Ku'ia Ahupua'a, Lahaina District, Island of Maui.* Honolulu, HI: Scientific Consultant Services, Inc., 2003. [No location available]

Morawski, Lauren and Michael F. Dega. *Archaeological Inventory Survey of a 7.65 Acre Property at Lot 10-H Ahupua'a of Hanaka'ō'ō, Lahaina District, Island of Maui, Hawai'i [TMK: (2) 4-4-06:056].* Honolulu, HI: Scientific Consultant Services, Inc., 2003. [SHPD ID: 2019LI81273]

Munekiyo & Hiraga, Inc. *Historic Resources Inventory Submittal, Maka'oi'oi Demolition*. Wailuku, HI: Munekiyo & Hiraga, Inc., 2003. [SHPD ID: 2019LI81049]

Munekiyo & Hiraga, Inc. *Maka'oi'oi (Honolua Plantation Managers Residence, Pineapple Hill Restaurant), Historical Report*. Wailuku, HI: Munekiyo & Hiraga, Inc., 2003. [SHPD ID: 2019LI81022]

O'Hare, Constance, Thomas K. Devereux, William H. Folk, and Hallett H. Hammatt. *Preservation Plan for Specific Sites in the Land Comprising Project District 2 at Kapalua, Honokahua and Nāpili 2 & 3 Ahupua'a Lahaina District of Maui*. Wailuku, HI: Cultural Surveys Hawai'i, Inc., 2003. [SHPD ID: 2019LI81002]

Rotunno-Hazuka, Lisa J. and Jeffrey Pantaleo. *Archaeological Monitoring Plan for the Renovations to the Lahaina-Kaiser Clinic, Pana'ewa Ahupua'a, Lahaina District, Island of Maui*. Wailuku, HI: Archaeological Services Hawaii, LLC, 2003. [SHPD ID: 2019LI80608]

Sinoto, Aki and Jeffrey Pantaleo. *Archaeological Inventory Survey of the Proposed Site for the New Lahaina Kingdom Hall Puunoa, Paunau Ahupua'a, Lahaina District, Maui Island TMK (2) 4-4-04:042 & 044)*. Wailuku, HI: Archaeological Services Hawaii, LLC, 2003. [SHPD ID: 2019LI80616]

Tomonari-Tuggle, M. J. *An Archaeological Reconnaissance Survey for 27 Wind Turbines in the Ukumehame Uplands, Island of Maui*. Honolulu, HI: International Archaeological Research Institute, Inc., 2003. [SHPD ID: 2019LI81627]

Tulchin, Jon and Hallett H. Hammatt. *Archaeological Assessment of a 0.2-Acre Parcel and Waterline, Māhinahina 4 Ahupua'a, Lahaina District, Island of Maui*. Wailuku, HI: Cultural Surveys Hawai'i, Inc., 2003. [SHPD ID: 2019LI81315]

2004

Ah Sam, Jessica A., Solomon H. Kailihiwa III, and Paul L. Cleghorn. *Archaeological Inventory Study and Cultural Impact Assessment for the Comfort Station Replacement During the Lahaina Pier Improvement Project, Lahaina, Maui [TMK (2) 4-6-01:001]*. Kailua, HI: Pacific Legacy, Inc., 2004.

Conte, Patty J. *Assessment of a Lot for Proposed Residential Construction, Kahana Ahupua'a, Lahaina District, Maui, Hawai'i*. Makawao, HI: CRM Solutions Hawai'i, Inc., 2004. [SHPD ID: 2019LI81300]

Dega, Michael F. and David B. Chaffee. *Archaeological Monitoring Plan for Construction at the Lahaina Shores, Moali'i Ahupua'a, Lahaina District, Maui*

Island, Hawai'i. Honolulu, HI: Scientific Consultant Services, Inc., 2004. [SHPD ID: 2019LI81373]

Dega, Michael F. and David B. Chaffee. *Archaeological Monitoring Plan for Construction Work on Approximately 25.3 Acres in Kapalua, Napili 2-3 Ahupua'a, Lahaina District, Maui Island, Hawai'i.* Honolulu, HI: Scientific Consultant Services, Inc., 2004. [SHPD ID: 2019LI81041]

Donham, Theresa K. *Archaeological Monitoring Plan for American Disabilities Act Improvements at the Lahaina Public Library, Paunau, Lahaina District, Maui, TMK: (2) 4-6-01:007 & 010.* Kīhei, HI: Akahele Archaeology, 2004. [SHPD ID: 2019LI81381]

Donham, Theresa K. *Archaeological Monitoring Plan for the Remodeling of a Dwelling at the Phleger Property, Halaka'a, Lahaina District, Maui TMK: (2) 4-6-05:014.* Kīhei, HI: Akahele Archaeology, 2004. [SHPD ID: 2019LI81558]

Fredericksen, Erik M. *An Archaeological Assessment for the Proposed Maui Preparatory Academy, Alaeloa Ahupua'a, Lahaina District, Island of Maui [TMK (2) 4-3-01: 01 por.].* Pukalani, HI: Xamanek Researches, 2004. [SHPD ID: 2019LI81053]

Fredericksen, Erik M. *An Archaeological Monitoring Plan for a Parcel of Land in Napili, Mailepai Ahupua'a, Lahaina District, Napili, Maui, TMK: (2) 4-3-15:014.* Pukalani, HI: Xamanek Researches, 2004. [SHPD ID: 2019LI81293]

Fredericksen, Erik M. *An Archaeological Monitoring Plan for the Dickenson Street Power Pole Replacement Project, Paunau Ahupua'a, Lahaina District, Island of Maui.* Pukalani, HI: Xamanek Researches, 2004. [SHPD ID: 2019LI81570]

Fredericksen, Erik M. *An Archaeological Monitoring Plan for the Proposed Kā'anapali Loop Road Project, Hanaka'ō'ō Ahupua'a, Lahaina District, Island of Maui.* Pukalani, HI: Xamanek Researches, 2004. [SHPD ID: 2019LI81268]

Fredericksen, Erik M. *An Archaeological Monitoring Report for the West Side Resource Center in Lahaina, Waine'e Ahupua'a, Lahaina District, Maui Island [TMK: (2) 4-6-15: por. of 1 and TMK: (2) 4-6-18: por. of 2].* Pukalani, HI: Xamanek Researches, 2004. [SHPD ID: 2019LI81535]

Fredericksen, Erik M. *Archaeological Assessment Report for a Portion of Land in Puako Ahupua'a, Lahaina District, Lahaina, Maui [TMK: (2) 4-6-08:053].* Pukalani, HI: Xamanek Researches, 2004. [SHPD ID: 2019LI81545]

Fredericksen, Erik M. *Archaeological Monitoring Report for a Portion of Land in Moali'i Ahupua'a, Lahaina District, Maui.* Pukalani, HI: Xamanek Researches, 2004. [SHPD ID: 2019LI81269]

Haun, Alan E. *Archaeological Site Documentation, Site 5401, Lands of Polanui and Pāhoa, Lahaina District, Island of Maui (TMK: 4-8-01:002, 4-7-01:001).* Kailua-Kona, HI: Haun and Associates, 2004. [SHPD ID: 2019LI81622]

Morawski, Lauren and Michael F. Dega. *Archaeological Inventory Survey Report of an Approximate 10-Acre Parcel in Kapalua in the Ahupua'a of Honokahua, Lahaina District (Formerly Kā'anapali), Island of Maui, Hawai'i.* Honolulu, HI: Scientific Consultant Services, Inc., 2004. [SHPD ID: 2019LI81017]

Pantaleo, Jeffrey and Paul Titchenal. *An Archaeological Inventory Survey Report for the Pulelehua Community Project TMK (2) 4-3-01:031 Por. Māhinahina 1, 2, 3, Māhinahina 4, and Kahana Ahupua'a, Lahaina and Kā'anapali Districts, Island of Maui.* Wailuku, HI: Archaeological Services Hawaii, LLC, 2004. [SHPD ID: 2019LI81072]

Rotunno-Hazuka, Lisa J. and Jeffrey Pantaleo. *Archaeological Monitoring Plan for the Construction of a Swimming Pool and Associated Utilities at the Allan Residence, Lahaina Ahupua'a, Lahaina District, Island of Maui.* Wailuku, HI: Archaeological Services Hawai'i, LLC, 2004. [SHPD ID: 2019LI80623]

Rotunno-Hazuka, Lisa J. and Jeffrey Pantaleo. *Archaeological Monitoring Plan For the Construction of an Accessory Dwelling at the Meston Residence at TMK (2) 4-6-07:030 Paunau Ahupua'a, Lahaina District, Island of Maui.* Wailuku, HI: Archaeological Services Hawaii, LLC, 2004. [SHPD ID: 2019LI81551]

Rotunno-Hazuka, Lisa J. and Jeffrey Pantaleo. *Archaeological Monitoring Plan for the Demolition of an Existing Single Family Residence & Pool Cover and Construction of a New Single Family Residence at TMK: (2) 4-5-04:048 Pu'unoa Ahupua'a, Lahaina District, Island of Maui.* Wailuku, HI: Archaeological Services Hawaii, LLC, 2004. [SHPD ID: 2019LI80625]

Rotunno-Hazuka, Lisa J. and Jeffrey Pantaleo. *Archaeological Monitoring Plan for the Demolition of an Existing Single Family Residence and Construction of a new Single Family Residence at TMK (2) 4-5-04:004, Pu'unoa Ahupua'a, Lahaina District, Island of Maui.* Wailuku, HI: Archaeological Services Hawaii, LLC, 2004. [SHPD ID: 2019LI80621]

2005

Bulgrin, Lon E. and Robert B. Rechtman. *An Archaeological Assessment Survey of TMK (2) 4-4-08:016 Hanaka'ō'ō Ahupua'a, Lahaina District, Island of Maui.* Rechtman Consulting, LLC, 2005.

Chaffee, D. and C. Monahan. *A Monitoring Plan for 3.054 Acres of Partially Developed Land in Honokōwai, Māhinahina 4 Ahupua'a, Lahaina District, Maui Island, Hawai'i.* Honolulu, HI: Scientific Consultant Services, Inc., 2005.

Chaffee, David B. and Michael F. Dega. *An Archaeological Monitoring Plan for Approximately 12,365 Foot sq. Property Located on Waine'e Street in Lahaina, Ahupua'a of Pana'ewa, Lahaina District, Maui Island, Hawai'i [TMK (2) 4-6-09:024].* Honolulu, HI: Scientific Consultant Services, Inc., 2005. [SHPD ID: 2019LI81580]

Chun, Allison and Michael F. Dega. *Addendum Archaeological Assessment Report on 0.13 Acres of Partially Developed land in Honokōwai, Māhinahina 4 Ahupua'a, Maui Island, Hawai'i.* Honolulu, HI: Scientific Consultant Services, Inc., 2005. [SHPD ID: 2019LI81043]

Conte, Patty J. *Archaeological Assessment Report for TMK (2) 4-3-03:043 Maile-pai Ahupua'a, Lahaina District, Island of Maui.* Makawao, HI: CRM Solutions Hawai'i, Inc., 2005. [SHPD ID: 2019LI81298]

Conte, Patty J. *Archaeological Monitoring Plan for Construction Within TMK (2) 4-5-14:013 Por. 8A, Lahaina District, Wahikuli Ahupua'a, Island of Maui.* Makawao, HI: CRM Solutions Hawai'i, Inc., 2005. [SHPD ID: 2019LI81348]

Conte, Patty J. *Archaeological Monitoring Plan for On and Off-Site Construction Related to the Proposed Amano Demo/Reconstruction, TMK (2) 4-5-12:008 Wahikuli Ahupua'a, Lahaina District, Island of Maui.* Makawao, HI: CRM Solutions Hawai'i, Inc., 2005. [SHPD ID: 2019LI81347]

Conte, Patty J. *Archaeological Monitoring Report for Construction, Lahaina District, Wahikuli Ahupua'a, Island of Maui.* Makawao, HI: CRM Solutions Hawai'i, Inc., 2005. [SHPD ID: 2019LI81345]

Dega, Michael F. *Archaeological Monitoring Plan for the Installation of a Septic System, Maui County Parks, Launiupoko Ahupua'a, Lahaina District, Maui Island, Hawai'i [TMK: (2) 4-7-01:17].* Honolulu, HI: Scientific Consultant Services, Inc., 2005. [SHPD ID: 2019LI81619]

Dega, Michael F. *Archaeological Monitoring Plan for the Maui Marriott Vacation Club, in the Ahupua'a of Hanaka'ō'ō, Lahaina District, Island of Maui, Hawai'i [TMK: (2) 4-4-13:001].* Honolulu, HI: Scientific Consultant Services, Inc., 2005. [SHPD ID: 2019LI80663]

Dockall, John E. and Hallett H. Hammatt. *An Archaeological Inventory Survey for a Proposed Town Center and Residential Village, Nāpili Ahupua'a, Lahaina District.* Wailuku, HI: Cultural Surveys Hawai'i, Inc., 2005. [SHPD ID: 2019LI81011]

Dockall, John E., Tanya L. Lee-Greig, and Hallett H. Hammatt. *An Archaeological Assessment of a Proposed Road Corridor for Maui Preparatory Academy, Alaeloa Ahupuaʻa, Lahaina District, Maui Island.* Wailuku, HI: Cultural Surveys Hawaiʻi, Inc., 2005. [SHPD ID: 2019LI81052]

Donham, Theresa K. *Archaeological Monitoring Report for American Disabilities Act Improvements at the Lahaina Public Library, Paunau, Lahaina District, Maui, TMK: (2) 4-6-01:007 & 010.* Kīhei, HI: Akahele Archaeology, 2005. [SHPD ID: 2019LI81403]

Fredericksen, Erik M. *A Preservation Plan for the Sites Contained within Kāʻanapali Coffee Estates Subdivision (aka Pioneer Farms Subdivision 1) Project Area, Hanakaʻōʻō Ahupuaʻa, Lahaina District, Island of Maui.* Pukalani, HI: Xamanek Researches, 2005. [SHPD ID: 2019LI81274]

Fredericksen, Erik M. *An Archaeological Monitoring Plan for a Portion of Land in Alaeloa Ahupuaʻa, Lahaina District, Maui TMK: (2) 4-5-014:032.* Pukalani, HI: Xamanek Researches, 2005. [SHPD ID: 2019LI81355]

Fredericksen, Erik M. *An Archaeological Monitoring Plan for the Proposed Lower Honoapiʻilani Highway Improvements Phase IV Project (Hoʻohui Road to Napilihau Street) in Kahana, Mailepai, and Alaeloa Ahupuaʻa, Napili, Lahaina District, Maui [F. A. P. No. STP 3080 (8)].* Pukalani, HI: Xamanek Researches, 2005. [SHPD ID: 2019LI81299]

Fredericksen, Erik M. *An Archaeological Monitoring Report for a Parcel of Land in Puako Ahupuaʻa, Lahaina District, Maui [TMK: (2) 4-6-008:022].* Pukalani, HI: Xamanek Researches, 2005. [SHPD ID: 2019LI81565]

Guerriero, Diane and Jeffrey *Pantaleo. Archaeological Inventory Survey Report of a 0.361 Acre Coastal Parcel, Waineʻe Ahupuaʻa, Lahaina District, Island of Maui.* Wailuku, HI: Archaeological Services Hawaii, LLC, 2005. [SHPD ID: 2019LI81560]

Guerriero, Diane, Lisa J. Rotunno-Hazuka, and Jeffrey Pantaleo. *Archaeological Assessment Report of a 0.428 Acre Parcel of Land at TMK 4-5-07:004 Kuholilea Ahupuaʻa, Lahaina District, Island of Maui.* Wailuku, HI: Archaeological Services Hawaii, LLC, 2005. [SHPD ID: 2019LI80606]

Guerriero, Diane, Lisa Rotunno-Hazuka, and Jeffrey Pantaleo. *Archaeological Assessment for the Royal Lahaina Resort Redevelopment Hanakaʻōʻō Ahupuaʻa, Lahaina District, Island of Maui.* Wailuku, HI: Archaeological Services Hawaii, LLC, 2005. [SHPD ID: 2019LI81261]

Havel, BreAnna and Michael F. Dega. *An Archaeological Assessment Report on 0.11 Acres of a Partially Developed Land in Honokōwai Ahupuaʻa, Lahaina District, Maui Island, Hawaiʻi [TMK 4-4-01:106].* Honolulu, HI: Scientific Consultant Services, Inc., 2005. [SHPD ID: 2019LI81285]

Havel, BreAnna and Michael F. Dega. *An Archaeological Assessment Report on 0.11 Acres of Partially Developed Land in Honokōwai Ahupuaʻa, Lahaina District, Maui Island, Hawaiʻi.* Honolulu, HI: Scientific Consultant Services, Inc., 2005. [SHPD ID: 2019LI81285]

Havel, BreAnna and Michael F. Dega. *Archaeological Monitoring Plan for the Maui Islander Project, Lahaina, Paunau Ahupuaʻa District, Maui Island, Hawaiʻi [TMK: 4-6-011:008].* Honolulu, HI: Scientific Consultant Services, Inc., 2005. [SHPD ID: 2019LI81582]

Kawachi, Carol. *Archaeological Monitoring Plan for Phase 1 of the Proposed Lahaina Watershed Flood Control Project Including Conservation District Use Application MA-3204 Board Permit, Polanui Ahupuaʻa, Lahaina District, Maui, Island TMK: (2) 4-8-01: por. 002, 018, 2005.* [SHPD ID: 2019LI81601]

Lee-Greig, Tanya L. and Hallett H. Hammatt. *Preservation Plan for Thirty-Three Historic Properties Located in and Adjacent to the Kapalua Mauka Project Area, Honokahua, Nāpili 2 & 3, and Nāpili 4-5 Ahupuaʻa, Lahaina District, Maui Island.* Wailuku, HI: Cultural Surveys Hawaiʻi, Inc., 2005. [SHPD ID: 2019LI80997]

Madeus, Jonas K., Tanya L. Lee-Greig, and Hallett H. Hammatt. *Archaeological Assessment of an 80-Acre Parcel in Kapalua, Honolua Ahupuaʻa, Lahaina District, Maui Island.* Wailuku, HI: Cultural Surveys Hawaiʻi, Inc., 2005. [SHPD ID: 2019LI80999]

Major, Maurice and P. Christiaan Klieger. *Historical Background and Archaeological Testing at Pikaneleʻs Kuleana in Lahaina, Maui: An Inventory Survey Report of LCA 310.3 (Royal Patent 1729.2, TMK (2) 4-6-07:013).* Honolulu, HI: Department of Anthropology, Bernice P. Bishop Museum, 1995. [SHPD ID: 2019LI81546; UH Call Number: DU629.L3 M36 1996]

McGerty, Leann and Robert L. Spear. *Cultural Impact Assessment on Two Parcels Incorporating the Royal Lahaina Hotel in Kāʻanapali, Hanakaʻōʻō Ahupuaʻa, Lahaina District, Maui Island, Hawaiʻi.* Honolulu, HI: Scientific Consultant Services, Inc., 2005. [SHPD ID: 2019LI80678]

Monahan, Christopher M. *An Archaeological Inventory Survey Report on Three Contiguous Parcels Measuring Approximately 25.3 Acres in Kapalua, Napili 2-3 Ahupuaʻa, Lahaina District, Maui Island, Hawaiʻi.* Honolulu, HI: Scientific Consultant Services, Inc., 2005. [SHPD ID: 2019LI81018]

Pickett, Jenny L. and Michael F. Dega. *An Archaeological Assessment for 16.8 Acres in Lahaina, Mākila Ahupua'a, Lahaina District, Maui Island, Hawai'i [TMK (2) 4-5-10:005 & 006 por.].* Honolulu, HI: Scientific Consultant Services, Inc., 2005. [SHPD ID: 2019LI80600]

Rechtman, Robert B. *Archaeological Monitoring Plan Associated with the Demolition of the Pioneer Mill, TMK (2) 4-5-09:007, Pana'ewa Ahupua'a, Lahaina District, Island of Maui.* Rechtman Consulting, LLC, 2005. [SHPD ID: 2019LI80603]

Rotunno-Hazuka, Lisa J. and Jeffrey Pantaleo. *Archaeological Monitoring Plan for All Improvements Related to the Proposed Construction of an Ohana and Garage at the Stiebinger Residence, Kau'aula Ahupua'a, Lahaina District, Island of Maui TMK (2) 4-6-06:005.* Wailuku, HI: Archaeological Services Hawaii, LLC, 2005. [SHPD ID: 2019LI81405]

Rotunno-Hazuka, Lisa J. and Jeffrey Pantaleo. *Archaeological Monitoring Plan for the Renovation and Revitalization of the Napili Kai Resort, Napili Ahupua'a, Lahaina District, Island of Maui.* Wailuku, HI: Archaeological Services Hawaii, LLC, 2005. [SHPD ID: 2019LI81067]

Tomonari-Tuggle, M. J. and Coral Rasmussen. *Preservation Plan for Site 50-50-09-5232, An Upland Heiau in Ukumehame Ahupua'a, Island of Maui TMK 4-8-01:1.* Honolulu, HI: International Archaeological Research Institute, Inc., 2005. [SHPD ID: 2019LI81629]

Webb, Erika L. *Inventory Survey of Honolua Plantation Shop Buildings Located at the Kapalua Central Resort, TMK (2) 4-2-4:024.* Honolulu, HI: Mason Architects, Inc., 2005. [SHPD ID: 2019LI81047]

2006

Collins, Sara L., Dennis Gosser, and Stephan D. Clark. *Archaeological Assessment of a Single Developed Parcel [TMK (2) 4-6-10:006] Lahaina, Island of Maui.* Honolulu, HI: Pacific Consulting Services, Inc., 2006. [No location available]

Conte, Patty J. *Archaeological Inventory Survey of the Stoops Property TMK (2) 4-1-01:018, Honolua Ahupua'a, Kā'anapali District, Maui, Hawai'i.* Makawao, HI: CRM Solutions Hawai'i, Inc., 2006. [SHPD ID: 2019LI81424]

Conte, Patty J. *Archaeological Monitoring Plan for On and Off-Site Construction Within and Related to TMK (2) 4-1-01:018, Honolua Ahupua'a, Kā'anapali District, Maui, Hawai'i.* Makawao, HI: CRM Solutions Hawai'i, Inc., 2006. [SHPD ID: 2019LI81424]

Conte, Patty J. *Archaeological Monitoring Plan for On and Off-Site Construction Within and Related to TMK (2) 4-5-13:006 Lahaina District, Pana'ewa Ahupua'a, Island of Maui.* Makawao, HI: CRM Solutions Hawai'i, Inc., 2006. [SHPD ID: 2019LI81349]

Conte, Patty J. *Archaeological Monitoring Plan for On and Off-Site Construction Within and Related to TMK (2) 4-5-14:073 Lahaina District, Wahikuli Ahupua'a, Island of Maui.* Makawao, HI: CRM Solutions Hawai'i, Inc., 2006. [SHPD ID: 2019LI81354]

Dega, Michael F. *A Preservation Plan for Multiple Archaeological Sites on Portions of a 570.3 Acre Property in the Launiupoko (Large Lot, Phase V) Subdivision No. 2, Launiupoko Ahupua'a, Lahaina District (Formerly Kā'anapali), Island of Maui [TMK (2) 4-7-01:02].* Honolulu, HI: Scientific Consultant Services, Inc., 2006. [SHPD ID: 2019LI81606]

Dega, Michael F. *An Addendum Archaeological Inventory Survey in Ukumehame Ahupua'a, Lahaina District, Island of Maui, Hawai'i [TMK (2) 4-9-02:008 por.].* Honolulu, HI: Scientific Consultant Services, Inc., 2006. [SHPD ID: 2019LI81645]

Dega, Michael F. and David B. Chaffee. *An Archaeological Monitoring Plan for a Private Residence Demolition in Lahaina, Moali'i Ahupua'a, Lahaina District, Maui Island, Hawai'i [TMK (2) 4-6-02:003].* Honolulu, HI: Scientific Consultant Services, Inc., 2006. [SHPD ID: 2019LI81394]

Fredericksen, Erik M. *An Archaeological Monitoring Report for Offsite Parking for the Lot 3 Temporary Parking Project, Kā'anapali, Hanaka'ō'ō Ahupua'a Lahaina District, Island of Maui.* Pukalani, HI: Xamanek Researches, 2006. [SHPD ID: 2019LI80660]

Hill, Robert R., Joseph Arnold, and Hallett H. Hammatt. *Archaeological Monitoring Report for a Dust Barrier Relocation at North Kā'anapali, Honokōwai Ahupua'a, Lahaina District, Island of Maui. TMK (2) 4-4-014:004 (por.)* Wailuku, HI: Cultural Surveys Hawai'i, Inc., 2006. [SHPD ID: 2019LI80658]

Hill, Robert R., Thomas K. Devereux, and Hallett H. Hammatt. *An Archaeological Assessment of a 9.650 Acre Parcel, 'Alaeloa Ahupua'a, Lahaina District, Maui Island, for the West Maui Village Project.* Wailuku, HI: Cultural Surveys Hawai'i, Inc., 2006. [SHPD ID: 2019LI81037]

McGerty, Leann and Robert L. Spear. *A Cultural Impact Assessment of Approximately 0.8 Acres of Land in Olowalu Ahupua'a, Wailuku District, Maui, Hawai'i [TMK (2) 4-9-003:45A].* Honolulu, HI: Scientific Consultant Services, Inc., 2006. [SHPD ID: 2019LI81636]

Pacheco, Robert. *A Cultural Impact Assessment for the Proposed Kāʻanapali Beach Restoration Project, Hanakaʻōʻō Ahupuaʻa, Lahaina District, Island of Maui, Hawaiʻi TMK (2) 4-4-008:001, 002, 003, 004, 005, 019, 022; 4-4-013:001, 002, 006, 007, 008.* Honolulu, HI: International Archaeology, LLC, 2006. [SHPD ID: 2019LI80681]

Pantaleo, Jeffrey. *Archaeological Inventory Report of a 1.65-Acre Parcel of Land Pūehuehue Iki Ahupuaʻa, Lahaina District, Island of Maui TMK (2) 4-7-04:001.* Wailuku, HI: Archaeological Services Hawaii, LLC, 2006. [SHPD ID: 2019LI81615]

Paraso, C. Kanani and Michael F. Dega. *An Archaeological Assessment of three parcels at the Hyatt Regency Maui Resort, Kāʻanapali, Hanakaʻōʻō Ahupuaʻa, Lahaina District, Maui Island, Hawaiʻi [TMK (2) 4-4-013:004, 005, 008];* Honolulu, HI: Scientific Consultant Services, Inc., 2006. [SHPD ID: 2019LI80041]

Paraso, C. Kanani and Michael F. Dega. *An Archaeological Inventory Survey of 633 Acres in the Launiupoko (Large Lot) Subdivision Nos. 3, 4, and 7, Launiupoko and Polanui Ahupuaʻa, Lahaina District (formerly Kāʻanapali), Island of Maui, Hawaiʻi [TMK (2) 4-8-01:2 por.].* Honolulu, HI: Scientific Consultant Services, Inc., 2006. [SHPD ID: 2019LI81600]

Pickett, Jenny L. and Michael F. Dega. *An Archaeological Inventory Survey of 583 Acres at Lipoa Point, Honolua Ahupuaʻa, Lahaina (Formerly Kāʻanapali) District, Maui Island, Hawaiʻi.* Honolulu, HI: Scientific Consultant Services, Inc., 2006. [SHPD ID: 2019LI81431]

Rechtman, Robert B. *Archaeological Monitoring Plan for the Subdivision and Development for the Subdivision and Development of TMK: (2) 4-4-08:016.* Rechtman Consulting, LLC, 2006. [SHPD ID: 2019LI80679]

Rechtman, Robert B. *Archaeological Monitoring Report Associated with the Demolition of the Pioneer Mill, Panaʻewa Ahupuaʻa, Lahaina District, Island of Maui.* Rechtman Consulting, LLC, 2006. [SHPD ID: 2019LI80602]

Rotunno-Hazuka, Lisa J. and Jeffrey Pantaleo, M.A. *Archaeological Preservation and Monitoring Plan for Site 50-50-03-4096 Feature 1 Located on a Residential Lot, TMK (2) 4-7-01:001 Pūehuehue Iki Ahupuaʻa, Lahaina District: Island of Maui.* Wailuku, HI: Archaeological Services Hawaii, LLC, 2006. [SHPD ID: 2019LI81591]

Rotunno-Hazuka, Lisa J. and Jeffrey Pantaleo. *Archaeological Monitoring Plan for All Ground Disturbing Activities Associated with the Construction of the Waineʻe Self Storage Facility located at TMK: (2) 4-5-07:004 Kuholilea Ahupuaʻa, Lahaina*

District, Island of Maui. Wailuku, HI: Archaeological Services Hawaii, LLC, 2006. [SHPD ID: 2019LI80607]

Rotunno-Hazuka, Lisa J. and Jeffrey Pantaleo. *Archaeological Monitoring Plan for All Improvements at the McFarland Residence TMK: (2) 4-5-13:003, Moali'i Ahupua'a Lahaina District, Island of Maui.* Wailuku, HI: Archaeological Services Hawaii, LLC, 2006. [SHPD ID: 2019LI81352]

Shefcheck, Donna M. and Michael F. Dega. *A Preservation Plan for Site 50-50-08-5968 and Site 50-50-08-5969 in Ukumehame Ahupua'a, Lahaina District, Island of Maui, Hawai'i [TMK: (2) 4-8-02:008 por.].* Honolulu, HI: Scientific Consultant Services, Inc., 2006. [SHPD ID: 2019LI81643]

Shefcheck, Donna M. and Michael F. Dega. *Site Report for a Previously Unrecorded Heiau in Launiupoko Ahupua'a, Lahaina District, Island of Maui, Hawai'i.* Honolulu, HI: Scientific Consultant Services, Inc., 2006. [SHPD ID: 2019LI81592]

2007

Collins, Sara L. *Archaeological Monitoring Plan for Ground-Altering Activities During the Grading and Excavations for Construction Associated with the Moku'ula/Mokuhinia Ecosystem Restoration Project, Phase I, Lahaina, Island of Maui.* Honolulu, HI: Pacific Consulting Services, Inc., 2007. [SHPD ID: 2019LI01493]

Conte, Patty J. *Archaeological Monitoring Plan for On and Off-Site Construction Related to the Proposed Kent Property Demo/Reconstruction, TMK (2) 4-5-12:010 Moali'i Ahupua'a, Lahaina District, Island of Maui.* Makawao, HI: CRM Solutions Hawai'i, Inc., 2007. [SHPD ID: 2019LI81346]

Conte, Patty J. *Archaeological Monitoring Report for Off-Site Construction (Mailepai Hui Land Lots 51-C-4-A, B & C) Lahaina District, Mailepai Ahupua'a, Island of Maui.* Makawao, HI: CRM Solutions Hawai'i, Inc., 2007. [SHPD ID: 2019LI81324]

Conte, Patty J. *Archaeological Monitoring Report for On and Off-Site Construction Within and Related to TMK (2) 4-5-14:073 Lahaina District, Wahikuli Ahupua'a, Island of Maui.* Makawao, HI: CRM Solutions Hawai'i, Inc., 2007. [SHPD ID: 2019LI81356]

Conte, Patty J. *Archaeological Monitoring Report within and Related to a Parcel on Front Street, Pana'ewa Ahupua'a, Lahaina District, Maui Island, TMK (2)*

4-5-13:006. Makawao, HI: CRM Solutions Hawaiʻi, Inc., 2007. [No location available]

Conte, Patty J. *Archaeological Preservation Plan for the Portion of Site #50-50-01-1756 Within TMK (2) 4-1-01:018 Honolua Ahupuaʻa, Kāʻanapali District, Maui, Hawaiʻi.* Makawao, HI: CRM Solutions Hawaiʻi, Inc., 2007. [SHPD ID: 2019LI81428]

Cordle, Shayna and Michael F. Dega. *An Archaeological Monitoring Report on Approximately 0.448-Acres for the Maui Marriott Vacation Club, Hanakaʻōʻō Ahupuaʻa, Lahaina District, Island of Maui, Hawaiʻi [TMK (2) 4-4-13:001].* Honolulu, HI: Scientific Consultant Services, Inc., 2007. [SHPD ID: 2019LI80029]

Cordle, Shayna, Jennifer Hunt, and Michael F. Dega. *An Archaeological Monitoring Report for a 12,365 Ft Sq. Property, Waineʻe St., Lahaina, Panaʻewa Ahupuaʻa, Lahaina District, Island of Maui, Hawaiʻi [TMK (2) 4-6-09:244].* Honolulu, HI: Scientific Consultant Services, Inc., 2007. [SHPD ID: 2019LI81566]

Dagher, Cathleen A. and Michael F. Dega. *An Archaeological Monitoring Plan for the Proposed Kapalua Coastal Trail Corridor Located in Kapalua and Honokōhau and Nāpili 2&3 Ahupuaʻa Lahaina District, Island of Maui, Hawaiʻi [TMK: (2) 4-2-Various].* Honolulu, HI: Scientific Consultant Services, Inc., 2007. [SHPD ID: 2019LI81421]

Fredericksen, Erik M. *An Archaeological Assessment Survey of a c. 5 Acre Portion of Land for the Proposed Temporary Off-Site Parking Project, Hanakaʻōʻō/Honokōwai Ahupuaʻa, Lahaina District, Maui Island [TMK: (2) 4-4-002: 003].* Pukalani, HI: Xamanek Researches, 2007. [No location available]

Hammatt, Hallett H. *An Archaeological Field Inspection of the Lahaina Bypass Highway, Phase 1A, Keawe Street Extension to Lahainaluna Road, and Current Condition of SIHP Number -2484.* Wailuku, HI: Cultural Surveys Hawaiʻi, Inc., 2007. [SHPD ID: 2019LI81366]

Hoerman, Rachel and Michael F. Dega. *An Archaeological Monitoring Plan for the Pavilion Restaurant Renovation at the Hyatt Regency Maui Resort and Spa, Kāʻanapali, Hanakaʻōʻō Ahupuaʻa, Lahaina District, Maui Island, Hawaiʻi.* Honolulu, HI: Scientific Consultant Services, Inc., 2007. [SHPD ID: 2019LI80666, 2019LI80665]

Johnston-OʻNeill, Emily and Michael F. Dega. *Archaeological Monitoring Plan for the Exterior Staircase Addition to the Convent Building at the Sacred Hearts Roman Catholic Property at 712 Waineʻe Street, Paunau Ahupuaʻa, Lahaina Dis-*

trict, Island of Maui TMK: (2) 4-6-10:001 (por.). Honolulu, HI: Scientific Consultant Services, Inc., 2007. [SHPD ID: 2019LI81541]

Lee-Greig, Tanya L. and Hallett H. Hammatt. *Addendum to An Archaeological Treatment Plan for no Adverse Effect the Honoapiʻilani Highway Realignment— Lahaina Bypass Section, Phase 1A, Keawe Street Extension to Lahainaluna Road, Panaʻewa Ahupuaʻa, Lahaina District, Maui Island, TMK (2) 4-5-031: 999 por., (2) 4-5-015:010 por., and (2) 4-5-021:022 por.* Wailuku, HI: Cultural Surveys Hawaiʻi, Inc., 2007. [SHPD ID: 2019LI81365, 2019LI81340]

Lee-Greig, Tanya L. and Hallett H. Hammatt. *Archaeological Monitoring Plan for the Puʻunēnē School and Lahainaluna High School Hawaiʻi Inter-Island DOE Cesspool Project, Island of Maui TMK (2) 4-6-018 and (2) 3-8-006.* Wailuku, HI: Cultural Surveys Hawaiʻi, Inc., 2007. [SHPD ID: 2019LI81526]

McGerty, Leann and Robert L. Spear. *A Cultural Impact Assessment for a portion of the Mauian Hotel Property, Nāpili Ahupuaʻa, Lahaina District, Maui Island, Hawaiʻi.* Honolulu, HI: Scientific Consultant Services, Inc., 2007. [SHPD ID: 2019LI81065]

McGerty, Leanne and Robert L. Spear. *Cultural Impact Assessment of a Parcel of Land in Lahaina Town, Alio Ahupuaʻa, Lahaina District, Maui Island, Hawaiʻi.* Honolulu, HI: Scientific Consultant Services, Inc., 2007. [SHPD ID: 2019LI81360]

Mooney, Kimberly M. and Paul L. Cleghorn. *Archaeological Monitoring Report for the Lahaina Small Boat Harbor Comfort Station Improvements, Lahaina, Maui.* Kailua, HI: Pacific Legacy, Inc., 2007. [SHPD ID: 2019LI81379]

Ogg, Randy and Michael F. Dega. *An Archaeological Assessment of Lahaina Wastewater Pump Station No. 1 Improvements, Honokōwai Ahupuaʻa, Lahaina District, Maui Island, Hawaiʻi [TMK: (2) 4-4-02:003 & (2) 4-4-02:029].* Honolulu, HI: Scientific Consultant Services, Inc., 2007. [SHPD ID: 2019LI81279]

Rogers, Scott. *An Archaeological Monitoring Plan for the Kāʻanapali—Hyatt Force Main Replacements, Kāʻanapali Resort Complex, Hanakaʻōʻō, Honokōwai Ahupuaʻa, Lahaina District, Island of Maui.* Pukalani, HI: Xamanek Researches, 2007. [SHPD ID: 2019LI80682]

Rotunno-Hazuka, Lisa J. and Jeffrey Pantaleo. *Archaeological Monitoring Plan for All Improvements Related to the Redevelopment of the Royal Lahaina Resort, Hanakaʻōʻō Ahupuaʻa; Lahaina District, Island of Maui, TMK:4-4-08:007& 013.* Wailuku, HI: Archaeological Services Hawaii, LLC, 2007. [SHPD ID: 2019LI80677]

Rotunno-Hazuka, Lisa J. and Jeffrey Pantaleo. *Archaeological Monitoring Plan for the Installation of a Grease Interceptor at TMK: (2) 4-5-02:009 Kelawea Ahupua'a, Lahaina District, Island of Maui.* Wailuku, HI: Archaeological Services Hawaii, LLC, 2007. [SHPD ID: 2019LI80646]

Shefcheck, Donna M. and Michael F. Dega. *An Archaeological Inventory Survey of 123.31 Acres in the Launiupoko (Large Lot) Subdivision 6 Launiupoko and Polanui Ahupua'a, Lahaina District (formerly Kā'anapali) Island of Maui, Hawai'i TMK (2) 4-8-01:002 por.).* Honolulu, HI: Scientific Consultant Services, Inc., 2007. [SHPD ID: 2019LI81596]

Spear, Robert L. *Field Inspection of a Sea Wall on the Brayton Property, 303 Front Street, Aholo/Kau'aula Ahupua'a, Lahaina District, Island of Maui, Hawai'i TMK: 4-6-3-05 (Seaward).* Honolulu, HI: Scientific Consultant Services, Inc., 2007. [SHPD ID: 2019LI81559]

Tome, Guerin and Michael F. Dega. *An Archaeological Inventory Survey for the Proposed Kapalua Coastal Trail Located in the Areas of Kapalua and Honokāhau, Honokahua and Nāpili 2 & 3.* Honolulu, HI: Scientific Consultant Services, Inc., 2007. [SHPD ID: 2019LI81433]

2008

Clark, Matthew R. and Robert B. Rechtman. *An Archaeological Inventory Survey of 333 Acres for the Proposed Expansion of the Kaheawa Wind Farm (TMK: 2-4-8:001: por. 001).* Rechtman Consulting, LLC, 2008. [SHPD ID: 2019LI81628]

Conte, Patty J. *Archaeological Monitoring Plan for On and Off-Site Construction Related to Pending and Future Improvements, Puunoa Ahupua'a, Lahaina District, Island of Maui.* Makawao, HI: CRM Solutions Hawai'i, Inc., 2008. [SHPD ID: 2019LI80599]

Cordle, Shayna and Michael F. Dega. *An Archaeological Monitoring Plan for 1.835 Acres in Napili, Napili 2-3 Ahupua'a, Lahaina District, Maui Island, Hawai'i.* Honolulu, HI: Scientific Consultant Services, Inc., 2008. ID: 2019LI81066]

Dagan, Colleen P. M. and Hallett H. Hammatt. *Archaeological Preservation Plan for SIHP 50-50-01-5672C and 50-50-01-5673H.* Wailuku, HI: Cultural Surveys Hawai'i, Inc., 2008. [SHPD ID: 2019LI81026]

Dagher, Cathleen A. and Michael F. Dega. *A Preservation Plan for Multiple Archaeological Sites Located in the Kapalua Coastal Trail Corridor in the areas of Nāpili, Kapalua, Honokahua, and Honolua, Ahupua'a of Nāpili 2 & 3, Honoka-*

hua, and Honolua, Lahaina District, Island of Maui, Hawaiʻi. Scientific Consultant Services, Inc.: Honolulu, HI, 2008. [SHPD ID: 2019LI79694]

Dagher, Cathleen A. and Michael F. Dega. *An Archaeological Monitoring Plan for the Proposed Kapalua Coastal Trail Located in the Areas of Nāpili, Kapalua, Honokahua, and Honolua, Ahupuaʻa of Nāpili 2 & 3, Honokahua, and Honolua, Lahaina district, Island of Maui, Hawaiʻi.* Honolulu, HI: Scientific Consultant Services, Inc., 2008. [SHPD ID: 2019LI81410]

Dega, Michael F. *Archaeological Inventory Survey of the Punakea Loop Corridor in Launiupoko and Polanui Ahupuaʻa, Lahaina District (formerly Kāʻanapali), island of Maui, Hawaiʻi [TMK: (2) 4-8-01:002 por. & 4-7-01:029 por.].* Honolulu, HI: Scientific Consultant Services, Inc., 2008. [SHPD ID: 2019LI81597]

Fredericksen, Erik M. *An Archaeological Monitoring Plan for a Detector Check Upgrade Project for the Lahaina Square Shopping Center, Waineʻe Ahupuaʻa, Lahaina District, Maui.* Pukalani, HI: Xamanek Researches, 2008. [SHPD ID: 2019LI80611]

Fredericksen, Erik M. and J. J. Frey. *An Archaeological Monitoring Report for the Kāʻanapali Shores Roadway Improvements Project, Honokōwai Ahupuaʻa, Lahaina District, Maui.* Pukalani, HI: Xamanek Researches, 2008. [SHPD ID: 2019LI81243]

Fredericksen, Erik M. and Jennifer J. Frey. *An Archaeological Inventory Survey of a portion of land in Mailepai Ahupuaʻa, Lahaina District, Maui Island.* Pukalani, HI: Xamanek Researches, 2008. [SHPD ID: 2019LI81302]

Fredericksen, Erik M. and Jennifer J. Frey. *An Archaeological Monitoring Report for the King Kamehameha III Elementary School Parking Lot Improvements Project, Puako Ahupuaʻa, Lahaina District TMK (2) 4-6-002:13.* Pukalani, HI: Xamanek Researches, 2008. [SHPD ID: 2019LI81374]

Fredericksen, Erik M. and Jennifer L. Frey. *An Archaeological Monitoring Report for the Kāʻanapali Shores Roadway Improvements Project, Honokōwai Ahupuaʻa, Lahaina District, Maui [TMK: (2) 4-4-001:097, and TMK (2) 4-4-001 (Right of Way)].* Pukalani, HI: Xamanek Researches, 2008. [SHPD ID: 2019LI81243]

Hill, Robert, Tanya Lee-Greig, and Hallett H. Hammatt. *An Archaeological Inventory Survey Report and Mitigation Plan for the Hawaiʻi State Department of Education Cesspool Conversion Project at the Lahainaluna High School, Panaʻewa Ahupuaʻa, Lahaina District, Maui Island, TMK (2) 4-6-18:005, 007, 012.* Wailuku, HI: Cultural Surveys Hawaiʻi, Inc., 2008. [No location available]

Hill, Robert R., Joseph Arnold, and Hallett H. Hammatt. *Archaeological Monitoring Report for Shoreline Improvements at Lot 3, North Kāʻanapali, Honokōwai Ahupuaʻa, Lahaina District, Maui Island [TMK (2) 4-4-014:005 (por.)].* Wailuku, HI: Cultural Surveys Hawaiʻi, Inc., 2008. [SHPD ID: 2019LI80653]

Hill, Robert R., Tanya Lee-Greig, and Hallett H. Hammatt. *Archaeological Monitoring Report for Shoreline Improvements at Lot 1, North Kāʻanapali, Honokōwai Ahupuaʻa, Lahaina District, Maui Island TMK: (2) 4-4-014:003 (por.).* Wailuku, HI: Cultural Surveys Hawaiʻi, Inc., 2008. [SHPD ID: 2019LI80657]

Hill, Robert R., Tanya L. Lee-Greig, and Hallett H. Hammatt. *Preservation Plan for a Fishing Koʻa, SIHP 50-50-03-6275, North Kāʻanapali, Lot 3, Honokōwai Ahupuaʻa, Maui Island [TMK (2) 4-4-014:005 por.].* Wailuku, HI: Cultural Surveys Hawaiʻi, Inc., 2008. [SHPD ID: 2019LI80654]

Hill, Robert R., Tanya L. Lee-Greig, and Hallett H. Hammatt. *Archaeological Monitoring Report for Dust Barrier Construction at Lot 3, North Kāʻanapali, Honokōwai Ahupuaʻa, Lahaina District, Island of Maui [TMK (2) 4-4-014:005 (por.)].* Wailuku, HI: Cultural Surveys Hawaiʻi, Inc., 2008. [SHPD ID: 2019LI80655]

Lee-Greig, Tanya L. and Hallett H. Hammatt. *Archaeological Inventory Survey Plan for Honoapiʻilani Highway Realignment Phase IA, Future Keawe Street Extension to Lahainaluna Road: Ikena Avenue Alignment with Modified Extension Kelawea, Paeohi, and Wahikuli Ahupuaʻa, Lahaina District, Maui Island TMK (2) 4-5-021, 010, 015, and 031: Multiple Parcels.* Wailuku, HI: Cultural Surveys Hawaiʻi, Inc., 2008. [SHPD ID: 2019LI81341]

Lee-Greig, Tanya, Robert Hill, and Hallett H. Hammatt. *An Archaeological Inventory Survey Report for the Lahaina Bypass Modified Alignment from Kahoma Stream to the Keawe Street Extension, Kelawea, Paeohi, and Wahikuli Ahupuaʻa, Lahaina District, Maui Island TMK (2) 4-5-021, 010, 015, and 031: Multiple Parcels.* Wailuku, HI: Cultural Surveys Hawaiʻi, Inc., 2008. [SHPD ID: 2019LI81368]

Lee-Greig, Tanya L., Robert Hill, and Hallett H. Hammatt. *An Archaeological Survey Report for the Realignment of a Section of the Honoapiʻilani Highway, Phase IA, Kelawea, Paeohi, and Wahikuli Ahupuaʻa, Lahaina District, Maui Island TMK (2) 4-5-021, 010, 015, and 031: Multiple Parcels.* Wailuku, HI: Cultural Surveys Hawaiʻi, Inc., 2008. [SHPD ID: 2019LI81361]

McCurdy, Todd D. and Hallett H. Hammatt. *Archaeological Literature Review and Field Inspection for Honoapiʻilani Highway Realignment (Lahaina Bypass), Phase 1B-1, Paunau Ahupuaʻa to Polanui Ahupuaʻa, Lahaina District, Maui Island*

TMK (2) 4-6-014:001-002, 4-6-018:002-003, 4-8-001:002 and 4-7-003:001. Wailuku, HI: Cultural Surveys Hawai'i, Inc., 2008. [SHPD ID: 2019LI81538]

Mooney, Kimberly M., Paul L. Cleghorn, and Elizabeth L. Kahahane. *Archaeological Inventory Survey for the Lahaina Pier Improvement Project Waine'e Ahupua'a, Lahaina District, Island of Maui.* Kailua, HI: Pacific Legacy, Inc., 2008. [SHPD ID: 2019LI81382]

Morawski, Lauren, Adam Johnson, Tomasi Patolo, and Michael F. Dega. *An Archaeological Inventory Survey of 520 Acres in the Launiupoko (Large Lot) Subdivision No. 1, Launiupoko Ahupua'a, Lahaina District (formerly Kā'anapali), Island of Maui, Hawai'i [TMK (2) 4-7-01:002 por.].* Honolulu, HI: Scientific Consultant Services, Inc., 2008. [SHPD ID: 2019LI81603]

Rotunno-Hazuka, Lisa J. and Jeffrey Pantaleo. *Final Archaeological Monitoring Report for All Ground Disturbing Activities Associated with the Development of a Residential Structure Located at TMK (2) 4-05-04:048 Pu'unoa Ahupua'a, Lahaina District, Island of Maui.* Wailuku, HI: Archaeological Services Hawaii, LLC, 2008. [SHPD ID: 2019LI80614]

Rotunno-Hazuka, Lisa J. and Jeffrey Pantaleo. *Final Archaeological Monitoring Report for All Ground Disturbing Activities Associated with the Development of a Residential Structure Located at TMK (2) 4-5-04:004, Pu'unoa Ahupua'a, Lahaina District, Island of Maui.* Wailuku, HI: Archaeological Services Hawaii, LLC, 2008. [SHPD ID: 2019LI80622]

Rotunno-Hazuka, Lisa J., Mia Watson, and Jeffrey Pantaleo. *Archaeological Monitoring Plan for the Repair and Installation of Underground Conduit at Front & Wharf Street, Lahaina and Waine'e Ahupua'a, Lahaina District, Island of Maui.* Wailuku, HI: Archaeological Services Hawaii, LLC, 2008. [SHPD ID: 2019LI81385]

Shefcheck, Donna M. and Michael F. Dega. *An Archaeological Inventory Survey of 122.84 Acres in the Launiupoko (Large Lot) Subdivision 6 Launiupoko and Polanui Ahupua'a, Lahaina District, Maui, Hawai'i [TMK (2) 4-7-01:029 por.].* Honolulu, HI: Scientific Consultant Services, Inc., 2008. [SHPD ID: 2019LI81593]

Shefcheck, Donna M. and Michael F. Dega. *An Archaeological Monitoring Plan for Lahaina Wastewater Pump Station No. 1 Improvements, Honokōwai Ahupua'a, Lahaina District Maui Island, Hawai'i [TMK (2) 4-4-02:033 and portions of 29 and 39].* Honolulu, HI: Scientific Consultant Services, Inc., 2008. [SHPD ID: 2019LI81253]

Shefcheck, Donna M. and Michael F. Dega. *An Archaeological Monitoring Plan for the Puunoa Subdivision No. 2, Lahaina, Pu'uiki Ahupua'a, Lahaina District,*

Island of Maui, Hawaiʻi. Honolulu, HI: Scientific Consultant Services, Inc., 2008. [SHPD ID: 2019LI80647]

Shefcheck, Donna M. and Michael F. Dega. *An Archaeological Monitoring Report for the Maui Islander Project, Lahaina, Paunau Ahupuaʻa, Lahaina District, Maui Island, Hawaiʻi [TMK: (2) 4-6-011:008].* Honolulu, HI: Scientific Consultant Services, Inc., 2008. [SHPD ID: 2019LI81576]

Tome, Guerin and Michael F. Dega. *An Archaeological Monitoring Plan for the Proposed Kapalua Coastal Trail Located in the areas of Nāpili, Kapalua, Honokahua, and Honolua, Ahupuaʻa of Nāpili 2&3, Honokahua, and Honolua, Lahaina District, Island of Maui, Hawaiʻi.* Honolulu, HI: Scientific Consultant Services, Inc., 2008. [SHPD ID: 2019LI81410]

Willman, Michael R., Tanya Lee-Greig, and Hallett H. Hammatt. *Addendum to Archaeological Monitoring Plan for the Puʻunēnē School and Lahainaluna High School Hawaiʻi Inter-Island DOE Cesspool Project, Island of Maui TMK (2) 4-6-18 and (2) 3-8-06.* Wailuku, HI: Cultural Surveys Hawaiʻi, Inc., 2008. [SHPD ID: 2019LI81524]

Wong, Charmaine and Michael F. Dega. *An Archaeological Assessment for the West Maui Hospital and Medical Center, Hanakaʻōʻō Ahupuaʻa, Lahaina (Kāʻanapali) District, Maui Island, Hawaiʻi, TMK: (2) 4-4-02:052.* Honolulu, HI: Scientific Consultant Services, Inc., 2008. [No location available]

2009

Cordle, Shayna, Cathleen A. Dagher, and Michael F. Dega. *An Archaeological Monitoring Report for Work on County Roadway (WTP T2008/0014) For the Lahaina Store Water Meter Replacement Project, Lahaina, Kuʻia Ahupuaʻa, Lahaina District, Island of Maui, Hawaiʻi [TMK: (2) 4-6-09:007],* 2009. Honolulu, HI: Scientific Consultant Services, Inc. [SHPD ID: 2019LI81563]

Dagher, Cathleen A. *Request for Information Pertaining to the Ukumehame Subdivision and the Impacts to Preserved Site 50-50-08-4438 Ukumehame Ahupuaʻa, Lahaina District, Island of Maui,* 2009. [SHPD ID: 2019LI81644]

Fredericksen, Erik M. *An Archaeological Monitoring Plan for the Kaahanui Place Electrical Improvements Project, Land of Puunoa, Lahaina District, Maui Island [TMK: (2) 4-5-04 por.].* Pukalani, HI: Xamanek Researches, 2009. [No location available]

Frey, Jennifer J. and Erik M. Fredericksen. *An Archaeological Monitoring Report for the King Kamehameha III Elementary School Campus Exterior Awning and Gutter Project, DOE Job No. P01090-06, Puako Ahupuaʻa, Lahaina District [TMK (2) 4-6-02:013, and (2) 4-6-02:014].* Pukalani, HI: Xamanek Researches, 2009. [SHPD ID: 2019LI81561]

Lee-Greig, Tanya L. and Hallett H. Hammatt. *An Archaeological Inventory Level Documentation for an Inadvertent Historic Property Discovery Identified During Pre-Construction Walk Through for the Lahaina Bypass Phase IA, Project: State Inventory of Historic properties 50-50-03-6277 (Lee-Greig et al. 2008).* Wailuku, HI: Cultural Surveys Hawaiʻi, Inc., 2009. [No location available]

Lee-Greig, Tanya L. and Hallett H. Hammatt. *Archaeological Monitoring Plan for the Lahaina Bypass Modified Alignment from Kahoma Stream to the Keawe Street Extension, Kelawea, Paeohi, and Wahikuli Ahupuaʻa, Lahaina District, Maui Island.* Wailuku, HI: Cultural Surveys Hawaiʻi, Inc., 2009. [SHPD ID: 2019LI81369]

McCurdy, Todd D. and Hallett H. Hammatt. *Archaeological Inventory Survey Documentation of Inadvertent Finds Identified during the Honoapiʻilani Highway Realignment (Lahaina Bypass) Phase 1B-1, Paunau Ahupuaʻa to Polanui Ahupuaʻa, Lahaina District, Maui Island TMK: (2) 4-6-014:001, 002; (2) 4-6-018:002, 003; (2) 4-8-001:002 and (2) 4-7-003:001.* Wailuku, HI: Cultural Surveys Hawaiʻi, Inc., 2009. [SHPD ID: 2019LI81536]

Oceanit. *Final Sampling Analysis Plan: Field Sampling and Quality Assurance Plans for the Mokuhinia Pond Site Investigation, Lahaina, Maui, Hawaiʻi.* Honolulu, HI: Oceanit, 2009. [SHPD ID: 2019LI81553]

Perzinski, David and Michael F. Dega. *An Archaeological Monitoring Report of the Construction at the Maui Marriott Vacation Club, Hanakaʻōʻō Ahupuaʻa, Lahaina District, Island of Maui, Hawaiʻi.* Honolulu, HI: Scientific Consultant Services, Inc., 2009. [No location available]

Rechtman, Robert B. and Ashton K. Dircks Ah Sam. *An Archaeological Inventory Survey for the Kaheawa Wind Power (KWP) Phase 2 Project Area [TMK (2) 3-6-001: por. 14 & (2) 4-8-01: Por. 001].* Rechtman Consulting, LLC, 2009. [SHPD ID: 2019LI80301]

Willman, Michael R., Robert R. Hill, Tanya L. Lee-Greig, and Hallett H. Hammatt. *Archaeological Monitoring Report for Sand Replenishment at Lots 1, 2, and 3, North Kāʻanapali, Honokōwai Ahupuaʻa, Lahaina District, Island of Maui*

[TMK (2) 4-4-014: 03, 04, 05 (por.)]. Wailuku, HI: Cultural Surveys Hawai'i, Inc., 2009. [SHPD ID: 2019LI80656]

2010

Dagher, Cathleen A. and Michael F. Dega. *Revised Preservation Plan for Site 50-50-08-4438, Ukumehame Ahupua'a, Lahaina District, Island of Maui, Hawai'i [TMK (2) 4-8-002:066; formerly (2) 4-9-002:009 por.].* Honolulu, HI: Scientific Consultant Services, Inc., 2010. [SHPD ID: 2019LI81625]

Kirkendall, Melissa, Kimberly M. Mooney, Elizabeth L. Kahahane, and Paul L. Cleghorn. *Archaeological Monitoring Plan for the Lahaina Pier Improvement Project, Waine'e Ahupua'a, Lahaina District, Island of Maui [TMK: (2) 4-6-01:001].* Kailua, HI: Pacific Legacy, Inc., 2010. [No location available]

Lee-Greig, Tanya, Constance O'Hare, Hallett H. Hammatt, Robert R. Hill, and Colleen Dagan. *Archaeological Data Recovery and Additional Testing at Land Commission Award 310: Pikanele's Kuleana at Pakala, Pakala Ahupua'a, Lahaina District, Maui Island.* Wailuku, HI: Cultural Surveys Hawai'i, Inc., 2010. [SHPD ID: 2019LI81573]

Madeus, Jonas K., Tanya Lee-Greig, and Hallett H. Hammatt. *An Archaeological Monitoring Report for the Lahaina Bypass Modified Alignment from the Lahainaluna Road Intersection to the Keawe Street Extension Kelawea, Paeohi, and Wahikuli Ahupua'a, Lahaina District, Maui Island TMK (2) 4-5-021, 010, 015, and 031: Multiple Parcels.* Wailuku, HI: Cultural Surveys Hawai'i, Inc., 2010. [SHPD ID: 2019LI81338]

McCurdy, Todd D. and Hallett H. Hammatt. *Addendum Report for Archaeological Inventory Survey Documentation of Inadvertent Finds Identified during the Honoapi'ilani Highway Realignment (Lahaina Bypass) Phase 1B-1, Paunau Ahupua'a to Polanui Ahupua'a, Lahaina District, Maui Island TMK (2) 4-6-014:001, 002: (2) 4-6-018:002, 003; (2) 4-8-001:002 and (2) 4-8-003:001.* Wailuku, HI: Cultural Surveys Hawai'i, Inc., 2010. [SHPD ID: 2019LI81537]

McCurdy, Todd D. and Hallett H. Hammatt. *An Archaeological Monitoring Plan for the Honoapi'ilani Highway Realignment (Lahaina Bypass), Phase 1B-1, Paunau Ahupua'a to Polanui Ahupua'a, Lahaina District, Maui Island TMK: (2) 4-6-014:001-002, 4-6-018:002-003, 4-7-001:002 and 4-7-003:001.* Wailuku, HI: Cultural Surveys Hawai'i, Inc., 2010. [SHPD ID: 2019LI81539]

McGerty, Leann and Robert L. Spear. *A Cultural Impact Assessment of Wastewater Pump Station No. 1 in Honokōwai Ahupua'a, Kā'anapali, Lahaina District, Maui*

Island, Hawai'i [TMK: (2) 4-4-02:003, (2) 4-4-02:029]. Honolulu, HI: Scientific Consultant Services, Inc., 2010. [SHPD ID: 2019LI81254]

Perzinski, David and Michael F. Dega. *An Archaeological Inventory Survey Report for a Bridge Replacement in Honolua, Honolua Ahupua'a, Lahaina District, Maui Island*. Honolulu, HI: Scientific Consultant Services, Inc., 2010. [SHPD ID: 2019LI81430]

Rotunno-Hazuka, Lisa J., Mia Watson, and Jeffrey Pantaleo. *Archaeological Monitoring Plan for the Improvements to a Commercial Restaurant Facility at TMK: (2) 4-5-07:034, Kā'anapali Ahupua'a, Lahaina District, Island of Maui*. Wailuku, HI: Archaeological Services Hawaii, LLC, 2010. [SHPD ID: 2019LI80610]

2011

Hunt, Jennifer, Lauren Morawski, and Michael F. Dega. *An Archaeological Monitoring Report for the Installation of New Sewer Lines and Force Mains and the Replacement of Waterlines for the County of Maui at Shaw, Front, and Dickenson Streets and Honoapi'ilani Highway in Lahaina AND The Installation of Underground Electrical Lines, Panels, and Meters at Armory Park/Kamehameha Iki Park on Front Street in Lahaina for Maui Parks and Recreation Division, Various Ahupua'a, Lahaina District, Island of Maui, Hawai'i [TMK (2) 4-6002:003, 005, 006, 007, 010, 012, 015, 016, and 027]*. Honolulu, HI: Scientific Consultant Services, Inc., 2011. [SHPD ID: 2019LI81393]

Perzinski, David and Michael F. Dega. *An Archaeological Inventory Survey of Three Contiguous Parcels of Land Totaling 0.417 Acres in Waine'e Ahupua'a, Lahaina District, Maui Island, Hawai'i*. Honolulu, HI: Scientific Consultant Services, Inc., 2011. [SHPD ID: 2019LI81543]

Six, Janet L. *Archaeological Monitoring Plan for Deck and Bar Repairs for: Leilani's on the Beach, Whalers Village Shopping Center, Building J 2435 Kā'anapali Parkway, Hanaka'ō'ō Ahupua'a, Lahaina District, Maui Island*. Pāhoa, HI: Sixth Sense Archaeological Consultants, LLC, 2011. [SHPD ID: 2019LI80676]

2012

Scientific Consultant Services, Inc. *An Archaeological Inventory Survey for Six Proposed Solar Voltaic Cell Sites Located in the Ahupua'a of Honokahua, Honokeana, and Honokōwai, Lahaina (Kā'anapali) District, Island of Maui, Hawai'i*. Honolulu, HI: Scientific Consultant Services, Inc., 2012. [SHPD ID: 2019LI81005]

2013

Chaffee, David B. and Michael F. Dega. *An Archaeological Monitoring Plan for the West Maui Recycled Water Expansion Project (Phase 2), Honokōwai Ahupuaʻa, Lahaina District, Maui Island, Hawaiʻi [TMK (2) 4-4-002:018 por].* Honolulu, HI: Scientific Consultant Services, Inc., 2013.

Dega, Michael F. *An Archaeological Inventory Survey Plan for Kāʻanapali Beach Hotel Beach Front Restaurant/Canoe Hale, Hanakaʻōʻō Ahupuaʻa, Lahaina District, Island of Maui, Hawaiʻi [TMK: (2) 4-4-008:003 por.].* Honolulu, HI: Scientific Consultant Services, Inc., 2013. [SHPD ID: 2019LI80674]

Medrano, Stephanie and Michael F. Dega. *An Archaeological Assessment for a 1.02-Acre Project Area in Lahaina, Kuʻia Ahupuaʻa, Lahaina District, Island of Maui, Hawaiʻi [TMK: (2) 4-6-009:036, 038, & 044].* Honolulu, HI: Scientific Consultant Services, Inc., 2013. [SHPD ID: 2019LI81581]

Perzinski, David. *Archaeological Field Inspection for the West Maui Recycled Water Expansion Project, Phase 2 County Job No. WW12-13, Lahaina, Maui, Hawaiʻi.* Honolulu, HI: Scientific Consultant Services, Inc., 2013. [No location available]

Perzinski, David and Michael F. Dega. *An Archaeological Assessment of a Seawall/ Revetment Structure in Honokōwai.* Honolulu, HI: Scientific Consultant Services, Inc., 2013. [SHPD ID: 2019LI81283]

Sea Engineering, Inc. *Final Environmental Assessment for Permanent Shore Protection of the Hololani Resort Condominiums Kahananui, Lahaina, Maui.* Honolulu, HI: Sea Engineering, Inc., 2013. [No location available]

2014

Chaffee, David B. and Michael F. Dega. *An Archaeological Monitoring Plan Covering Three Parcels at the Hyatt Regency Maui Resort Kāʻanapali, Hanakaʻōʻō Ahupuaʻa, Lahaina District, Maui Island, Hawaiʻi [TMK (2) 4-4-13:005, 008, 004].* Honolulu, HI: Scientific Consultant Services, Inc., 2014.

Chaffee, David B. and Michael F. Dega. *An Archaeological Monitoring Plan for Kāʻanapali Beach Hotel Beach Front, Restaurant/Canoe Hale, Hanakaʻōʻō Ahupuaʻa, Lahaina District, Island of Maui, Hawaiʻi.* Honolulu, HI: Scientific Consultant Services, Inc., 2014.

Chaffee, David B. and Michael F. Dega. *An Archaeological Monitoring Plan for the Maui Countywide Wastewater Pump Station Renovations, Phase II Project at Multiple Locations, Hanakaʻōʻō Ahupuaʻa and Mākila Ahupuaʻa, Lahaina District,*

Maui Island, Hawai'i [TMK: (2) 4-4-013:003, por. and 4-6-028:054]. Honolulu, HI: Scientific Consultant Services, Inc., 2014.

Dagher, Cathleen A. and Michael F. Dega. *An Archaeological Assessment of the Kā'anapali Beach Hotel Beach Front Restaurant/Canoe Hale, Hanaka'ō'ō Ahupua'a, Lahaina District, Island of Maui, Hawai'i [TMK: (2) 4-4-08:003].* Honolulu, HI: Scientific Consultant Services, Inc., 2014. [SHPD ID: 2019LI81259]

Folio, Katie M. and Hallett H. Hammatt. *An Archaeological Monitoring Plan for Proposed Improvements at the Feast of Lele, Waiokama Ahupua'a, Lahaina District, Island of Maui TMK: (2) 4-6-002:007 (por.).* Wailuku, HI: Cultural Surveys Hawai'i, Inc., 2014. [SHPD ID: 2019LI81372]

Haun, Alan E. and Dave Henry. *Final Archaeological Monitoring Plan, TMK (2) 4-5-13:016, Wahikuli Ahupua'a, Lahaina District, Island of Maui.* Kailua-Kona, HI: Haun and Associates, 2014. [SHPD ID: 2019LI81350]

Lee-Greig, Tanya L. and Hallett H. Hammatt. *An Archaeological Monitoring Plan for Whalers Village Renovation and Expansion Project, Hanaka'ō'ō Ahupua'a, Lahaina District, Maui Island.* Wailuku, HI: Cultural Surveys Hawai'i, Inc., 2014. [SHPD ID: 2019LI80675]

Lee-Greig, Tanya L. and Hallett H. Hammatt. *Archaeological Assessment for the Proposed Westin Maui Resort & Spa Master Plan Improvements, Hanaka'ō'ō Ahupua'a, Lahaina District, Island of Maui, TMK (2) 4-4-008:019.* Wailuku, HI: Cultural Surveys Hawai'i, Inc., 2014. [SHPD ID: 2019LI80684]

Lee-Greig, Tanya L. and Hallett H. Hammatt. *Archaeological Inventory Survey Plan for the Proposed Mokuhinia Ecosystem Restoration Project Waiokama and Lower Waine'e Ahupua'a, Lahaina District, Maui Island.* Wailuku, HI: Cultural Surveys Hawai'i, Inc., 2014. [SHPD ID: 2019LI81554]

Lee-Greig, Tanya L. and Hallett H. Hammatt. *Archaeological Monitoring Plan for the Honoapi'ilani Highway Safety Improvements at Kā'anapali Parkway and Halelo Street Hanaka'ō'ō Ahupua'a, Lahaina District, Maui Island [TMK (2) 4-4-006:999 por; 4-4-009:036 por.).* Wailuku, HI: Cultural Surveys Hawai'i, Inc., 2014. [SHPD ID: 2019LI81271]

Madeus, Jonas K. and Hallett H. Hammatt. *An Archaeological Monitoring Plan for the Proposed Hololani Resort Condominiums Shoreline Protection Project in Kahananui Ahupua'a, Lahaina District, Maui Island TMK: (2) 4-3-010:009 por.* Wailuku, HI: Cultural Surveys Hawai'i, Inc., 2014. [SHPD ID: 2019LI81312]

Perzinski, David and Michael F. Dega. *Archaeological Assessment for the West Maui Well No. 2 Exploratory, DWS Job No. 11-06, Kahana Ahupua'a, Lahaina*

(Kāʻanapali) District, Maui, Hawaiʻi. Honolulu, HI: Scientific Consultant Services, Inc., 2014. [SHPD ID: 2019LI81057]

Perzinski, David and Michael F. Dega. *Archaeological Monitoring Report for Lahaina No. 3 Force Main Replacement Project Wahikuli and Hanakaʻōʻō Ahupuaʻa, Lahaina District, Island of Maui, Hawaiʻi [TMK (2) 4-4-013].* Honolulu, HI: Scientific Consultant Services, Inc., 2014. [SHPD ID: 2019LI80661]

Wong, Charmaine and Michael F. Dega. *An Archaeological Assessment for the West Maui Hospital and Medical Center, Hanakaʻōʻō Ahupuaʻa, Lahaina (Kāʻanapali) district, Maui Island, Hawaiʻi [TMK: (2) 4-4-02:052].* Honolulu, HI: Scientific Consultant Services, Inc., 2014. [SHPD ID: 2019LI81245]

2015

Andricci, Nicole and Michael F. Dega. *AAAAA Rent-A-Space Extension Project Honokōwai, Māhinahina 4 Ahupuaʻa Lahaina (Kāʻanapali) District, Maui Island Hawaii [TMK (2) 4-4-01:026].* Honolulu, HI: Scientific Consultant Services, Inc., 2015.

Andricci, Nicole and Michael F. Dega. *Archaeological Assessment of a 15.7 Acre Section of Undeveloped Land and a Proposed Road Extension, Kuʻia Ahupuaʻa, Lahaina District, Island of Maui, Hawaiʻi [TMK (2) 4-6-018:003 por.].* Honolulu, HI: Scientific Consultant Services, Inc., 2015.

Bassford, B. A. and Michael F. Dega. *Burial Site Component of an Archaeological Data Recovery and Preservation Plan for Site 50-50-08-8284 at Camp Olowalu in Olowalu, Olowalu Ahupuaʻa, Lahaina District, Maui Island, Hawaiʻi [TMK (2) 4-8-03:084 por.].* Honolulu, HI: Scientific Consultant Services, Inc., 2015. [No location available]

Dagher, Cathleen A. and Michael F. Dega. *An Archaeological Monitoring Plan for the Napili Culvert Replacement Project, Nāpili 4 and 5 Ahupuaʻa, Lahaina (Kāʻanapali) District, Island of Maui, Hawaiʻi.* Honolulu, HI: Scientific Consultant Services, Inc., 2015. [SHPD ID: 2019LI81056]

Dagher, Cathleen A. and Michael F. Dega. *An Archaeological Monitoring Plan for the Napili No. 5 & 6 WWPS Force Main Replacement Honokahua Ahupuaʻa, Lahaina (Kāʻanapali) District, Island of Maui, Hawaiʻi [TMK (2) 4-2-04: portion of 48 (Lot 3-A-1 of Kapalua Makai Subdivision No. 4) and TMK (2) 4-2-04: portion of 59 (Lot A-1-A-2 of Kapalua Development (Large-Lot) Subdivision).* Honolulu, HI: Scientific Consultant Services, Inc., 2015. [SHPD ID: 2019LI81016]

Dagher, Cathleen A. and Michael F. Dega. *An Archaeological Monitoring Plan for the Poseley Residence, Olowalu Ahupuaʻa, Lahaina District, Island of Maui,*

Hawaiʻi [TMK: (2) 4-8-03:047 and portions of 001 and 084 (Easement G)]. Honolulu, HI: Scientific Consultant Services, Inc., 2015. [SHPD ID: 2019LI81660]

Dega, Michael F. *An Archaeological Monitoring Plan for Improvements at D. T. Fleming Beach Park for the County of Maui, Department of Parks and Recreation, Honokahua Ahupuaʻa [sic], Lahaina District, Island of Maui, Hawaiʻi*. Honolulu, HI: Scientific Consultant Services, Inc., 2015. [SHPD ID: 2019LI81042]

Dega, Michael F. *An Archaeological Monitoring Plan for Improvements at Honokōwai Beach Park for the County of Maui, Department of Parks and Recreation, Honokōwai Ahupuaʻa, Lahaina District, Island of Maui, Hawaiʻi [TMK (2) 4-4-01:046 por. & 047 por]*. Honolulu, HI: Scientific Consultant Services, Inc., 2015. [SHPD ID: 2019LI81042]

Dega, Michael F. *An Archaeological Monitoring Plan for the West Maui Recycled Water Expansion Project (Phase 2), Honokōwai Ahupuaʻa, Lahaina District, Maui Island, Hawaiʻi*. Honolulu, HI: Scientific Consultant Services, Inc., 2015. [SHPD ID: 2019LI81246]

OʻDay, Patrick and David Byerly. *Archaeological Inventory Survey of Proposed Fenceline Corridor for the West Maui Forest Reserve, Kuʻia, Mākila, Pāhoa, Halakaʻa, Polaiki, Launiupoko, and Olowalu Ahupuaʻa, Lahaina District, Maui Island, Hawaiʻi*. Kailua, HI: Garcia & Associates, 2015. [SHPD ID: 2019LI81533]

Pacheco, Robert. *An Archaeological Literature Review for the Proposed Kāʻanapali Beach Restoration Project, Hanakaʻōʻō Ahupuaʻa, Lahaina District, Island of Maui, Hawaiʻi TMK (2) 4-4-008:001, 002, 003, 004, 005, 019, 022; 4-4-013:001, 002, 006, 007, 008*. Honolulu, HI: International Archaeology, LLC, 2015. [SHPD ID: 2019LI81260]

Perzinski, David and Michael F. Dega. *An Archaeological Monitoring Report for the Installation of Subsurface Utilities in Nāpili, Kapalua, Honokahua Ahupuaʻa, Lahaina District, Island of Maui, Hawaiʻi*. Honolulu, HI: Scientific Consultant Services, Inc., 2015. [SHPD ID: 2019LI81034]

Rotunno-Hazuka, Lisa J. and Jeffrey Pantaleo. *Final Archaeological Monitoring Plan for the Installation of a New Water Service and Relocated Power Pole Along Kalena Street Kelawea Ahupuaʻa, Lahaina District, Island of Maui*. Wailuku, HI: Archaeological Services Hawaii, LLC, 2015. [No location available]

2016

Andricci, Nicole and Michael F. Dega. *An Archaeological Monitoring Plan for a Residential Parcel 33 at 572 Waineʻe Street, Waineʻe Ahupuaʻa, Lahaina District,*

Maui Island, Hawaiʻi [TMK (2) 4-6-12:033]. Honolulu, HI: Scientific Consultant Services, Inc., 2016.

Dagher, Cathleen A. and Michael F. Dega. *Archaeological Field Inspection Results and Recommendations for the Proposed Maui Police Department Communications Facility at Lahainaluna Water Treatment Site, Panaʻewa Ahupuaʻa, Lahaina District, Maui Island, Hawaiʻi [TMK: (2) 4-6-18:012 por.].* Honolulu, HI: Scientific Consultant Services, Inc., 2016. [SHPD ID: 2019LI81527]

Dagher, Cathleen A. and Michael F. Dega. *Archaeological Field Inspection Results and Recommendations for the Proposed Maui Police Department Communications Facility at Māhinahina Water Treatment Plant, Māhinahina Ahupuaʻa, Lahaina District, Maui Island, Hawaiʻi.* Honolulu, HI: Scientific Consultant Services, Inc., 2016. [SHPD ID: 2019LI81036]

Desilets, Michael and Patrick OʻDay. *Preservation Plan for Proposed Fenceline Corridor for the West Maui Forest Reserve, Kuʻia, Mākila, Pāhoa, Halakaʻa, Polaiki, Launiupoko, and Olowalu Ahupuaʻa, Lahaina District, Maui Island, Hawaiʻi.* Kailua, HI: Garcia & Associates, 2016. [SHPD ID: 2019LI81528]

Folio, Katie M. and Hallett H. Hammatt. *Archaeological Monitoring Plan for the Special Use Permit Application for the Napili Point 1 AOAO (SMX 2015/0465) and Napili Point II (SMX 2015/0472) Project, Honokeana Ahupuaʻa, Lahaina District, Island of Maui, Napili Point I.* Wailuku, HI: Cultural Surveys Hawaiʻi, Inc., 2016. [SHPD ID: 2019LI81068]

Folio, Katie M. and Hallett H. Hammatt. *Archaeological Monitoring Report for the Special Use Permit Application for the Napili Point I (SMX 2015/0465) and Napili Point II (SMX 2015/0472) Project, Honokeana Ahupuaʻa, Lahaina District, Island of Maui, Napili Point I TMK: (2) 4-3-002:021 (por.), Napili Point II.* Wailuku, HI: Cultural Surveys Hawaiʻi, Inc., 2016. [SHPD ID: 2019LI81068]

Wasson, Eugene C. IV and Michael F. Dega. *An Archaeological Monitoring Report for the Lahaina No. 4. Force Main Replacement Project, in Lahaina, Wahikuli Ahupuaʻa, Lahaina District, Island of Maui, Hawaiʻi.* Honolulu, HI: Scientific Consultant Services, Inc., 2016. [SHPD ID: 2019LI80628]

2017

Andricci, Nicole and Michael F. Dega. *An Archaeological Assessment for the Lahaina Square Redevelopment Project, Lahaina, Waineʻe Ahupuaʻa, District of Lahaina, Island of Maui, Hawaiʻi.* Honolulu, HI: Scientific Consultant Services, Inc., 2017. [SHPD ID: 2019LI80016]

Dagher, Cathleen A. and Michael F. Dega. *A Preservation Plan for the "Brick Palace" (A Component of State Site 50-50-03-3001) Within the Proposed Lahaina Harbor Complete Streets Project Area, Lahaina, Paunau Ahupuaʻa, Lahaina District, Island of Maui, Hawaiʻi [TMK (2) 4-6-01:004].* Honolulu, HI: Scientific Consultant Services, Inc., 2017. [SHPD ID: 2019LI81386]

Dega, Michael F. *An Archaeological Monitoring Plan for the Ulupono Center Project, Lahaina, Panaʻewa Ahupuaʻa, Lahaina District, Hawaiʻi, TMK (2) 4-5-10:054.* Honolulu, HI: Scientific Consultant Services Inc., 2017. [SHPD ID: 2019LI80597]

Lash, Erik and Michael F. Dega. *An Archaeological Monitoring Plan for the Proposed Lahaina Harbor Complete Streets Project on Approximately 3.11 Acres (1.26 Hectares) in Lahaina, Paunau Ahupuaʻa, Lahaina District, Island of Maui, Hawaiʻi [TMK (2) 4-6-001:001, 004, 007, 009, 010, 012, and Adjacent Roadways].* Honolulu, HI: Scientific Consultant Services, Inc., 2017. [SHPD ID: 2019LI81388]

Medeiros, Colleen and Hallett H. Hammatt. *Archaeological Monitoring Report for the Kāʻanapali North Beach Development Area, Lot 3, Site Excavation, Honokōwai Ahupuaʻa, Lahaina District, Maui Island.* Wailuku, HI: Cultural Surveys Hawaiʻi, Inc., 2017. [SHPD ID: 2019LI80652]

Wiley, Tiffany E. and Michael F. Dega. *Addendum to an Archaeological Monitoring Plan for the Poseley Residence, Olowalu Ahupuaʻa, Lahaina District, Island of Maui, Hawaiʻi [TMK (2) 4-8-003:047, and portions of 001 and 084 (Easement G)].* Honolulu, HI: Scientific Consultant Services, Inc., 2017. [No location available]

2018

Dagher, Cathleen A. and Michael F. Dega. *Archaeological Monitoring Plan for the Maui Sands Sea Wall Repair Project, Moʻomuku ʻili, Honokōwai Ahupuaʻa, Lahaina (Kāʻanapali) District, Island of Maui, Hawaiʻi.* Honolulu, HI: Scientific Consultant Services, Inc., 2018. [No location available]

Kehajit, Chonnikarn and Michael F. Dega. *Archaeological Assessment for shoreline mitigation at the Hyatt Regency Maui Resort, Hanakaʻōʻō Ahupuaʻa, Lahaina District, Island of Maui, Hawaiʻi.* Honolulu, HI: Scientific Consultant Services, Inc., 2018. [No location available]

Kehajit, Chonnikarn and Michael F. Dega. *Archaeological Monitoring Plan for 1191 Front Street Replacement of an Existing Water Supply Project, Lahaina,*

Wahikuli Ahupuaʻa, Lahaina District, Island of Maui, Hawaiʻi. Honolulu, HI: Scientific Consultant Services, Inc., 2018. [SHPD ID: 2022LI00191]

Lyman, Kepa and Michael F. Dega. *Addendum—Archaeological Monitoring Plan for Lahaina Wastewater Pump Station No. 1 Improvements Honokōwai Ahupuaʻa, Lahaina District, Maui Island, Hawaiʻi [TMK (2) 4-4-002:33 and portions of 29 & 39].* Honolulu, HI: Scientific Consultant Services, Inc., 2018. [No location available]

Madeus, Jonas K., Josephine M. Yucha, and Hallett H. Hammatt. *Archaeological Monitoring Report for Improvements at Feast of Lele, Waiokama Ahupuaʻa, Lahaina District, Maui Island, TMK (2) 4-6-002:007 (por.).* Wailuku, HI: Cultural Surveys Hawaiʻi, Inc., 2018. [No location available]

Pestana, Elizabeth and Michael F. Dega. *Archaeological Inventory Survey of a 5.18 Acre Parcel in Kahana, Kahana Ahupuaʻa, Kāʻanapali District, Island of Maui, Hawaiʻi [TMK: (2)-4-3-15:069].* Honolulu, HI: Scientific Consultant Services, Inc., 2018. [SHPD ID: 2019LI81301]

Rotunno-Hazuka, Lisa J. and Jeffrey Pantaleo. *Final Archaeological Monitoring Plan for Demolition and New Construction along Front Street, Paunau Ahupuaʻa, Lahaina District, Kula Moku, Island of Maui.* Wailuku, HI: Archaeological Services Hawaii, LLC, 2018. [SHPD ID: 2019LI80633]

Six, Janet L. *A Final Archaeological Assessment Report for Maui County Work on County Roadway (WTP T20160044) and grading and grubbing (GT20160132) Proposed Sunset Terrace Lot Beautification Project, Honokōwai Ahupuaʻa, Lahaina District Maui Island, TMK (2) 4-4-02:029 and 034 (por.).* Pāhoa, HI: Sixth Sense Archaeological Consultants, LLC, 2018. [SHPD ID: 2019LI81282]

Six, Janet L. *Final Archaeological Monitoring Plan for Maui County Work on County Roadway (WTP T20160044) and Grading and Grubbing (GT2016132) Proposed Sunset Terrace Lot Beautification Project Honokōwai Ahupuaʻa, Lahaina Project Honokōwai Ahupuaʻa, Lahaina District, Maui Island, Hawaiʻi.* Pāhoa, HI: Sixth Sense Archaeological Consultants, LLC, 2018. [SHPD ID: 2019LI81282]

Six, Janet L. *Final Archaeological Monitoring Plan for Special Management Area Application (SMX2017/0098) for the Proposed Kahana Beach Resort DCDA Upgrade, Kahana Ahupuaʻa, Lahaina District, Island of Maui.* Pāhoa, HI: Sixth Sense Archaeological Consultants, LLC, 2018. [SHPD ID: 2019LI81303]

Six, Janet L. *Final Archaeological Monitoring Plan for Work on County Roadway Permit Application (WTP T2017-0055) Installation Communication Utilities, West Maui Village, Kohi & Napilihau St., Napili, ʻAlaeloa Ahupuaʻa, Kāʻanapali District, Island of Maui.* Pāhoa, HI: Sixth Sense Archaeological Consultants, LLC, 2018. [SHPD ID: 2019LI81317]

Yucha, Josephine M. and Hallett H. Hammatt. *Archaeological Monitoring Plan for the Sheraton Maui Resort & Spa Sewer Improvements Project, Hanakaʻōʻō Ahupuaʻa, Lahaina District, Maui Island, TMKs: (2) 4-4-08:005 and 011 (pors).* Wailuku, HI: Cultural Surveys Hawaiʻi, Inc., 2018. [SHPD ID: 2019LI80670]

Yucha, Josephine M. and Hallett H. Hammatt. *Archaeological Monitoring Report for the Sheraton Maui Sewer Improvements Project, Hanakaʻōʻō Ahupuaʻa, Lahaina District, Maui Island, TMKs: (2) 4-4-008:005 and 011 (pors.).* Wailuku, HI: Cultural Surveys Hawaiʻi, Inc., 2018. [SHPD ID: 2019LI81258]

Yucha, Trevor M. and Hallett H. Hammatt. *Archaeological Monitoring Plan for the Westin Maui Resort & Spa Master Plan Improvements, Hanakaʻōʻō Ahupuaʻa, Lahaina District, Island of Maui, TMK (2) 4-4-08:019.* Wailuku, HI: Cultural Surveys Hawaiʻi, Inc., 2018. [SHPD ID: 2019LI80683]

2019

Dagher, Cathleen A. and Michael F. Dega. *An Archaeological Monitoring Plan for Olowalu Lot 24, Olowalu Ahupuaʻa, Lahaina District, Island of Maui, Hawaiʻi [TMK: (2) 4-8-03:107].* Honolulu, HI: Scientific Consultant Services, Inc., 2019. [SHPD ID: 2019LI05336]

Fredericksen, Erik M. *An Archaeological Monitoring Plan for the Emerald Plaza II Project, Land of Moaliʻi, Lahaina District, Island of Maui, TMK: (2) 4-5-10:052.* Pukalani, HI: Xamanek Researches, 2019. [No location available]

Frey, Jennifer J., Josephine M. Yucha, and Hallett H. Hammatt. *Archaeological Monitoring Report for the Westin Maui Resort & Spa Master Plan Improvements Project, Parking Garage, Lobby, and Porte Cochere Driveway, Hanakaʻōʻō Ahupuaʻa, Lahaina District, Island of Maui, TMK (2) 4-4-008:019.* Wailuku, HI: Cultural Surveys Hawaiʻi, Inc., 2019. [SHPD ID: 2019LI80683]

Frey, Jennifer J., Ryan Luskin, Angela L. Yates, and Hallett H. Hammatt. *Archaeological Monitoring Report for the Hololani Resort Condominiums Shoreline Protection Project, Kahana Ahupuaʻa, Lahaina District, Maui Island.* Wailuku, HI: Cultural Surveys Hawaiʻi, Inc., 2019. [SHPD ID: 2019LI81312]

Yeomans, Sarah K. *Archaeological Monitoring Plan Parking Lot Drainage System Installation, Panaʻewa Ahupuaʻa, Lahaina District, Island of Maui, Hawaiʻi.* Honolulu, HI: Scientific Consultant Services, Inc., 2019. [SHPD ID: 2019LI80640]

Yucha, Josephine M. and Hallett H. Hammatt. *Archaeological Monitoring Plan for the Lahaina Intermediate School Campus Fire Alarm Replacement Project,*

Pana'ewa and Ku'ia Ahupua'a, Lahaina District, Maui Island TMK (2) 4-6-18:013 por. Wailuku, HI: Cultural Surveys Hawai'i, Inc., 2019. [No location available]

2020

Dagher, Cathleen A. and Michael F. Dega. *An Archaeological Monitoring Plan for the Nāpili No. 3 WWPS Force Main Replacement, Lower Honoapi'ilani Road Right-of-Way, Kahana Ahupua'a, Lahaina (Kā'anapali) District Island of Maui, Hawai'i. [TMK (2) 4-2-05:999 and 4-3-10:999].* Honolulu, HI: Scientific Consultant Services, Inc., 2020. [SHPD ID: 2021LI00158]

Dagher, Cathleen A. and Michael F. Dega. *An Archaeological Monitoring Plan for the Nāpili No. 4 WWPS Force Main Replacement, Lower Honoapi'ilani Road Right-of-Way, Honokeana and 'Alaeloa Ahupua'a, Lahaina, (Kā'anapali) District, Island of Maui, Hawai'i.* Honolulu, HI: Scientific Consultant Services, Inc., 2020. [SHPD ID: 2021LI00158]

Dagher, Cathleen A. and Michael F. Dega. *Archaeological Monitoring Plan for 790 Front Street Waterline (WTP T2017-00280) Lahaina, Paunau Ahupua'a, Lahaina District, Island of Maui, Hawai'i [TMK: (2) 4-6-09:999].* Honolulu, HI: Scientific Consultant Services, Inc., 2020. [SHPD ID: 2022LI00633]

Lyman, Kepa and Michael F. Dega. *Archaeological Monitoring Plan for the Hanaka'ō'ō Beach Park Parking Improvements, Hanaka'ō'ō Ahupua'a, Lahaina (Kā'anapali) District, Island of Maui.* Honolulu, HI: Scientific Consultant Services, Inc., 2020. [SHPD ID: 2021LI00062]

Yates and Hallett H. Hammatt. *Archaeological Monitoring Plan for the Kā'anapali 2020 Master Plan, Kā'anapali Coffee Farms Subdivision Phase II Project, Hanaka'ō'ō and Honokōwai Ahupua'a, Lahaina District, Maui Island, TMK (2) 4-4-02:002.* Wailuku, HI: Cultural Surveys Hawai'i, Inc., 2020. [SHPD ID: 2021LI00326, 2022LI00365]

Yucha, Josephine M. and Hallett H. Hammatt. *Archaeological Monitoring Plan for the Valley Isle Resort Renovation Project, Kahana Ahupua'a, Lahaina District, Maui Island, TMK: (2) 4-3-10:004.* Wailuku, HI: Cultural Surveys Hawai'i, Inc., 2020. [SHPD ID: 2021LI00211]

2021

Chong Jin and Michael F. Dega. *Archaeological Monitoring Report for the Kapalua Sinkhole Remediation and Native Plant Restoration Project, Nāpili 2-3 Ahupua'a,*

Lahaina District, Island of Maui [TMK: (2) 4-2-04:025 and (2) 4-2-04:059]. Honolulu, HI: Scientific Consultant Services, Inc., 2021. [SHPD ID: 2022LI00634]

Chong Jin, Garcia Alondra, and Michael F. Dega. *Archaeological Monitoring Plan for 7,804 sq. ft. Parcel at 432 Ilikahi Street, Paunau Ahupuaʻa, Lahaina District, Island of Maui, Hawaiʻi [TMK: (2) 4-6-06:056 por.].* Honolulu, HI: Scientific Consultant Services, Inc., 2021. [SHPD ID: 2021LI00125]

Frey, Jennifer J., Josephine M. Yucha, and Hallett H. Hammatt. *Archaeological Monitoring Report for the Valley Isle Resort Renovation Project, Kahana Ahupuaʻa, Lahaina District, Maui Island, TMK: (2) 4-3-10:004.* Wailuku, HI: Cultural Surveys Hawaiʻi, Inc., 2021. [SHPD ID: 2022LI00135]

Gallo and Michael F. Dega. *Archaeological Assessment for a New Farm Dwelling for Mākila Ranches, Lot 4, Polanui Ahupuaʻa, Lahaina District, Island of Maui, Hawaiʻi [TMK: (2) 4-7-14:004 por.].* Honolulu, HI: Scientific Consultant Services, Inc., 2021. [SHPD ID: 2022LI00382]

Lee and Michael F. Dega. *An Archaeological Assessment for a New Wastewater System at the Olowalu Plantation Manager's House in Olowalu, Olowalu Ahupuaʻa, Lahaina District, Island of Maui, Hawaiʻi [TMK: (2) 4-8-03:005 por.].* Honolulu, HI: Scientific Consultant Services, Inc., 2021. [SHPD ID: 2021LI00436]

Stankov, Pavel and Michael F. Dega. *Archaeological Monitoring Plan for the Renovations and Landscaping at the Stakelbeck Property at Olowalu Ahupuaʻa, Lahaina District, Island of Maui, Hawaiʻi [TMK (2) 4-8-03:002 por.].* Honolulu, HI: Scientific Consultant Services, Inc., 2021. [SHPD ID: 2021LI00103]

Yucha, Josephine M., Jennifer Frey, and Hallett H. Hammatt. *Burial Site Component of an Archaeological Data Recovery Plan for SIHP # 50-50-03-8842 at the Westin Maui Resort & Spa Improvements Project, Phase III, Hanakaʻōʻō Ahupuaʻa, Lahaina District, Maui, TMK: (2) 4-4-08:019.* Wailuku, HI: Cultural Surveys Hawaiʻi, Inc., 2021. [SHPD ID: 2021LI00104]

2022

Chong Jin and Michael F. Dega. *Archaeological Assessment for the Launiupoko Water System Line Extension to Waineʻe Project, Pūehuehu Nui and Pāhoa Ahupuaʻa, Lahaina District, Island of Maui, Hawaiʻi [TMK: (2) 4-6-013: portion of 022; 4-7-002: portion of 004; 4-7-003: portion of 031].* Honolulu, HI: Scientific Consultant Services, Inc., 2022. [SHPD ID: 2022LI00556]

Dagher, Cathleen A. and Michael F. Dega. *Archaeological Inventory Survey for the Proposed West Maui Water Source Development Project Māhinahina Well (State Well No. 6-5638-004) (West Maui Well No. 1) and the Kahana Well (State Well No. 6-5738-002) (West Maui Well No. 2), Honokōwai, Māhinahina, and Māhinahina 1, 2, 3 Ahupuaʻa, Lahaina (Kāʻanapali) District, Island of Maui, Hawaiʻi [TMK: (2) 4-3-01:017, (2) 4-3-01:084; (2) 4-4-02:014, 015, and 018; and (2) 4-4-004:009, 011, 017, and 019].* Honolulu, HI: Scientific Consultant Services, Inc., 2022. [SHPD ID: 2022LI00356]

Madeus, Jonas K. et al. *Archaeological Inventory Survey for the Villages of Leialiʻi, Phase 1-B Subdivision and Related Improvements Project, Wahikuli Ahupuaʻa, Lahaina District, Maui Island, TMKs: (2) 4-5-021:010 por., 014 por., 020, and 021 por.; (2) 4-5-36:109, 110, and 112; and Honoapiʻilani Highway Right-of-Way.* Wailuku, HI: Cultural Surveys Hawaiʻi, Inc., 2022. [SHPD ID: 2022LI00589]

Mason Architects, Inc. *Reconnaissance Level Survey, Honokōwai Reservoir for the West Maui Recycled Water and Kāʻanapali Resort R-1 Water Distribution Expansion Project. TMK (2) 4-4-02:019.* Honolulu, HI: Mason Architects, Inc., 2022. [SHPD ID: 2023LI00017]

Mulrooney et al. *Archaeological Inventory Survey Report for the Kahana Solar Project in Ahupuaʻa of Kahana and Māhinahina 1-3, Moku of Kāʻanapali (Lahaina Modern Tax District), Island of Maui [TMK: (2) 4-3-01:017 por.; (2) 4-3-01:082 por.; (2) 4-3-01:084 por.].* Kailua, HI: Pacific Legacy, Inc., 2022.

Yucha, Josephine M. et al. *Archaeological Inventory Survey for the Puʻukoliʻi Village Mauka Project, Hanakaʻōʻō Ahupuaʻa, Lahaina District, Maui Island, TMKs: (2) 4-4-02:002, 048, and 053 por., (2) 4-4-06:070, 086 and 087 por., and (2) 4-4-15:034 through 072.* Wailuku, HI: Cultural Surveys Hawaiʻi, Inc., 2022. [SHPD ID: 2023LI00110]

2023

Fredericksen, Erik M. *Archaeological Inventory Survey for the Proposed Lahaina Cannery Fuel Station Project, Land of Moaliʻi, Lahaina District, Island of Maui [TMK: (2) 4-5-11: 004 Por.].* Pukalani, HI: Xamanek Researches, 2023. [SHPD ID: 2023LI00137]

Fredericksen, Erik M. and J. J. Frey. *Burial Site Component of an Archaeological Data Recovery Plan for Inadvertently Discovered Human Skeletal Remains, Site 50-50-03-08973, Located in Previously Imported Sand Fill During Utilities Installation for the Lahaina Cannery Fuel Station Project, Ahupuaʻa of Moaliʻi, Lahaina*

District, Island of Maui [TMK: (2) 4-5-11:004 por.]. Pukalani, HI: Xamanek Researches, 2023. [SHPD ID: 2023LI00074]

Lee-Greig, Tanya L. *Archaeological Monitoring Plan for the Traffic Signal Improvements at Pāpalaua Street/Waineʻe Street Intersection, Federal Aid Project No. STP-3020 (001) Aki and Uhao Ahupuaʻa (Paunau Modern Ahupuaʻa), Lahaina Moku and Modern Tax District, Mokupuni of Maui [TMK: (2) 4-5-002:999 ROW, 4-5-006:999 ROW, 4-5-006:004, and 4-5-006:015].* Honolulu, HI: Aina Archaeology, 2023. [SHPD ID: 2023LI00149].

Yucha, Josephine M. and Hallett H. Hammatt. *Archaeological Monitoring Plan for the Puʻukoliʻi Village Mauka Project, Hanakaʻōʻō Ahupuaʻa, Lahaina District, Maui Island, TMKs: (2) 4-4-02:002, 048, and 053 por., (2) 4-4-06:070, 086 and 087 por., and (2) 4-4-15:034 through 072. 24:026 (por.).* Wailuku, HI: Cultural Surveys Hawaiʻi, Inc., 2023. [SHPD ID: 2023LI00111]

Yucha, Josephine M. and Hallett H. Hammatt. *Archaeological Monitoring Plan for the Villages of Leialiʻi, Village 1-B Subdivision and Related Improvements Project, Wahikuli Ahupuaʻa, Lahaina District, Maui Island, TMKs: (2) 4-5-021:010 por., 014 por., 015 por., 020, and 021 por.; (2) 4-5-36:109, 110, and 112; and Honoapiʻilani Highway Right-of-Way.* Wailuku, HI: Cultural Surveys Hawaiʻi, Inc., 2022. [SHPD ID: 2023LI00106]

NONE

Knecht, Daniel P. and Timothy M. Rieth. *Archaeological Monitoring Plan for the Lahainaluna High School New Classroom Building Project, Panaʻewa Ahupuaʻa, Lahaina District, Maui.* Honolulu, HI: International Archaeology, LLC. [No location available]

PUBLICATIONS BY COMPANY
Publications without companies are listed at the end

AINA ARCHAEOLOGY

Lee-Greig, Tanya L. *Archaeological Monitoring Plan for the Traffic Signal Improvements at Pāpalaua Street/Waineʻe Street Intersection, Federal Aid Project No. STP-3020 (001) Aki and Uhao Ahupuaʻa (Paunau Modern Ahupuaʻa), Lahaina Moku and Modern Tax District, Mokupuni of Maui [TMK: (2) 4-5-002:999 ROW, 4-5-006:999 ROW, 4-5-006:004, and 4-5-006:015].* Honolulu, HI: Aina Archaeology, 2023. [SHPD ID: 2023LI00149].

AKAHELE ARCHAEOLOGY

Donham, Theresa K. *Archaeological Monitoring Plan for American Disabilities Act Improvements at the Lahaina Public Library, Paunau, Lahaina District, Maui, TMK: (2) 4-6-01:007 & 010.* Kīhei, HI: Akahele Archaeology, 2004. [SHPD ID: 2019LI81381]

Donham, Theresa K. *Archaeological Monitoring Plan for Construction of a Pool & Spa at the Hurlock Property, Moaliʻi, Lahaina District, Maui, TMK: (2) 4-5-13:004.* Kīhei, HI: Akahele Archaeology, 2003. [SHPD ID: 2019LI81351]

Donham, Theresa K. *Archaeological Monitoring Plan for the Remodeling of a Dwelling at the Phleger Property, Halakaʻa, Lahaina District, Maui TMK: (2) 4-6-05:014.* Kīhei, HI: Akahele Archaeology, 2004. [SHPD ID: 2019LI81558]

Donham, Theresa K. *Archaeological Monitoring Report for American Disabilities Act Improvements at the Lahaina Public Library, Paunau, Lahaina District, Maui, TMK: (2) 4-6-01:007 & 010.* Kīhei, HI: Akahele Archaeology, 2005. [SHPD ID: 2019LI81403]

Aki Sinoto Consulting

Aki Sinoto Consulting. *Archaeological Monitoring During the Renovation of the Lahaina Center Parking Structure, Lahaina, Maui.* Honolulu, HI: Aki Sinoto Consulting, 1995.

Aki Sinoto Consulting. *Archaeological Monitoring Plan for Utility Trenching at the Lahaina Shopping Center, Paunau, Lahaina, Maui.* Honolulu, HI: Aki Sinoto Consulting, 1996.

Burgett, Berdena and Robert L. Spear. *An Archaeological Inventory Survey of an 8.8 Acre Parcel in the Land of Kainehi, Lahaina District, Paunau Ahupuaʻa, Island of Maui.* Honolulu, HI: Aki Sinoto Consulting, 1994.

Sinoto, Aki and Jeffrey Pantaleo. *Archaeological Inventory Survey of TMK (2) 4-4-01:002, 11, and 12 (Revised Final 9-92).* Honolulu, HI: Aki Sinoto Consulting, 1991. [No location available]

Sinoto, Aki. *An Archaeological Assessment of the Native Plant Conservatory Project, Ukumehame Firing Range, Ukumehame, Lahaina, Maui TMK (2) 4-8-2:047.* Honolulu, HI: Aki Sinoto Consulting, 1997. [SHPD ID: 2019LI81624]

Archaeological Consultants of Hawaii, Inc.

Kennedy, Joseph. *Archaeological Inventory Survey and Subsurface Testing Report for TMK: (2) 4-3-01:031, Located at Kahana Ahupuaʻa, Island of Maui,* Revised May 1992, 1992. [SHPD ID: 2019LI81051]

Kennedy, Joseph. *Archaeological Inventory Survey of Kahana, Maui.* Haleʻiwa, HI: Archaeological Consultants of Hawaii, 1985. [No location available]

Kennedy, Joseph. *Archaeological Inventory Survey of TMK (2) 4-3-02:068 & 069, Located at Napili, Island of Maui.* Haleʻiwa, HI: Archaeological Consultants of Hawaii, 1990. [SHPD ID: 2019LI81061]

Kennedy, Joseph. *Archaeological Inventory Survey Report for TMK (2) 4-3-01:31, located at Kahana, Island of Maui.* Haleʻiwa, HI: Archaeological Consultants of Hawaii, 1991. [SHPD ID: 2019LI81069]

Kennedy, Joseph. *Archaeological Report Concerning Subsurface Testing at TMK: (2) 4-6-08:012, Lahaina Maui.* Haleʻiwa, HI: Archaeological Consultants of Hawaii, 1989. [SHPD ID: 2019LI81544]

Kennedy, Joseph. *Archaeological Walk Through Examination of Quarry Site located Mauka of Honoapi'ilani Highway near Lipoa Point, Honolua, Maui.* Hale'iwa, HI: Archaeological Consultants of Hawaii, 1988. [SHPD ID: 2019LI81425]

Kennedy, Joseph. *Hawea Point Residential Project: Archaeological Review, Survey, and Assessments.* Hale'iwa, HI: Archaeological Consultants of Hawaii, 1990. [SHPD ID: 2019LI81416]

Kennedy, Joseph and Tim Denham. *Archaeological Inventory Survey and Subsurface Testing Report for TMK (2) 4-3-01:031, located at Kahana Ahupua'a, Maui.* Hale'iwa, HI: Archaeological Consultants of Hawaii, 1992.

Moore, James R. and Joseph Kennedy. *An Archaeological Inventory Survey with Subsurface Testing Report for Portions of the Proposed Kahana Ridge Subdivision Located at TMK: (2) 4-3-05:016 & 018, in Kahana Ahupua'a, Lahaina District, Island of Maui.* Hale'iwa, HI: Archaeological Consultants of Hawaii, 1994. [SHPD ID: 2019LI81329]

ARCHAEOLOGICAL RESEARCH CENTER HAWAI'I, INC.

Ching, Francis K. W. *Archaeological Assessment of the Property on Which the Proposed Marriott Kā'anapali Hotel is to be Built, Kā'anapali, Maui Island.* Lāwa'i, HI: Archaeological Research Center Hawai'i, 1979. [SHPD ID: 2019LI81267]

Davis, Bertell D. *Archaeological Surface Survey, Honokōwai Gulch, Kā'anapali, Maui Island.* Lāwa'i, HI: Archaeological Research Center Hawai'i, 1977. [SHPD ID: 2019LI81277]

Davis, Bertell D. *Preliminary Report, Mala Wharf Burials, Phase 1, Mala, Lahaina, Maui Island.* Lāwa'i, HI: Archaeological Research Center Hawai'i, 1977. [No location available]

Griffin, Bion P. and George W. Lovelace, eds. *Survey and Salvage—Honoapi'ilani Highway: The Archaeology of Kā'anapali from Honokōwai to 'Alaeloa Ahupua'a.* Lāwa'i, HI: Archaeological Research Center Hawai'i, Inc., 1977. [UH Call Number: DU628.M3 A7 1977]

Hammatt, Hallett H. *Archaeological Investigation and Monitoring, Mala Wharf Boat-Launch Ramp Area, Lahaina, Maui Island.* Lāwa'i, HI: Archaeological Research Center Hawai'i, Inc., 1978. [SHPD ID: 2019LI81387; UH Call Number: GN486 .H35]

Hammatt, Hallett H. *Archaeological Reconnaissance at the Proposed Hyatt Regency Site, Hanaka'ō'ō, Kā'anapali, Maui Island, Tax Map Key; 4-4-06:31 Lot 60, ARCH*

14-129. Lāwaʻi, HI: Archaeological Research Center Hawaiʻi, 1978. [SHPD ID: 2019LI81264; UH Call Number: GN486 .H35]

Olson, Larry G. *Appendix II—A Geoarchaeological Report of Site 225, Māhinahina Gulch, Maui, Hawaiʻi*. Lāwaʻi, HI: Archaeological Research Center Hawaiʻi, 1977. [No location available]

Archaeological Services Hawaii, LLC

Guerriero, Diane and Jeffrey *Pantaleo. Archaeological Inventory Survey Report of a 0.361 Acre Coastal Parcel, Waineʻe Ahupuaʻa, Lahaina District, Island of Maui*. Wailuku, HI: Archaeological Services Hawaii, LLC, 2005. [SHPD ID: 2019LI81560]

Guerriero, Diane, Lisa J. Rotunno-Hazuka, and Jeffrey Pantaleo. *Archaeological Assessment Report of a 0.428 Acre Parcel of Land at TMK 4-5-07:004 Kuholilea Ahupuaʻa, Lahaina District, Island of Maui*. Wailuku, HI: Archaeological Services Hawaii, LLC, 2005. [SHPD ID: 2019LI80606]

Guerriero, Diane, Lisa Rotunno-Hazuka, and Jeffrey Pantaleo. *Archaeological Assessment for the Royal Lahaina Resort Redevelopment Hanakaʻōʻō Ahupuaʻa, Lahaina District, Island of Maui*. Wailuku, HI: Archaeological Services Hawaii, LLC, 2005. [SHPD ID: 2019LI81261]

Pantaleo, Jeffrey. *Archaeological Inventory Report of a 1.65-Acre Parcel of Land Pūehuehue Iki Ahupuaʻa, Lahaina District, Island of Maui TMK (2) 4-7-04:001*. Wailuku, HI: Archaeological Services Hawaii, LLC, 2006. [SHPD ID: 2019LI81615]

Pantaleo, Jeffrey and Paul Titchenal. *An Archaeological Inventory Survey Report for the Pulelehua Community Project TMK (2) 4-3-01:031 Por. Māhinahina 1, 2, 3, Māhinahina 4, and Kahana Ahupuaʻa, Lahaina and Kāʻanapali Districts, Island of Maui*. Wailuku, HI: Archaeological Services Hawaii, LLC, 2004. [SHPD ID: 2019LI81072]

Rotunno-Hazuka, Lisa J. *Archaeological Assessment for the Proposed Well Site in Launiupoko, Lahaina, Maui TMK 4-7-02:001 Lot B*. Wailuku, HI: Archaeological Services Hawaii, LLC, 1997. [SHPD ID: 2019LI81617]

Rotunno-Hazuka, Lisa J. and Jeffrey Pantaleo, M.A. *Archaeological Preservation and Monitoring Plan for Site 50-50-03-4096 Feature 1 Located on a Residential Lot, TMK (2) 4-7-01:001 Pūehuehue Iki Ahupuaʻa, Lahaina District: Island of Maui*. Wailuku, HI: Archaeological Services Hawaii, LLC, 2006. [SHPD ID: 2019LI81591]

Rotunno-Hazuka, Lisa J. and Jeffrey Pantaleo. *Archaeological Monitoring Plan for a Waterline Installation at TMK: (2) 4-5-01:045 Old Lahaina Center, Papalua Street, Pana'ewa Ahupua'a, Lahaina District, Island of Maui*. Wailuku, HI: Archaeological Services Hawaii, LLC, 2002. [SHPD ID: 2019LI80638]

Rotunno-Hazuka, Lisa J. and Jeffrey Pantaleo. *Archaeological Monitoring Plan for All Ground Disturbing Activities Associated with the Construction of the Waine'e Self Storage Facility located at TMK: (2) 4-5-07:004 Kuholilea Ahupua'a, Lahaina District, Island of Maui*. Wailuku, HI: Archaeological Services Hawaii, LLC, 2006. [SHPD ID: 2019LI80607]

Rotunno-Hazuka, Lisa J. and Jeffrey Pantaleo. *Archaeological Monitoring Plan for All Improvements at the McFarland Residence TMK: (2) 4-5-13:003, Moali'i Ahupua'a Lahaina District, Island of Maui*. Wailuku, HI: Archaeological Services Hawaii, LLC, 2006. [SHPD ID: 2019LI81352]

Rotunno-Hazuka, Lisa J. and Jeffrey Pantaleo. *Archaeological Monitoring Plan for All Improvements Related to the Proposed Construction of an Ohana and Garage at the Stiebinger Residence, Kau'aula Ahupua'a, Lahaina District, Island of Maui TMK (2) 4-6-06:005*. Wailuku, HI: Archaeological Services Hawaii, LLC, 2005. [SHPD ID: 2019LI81405]

Rotunno-Hazuka, Lisa J. and Jeffrey Pantaleo. *Archaeological Monitoring Plan for All Improvements Related to the Redevelopment of the Royal Lahaina Resort, Hanaka'ō'ō Ahupua'a; Lahaina District, Island of Maui, TMK:4-4-08:007& 013*. Wailuku, HI: Archaeological Services Hawaii, LLC, 2007. [SHPD ID: 2019LI80677]

Rotunno-Hazuka, Lisa J. and Jeffrey Pantaleo. *Archaeological Monitoring Plan for Pool Installation at TMK (2) 4-5-04:037 Lahilahi Street, Ku'ia Ahupua'a, Lahaina District, Island of Maui*. Wailuku, HI: Archaeological Services Hawaii, LLC, 2002. [SHPD ID: 2019LI80627]

Rotunno-Hazuka, Lisa J. and Jeffrey Pantaleo. *Archaeological Monitoring Plan for the Construction of a Swimming Pool and Associated Utilities at the Allan Residence, Lahaina Ahupua'a, Lahaina District, Island of Maui*. Wailuku, HI: Archaeological Services Hawai'i, LLC, 2004. [SHPD ID: 2019LI80623]

Rotunno-Hazuka, Lisa J. and Jeffrey Pantaleo. *Archaeological Monitoring Plan For the Construction of an Accessory Dwelling at the Meston Residence at TMK (2) 4-6-07:030 Paunau Ahupua'a, Lahaina District, Island of Maui*. Wailuku, HI: Archaeological Services Hawaii, LLC, 2004. [SHPD ID: 2019LI81551]

Rotunno-Hazuka, Lisa J. and Jeffrey Pantaleo. *Archaeological Monitoring Plan for the Demolition of an Existing Single Family Residence & Pool Cover and*

Construction of a New Single Family Residence at TMK: (2) 4-5-04:048 Puʻunoa Ahupuaʻa, Lahaina District, Island of Maui. Wailuku, HI: Archaeological Services Hawaii, LLC, 2004. [SHPD ID: 2019LI80625]

Rotunno-Hazuka, Lisa J. and Jeffrey Pantaleo. *Archaeological Monitoring Plan for the Demolition of an Existing Single Family Residence and Construction of a new Single Family Residence at TMK (2) 4-5-04:004, Puʻunoa Ahupuaʻa, Lahaina District, Island of Maui.* Wailuku, HI: Archaeological Services Hawaii, LLC, 2004. [SHPD ID: 2019LI80621]

Rotunno-Hazuka, Lisa J. and Jeffrey Pantaleo. *Archaeological Monitoring Plan for the Installation of a Grease Interceptor at TMK: (2) 4-5-02:009 Kelawea Ahupuaʻa, Lahaina District, Island of Maui.* Wailuku, HI: Archaeological Services Hawaii, LLC, 2007. [SHPD ID: 2019LI80646]

Rotunno-Hazuka, Lisa J. and Jeffrey Pantaleo. *Archaeological Monitoring Plan for the Renovation and Revitalization of the Napili Kai Resort, Napili Ahupuaʻa, Lahaina District, Island of Maui.* Wailuku, HI: Archaeological Services Hawaii, LLC, 2005. [SHPD ID: 2019LI81067]

Rotunno-Hazuka, Lisa J. and Jeffrey Pantaleo. *Archaeological Monitoring Plan for the Renovations to the Lahaina-Kaiser Clinic, Panaʻewa Ahupuaʻa, Lahaina District, Island of Maui.* Wailuku, HI: Archaeological Services Hawaii, LLC, 2003. [SHPD ID: 2019LI80608]

Rotunno-Hazuka, Lisa J. and Jeffrey Pantaleo. *Final Archaeological Monitoring Plan for Demolition and New Construction along Front Street, Paunau Ahupuaʻa, Lahaina District, Kula Moku, Island of Maui.* Wailuku, HI: Archaeological Services Hawaii, LLC, 2018. [SHPD ID: 2019LI80633]

Rotunno-Hazuka, Lisa J. and Jeffrey Pantaleo. *Final Archaeological Monitoring Plan for the Installation of a New Water Service and Relocated Power Pole Along Kalena Street Kelawea Ahupuaʻa, Lahaina District, Island of Maui.* Wailuku, HI: Archaeological Services Hawaii, LLC, 2015. [No location available]

Rotunno-Hazuka, Lisa J. and Jeffrey Pantaleo. *Final Archaeological Monitoring Report for All Ground Disturbing Activities Associated with the Development of a Residential Structure Located at TMK (2) 4-05-04:048 Puʻunoa Ahupuaʻa, Lahaina District, Island of Maui.* Wailuku, HI: Archaeological Services Hawaii, LLC, 2008. [SHPD ID: 2019LI80614]

Rotunno-Hazuka, Lisa J. and Jeffrey Pantaleo. *Final Archaeological Monitoring Report for All Ground Disturbing Activities Associated with the Development of a Residential Structure Located at TMK (2) 4-5-04:004, Puʻunoa Ahupuaʻa, Lahaina*

District, Island of Maui. Wailuku, HI: Archaeological Services Hawaii, LLC, 2008. [SHPD ID: 2019LI80622]

Rotunno-Hazuka, Lisa J., Mia Watson, and Jeffrey Pantaleo. *Archaeological Monitoring Plan for the Improvements to a Commercial Restaurant Facility at TMK: (2) 4-5-07:034, Kāʻanapali Ahupuaʻa, Lahaina District, Island of Maui.* Wailuku, HI: Archaeological Services Hawaii, LLC, 2010. [SHPD ID: 2019LI80610]

Rotunno-Hazuka, Lisa J., Mia Watson, and Jeffrey Pantaleo. *Archaeological Monitoring Plan for the Repair and Installation of Underground Conduit at Front & Wharf Street, Lahaina and Waineʻe Ahupuaʻa, Lahaina District, Island of Maui.* Wailuku, HI: Archaeological Services Hawaii, LLC, 2008. [SHPD ID: 2019LI81385]

Sinoto, Aki and Jeffrey Pantaleo. *Archaeological Inventory Survey of the Proposed Site for the New Lahaina Kingdom Hall Puunoa, Paunau Ahupuaʻa, Lahaina District, Maui Island TMK (2) 4-4-04:042 & 044).* Wailuku, HI: Archaeological Services Hawaii, LLC, 2003. [SHPD ID: 2019LI80616]

Bernice P. Bishop Museum

Chapman, P. S. and P. V. Kirch. *Archaeological Excavations at Seven Sites, Southeast Maui, Hawaiian Islands.* Honolulu, HI: Department of Anthropology, Bernice P. Bishop Museum, 1979. [UH Call Number: DU624.A1 B47 no.79-1]

Cleghorn, Paul L. *A Progress Report upon Completion of Fieldwork at the Seamen's Hospital, Lahaina, Maui (Phase 1).* Honolulu, HI: Department of Anthropology, Bernice P. Bishop Museum, 1975. [UH Call Number: DU629.L3 C54 1975]

Cleghorn, Paul L. *Phase 1 Archaeological Research at the Seamen's Hospital (Site D5-10), Lahaina, Maui.* Honolulu, HI: Department of Anthropology, Bernice P. Bishop Museum, 1975. [UH Call Number: DU629.L3 C544 1975]

Connolly, Robert D. III. *Phase I Archaeological Survey of Kahoma Stream Flood-Control-Project Area, Lahaina, Maui.* Honolulu, HI: Department of Anthropology, Bernice P. Bishop Museum, 1974.

Dobyns, Susan and Jane Allen-Wheeler. *Archaeological Monitoring at the Site of the Kāʻanapali Aliʻi Condominium, Island of Maui.* Honolulu, HI: Department of Anthropology, Bernice P. Bishop Museum, 1982. [SHPD ID: 2019LI80673]

Hommon, Robert J. *Report on a Walk Through Survey of the Kahoma Stream Flood Control Project Area.* Honolulu, HI: Department of Anthropology, Bernice P. Bishop Museum, 1973.

Kaschko, Michael W. *Archaeological Survey of the Honolua Development Area, Maui.* Department of Anthropology, Honolulu, HI: Bernice P. Bishop Museum, 1973. [SHPD ID: 2019LI81019]

Kaschko, Michael W. *Archaeological Walk-Through Survey of Specified Areas in the Wailuku Flood Prevention Project and the Honolua Watershed, Maui.* Honolulu, HI: Department of Anthropology, Bernice P. Bishop Museum, 1974. [SHPD ID: 2019LI81443]

Kirch, Patrick V. *Archaeological Excavations at Site D13-1, Hawea Point, Maui, Hawaiian Islands.* Honolulu, HI: Department of Anthropology, Bernice P. Bishop Museum, 1973. [SHPD ID: 2019LI81021; UH Call Number: DU629. H393 K57 1973]

Kirch, Patrick V. *Archaeological Survey of the Honolua Development Area, Maui.* Honolulu, HI: Department of Anthropology, Bernice P. Bishop Museum, 1973. [SHPD ID: 2019LI81019; UH Call Number: DU629.K374 K57 1973]

Klieger, Paul Christiaan and Lonnie Somer. *Emergency Mitigation at Maluʻulu o Lele Park, Lahaina, Maui, Hawaiʻi, Site of Mokuʻula, Residence of King Kamehameha III (Site 50-50-03-2967; TMK (2) 4-6-7 Parcel 002: BPBM 50-MA-D5-12).* Honolulu, HI: Department of Anthropology, Bernice P. Bishop Museum, 1989. [SHPD ID: 2019LI81550]

Klieger, Paul Christiaan and Susan A. Lebo. *Archaeological Inventory Survey of Waiōlaʻi and Waiokila Catchments, Kahakuloa, West Maui, Hawaiʻi.* Honolulu, HI: Department of Anthropology, Bernice P. Bishop Museum, 1995. [No location available]

Komori, Eric K. *Archaeological Investigations at Kahana Gulch, Lahaina District, Maui.* Honolulu, HI: Department of Anthropology, Bernice P. Bishop Museum, 1983. [SHPD ID: 2019LI81070; UH Call Number: DU629.K343 K66 1983]

Kurashina, Hiro and Aki Sinoto. *Archaeological Reconnaissance of the Proposed Shopping Center at Lahaina, Maui, Hawaiʻi, TMK: (2) 4-5-02:009.* Honolulu, HI: Department of Anthropology, Bernice P. Bishop Museum, 1984. [SHPD ID: 2019LI80648; UH Call Number: DU629.L3 K87 1984]

Major, Maurice. *Ridgetops and Gulch Bottoms: An Archaeological Inventory Survey of Waiōlaʻi and Waiokila Catchments, Kahakuloa, West Maui, Hawaiʻi. TMK (2) 3-1-01:003.* Honolulu, HI: Department of Anthropology, Bernice P. Bishop Museum, 1996. [SHPD ID: 2019LI80145]

Major, Maurice and P. Christiaan Klieger. *Historical Background and Archaeological Testing at Pikanele's Kuleana in Lahaina, Maui: An Inventory Survey*

Report of LCA 310.3 (Royal Patent 1729.2, TMK (2) 4-6-07:013). Honolulu, HI: Department of Anthropology, Bernice P. Bishop Museum, 1995. [SHPD ID: 2019LI81546; UH Call Number: DU629.L3 M36 1996]

Major, Maurice, P. Christiaan Klieger, and Susan A. Lebo. *Historical Background and Archaeological Testing at Pikanele's Kuleana in Lahaina, Maui: An Inventory Survey Report of LCA 310.3 (Royal Patent 1729.2, TMK (2) 4-6-07:013*. Honolulu, HI: Department of Anthropology, Bernice P. Bishop Museum, 1996. [SHPD ID: 2019LI81546]

Moore, Kenneth R. *Archaeological Survey of Honolua Valley, Maui*. Honolulu, HI: Department of Anthropology, Bernice P. Bishop Museum, 1974. [SHPD ID: 2019LI81436; UH Call Number: DU629.H69 M66 1974]

Pantaleo, Jeffrey. *Archaeological Survey of the Proposed Lahainaluna Reservoir and Treatment Facility, Lahaina, Maui*. Honolulu, HI: Public Archaeology Section, Applied Research Group, Bernice P. Bishop Museum, 1991. [SHPD ID: 2019LI81530]

Riford, Mary F. and Paul L. *Cleghorn. Documentary Assessment of Archaeological Potential of Ten Prospective Power Plant Sites on Maui*. Honolulu, HI: Public Archaeology Section, Bernice P. Bishop Museum, 1989. [SHPD ID: 2022LI00168]

Sinoto, Aki. *An Archaeological Reconnaissance of the Mala Wharf Boat Launch Ramp Area, Lahaina, Maui*. Honolulu, HI: Department of Anthropology, Bernice P. Bishop Museum, 1975. [SHPD ID: 2019LI80624; UH Call Number: DU629.M353 S56 1975]

Sinoto, Aki. *Field Examination of Six Sites in the Honolua Watershed, Maui*. Honolulu, HI: Department of Anthropology, Bernice P. Bishop Museum, 1975. [SHPD ID: 2019LI81435; UH Call Number: DU629.H69 S56 1975]

Sinoto, Aki. *Proposed Kai Ala Subdivision, Kā'anapali, Maui*. Honolulu, HI: Bernice P. Bishop Museum, 1990. [SHPD ID: 2019LI81265]

Weisler, M. *Field Inspection of Hanaka'ō'ō Construction Site, Maui*. Honolulu, HI: Department of Anthropology, Bernice P. Bishop Museum, 1983. [No location available]

CHINIAGO, INC.

Barrera, William Jr. *Honoapi'ilani Highway, Maui: Archaeological Reconnaissance*. Honolulu, HI: Chiniago, Inc., 1988.

Barrera, William Jr. *North Beach, Maui: Archaeological Reconnaissance.* Honolulu, HI: Chiniago, Inc., 1986. [SHPD ID: 2019LI81288]

Community Planning Inc.

Community Planning, Inc. *Lahaina Historical Restoration and Preservation.* Community Planning Inc., 1961. [UH Call Number: DU629.L3 M3]

CRM Solutions Hawai'i, Inc.

Conte, Patty J. *Archaeological Assessment Report for TMK (2) 4-3-03:043 Mailepai Ahupua'a, Lahaina District, Island of Maui.* Makawao, HI: CRM Solutions Hawai'i, Inc., 2005. [SHPD ID: 2019LI81298]

Conte, Patty J. *Archaeological Inventory Survey of the Stoops Property TMK (2) 4-1-01:018, Honolua Ahupua'a, Kā'anapali District, Maui, Hawai'i.* Makawao, HI: CRM Solutions Hawai'i, Inc., 2006. [SHPD ID: 2019LI81424]

Conte, Patty J. *Archaeological Monitoring Plan for Construction Within TMK (2) 4-5-14:013 Por. 8A, Lahaina District, Wahikuli Ahupua'a, Island of Maui.* Makawao, HI: CRM Solutions Hawai'i, Inc., 2005. [SHPD ID: 2019LI81348]

Conte, Patty J. *Archaeological Monitoring Plan for On and Off-Site Construction Related to Pending and Future Improvements, Puunoa Ahupua'a, Lahaina District, Island of Maui.* Makawao, HI: CRM Solutions Hawai'i, Inc., 2008. [SHPD ID: 2019LI80599]

Conte, Patty J. *Archaeological Monitoring Plan for On and Off-Site Construction related to the Proposed Amano Demo/Reconstruction, TMK (2) 4-5-12:008 Wahikuli Ahupua'a, Lahaina District, Island of Maui.* Makawao, HI: CRM Solutions Hawai'i, Inc., 2005. [SHPD ID: 2019LI81347]

Conte, Patty J. *Archaeological Monitoring Plan for On and Off-Site Construction Related to the Proposed Kent Property Demo/Reconstruction, TMK (2) 4-5-12:010 Moali'i Ahupua'a, Lahaina District, Island of Maui.* Makawao, HI: CRM Solutions Hawai'i, Inc., 2007. [SHPD ID: 2019LI81346]

Conte, Patty J. *Archaeological Monitoring Plan for On and Off-Site Construction Within and Related to TMK (2) 4-1-01:018, Honolua Ahupua'a, Kā'anapali District, Maui, Hawai'i.* Makawao, HI: CRM Solutions Hawai'i, Inc., 2006. [SHPD ID: 2019LI81424]

Conte, Patty J. *Archaeological Monitoring Plan for On and Off-Site Construction Within and Related to TMK (2) 4-5-13:006 Lahaina District, Pana'ewa Ahupua'a,*

Island of Maui. Makawao, HI: CRM Solutions Hawai'i, Inc., 2006. [SHPD ID: 2019LI81349]

Conte, Patty J. *Archaeological Monitoring Plan for On and Off-Site Construction Within and Related to TMK (2) 4-5-14:073 Lahaina District, Wahikuli Ahupua'a, Island of Maui*. Makawao, HI: CRM Solutions Hawai'i, Inc., 2006. [SHPD ID: 2019LI81354]

Conte, Patty J. *Archaeological Monitoring Report for Construction, Lahaina District, Wahikuli Ahupua'a, Island of Maui*. Makawao, HI: CRM Solutions Hawai'i, Inc., 2005. [SHPD ID: 2019LI81345]

Conte, Patty J. *Archaeological Monitoring Report for Off-Site Construction (Mailepai Hui Land Lots 51-C-4-A, B & C) Lahaina District, Mailepai Ahupua'a, Island of Maui*. Makawao, HI: CRM Solutions Hawai'i, Inc., 2007. [SHPD ID: 2019LI81324]

Conte, Patty J. *Archaeological Monitoring Report for On and Off-Site Construction Within and Related to TMK (2) 4-5-14:073 Lahaina District, Wahikuli Ahupua'a, Island of Maui*. Makawao, HI: CRM Solutions Hawai'i, Inc., 2007. [SHPD ID: 2019LI81356]

Conte, Patty J. *Archaeological Monitoring Report Within and Related to a Parcel on Front Street, Pana'ewa Ahupua'a, Lahaina District, Maui Island, TMK (2) 4-5-13:006*. Makawao, HI: CRM Solutions Hawai'i, Inc., 2007. [No location available]

Conte, Patty J. *Archaeological Preservation Plan for the Portion of Site #50-50-01-1756 Within TMK (2) 4-1-01:018 Honolua Ahupua'a, Kā'anapali District, Maui, Hawai'i*. Makawao, HI: CRM Solutions Hawai'i, Inc., 2007. [SHPD ID: 2019LI81428]

Conte, Patty J. *Assessment of a Lot for Proposed Residential Construction, Kahana Ahupua'a, Lahaina District, Maui, Hawai'i*. Makawao, HI: CRM Solutions Hawai'i, Inc., 2004. [SHPD ID: 2019LI81300]

CULTURAL SURVEYS HAWAI'I, INC.

Dagan, Colleen P. M. and Hallett H. Hammatt. *Archaeological Preservation Plan for SIHP 50-50-01-5672C and 50-50-01-5673H*. Wailuku, HI: Cultural Surveys Hawai'i, Inc., 2008. [SHPD ID: 2019LI81026]

Devereux, Thomas K., Ian A. Masterson, Melody Heidel, Victoria Creed, Leilani Pyle, and Hallett H. Hammatt. *Archaeological Inventory Survey and Subsurface Testing of a 440 Acre Parcel, Ahupua'a of Ukumehame, Lahaina Dis-*

trict, Island of Maui. Wailuku, HI: Cultural Surveys Hawai'i, Inc., 1999. [SHPD ID: 2019LI81639]

Devereux, Thomas K., William H. Folk, and Hallett H. Hammatt. *Archaeological Survey of the Lands Comprising Project District 2 at Kapalua, Honokahua, and Nāpili 2 & 3 Ahupua'a Lahaina District of Maui.* Wailuku, HI: Cultural Surveys Hawai'i, Inc., 2001. [SHPD ID: 2019LI81007]

Dockall, John E. and Hallett H. Hammatt. *An Archaeological Inventory Survey for a Proposed Town Center and Residential Village, Nāpili Ahupua'a, Lahaina District.* Wailuku, HI: Cultural Surveys Hawai'i, Inc., 2005. [SHPD ID: 2019LI81011]

Dockall, John E., Tanya L. Lee-Greig, and Hallett H. Hammatt. *An Archaeological Assessment of a Proposed Road Corridor for Maui Preparatory Academy, Alaeloa Ahupua'a, Lahaina District, Maui Island.* Wailuku, HI: Cultural Surveys Hawai'i, Inc., 2005. [SHPD ID: 2019LI81052]

Folio, Katie M. and Hallett H. Hammatt. *An Archaeological Monitoring Plan for Proposed Improvements at the Feast of Lele, Waiokama Ahupua'a, Lahaina District, Island of Maui TMK: (2) 4-6-002:007 (por.).* Wailuku, HI: Cultural Surveys Hawai'i, Inc., 2014. [SHPD ID: 2019LI81372]

Folio, Katie M. and Hallett H. Hammatt. *Archaeological Monitoring Plan for the Special Use Permit Application for the Napili Point 1 AOAO (SMX 2015/0465) and Napili Point II (SMX 2015/0472) Project, Honokeana Ahupua'a, Lahaina District, Island of Maui, Napili Point I.* Wailuku, HI: Cultural Surveys Hawai'i, Inc., 2016. [SHPD ID: 2019LI81068]

Folio, Katie M. and Hallett H. Hammatt. *Archaeological Monitoring Report for the Special Use Permit Application for the Napili Point I (SMX 2015/0465) and Napili Point II (SMX 2015/0472) Project, Honokeana Ahupua'a, Lahaina District, Island of Maui, Napili Point I TMK: (2) 4-3-002:021 (por.), Napili Point II.* Wailuku, HI: Cultural Surveys Hawai'i, Inc., 2016. [SHPD ID: 2019LI81068]

Folk, William. *Letter to Noel Kennett Re: End of Fieldwork of Archaeological Monitoring at Mala Wharf for an Electrical Line.* Wailuku, HI: Cultural Surveys Hawai'i, Inc., 1993. [SHPD ID: 2019LI80619]

Frey, Jennifer J., Josephine M. Yucha, and Hallett H. Hammatt. *Archaeological Monitoring Report for the Valley Isle Resort Renovation Project, Kahana Ahupua'a, Lahaina District, Maui Island, TMK: (2) 4-3-10:004.* Wailuku, HI: Cultural Surveys Hawai'i, Inc., 2021. [SHPD ID: 2022LI00135]

Frey, Jennifer J., Josephine M. Yucha, and Hallett H. Hammatt. *Archaeological Monitoring Report for the Westin Maui Resort & Spa Master Plan Improvements Project, Parking Garage, Lobby, and Porte Cochere Driveway, Hanaka'ō'ō Ahupua'a, Lahaina District, Island of Maui, TMK (2) 4-4-008:019.* Wailuku, HI: Cultural Surveys Hawai'i, Inc., 2019. [SHPD ID: 2019LI80683]

Frey, Jennifer J., Ryan Luskin, Angela L. Yates, and Hallett H. Hammatt. *Archaeological Monitoring Report for the Hololani Resort Condominiums Shoreline Protection Project, Kahana Ahupua'a, Lahaina District, Maui Island.* Wailuku, HI: Cultural Surveys Hawai'i, Inc., 2019. [SHPD ID: 2019LI81312]

Hammatt, Hallett H. *An Archaeological Field Inspection of the Lahaina Bypass Highway, Phase 1A, Keawe Street Extension to Lahainaluna Road, and Current Condition of SIHP Number -2484.* Wailuku, HI: Cultural Surveys Hawai'i, Inc., 2007. [SHPD ID: 2019LI81366]

Hammatt, Hallett H. *Archaeological Preservation Plan for 10 Sites Within for 440 Acre Parcel, Ahupua'a of Ukumehame, Lahaina District, Island of Maui.* Wailuku, HI: Cultural Surveys Hawai'i, Inc., 2000. [SHPD ID: 2019LI81626]

Hammatt, Hallett H. *Lahaina (Front Street) Archaeological Test Excavations, TMK 4-5-3:012, Island of Maui.* Wailuku, HI: Cultural Surveys Hawai'i, Inc., 2003. [SHPD ID: 2019LI80649]

Hammatt, Hallett H. *Restoration Plan for Pole 69 (Original Location) at Ukumehame Gulch, Ma'alaea to Lahaina Third 69 KV Transmission Line.* Wailuku, HI: Cultural Surveys Hawai'i, Inc., 1996. [SHPD ID: 2019LI81632]

Hammatt, Hallett H. and David W. Shideler. *Draft Proposal for an Archaeological Mitigation Plan at the Lahaina Courthouse, Lahaina, Lahaina District, Maui Island, Hawai'i.* Wailuku, HI: Cultural Surveys Hawai'i, Inc., 1999. [SHPD ID: 2019LI81400]

Hammatt, Hallett H. and David W. Shideler. *Preservation Plan for Four Sites (50-50-01-5234, A Water Exploration Tunnel; -5235, A Petroglyph; -5425, A Historic Trail, and -5426, A Pre-Contact Habitation Site) Located Within a 400-Acre Parcel at Honolua Ahupua'a.* Wailuku, HI: Cultural Surveys Hawai'i, Inc., 2003. [SHPD ID: 2019LI81003]

Hammatt, Hallett H. and David W. Shideler. *Written Findings of Archaeological Monitoring at the Lahaina Courthouse, Lahaina, Lahaina District, Maui Island, Hawai'i.* Wailuku, HI: Cultural Surveys Hawai'i, Inc., 1998. [SHPD ID: 2019LI81401]

Hammatt, Hallett H. and Rodney Chiogioji. *Archaeological Monitoring Plan for a ½-Acre parcel in Napili 2-3 Ahupua'a, Lahaina District, Island of Maui.* Wailuku, HI: Cultural Surveys Hawai'i, Inc., 2002. [SHPD ID: 2019LI81063]

Hammatt, Hallett H., David W. Shideler, and Tony Bush. *Archaeological Inventory Survey of an Approximately 400-Acre Parcel at Honolua Ahupua'a Lahaina District of Maui.* Wailuku, HI: Cultural Surveys Hawai'i, Inc., 2003. [SHPD ID: 2019LI80993]

Heidel, Melody, William H. Folk, and Hallett H. Hammatt. *An Archaeological Inventory Survey for Waiola Church, Ahupua'a of Waine'e, Lahaina District, Island of Maui.* Wailuku, HI: Cultural Surveys Hawai'i, Inc., 1994. [SHPD ID: 2019LI81552]

Hill, Robert, Tanya Lee-Greig, and Hallett H. Hammatt. *An Archaeological Inventory Survey Report and Mitigation Plan for the Hawai'i State Department of Education Cesspool Conversion Project at the Lahainaluna High School, Pana'ewa Ahupua'a, Lahaina District, Maui Island, TMK (2) 4-6-18:005, 007, 012.* Wailuku, HI: Cultural Surveys Hawai'i, Inc., 2008. [No location available]

Hill, Robert R., Joseph Arnold, and Hallett H. Hammatt. *Archaeological Monitoring Report for a Dust Barrier Relocation at North Kā'anapali, Honokōwai Ahupua'a, Lahaina District, Island of Maui. TMK (2) 4-4-014:004 (por.)* Wailuku, HI: Cultural Surveys Hawai'i, Inc., 2006. [SHPD ID: 2019LI80658]

Hill, Robert R., Joseph Arnold, and Hallett H. Hammatt. *Archaeological Monitoring Report for Shoreline Improvements at Lot 3, North Kā'anapali, Honokōwai Ahupua'a, Lahaina District, Maui Island [TMK (2) 4-4-014:005 (por.)].* Wailuku, HI: Cultural Surveys Hawai'i, Inc., 2008. [SHPD ID: 2019LI80653]

Hill, Robert R., Tanya L. Lee-Greig, and Hallett H. Hammatt. *Preservation Plan for a Fishing Ko'a, SIHP 50-50-03-6275, North Kā'anapali, Lot 3, Honokōwai Ahupua'a, Maui Island [TMK (2) 4-4-014:005 por.].* Wailuku, HI: Cultural Surveys Hawai'i, Inc., 2008. [SHPD ID: 2019LI80654]

Hill, Robert R., Tanya L. Lee-Greig, and Hallett H. Hammatt. *Archaeological Monitoring Report for Dust Barrier Construction at Lot 3, North Kā'anapali, Honokōwai Ahupua'a, Lahaina District, Island of Maui [TMK (2) 4-4-014:005 (por.)].* Wailuku, HI: Cultural Surveys Hawai'i, Inc., 2008. [SHPD ID: 2019LI80655]

Hill, Robert R., Tanya Lee-Greig, and Hallett H. Hammatt. *Archaeological Monitoring Report for Shoreline Improvements at Lot 1, North Kā'anapali, Honokōwai Ahupua'a, Lahaina District, Maui Island TMK: (2) 4-4-014:003 (por.).* Wailuku, HI: Cultural Surveys Hawai'i, Inc., 2008. [SHPD ID: 2019LI80657]

Hill, Robert R., Thomas K. Devereux, and Hallett H. Hammatt. *An Archae-ological Assessment of a 9.650 Acre Parcel, ʻAlaeloa Ahupuaʻa, Lahaina District, Maui Island, for the West Maui Village Project.* Wailuku, HI: Cultural Surveys Hawaiʻi, Inc., 2006. [SHPD ID: 2019LI81037]

Lee-Greig, Tanya, Constance OʻHare, Hallett H. Hammatt, Robert R. Hill, and Colleen Dagan. *Archaeological Data Recovery and Additional Testing at Land Commission Award 310: Pikaneleʻs Kuleana at Pakala, Pakala Ahupuaʻa, Lahaina District, Maui Island.* Wailuku, HI: Cultural Surveys Hawaiʻi, Inc., 2010. [SHPD ID: 2019LI81573]

Lee-Greig, Tanya, Robert Hill, and Hallett H. Hammatt. *An Archaeological Inventory Survey Report for the Lahaina Bypass Modified Alignment from Kahoma Stream to the Keawe Street Extension, Kelawea, Paeohi, and Wahikuli Ahupuaʻa, Lahaina District, Maui Island TMK (2) 4-5-021, 010, 015, and 031: Multiple Parcels.* Wailuku, HI: Cultural Surveys Hawaiʻi, Inc., 2008. [SHPD ID: 2019LI81368]

Lee-Greig, Tanya L. and Hallett H. Hammatt. *Addendum to An Archaeological Treatment Plan for no Adverse Effect the Honoapiʻilani Highway Realignment—Lahaina Bypass Section, Phase 1A, Keawe Street Extension to Lahainaluna Road, Panaʻewa Ahupuaʻa, Lahaina District, Maui Island, TMK (2) 4-5-031: 999 por., (2) 4-5-015:010 por., and (2) 4-5-021:022 por.* Wailuku, HI: Cultural Surveys Hawaiʻi, Inc., 2007. [SHPD ID: 2019LI81365, 2019LI81340]

Lee-Greig, Tanya L. and Hallett H. Hammatt. *An Archaeological Inventory Level Documentation for an Inadvertent Historic Property Discovery Identified During Pre-Construction Walk Through for the Lahaina Bypass Phase IA, Project: State Inventory of Historic properties 50-50-03-6277 (Lee-Greig et al. 2008).* Wailuku, HI: Cultural Surveys Hawaiʻi, Inc., 2009. [No location available]

Lee-Greig, Tanya L. and Hallett H. Hammatt. *An Archaeological Monitoring Plan for Whalers Village Renovation and Expansion Project, Hanakaʻōʻō Ahupuaʻa, Lahaina District, Maui Island.* Wailuku, HI: Cultural Surveys Hawaiʻi, Inc., 2014. [SHPD ID: 2019LI80675]

Lee-Greig, Tanya L. and Hallett H. Hammatt. *Archaeological Assessment for the Proposed Westin Maui Resort & Spa Master Plan Improvements, Hanakaʻōʻō Ahupuaʻa, Lahaina District, Island of Maui, TMK (2) 4-4-008:019.* Wailuku, HI: Cultural Surveys Hawaiʻi, Inc., 2014. [SHPD ID: 2019LI80684]

Lee-Greig, Tanya L. and Hallett H. Hammatt. *Archaeological Inventory Survey Plan for Honoapiʻilani Highway Realignment Phase IA, Future Keawe Street Extension to Lahainaluna Road: Ikena Avenue Alignment with Modified Extension Kelawea, Paeohi, and Wahikuli Ahupuaʻa, Lahaina District, Maui Island TMK*

(2) 4-5-021, 010, 015, and 031: Multiple Parcels. Wailuku, HI: Cultural Surveys Hawai'i, Inc., 2008. [SHPD ID: 2019LI81341]

Lee-Greig, Tanya L. and Hallett H. Hammatt. *Archaeological Inventory Survey Plan for the Proposed Mokuhinia Ecosystem Restoration Project Waiokama and Lower Waine'e Ahupua'a, Lahaina District, Maui Island.* Wailuku, HI: Cultural Surveys Hawai'i, Inc., 2014. [SHPD ID: 2019LI81554]

Lee-Greig, Tanya L. and Hallett H. Hammatt. *Archaeological Monitoring Plan for the Honoapi'ilani Highway Safety Improvements at Kā'anapali Parkway and Halelo Street Hanaka'ō'ō Ahupua'a, Lahaina District, Maui Island [TMK (2) 4-4-006:999 por; 4-4-009:036 por.).* Wailuku, HI: Cultural Surveys Hawai'i, Inc., 2014. [SHPD ID: 2019LI81271]

Lee-Greig, Tanya L. and Hallett H. Hammatt. *Archaeological Monitoring Plan for the Lahaina Bypass Modified Alignment from Kahoma Stream to the Keawe Street Extension, Kelawea, Paeohi, and Wahikuli Ahupua'a, Lahaina District, Maui Island.* Wailuku, HI: Cultural Surveys Hawai'i, Inc., 2009. [SHPD ID: 2019LI81369]

Lee-Greig, Tanya L. and Hallett H. Hammatt. *Archaeological Monitoring Plan for the Pu'unēnē School and Lahainaluna High School Hawai'i Inter-Island DOE Cesspool Project, Island of Maui TMK (2) 4-6-018 and (2) 3-8-006.* Wailuku, HI: Cultural Surveys Hawai'i, Inc., 2007. [SHPD ID: 2019LI81526]

Lee-Greig, Tanya L. and Hallett H. Hammatt. *Preservation Plan for Thirty-Three Historic Properties Located in and Adjacent to the Kapalua Mauka Project Area, Honokahua, Nāpili 2 & 3, and Nāpili 4-5 Ahupua'a, Lahaina District, Maui Island.* Wailuku, HI: Cultural Surveys Hawai'i, Inc., 2005. [SHPD ID: 2019LI80997]

Lee-Greig, Tanya L., Robert Hill, and Hallett H. Hammatt. *An Archaeological Survey Report for the Realignment of a Section of the Honoapi'ilani Highway, Phase IA, Kelawea, Paeohi, and Wahikuli Ahupua'a, Lahaina District, Maui Island TMK (2) 4-5-021, 010, 015, and 031: Multiple Parcels.* Wailuku, HI: Cultural Surveys Hawai'i, Inc., 2008. [SHPD ID: 2019LI81361]

Madeus, Jonas K. and Hallett H. Hammatt. *An Archaeological Monitoring Plan for the Proposed Hololani Resort Condominiums Shoreline Protection Project in Kahananui Ahupua'a, Lahaina District, Maui Island TMK: (2) 4-3-010:009 por.* Wailuku, HI: Cultural Surveys Hawai'i, Inc., 2014. [SHPD ID: 2019LI81312]

Madeus, Jonas K. et al. *Archaeological Inventory Survey for the Villages of Leia-li'i, Phase 1-B Subdivision and Related Improvements Project, Wahikuli Ahupua'a, Lahaina District, Maui Island, TMKs: (2) 4-5-021:010 por., 014 por., 020, and*

021 por.; (2) 4-5-36:109, 110, and 112; and Honoapi'ilani Highway Right-of-Way. Wailuku, HI: Cultural Surveys Hawai'i, Inc., 2022. [SHPD ID: 2022LI00589]

Madeus, Jonas K., Josephine M. Yucha, and Hallett H. Hammatt. *Archaeological Monitoring Report for Improvements at Feast of Lele, Waiokama Ahupua'a, Lahaina District, Maui Island, TMK (2) 4-6-002:007 (por.).* Wailuku, HI: Cultural Surveys Hawai'i, Inc., 2018. [No location available]

Madeus, Jonas K., Tanya L. Lee-Greig, and Hallett H. Hammatt. *Archaeological Assessment of an 80-Acre Parcel in Kapalua, Honolua Ahupua'a, Lahaina District, Maui Island.* Wailuku, HI: Cultural Surveys Hawai'i, Inc., 2005. [SHPD ID: 2019LI80999]

Madeus, Jonas K., Tanya Lee-Greig, and Hallett H. Hammatt. *An Archaeological Monitoring Report for the Lahaina Bypass Modified Alignment from the Lahainaluna Road Intersection to the Keawe Street Extension Kelawea, Paeohi, and Wahikuli Ahupua'a, Lahaina District, Maui Island TMK (2) 4-5-021, 010, 015, and 031: Multiple Parcels.* Wailuku, HI: Cultural Surveys Hawai'i, Inc., 2010. [SHPD ID: 2019LI81338]

Masterson, Ian and Hallett H. Hammatt. *An Addendum Report for the New Alignment Section between Points 14D, 15, and 16 along the Proposed Ma'alaea-Lahaina Third 69 kV Transmission Line, Maui.* Wailuku, HI: Cultural Surveys Hawai'i, Inc., 1995. [SHPD ID: 2019LI81633]

Masterson, Ian and Hallett H. Hammatt. *Report on the Completed Reconstruction of Walls at Hiki'i Heiau Ukumehame Ahupua'a, Island of Maui.* Wailuku, HI: Cultural Surveys Hawai'i, Inc., 1999. [SHPD ID: 2019LI81631]

McCurdy, Todd D. and Hallett H. Hammatt. *Addendum Report for Archaeological Inventory Survey Documentation of Inadvertent Finds Identified during the Honoapi'ilani Highway Realignment (Lahaina Bypass) Phase 1B-1, Paunau Ahupua'a to Polanui Ahupua'a, Lahaina District, Maui Island TMK (2) 4-6-014:001, 002: (2) 4-6-018:002, 003; (2) 4-8-001:002 and (2) 4-8-003:001.* Wailuku, HI: Cultural Surveys Hawai'i, Inc., 2010. [SHPD ID: 2019LI81537]

McCurdy, Todd D. and Hallett H. Hammatt. *An Archaeological Monitoring Plan for the Honoapi'ilani Highway Realignment (Lahaina Bypass), Phase 1B-1, Paunau Ahupua'a to Polanui Ahupua'a, Lahaina District, Maui Island TMK: (2) 4-6-014:001-002, 4-6-018:002-003, 4-7-001:002 and 4-7-003:001.* Wailuku, HI: Cultural Surveys Hawai'i, Inc., 2010. [SHPD ID: 2019LI81539]

McCurdy, Todd D. and Hallett H. Hammatt. *Archaeological Inventory Survey Documentation of Inadvertent Finds Identified during the Honoapi'ilani Highway Realignment (Lahaina Bypass) Phase 1B-1, Paunau Ahupua'a to Polanui Ahupua'a,*

Lahaina District, Maui Island TMK: (2) 4-6-014:001, 002; (2) 4-6-018:002, 003; (2) 4-8-001:002 and (2) 4-7-003:001. Wailuku, HI: Cultural Surveys Hawai'i, Inc., 2009. [SHPD ID: 2019LI81536]

McCurdy, Todd D. and Hallett H. Hammatt. *Archaeological Literature Review and Field Inspection for Honoapi'ilani Highway Realignment (Lahaina Bypass), Phase 1B-1, Paunau Ahupua'a to Polanui Ahupua'a, Lahaina District, Maui Island TMK (2) 4-6-014:001-002, 4-6-018:002-003, 4-8-001:002 and 4-7-003:001.* Wailuku, HI: Cultural Surveys Hawai'i, Inc., 2008. [SHPD ID: 2019LI81538]

Medeiros, Colleen and Hallett H. Hammatt. *Archaeological Monitoring Report for the Kā'anapali North Beach Development Area, Lot 3, Site Excavation, Honokōwai Ahupua'a, Lahaina District, Maui Island.* Wailuku, HI: Cultural Surveys Hawai'i, Inc., 2017. [SHPD ID: 2019LI80652]

O'Hare, Constance, Thomas K. Devereux, William H. Folk, and Hallett H. Hammatt. *Preservation Plan for Specific Sites in the Land Comprising Project District 2 at Kapalua, Honokahua and Nāpili 2 & 3 Ahupua'a Lahaina District of Maui.* Wailuku, HI: Cultural Surveys Hawai'i, Inc., 2003. [SHPD ID: 2019LI81002]

Tulchin, Jon and Hallett H. Hammatt. *Archaeological Assessment of a 0.2-Acre Parcel and Waterline, Māhinahina 4 Ahupua'a, Lahaina District, Island of Maui.* Wailuku, HI: Cultural Surveys Hawai'i, Inc., 2003. [SHPD ID: 2019LI81315]

Willman, Michael R., Robert R. Hill, Tanya L. Lee-Greig, and Hallett H. Hammatt. *Archaeological Monitoring Report for Sand Replenishment at Lots 1, 2, and 3, North Kā'anapali, Honokōwai Ahupua'a, Lahaina District, Island of Maui [TMK (2) 4-4-014: 03, 04, 05 (por.)].* Wailuku, HI: Cultural Surveys Hawai'i, Inc., 2009. [SHPD ID: 2019LI80656]

Willman, Michael R., Tanya Lee-Greig, and Hallett H. Hammatt. *Addendum to Archaeological Monitoring Plan for the Pu'unēnē School and Lahainaluna High School Hawai'i Inter-Island DOE Cesspool Project, Island of Maui TMK (2) 4-6-18 and (2) 3-8-06.* Wailuku, HI: Cultural Surveys Hawai'i, Inc., 2008. [SHPD ID: 2019LI81524]

Yates and Hallett H. Hammatt. *Archaeological Monitoring Plan for the Kā'anapali 2020 Master Plan, Kā'anapali Coffee Farms Subdivision Phase II Project, Hanaka'ō'ō and Honokōwai Ahupua'a, Lahaina District, Maui Island, TMK (2) 4-4-02:002.* Wailuku, HI: Cultural Surveys Hawai'i, Inc., 2020. [SHPD ID: 2021LI00326, 2022LI00365]

Yucha, Josephine M. and Hallett H. Hammatt. *Archaeological Monitoring Plan for the Lahaina Intermediate School Campus Fire Alarm Replacement Project,*

Panaʻewa and Kuʻia Ahupuaʻa, Lahaina District, Maui Island TMK (2) 4-6-18:013 por. Wailuku, HI: Cultural Surveys Hawaiʻi, Inc., 2019. [No location available]

Yucha, Josephine M. and Hallett H. Hammatt. *Archaeological Monitoring Plan for the Puʻukoliʻi Village Mauka Project, Hanakaʻōʻō Ahupuaʻa, Lahaina District, Maui Island, TMKs: (2) 4-4-02:002, 048, and 053 por., (2) 4-4-06:070, 086 and 087 por., and (2) 4-4-15:034 through 072. 24:026 (por.).* Wailuku, HI: Cultural Surveys Hawaiʻi, Inc., 2023. [SHPD ID: 2023LI00111]

Yucha, Josephine M. and Hallett H. Hammatt. *Archaeological Monitoring Plan for the Sheraton Maui Resort & Spa Sewer Improvements Project, Hanakaʻōʻō Ahupuaʻa, Lahaina District, Maui Island, TMKs: (2) 4-4-08:005 and 011 (pors).* Wailuku, HI: Cultural Surveys Hawaiʻi, Inc., 2018. [SHPD ID: 2019LI80670]

Yucha, Josephine M. and Hallett H. Hammatt. *Archaeological Monitoring Plan for the Valley Isle Resort Renovation Project, Kahana Ahupuaʻa, Lahaina District, Maui Island, TMK: (2) 4-3-10:004.* Wailuku, HI: Cultural Surveys Hawaiʻi, Inc., 2020. [SHPD ID: 2021LI00211]

Yucha, Josephine M. and Hallett H. Hammatt. *Archaeological Monitoring Plan for the Villages of Leialiʻi, Village 1-B Subdivision and Related Improvements Project, Wahikuli Ahupuaʻa, Lahaina District, Maui Island, TMKs: (2) 4-5-021:010 por., 014 por., 015 por., 020, and 021 por.; (2) 4-5-36:109, 110, and 112; and Honoapiʻilani Highway Right-of-Way.* Wailuku, HI: Cultural Surveys Hawaiʻi, Inc., 2022. [SHPD ID: 2023LI00106]

Yucha, Josephine M. and Hallett H. Hammatt. *Archaeological Monitoring Report for the Sheraton Maui Sewer Improvements Project, Hanakaʻōʻō Ahupuaʻa, Lahaina District, Maui Island, TMKs: (2) 4-4-008:005 and 011 (pors.).* Wailuku, HI: Cultural Surveys Hawaiʻi, Inc., 2018. [SHPD ID: 2019LI81258]

Yucha, Josephine M. et al. *Archaeological Inventory Survey for the Puʻukoliʻi Village Mauka Project, Hanakaʻōʻō Ahupuaʻa, Lahaina District, Maui Island, TMKs: (2) 4-4-02:002, 048, and 053 por., (2) 4-4-06:070, 086 and 087 por., and (2) 4-4-15:034 through 072.* Wailuku, HI: Cultural Surveys Hawaiʻi, Inc., 2022. [SHPD ID: 2023LI00110]

Yucha, Josephine M., Jennifer Frey, and Hallett H. Hammatt. *Burial Site Component of an Archaeological Data Recovery Plan for SIHP # 50-50-03-8842 at the Westin Maui Resort & Spa Improvements Project, Phase III, Hanakaʻōʻō Ahupuaʻa, Lahaina District, Maui, TMK: (2) 4-4-08:019.* Wailuku, HI: Cultural Surveys Hawaiʻi, Inc., 2021. [SHPD ID: 2021LI00104]

Yucha, Trevor M. and Hallett H. Hammatt. *Archaeological Monitoring Plan for the Westin Maui Resort & Spa Master Plan Improvements, Hanakaʻōʻō Ahupuaʻa,*

Lahaina District, Island of Maui, TMK (2) 4-4-08:019. Wailuku, HI: Cultural Surveys Hawai'i, Inc., 2018. [SHPD ID: 2019LI80683]

GARCIA & ASSOCIATES

Desilets, Michael and Patrick O'Day. *Preservation Plan for Proposed Fenceline Corridor for the West Maui Forest Reserve, Ku'ia, Mākila, Pāhoa, Halaka'a, Polaiki, Launiupoko, and Olowalu Ahupua'a, Lahaina District, Maui Island, Hawai'i.* Kailua, HI: Garcia & Associates, 2016. [SHPD ID: 2019LI81528]

O'Day, Patrick and David Byerly. *Archaeological Inventory Survey of Proposed Fenceline Corridor for the West Maui Forest Reserve, Ku'ia, Mākila, Pāhoa, Halaka'a, Polaiki, Launiupoko, and Olowalu Ahupua'a, Lahaina District, Maui Island, Hawai'i.* Kailua, HI: Garcia & Associates, 2015. [SHPD ID: 2019LI81533]

HAUN AND ASSOCIATES

Haun, Alan E. *Archaeological Assessment TMK (2) 4-7-02:005 Land of Pāhoa, Lahaina District, Island of Maui.* Kailua-Kona, HI: Haun and Associates, 2001. [SHPD ID: 2019LI81616]

Haun, Alan E. *Archaeological Assessment, Lands of Polanui, Polaiki, and Launiupoko, Lahaina District, Island of Maui.* Kailua-Kona, HI: Haun and Associates, 2002. [SHPD ID: 2019LI81608]

Haun, Alan E. *Archaeological Inventory Survey Kaua'ula Development Parcel, Lands of Pūehuehu Iki, Pāhoa, and Pola Nui, Lahaina District, Island of Maui.* Kailua-Kona, HI: Haun and Associates, 1999. [No location available]

Haun, Alan E. *Archaeological Site Documentation, Site 5401, Lands of Polanui and Pāhoa, Lahaina District, Island of Maui (TMK: 4-8-01:002, 4-7-01:001).* Kailua-Kona, HI: Haun and Associates, 2004. [SHPD ID: 2019LI81622]

Haun, Alan E. and Dave Henry. *Archaeological Inventory Survey, Proposed 124-Acre Mākila Subdivision, Lands of Launiupoko, Polanui and Pūehuehu Nui, Lahaina District, Island of Maui (TMK: 4-7-01: por. 1 and TMK 4-7-04: Por. 4).* Kailua-Kona, HI: Haun and Associates, 2001. [SHPD ID: 2019LI81623]

Haun, Alan E. and Dave Henry. *Archaeological Inventory Survey, TMK 4-6-7:010 'Ili of Pakala, Land of Puako District, Island of Maui.* Kailua-Kona, HI: Haun and Associates, 2001. [SHPD ID: 2019LI81555]

Haun, Alan E. and Dave Henry. *Final Archaeological Monitoring Plan, TMK (2) 4-5-13:016, Wahikuli Ahupua'a, Lahaina District, Island of Maui.* Kailua-Kona, HI: Haun and Associates, 2014. [SHPD ID: 2019LI81350]

Haun, Alan E. and Dave Henry with Maria E. K. Orr. *Archaeological Inventory Survey Portion of TMK 4-7-01:002, Land of Launiupoko, Lahaina District, Island of Maui.* Kailua-Kona, HI: Haun and Associates, 2001. [SHPD ID: 2019LI81599]

Haun, Alan E. and Jack D. Henry. *Archaeological Site Preservation Plan Kau'aula Development Parcel, Lands of Pūehuehu Iki, Pāhoa, and Polanui Ahupua'a, Lahaina District, Island of Maui [TMK (2) 4-7-02:04, 05, & 07, (2) 4-7-03:por. 01].* Kailua-Kona, HI: Haun and Associates, 2003. [SHPD ID: 2019LI81618]

Haun, Alan E. and Jack D. Henry. *Archaeological Site Preservation Plan, Kaua'ula Development Parcel, Lands of Pūehuehu Iki, Pāhoa, and Polo Nui, Lahaina District, Island of Maui [TMK: (2) 4-7-03:001].* Kailua-Kona, HI: Haun and Associates, 2000. [SHPD ID: 2019LI81613]

HAWAI'I MARINE RESEARCH, INC.

Ahlo, Hamilton M. and Maurice E. Morgenstein. *Archaeological Test Excavations Near the Mouth of Kahoma Stream, Lahaina, Maui.* Honolulu, HI: Hawai'i Marine Research, 1979.

Joerger, Pauline King and Michael W. Kaschko. *A Cultural Historical Overview of the Kahoma Stream Flood Control Project, Lahaina, Maui and Ma'alaea Small Boat Harbor Project, Ma'alaea, Maui.* Honolulu, HI: Hawai'i Marine Research, Inc., 1979. [SHPD ID: 2019LI80298; UH Call Number: DU629.L3 J63]

HAWAI'I STATE GOVERNMENT

Donham, Theresa K. *Field Inspection of a Proposed Culvert Location, USDA-SCS Lahaina Watershed Project, Pola Nui, Lahaina District, Maui [TMK (2) 4-7-01:018].* Wailuku, HI: State Historic Preservation Division, Maui Section, 1991. [SHPD ID: 2019LI81607]

Hart, Christopher. *Final Report of the Preparation for Exhibit of King Kamehameha I's "Brick Palace" at Lahaina, Maui, Hawai'i.* Maui Historic Commission, 1970.

Keau, Charles. *Archaeological Reconnaissance (Surface Survey) for Hanaka'ō'ō (Hahakea) Beach Park. Includes cover letter: An Archaeological Reconnaissance of*

Hahakea Beach Park, Hanaka'ō'ō, Maui. TMK: 4-4-06:33 by Earl Neller. State Historic Preservation Office, March 1982. [SHPD ID: 2019LI81272; UH Call Number: DU629.H364 K43 1981]

Lum, Francis. *Amendment to Testing at Kahana Desilting Basin, Holoua [Honolua?] Watershed, Lahaina District, Maui, Hawai'i, Francis Lum, Soil Conservation Service.* Soil Conservation Service, 1983. [SHPD ID: 2019LI81058]

Neller, Earl. *An Archaeological Reconnaissance of Hahakea Beach Park, Hanaka'ō'ō, Maui.* Honolulu, HI: State of Hawai'i Preservation Office, 1982. [SHPD ID: 2019LI81272; UH Call Number: DU629.H364 N45 1982]

International Archaeological Research Institute, Inc.

Athens, J. Stephen. *Archaeological Monitoring Plan, Trenching at Taco Bell, Lahaina, Kā'anapali Ahupua'a, Lahaina District, Maui [TMK (2) 4-5-07:034].* Honolulu, HI: International Archaeological Research Institute, Inc., 1999.

Goodwin, Conrad and Spencer Leinewebber. *Archaeological Inventory Survey Report, Pioneer Mil Company, Ltd. Sugar Enterprise Lands, Site No. 50-50-03-4420, Villages of Leiali'i Project, Lahaina, Maui Hawai'i.* Honolulu, HI: International Archaeological Research Institute, Inc., 1997. [SHPD ID: 2019LI81363]

Liston, Jolie. *Archaeological Monitoring of Trenching Activities at Taco Bell, Lahaina, Maui.* Honolulu, HI: International Archaeological Research Institute, Inc., 1999. [SHPD ID: 2019LI80605]

Magnuson, Carol M. *Supplemental Archaeological Survey of Turbine Pad Alignments, Kaheawa Pastures, Upland Ukumehame Ahupua'a, Maui.* Honolulu, HI: International Archaeological Research Institute, Inc., 2003. [SHPD ID: 2019LI81630]

Tomonari-Tuggle, M. J. *An Archaeological Reconnaissance Survey for 27 Wind Turbines in the Ukumehame Uplands, Island of Maui.* Honolulu, HI: International Archaeological Research Institute, Inc., 2003. [SHPD ID: 2019LI81627]

Tomonari-Tuggle, M. J. and Coral Rasmussen. *Preservation Plan for Site 50-50-09-5232, An Upland Heiau in Ukumehame Ahupua'a, Island of Maui TMK 4-8-01:1.* Honolulu, HI: International Archaeological Research Institute, Inc., 2005. [SHPD ID: 2019LI81629]

Tomonari-Tuggle, M. J. and H. D. Tuggle. *Archaeological Survey of Two Demonstration Trails of the Hawai'i Statewide Trail and Access System.* Honolulu, HI: International Archaeological Research Institute, Inc., 1991. [SHPD ID: 2019LI79001; UH Call Number: DU628.M3 T66 1991]

International Archaeology, LLC

Knecht, Daniel P. and Timothy M. Rieth. *Archaeological Monitoring Plan for the Lahainaluna High School New Classroom Building Project, Pana'ewa Ahupua'a, Lahaina District, Maui.* Honolulu, HI: International Archaeology, LLC. [No location available]

Pacheco, Robert. *A Cultural Impact Assessment for the Proposed Kā'anapali Beach Restoration Project, Hanaka'ō'ō Ahupua'a, Lahaina District, Island of Maui, Hawai'i TMK (2) 4-4-008:001, 002, 003, 004, 005, 019, 022; 4-4-013:001, 002, 006, 007, 008.* Honolulu, HI: International Archaeology, LLC, 2006. [SHPD ID: 2019LI80681]

Pacheco, Robert. *An Archaeological Literature Review for the Proposed Kā'anapali Beach Restoration Project, Hanaka'ō'ō Ahupua'a, Lahaina District, Island of Maui, Hawai'i TMK (2) 4-4-008:001, 002, 003, 004, 005, 019, 022; 4-4-013:001, 002, 006, 007, 008.* Honolulu, HI: International Archaeology, LLC, 2015. [SHPD ID: 2019LI81260]

John Carl Warnecke and Associates

John Carl Warnecke and Associates. *Lahaina Small Boat Harbor Study.* San Francisco, CA: John Carl Warnecke and Associates, Architects and Planning Consultants, 1965. [SHPD ID: 2019LI81397]

Lahaina Restoration Foundation

Windley, Larry. *Recommended Action Plan for the Preservation/Restoration of the Hale Pa'ahao Prison Site, Lahaina.* Lahaina, HI: Lahaina Restoration Foundation, 1967. [SHPD ID: 2019LI81257]

Launiupoko Associates

Launiupoko Associates, LLC. *Archaeological Preservation Plan, Mahanalua Nui Subdivision.* Launiupoko Associates, 1998. [SHPD ID: 2019LI81602]

Mason Architects [formerly Spencer Mason Architects]

Mason Architects, Inc. *Reconnaissance Level Survey, Honokōwai Reservoir for the West Maui Recycled Water and Kā'anapali Resort R-1 Water Distribution Expansion Project. TMK (2) 4-4-02:019.* Honolulu, HI: Mason Architects, Inc., 2022. [SHPD ID: 2023LI00017]

Michael T. Munekiyo Consulting, Inc.

Munekiyo, Michael T. *Redevelopment of ABC Store at 726 Front Street, Application for Historic District Approval.* Wailuku, HI: Michael T. Munekiyo Consulting, Inc., 1993. [SHPD ID: 2019LI81540]

Munekiyo & Hiraga, Inc.

Munekiyo & Hiraga, Inc. *Historic Resources Inventory Submittal, Maka'oi'oi Demolition.* Wailuku, HI: Munekiyo & Hiraga, Inc., 2003. [SHPD ID: 2019LI81049]

Munekiyo & Hiraga, Inc. *Maka'oi'oi (Honolua Plantation Managers Residence, Pineapple Hill Restaurant), Historical Report.* Wailuku, HI: Munekiyo & Hiraga, Inc., 2003. [SHPD ID: 2019LI81022]

Oceanit

Oceanit. *Final Sampling Analysis Plan: Field Sampling and Quality Assurance Plans for the Mokuhinia Pond Site Investigation, Lahaina, Maui, Hawai'i.* Honolulu, HI: Oceanit, 2009. [SHPD ID: 2019LI81553]

Olowalu Elua Associates, LLC

Olowalu Elua Associates, LLC. *Archaeological Mitigation and Preservation Plan, Makai Portion (Phase 1), Olowalu Ahupua'a, Lahaina District, Maui Island.* Olowalu, HI: Olowalu Elua Associates, LLC, 2001.

Olowalu Elua Associates, LLC. *Archaeological Preservation Plan, Mauka Portion (Phase 2), Olowalu Ahupua'a, Lahaina District, Maui Island.* Olowalu, HI: Olowalu Elua Associates, LLC, 2002. [SHPD ID: 2019LI00099]

Olowalu Elua Associates, LLC. *Monitoring Plan for Sites 50-50-08-4820 and 50-50-08-4821; Olowalu Ahupua'a, Lahaina District; Island of Maui [TMK (2) 4-8-003: portion of 10].* Olowalu, HI: Olowalu Elua Associates, LLC, 2002. [No location available]

Pacific Consulting Services, Inc.

Collins, Sara L. *Archaeological Monitoring Plan for Ground-Altering Activities During the Grading and Excavations for Construction Associated with the Moku'ula/*

Mokuhinia Ecosystem Restoration Project, Phase I, Lahaina, Island of Maui. Honolulu, HI: Pacific Consulting Services, Inc., 2007. [SHPD ID: 2019LI01493]

Collins, Sara L., Dennis Gosser, and Stephan D. Clark. *Archaeological Assessment of a Single Developed Parcel [TMK (2) 4-6-10:006] Lahaina, Island of Maui.* Honolulu, HI: Pacific Consulting Services, Inc., 2006. [No location available]

PACIFIC LEGACY, INC.

Ah Sam, Jessica A., Solomon H. Kailihiwa III, and Paul L. Cleghorn. *Archaeological Inventory Study and Cultural Impact Assessment for the Comfort Station Replacement During the Lahaina Pier Improvement Project, Lahaina, Maui [TMK (2) 4-6-01:001].* Kailua, HI: Pacific Legacy, Inc., 2004.

Kirkendall, Melissa, Kimberly M. Mooney, Elizabeth L. Kahahane, and Paul L. Cleghorn. *Archaeological Monitoring Plan for the Lahaina Pier Improvement Project, Waineʻe Ahupuaʻa, Lahaina District, Island of Maui [TMK: (2) 4-6-01:001].* Kailua, HI: Pacific Legacy, Inc., 2010. [No location available]

Mooney, Kimberly M. and Paul L. Cleghorn. *Archaeological Monitoring Report for the Lahaina Small Boat Harbor Comfort Station Improvements, Lahaina, Maui.* Kailua, HI: Pacific Legacy, Inc., 2007. [SHPD ID: 2019LI81379]

Mooney, Kimberly M., Paul L. Cleghorn, and Elizabeth L. Kahahane. *Archaeological Inventory Survey for the Lahaina Pier Improvement Project Waineʻe Ahupuaʻa, Lahaina District, Island of Maui.* Kailua, HI: Pacific Legacy, Inc., 2008. [SHPD ID: 2019LI81382]

Mulrooney et al. *Archaeological Inventory Survey Report for the Kahana Solar Project in Ahupuaʻa of Kahana and Māhinahina 1-3, Moku of Kāʻanapali (Lahaina Modern Tax District), Island of Maui [TMK: (2) 4-3-01:017 por.; (2) 4-3-01:082 por.; (2) 4-3-01:084 por.].* Kailua, HI: Pacific Legacy, Inc., 2022

PAUL H. ROSENDAHL, PH.D., INC.

Donham, Theresa K. *Addendum Report: Additional Subsurface Testing of Area III, Subsurface Archaeological Testing, Revised Ritz-Carlton Kapalua Hotel Project Site, Areas I, II, and III, Land of Honokahua, Lahaina District, Island of Maui.* Hilo, HI: Paul H. Rosendahl, Ph.D., Inc., 1989. [SHPD ID: 2019LI81414]

Donham, Theresa K. *Archaeological Survey Test Excavations Kapalua Hotel Development Site 2-H, Kapalua Bay Resort, Land of Honokahua, Lahaina, Island of Maui.* Hilo, HI: Paul H. Rosendahl, Ph.D., Inc., 1986. [2019LI80998]

Donham, Theresa K. *Interim Report: Kapalua Mitigation Program Data Recovery Excavations at the Honokahua Burial Site, Land of Honokahua, Lahaina District, Island of Maui.* Hilo, HI: Paul H. Rosendahl, Ph.D., Inc., 1989. [SHPD ID: 2019LI81417]

Ferguson, Lee, Arne Carlson, and Berdena Burgett. *Subsurface Archaeological Testing, Revised Ritz-Carlton Kapalua Hotel Project Site, Areas I, II and III.* Hilo, HI: Paul H. Rosendahl, Ph.D., Inc., 1989. [SHPD ID: 2019LI81006]

Graves, Donna and Susan Goodfellow. *Archaeological Inventory Survey, Launiupoko Golf Course, Land of Launiupoko, Lahaina District, Island of Maui.* Hilo, HI: Paul H. Rosendahl, Ph.D., Inc., 1991. [SHPD ID: 2019LI81595, 2019LI81610]

Guerriero, Diane A., Charvet-Pond, and S. Goodfellow. *Archaeological Monitoring and Data Recovery, Kapalua Ritz-Carlton Hotel Site, Land of Honokahua, Lahaina District, Island of Maui [TMK: (2) 4-2-01:004, 005, por. 012, 013, por. 018, 034].* Hilo, HI: Paul H. Rosendahl, Ph.D., Inc., 1993. [No location available]

Jensen, Peter A. and Jenny O'Claray. *Supplemental Archaeological Survey, Lahaina Master Planned Project Offsite Sewer, Water Improvements, and Cane Haul Road.* Hilo, HI: Paul H. Rosendahl, Ph.D., Inc., 1991. [SHPD ID: 2019LI81419]

Jensen, Peter M. *Archaeological Inventory Survey Honoapi'ilani Highway Realignment Project Lahaina Bypass Section—Modified Corridor Alignment, Lands of Honokōwai, Hanaka'ō'ō, Wahikuli, Pana'ewa, Ku'ia, Halaka'a, Pūehuehu Nui, Pāhoa, Polanui, and Launiupoko, Lahaina District, Island of Maui.* Hilo, HI: Paul H. Rosendahl, Ph.D., Inc., 1991. [SHPD ID: 2019LI81242]

Jensen, Peter M. *Archaeological Inventory Survey Lahaina Bypass Highway New Connector Roads Project Area, Ahupua'a of Hanaka'ō'ō and Paunau, Lahaina District, Island of Maui.* Hilo, HI: Paul H. Rosendahl, Ph.D., Inc., 1994. [SHPD ID: 2019LI81611]

Jensen, Peter M. *Archaeological Inventory Survey Lahaina Master Planned Project Site: Land of Wahikuli, Lahaina District, Island of Maui.* Hilo, HI: Paul H. Rosendahl, Ph.D., Inc., 1989. [SHPD ID: 2019LI80636]

Jensen, Peter M. *Archaeological Inventory Survey South Beach Mauka Development Site, Ahupua'a of Hanaka'ō'ō, Lahaina District, Island of Maui.* Hilo, HI: Paul H. Rosendahl, Ph.D., Inc., 1990. [SHPD ID: 2019LI81262; UH Call Number: DU628.M3 J46 1990]

Jensen, Peter M. *Letter Report: Additional Field Survey Lahaina Bypass Section, Modified Corridor Alignment, Honoapi'ilani Highway Realignment Project, Lands of Pāhoa and Polanui, Lahaina District, Island of Maui [TMK: (2) 4-7-01, 02].* Hilo, HI: Paul H. Rosendahl, Ph.D., Inc., 1992. [SHPD ID: 2019LI81609]

Jensen, Peter M. and G. Mehalchick. *Archaeological Inventory Survey North Beach Mauka (Kāʻanapali) Site, Ahupuaʻa of Hanakaʻōʻō, Lahaina District, Island of Maui.* Hilo, HI: Paul H. Rosendahl, Ph.D., Inc., 1993. [UH Call Number: DU628.M3 J46 1989]

Jensen, Peter M. and Gemma Mahalchick. *Archaeological Inventory Survey, The Puʻukoliʻi Village Project Area, Ahupuaʻa of Hanakaʻōʻō, Lahaina District, Island of Maui.* Hilo, HI: Paul H. Rosendahl, Ph.D., Inc., 1992. [SHPD ID: 2019LI81252]

OʻClaray, Jenny. *Additional Field Work for Drainage 11 Kapalua Plantation Estates Project Area, Lands of Honokahua, Honolua, Napili 2-2 Lahaina District, Island of Maui.* Hilo, HI: Paul H. Rosendahl, Ph.D., Inc., 1991. [SHPD ID: 2019LI81415]

Pietrusewsky, Michael, Michele T. Douglas, Patricia A. Kalima, and Rona M. Ikehara. *Human Skeletal and Dental Remains from the Honokahua Burial Site, Land of Honokahua, Lahaina District, Island of Maui, Hawaiʻi.* Hilo, HI: Paul H. Rosendahl, Ph.D., Inc., 1991. [Call Number, DU629.H67 H86 1991a]

Rogers, Donnell J. and Paul H. Rosendahl. *Archaeological Survey and Recording Iliilikea and Maiu Heiau on the North Coast of Maui, Land of Honokōhau, Lahaina District, Island of Maui.* Hilo, HI: Paul H. Rosendahl, Ph.D., Inc., 1992. [SHPD ID: 2019LI81440]

Rosendahl, Margaret L. K. *Archaeological Field Inspection, Sheraton Maui Master Plan Project Area, Lands of Honokōwai and Hanakaʻōʻō, Lahaina District, Island of Maui.* Hilo, HI: Paul H. Rosendahl, Ph.D., Inc., 1986. [No location available]

Rosendahl, Margaret L. K. *Subsurface Archaeological Reconnaissance Survey, North Beach Development Site, Ahupuaʻa of Hanakaʻōʻō, Lahaina District, Island of Maui.* Hilo, HI: Paul H. Rosendahl, Ph.D., Inc., 1987. [SHPD ID: 2019LI81244]

Rosendahl, Paul H. *A Plan for Archaeological Monitoring of Shoreline Construction, Kāʻanapali North Beach Development Site, Ahupuaʻa of Hanakaʻōʻō, Lahaina District, Island of Maui.* Hilo, HI: Paul H. Rosendahl, Ph.D., Inc., 1987. [SHPD ID: 2019LI80659]

Rosendahl, Paul H. *Additional Inventory Survey for Drainage Easement 11 Kapalua Plantation Estates Project Area, Lands of Honokahua, Honolua, and Napili 2-3, Lahaina District, Island of Maui.* Hilo, HI: Paul H. Rosendahl, Ph.D., Inc., 1991. [SHPD ID: 2019LI80996]

Rosendahl, Paul H. *Archaeological Field Inspection Hawea Point Residence Site; Hawea Point, Lands of Napili 2 & 3 Lahaina District, Island of Maui.* Hilo, HI: Paul H. Rosendahl, Ph.D., Inc., 1988. [SHPD ID: 2019LI81001]

Rosendahl, Paul H. *Archaeological Monitoring Plan, Mala Village Subdivision, Land of Puʻunoa, Lahaina District, Island of Maui [TMK: (2) 4-5-04:008, 009, 059, 060, 061, 062].* Hilo, HI: Paul H. Rosendahl, Ph.D., Inc., 2002. [SHPD ID: 2019LI80615]

Rosendahl, Paul H. *Archaeological Reconnaissance Survey, The Cottages Project Area Kapalua Development Site 2-A, Lands of Honokahua and Napili 2 & 3, Lahaina District, Island of Maui.* Hilo, HI: Paul H. Rosendahl, Ph.D., Inc., 1988. [SHPD ID: 2019LI81009]

Rosendahl, Paul H. *Archaeological Treatment Plan for No Adverse Effect, Lahaina Bypass Highway Project, Lands of Honokōwai, Hanakaʻōʻō, Wahikuli, Panaʻewa, Kuʻia, Halakaʻa, Pūehuehu Nui, Pāhoa, Polanui, and Launiupoko, Lahaina District, Island of Maui.* Hilo, HI: Paul H. Rosendahl, Ph.D., Inc., 1994. [SHPD ID: 2019LI81439]

Rosendahl, Paul H. *Phase I Monitoring Plan: Archaeological Mitigation Program, Ritz-Carlton Hotel Project Site, Land of Honokahua, Lahaina District, Island of Maui. PHRI Memo 857-070390.* Hilo, HI: Paul H. Rosendahl, Ph.D., Inc., 1990. [No location available]

Rosendahl, Paul H. *PHRI Status Reports on Honokahua.* Hilo, HI: Paul H. Rosendahl, Ph.D., Inc., 1987. [SHPD ID: 2019LI81004]

Rosendahl, Paul H. *Subsurface Reconnaissance Testing, Kapalua Place Project Area, Kapalua Development Site 2-A, Lands of Honokahua and Napili 2 & 3, Lahaina District, Island of Maui.* Hilo, HI: Paul H. Rosendahl, Ph.D., Inc., 1988. [SHPD ID: 2019LI81000]

Smith, Helen Wong. *Historical Documentary Research in Archaeological Inventory Survey, Lahaina Master Planned Project Site, Land of Wahikuli, Lahaina District, Island of Maui.* Hilo, HI: Paul H. Rosendahl, Ph.D., Inc., 1989. [No location available]

Walker, Alan T. and Paul H. Rosendahl. *Testing of Cultural Remains Associated with the Kahana Desilting Basin, Honolua Watershed, Land of Kahana, Lahaina District, County of Maui, Hawaiʻi.* Hilo, HI: Paul H. Rosendahl, Ph.D., Inc., 1985. [SHPD ID: 2019LI81071; UH Call Number: DU629.K343 W35 1985]

Rechtman Consulting, LLC

Bulgrin, Lon E. and Robert B. Rechtman. *An Archaeological Assessment Survey of TMK (2) 4-4-08:016 Hanaka'ō'ō Ahupua'a, Lahaina District, Island of Maui.* Rechtman Consulting, LLC, 2005.

Clark, Matthew R. and Robert B. Rechtman. *An Archaeological Inventory Survey of 333 Acres for the Proposed Expansion of the Kaheawa Wind Farm (TMK: 2-4-8:001: por. 001).* Rechtman Consulting, LLC, 2008. [SHPD ID: 2019LI81628]

Rechtman, Robert B. *Archaeological Monitoring Plan Associated with the Demolition of the Pioneer Mill, TMK (2) 4-5-09:007, Pana'ewa Ahupua'a, Lahaina District, Island of Maui.* Rechtman Consulting, LLC, 2005. [SHPD ID: 2019LI80603]

Rechtman, Robert B. *Archaeological Monitoring Plan for the Subdivision and Development for the Subdivision and Development of TMK: (2) 4-4-08:016.* Rechtman Consulting, LLC, 2006. [SHPD ID: 2019LI80679]

Rechtman, Robert B. *Archaeological Monitoring Report Associated with the Demolition of the Pioneer Mill, Pana'ewa Ahupua'a, Lahaina District, Island of Maui.* Rechtman Consulting, LLC, 2006. [SHPD ID: 2019LI80602]

Rechtman, Robert B. and Ashton K. Dircks Ah Sam. *An Archaeological Inventory Survey for the Kaheawa Wind Power (KWP) Phase 2 Project Area [TMK (2) 3-6-001:por. 14 & (2) 4-8-01: Por. 001].* Rechtman Consulting, LLC, 2009. [SHPD ID: 2019LI80301]

Science Management, Inc.

Hommon, Robert J. *An Archaeological Reconnaissance Survey of an Area Near Waine'e Village, West Maui.* Hawai'i: Science Management, Inc., 1982. [SHPD ID: 2019LI81389; UH Call Number: DU629.W346 H66 1982]

Hommon, Robert J. *An Archaeological Reconnaissance Survey of the North Beach Mauka and South Beach Beach Mauka Areas, Hanaka'ō'ō, West Maui.* Hawai'i: Science Management, Inc., 1982. [No location available]

Hommon, Robert J. and Hamilton M. Ahlo, Jr. *An Archaeological Reconnaissance Survey of the Site of a Proposed Airstrip at Māhinahina, West Maui.* Science Management, Inc., 1982. [SHPD ID: 2019LI81050; UH Call Number: DU629.M345 H66 1982]

SCIENTIFIC CONSULTANT SERVICES, INC.

Andricci, Nicole and Michael F. Dega. *AAAAA Rent-A-Space Extension Project Honokōwai, Māhinahina 4 Ahupuaʻa Lahaina (Kāʻanapali) District, Maui Island Hawaii [TMK (2) 4-4-01:026].* Honolulu, HI: Scientific Consultant Services, Inc., 2015.

Andricci, Nicole and Michael F. Dega. *An Archaeological Assessment for the Lahaina Square Redevelopment Project, Lahaina, Waineʻe Ahupuaʻa, District of Lahaina, Island of Maui, Hawaiʻi.* Honolulu, HI: Scientific Consultant Services, Inc., 2017. [SHPD ID: 2019LI80016]

Andricci, Nicole and Michael F. Dega. *An Archaeological Monitoring Plan for a Residential Parcel 33 at 572 Waineʻe Street, Waineʻe Ahupuaʻa, Lahaina District, Maui Island, Hawaiʻi [TMK (2) 4-6-12:033].* Honolulu, HI: Scientific Consultant Services, Inc., 2016.

Andricci, Nicole and Michael F. Dega. *Archaeological Assessment of a 15.7 Acre Section of Undeveloped Land and a Proposed Road Extension, Kuʻia Ahupuaʻa, Lahaina District, Island of Maui, Hawaiʻi [TMK (2) 4-6-018:003 por.].* Honolulu, HI: Scientific Consultant Services, Inc., 2015.

Bassford, B. A. and Michael F. Dega. *Burial Site Component of an Archaeological Data Recovery and Preservation Plan for Site 50-50-08-8284 at Camp Olowalu in Olowalu, Olowalu Ahupuaʻa, Lahaina District, Maui Island, Hawaiʻi [TMK (2) 4-8-03:084 por.].* Honolulu, HI: Scientific Consultant Services, Inc., 2015. [No location available]

Buffum, Amy and Michael F. Dega. *An Archaeological Monitoring Report for Construction work at Honokōwai, Māhinahina Ahupuaʻa, Kāʻanapali District, Maui Island, Hawaii.* Honolulu, HI: Scientific Consultant Services, Inc., 2002.

Calis, Irene. *Archaeological Monitoring Report: Parking Lot Drainage System Installation, Panaʻewa Ahupuaʻa, Lahaina District, Island of Maui, Hawaiʻi.* Honolulu, HI: Scientific Consultant Services, Inc., 2002. [SHPD ID: 2019LI80642]

Chaffee, D. and C. Monahan. *A Monitoring Plan for 3.054 Acres of Partially Developed Land in Honokōwai, Māhinahina 4 Ahupuaʻa, Lahaina District, Maui Island, Hawaiʻi.* Honolulu, HI: Scientific Consultant Services, Inc., 2005.

Chaffee, David B. and Michael F. Dega. *An Archaeological Monitoring Plan Covering Three Parcels at the Hyatt Regency Maui Resort Kāʻanapali, Hanakaʻōʻō Ahupuaʻa, Lahaina District, Maui Island, Hawaiʻi [TMK (2) 4-4-13:005, 008, 004].* Honolulu, HI: Scientific Consultant Services, Inc., 2014.

Chaffee, David B. and Michael F. Dega. *An Archaeological Monitoring Plan for Approximately 12,365 Foot sq. Property Located on Waineʻe Street in Lahaina, Ahupuaʻa of Panaʻewa, Lahaina District, Maui Island, Hawaiʻi [TMK (2) 4-6-09:024].* Honolulu, HI: Scientific Consultant Services, Inc., 2005. [SHPD ID: 2019LI81580]

Chaffee, David B. and Michael F. Dega. *An Archaeological Monitoring Plan for Kāʻanapali Beach Hotel Beach Front, Restaurant/Canoe Hale, Hanakaʻōʻō Ahupuaʻa, Lahaina District, Island of Maui, Hawaiʻi.* Honolulu, HI: Scientific Consultant Services, Inc., 2014.

Chaffee, David B. and Michael F. Dega. *An Archaeological Monitoring Plan for Subdivision Construction of a 450-Acre Parcel of Land, Ahupuaʻa of Ukumehame, Lahaina District, Island of Maui, Hawaiʻi [TMK (2) 4-8-02:09].* Honolulu, HI: Scientific Consultant Services, Inc., 2003.

Chaffee, David B. and Michael F. Dega. *An Archaeological Monitoring Plan for the Maui Countywide Wastewater Pump Station Renovations, Phase II Project at Multiple Locations, Hanakaʻōʻō Ahupuaʻa and Mākila Ahupuaʻa, Lahaina District, Maui Island, Hawaiʻi [TMK: (2) 4-4-013:003, por. and 4-6-028:054].* Honolulu, HI: Scientific Consultant Services, Inc., 2014.

Chaffee, David B. and Michael F. Dega. *An Archaeological Monitoring Plan for the West Maui Recycled Water Expansion Project (Phase 2), Honokōwai Ahupuaʻa, Lahaina District, Maui Island, Hawaiʻi [TMK (2) 4-4-002:018 por].* Honolulu, HI: Scientific Consultant Services, Inc., 2013.

Chaffee, David B. and Robert L. Spear. *An Archaeological Monitoring Plan for Construction Activities on a 13,237 Square Foot Parcel in ʻAlaeloa Ahupuaʻa, Lahaina District, Maui Island, Hawaii.* Honolulu, HI: Scientific Consultant Services, Inc., 2001.

Chong Jin and Michael F. Dega. *Archaeological Assessment for the Launiupoko Water System Line Extension to Waineʻe Project, Pūehuehu Nui and Pāhoa Ahupuaʻa, Lahaina District, Island of Maui, Hawaiʻi [TMK: (2) 4-6-013: portion of 022; 4-7-002: portion of 004; 4-7-003: portion of 031].* Honolulu, HI: Scientific Consultant Services, Inc., 2022. [SHPD ID: 2022LI00556]

Chong Jin and Michael F. Dega. *Archaeological Monitoring Report for the Kapalua Sinkhole Remediation and Native Plant Restoration Project, Nāpili 2-3 Ahupuaʻa, Lahaina District, Island of Maui [TMK: (2) 4-2-04:025 and (2) 4-2-04:059].* Honolulu, HI: Scientific Consultant Services, Inc., 2021. [SHPD ID: 2022LI00634]

Chong Jin, Garcia Alondra, and Michael F. Dega. *Archaeological Monitoring Plan for 7,804 sq. ft. Parcel at 432 Ilikahi Street, Paunau Ahupuaʻa, Lahaina Dis-*

trict, Island of Maui, Hawaiʻi [TMK: (2) 4-6-06:056 por.]. Honolulu, HI: Scientific Consultant Services, Inc., 2021. [SHPD ID: 2021LI00125]

Chun, Allison and Michael F. Dega. *Addendum Archaeological Assessment Report on 0.13 Acres of Partially Developed land in Honokōwai, Māhinahina 4 Ahupuaʻa, Maui Island, Hawaiʻi.* Honolulu, HI: Scientific Consultant Services, Inc., 2005. [SHPD ID: 2019LI81043]

Cordle, Shayna and Michael F. Dega. *An Archaeological Monitoring Plan for 1.835 Acres in Napili, Napili 2-3 Ahupuaʻa, Lahaina District, Maui Island, Hawaiʻi.* Honolulu, HI: Scientific Consultant Services, Inc., 2008. ID: 2019LI81066]

Cordle, Shayna and Michael F. Dega. *An Archaeological Monitoring Report on Approximately 0.448-Acres for the Maui Marriott Vacation Club, Hanakaʻōʻō Ahupuaʻa, Lahaina District, Island of Maui, Hawaiʻi [TMK (2) 4-4-13:001].* Honolulu, HI: Scientific Consultant Services, Inc., 2007. [SHPD ID: 2019LI80029]

Cordle, Shayna, Cathleen A. Dagher, and Michael F. Dega. *An Archaeological Monitoring Report for Work on County Roadway (WTP T2008/0014) For the Lahaina Store Water Meter Replacement Project, Lahaina, Kuʻia Ahupuaʻa, Lahaina District, Island of Maui, Hawaiʻi [TMK: (2) 4-6-09:007],* 2009. Honolulu, HI: Scientific Consultant Services, Inc. [SHPD ID: 2019LI81563]

Cordle, Shayna, Jennifer Hunt, and Michael F. Dega. *An Archaeological Monitoring Report for a 12,365 Ft Sq. Property, Waineʻe St., Lahaina, Panaʻewa Ahupuaʻa, Lahaina District, Island of Maui, Hawaiʻi [TMK (2) 4-6-09:244].* Honolulu, HI: Scientific Consultant Services, Inc., 2007. [SHPD ID: 2019LI81566]

Dagher, Cathleen A. and Michael F. Dega. *A Preservation Plan for Multiple Archaeological Sites Located in the Kapalua Coastal Trail Corridor in the areas of Nāpili, Kapalua, Honokahua, and Honolua, Ahupuaʻa of Nāpili 2 & 3, Honokahua, and Honolua, Lahaina District, Island of Maui, Hawaiʻi.* Scientific Consultant Services, Inc.: Honolulu, HI, 2008. [SHPD ID: 2019LI79694]

Dagher, Cathleen A. and Michael F. Dega. *A Preservation Plan for the "Brick Palace" (A Component of State Site 50-50-03-3001) Within the Proposed Lahaina Harbor Complete Streets Project Area, Lahaina, Paunau Ahupuaʻa, Lahaina District, Island of Maui, Hawaiʻi [TMK (2) 4-6-01:004].* Honolulu, HI: Scientific Consultant Services, Inc., 2017. [SHPD ID: 2019LI81386]

Dagher, Cathleen A. and Michael F. Dega. *An Archaeological Assessment of the Kāʻanapali Beach Hotel Beach Front Restaurant/Canoe Hale, Hanakaʻōʻō Ahupuaʻa, Lahaina District, Island of Maui, Hawaiʻi [TMK: (2) 4-4-08:003].* Honolulu, HI: Scientific Consultant Services, Inc., 2014. [SHPD ID: 2019LI81259]

Dagher, Cathleen A. and Michael F. Dega. *An Archaeological Monitoring Plan for Olowalu Lot 24, Olowalu Ahupuaʻa, Lahaina District, Island of Maui, Hawaiʻi [TMK: (2) 4-8-03:107].* Honolulu, HI: Scientific Consultant Services, Inc., 2019. [SHPD ID: 2019LI05336]

Dagher, Cathleen A. and Michael F. Dega. *An Archaeological Monitoring Plan for the Napili Culvert Replacement Project, Nāpili 4 and 5 Ahupuaʻa, Lahaina (Kāʻanapali) District, Island of Maui, Hawaiʻi.* Honolulu, HI: Scientific Consultant Services, Inc., 2015. [SHPD ID: 2019LI81056]

Dagher, Cathleen A. and Michael F. Dega. *An Archaeological Monitoring Plan for the Nāpili No. 3 WWPS Force Main Replacement, Lower Honoapiʻilani Road Right-of-Way, Kahana Ahupuaʻa, Lahaina (Kāʻanapali) District Island of Maui, Hawaiʻi. [TMK (2) 4-2-05:999 and 4-3-10:999].* Honolulu, HI: Scientific Consultant Services, Inc., 2020. [SHPD ID: 2021LI00158]

Dagher, Cathleen A. and Michael F. Dega. *An Archaeological Monitoring Plan for the Nāpili No. 4 WWPS Force Main Replacement, Lower Honoapiʻilani Road Right-of-Way, Honokeana and ʻAlaeloa Ahupuaʻa, Lahaina, (Kāʻanapali) District, Island of Maui, Hawaiʻi.* Honolulu, HI: Scientific Consultant Services, Inc., 2020. [SHPD ID: 2021LI00158]

Dagher, Cathleen A. and Michael F. Dega. *An Archaeological Monitoring Plan for the Napili No. 5 & 6 WWPS Force Main Replacement Honokahua Ahupuaʻa, Lahaina (Kāʻanapali) District, Island of Maui, Hawaiʻi [TMK (2) 4-2-04: portion of 48 (Lot 3-A-1 of Kapalua Makai Subdivision No. 4) and TMK (2) 4-2-04: portion of 59 (Lot A-1-A-2 of Kapalua Development (Large-Lot) Subdivision).* Honolulu, HI: Scientific Consultant Services, Inc., 2015. [SHPD ID: 2019LI81016]

Dagher, Cathleen A. and Michael F. Dega. *An Archaeological Monitoring Plan for the Poseley Residence, Olowalu Ahupuaʻa, Lahaina District, Island of Maui, Hawaiʻi [TMK: (2) 4-8-03:047 and portions of 001 and 084 (Easement G)].* Honolulu, HI: Scientific Consultant Services, Inc., 2015. [SHPD ID: 2019LI81660]

Dagher, Cathleen A. and Michael F. Dega. *An Archaeological Monitoring Plan for the Proposed Kapalua Coastal Trail Corridor Located in Kapalua and Honokōhau and Nāpili 2&3 Ahupuaʻa Lahaina District, Island of Maui, Hawaiʻi [TMK: (2) 4-2-Various].* Honolulu, HI: Scientific Consultant Services, Inc., 2007. [SHPD ID: 2019LI81421]

Dagher, Cathleen A. and Michael F. Dega. *An Archaeological Monitoring Plan for the Proposed Kapalua Coastal Trail Located in the Areas of Nāpili, Kapalua, Honokahua, and Honolua, Ahupuaʻa of Nāpili 2 & 3, Honokahua, and Honolua,*

Lahaina district, Island of Maui, Hawai'i. Honolulu, HI: Scientific Consultant Services, Inc., 2008. [SHPD ID: 2019LI81410]

Dagher, Cathleen A. and Michael F. Dega. *Archaeological Field Inspection Results and Recommendations for the Proposed Maui Police Department Communications Facility at Lahainaluna Water Treatment Site, Pana'ewa Ahupua'a, Lahaina District, Maui Island, Hawai'i [TMK: (2) 4-6-18:012 por.].* Honolulu, HI: Scientific Consultant Services, Inc., 2016. [SHPD ID: 2019LI81527]

Dagher, Cathleen A. and Michael F. Dega. *Archaeological Field Inspection Results and Recommendations for the Proposed Maui Police Department Communications Facility at Māhinahina Water Treatment Plant, Māhinahina Ahupua'a, Lahaina District, Maui Island, Hawai'i.* Honolulu, HI: Scientific Consultant Services, Inc., 2016. [SHPD ID: 2019LI81036]

Dagher, Cathleen A. and Michael F. Dega. *Archaeological Inventory Survey for the Proposed West Maui Water Source Development Project Māhinahina Well (State Well No. 6-5638-004) (West Maui Well No. 1) and the Kahana Well (State Well No. 6-5738-002) (West Maui Well No. 2), Honokōwai, Māhinahina, and Māhinahina 1, 2, 3 Ahupua'a, Lahaina (Kā'anapali) District, Island of Maui, Hawai'i [TMK: (2) 4-3-01:017, (2) 4-3-01:084; (2) 4-4-02:014, 015, and 018; and (2) 4-4-004:009, 011, 017, and 019].* Honolulu, HI: Scientific Consultant Services, Inc., 2022. [SHPD ID: 2022LI00356]

Dagher, Cathleen A. and Michael F. Dega. *Archaeological Monitoring Plan for 790 Front Street Waterline (WTP T2017-00280) Lahaina, Paunau Ahupua'a, Lahaina District, Island of Maui, Hawai'i [TMK: (2) 4-6-09:999].* Honolulu, HI: Scientific Consultant Services, Inc., 2020. [SHPD ID: 2022LI00633]

Dagher, Cathleen A. and Michael F. Dega. *Archaeological Monitoring Plan for the Maui Sands Sea Wall Repair Project, Mo'omuku 'ili, Honokōwai Ahupua'a, Lahaina (Kā'anapali) District, Island of Maui, Hawai'i.* Honolulu, HI: Scientific Consultant Services, Inc., 2018. [No location available]

Dagher, Cathleen A. and Michael F. Dega. *Revised Preservation Plan for Site 50-50-08-4438, Ukumehame Ahupua'a, Lahaina District, Island of Maui, Hawai'i [TMK (2) 4-8-002:066; formerly (2) 4-9-002:009 por.].* Honolulu, HI: Scientific Consultant Services, Inc., 2010. [SHPD ID: 2019LI81625]

Dega, Michael F. *A Preservation Plan for Multiple Archaeological Sites on Portions of a 570.3 Acre Property in the Launiupoko (Large Lot, Phase V) Subdivision No. 2, Launiupoko Ahupua'a, Lahaina District (Formerly Kā'anapali), Island of Maui [TMK (2) 4-7-01:02].* Honolulu, HI: Scientific Consultant Services, Inc., 2006. [SHPD ID: 2019LI81606]

Dega, Michael F. *An Addendum Archaeological Inventory Survey in Ukume-hame Ahupuaʻa, Lahaina District, Island of Maui, Hawaiʻi [TMK (2) 4-9-02:008 por.].* Honolulu, HI: Scientific Consultant Services, Inc., 2006. [SHPD ID: 2019LI81645]

Dega, Michael F. *An Archaeological Inventory Survey Plan for Kāʻanapali Beach Hotel Beach Front Restaurant/Canoe Hale, Hanakaʻōʻō Ahupuaʻa, Lahaina District, Island of Maui, Hawaiʻi [TMK: (2) 4-4-008:003 por.].* Honolulu, HI: Scientific Consultant Services, Inc., 2013. [SHPD ID: 2019LI80674]

Dega, Michael F. *An Archaeological Monitoring plan for Construction Work at Honokōwai, Māhinahina Ahupuaʻa, Kāʻanapali District, Maui Island, Hawaiʻi.* Honolulu, HI: Scientific Consultant Services, Inc., 2000. [SHPD ID: 2019LI81247]

Dega, Michael F. *An Archaeological Monitoring Plan for Improvements at D. T. Fleming Beach Park for the County of Maui, Department of Parks and Recreation, Honokahua Ahupuaʻa [sic], Lahaina District, Island of Maui, Hawaiʻi.* Honolulu, HI: Scientific Consultant Services, Inc., 2015. [SHPD ID: 2019LI81042]

Dega, Michael F. *An Archaeological Monitoring Plan for Improvements at Honokōwai Beach Park for the County of Maui, Department of Parks and Recreation, Honokōwai Ahupuaʻa, Lahaina District, Island of Maui, Hawaiʻi [TMK (2) 4-4-01:046 por. & 047 por].* Honolulu, HI: Scientific Consultant Services, Inc., 2015. [SHPD ID: 2019LI81042]

Dega, Michael F. *An Archaeological Monitoring Plan for the Ulupono Center Project, Lahaina, Panaʻewa Ahupuaʻa, Lahaina District, Hawaiʻi, TMK (2) 4-5-10:054.* Honolulu, HI: Scientific Consultant Services Inc., 2017. [SHPD ID: 2019LI80597]

Dega, Michael F. *An Archaeological Monitoring Plan for the West Maui Recycled Water Expansion Project (Phase 2), Honokōwai Ahupuaʻa, Lahaina District, Maui Island, Hawaiʻi.* Honolulu, HI: Scientific Consultant Services, Inc., 2015. [SHPD ID: 2019LI81246]

Dega, Michael F. *Archaeological Inventory Survey of a 3-Acre Parcel in Kahana-Kai, Kahana Ahupuaʻa, Kāʻanapali District, Island of Maui, Hawaiʻi.* Honolulu, HI: Scientific Consultant Services, Inc., 2001. [SHPD ID: 2019LI81327]

Dega, Michael F. *Archaeological Inventory Survey of the Punakea Loop Corridor in Launiupoko and Polanui Ahupuaʻa, Lahaina District (formerly Kāʻanapali), island of Maui, Hawaiʻi [TMK: (2) 4-8-01:002 por. & 4-7-01:029 por.].* Honolulu, HI: Scientific Consultant Services, Inc., 2008. [SHPD ID: 2019LI81597]

Dega, Michael F. *Archaeological Monitoring Plan for Limited Construction Work in Lahaina, Kuʻia Ahupuaʻa, Lahaina District, Island of Maui, Hawaiʻi.* Honolulu, HI: Scientific Consultant Services, Inc., 2003. [SHPD ID: 2019LI80641]

Dega, Michael F. *Archaeological Monitoring Plan for the Front Street Waterline Replacement Project, Panaʻewa Ahupuaʻa, Lahaina District, Island of Maui, Hawaiʻi [TMK (2) 4-5-04, 05, and 08].* Honolulu, HI: Scientific Consultant Services, Inc., 2002. [SHPD ID: 2019LI80631]

Dega, Michael F. *Archaeological Monitoring Plan for the Installation of a Septic System, Maui County Parks, Launiupoko Ahupuaʻa, Lahaina District, Maui Island, Hawaiʻi [TMK: (2) 4-7-01:17].* Honolulu, HI: Scientific Consultant Services, Inc., 2005. [SHPD ID: 2019LI81619]

Dega, Michael F. *Archaeological Monitoring Plan for the Maui Marriott Vacation Club, in the Ahupuaʻa of Hanakaʻōʻō, Lahaina District, Island of Maui, Hawaiʻi [TMK: (2) 4-4-13:001].* Honolulu, HI: Scientific Consultant Services, Inc., 2005. [SHPD ID: 2019LI80663]

Dega, Michael F. and David B. Chaffee. *An Archaeological Monitoring Plan for a Private Residence Demolition in Lahaina, Moaliʻi Ahupuaʻa, Lahaina District, Maui Island, Hawaiʻi [TMK (2) 4-6-02:003].* Honolulu, HI: Scientific Consultant Services, Inc., 2006. [SHPD ID: 2019LI81394]

Dega, Michael F. and David B. Chaffee. *Archaeological Monitoring Plan for Construction at the Lahaina Shores, Moaliʻi Ahupuaʻa, Lahaina District, Maui Island, Hawaiʻi.* Honolulu, HI: Scientific Consultant Services, Inc., 2004. [SHPD ID: 2019LI81373]

Dega, Michael F. and David B. Chaffee. *Archaeological Monitoring Plan for Construction Work on Approximately 25.3 Acres in Kapalua, Napili 2-3 Ahupuaʻa, Lahaina District, Maui Island, Hawaiʻi.* Honolulu, HI: Scientific Consultant Services, Inc., 2004. [SHPD ID: 2019LI81041]

Dega, Michael F. and Mary Sullivan. *Archaeological Monitoring Plan for Construction at the Lahaina Store, Lahaina, Kuʻia Ahupuaʻa, Lahaina District, Island of Maui, Hawaiʻi [TMK: (2) 4-6-09:007 & 062].* Honolulu, HI: Scientific Consultant Services, Inc., 2002. [SHPD ID: 2019LI81578]

Gallo and Michael F. Dega. *Archaeological Assessment for a New Farm Dwelling for Mākila Ranches, Lot 4, Polanui Ahupuaʻa, Lahaina District, Island of Maui, Hawaiʻi [TMK: (2) 4-7-14:004 por.].* Honolulu, HI: Scientific Consultant Services, Inc., 2021. [SHPD ID: 2022LI00382]

Havel, BreAnna and Michael F. Dega. *An Archaeological Assessment Report on 0.11 Acres of a Partially Developed Land in Honokōwai Ahupuaʻa, Lahaina District, Maui Island, Hawaiʻi [TMK 4-4-01:106]*. Honolulu, HI: Scientific Consultant Services, Inc., 2005. [SHPD ID: 2019LI81285]

Havel, BreAnna and Michael F. Dega. *An Archaeological Assessment Report on 0.11 Acres of Partially Developed Land in Honokōwai Ahupuaʻa, Lahaina District, Maui Island, Hawaiʻi.* Honolulu, HI: Scientific Consultant Services, Inc., 2005. [SHPD ID: 2019LI81285]

Havel, BreAnna and Michael F. Dega. *Archaeological Monitoring Plan for the Maui Islander Project, Lahaina, Paunau Ahupuaʻa District, Maui Island, Hawaiʻi [TMK: 4-6-011:008]*. Honolulu, HI: Scientific Consultant Services, Inc., 2005. [SHPD ID: 2019LI81582]

Hoerman, Rachel and Michael F. Dega. *An Archaeological Monitoring Plan for the Pavilion Restaurant Renovation at the Hyatt Regency Maui Resort and Spa, Kāʻanapali, Hanakaʻōʻō Ahupuaʻa, Lahaina District, Maui Island, Hawaiʻi.* Honolulu, HI: Scientific Consultant Services, Inc., 2007. [SHPD ID: 2019LI80666, 2019LI80665]

Hunt, Jennifer, Lauren Morawski, and Michael F. Dega. *An Archaeological Monitoring Report for the Installation of New Sewer Lines and Force Mains and the Replacement of Waterlines for the County of Maui at Shaw, Front, and Dickenson Streets and Honoapiʻilani Highway in Lahaina AND The Installation of Underground Electrical Lines, Panels, and Meters at Armory Park/Kamehameha Iki Park on Front Street in Lahaina for Maui Parks and Recreation Division, Various Ahupuaʻa, Lahaina District, Island of Maui, Hawaiʻi [TMK (2) 4-6002:003, 005, 006, 007, 010, 012, 015, 016, and 027]*. Honolulu, HI: Scientific Consultant Services, Inc., 2011. [SHPD ID: 2019LI81393]

Johnston-OʻNeill, Emily and Michael F. Dega. *Archaeological Monitoring Plan for the Exterior Staircase Addition to the Convent Building at the Sacred Hearts Roman Catholic Property at 712 Waineʻe Street, Paunau Ahupuaʻa, Lahaina District, Island of Maui TMK: (2) 4-6-10:001 (por.).* Honolulu, HI: Scientific Consultant Services, Inc., 2007. [SHPD ID: 2019LI81541]

Kehajit, Chonnikarn and Michael F. Dega. *Archaeological Assessment for shoreline mitigation at the Hyatt Regency Maui Resort, Hanakaʻōʻō Ahupuaʻa, Lahaina District, Island of Maui, Hawaiʻi.* Honolulu, HI: Scientific Consultant Services, Inc., 2018. [No location available]

Kehajit, Chonnikarn and Michael F. Dega. *Archaeological Monitoring Plan for 1191 Front Street Replacement of an Existing Water Supply Project, Lahaina,*

Wahikuli Ahupua'a, Lahaina District, Island of Maui, Hawai'i. Honolulu, HI: Scientific Consultant Services, Inc., 2018. [SHPD ID: 2022LI00191]

Lash, Erik and Michael F. Dega. *An Archaeological Monitoring Plan for the Proposed Lahaina Harbor Complete Streets Project on Approximately 3.11 Acres (1.26 Hectares) in Lahaina, Paunau Ahupua'a, Lahaina District, Island of Maui, Hawai'i [TMK (2) 4-6-001:001, 004, 007, 009, 010, 012, and Adjacent Roadways]*. Honolulu, HI: Scientific Consultant Services, Inc., 2017. [SHPD ID: 2019LI81388]

Lee and Michael F. Dega. *An Archaeological Assessment for a New Wastewater System at the Olowalu Plantation Manager's House in Olowalu, Olowalu Ahupua'a, Lahaina District, Island of Maui, Hawai'i [TMK: (2) 4-8-03:005 por.]*. Honolulu, HI: Scientific Consultant Services, Inc., 2021. [SHPD ID: 2021LI00436]

Lyman, Kepa and Michael F. Dega. *Addendum—Archaeological Monitoring Plan for Lahaina Wastewater Pump Station No. 1 Improvements Honokōwai Ahupua'a, Lahaina District, Maui Island, Hawai'i [TMK (2) 4-4-002:33 and portions of 29 & 39]*. Honolulu, HI: Scientific Consultant Services, Inc., 2018. [No location available]

Lyman, Kepa and Michael F. *Dega. Archaeological Monitoring Plan for the Hanaka'ō'ō Beach Park Parking Improvements, Hanaka'ō'ō Ahupua'a, Lahaina (Kā'anapali) District, Island of Maui*. Honolulu, HI: Scientific Consultant Services, Inc., 2020. [SHPD ID: 2021LI00062]

McGerty, Leann and Robert L. Spear. *A Cultural Impact Assessment for a portion of the Mauian Hotel Property, Nāpili Ahupua'a, Lahaina District, Maui Island, Hawai'i*. Honolulu, HI: Scientific Consultant Services, Inc., 2007. [SHPD ID: 2019LI81065]

McGerty, Leann and Robert L. Spear. *A Cultural Impact Assessment for Maui Marriott Ocean Club, Situated in the Ahupua'a of Hanaka'ō'ō, Lahaina District, Island of Maui, Hawai'i*. Honolulu, HI: Scientific Consultant Services, Inc., 2002. [SHPD ID: 2019LI80664]

McGerty, Leann and Robert L. Spear. *A Cultural Impact Assessment of Approximately 0.8 Acres of Land in Olowalu Ahupua'a, Wailuku District, Maui, Hawai'i [TMK (2) 4-9-003:45A]*. Honolulu, HI: Scientific Consultant Services, Inc., 2006. [SHPD ID: 2019LI81636]

McGerty, Leann and Robert L. Spear. *A Cultural Impact Assessment of Wastewater Pump Station No. 1 in Honokōwai Ahupua'a, Kā'anapali, Lahaina District, Maui*

Island, Hawai'i [TMK: (2) 4-4-02:003, (2) 4-4-02:029]. Honolulu, HI: Scientific Consultant Services, Inc., 2010. [SHPD ID: 2019LI81254]

McGerty, Leann and Robert L. Spear. *A Cultural Impact Assessment on a Piece of Property Located in Kā'anapali, Hanaka'ō'ō Ahupua'a, Lahaina District, Maui Island, Hawai'i [TMK: (2) 4-4-06:056].* Scientific Consultant Services, Inc.: Honolulu, HI, 2003. [SHPD ID: 2019LI81266]

McGerty, Leann and Robert L. Spear. *An Archaeological Inventory Survey at the Maui Marriott Ocean Club, in the Ahupua'a of Hanaka'ō'ō, Lahaina District, Island of Maui, Hawai'i.* Honolulu, HI: Scientific Consultant Services, Inc., 2002. [SHPD ID: 2019LI80107]

McGerty, Leann and Robert L. Spear. *Cultural Impact Assessment on Two Parcels Incorporating the Royal Lahaina Hotel in Kā'anapali, Hanaka'ō'ō Ahupua'a, Lahaina District, Maui Island, Hawai'i.* Honolulu, HI: Scientific Consultant Services, Inc., 2005. [SHPD ID: 2019LI80678]

McGerty, Leanne and Robert L. Spear. *Cultural Impact Assessment of a Parcel of Land in Lahaina Town, Alio Ahupua'a, Lahaina District, Maui Island, Hawai'i.* Honolulu, HI: Scientific Consultant Services, Inc., 2007. [SHPD ID: 2019LI81360]

Medrano, Stephanie and Michael F. Dega. *An Archaeological Assessment for a 1.02-Acre Project Area in Lahaina, Ku'ia Ahupua'a, Lahaina District, Island of Maui, Hawai'i [TMK: (2) 4-6-009:036, 038, & 044].* Honolulu, HI: Scientific Consultant Services, Inc., 2013. [SHPD ID: 2019LI81581]

Monahan, Christopher M. *An Archaeological Assessment Report on 17.746 Acres of Land (Lahaina Business Park, Phase II) on an Undeveloped Lot in Lahaina, Moali'i Ahupua'a, Lahaina District, Maui Island, Hawai'i [TMK: (2) 4-5-10:007].* Honolulu, HI: Scientific Consultant Services, Inc., 2003. [SHPD ID: 2019LI80604]

Monahan, Christopher M. *An Archaeological Assessment Report on 3.054 Acres of Partially Developed Land in Honokōwai, Māhinahina 4 Ahupua'a, Lahaina District, Maui Island, Hawai'i [TMK (2) 4-3-06:002 and 069].* Honolulu, HI: Scientific Consultant Services, Inc., 2003. [SHPD ID: 2019LI81314, 2019LI81304]

Monahan, Christopher M. *An Archaeological Inventory Survey Report on Three Contiguous Parcels Measuring Approximately 25.3 Acres in Kapalua, Napili 2-3 Ahupua'a, Lahaina District, Maui Island, Hawai'i.* Honolulu, HI: Scientific Consultant Services, Inc., 2005. [SHPD ID: 2019LI81018]

Monahan, Christopher M., Lauren Morawski, and Michael F. Dega. *Archaeological Monitoring Plan for Pool Installation at TMK (2) 4-5-04:037 Lahilahi*

Street, Kuʻia Ahupuaʻa, Lahaina District, Island of Maui. Honolulu, HI: Scientific Consultant Services, Inc., 2003. [No location available]

Morawski, Lauren and Michael F. Dega. *Archaeological Inventory Survey of a 7.65 Acre Property at Lot 10-H Ahupuaʻa of Hanakaʻōʻō, Lahaina District, Island of Maui, Hawaiʻi [TMK: (2) 4-4-06:056].* Honolulu, HI: Scientific Consultant Services, Inc., 2003. [SHPD ID: 2019LI81273]

Morawski, Lauren and Michael F. Dega. *Archaeological Inventory Survey Report of an Approximate 10-Acre Parcel in Kapalua in the Ahupuaʻa of Honokahua, Lahaina District (Formerly Kāʻanapali), Island of Maui, Hawaiʻi.* Honolulu, HI: Scientific Consultant Services, Inc., 2004. [SHPD ID: 2019LI81017]

Morawski, Lauren, Adam Johnson, Tomasi Patolo, and Michael F. Dega. *An Archaeological Inventory Survey of 520 Acres in the Launiupoko (Large Lot) Subdivision No. 1, Launiupoko Ahupuaʻa, Lahaina District (formerly Kāʻanapali), Island of Maui, Hawaiʻi [TMK (2) 4-7-01:002 por.].* Honolulu, HI: Scientific Consultant Services, Inc., 2008. [SHPD ID: 2019LI81603]

Ogg, Randy and Michael F. Dega. *An Archaeological Assessment of Lahaina Wastewater Pump Station No. 1 Improvements, Honokōwai Ahupuaʻa, Lahaina District, Maui Island, Hawaiʻi [TMK: (2) 4-4-02:003 & (2) 4-4-02:029].* Honolulu, HI: Scientific Consultant Services, Inc., 2007. [SHPD ID: 2019LI81279]

Paraso, C. Kanani and Michael F. Dega. *An Archaeological Assessment of three parcels at the Hyatt Regency Maui Resort, Kāʻanapali, Hanakaʻōʻō Ahupuaʻa, Lahaina District, Maui Island, Hawaiʻi [TMK (2) 4-4-013:004, 005, 008];* Honolulu, HI: Scientific Consultant Services, Inc., 2006. [SHPD ID: 2019LI80041]

Paraso, C. Kanani and Michael F. Dega. *An Archaeological Inventory Survey of 633 Acres in the Launiupoko (Large Lot) Subdivision Nos. 3, 4, and 7, Launiupoko and Polanui Ahupuaʻa, Lahaina District (formerly Kāʻanapali), Island of Maui, Hawaiʻi [TMK (2) 4-8-01:2 por.].* Honolulu, HI: Scientific Consultant Services, Inc., 2006. [SHPD ID: 2019LI81600]

Perzinski, David. *Archaeological Field Inspection for the West Maui Recycled Water Expansion Project, Phase 2 County Job No. WW12-13, Lahaina, Maui, Hawaiʻi.* Honolulu, HI: Scientific Consultant Services, Inc., 2013. [No location available]

Perzinski, David and Michael F. Dega. *An Archaeological Assessment of a Seawall/ Revetment Structure in Honokōwai.* Honolulu, HI: Scientific Consultant Services, Inc., 2013. [SHPD ID: 2019LI81283]

Perzinski, David and Michael F. Dega. *An Archaeological Inventory Survey of Three Contiguous Parcels of Land Totaling 0.417 Acres in Waineʻe Ahupuaʻa,*

Lahaina District, Maui Island, Hawai'i. Honolulu, HI: Scientific Consultant Services, Inc., 2011. [SHPD ID: 2019LI81543]

Perzinski, David and Michael F. Dega. *An Archaeological Inventory Survey Report for a Bridge Replacement in Honolua, Honolua Ahupua'a, Lahaina District, Maui Island.* Honolulu, HI: Scientific Consultant Services, Inc., 2010. [SHPD ID: 2019LI81430]

Perzinski, David and Michael F. Dega. *An Archaeological Monitoring Report for the Installation of Subsurface Utilities in Nāpili, Kapalua, Honokahua Ahupua'a, Lahaina District, Island of Maui, Hawai'i.* Honolulu, HI: Scientific Consultant Services, Inc., 2015. [SHPD ID: 2019LI81034]

Perzinski, David and Michael F. Dega. *An Archaeological Monitoring Report of the Construction at the Maui Marriott Vacation Club, Hanaka'ō'ō Ahupua'a, Lahaina District, Island of Maui, Hawai'i.* Honolulu, HI: Scientific Consultant Services, Inc., 2009. [No location available]

Perzinski, David and Michael F. Dega. *Archaeological Assessment for the West Maui Well No. 2 Exploratory, DWS Job No. 11-06, Kahana Ahupua'a, Lahaina (Kā'anapali) District, Maui, Hawai'i.* Honolulu, HI: Scientific Consultant Services, Inc., 2014. [SHPD ID: 2019LI81057]

Perzinski, David and Michael F. Dega. *Archaeological Monitoring Report for Lahaina No. 3 Force Main Replacement Project Wahikuli and Hanaka'ō'ō Ahupua'a, Lahaina District, Island of Maui, Hawai'i [TMK (2) 4-4-013].* Honolulu, HI: Scientific Consultant Services, Inc., 2014. [SHPD ID: 2019LI80661]

Pestana, Elizabeth and Michael F. Dega. *Archaeological Inventory Survey of a 5.18 Acre Parcel in Kahana, Kahana Ahupua'a, Kā'anapali District, Island of Maui, Hawai'i [TMK: (2)-4-3-15:069].* Honolulu, HI: Scientific Consultant Services, Inc., 2018. [SHPD ID: 2019LI81301]

Pickett, Jenny L. and Michael F. Dega. *An Archaeological Assessment for 16.8 Acres in Lahaina, Mākila Ahupua'a, Lahaina District, Maui Island, Hawai'i [TMK (2) 4-5-10:005 & 006 por.].* Honolulu, HI: Scientific Consultant Services, Inc., 2005. [SHPD ID: 2019LI80600]

Pickett, Jenny L. and Michael F. Dega. *An Archaeological Inventory Survey of 583 Acres at Lipoa Point, Honolua Ahupua'a, Lahaina (Formerly Kā'anapali) District, Maui Island, Hawai'i.* Honolulu, HI: Scientific Consultant Services, Inc., 2006. [SHPD ID: 2019LI81431]

Scientific Consultant Services, Inc. *An Archaeological Inventory Survey for Six Proposed Solar Voltaic Cell Sites Located in the Ahupua'a of Honokahua, Honokeana, and Honokōwai, Lahaina (Kāʻanapali) District, Island of Maui, Hawaiʻi.* Hono-lulu, HI: Scientific Consultant Services, Inc., 2012. [SHPD ID: 2019LI81005]

Shefcheck, Donna M. and Michael F. Dega. *A Preservation Plan for Site 50-50-08-5968 and Site 50-50-08-5969 in Ukumehame Ahupuaʻa, Lahaina District, Island of Maui, Hawaiʻi [TMK: (2) 4-8-02:008 por.].* Honolulu, HI: Scientific Consultant Services, Inc., 2006. [SHPD ID: 2019LI81643]

Shefcheck, Donna M. and Michael F. Dega. *An Archaeological Inventory Survey of 122.84 Acres in the Launiupoko (Large Lot) Subdivision 6 Launiupoko and Polanui Ahupuaʻa, Lahaina District, Maui, Hawaiʻi [TMK (2) 4-7-01:029 por.].* Hono-lulu, HI: Scientific Consultant Services, Inc., 2008. [SHPD ID: 2019LI81593]

Shefcheck, Donna M. and Michael F. Dega. *An Archaeological Inventory Survey of 123.31 Acres in the Launiupoko (Large Lot) Subdivision 6 Launiupoko and Polanui Ahupuaʻa, Lahaina District (formerly Kāʻanapali) Island of Maui, Hawaiʻi TMK (2) 4-8-01:002 por.).* Honolulu, HI: Scientific Consultant Services, Inc., 2007. [SHPD ID: 2019LI81596]

Shefcheck, Donna M. and Michael F. Dega. *An Archaeological Monitoring Plan for Lahaina Wastewater Pump Station No. 1 Improvements, Honokōwai Ahupuaʻa, Lahaina District Maui Island, Hawaiʻi [TMK (2) 4-4-02:033 and portions of 29 and 39].* Honolulu, HI: Scientific Consultant Services, Inc., 2008. [SHPD ID: 2019LI81253]

Shefcheck, Donna M. and Michael F. Dega. *An Archaeological Monitoring Plan for the Puunoa Subdivision No. 2, Lahaina, Puʻuiki Ahupuaʻa, Lahaina District, Island of Maui, Hawaiʻi.* Honolulu, HI: Scientific Consultant Services, Inc., 2008. [SHPD ID: 2019LI80647]

Shefcheck, Donna M. and Michael F. Dega. *An Archaeological Monitoring Report for the Maui Islander Project, Lahaina, Paunau Ahupuaʻa, Lahaina District, Maui Island, Hawaiʻi [TMK: (2) 4-6-011:008].* Honolulu, HI: Scientific Consultant Services, Inc., 2008. [SHPD ID: 2019LI81576]

Shefcheck, Donna M. and Michael F. Dega. *Site Report for a Previously Unre-corded Heiau in Launiupoko Ahupuaʻa, Lahaina District, Island of Maui, Hawaiʻi.* Honolulu, HI: Scientific Consultant Services, Inc., 2006. [SHPD ID: 2019LI81592]

Spear, Robert L. *Field Inspection of a Sea Wall on the Brayton Property, 303 Front Street, Aholo/Kauʻaula Ahupuaʻa, Lahaina District, Island of Maui, Hawaiʻi TMK: 4-6-3-05 (Seaward).* Honolulu, HI: Scientific Consultant Services, Inc., 2007. [SHPD ID: 2019LI81559]

Stankov, Pavel and Michael F. Dega. *Archaeological Monitoring Plan for the Renovations and Landscaping at the Stakelbeck Property at Olowalu Ahupuaʻa, Lahaina District, Island of Maui, Hawaiʻi [TMK (2) 4-8-03:002 por.]*. Honolulu, HI: Scientific Consultant Services, Inc., 2021. [SHPD ID: 2021LI00103]

Tome, Guerin and Michael F. Dega. *An Archaeological Inventory Survey for the Proposed Kapalua Coastal Trail Located in the Areas of Kapalua and Honokāhau, Honokahua and Nāpili 2 & 3*. Honolulu, HI: Scientific Consultant Services, Inc., 2007. [SHPD ID: 2019LI81433]

Tome, Guerin and Michael F. Dega. *An Archaeological Monitoring Plan for the Proposed Kapalua Coastal Trail Located in the areas of Nāpili, Kapalua, Honokahua, and Honolua, Ahupuaʻa of Nāpili 2&3, Honokahua, and Honolua, Lahaina District, Island of Maui, Hawaiʻi*. Honolulu, HI: Scientific Consultant Services, Inc., 2008. [SHPD ID: 2019LI81410]

Tome, Guerin, Irene Calis, and Michael F. Dega. *An Archaeological Inventory Survey in Honolua, Honolua Ahupuaʻa, Lahaina District, Island of Maui, Hawaiʻi [TMK: (2) 4-1-01:005]*. Honolulu, HI: Scientific Consultant Services, Inc., 2002. [SHPD ID: 2019LI81423]

Wasson, Eugene C. IV and Michael F. Dega. *An Archaeological Monitoring Report for the Lahaina No. 4. Force Main Replacement Project, in Lahaina, Wahikuli Ahupuaʻa, Lahaina District, Island of Maui, Hawaiʻi*. Honolulu, HI: Scientific Consultant Services, Inc., 2016. [SHPD ID: 2019LI80628]

Wiley, Tiffany E. and Michael F. Dega. *Addendum to an Archaeological Monitoring Plan for the Poseley Residence, Olowalu Ahupuaʻa, Lahaina District, Island of Maui, Hawaiʻi [TMK (2) 4-8-003:047, and portions of 001 and 084 (Easement G)]*. Honolulu, HI: Scientific Consultant Services, Inc., 2017. [No location available]

Wong, Charmaine and Michael F. Dega. *An Archaeological Assessment for the West Maui Hospital and Medical Center, Hanakaʻōʻō Ahupuaʻa, Lahaina (Kāʻanapali) district, Maui Island, Hawaiʻi [TMK: (2) 4-4-02:052]*. Honolulu, HI: Scientific Consultant Services, Inc., 2014. [SHPD ID: 2019LI81245]

Wong, Charmaine and Michael F. Dega. *An Archaeological Assessment for the West Maui Hospital and Medical Center, Hanakaʻōʻō Ahupuaʻa, Lahaina (Kāʻanapali) District, Maui Island, Hawaiʻi, TMK: (2) 4-4-02:052*. Honolulu, HI: Scientific Consultant Services, Inc., 2008. [No location available]

Yeomans, Sarah K. *Archaeological Monitoring Plan Parking Lot Drainage System Installation, Panaʻewa Ahupuaʻa, Lahaina District, Island of Maui, Hawaiʻi*. Honolulu, HI: Scientific Consultant Services, Inc., 2019. [SHPD ID: 2019LI80640]

SEA ENGINEERING, INC.

Sea Engineering, Inc. *Final Environmental Assessment for Permanent Shore Protection of the Hololani Resort Condominiums Kahananui, Lahaina, Maui.* Honolulu, HI: Sea Engineering, Inc., 2013. [No location available]

SIXTH SENSE ARCHAEOLOGICAL CONSULTANTS, LLC

Six, Janet L. *A Final Archaeological Assessment Report for Maui County Work on County Roadway (WTP T20160044) and grading and grubbing (GT20160132) Proposed Sunset Terrace Lot Beautification Project, Honokōwai Ahupuaʻa, Lahaina District Maui Island, TMK (2) 4-4-02:029 and 034 (por.).* Pāhoa, HI: Sixth Sense Archaeological Consultants, LLC, 2018. [SHPD ID: 2019LI81282]

Six, Janet L. *Archaeological Monitoring Plan for Deck and Bar Repairs for: Leilaniʻs on the Beach, Whalers Village Shopping Center, Building J 2435 Kāʻanapali Parkway, Hanakaʻōʻō Ahupuaʻa, Lahaina District, Maui Island.* Pāhoa, HI: Sixth Sense Archaeological Consultants, LLC, 2011. [SHPD ID: 2019LI80676]

Six, Janet L. *Final Archaeological Monitoring Plan for Maui County Work on County Roadway (WTP T20160044) and Grading and Grubbing (GT2016132) Proposed Sunset Terrace Lot Beautification Project Honokōwai Ahupuaʻa, Lahaina Project Honokōwai Ahupuaʻa, Lahaina District, Maui Island, Hawaiʻi.* Pāhoa, HI: Sixth Sense Archaeological Consultants, LLC, 2018. [SHPD ID: 2019LI81282]

Six, Janet L. *Final Archaeological Monitoring Plan for Special Management Area Application (SMX2017/0098) for the Proposed Kahana Beach Resort DCDA Upgrade, Kahana Ahupuaʻa, Lahaina District, Island of Maui.* Pāhoa, HI: Sixth Sense Archaeological Consultants, LLC, 2018. [SHPD ID: 2019LI81303]

Six, Janet L. *Final Archaeological Monitoring Plan for Work on County Roadway Permit Application (WTP T2017-0055) Installation Communication Utilities, West Maui Village, Kohi & Napilihau St., Napili, ʻAlaeloa Ahupuaʻa, Kāʻanapali District, Island of Maui.* Pāhoa, HI: Sixth Sense Archaeological Consultants, LLC, 2018. [SHPD ID: 2019LI81317]

SPENCER MASON ARCHITECTS

Spencer Mason Architects. *Historic Site Survey for Lahainaluna Road and Waineʻe Street Widening Projects.* Honolulu, HI: Spencer Mason Architects, 1988. [SHPD ID: 2019LI81432]

Spencer Mason Architects. *Historic Structures Report: Old Lahaina Courthouse.* Honolulu, HI: Spencer Mason Architects, 1996. [SHPD ID: 2019LI81378]

Spencer Mason Architects. *Various Historic Site Survey for Lahainaluna Road and Waine'e Street Widening Projects.* Honolulu, HI: Spencer Mason Architects, 1988. [SHPD ID: 2019LI81432]

Webb, Erika L. *Inventory Survey of Honolua Plantation Shop Buildings Located at the Kapalua Central Resort, TMK (2) 4-2-4:024.* Honolulu, HI: Mason Architects, Inc., 2005. [SHPD ID: 2019LI81047]

University of Hawai'i at Mānoa

Pietrusewsky, Michael and Michele T. Douglas. *An Analysis of Additional Historic Human Skeletal Remains from the Kahoma Stream Flood Control Project, 1989, Lahaina, Maui.* Honolulu, HI: University of Hawai'i at Mānoa, 1990. [SHPD ID: DU629.L3 P54 1990]

Pietrusewsky, Michael, Michele T. Douglas, and Rona Ikehara. *An Osteological Study of Human Remains from the Kahoma Stream Flood Control Project, Lahaina, Maui.* Honolulu, HI: University of Hawai'i at Mānoa, 1989. [UH Call Number: DU629.K76 P54 1989]

Xamanek Researches

Fredericksen et al. *An Archaeological Inventory Survey of a 9.976 Acre parcel in the Kahana/Mailepai/Alaeloa District, Lahaina District, Maui, Hawai'i.* Pukalani, HI: Xamanek Researches, 1990. [SHPD ID: 2019LI81060]

Fredericksen, Demaris. *Monitoring Report for the Sheraton-Maui Redevelopment Project, Hanaka'ō'ō Ahupua'a, Lahaina District, Maui Island.* Pukalani, HI: Xamanek Researches, 1998. [SHPD ID: 2019LI81263]

Fredericksen, Demaris L. *Monitoring Report for the Sheraton-Maui Redevelopment Project Hanaka'ō'ō Ahupua'a, Lahaina District, Maui Island [TMK: (2) 4-4-08:005].* Pukalani, HI: Xamanek Researches, 1998. [SHPD ID: 2019LI81263]

Fredericksen, Demaris L. and Erik M. Fredericksen. *An Archaeological Inventory Survey of a portion of land in Nāpili 2-3 Ahupua'a, Lahaina District, Island of Maui [TMK: (2) 4-2-07: Parcels 007 and 008].* Pukalani, HI: Xamanek Researches, 2003. [SHPD ID: 2019LI81044]

Fredericksen, Demaris L. and Erik M. Fredericksen. *An Archaeological Inventory Survey of the Proposed Sandwich Isles Communications, Inc. Fiber Optics Landing*

Location near the Lahaina Post Office, Wahikuli Ahupuaʻa, Lahaina District, Island of Maui (TMK: 4-5-21:015). Pukalani, HI: Xamanek Researches, 2003. [SHPD ID: 2019LI81336]

Fredericksen, Demaris L. and Erik M. Fredericksen. *Archaeological Inventory Survey (Phase 1) in the ʻIli of Pakala, Puako Ahupuaʻa, Lahaina District, Maui Island [TMK: (2) 4-6-07:007]*. Xamanek Researches: Pukalani, HI, 1999. [SHPD ID: 2019LI81547]

Fredericksen, Demaris L. and Erik M. Fredericksen. *Archaeological Inventory Survey for Kahana-Kai Subdivision, Kahana Ahupuaʻa, Lahaina [Kāʻanapali] District, Maui Island*. Pukalani, HI: Xamanek Researches, 1995. [SHPD ID: 2019LI81330]

Fredericksen, Demaris L. and Erik M. Fredericksen. *Archaeological Inventory Survey of a 24-Acre Parcel, Kapalua Lot 19, Located in Napili 2-3 Ahupuaʻa, Lahaina District, Maui Island [TMK: (2) 4-2-04: por. 024]*. Pukalani, HI: Xamanek Researches, 2000. [SHPD ID: 2019LI81025]

Fredericksen, Demaris L. and Erik M. Fredericksen. *Archaeological Inventory Survey of Makai Portion (Phase 1) of Olowalu Development Parcel, Olowalu Ahupuaʻa, Lahaina District, Maui Island [TMK: (2) 4-8-03: por. 05]*. Pukalani, HI: Xamanek Researches, 2000. [SHPD ID: 2019LI81638]

Fredericksen, Demaris L. and Walter M. Fredericksen. *Archaeological Monitoring Plan for the Sheraton-Maui Redevelopment Project, Ahupuaʻa of Hanakaʻōʻō, Lahaina District, Maui Island*. Pukalani, HI: Xamanek Researches, 1995. [SHPD ID: 2019LI80672]

Fredericksen, Demaris L., Walter M. Fredericksen, and Erik M. Fredericksen. *Archaeological Inventory Survey of a 9.976 Acre Parcel in the Kahana/Mailepai/Akeloa Lands, Lahaina District, Maui, Hawaiʻi*. Pukalani, HI: Xamanek Researches, 1990. [SHPD ID: 2019LI81060]

Fredericksen, Erik M. *A Preliminary Report Summarizing Results of Field Research for an Archaeological Inventory Survey to Satisfy Requirements of SHPD at [TMK: (2) 4-2-04: por. 024] located in Honokahua Ahupuaʻa, Lahaina District, Island of Maui, Hawaiʻi*. Pukalani, HI: Xamanek Researches, 2003.

Fredericksen, Erik M. *A Preservation Plan for the Sites Contained within Kāʻanapali Coffee Estates Subdivision (aka Pioneer Farms Subdivision 1) Project Area, Hanakaʻōʻō Ahupuaʻa, Lahaina District, Island of Maui*. Pukalani, HI: Xamanek Researches, 2005. [SHPD ID: 2019LI81274]

Fredericksen, Erik M. *An Archaeological Assessment for the Proposed Maui Preparatory Academy, Alaeloa Ahupuaʻa, Lahaina District, Island of Maui [TMK (2) 4-3-01: 01 por.].* Pukalani, HI: Xamanek Researches, 2004. [SHPD ID: 2019LI81053]

Fredericksen, Erik M. *An Archaeological Assessment Survey of a c. 5 Acre Portion of Land for the Proposed Temporary Off-Site Parking Project, Hanakaʻōʻō/Honokōwai Ahupuaʻa, Lahaina District, Maui Island [TMK: (2) 4-4-002: 003].* Pukalani, HI: Xamanek Researches, 2007. [No location available]

Fredericksen, Erik M. *An Archaeological Monitoring Plan for a Detector Check Upgrade Project for the Lahaina Square Shopping Center, Waineʻe Ahupuaʻa, Lahaina District, Maui.* Pukalani, HI: Xamanek Researches, 2008. [SHPD ID: 2019LI80611]

Fredericksen, Erik M. *An Archaeological Monitoring Plan for a parcel of land in Napili, Mailepai Ahupuaʻa, Lahaina District, Napili, Maui, TMK: (2) 4-3-15:014.* Pukalani, HI: Xamanek Researches, 2004. [SHPD ID: 2019LI81293]

Fredericksen, Erik M. *An Archaeological Monitoring Plan for a Portion of Land in Alaeloa Ahupuaʻa, Lahaina District, Maui TMK: (2) 4-5-014:032.* Pukalani, HI: Xamanek Researches, 2005. [SHPD ID: 2019LI81355]

Fredericksen, Erik M. *An Archaeological Monitoring Plan for an Inventory Survey Concurrent with Construction Activities on a Parcel of Land in Puako Ahupuaʻa, Lahaina District, Lahaina, Maui [TMK: (2) 4-6-08:48 and 53].* Pukalani, HI: Xamanek Researches, 2003. [SHPD ID: 2019LI81569]

Fredericksen, Erik M. *An Archaeological Monitoring Plan for the Dickenson Street Power Pole Replacement Project, Paunau Ahupuaʻa, Lahaina District, Island of Maui.* Pukalani, HI: Xamanek Researches, 2004. [SHPD ID: 2019LI81570]

Fredericksen, Erik M. *An Archaeological Monitoring Plan for the Emerald Plaza II Project, Land of Moaliʻi, Lahaina District, Island of Maui, TMK: (2) 4-5-10:052.* Pukalani, HI: Xamanek Researches, 2019. [No location available]

Fredericksen, Erik M. *An Archaeological Monitoring Plan for the Kaahanui Place Electrical Improvements Project, Land of Puunoa, Lahaina District, Maui Island [TMK: (2) 4-5-04 por.].* Pukalani, HI: Xamanek Researches, 2009. [No location available]

Fredericksen, Erik M. *An Archaeological Monitoring Plan for the Proposed Kāʻanapali Loop Road Project, Hanakaʻōʻō Ahupuaʻa, Lahaina District, Island of Maui.* Pukalani, HI: Xamanek Researches, 2004. [SHPD ID: 2019LI81268]

Fredericksen, Erik M. *An Archaeological Monitoring Plan for the Proposed Lower Honoapiʻilani Highway Improvements Phase IV Project (Hoʻohui Road to Napilihau Street) in Kahana, Mailepai, and Alaeloa Ahupuaʻa, Napili, Lahaina District, Maui [F. A. P. No. STP 3080 (8)]*. Pukalani, HI: Xamanek Researches, 2005. [SHPD ID: 2019LI81299]

Fredericksen, Erik M. *An Archaeological Monitoring Plan for the West Side Resource Center in Lahaina, Waineʻe Ahupuaʻa, Lahaina District, Maui Island (TMK: 4-6-15: por. of 1 and 4-6-18: por. of 2)*. Pukalani, HI: Xamanek Researches, 2002. [SHPD ID: 2019LI81534]

Fredericksen, Erik M. *An Archaeological Monitoring Report for a Parcel of Land in Puako Ahupuaʻa, Lahaina District, Maui [TMK: (2) 4-6-008:022]*. Pukalani, HI: Xamanek Researches, 2005. [SHPD ID: 2019LI81565]

Fredericksen, Erik M. *An Archaeological Monitoring Report for Offsite Parking for the Lot 3 Temporary Parking Project, Kāʻanapali, Hanakaʻōʻō Ahupuaʻa Lahaina District, Island of Maui*. Pukalani, HI: Xamanek Researches, 2006. [SHPD ID: 2019LI80660]

Fredericksen, Erik M. *An Archaeological Monitoring Report for the West Side Resource Center in Lahaina, Waineʻe Ahupuaʻa, Lahaina District, Maui Island [TMK: (2) 4-6-15: por. of 1 and TMK: (2) 4-6-18: por. of 2]*. Pukalani, HI: Xamanek Researches, 2004. [SHPD ID: 2019LI81535]

Fredericksen, Erik M. *Archaeological Assessment Report for a Portion of Land in Puako Ahupuaʻa, Lahaina District, Lahaina, Maui [TMK: (2) 4-6-08:053]*. Pukalani, HI: Xamanek Researches, 2004. [SHPD ID: 2019LI81545]

Fredericksen, Erik M. *Archaeological Inventory Survey for the Proposed Lahaina Cannery Fuel Station Project, Land of Moaliʻi, Lahaina District, Island of Maui [TMK: (2) 4-5-11: 004 Por.]*. Pukalani, HI: Xamanek Researches, 2023. [SHPD ID: 2023LI00137]

Fredericksen, Erik M. *Archaeological Monitoring Plan for a Parcel of Land in the ʻIli of Pakala, Puako Ahupuaʻa, Lahaina District, Island of Maui [TMK: (2) 4-6-07:003]*. Xamanek Researches: Pukalani, HI, 1998. [SHPD ID: 2019LI81549]

Fredericksen, Erik M. *Archaeological Monitoring Plan for a Water Lateral and Sewer Lateral Installation Project for a Parcel of Land in Lahaina, Moaliʻi Ahupuaʻa, Lahaina District, Maui*. Pukalani, HI: Xamanek Researches, 2003. [SHPD ID: 2019LI81270]

Fredericksen, Erik M. *Archaeological Monitoring Plan for Improvements at 815 Front Street, Paunau Ahupua'a, Lahaina District, Maui.* Pukalani, HI: Xamanek Researches, 2001. [SHPD ID: 2019LI80644]

Fredericksen, Erik M. *Archaeological Monitoring Plan for Lot 29 (Site 29) Honokahua and Napili 2-3 Ahupua'a, Lahaina District, Maui, Hawai'i.* Pukalani, HI: Xamanek Researches, 1999. [SHPD ID: 2019LI81028]

Fredericksen, Erik M. *Archaeological Monitoring Plan for Sewer Lateral Installation Project at 460 Alio Street, Land of Nalehu, Mākila Ahupua'a, Lahaina District, Maui [TMK (2) 4-6-06:031].* Pukalani, HI: Xamanek Researches, 2003. [SHPD ID: 2019LI81270]

Fredericksen, Erik M. *Archaeological Monitoring Plan for the King Kamehameha III Elementary School Building B, Building D, and PT 201 Restroom Renovation Project, Puako Ahupua'a, Lahaina District, Maui [TMK: (2) 4-6-02:013 & 014].* Pukalani, HI: Xamanek Researches, 2001. [SHPD ID: 2019LI81392]

Fredericksen, Erik M. *Archaeological Monitoring Plan for the Proposed Plantation Inn Improvements Project (GPC 2002/43), Pana'ewa Ahupua'a, Lahaina District, Maui [TMK: (2) 4-6-009: 036, 037 and 044].* Pukalani, HI: Xamanek Researches, 2002. [SHPD ID: 2019LI81579]

Fredericksen, Erik M. *Archaeological Monitoring Plan for the Sabia Building Development and Improvement Project at 816A Front Street, Paunau Ahupua'a, Lahaina District, Maui.* Pukalani, HI: Xamanek Researches, 2000. [SHPD ID: 2019LI80617]

Fredericksen, Erik M. *Archaeological Monitoring Plan for the Wharf Street Accessibility Improvements at Lahaina Harbor—Electrical Underground Work Project, Puako Ahupua'a, Lahaina District, Maui [TMK: (2) 4-6-01 and 4-6-01: Portion of Parcel 1].* Pukalani, HI: Xamanek Researches, 2002. [SHPD ID: 2019LI81402]

Fredericksen, Erik M. *Archaeological Monitoring Plan on a 1.3 Acre of Land on the Olowalu Makai Project Area, Olowalu Ahupua'a, Lahaina District, Maui [TMK: (2) 4-9-03:044].* Pukalani, HI: Xamanek Researches, 2001. [SHPD ID: 2019LI81635]

Fredericksen, Erik M. *Archaeological Monitoring Report for a 1.3 Acre of Land on the Olowalu Makai Project Area, Olowalu Ahupua'a, Lahaina District, Maui (TMK 2-4-8-03:44).* Pukalani, HI: Xamanek Researches, 2003. [SHPD ID: 2019LI81637]

Fredericksen, Erik M. *Archaeological Monitoring Report for a Portion of Land in Moaliʻi Ahupuaʻa, Lahaina District, Maui.* Pukalani, HI: Xamanek Researches, 2004. [SHPD ID: 2019LI81269]

Fredericksen, Erik M. *Archaeological Monitoring Report for the Coconut Grove Development (Site 29), Honokahua and Napili 2-3 Ahupuaʻa Lahiana District, Island of Maui.* Pukalani, HI: Xamanek Researches, 2001. [SHPD ID: 2019LI17106]

Fredericksen, Erik M. *Archaeological Monitoring Report for the Proposed Plantation Inn Improvements Project (GPC2002/43) Panaʻewa Ahupuaʻa, Lahaina District, Maui, TMK: (2) 4-6-09:036, 037, and 044.* Pukalani, HI: Xamanek Researches, 2003. [SHPD ID: 2019LI81574]

Fredericksen, Erik M. *Archaeological Monitoring Report for the Verizon Hawaii, Inc. Equipment Installation project at TMK: (2) 4-2-04:021 Ritz-Carlton, Kapalua, Honokahua Ahupuaʻa, Lahaina District, Maui, Hawaiʻi.* Pukalani, HI: Xamanek Researches, 2001. [SHPD ID: 2019LI81014, 2019LI81029]

Fredericksen, Erik M. *Archaeological Monitoring Report on the Pioneer Inn Swimming Pool Construction Project.* Pukalani, HI: Xamanek Researches, 1997. [SHPD ID: 2019LI81383]

Fredericksen, Erik M. *Archaeological Reconnaissance Report for the County of Maui Honokōhau Water System Improvements Project, Lahaina District, Maui Island.* Pukalani, HI: Xamanek Researches, 1998. [SHPD ID: 2019LI80994]

Fredericksen, Erik M. *Preservation Plan for Possible Burial Features Contained Within Sites 50-50-01-5139, 5142, 5157 and 5158 Located on the Kapalua Mauka Project area, Honokahua and Napili 2 & 3 Ahupuaʻa, Lahaina District, Island of Maui.* Pukalani, HI: Xamanek Researches, 2003. [SHPD ID: 2019LI81407]

Fredericksen, Erik M. and Demaris Fredericksen. *Archaeological Inventory Survey for the Proposed Honokōhau Water System Improvement Project, Honokōhau Ahupuaʻa, Kāʻanapali District, Maui Island. DRAFT.* Pukalani, HI: Xamanek Researches, 1999. [SHPD ID: 2019LI80995]

Fredericksen, Erik M. and Demaris Fredericksen. *Archaeological Inventory Survey Report for Portion of Land in Puako Ahupuaʻa, Lahaina District, Lahaina, Maui, [TMK: (2) 4-6-08:53 and 48].* Pukalani, HI: Xamanek Researches, 2002. [SHPD ID: 2019LI81571]

Fredericksen, Erik M. and Demaris L. Fredericksen. *Additional Archaeological Inventory Survey Level Work for Site 50-50-03-4797, Lower Honoapiʻilani Road Improvements Project Corridor; Alaeloa, Mailepai and Kahana Ahupuaʻa, Lahaina*

District, Maui Island [TMK (2) 4-3-15]. Pukalani, HI: Xamanek Researches, 2001. [SHPD ID: 2021LI00221]

Fredericksen, Erik M. and Demaris L. Fredericksen. *An Archaeological Inventory Survey (Phase 2) of a New Alignment for the Honokōhau Waterline Project, Honokōhau, Ahupuaʻa, Kāʻanapali District, Island of Maui.* Pukalani, HI: Xamanek Researches, 2002. [SHPD ID: 2019LI81426]

Fredericksen, Erik M. and Demaris L. Fredericksen. *An Archaeological Inventory Survey of Honoapiʻilani Highway Corridor from Alaelae Point to Honolua Bay, Honolua and Honokahua Ahupuaʻa, Lahaina District, Maui Island.* Pukalani, HI: Xamanek Researches, 2000. [SHPD ID: 2019LI81045]

Fredericksen, Erik M. and Demaris L. Fredericksen. *An Archaeological Inventory Survey of the Lahaina Watershed Flood Control Project Area, Lands of Polanui, Paha, Pueuehunui, Lahaina District, Maui Island (TMK: 4-6-13:016, 18, 26; TMK 4-7-01, 02).* Pukalani, HI: Xamanek Researches, 2003. [SHPD ID: 2019LI81442]

Fredericksen, Erik M. and Demaris L. Fredericksen. *Archaeological Inventory Survey for the Proposed Golf Academy Project Kapalua, Maui, Hawaiʻi, TMK 4-2-04: por. 24.* Pukalani, HI: Xamanek Researches, 1998. [SHPD ID: 2019LI81012]

Fredericksen, Erik M. and Demaris L. Fredericksen. *Archaeological Inventory Survey of 475 Acres in Kapalua District 2 Project Area, Located in Napili and Honokahua Ahupuaʻa, Lahaina District, Maui Island, TMK: (2) 4-2-01: por. 1.* Pukalani, HI: Xamanek Researches, 2002. [SHPD ID: 2021LI00311]

Fredericksen, Erik M. and Demaris L. Fredericksen. *Archaeological Inventory Survey of the Lower Honoapiʻilani Road Improvements Project Corridor (TMK 4-3-03; 4-3-05; 4-3-10; 4-3-15) Lahaina District, Maui Island.* Pukalani, HI: Xamanek Researches, 1999. [SHPD ID: 2021LI00220]

Fredericksen, Erik M. and Demaris L. Fredericksen. *Archaeological Inventory Survey of the Lower Honoapiʻilani Road Improvements Project Corridor.* Pukalani, HI: Xamanek Researches, 1999. [SHPD ID: 2021LI00220]

Fredericksen, Erik M. and J. J. Frey. *An Archaeological Monitoring Report for the Kāʻanapali Shores Roadway Improvements Project, Honokōwai Ahupuaʻa, Lahaina District, Maui.* Pukalani, HI: Xamanek Researches, 2008. [SHPD ID: 2019LI81243]

Fredericksen, Erik M. and J. J. Frey. *Burial Site Component of an Archaeological Data Recovery Plan for Inadvertently Discovered Human Skeletal Remains, Site 50-50-03-08973, Located in Previously Imported Sand Fill During Utilities Installa-*

tion for the Lahaina Cannery Fuel Station Project, Ahupuaʻa of Moaliʻi, Lahaina
District, Island of Maui [TMK: (2) 4-5-11:004 por.]*. Pukalani, HI: Xamanek
Researches, 2023. [SHPD ID: 2023LI00074]

Fredericksen, Erik M. and Jennifer J. Frey. *An Archaeological Inventory Survey of
a Portion of Land in Mailepai Ahupuaʻa, Lahaina District, Maui Island*. Pukalani,
HI: Xamanek Researches, 2008. [SHPD ID: 2019LI81302]

Fredericksen, Erik M. and Jennifer J. Frey. *An Archaeological Monitoring Report
for the King Kamehameha III Elementary School Parking Lot Improvements Project,
Puako Ahupuaʻa, Lahaina District TMK (2) 4-6-002:13*. Pukalani, HI: Xamanek
Researches, 2008. [SHPD ID: 2019LI81374]

Fredericksen, Erik M. and Jennifer L. Frey. *An Archaeological Monitoring Report
for the Kāʻanapali Shores Roadway Improvements Project, Honokōwai Ahupuaʻa,
Lahaina District, Maui [TMK: (2) 4-4-001:097, and TMK (2) 4-4-001 (Right of
Way)]*. Pukalani, HI: Xamanek Researches, 2008. [SHPD ID: 2019LI81243]

Fredericksen, Erik M., Demaris Fredericksen, and W. M. Fredericksen. *An
Archaeological Inventory Survey at Honokōwai Beach Park, Honokōwai Ahupuaʻa,
Lahaina District, Maui Island*. Pukalani, HI: Xamanek Researches, 1994. [No
location available]

Fredericksen, Erik M., Demaris L. Fredericksen, and Walter M. Fredericksen.
*An Archaeological Inventory Survey of a 12.2 Acre Parcel. Honokahua and Napili
2-3 Ahupuaʻa, Lahaina District Maui Island*. Pukalani, HI: Xamanek Researches,
1994. [SHPD ID: 2019LI81030]

Fredericksen, Erik M., Walter M. Fredericksen, and Demaris L. Fredericksen. *Additional Archaeological Inventory Survey Subsurface testing at Kapalua
Bay Hotel [TMK (2) 4-2-04:26], Honokahua and Napili 2-3 Ahupuaʻa, Lahaina
District, Maui Island*. Pukalani, HI: Xamanek Researches, 1996. [SHPD ID:
2019LI81024]

Fredericksen, Walter M. *An Historic and Traditional Land Use Study Utilizing
Oral History Interviews for Assessing Cultural Impacts, for the Kapalua Project
2 and Expanded Project 2, Kapalua, Maui, Hawaiʻi*. Pukalani, HI: Xamanek
Researches, 2001. [No location available]

Fredericksen, Walter M. *Archaeological Monitoring Report for the Remodeling
Project of the Lahaina Yacht Club, 835 Front Street, Paunau Ahupuaʻa, Lahaina
District, Island of Maui*. Pukalani, HI: Xamanek Researches, 2002. [SHPD ID:
2019LI80645]

Fredericksen, Walter M. and Demaris Fredericksen. *Archaeological Monitoring Report for The Kai Ala Subdivision, Ahupuaʻa of Hanakaoʻo, Lahaina District, Island of Maui.* Pukalani, HI: Xamanek Researches, 1996. [SHPD ID: 2019LI81251]

Fredericksen, Walter M. and Demaris L. Fredericksen. *An Archaeological Inventory Survey on a Parcel of Land Located in the Ahupuaʻa of Paunau, Lahaina District, Island of Maui TMK (2) 4-6-09:012.* Pukalani, HI: Xamanek Researches, 1993. [SHPD ID: 2022LI00237]

Fredericksen, Walter M. and Demaris L. Fredericksen. *Archaeological Data Recovery Report on the Plantation Inn Site, Lahaina, Maui, Hawaiʻi.* Pukalani, HI: Xamanek Researches, 1990. [SHPD ID: 2019LI81589; UH Call Number: DU629.L3 F738 1990a]

Fredericksen, Walter M. and Demaris L. Fredericksen. *Archaeological Data Recovery Report on the Plantation Inn Site, Lahaina, Maui, Hawaiʻi.* Pukalani, HI: Xamanek Researches, 1993. [SHPD ID: 2019LI81589]

Fredericksen, Walter M. and Demaris L. Fredericksen. *Report on the Archaeological Excavation Conducted at Hale Paʻi Site, 1981–1982.* Pukalani, HI: Xamanek Researches, 1988. [SHPD ID: 2019LI81532]

Fredericksen, Walter M. Jr. and Demaris L. Fredericksen. *Report on the Excavation of the Outbuildings Adjacent to the Baldwin House, Undertaken for the Lahaina Restoration Foundation, Lahaina, Maui, Hawaiʻi.* Pukalani, HI: Xamanek Researches, 1978. [SHPD ID: 2019LI81568]

Fredericksen, Walter M., Demaris Fredericksen, and Erik M. Fredericksen. *Report on the Archaeological Inventory Survey at Historic Site #15, Lahaina Maui, Hawaiʻi.* Pukalani, HI: Xamanek Researches, 1988. [SHPD ID: 2019LI81406]

Fredericksen, Walter M., Demaris L. Fredericksen, and Erik M. Fredericksen. *An Archaeological Inventory Survey of a Parcel of Land Adjacent to Malu-Ulu-o-Lele Park, Lahaina, Maui, Hawaiʻi.* Pukalani, HI: Xamanek Researches, 1989. [SHPD ID: 2019LI81548]

Fredericksen, Walter M., Demaris L. Fredericksen, and Erik M. Fredericksen. *An Archaeological Inventory Survey of the Plantation Inn Site, Lahaina, Maui, Hawaiʻi.* Pukalani, HI: Xamanek Researches, 1989. [SHPD ID: 2019LI81588]

Fredericksen, Walter M., Demaris L. Fredericksen, and Erik M. Fredericksen. *Archaeological Data Recovery Report on the AUS Site, Lahaina, Maui, Hawaiʻi.* Pukalani, HI: Xamanek Researches, 1989. [SHPD ID: 2019LI81562]

Fredericksen, Walter M., Demaris L. Fredericksen, and Erik M. Fredericksen. *The AUS Site: H. S. #50-03-1797 A Preliminary Archaeological Inventory Survey Report.* Pukalani, HI: Xamanek Researches, 1989. [No location available]

Frey, Jennifer J. and Erik M. Fredericksen. *An Archaeological Monitoring Report for the King Kamehameha III Elementary School Campus Exterior Awning and Gutter Project, DOE Job No. P01090-06, Puako Ahupuaʻa, Lahaina District [TMK (2) 4-6-02:013, and (2) 4-6-02:014].* Pukalani, HI: Xamanek Researches, 2009. [SHPD ID: 2019LI81561]

Rogers, Scott. *An Archaeological Monitoring Plan for the Kāʻanapali—Hyatt Force Main Replacements, Kāʻanapali Resort Complex, Hanakaʻōʻō, Honokōwai Ahupuaʻa, Lahaina District, Island of Maui.* Pukalani, HI: Xamanek Researches, 2007. [SHPD ID: 2019LI80682]

ZZ-No Publisher Designated

Athens, J. Stephen. *Archaeological Reconnaissance at Honokahua Well B, Lahaina District, West Maui,* 1985.

Chapman, Phillips, Brandt and Associates. *Lahaina Banyan Courtyard Preliminary Development and Restoration Plans,* 1972. [SHPD ID: 2019LI81398]

Cliver, Blaine E., *Architectural Restorationalist. Architecturally speaking… The Baldwin House,* Lahaina, Maui, 1966. [SHPD ID: 2019LI81038]

Dagher, Cathleen A. *Request for Information Pertaining to the Ukumehame Subdivision and the Impacts to Preserved Site 50-50-08-4438 Ukumehame Ahupuaʻa, Lahaina District, Island of Maui,* 2009. [SHPD ID: 2019LI81644]

Duensing, Dawn E. and Michael W. Foley. *Lahaina Design Guidelines, Lahaina Town, Maui, Hawaiʻi,* 2003. [SHPD ID: 2019LI81377]

Fox, Robert M. *Site Survey & Inventory, Hale Paʻi o Lahainaluna.* Honolulu, HI: AIA, 1977. [SHPD ID: 2019LI81590]

Fredericksen, Walter M. and Demaris L. Fredericksen. *Report on the Archaeological Excavation of the "Brick Palace" of King Kamehameha I at Lahaina, Maui, Hawaiʻi,* 1965. [SHPD ID: 2019LI81384; UH Call Number: DU629.L3 F74]

Frost, Lockwood H. *A Report and Recommendations on the Restoration and Preservation of Hale Aloha, Lahaina, Maui,* 1973. [No location available]

Haun, A. E. *Subsurface Archaeological Reconnaissance Survey, Lahaina Cannery Makai and Mauka Parcels, Land of Moaliʻi, Lahaina District, Island of Maui,* 1988. [SHPD ID: 2019LI80612]

Haun, Alan E. and Jack D. Henry. *Archaeological Data Recovery Plan Sites 4141 and 4143, Land of Honolua, Lahaina District, Island of Maui*, 2002. [SHPD ID: 2019LI81010]

Kawachi, Carol. *Archaeological Monitoring Plan for Phase 1 of the Proposed Lahaina Watershed Flood Control Project Including Conservation District Use Application MA-3204 Board Permit, Polanui Ahupuaʻa, Lahaina District, Maui, Island TMK: (2) 4-8-01: por. 002, 018, 2005*. [SHPD ID: 2019LI81601]

Kennedy, Joseph. *Archaeological Inventory Survey and Subsurface Testing Report for a Property Located at TMK: 4-3-03:108 and 110, ʻAlaeloa Ahupuaʻa, Lahaina District, on the Island of Maui*, 1992. [SHPD ID: 2022LI00219]

Kennedy, Joseph. *Archaeological Inventory Survey Report for TMK: (2) 4-3-01:031; Located at Kahana, Island of Maui*. 1990. [SHPD ID: 2019LI81054]

Kennedy, Joseph. *Archaeological Investigations at Kahana, Maui*, 1986. [No location available]

Kennedy, Joseph. *Archaeological Walk Through Reconnaissance of (2)4-3-01:001 Napili Fire Station, TMK (2) 4-3-01:001 (por.)*, 1989. [SHPD ID: 2019LI81054]

Kennedy, Joseph. *Field Inspection: Stone Building at Kahana*, Maui, 1986. [SHPD ID: 2019LI81332]

Ladd, Edmund J. *Archaeological Survey Report*, 1980. [No location available]

McGerty, Leann and Robert L. Spear. *An Inventory Survey of a 3.3 Acre Parcel in Māhinahina 4 Ahupuaʻa, Lahaina District, Island of Maui, Hawaiʻi [TMK (2) 4-3-06:003]*, 1996. [SHPD ID: 2019LI81305]

Nagata, Ralston H. *CDUA-MA-5/12/82-1407, Land Clearing and Planting of Commercially Valuable Tree Species at Kahakuloa, Wailuku, Maui. Memorandum to: Roger Evans, Planning Office from DLNR, Division of State Parks*, 1983. [No location available]

Nagata, Ralston H. and Martha Yent. *CDUA: MA-1436, Taro Planting at Kahakuloa Valley, Wailuku, Maui. Memorandum to Mr. Roger Evans, Planning Office from DLNR, Division of State Parks*, 1982. [UH Call Number: DU629. K344 N34 1982]

Neller, Earl. *An Archaeological Reconnaissance Along the Coast at Ukumehame, Maui*, 1982. [SHPD ID: 2019LI81640; UH Call Number: DU629.U38 N45 1982]

Pantaleo, Jeffrey. *Archaeological Monitoring Plan Phase 2 of the Proposed Lahaina Watershed Flood Control Project, Polanui and Pāhoa Ahupuaʻa, Lahaina District,*

Maui Island [TMK (2) 4-8-001: por. 02; 4-7-02:por. 4, 5, 7], 1991. [No location available]

Peterson, Charles E. *Notes on the Lahaina Court and Custom House, Lahaina, Maui, Hawaiʻi, Built 1859*, 1966. [SHPD ID: 2019LI81376]

Pyle, Dorothy. "The Intriguing Seamen's Hospital." *The Hawaiian Journal of History*, vol. 8, 1974, pp. 121–135 [UH Call Number: DU620 .H44]

Silva, C. L. *Appendix A: Preliminary Historical Documentary Research, in Archaeological Survey Test Excavations, Kapalua Hotel Development Site 2-H, Kapalua Bay Resort, Land of Honokahua, Lahaina District, Island of Maui. PHRI Report 224-052286*, 1986. [No location available]

Spriggs, Matthew. *Trip Report: Makaluapuna Point, Honokahua, Lahaina District, Maui*, 1989. [SHPD ID: 2019LI81413; UH Call Number: DU629.M356 S67 1989]

Tourtellotte, Perry A. *Archaeological Inspection Report for Rainbow Ranch*, 1988. [SHPD ID: 2019LI81059]

Walton, Beth. *A Preliminary Report on an Archaeological Survey of the Portion of Piilani Highway from Stake 195+00 to Stake 250+00*, 1972. [SHPD ID: 2019LI79374]

Watanabe, Farley. *Archaeological Site Investigation Kahoma Stream Flood Control Project TMK (2) 4-5-15:008.* Honolulu, HI: Army Corps of Engineers, 1987. [SHPD ID: 2019LI81342]tions by Year

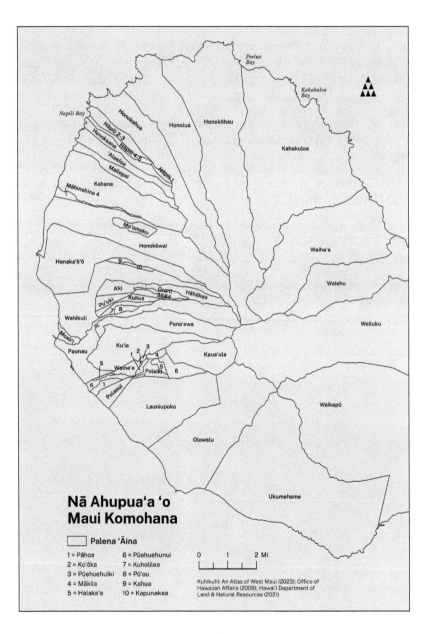

Nā Ahupua'a 'o
Maui Komohana

☐ Palena 'Āina

1 = Pāhoa   6 = Pūehuehunui
2 = Ko'ōka   7 = Kuholilea
3 = Pūehuehuiki 8 = Pū'ou
4 = Mākila   9 = Kahua
5 = Halaka'a   10 = Kapunakea

0   1   2 Mi

Kuhikuhi: An Atlas of West Maui (2023); Office of
Hawaiian Affairs (2009); Hawai'i Department of
Land & Natural Resources (2021)

AHOLO

Spear, Robert L. *Field Inspection of a Sea Wall on the Brayton Property, 303 Front Street, Aholo/Kau'aula Ahupua'a, Lahaina District, Island of Maui, Hawai'i TMK: 4-6-3-05 (Seaward)*. Honolulu, HI: Scientific Consultant Services, Inc., 2007. [SHPD ID: 2019LI81559]

AKELOA

Fredericksen, Demaris L., Walter M. Fredericksen, and Erik M. Fredericksen. *Archaeological Inventory Survey of a 9.976 Acre Parcel in the Kahana/Mailepai/Akeloa Lands, Lahaina District, Maui, Hawai'i*. Pukalani, HI: Xamanek Researches, 1990. [SHPD ID: 2019LI81060]

ALIO

McGerty, Leanne and Robert L. Spear. *Cultural Impact Assessment of a Parcel of Land in Lahaina Town, Alio Ahupua'a, Lahaina District, Maui Island, Hawai'i*. Honolulu, HI: Scientific Consultant Services, Inc., 2007. [SHPD ID: 2019LI81360]

HALAKA'A

Desilets, Michael and Patrick O'Day. *Preservation Plan for Proposed Fenceline Corridor for the West Maui Forest Reserve, Ku'ia, Mākila, Pāhoa, Halaka'a, Polaiki, Launiupoko, and Olowalu Ahupua'a, Lahaina District, Maui Island, Hawai'i*. Kailua, HI: Garcia & Associates, 2016. [SHPD ID: 2019LI81528]

Donham, Theresa K. *Archaeological Monitoring Plan for the Remodeling of a Dwelling at the Phleger Property, Halaka'a, Lahaina District, Maui TMK: (2) 4-6-05:014*. Kīhei, HI: Akahele Archaeology, 2004. [SHPD ID: 2019LI81558]

Fredericksen, Erik M. and Demaris L. Fredericksen. *An Archaeological Inventory Survey of the Lahaina Watershed Flood Control Project Area, Lands of Polanui, Paha, Pueuehunui, Lahaina District, Maui Island (TMK: 4-6-13:016, 18, 26; TMK 4-7-01, 02)*. Pukalani, HI: Xamanek Researches, 2003. [SHPD ID: 2019LI81442]

Jensen, Peter M. *Archaeological Inventory Survey Honoapi'ilani Highway Realignment Project Lahaina Bypass Section—Modified Corridor Alignment, Lands of Honokōwai, Hanaka'ō'ō, Wahikuli, Pana'ewa, Ku'ia, Halaka'a, Pūehuehu Nui, Pāhoa, Polanui, and Launiupoko, Lahaina District, Island of Maui*. Hilo, HI: Paul H. Rosendahl, Ph.D., Inc., 1991. [SHPD ID: 2019LI81242]

McCurdy, Todd D. and Hallett H. Hammatt. *Addendum Report for Archaeological Inventory Survey Documentation of Inadvertent Finds Identified during the Honoapiʻilani Highway Realignment (Lahaina Bypass) Phase 1B-1, Paunau Ahupuaʻa to Polanui Ahupuaʻa, Lahaina District, Maui Island TMK (2) 4-6-014:001, 002: (2) 4-6-018:002, 003; (2) 4-8-001:002 and (2) 4-8-003:001.* Wailuku, HI: Cultural Surveys Hawaiʻi, Inc., 2010. [SHPD ID: 2019LI81537]

McCurdy, Todd D. and Hallett H. Hammatt. *An Archaeological Monitoring Plan for the Honoapiʻilani Highway Realignment (Lahaina Bypass), Phase 1B-1, Paunau Ahupuaʻa to Polanui Ahupuaʻa, Lahaina District, Maui Island TMK: (2) 4-6-014:001-002, 4-6-018:002-003, 4-7-001:002 and 4-7-003:001.* Wailuku, HI: Cultural Surveys Hawaiʻi, Inc., 2010. [SHPD ID: 2019LI81539]

McCurdy, Todd D. and Hallett H. Hammatt. *Archaeological Inventory Survey Documentation of Inadvertent Finds Identified during the Honoapiʻilani Highway Realignment (Lahaina Bypass) Phase 1B-1, Paunau Ahupuaʻa to Polanui Ahupuaʻa, Lahaina District, Maui Island TMK: (2) 4-6-014:001, 002; (2) 4-6-018:002, 003; (2) 4-8-001:002 and (2) 4-7-003:001.* Wailuku, HI: Cultural Surveys Hawaiʻi, Inc., 2009. [SHPD ID: 2019LI81536]

McCurdy, Todd D. and Hallett H. Hammatt. *Archaeological Literature Review and Field Inspection for Honoapiʻilani Highway Realignment (Lahaina Bypass), Phase 1B-1, Paunau Ahupuaʻa to Polanui Ahupuaʻa, Lahaina District, Maui Island TMK (2) 4-6-014:001-002, 4-6-018:002-003, 4-8-001:002 and 4-7-003:001.* Wailuku, HI: Cultural Surveys Hawaiʻi, Inc., 2008. [SHPD ID: 2019LI81538]

Rosendahl, Paul H. *Archaeological Treatment Plan for No Adverse Effect, Lahaina Bypass Highway Project, Lands of Honokōwai, Hanakaʻōʻō, Wahikuli, Panaʻewa, Kuʻia, Halakaʻa, Pūehuehu Nui, Pāhoa, Polanui, and Launiupoko, Lahaina District, Island of Maui.* Hilo, HI: Paul H. Rosendahl, Ph.D., Inc., 1994. [SHPD ID: 2019LI81439]

Hanakaʻōʻō

Bulgrin, Lon E. and Robert B. Rechtman. *An Archaeological Assessment Survey of TMK (2) 4-4-08:016 Hanakaʻōʻō Ahupuaʻa, Lahaina District, Island of Maui.* Rechtman Consulting, LLC, 2005.

Chaffee, David B. and Michael F. Dega. *An Archaeological Monitoring Plan Covering Three Parcels at the Hyatt Regency Maui Resort Kāʻanapali, Hanakaʻōʻō Ahupuaʻa, Lahaina District, Maui Island, Hawaiʻi [TMK (2) 4-4-13:005, 008, 004].* Honolulu, HI: Scientific Consultant Services, Inc., 2014.

Chaffee, David B. and Michael F. Dega. *An Archaeological Monitoring Plan for Kāʻanapali Beach Hotel Beach Front, Restaurant/Canoe Hale, Hanakaʻōʻō Ahupuaʻa, Lahaina District, Island of Maui, Hawaiʻi.* Honolulu, HI: Scientific Consultant Services, Inc., 2014.

Chaffee, David B. and Michael F. Dega. *An Archaeological Monitoring Plan for the Maui Countywide Wastewater Pump Station Renovations, Phase II Project at Multiple Locations, Hanakaʻōʻō Ahupuaʻa and Mākila Ahupuaʻa, Lahaina District, Maui Island, Hawaiʻi [TMK: (2) 4-4-013:003, por. and 4-6-028:054].* Honolulu, HI: Scientific Consultant Services, Inc., 2014.

Ching, Francis K. W. *Archaeological Assessment of the Property on Which the Proposed Marriott Kāʻanapali Hotel is to be Built, Kāʻanapali, Maui Island.* Lāwaʻi, HI: Archaeological Research Center Hawaiʻi, 1979. [SHPD ID: 2019LI81267]

Cordle, Shayna and Michael F. Dega. *An Archaeological Monitoring Report on Approximately 0.448-Acres for the Maui Marriott Vacation Club, Hanakaʻōʻō Ahupuaʻa, Lahaina District, Island of Maui, Hawaiʻi [TMK (2) 4-4-13:001].* Honolulu, HI: Scientific Consultant Services, Inc., 2007. [SHPD ID: 2019LI80029]

Dagher, Cathleen A. and Michael F. Dega. *An Archaeological Assessment of the Kāʻanapali Beach Hotel Beach Front Restaurant/Canoe Hale, Hanakaʻōʻō Ahupuaʻa, Lahaina District, Island of Maui, Hawaiʻi [TMK: (2) 4-4-08:003].* Honolulu, HI: Scientific Consultant Services, Inc., 2014. [SHPD ID: 2019LI81259]

Dega, Michael F. *An Archaeological Inventory Survey Plan for Kāʻanapali Beach Hotel Beach Front Restaurant/Canoe Hale, Hanakaʻōʻō Ahupuaʻa, Lahaina District, Island of Maui, Hawaiʻi [TMK: (2) 4-4-008:003 por.].* Honolulu, HI: Scientific Consultant Services, Inc., 2013. [SHPD ID: 2019LI80674]

Dega, Michael F. *Archaeological Monitoring Plan for the Maui Marriott Vacation Club, in the Ahupuaʻa of Hanakaʻōʻō, Lahaina District, Island of Maui, Hawaiʻi [TMK: (2) 4-4-13:001].* Honolulu, HI: Scientific Consultant Services, Inc., 2005. [SHPD ID: 2019LI80663]

Dobyns, Susan and Jane Allen-Wheeler. *Archaeological Monitoring at the Site of the Kāʻanapali Aliʻi Condominium, Island of Maui.* Honolulu, HI: Department of Anthropology, Bernice P. Bishop Museum, 1982. [SHPD ID: 2019LI80673]

Fredericksen, Demaris. *Monitoring Report for the Sheraton-Maui Redevelopment Project, Hanakaʻōʻō Ahupuaʻa, Lahaina District, Maui Island.* Pukalani, HI: Xamanek Researches, 1998. [SHPD ID: 2019LI81263]

Fredericksen, Demaris L. *Monitoring Report for the Sheraton-Maui Redevelopment Project Hanaka'ō'ō Ahupua'a, Lahaina District, Maui Island [TMK: (2) 4-4-08:005].* Pukalani, HI: Xamanek Researches, 1998. [SHPD ID: 2019LI81263]

Fredericksen, Demaris L. and Walter M. Fredericksen. *Archaeological Monitoring Plan for the Sheraton-Maui Redevelopment Project, Ahupua'a of Hanaka'ō'ō, Lahaina District, Maui Island.* Pukalani, HI: Xamanek Researches, 1995. [SHPD ID: 2019LI80672]

Fredericksen, Erik M. *A Preservation Plan for the Sites Contained within Kā'anapali Coffee Estates Subdivision (aka Pioneer Farms Subdivision 1) Project Area, Hanaka'ō'ō Ahupua'a, Lahaina District, Island of Maui.* Pukalani, HI: Xamanek Researches, 2005. [SHPD ID: 2019LI81274]

Fredericksen, Erik M. *An Archaeological Assessment Survey of a c. 5 Acre Portion of Land for the Proposed Temporary Off-Site Parking Project, Hanaka'ō'ō/Honokōwai Ahupua'a, Lahaina District, Maui Island [TMK: (2) 4-4-002: 003].* Pukalani, HI: Xamanek Researches, 2007. [No location available]

Fredericksen, Erik M. *An Archaeological Monitoring Plan for the Proposed Kā'anapali Loop Road Project, Hanaka'ō'ō Ahupua'a, Lahaina District, Island of Maui.* Pukalani, HI: Xamanek Researches, 2004. [SHPD ID: 2019LI81268]

Fredericksen, Erik M. *An Archaeological Monitoring Report for Offsite Parking for the Lot 3 Temporary Parking Project, Kā'anapali, Hanaka'ō'ō Ahupua'a Lahaina District, Island of Maui.* Pukalani, HI: Xamanek Researches, 2006. [SHPD ID: 2019LI80660]

Fredericksen, Walter M. and Demaris Fredericksen. *Archaeological Monitoring Report for The Kai Ala Subdivision, Ahupua'a of Hanakao'o, Lahaina District, Island of Maui.* Pukalani, HI: Xamanek Researches, 1996. [SHPD ID: 2019LI81251]

Frey, Jennifer J., Josephine M. Yucha, and Hallett H. Hammatt. *Archaeological Monitoring Report for the Westin Maui Resort & Spa Master Plan Improvements Project, Parking Garage, Lobby, and Porte Cochere Driveway, Hanaka'ō'ō Ahupua'a, Lahaina District, Island of Maui, TMK (2) 4-4-008:019.* Wailuku, HI: Cultural Surveys Hawai'i, Inc., 2019. [SHPD ID: 2019LI80683]

Graves, Donna and Susan Goodfellow. *Archaeological Inventory Survey, Launiupoko Golf Course, Land of Launiupoko, Lahaina District, Island of Maui.* Hilo, HI: Paul H. Rosendahl, Ph.D., Inc., 1991. [SHPD ID: 2019LI81595, 2019LI81610]

Guerriero, Diane, Lisa Rotunno-Hazuka, and Jeffrey Pantaleo. *Archaeological Assessment for the Royal Lahaina Resort Redevelopment Hanaka'ō'ō Ahupua'a, Lahaina District, Island of Maui.* Wailuku, HI: Archaeological Services Hawaii, LLC, 2005. [SHPD ID: 2019LI81261]

Hammatt, Hallett H. *Archaeological Reconnaissance at the Proposed Hyatt Regency Site, Hanaka'ō'ō, Kā'anapali, Maui Island, Tax Map Key; 4-4-06:31 Lot 60, ARCH 14-129.* Lāwa'i, HI: Archaeological Research Center Hawai'i, 1978. [SHPD ID: 2019LI81264; UH Call Number: GN486 .H35]

Hoerman, Rachel and Michael F. Dega. *An Archaeological Monitoring Plan for the Pavilion Restaurant Renovation at the Hyatt Regency Maui Resort and Spa, Kā'anapali, Hanaka'ō'ō Ahupua'a, Lahaina District, Maui Island, Hawai'i.* Honolulu, HI: Scientific Consultant Services, Inc., 2007. [SHPD ID: 2019LI80666, 2019LI80665]

Hommon, Robert J. *An Archaeological Reconnaissance Survey of the North Beach Mauka and South Beach Beach Mauka Areas, Hanaka'ō'ō, West Maui.* Hawai'i: Science Management, Inc., 1982. [No location available]

Jensen, Peter M. *Archaeological Inventory Survey Honoapi'ilani Highway Realignment Project Lahaina Bypass Section—Modified Corridor Alignment, Lands of Honokōwai, Hanaka'ō'ō, Wahikuli, Pana'ewa, Ku'ia, Halaka'a, Pūehuehu Nui, Pāhoa, Polanui, and Launiupoko, Lahaina District, Island of Maui.* Hilo, HI: Paul H. Rosendahl, Ph.D., Inc., 1991. [SHPD ID: 2019LI81242]

Jensen, Peter M. *Archaeological Inventory Survey Lahaina Bypass Highway New Connector Roads Project Area, Ahupua'a of Hanaka'ō'ō and Paunau, Lahaina District, Island of Maui.* Hilo, HI: Paul H. Rosendahl, Ph.D., Inc., 1994. [SHPD ID: 2019LI81611]

Jensen, Peter M. *Archaeological Inventory Survey South Beach Mauka Development Site, Ahupua'a of Hanaka'ō'ō, Lahaina District, Island of Maui.* Hilo, HI: Paul H. Rosendahl, Ph.D., Inc., 1990. [SHPD ID: 2019LI81262; UH Call Number: DU628.M3 J46 1990]

Jensen, Peter M. and G. Mehalchick. *Archaeological Inventory Survey North Beach Mauka (Kā'anapali) Site, Ahupua'a of Hanaka'ō'ō, Lahaina District, Island of Maui.* Hilo, HI: Paul H. Rosendahl, Ph.D., Inc., 1993. [UH Call Number: DU628.M3 J46 1989]

Jensen, Peter M. and Gemma Mahalchick. *Archaeological Inventory Survey, The Pu'ukoli'i Village Project Area, Ahupua'a of Hanaka'ō'ō, Lahaina District, Island of Maui.* Hilo, HI: Paul H. Rosendahl, Ph.D., Inc., 1992. [SHPD ID: 2019LI81252]

Keau, Charles. *Archaeological Reconnaissance (Surface Survey) for Hanakaʻōʻō (Hahakea) Beach Park. Includes cover letter: An Archaeological Reconnaissance of Hahakea Beach Park, Hanakaʻōʻō, Maui. TMK: 4-4-06:33 by Earl Neller.* State Historic Preservation Office, March 1982. [SHPD ID: 2019LI81272; UH Call Number: DU629.H364 K43 1981]

Kehajit, Chonnikarn and Michael F. Dega. *Archaeological Assessment for shoreline mitigation at the Hyatt Regency Maui Resort, Hanakaʻōʻō Ahupuaʻa, Lahaina District, Island of Maui, Hawaiʻi.* Honolulu, HI: Scientific Consultant Services, Inc., 2018. [No location available]

Lee-Greig, Tanya L. and Hallett H. Hammatt. *An Archaeological Inventory Level Documentation for an Inadvertent Historic Property Discovery Identified During Pre-Construction Walk Through for the Lahaina Bypass Phase IA, Project: State Inventory of Historic properties 50-50-03-6277 (Lee-Greig et al. 2008).* Wailuku, HI: Cultural Surveys Hawaiʻi, Inc., 2009. [No location available]

Lee-Greig, Tanya L. and Hallett H. Hammatt. *An Archaeological Monitoring Plan for Whalers Village Renovation and Expansion Project, Hanakaʻōʻō Ahupuaʻa, Lahaina District, Maui Island.* Wailuku, HI: Cultural Surveys Hawaiʻi, Inc., 2014. [SHPD ID: 2019LI80675]

Lee-Greig, Tanya L. and Hallett H. Hammatt. *Archaeological Assessment for the Proposed Westin Maui Resort & Spa Master Plan Improvements, Hanakaʻōʻō Ahupuaʻa, Lahaina District, Island of Maui, TMK (2) 4-4-008:019.* Wailuku, HI: Cultural Surveys Hawaiʻi, Inc., 2014. [SHPD ID: 2019LI80684]

Lee-Greig, Tanya L. and Hallett H. Hammatt. *Archaeological Monitoring Plan for the Honoapiʻilani Highway Safety Improvements at Kāʻanapali Parkway and Halelo Street Hanakaʻōʻō Ahupuaʻa, Lahaina District, Maui Island [TMK (2) 4-4-006:999 por; 4-4-009:036 por.).* Wailuku, HI: Cultural Surveys Hawaiʻi, Inc., 2014. [SHPD ID: 2019LI81271]

Lyman, Kepa and Michael F. *Dega. Archaeological Monitoring Plan for the Hanakaʻōʻō Beach Park Parking Improvements, Hanakaʻōʻō Ahupuaʻa, Lahaina (Kāʻanapali) District, Island of Maui.* Honolulu, HI: Scientific Consultant Services, Inc., 2020. [SHPD ID: 2021LI00062]

McGerty, Leann and Robert L. Spear. *A Cultural Impact Assessment for Maui Marriott Ocean Club, Situated in the Ahupuaʻa of Hanakaʻōʻō, Lahaina District, Island of Maui, Hawaiʻi.* Honolulu, HI: Scientific Consultant Services, Inc., 2002. [SHPD ID: 2019LI80664]

McGerty, Leann and Robert L. Spear. *A Cultural Impact Assessment on a Piece of Property Located in Kāʻanapali, Hanakaʻōʻō Ahupuaʻa, Lahaina District, Maui*

Island, Hawaiʻi [TMK: (2) 4-4-06:056]. Scientific Consultant Services, Inc.: Honolulu, HI, 2003. [SHPD ID: 2019LI81266]

McGerty, Leann and Robert L. Spear. *An Archaeological Inventory Survey at the Maui Marriott Ocean Club, in the Ahupuaʻa of Hanakaʻōʻō, Lahaina District, Island of Maui, Hawaiʻi.* Honolulu, HI: Scientific Consultant Services, Inc., 2002. [SHPD ID: 2019LI80107]

McGerty, Leann and Robert L. Spear. *Cultural Impact Assessment on Two Parcels Incorporating the Royal Lahaina Hotel in Kāʻanapali, Hanakaʻōʻō Ahupuaʻa, Lahaina District, Maui Island, Hawaiʻi.* Honolulu, HI: Scientific Consultant Services, Inc., 2005. [SHPD ID: 2019LI80678]

Morawski, Lauren and Michael F. Dega. *Archaeological Inventory Survey of a 7.65 Acre Property at Lot 10-H Ahupuaʻa of Hanakaʻōʻō, Lahaina District, Island of Maui, Hawaiʻi [TMK: (2) 4-4-06:056].* Honolulu, HI: Scientific Consultant Services, Inc., 2003. [SHPD ID: 2019LI81273]

Neller, Earl. *An Archaeological Reconnaissance of Hahakea Beach Park, Hanakaʻōʻō, Maui.* Honolulu, HI: State of Hawaiʻi Preservation Office, 1982. [SHPD ID: 2019LI81272; UH Call Number: DU629.H364 N45 1982]

Pacheco, Robert. *A Cultural Impact Assessment for the Proposed Kāʻanapali Beach Restoration Project, Hanakaʻōʻō Ahupuaʻa, Lahaina District, Island of Maui, Hawaiʻi TMK (2) 4-4-008:001, 002, 003, 004, 005, 019, 022; 4-4-013:001, 002, 006, 007, 008.* Honolulu, HI: International Archaeology, LLC, 2006. [SHPD ID: 2019LI80681]

Pacheco, Robert. *An Archaeological Literature Review for the Proposed Kāʻanapali Beach Restoration Project, Hanakaʻōʻō Ahupuaʻa, Lahaina District, Island of Maui, Hawaiʻi TMK (2) 4-4-008:001, 002, 003, 004, 005, 019, 022; 4-4-013:001, 002, 006, 007, 008.* Honolulu, HI: International Archaeology, LLC, 2015. [SHPD ID: 2019LI81260]

Paraso, C. Kanani and Michael F. Dega. *An Archaeological Inventory Survey of 633 Acres in the Launiupoko (Large Lot) Subdivision Nos. 3, 4, and 7, Launiupoko and Polanui Ahupuaʻa, Lahaina District (formerly Kāʻanapali), Island of Maui, Hawaiʻi [TMK (2) 4-8-01:2 por.].* Honolulu, HI: Scientific Consultant Services, Inc., 2006. [SHPD ID: 2019LI81600]

Perzinski, David and Michael F. Dega. *An Archaeological Monitoring Report of the Construction at the Maui Marriott Vacation Club, Hanakaʻōʻō Ahupuaʻa, Lahaina District, Island of Maui, Hawaiʻi.* Honolulu, HI: Scientific Consultant Services, Inc., 2009. [No location available]

Perzinski, David and Michael F. Dega. *Archaeological Monitoring Report for Lahaina No. 3 Force Main Replacement Project Wahikuli and Hanakaʻōʻō Ahupuaʻa, Lahaina District, Island of Maui, Hawaiʻi [TMK (2) 4-4-013].* Honolulu, HI: Scientific Consultant Services, Inc., 2014. [SHPD ID: 2019LI80661]

Rechtman, Robert B. *Archaeological Monitoring Plan for the Subdivision and Development for the Subdivision and Development of TMK: (2) 4-4-08:016.* Rechtman Consulting, LLC, 2006. [SHPD ID: 2019LI80679]

Rogers, Scott. *An Archaeological Monitoring Plan for the Kāʻanapali—Hyatt Force Main Replacements, Kāʻanapali Resort Complex, Hanakaʻōʻō, Honokōwai Ahupuaʻa, Lahaina District, Island of Maui.* Pukalani, HI: Xamanek Researches, 2007. [SHPD ID: 2019LI80682]

Rosendahl, Margaret L. K. *Archaeological Field Inspection, Sheraton Maui Master Plan Project Area, Lands of Honokōwai and Hanakaʻōʻō, Lahaina District, Island of Maui.* Hilo, HI: Paul H. Rosendahl, Ph.D., Inc., 1986. [No location available]

Rosendahl, Margaret L. K. *Subsurface Archaeological Reconnaissance Survey, North Beach Development Site, Ahupuaʻa of Hanakaʻōʻō, Lahaina Eistrict, Island of Maui.* Hilo, HI: Paul H. Rosendahl, Ph.D., Inc., 1987. [SHPD ID: 2019LI81244]

Rosendahl, Paul H. *A Plan for Archaeological Monitoring of Shoreline Construction, Kāʻanapali North Beach Development Site, Ahupuaʻa of Hanakaʻōʻō, Lahaina District, Island of Maui.* Hilo, HI: Paul H. Rosendahl, Ph.D., Inc., 1987. [SHPD ID: 2019LI80659]

Rosendahl, Paul H. *Archaeological Treatment Plan for No Adverse Effect, Lahaina Bypass Highway Project, Lands of Honokōwai, Hanakaʻōʻō, Wahikuli, Panaʻewa, Kuʻia, Halakaʻa, Pūehuehu Nui, Pāhoa, Polanui, and Launiupoko, Lahaina District, Island of Maui.* Hilo, HI: Paul H. Rosendahl, Ph.D., Inc., 1994. [SHPD ID: 2019LI81439]

Rotunno-Hazuka, Lisa J. and Jeffrey Pantaleo. *Archaeological Monitoring Plan for All Improvements Related to the Redevelopment of the Royal Lahaina Resort, Hanakaʻōʻō Ahupuaʻa; Lahaina District, Island of Maui, TMK:4-4-08:007& 013.* Wailuku, HI: Archaeological Services Hawaii, LLC, 2007. [SHPD ID: 2019LI80677]

Six, Janet L. *Archaeological Monitoring Plan for Deck and Bar Repairs for: Leilaniʻs on the Beach, Whalers Village Shopping Center, Building J 2435 Kāʻanapali Parkway, Hanakaʻōʻō Ahupuaʻa, Lahaina District, Maui Island.* Pāhoa, HI: Sixth Sense Archaeological Consultants, LLC, 2011. [SHPD ID: 2019LI80676]

Weisler, M. *Field Inspection of Hanakaʻōʻō Construction Site, Maui.* Honolulu, HI: Department of Anthropology, Bernice P. Bishop Museum, 1983. [No location available]

Wong, Charmaine and Michael F. Dega. *An Archaeological Assessment for the West Maui Hospital and Medical Center, Hanakaʻōʻō Ahupuaʻa, Lahaina (Kāʻanapali) district, Maui Island, Hawaiʻi [TMK: (2) 4-4-02:052].* Honolulu, HI: Scientific Consultant Services, Inc., 2014. [SHPD ID: 2019LI81245]

Wong, Charmaine and Michael F. Dega. *An Archaeological Assessment for the West Maui Hospital and Medical Center, Hanakaʻōʻō Ahupuaʻa, Lahaina (Kāʻanapali) District, Maui Island, Hawaiʻi, TMK: (2) 4-4-02:052.* Honolulu, HI: Scientific Consultant Services, Inc., 2008. [No location available]

Yates and Hallett H. Hammatt. *Archaeological Monitoring Plan for the Kāʻanapali 2020 Master Plan, Kāʻanapali Coffee Farms Subdivision Phase II Project, Hanakaʻōʻō and Honokōwai Ahupuaʻa, Lahaina District, Maui Island, TMK (2) 4-4-02:002.* Wailuku, HI: Cultural Surveys Hawaiʻi, Inc., 2020. [SHPD ID: 2021LI00326, 2022LI00365]

Yucha, Josephine M. and Hallett H. Hammatt. *Archaeological Monitoring Plan for the Puʻukoliʻi Village Mauka Project, Hanakaʻōʻō Ahupuaʻa, Lahaina District, Maui Island, TMKs: (2) 4-4-02:002, 048, and 053 por., (2) 4-4-06:070, 086 and 087 por., and (2) 4-4-15:034 through 072. 24:026 (por.).* Wailuku, HI: Cultural Surveys Hawaiʻi, Inc., 2023. [SHPD ID: 2023LI00111]

Yucha, Josephine M. and Hallett H. Hammatt. *Archaeological Monitoring Plan for the Sheraton Maui Resort & Spa Sewer Improvements Project, Hanakaʻōʻō Ahupuaʻa, Lahaina District, Maui Island, TMKs: (2) 4-4-08:005 and 011 (pors).* Wailuku, HI: Cultural Surveys Hawaiʻi, Inc., 2018. [SHPD ID: 2019LI80670]

Yucha, Josephine M. and Hallett H. Hammatt. *Archaeological Monitoring Report for the Sheraton Maui Sewer Improvements Project, Hanakaʻōʻō Ahupuaʻa, Lahaina District, Maui Island, TMKs: (2) 4-4-008:005 and 011 (pors.).* Wailuku, HI: Cultural Surveys Hawaiʻi, Inc., 2018. [SHPD ID: 2019LI81258]

Yucha, Josephine M. et al. *Archaeological Inventory Survey for the Puʻukoliʻi Village Mauka Project, Hanakaʻōʻō Ahupuaʻa, Lahaina District, Maui Island, TMKs: (2) 4-4-02:002, 048, and 053 por., (2) 4-4-06:070, 086 and 087 por., and (2) 4-4-15:034 through 072.* Wailuku, HI: Cultural Surveys Hawaiʻi, Inc., 2022. [SHPD ID: 2023LI00110]

Yucha, Josephine M., Jennifer Frey, and Hallett H. Hammatt. *Burial Site Component of an Archaeological Data Recovery Plan for SIHP # 50-50-03-8842 at the Westin Maui Resort & Spa Improvements Project, Phase III, Hanakaʻōʻō Ahupuaʻa,*

Lahaina District, Maui, TMK: (2) 4-4-08:019. Wailuku, HI: Cultural Surveys Hawaiʻi, Inc., 2021. [SHPD ID: 2021LI00104]

Yucha, Trevor M. and Hallett H. Hammatt. *Archaeological Monitoring Plan for the Westin Maui Resort & Spa Master Plan Improvements, Hanakaʻōʻō Ahupuaʻa, Lahaina District, Island of Maui, TMK (2) 4-4-08:019.* Wailuku, HI: Cultural Surveys Hawaiʻi, Inc., 2018. [SHPD ID: 2019LI80683]

HAWEA

Kennedy, Joseph. *Hawea Point Residential Project: Archaeological Review, Survey, and Assessments.* Haleʻiwa, HI: Archaeological Consultants of Hawaii, 1990. [SHPD ID: 2019LI81416]

Ladd, Edmund J. *Archaeological Survey Report,* 1980. [No location available]

Rosendahl, Paul H. *Archaeological Field Inspection Hawea Point Residence Site; Hawea Point, Lands of Napili 2 & 3 Lahaina District, Island of Maui.* Hilo, HI: Paul H. Rosendahl, Ph.D., Inc., 1988. [SHPD ID: 2019LI81001]

HONOKAHUA

Athens, J. Stephen. *Archaeological Reconnaissance at Honokahua Well B, Lahaina District, West Maui,* 1985.

Dagan, Colleen P. M. and Hallett H. Hammatt. *Archaeological Preservation Plan for SIHP 50-50-01-5672C and 50-50-01-5673H.* Wailuku, HI: Cultural Surveys Hawaiʻi, Inc., 2008. [SHPD ID: 2019LI81026]

Dagher, Cathleen A. and Michael F. Dega. *A Preservation Plan for Multiple Archaeological Sites Located in the Kapalua Coastal Trail Corridor in the areas of Nāpili, Kapalua, Honokahua, and Honolua, Ahupuaʻa of Nāpili 2 & 3, Honokahua, and Honolua, Lahaina District, Island of Maui, Hawaiʻi.* Scientific Consultant Services, Inc.: Honolulu, HI, 2008. [SHPD ID: 2019LI79694]

Dagher, Cathleen A. and Michael F. Dega. *An Archaeological Monitoring Plan for the Napili No. 5 & 6 WWPS Force Main Replacement Honokahua Ahupuaʻa, Lahaina (Kāʻanapali) District, Island of Maui, Hawaiʻi [TMK (2) 4-2-04: portion of 48 (Lot 3-A-1 of Kapalua Makai Subdivision No. 4) and TMK (2) 4-2-04: portion of 59 (Lot A-1-A-2 of Kapalua Development (Large-Lot) Subdivision).* Honolulu, HI: Scientific Consultant Services, Inc., 2015. [SHPD ID: 2019LI81016]

Dagher, Cathleen A. and Michael F. Dega. *An Archaeological Monitoring Plan for the Proposed Kapalua Coastal Trail Located in the Areas of Nāpili, Kapalua,*

Honokahua, and Honolua, Ahupuaʻa of Nāpili 2 & 3, Honokahua, and Honolua, Lahaina district, Island of Maui, Hawaiʻi. Honolulu, HI: Scientific Consultant Services, Inc., 2008. [SHPD ID: 2019LI81410]

Dega, Michael F. *An Archaeological Monitoring Plan for Improvements at D. T. Fleming Beach Park for the County of Maui, Department of Parks and Recreation, Honokahua Ahupuaʻa [sic], Lahaina District, Island of Maui, Hawaiʻi.* Honolulu, HI: Scientific Consultant Services, Inc., 2015. [SHPD ID: 2019LI81042]

Devereux, Thomas K., William H. Folk, and Hallett H. Hammatt. *Archaeological Survey of the Lands Comprising Project District 2 at Kapalua, Honokahua, and Nāpili 2 & 3 Ahupuaʻa Lahaina District of Maui.* Wailuku, HI: Cultural Surveys Hawaiʻi, Inc., 2001. [SHPD ID: 2019LI81007]

Donham, Theresa K. *Addendum Report: Additional Subsurface Testing of Area III, Subsurface Archaeological Testing, Revised Ritz-Carlton Kapalua Hotel Project Site, Areas I, II, and III, Land of Honokahua, Lahaina District, Island of Maui.* Hilo, HI: Paul H. Rosendahl, Ph.D., Inc., 1989. [SHPD ID: 2019LI81414]

Donham, Theresa K. *Archaeological Survey Test Excavations Kapalua Hotel Development Site 2-H, Kapalua Bay Resort, Land of Honokahua, Lahaina, Island of Maui.* Hilo, HI: Paul H. Rosendahl, Ph.D., Inc., 1986. [2019LI80998]

Donham, Theresa K. *Interim Report: Kapalua Mitigation Program Data Recovery Excavations at the Honokahua Burial Site, Land of Honokahua, Lahaina District, Island of Maui.* Hilo, HI: Paul H. Rosendahl, Ph.D., Inc., 1989. [SHPD ID: 2019LI81417]

Ferguson, Lee, Arne Carlson, and Berdena Burgett. *Subsurface Archaeological Testing, Revised Ritz-Carlton Kapalua Hotel Project Site, Areas I, II and III.* Hilo, HI: Paul H. Rosendahl, Ph.D., Inc., 1989. [SHPD ID: 2019LI81006]

Fredericksen, Erik M. *A Preliminary Report Summarizing Results of Field Research for an Archaeological Inventory Survey to Satisfy Requirements of SHPD at [TMK: (2) 4-2-04:por. 024] located in Honokahua Ahupuaʻa, Lahaina District, Island of Maui, Hawaiʻi.* Pukalani, HI: Xamanek Researches, 2003.

Fredericksen, Erik M. *Archaeological Monitoring Plan for Lot 29 (Site 29) Honokahua and Napili 2-3 Ahupuaʻa, Lahaina District, Maui, Hawaiʻi.* Pukalani, HI: Xamanek Researches, 1999. [SHPD ID: 2019LI81028]

Fredericksen, Erik M. *Archaeological Monitoring Report for the Coconut Grove Development (Site 29), Honokahua and Napili 2-3 Ahupuaʻa Lahiana District, Island of Maui.* Pukalani, HI: Xamanek Researches, 2001. [SHPD ID: 2019LI17106]

Fredericksen, Erik M. *Archaeological Monitoring Report for the Verizon Hawaii, Inc. Equipment Installation project at TMK: (2) 4-2-04:021 Ritz-Carlton, Kapalua, Honokahua Ahupuaʻa, Lahaina District, Maui, Hawaiʻi.* Pukalani, HI: Xamanek Researches, 2001. [SHPD ID: 2019LI81014, 2019LI81029]

Fredericksen, Erik M. *Preservation Plan for Possible Burial Features Contained Within Sites 50-50-01-5139, 5142, 5157 and 5158 Located on the Kapalua Mauka Project area, Honokahua and Napili 2 & 3 Ahupuaʻa, Lahaina District, Island of Maui.* Pukalani, HI: Xamanek Researches, 2003. [SHPD ID: 2019LI81407]

Fredericksen, Erik M. and Demaris L. Fredericksen. *An Archaeological Inventory Survey of Honoapiʻilani Highway Corridor from Alaelae Point to Honolua Bay, Honolua and Honokahua Ahupuaʻa, Lahaina District, Maui Island.* Pukalani, HI: Xamanek Researches, 2000. [SHPD ID: 2019LI81045]

Fredericksen, Erik M. and Demaris L. Fredericksen. *Archaeological Inventory Survey of 475 Acres in Kapalua District 2 Project Area, Located in Napili and Honokahua Ahupuaʻa, Lahaina District, Maui Island, TMK: (2) 4-2-01: por. 1.* Pukalani, HI: Xamanek Researches, 2002. [SHPD ID: 2021LI00311]

Fredericksen, Erik M., Demaris L. Fredericksen, and Walter M. Fredericksen. *An Archaeological Inventory Survey of a 12.2 Acre Parcel. Honokahua and Napili 2-3 Ahupuaʻa, Lahaina District Maui Island.* Pukalani, HI: Xamanek Researches, 1994. [SHPD ID: 2019LI81030]

Fredericksen, Erik M., Walter M. Fredericksen, and Demaris L. Fredericksen. *Additional Archaeological Inventory Survey Subsurface testing at Kapalua Bay Hotel [TMK (2) 4-2-04:26], Honokahua and Napili 2-3 Ahupuaʻa, Lahaina District, Maui Island.* Pukalani, HI: Xamanek Researches, 1996. [SHPD ID: 2019LI81024]

Guerriero, Diane A., Charvet-Pond, and S. Goodfellow. *Archaeological Monitoring and Data Recovery, Kapalua Ritz-Carlton Hotel Site, Land of Honokahua, Lahaina District, Island of Maui [TMK: (2) 4-2-01:004, 005, por. 012, 013, por. 018, 034].* Hilo, HI: Paul H. Rosendahl, Ph.D., Inc., 1993. [No location available]

Haun, Alan E. and Jack D. Henry. *Archaeological Data Recovery Plan Sites 4141 and 4143, Land of Honolua, Lahaina District, Island of Maui,* 2002. [SHPD ID: 2019LI81010]

Lee-Greig, Tanya L. and Hallett H. Hammatt. *Preservation Plan for Thirty-Three Historic Properties Located in and Adjacent to the Kapalua Mauka Project Area, Honokahua, Nāpili 2 & 3, and Nāpili 4-5 Ahupuaʻa, Lahaina District, Maui Island.* Wailuku, HI: Cultural Surveys Hawaiʻi, Inc., 2005. [SHPD ID: 2019LI80997]

Morawski, Lauren and Michael F. Dega. *Archaeological Inventory Survey Report of an Approximate 10-Acre Parcel in Kapalua in the Ahupuaʻa of Honokahua, Lahaina District (Formerly Kāʻanapali), Island of Maui, Hawaiʻi.* Honolulu, HI: Scientific Consultant Services, Inc., 2004. [SHPD ID: 2019LI81017]

Munekiyo & Hiraga, Inc. *Makaʻoiʻoi (Honolua Plantation Managers Residence, Pineapple Hill Restaurant), Historical Report.* Wailuku, HI: Munekiyo & Hiraga, Inc., 2003. [SHPD ID: 2019LI81022]

OʻClaray, Jenny. *Additional Field Work for Drainage 11 Kapalua Plantation Estates Project Area, Lands of Honokahua, Honolua, Napili 2-2 Lahaina District, Island of Maui.* Hilo, HI: Paul H. Rosendahl, Ph.D., Inc., 1991. [SHPD ID: 2019LI81415]

OʻHare, Constance, Thomas K. Devereux, William H. Folk, and Hallett H. Hammatt. *Preservation Plan for Specific Sites in the Land Comprising Project District 2 at Kapalua, Honokahua and Nāpili 2 & 3 Ahupuaʻa Lahaina District of Maui.* Wailuku, HI: Cultural Surveys Hawaiʻi, Inc., 2003. [SHPD ID: 2019LI81002]

Perzinski, David and Michael F. Dega. *An Archaeological Monitoring Report for the Installation of Subsurface Utilities in Nāpili, Kapalua, Honokahua Ahupuaʻa, Lahaina District, Island of Maui, Hawaiʻi.* Honolulu, HI: Scientific Consultant Services, Inc., 2015. [SHPD ID: 2019LI81034]

Pietrusewsky, Michael, Michele T. Douglas, Patricia A. Kalima, and Rona M. Ikehara. *Human Skeletal and Dental Remains from the Honokahua Burial Site, Land of Honokahua, Lahaina District, Island of Maui, Hawaiʻi.* Hilo, HI: Paul H. Rosendahl, Ph.D., Inc., 1991. [Call Number, DU629.H67 H86 1991a]

Rosendahl, Paul H. *Additional Inventory Survey for Drainage Easement 11 Kapalua Plantation Estates Project Area, Lands of Honokahua, Honolua, and Napili 2-3, Lahaina District, Island of Maui.* Hilo, HI: Paul H. Rosendahl, Ph.D., Inc., 1991. [SHPD ID: 2019LI80996]

Rosendahl, Paul H. *Archaeological Reconnaissance Survey, The Cottages Project Area Kapalua Development Site 2-A, Lands of Honokahua and Napili 2 & 3, Lahaina District, Island of Maui.* Hilo, HI: Paul H. Rosendahl, Ph.D., Inc., 1988. [SHPD ID: 2019LI81009]

Rosendahl, Paul H. *Phase I Monitoring Plan: Archaeological Mitigation Program, Ritz-Carlton Hotel Project Site, Land of Honokahua, Lahaina District, Island of Maui. PHRI Memo 857-070390.* Hilo, HI: Paul H. Rosendahl, Ph.D., Inc., 1990. [No location available]

Rosendahl, Paul H. *PHRI Status Reports on Honokahua.* Hilo, HI: Paul H. Rosendahl, Ph.D., Inc., 1987. [SHPD ID: 2019LI81004]

Rosendahl, Paul H. *Subsurface Reconnaissance Testing, Kapalua Place Project Area, Kapalua Development Site 2-A, Lands of Honokahua and Napili 2 & 3, Lahaina District, Island of Maui.* Hilo, HI: Paul H. Rosendahl, Ph.D., Inc., 1988. [SHPD ID: 2019LI81000]

Scientific Consultant Services, Inc. *An Archaeological Inventory Survey for Six Proposed Solar Voltaic Cell Sites Located in the Ahupuaʻa of Honokahua, Honokeana, and Honokōwai, Lahaina (Kāʻanapali) District, Island of Maui, Hawaiʻi.* Honolulu, HI: Scientific Consultant Services, Inc., 2012. [SHPD ID: 2019LI81005]

Spriggs, Matthew. *Trip Report: Makaluapuna Point, Honokahua, Lahaina District, Maui, 1989.* [SHPD ID: 2019LI81413; UH Call Number: DU629.M356 S67 1989]

Tome, Guerin and Michael F. Dega. *An Archaeological Inventory Survey for the Proposed Kapalua Coastal Trail Located in the Areas of Kapalua and Honokāhau, Honokahua and Nāpili 2 & 3.* Honolulu, HI: Scientific Consultant Services, Inc., 2007. [SHPD ID: 2019LI81433]

Tome, Guerin and Michael F. Dega. *An Archaeological Monitoring Plan for the Proposed Kapalua Coastal Trail Located in the areas of Nāpili, Kapalua, Honokahua, and Honolua, Ahupuaʻa of Nāpili 2&3, Honokahua, and Honolua, Lahaina District, Island of Maui, Hawaiʻi.* Honolulu, HI: Scientific Consultant Services, Inc., 2008. [SHPD ID: 2019LI81410]

Honokeana

Dagher, Cathleen A. and Michael F. Dega. *An Archaeological Monitoring Plan for the Nāpili No. 4 WWPS Force Main Replacement, Lower Honoapiʻilani Road Right-of-Way, Honokeana and ʻAlaeloa Ahupuaʻa, Lahaina, (Kāʻanapali) District, Island of Maui, Hawaiʻi.* Honolulu, HI: Scientific Consultant Services, Inc., 2020. [SHPD ID: 2021LI00158]

Folio, Katie M. and Hallett H. Hammatt. *Archaeological Monitoring Plan for the Special Use Permit Application for the Napili Point 1 AOAO (SMX 2015/0465) and Napili Point II (SMX 2015/0472) Project, Honokeana Ahupuaʻa, Lahaina District, Island of Maui, Napili Point I.* Wailuku, HI: Cultural Surveys Hawaiʻi, Inc., 2016. [SHPD ID: 2019LI81068]

Folio, Katie M. and Hallett H. Hammatt. *Archaeological Monitoring Report for the Special Use Permit Application for the Napili Point I (SMX 2015/0465) and Napili Point II (SMX 2015/0472) Project, Honokeana Ahupuaʻa, Lahaina District, Island of Maui, Napili Point I TMK: (2) 4-3-002:021 (por.), Napili Point II.* Wailuku, HI: Cultural Surveys Hawaiʻi, Inc., 2016. [SHPD ID: 2019LI81068]

Medeiros, Colleen and Hallett H. Hammatt. *Archaeological Monitoring Report for the Kāʻanapali North Beach Development Area, Lot 3, Site Excavation, Honokōwai Ahupuaʻa, Lahaina District, Maui Island.* Wailuku, HI: Cultural Surveys Hawaiʻi, Inc., 2017. [SHPD ID: 2019LI80652]

Scientific Consultant Services, Inc. *An Archaeological Inventory Survey for Six Proposed Solar Voltaic Cell Sites Located in the Ahupuaʻa of Honokahua, Honokeana, and Honokōwai, Lahaina (Kāʻanapali) District, Island of Maui, Hawaiʻi.* Honolulu, HI: Scientific Consultant Services, Inc., 2012. [SHPD ID: 2019LI81005]

Sinoto, Aki. *Field Examination of Six Sites in the Honolua Watershed, Maui.* Honolulu, HI: Department of Anthropology, Bernice P. Bishop Museum, 1975. [SHPD ID: 2019LI81435; UH Call Number: DU629.H69 S56 1975]

HONOKŌHAU

Dagher, Cathleen A. and Michael F. Dega. *An Archaeological Monitoring Plan for the Proposed Kapalua Coastal Trail Corridor Located in Kapalua and Honokōhau and Nāpili 2&3 Ahupuaʻa Lahaina District, Island of Maui, Hawaiʻi [TMK: (2) 4-2-Various].* Honolulu, HI: Scientific Consultant Services, Inc., 2007. [SHPD ID: 2019LI81421]

Dagher, Cathleen A. and Michael F. Dega. *An Archaeological Monitoring Plan for the Proposed Kapalua Coastal Trail Located in the Areas of Nāpili, Kapalua, Honokahua, and Honolua, Ahupuaʻa of Nāpili 2 & 3, Honokahua, and Honolua, Lahaina district, Island of Maui, Hawaiʻi.* Honolulu, HI: Scientific Consultant Services, Inc., 2008. [SHPD ID: 2019LI81410]

Fredericksen, Erik M. *Archaeological Reconnaissance Report for the County of Maui Honokōhau Water System Improvements Project, Lahaina District, Maui Island.* Pukalani, HI: Xamanek Researches, 1998. [SHPD ID: 2019LI80994]

Fredericksen, Erik M. and Demaris Fredericksen. *Archaeological Inventory Survey for the Proposed Honokōhau Water System Improvement Project, Honokōhau Ahupuaʻa, Kāʻanapali District, Maui Island. DRAFT.* Pukalani, HI: Xamanek Researches, 1999. [SHPD ID: 2019LI80995]

Fredericksen, Erik M. and Demaris L. Fredericksen. *An Archaeological Inventory Survey (Phase 2) of a New Alignment for the Honokōhau Waterline Project, Honokōhau, Ahupua'a, Kā'anapali District, Island of Maui.* Pukalani, HI: Xamanek Researches, 2002. [SHPD ID: 2019LI81426]

Rogers, Donnell J. and Paul H. Rosendahl. *Archaeological Survey and Recording Iliilikea and Maiu Heiau on the North Coast of Maui, Land of Honokōhau, Lahaina District, Island of Maui.* Hilo, HI: Paul H. Rosendahl, Ph.D., Inc., 1992. [SHPD ID: 2019LI81440]

Tome, Guerin and Michael F. Dega. *An Archaeological Inventory Survey for the Proposed Kapalua Coastal Trail Located in the Areas of Kapalua and Honokāhau, Honokahua and Nāpili 2 & 3.* Honolulu, HI: Scientific Consultant Services, Inc., 2007. [SHPD ID: 2019LI81433]

HONOKŌWAI

Andricci, Nicole and Michael F. Dega. *AAAAA Rent-A-Space Extension Project Honokōwai, Māhinahina 4 Ahupua'a Lahaina (Kā'anapali) District, Maui Island Hawaii [TMK (2) 4-4-01:026].* Honolulu, HI: Scientific Consultant Services, Inc., 215.

Chaffee, D. and C. Monahan. *A Monitoring Plan for 3.054 Acres of Partially Developed Land in Honokōwai, Māhinahina 4 Ahupua'a, Lahaina District, Maui Island, Hawai'i.* Honolulu, HI: Scientific Consultant Services, Inc., 2005.

Chaffee, David B. and Michael F. Dega. *An Archaeological Monitoring Plan for the West Maui Recycled Water Expansion Project (Phase 2), Honokōwai Ahupua'a, Lahaina District, Maui Island, Hawai'i [TMK (2) 4-4-002:018 por].* Honolulu, HI: Scientific Consultant Services, Inc., 2013.

Chun, Allison and Michael F. Dega. *Addendum Archaeological Assessment Report on 0.13 Acres of Partially Developed land in Honokōwai, Māhinahina 4 Ahupua'a, Maui Island, Hawai'i.* Honolulu, HI: Scientific Consultant Services, Inc., 2005. [SHPD ID: 2019LI81043]

Dagher, Cathleen A. and Michael F. Dega. *Archaeological Inventory Survey for the Proposed West Maui Water Source Development Project Māhinahina Well (State Well No. 6-5638-004) (West Maui Well No. 1) and the Kahana Well (State Well No. 6-5738-002) (West Maui Well No. 2), Honokōwai, Māhinahina, and Māhinahina 1, 2, 3 Ahupua'a, Lahaina (Kā'anapali) District, Island of Maui, Hawai'i [TMK: (2) 4-3-01:017, (2) 4-3-01:084; (2) 4-4-02:014, 015, and 018; and (2) 4-4-004:009,*

011, 017, and 019]. Honolulu, HI: Scientific Consultant Services, Inc., 2022. [SHPD ID: 2022LI00356]

Dagher, Cathleen A. and Michael F. Dega. *Archaeological Monitoring Plan for the Maui Sands Sea Wall Repair Project, Moʻomuku ʻili, Honokōwai Ahupuaʻa, Lahaina (Kāʻanapali) District, Island of Maui, Hawaiʻi.* Honolulu, HI: Scientific Consultant Services, Inc., 2018. [No location available]

Davis, Bertell D. *Archaeological Surface Survey, Honokōwai Gulch, Kāʻanapali, Maui Island.* Lāwaʻi, HI: Archaeological Research Center Hawaiʻi, 1977. [SHPD ID: 2019LI81277]

Dega, Michael F. *An Archaeological Monitoring Plan for Improvements at Honokōwai Beach Park for the County of Maui, Department of Parks and Recreation, Honokōwai Ahupuaʻa, Lahaina District, Island of Maui, Hawaiʻi [TMK (2) 4-4-01:046 por. & 047 por].* Honolulu, HI: Scientific Consultant Services, Inc., 2015. [SHPD ID: 2019LI81042]

Dega, Michael F. *An Archaeological Monitoring Plan for the West Maui Recycled Water Expansion Project (Phase 2), Honokōwai Ahupuaʻa, Lahaina District, Maui Island, Hawaiʻi.* Honolulu, HI: Scientific Consultant Services, Inc., 2015. [SHPD ID: 2019LI81246]

Fredericksen, Erik M. *An Archaeological Assessment Survey of a c. 5 Acre Portion of Land for the Proposed Temporary Off-Site Parking Project, Hanakaʻōʻō/Honokōwai Ahupuaʻa, Lahaina District, Maui Island [TMK: (2) 4-4-002: 003].* Pukalani, HI: Xamanek Researches, 2007. [No location available]

Fredericksen, Erik M. and J. J. Frey. *An Archaeological Monitoring Report for the Kāʻanapali Shores Roadway Improvements Project, Honokōwai Ahupuaʻa, Lahaina District, Maui.* Pukalani, HI: Xamanek Researches, 2008. [SHPD ID: 2019LI81243]

Fredericksen, Erik M. and Jennifer L. Frey. *An Archaeological Monitoring Report for the Kāʻanapali Shores Roadway Improvements Project, Honokōwai Ahupuaʻa, Lahaina District, Maui [TMK: (2) 4-4-001:097, and TMK (2) 4-4-001 (Right of Way)].* Pukalani, HI: Xamanek Researches, 2008. [SHPD ID: 2019LI81243]

Fredericksen, Erik M., Demaris Fredericksen, and W. M. Fredericksen. *An Archaeological Inventory Survey at Honokōwai Beach Park, Honokōwai Ahupuaʻa, Lahaina District, Maui Island.* Pukalani, HI: Xamanek Researches, 1994. [No location available]

Griffin, Bion P. and George W. Lovelace, eds. *Survey and Salvage—Honoapiʻilani Highway: The Archaeology of Kāʻanapali from Honokōwai to ʻAlaeloa Ahupuaʻa.*

Lāwaʻi, HI: Archaeological Research Center Hawaiʻi, Inc., 1977. [UH Call Number: DU628.M3 A7 1977]

Havel, BreAnna and Michael F. Dega. *An Archaeological Assessment Report on 0.11 Acres of a Partially Developed Land in Honokōwai Ahupuaʻa, Lahaina District, Maui Island, Hawaiʻi [TMK 4-4-01:106]*. Honolulu, HI: Scientific Consultant Services, Inc., 2005. [SHPD ID: 2019LI81285]

Havel, BreAnna and Michael F. Dega. *An Archaeological Assessment Report on 0.11 Acres of Partially Developed Land in Honokōwai Ahupuaʻa, Lahaina District, Maui Island, Hawaiʻi*. Honolulu, HI: Scientific Consultant Services, Inc., 2005. [SHPD ID: 2019LI81285]

Hill, Robert R., Joseph Arnold, and Hallett H. Hammatt. *Archaeological Monitoring Report for a Dust Barrier Relocation at North Kāʻanapali, Honokōwai Ahupuaʻa, Lahaina District, Island of Maui. TMK (2) 4-4-014:004 (por.)* Wailuku, HI: Cultural Surveys Hawaiʻi, Inc., 2006. [SHPD ID: 2019LI80658]

Hill, Robert R., Joseph Arnold, and Hallett H. Hammatt. *Archaeological Monitoring Report for Shoreline Improvements at Lot 3, North Kāʻanapali, Honokōwai Ahupuaʻa, Lahaina District, Maui Island [TMK (2) 4-4-014:005 (por.)]*. Wailuku, HI: Cultural Surveys Hawaiʻi, Inc., 2008. [SHPD ID: 2019LI80653]

Hill, Robert R., Tanya L. Lee-Greig, and Hallett H. Hammatt. *Preservation Plan for a Fishing Koʻa, SIHP 50-50-03-6275, North Kāʻanapali, Lot 3, Honokōwai Ahupuaʻa, Maui Island [TMK (2) 4-4-014:005 por.]*. Wailuku, HI: Cultural Surveys Hawaiʻi, Inc., 2008. [SHPD ID: 2019LI80654]

Hill, Robert R., Tanya L. Lee-Greig, and Hallett H. Hammatt. *Archaeological Monitoring Report for Dust Barrier Construction at Lot 3, North Kāʻanapali, Honokōwai Ahupuaʻa, Lahaina District, Island of Maui [TMK (2) 4-4-014:005 (por.)]*. Wailuku, HI: Cultural Surveys Hawaiʻi, Inc., 2008. [SHPD ID: 2019LI80655]

Hill, Robert R., Tanya Lee-Greig, and Hallett H. Hammatt. *Archaeological Monitoring Report for Shoreline Improvements at Lot 1, North Kāʻanapali, Honokōwai Ahupuaʻa, Lahaina District, Maui Island TMK: (2) 4-4-014:003 (por.)*. Wailuku, HI: Cultural Surveys Hawaiʻi, Inc., 2008. [SHPD ID: 2019LI80657]

Jensen, Peter M. *Archaeological Inventory Survey Honoapiʻilani Highway Realignment Project Lahaina Bypass Section—Modified Corridor Alignment, Lands of Honokōwai, Hanakaʻōʻō, Wahikuli, Panaʻewa, Kuʻia, Halakaʻa, Pūehuehu Nui, Pāhoa, Polanui, and Launiupoko, Lahaina District, Island of Maui*. Hilo, HI: Paul H. Rosendahl, Ph.D., Inc., 1991. [SHPD ID: 2019LI81242]

Kaschko, Michael W. *Archaeological Walk-Through Survey of Specified Areas in the Wailuku Flood Prevention Project and the Honolua Watershed, Maui.* Honolulu, HI: Department of Anthropology, Bernice P. Bishop Museum, 1974. [SHPD ID: 2019LI81443]

Lyman, Kepa and Michael F. Dega. *Addendum—Archaeological Monitoring Plan for Lahaina Wastewater Pump Station No. 1 Improvements Honokōwai Ahupuaʻa, Lahaina District, Maui Island, Hawaiʻi [TMK (2) 4-4-002:33 and portions of 29 & 39].* Honolulu, HI: Scientific Consultant Services, Inc., 2018. [No location available]

McGerty, Leann and Robert L. Spear. *A Cultural Impact Assessment of Wastewater Pump Station No. 1 in Honokōwai Ahupuaʻa, Kāʻanapali, Lahaina District, Maui Island, Hawaiʻi [TMK: (2) 4-4-02:003, (2) 4-4-02:029].* Honolulu, HI: Scientific Consultant Services, Inc., 2010. [SHPD ID: 2019LI81254]

Medeiros, Colleen and Hallett H. Hammatt. *Archaeological Monitoring Report for the Kāʻanapali North Beach Development Area, Lot 3, Site Excavation, Honokōwai Ahupuaʻa, Lahaina District, Maui Island.* Wailuku, HI: Cultural Surveys Hawaiʻi, Inc., 2017. [SHPD ID: 2019LI80652]

Monahan, Christopher M. *An Archaeological Assessment Report on 3.054 Acres of Partially Developed Land in Honokōwai, Māhinahina 4 Ahupuaʻa, Lahaina District, Maui Island, Hawaiʻi [TMK (2) 4-3-06:002 and 069].* Honolulu, HI: Scientific Consultant Services, Inc., 2003. [SHPD ID: 2019LI81314, 2019LI81304]

Ogg, Randy and Michael F. Dega. *An Archaeological Assessment of Lahaina Wastewater Pump Station No. 1 Improvements, Honokōwai Ahupuaʻa, Lahaina District, Maui Island, Hawaiʻi [TMK: (2) 4-4-02:003 & (2) 4-4-02:029].* Honolulu, HI: Scientific Consultant Services, Inc., 2007. [SHPD ID: 2019LI81279]

Perzinski, David and Michael F. Dega. *An Archaeological Assessment of a Seawall/Revetment Structure in Honokōwai.* Honolulu, HI: Scientific Consultant Services, Inc., 2013. [SHPD ID: 2019LI81283]

Rogers, Scott. *An Archaeological Monitoring Plan for the Kāʻanapali—Hyatt Force Main Replacements, Kāʻanapali Resort Complex, Hanakaʻōʻō, Honokōwai Ahupuaʻa, Lahaina District, Island of Maui.* Pukalani, HI: Xamanek Researches, 2007. [SHPD ID: 2019LI80682]

Rosendahl, Margaret L. K. *Archaeological Field Inspection, Sheraton Maui Master Plan Project Area, Lands of Honokōwai and Hanakaʻōʻō, Lahaina District, Island of Maui.* Hilo, HI: Paul H. Rosendahl, Ph.D., Inc., 1986. [No location available]

Shefcheck, Donna M. and Michael F. Dega. *An Archaeological Monitoring Plan for Lahaina Wastewater Pump Station No. 1 Improvements, Honokōwai Ahupuaʻa, Lahaina District Maui Island, Hawaiʻi [TMK (2) 4-4-02:033 and portions of 29 and 39].* Honolulu, HI: Scientific Consultant Services, Inc., 2008. [SHPD ID: 2019LI81253]

Sinoto, Aki. *Field Examination of Six Sites in the Honolua Watershed, Maui.* Honolulu, HI: Department of Anthropology, Bernice P. Bishop Museum, 1975. [SHPD ID: 2019LI81435; UH Call Number: DU629.H69 S56 1975]

Six, Janet L. *A Final Archaeological Assessment Report for Maui County Work on County Roadway (WTP T20160044) and grading and grubbing (GT20160132) Proposed Sunset Terrace Lot Beautification Project, Honokōwai Ahupuaʻa, Lahaina District Maui Island, TMK (2) 4-4-02:029 and 034 (por.).* Pāhoa, HI: Sixth Sense Archaeological Consultants, LLC, 2018. [SHPD ID: 2019LI81282]

Six, Janet L. *Final Archaeological Monitoring Plan for Maui County Work on County Roadway (WTP T20160044) and Grading and Grubbing (GT2016132) Proposed Sunset Terrace Lot Beautification Project Honokōwai Ahupuaʻa, Lahaina Project Honokōwai Ahupuaʻa, Lahaina District, Maui Island, Hawaiʻi.* Pāhoa, HI: Sixth Sense Archaeological Consultants, LLC, 2018. [SHPD ID: 2019LI81282]

Willman, Michael R., Robert R. Hill, Tanya L. Lee-Greig, and Hallett H. Hammatt. *Archaeological Monitoring Report for Sand Replenishment at Lots 1, 2, and 3, North Kāʻanapali, Honokōwai Ahupuaʻa, Lahaina District, Island of Maui [TMK (2) 4-4-014: 03, 04, 05 (por.)].* Wailuku, HI: Cultural Surveys Hawaiʻi, Inc., 2009. [SHPD ID: 2019LI80656]

Yates and Hallett H. Hammatt. *Archaeological Monitoring Plan for the Kāʻanapali 2020 Master Plan, Kāʻanapali Coffee Farms Subdivision Phase II Project, Hanakaʻōʻō and Honokōwai Ahupuaʻa, Lahaina District, Maui Island, TMK (2) 4-4-02:002.* Wailuku, HI: Cultural Surveys Hawaiʻi, Inc., 2020. [SHPD ID: 2021LI00326, 2022LI00365]

Launiupoko

Jensen, Peter M. *Archaeological Inventory Survey Honoapiʻilani Highway Realignment Project Lahaina Bypass Section—Modified Corridor Alignment, Lands of Honokōwai, Hanakaʻōʻō, Wahikuli, Panaʻewa, Kuʻia, Halakaʻa, Pūehuehu Nui, Pāhoa, Polanui, and Launiupoko, Lahaina District, Island of Maui.* Hilo, HI: Paul H. Rosendahl, Ph.D., Inc., 1991. [SHPD ID: 2019LI81242]

Honolua

Conte, Patty J. *Archaeological Inventory Survey of the Stoops Property TMK (2) 4-1-01:018, Honolua Ahupuaʻa, Kāʻanapali District, Maui, Hawaiʻi.* Makawao, HI: CRM Solutions Hawaiʻi, Inc., 2006. [SHPD ID: 2019LI81424]

Conte, Patty J. *Archaeological Monitoring Plan for On and Off-Site Construction Within and Related to TMK (2) 4-1-01:018, Honolua Ahupuaʻa, Kāʻanapali District, Maui, Hawaiʻi.* Makawao, HI: CRM Solutions Hawaiʻi, Inc., 2006. [SHPD ID: 2019LI81424]

Conte, Patty J. *Archaeological Preservation Plan for the Portion of Site #50-50-01-1756 Within TMK (2) 4-1-01:018 Honolua Ahupuaʻa, Kāʻanapali District, Maui, Hawaiʻi.* Makawao, HI: CRM Solutions Hawaiʻi, Inc., 2007. [SHPD ID: 2019LI81428]

Hammatt, Hallett H. and David W. Shideler. *Preservation Plan for Four Sites (50-50-01-5234, A Water Exploration Tunnel; -5235, A Petroglyph; -5425, A Historic Trail, and -5426, A Pre-Contact Habitation Site) Located Within a 400-Acre Parcel at Honolua Ahupuaʻa.* Wailuku, HI: Cultural Surveys Hawaiʻi, Inc., 2003. [SHPD ID: 2019LI81003]

Hammatt, Hallett H., David W. Shideler, and Tony Bush. *Archaeological Inventory Survey of an Approximately 400-Acre Parcel at Honolua Ahupuaʻa Lahaina District of Maui.* Wailuku, HI: Cultural Surveys Hawaiʻi, Inc., 2003. [SHPD ID: 2019LI80993]

Kaschko, Michael W. *Archaeological Survey of the Honolua Development Area, Maui.* Department of Anthropology, Honolulu, HI: Bernice P. Bishop Museum, 1973. [SHPD ID: 2019LI81019]

Kaschko, Michael W. *Archaeological Walk-Through Survey of Specified Areas in the Wailuku Flood Prevention Project and the Honolua Watershed, Maui.* Honolulu, HI: Department of Anthropology, Bernice P. Bishop Museum, 1974. [SHPD ID: 2019LI81443]

Kennedy, Joseph. *Archaeological Walk Through Examination of Quarry Site located Mauka of Honoapiʻilani Highway near Lipoa Point, Honolua, Maui.* Haleʻiwa, HI: Archaeological Consultants of Hawaii, 1988. [SHPD ID: 2019LI81425]

Lee-Greig, Tanya L. and Hallett H. Hammatt. *Preservation Plan for Thirty-Three Historic Properties Located in and Adjacent to the Kapalua Mauka Project Area, Honokahua, Nāpili 2 & 3, and Nāpili 4-5 Ahupuaʻa, Lahaina District, Maui Island.* Wailuku, HI: Cultural Surveys Hawaiʻi, Inc., 2005. [SHPD ID: 2019LI80997]

Lum, Francis. *Amendment to Testing at Kahana Desilting Basin, Holoua [Honolua?] Watershed, Lahaina District, Maui, Hawaiʻi, Francis Lum, Soil Conservation Service.* Soil Conservation Service, 1983. [SHPD ID: 2019LI81058]

Madeus, Jonas K., Tanya L. Lee-Greig, and Hallett H. Hammatt. *Archaeological Assessment of an 80-Acre Parcel in Kapalua, Honolua Ahupuaʻa, Lahaina District, Maui Island.* Wailuku, HI: Cultural Surveys Hawaiʻi, Inc., 2005. [SHPD ID: 2019LI80999]

Moore, Kenneth R. *Archaeological Survey of Honolua Valley, Maui.* Honolulu, HI: Department of Anthropology, Bernice P. Bishop Museum, 1974. [SHPD ID: 2019LI81436; UH Call Number: DU629.H69 M66 1974]

OʻClaray, Jenny. *Additional Field Work for Drainage 11 Kapalua Plantation Estates Project Area, Lands of Honokahua, Honolua, Napili 2-2 Lahaina District, Island of Maui.* Hilo, HI: Paul H. Rosendahl, Ph.D., Inc., 1991. [SHPD ID: 2019LI81415]

Perzinski, David and Michael F. Dega. *An Archaeological Inventory Survey Report for a Bridge Replacement in Honolua, Honolua Ahupuaʻa, Lahaina District, Maui Island.* Honolulu, HI: Scientific Consultant Services, Inc., 2010. [SHPD ID: 2019LI81430]

Pickett, Jenny L. and Michael F. Dega. *An Archaeological Inventory Survey of 583 Acres at Lipoa Point, Honolua Ahupuaʻa, Lahaina (Formerly Kāʻanapali) District, Maui Island, Hawaiʻi.* Honolulu, HI: Scientific Consultant Services, Inc., 2006. [SHPD ID: 2019LI81431]

Rosendahl, Paul H. *Additional Inventory Survey for Drainage Easement 11 Kapalua Plantation Estates Project Area, Lands of Honokahua, Honolua, and Napili 2-3, Lahaina District, Island of Maui.* Hilo, HI: Paul H. Rosendahl, Ph.D., Inc., 1991. [SHPD ID: 2019LI80996]

Sinoto, Aki. *Field Examination of Six Sites in the Honolua Watershed, Maui.* Honolulu, HI: Department of Anthropology, Bernice P. Bishop Museum, 1975. [SHPD ID: 2019LI81435; UH Call Number: DU629.H69 S56 1975]

Tome, Guerin and Michael F. Dega. *An Archaeological Monitoring Plan for the Proposed Kapalua Coastal Trail Located in the areas of Nāpili, Kapalua, Honokahua, and Honolua, Ahupuaʻa of Nāpili 2&3, Honokahua, and Honolua, Lahaina District, Island of Maui, Hawaiʻi.* Honolulu, HI: Scientific Consultant Services, Inc., 2008. [SHPD ID: 2019LI81410]

Tome, Guerin, Irene Calis, and Michael F. Dega. *An Archaeological Inventory Survey in Honolua, Honolua Ahupuaʻa, Lahaina District, Island of Maui, Hawaiʻi [TMK: (2) 4-1-01:005].* Honolulu, HI: Scientific Consultant Services, Inc., 2002. [SHPD ID: 2019LI81423]

'ALAELOA

Chaffee, David B. and Robert L. Spear. *An Archaeological Monitoring Plan for Construction Activities on a 13,237 Square Foot Parcel in 'Alaeloa Ahupua'a, Lahaina District, Maui Island, Hawaii.* Honolulu, HI: Scientific Consultant Services, Inc., 2001.

Dagher, Cathleen A. and Michael F. Dega. *An Archaeological Monitoring Plan for the Nāpili No. 4 WWPS Force Main Replacement, Lower Honoapi'ilani Road Right-of-Way, Honokeana and 'Alaeloa Ahupua'a, Lahaina, (Kā'anapali) District, Island of Maui, Hawai'i.* Honolulu, HI: Scientific Consultant Services, Inc., 2020. [SHPD ID: 2021LI00158]

Dockall, John E., Tanya L. Lee-Greig, and Hallett H. Hammatt. *An Archaeological Assessment of a Proposed Road Corridor for Maui Preparatory Academy, Alaeloa Ahupua'a, Lahaina District, Maui Island.* Wailuku, HI: Cultural Surveys Hawai'i, Inc., 2005. [SHPD ID: 2019LI81052]

Fredericksen et al. *An Archaeological Inventory Survey of a 9.976 Acre parcel in the Kahana/Mailepai/Alaeloa District, Lahaina District, Maui, Hawai'i.* Pukalani, HI: Xamanek Researches, 1990. [SHPD ID: 2019LI81060]

Fredericksen, Erik M. *An Archaeological Assessment for the Proposed Maui Preparatory Academy, Alaeloa Ahupua'a, Lahaina District, Island of Maui [TMK (2) 4-3-01: 01 por.].* Pukalani, HI: Xamanek Researches, 2004. [SHPD ID: 2019LI81053]

Fredericksen, Erik M. *An Archaeological Monitoring Plan for a Portion of Land in Alaeloa Ahupua'a, Lahaina District, Maui [TMK: (2) 4-5-014:032].* Pukalani, HI: Xamanek Researches, 2005. [SHPD ID: 2019LI81355]

Fredericksen, Erik M. and Demaris L. Fredericksen. *Additional Archaeological Inventory Survey Level Work for Site 50-50-03-4797, Lower Honoapi'ilani Road Improvements Project Corridor; Alaeloa, Mailepai and Kahana Ahupua'a, Lahaina District, Maui Island [TMK (2) 4-3-15].* Pukalani, HI: Xamanek Researches, 2001. [SHPD ID: 2021LI00221]

Griffin, Bion P. and George W. Lovelace, eds. *Survey and Salvage—Honoapi'ilani Highway: The Archaeology of Kā'anapali from Honokōwai to 'Alaeloa Ahupua'a.* Lāwa'i, HI: Archaeological Research Center Hawai'i, Inc., 1977. [UH Call Number: DU628.M3 A7 1977]

Hill, Robert R., Thomas K. Devereux, and Hallett H. Hammatt. *An Archaeological Assessment of a 9.650 Acre Parcel, 'Alaeloa Ahupua'a, Lahaina District, Maui Island, for the West Maui Village Project.* Wailuku, HI: Cultural Surveys Hawai'i, Inc., 2006. [SHPD ID: 2019LI81037]

Kennedy, Joseph. *Archaeological Inventory Survey and Subsurface Testing Report for a Property Located at TMK: 4-3-03:108 and 110, ʻAlaeloa Ahupuaʻa, Lahaina District, on the Island of Maui,* 1992. [SHPD ID: 2022LI00219]

Kennedy, Joseph and Tim Denham. *Archaeological Inventory Survey and Subsurface Testing Report for TMK(2) 4-3-01:031, located at Kahana Ahupuaʻa, Maui.* Haleʻiwa, HI: Archaeological Consultants of Hawaii, 1992.

Six, Janet L. *Final Archaeological Monitoring Plan for Work on County Roadway Permit Application (WTP T2017-0055) Installation Communication Utilities, West Maui Village, Kohi & Napilihau St., Napili, ʻAlaeloa Ahupuaʻa, Kāʻanapali District, Island of Maui.* Pāhoa, HI: Sixth Sense Archaeological Consultants, LLC, 2018. [SHPD ID: 2019LI81317]

Kahakuloa

Klieger, Paul Christiaan and Susan A. Lebo. *Archaeological Inventory Survey of Waiōlaʻi and Waiokila Catchments, Kahakuloa, West Maui, Hawaiʻi.* Honolulu, HI: Department of Anthropology, Bernice P. Bishop Museum, 1995. [No location available]

Major, Maurice. *Ridgetops and Gulch Bottoms: An Archaeological Inventory Survey of Waiōlaʻi and Waiokila Catchments, Kahakuloa, West Maui, Hawaiʻi. TMK (2) 3-1-01:003.* Honolulu, HI: Department of Anthropology, Bernice P. Bishop Museum, 1996. [SHPD ID: 2019LI80145]

Nagata, Ralston H. *CDUA-MA-5/12/82-1407, Land Clearing and Planting of Commercially Valuable Tree Species at Kahakuloa, Wailuku, Maui. Memorandum to: Roger Evans, Planning Office from DLNR, Division of State Parks,* 1983. [No location available]

Nagata, Ralston H. and Martha Yent. *CDUA: MA-1436, Taro Planting at Kahakuloa Valley, Wailuku, Maui. Memorandum to Mr. Roger Evans, Planning Office from DLNR, Division of State Parks,* 1982. [UH Call Number: DU629. K344 N34 1982]

Kahana

Conte, Patty J. *Assessment of a Lot for Proposed Residential Construction, Kahana Ahupuaʻa, Lahaina District, Maui, Hawaiʻi.* Makawao, HI: CRM Solutions Hawaiʻi, Inc., 2004. [SHPD ID: 2019LI81300]

Dagher, Cathleen A. and Michael F. Dega. *An Archaeological Monitoring Plan for the Nāpili No. 3 WWPS Force Main Replacement, Lower Honoapi'ilani Road Right-of-Way, Kahana Ahupua'a, Lahaina (Kā'anapali) District Island of Maui, Hawai'i. [TMK (2) 4-2-05:999 and 4-3-10:999].* Honolulu, HI: Scientific Consultant Services, Inc., 2020. [SHPD ID: 2021LI00158]

Dega, Michael F. *Archaeological Inventory Survey of a 3-Acre Parcel in Kahana-Kai, Kahana Ahupua'a, Kā'anapali District, Island of Maui, Hawai'i.* Honolulu, HI: Scientific Consultant Services, Inc., 2001. [SHPD ID: 2019LI81327]

Fredericksen et al. *An Archaeological Inventory Survey of a 9.976 Acre parcel in the Kahana/Mailepai/Alaeloa District, Lahaina District, Maui, Hawai'i.* Pukalani, HI: Xamanek Researches, 1990. [SHPD ID: 2019LI81060]

Fredericksen, Demaris L. and Erik M. Fredericksen. *Archaeological Inventory Survey for Kahana-Kai Subdivision, Kahana Ahupua'a, Lahaina [Kā'anapali] District, Maui Island.* Pukalani, HI: Xamanek Researches, 1995. [SHPD ID: 2019LI81330]

Fredericksen, Demaris L., Walter M. Fredericksen, and Erik M. Fredericksen. *Archaeological Inventory Survey of a 9.976 Acre Parcel in the Kahana/Mailepai/Akeloa Lands, Lahaina District, Maui, Hawai'i.* Pukalani, HI: Xamanek Researches, 1990. [SHPD ID: 2019LI81060]

Fredericksen, Erik M. *An Archaeological Monitoring Plan for the Proposed Lower Honoapi'ilani Highway Improvements Phase IV Project (Ho'ohui Road to Napilihau Street) in Kahana, Mailepai, and Alaeloa Ahupua'a, Napili, Lahaina District, Maui [F. A. P. No. STP 3080 (8)].* Pukalani, HI: Xamanek Researches, 2005. [SHPD ID: 2019LI81299]

Fredericksen, Erik M. and Demaris L. Fredericksen. *Additional Archaeological Inventory Survey Level Work for Site 50-50-03-4797, Lower Honoapi'ilani Road Improvements Project Corridor; Alaeloa, Mailepai and Kahana Ahupua'a, Lahaina District, Maui Island [TMK (2) 4-3-15].* Pukalani, HI: Xamanek Researches, 2001. [SHPD ID: 2021LI00221]

Frey, Jennifer J., Josephine M. Yucha, and Hallett H. Hammatt. *Archaeological Monitoring Report for the Valley Isle Resort Renovation Project, Kahana Ahupua'a, Lahaina District, Maui Island [TMK: (2) 4-3-10:004].* Wailuku, HI: Cultural Surveys Hawai'i, Inc., 2021. [SHPD ID: 2022LI00135]

Frey, Jennifer J., Ryan Luskin, Angela L. Yates, and Hallett H. Hammatt. *Archaeological Monitoring Report for the Hololani Resort Condominiums Shoreline Protection Project, Kahana Ahupua'a, Lahaina District, Maui Island.* Wailuku, HI: Cultural Surveys Hawai'i, Inc., 2019. [SHPD ID: 2019LI81312]

Hommon, Robert J. and Hamilton M. Ahlo, Jr. *An Archaeological Reconnaissance Survey of the Site of a Proposed Airstrip at Māhinahina, West Maui.* Science Management, Inc., 1982. [SHPD ID: 2019LI81050; UH Call Number: DU629. M345 H66 1982]

Kaschko, Michael W. *Archaeological Walk-Through Survey of Specified Areas in the Wailuku Flood Prevention Project and the Honolua Watershed, Maui.* Honolulu, HI: Department of Anthropology, Bernice P. Bishop Museum, 1974. [SHPD ID: 2019LI81443]

Kennedy, Joseph. *Archaeological Inventory Survey and Subsurface Testing Report for TMK: (2) 4-3-01:031, Located at Kahana Ahupuaʻa, Island of Maui,* Revised May 1992, 1992. [SHPD ID: 2019LI81051]

Kennedy, Joseph. *Archaeological Inventory Survey of Kahana, Maui.* Haleʻiwa, HI: Archaeological Consultants of Hawaii, 1985. [No location available]

Kennedy, Joseph. *Archaeological Inventory Survey Report for TMK (2) 4-3-01:31, located at Kahana, Island of Maui.* Haleʻiwa, HI: Archaeological Consultants of Hawaii, 1991. [SHPD ID: 2019LI81069]

Kennedy, Joseph. *Archaeological Inventory Survey Report for TMK: (2) 4-3-01:031; Located at Kahana, Island of Maui.* 1990. [SHPD ID: 2019LI81054]

Kennedy, Joseph. *Archaeological Investigations at Kahana, Maui,* 1986. [No location available]

Kennedy, Joseph. *Field Inspection: Stone Building at Kahana,* Maui, 1986. [SHPD ID: 2019LI81332]

Kennedy, Joseph and Tim Denham. *Archaeological Inventory Survey and Subsurface Testing Report for TMK(2) 4-3-01:031, located at Kahana Ahupuaʻa, Maui.* Haleʻiwa, HI: Archaeological Consultants of Hawaii, 1992.

Komori, Eric K. *Archaeological Investigations at Kahana Gulch, Lahaina District, Maui.* Honolulu, HI: Department of Anthropology, Bernice P. Bishop Museum, 1983. [SHPD ID: 2019LI81070; UH Call Number: DU629.K343 K66 1983]

Madeus, Jonas K. and Hallett H. Hammatt. *An Archaeological Monitoring Plan for the Proposed Hololani Resort Condominiums Shoreline Protection Project in Kahananui Ahupuaʻa, Lahaina District, Maui Island TMK: (2) 4-3-010:009 por.* Wailuku, HI: Cultural Surveys Hawaiʻi, Inc., 2014. [SHPD ID: 2019LI81312]

Moore, James R. and Joseph Kennedy. *An Archaeological Inventory Survey with Subsurface Testing Report for Portions of the Proposed Kahana Ridge Subdivision*

Located at TMK: (2) 4-3-05:016 & 018, in Kahana Ahupuaʻa, Lahaina District, Island of Maui. Haleʻiwa, HI: Archaeological Consultants of Hawaii, 1994. [SHPD ID: 2019LI81329]

Mulrooney et al. *Archaeological Inventory Survey Report for the Kahana Solar Project in Ahupuaʻa of Kahana and Māhinahina 1-3, Moku of Kāʻanapali (Lahaina Modern Tax District), Island of Maui [TMK: (2) 4-3-01:017 por.; (2) 4-3-01:082 por.; (2) 4-3-01:084 por.].* Kailua, HI: Pacific Legacy, Inc., 2022

Pantaleo, Jeffrey and Paul Titchenal. *An Archaeological Inventory Survey Report for the Pulelehua Community Project TMK (2) 4-3-01:031 Por. Māhinahina 1, 2, 3, Māhinahina 4, and Kahana Ahupuaʻa, Lahaina and Kāʻanapali Districts, Island of Maui.* Wailuku, HI: Archaeological Services Hawaii, LLC, 2004. [SHPD ID: 2019LI81072]

Perzinski, David and Michael F. Dega. *Archaeological Assessment for the West Maui Well No. 2 Exploratory, DWS Job No. 11-06, Kahana Ahupuaʻa, Lahaina (Kāʻanapali) District, Maui, Hawaiʻi.* Honolulu, HI: Scientific Consultant Services, Inc., 2014. [SHPD ID: 2019LI81057]

Pestana, Elizabeth and Michael F. Dega. *Archaeological Inventory Survey of a 5.18 Acre Parcel in Kahana, Kahana Ahupuaʻa, Kāʻanapali District, Island of Maui, Hawaiʻi [TMK: (2)-4-3-15:069].* Honolulu, HI: Scientific Consultant Services, Inc., 2018. [SHPD ID: 2019LI81301]

Sea Engineering, Inc. *Final Environmental Assessment for Permanent Shore Protection of the Hololani Resort Condominiums Kahananui, Lahaina, Maui.* Honolulu, HI: Sea Engineering, Inc., 2013. [No location available]

Six, Janet L. *Final Archaeological Monitoring Plan for Special Management Area Application (SMX2017/0098) for the Proposed Kahana Beach Resort DCDA Upgrade, Kahana Ahupuaʻa, Lahaina District, Island of Maui.* Pāhoa, HI: Sixth Sense Archaeological Consultants, LLC, 2018. [SHPD ID: 2019LI81303]

Walker, Alan T. and Paul H. Rosendahl. *Testing of Cultural Remains Associated with the Kahana Desilting Basin, Honolua Watershed, Land of Kahana, Lahaina District, County of Maui, Hawaiʻi.* Hilo, HI: Paul H. Rosendahl, Ph.D., Inc., 1985. [SHPD ID: 2019LI81071; UH Call Number: DU629.K343 W35 1985]

Yucha, Josephine M. and Hallett H. Hammatt. *Archaeological Monitoring Plan for the Valley Isle Resort Renovation Project, Kahana Ahupuaʻa, Lahaina District, Maui Island, TMK: (2) 4-3-10:004.* Wailuku, HI: Cultural Surveys Hawaiʻi, Inc., 2020. [SHPD ID: 2021LI00211]

KĀʻANAPALI

Athens, J. Stephen. *Archaeological Monitoring Plan, Trenching at Taco Bell, Lahaina, Kāʻanapali Ahupuaʻa, Lahaina District, Maui [TMK (2) 4-5-07:034].* Honolulu, HI: International Archaeological Research Institute, Inc., 1999.

Rotunno-Hazuka, Lisa J., Mia Watson, and Jeffrey Pantaleo. *Archaeological Monitoring Plan for the Improvements to a Commercial Restaurant Facility at TMK: (2) 4-5-07:034, Kāʻanapali Ahupuaʻa, Lahaina District, Island of Maui.* Wailuku, HI: Archaeological Services Hawaii, LLC, 2010. [SHPD ID: 2019LI80610]

KAPALUA

Dagher, Cathleen A. and Michael F. Dega. *An Archaeological Monitoring Plan for the Proposed Kapalua Coastal Trail Corridor Located in Kapalua and Honokōhau and Nāpili 2&3 Ahupuaʻa Lahaina District, Island of Maui, Hawaiʻi [TMK: (2) 4-2-Various].* Honolulu, HI: Scientific Consultant Services, Inc., 2007. [SHPD ID: 2019LI81421]

Dagher, Cathleen A. and Michael F. Dega. *An Archaeological Monitoring Plan for the Proposed Kapalua Coastal Trail Located in the Areas of Nāpili, Kapalua, Honokahua, and Honolua, Ahupuaʻa of Nāpili 2 & 3, Honokahua, and Honolua, Lahaina district, Island of Maui, Hawaiʻi.* Honolulu, HI: Scientific Consultant Services, Inc., 2008. [SHPD ID: 2019LI81410]

Dega, Michael F. and David B. Chaffee. *Archaeological Monitoring Plan for Construction Work on Approximately 25.3 Acres in Kapalua, Napili 2-3 Ahupuaʻa, Lahaina District, Maui Island, Hawaiʻi.* Honolulu, HI: Scientific Consultant Services, Inc., 2004. [SHPD ID: 2019LI81041]

Devereux, Thomas K., William H. Folk, and Hallett H. Hammatt. *Archaeological Survey of the Lands Comprising Project District 2 at Kapalua, Honokahua, and Nāpili 2 & 3 Ahupuaʻa Lahaina District of Maui.* Wailuku, HI: Cultural Surveys Hawaiʻi, Inc., 2001. [SHPD ID: 2019LI81007]

Donham, Theresa K. *Archaeological Survey Test Excavations Kapalua Hotel Development Site 2-H, Kapalua Bay Resort, Land of Honokahua, Lahaina, Island of Maui.* Hilo, HI: Paul H. Rosendahl, Ph.D., Inc., 1986. [2019LI80998]

Donham, Theresa K. *Interim Report: Kapalua Mitigation Program Data Recovery Excavations at the Honokahua Burial Site, Land of Honokahua, Lahaina District,*

Island of Maui. Hilo, HI: Paul H. Rosendahl, Ph.D., Inc., 1989. [SHPD ID: 2019LI81417]

Fredericksen, Demaris L. and Erik M. Fredericksen. *Archaeological Inventory Survey of a 24-Acre Parcel, Kapalua Lot 19, Located in Napili 2-3 Ahupua'a, Lahaina District, Maui Island [TMK: (2) 4-2-04: por. 024]*. Pukalani, HI: Xamanek Researches, 2000. [SHPD ID: 2019LI81025]

Fredericksen, Erik M. *Archaeological Monitoring Report for the Verizon Hawaii, Inc. Equipment Installation project at TMK: (2) 4-2-04:021 Ritz-Carlton, Kapalua, Honokahua Ahupua'a, Lahaina District, Maui, Hawai'i*. Pukalani, HI: Xamanek Researches, 2001. [SHPD ID: 2019LI81014, 2019LI81029]

Fredericksen, Erik M. and Demaris L. Fredericksen. *Archaeological Inventory Survey for the Proposed Golf Academy Project Kapalua, Maui, Hawai'i, TMK 4-2-04: por. 24*. Pukalani, HI: Xamanek Researches, 1998. [SHPD ID: 2019LI81012]

Fredericksen, Erik M., Walter M. Fredericksen, and Demaris L. Fredericksen. *Additional Archaeological Inventory Survey Subsurface testing at Kapalua Bay Hotel [TMK (2) 4-2-04:26], Honokahua and Napili 2-3 Ahupua'a, Lahaina District, Maui Island*. Pukalani, HI: Xamanek Researches, 1996. [SHPD ID: 2019LI81024]

Fredericksen, Walter M. *An Historic and Traditional Land Use Study Utilizing Oral History Interviews for Assessing Cultural Impacts, for the Kapalua Project 2 and Expanded Project 2, Kapalua, Maui, Hawai'i*. Pukalani, HI: Xamanek Researches, 2001. [No location available]

Madeus, Jonas K., Tanya L. Lee-Greig, and Hallett H. Hammatt. *Archaeological Assessment of an 80-Acre Parcel in Kapalua, Honolua Ahupua'a, Lahaina District, Maui Island*. Wailuku, HI: Cultural Surveys Hawai'i, Inc., 2005. [SHPD ID: 2019LI80999]

Monahan, Christopher M. *An Archaeological Inventory Survey Report on Three Contiguous Parcels Measuring Approximately 25.3 Acres in Kapalua, Napili 2-3 Ahupua'a, Lahaina District, Maui Island, Hawai'i*. Honolulu, HI: Scientific Consultant Services, Inc., 2005. [SHPD ID: 2019LI81018]

Morawski, Lauren and Michael F. Dega. *Archaeological Inventory Survey Report of an Approximate 10-Acre Parcel in Kapalua in the Ahupua'a of Honokahua, Lahaina District (Formerly Kā'anapali), Island of Maui, Hawai'i*. Honolulu, HI: Scientific Consultant Services, Inc., 2004. [SHPD ID: 2019LI81017]

Munekiyo & Hiraga, Inc. *Historic Resources Inventory Submittal, Makaʻoiʻoi Demolition.* Wailuku, HI: Munekiyo & Hiraga, Inc., 2003. [SHPD ID: 2019LI81049]

OʻHare, Constance, Thomas K. Devereux, William H. Folk, and Hallett H. Hammatt. *Preservation Plan for Specific Sites in the Land Comprising Project District 2 at Kapalua, Honokahua and Nāpili 2 & 3 Ahupuaʻa Lahaina District of Maui.* Wailuku, HI: Cultural Surveys Hawaiʻi, Inc., 2003. [SHPD ID: 2019LI81002]

Silva, C. L. *Appendix A: Preliminary Historical Documentary Research, in Archaeological Survey Test Excavations, Kapalua Hotel Development Site 2-H, Kapalua Bay Resort, Land of Honokahua, Lahaina District, Island of Maui. PHRI Report 224-052286,* 1986. [No location available]

Tome, Guerin and Michael F. Dega. *An Archaeological Inventory Survey for the Proposed Kapalua Coastal Trail Located in the Areas of Kapalua and Honokāhau, Honokahua and Nāpili 2 & 3.* Honolulu, HI: Scientific Consultant Services, Inc., 2007. [SHPD ID: 2019LI81433]

Tome, Guerin and Michael F. Dega. *An Archaeological Monitoring Plan for the Proposed Kapalua Coastal Trail Located in the areas of Nāpili, Kapalua, Honokahua, and Honolua, Ahupuaʻa of Nāpili 2&3, Honokahua, and Honolua, Lahaina District, Island of Maui, Hawaiʻi.* Honolulu, HI: Scientific Consultant Services, Inc., 2008. [SHPD ID: 2019LI81410]

Webb, Erika L. *Inventory Survey of Honolua Plantation Shop Buildings Located at the Kapalua Central Resort, TMK (2) 4-2-4:024.* Honolulu, HI: Mason Architects, Inc., 2005. [SHPD ID: 2019LI81047]

Kauaʻula

Rotunno-Hazuka, Lisa J. and Jeffrey Pantaleo. *Archaeological Monitoring Plan for All Improvements Related to the Proposed Construction of an Ohana and Garage at the Stiebinger Residence, Kauʻaula Ahupuaʻa, Lahaina District, Island of Maui TMK (2) 4-6-06:005.* Wailuku, HI: Archaeological Services Hawaii, LLC, 2005. [SHPD ID: 2019LI81405]

Spear, Robert L. *Field Inspection of a Sea Wall on the Brayton Property, 303 Front Street, Aholo/Kauʻaula Ahupuaʻa, Lahaina District, Island of Maui, Hawaiʻi TMK: 4-6-3-05 (Seaward).* Honolulu, HI: Scientific Consultant Services, Inc., 2007. [SHPD ID: 2019LI81559]

KELAWEA

Lee-Greig, Tanya L. and Hallett H. Hammatt. *Archaeological Inventory Survey Plan for Honoapiʻilani Highway Realignment Phase IA, Future Keawe Street Extension to Lahainaluna Road: Ikena Avenue Alignment with Modified Extension Kelawea, Paeohi, and Wahikuli Ahupuaʻa, Lahaina District, Maui Island TMK (2) 4-5-021, 010, 015, and 031: Multiple Parcels.* Wailuku, HI: Cultural Surveys Hawaiʻi, Inc., 2008. [SHPD ID: 2019LI81341]

Lee-Greig, Tanya L. and Hallett H. Hammatt. *Archaeological Monitoring Plan for the Lahaina Bypass Modified Alignment from Kahoma Stream to the Keawe Street Extension, Kelawea, Paeohi, and Wahikuli Ahupuaʻa, Lahaina District, Maui Island.* Wailuku, HI: Cultural Surveys Hawaiʻi, Inc., 2009. [SHPD ID: 2019LI81369]

Lee-Greig, Tanya L., Robert Hill, and Hallett H. Hammatt. *An Archaeological Survey Report for the Realignment of a Section of the Honoapiʻilani Highway, Phase IA, Kelawea, Paeohi, and Wahikuli Ahupuaʻa, Lahaina District, Maui Island TMK (2) 4-5-021, 010, 015, and 031: Multiple Parcels.* Wailuku, HI: Cultural Surveys Hawaiʻi, Inc., 2008. [SHPD ID: 2019LI81361]

Madeus, Jonas K., Tanya Lee-Greig, and Hallett H. Hammatt. *An Archaeological Monitoring Report for the Lahaina Bypass Modified Alignment from the Lahainaluna Road Intersection to the Keawe Street Extension Kelawea, Paeohi, and Wahikuli Ahupuaʻa, Lahaina District, Maui Island TMK (2) 4-5-021, 010, 015, and 031: Multiple Parcels.* Wailuku, HI: Cultural Surveys Hawaiʻi, Inc., 2010. [SHPD ID: 2019LI81338]

Rotunno-Hazuka, Lisa J. and Jeffrey Pantaleo. *Archaeological Monitoring Plan for the Installation of a Grease Interceptor at TMK: (2) 4-5-02:009 Kelawea Ahupuaʻa, Lahaina District, Island of Maui.* Wailuku, HI: Archaeological Services Hawaii, LLC, 2007. [SHPD ID: 2019LI80646]

Rotunno-Hazuka, Lisa J. and Jeffrey Pantaleo. *Final Archaeological Monitoring Plan for the Installation of a New Water Service and Relocated Power Pole Along Kalena Street Kelawea Ahupuaʻa, Lahaina District, Island of Maui.* Wailuku, HI: Archaeological Services Hawaii, LLC, 2015. [No location available]

KUHOLILEA

Guerriero, Diane, Lisa J. Rotunno-Hazuka, and Jeffrey Pantaleo. *Archaeological Assessment Report of a 0.428 Acre Parcel of Land at TMK 4-5-07:004 Kuholilea*

Ahupuaʻa, Lahaina District, Island of Maui. Wailuku, HI: Archaeological Services Hawaii, LLC, 2005. [SHPD ID: 2019LI80606]

Rotunno-Hazuka, Lisa J. and Jeffrey Pantaleo. *Archaeological Monitoring Plan for All Ground Disturbing Activities Associated with the Construction of the Waineʻe Self Storage Facility located at TMK: (2) 4-5-07:004 Kuholilea Ahupuaʻa, Lahaina District, Island of Maui.* Wailuku, HI: Archaeological Services Hawaii, LLC, 2006. [SHPD ID: 2019LI80607]

Kuhua 1

Kurashina, Hiro and Aki Sinoto. *Archaeological Reconnaissance of the Proposed Shopping Center at Lahaina, Maui, Hawaiʻi, TMK: (2) 4-5-02:009.* Honolulu, HI: Department of Anthropology, Bernice P. Bishop Museum, 1984. [SHPD ID: 2019LI80648; UH Call Number: DU629.L3 K87 1984]

Kuhua 2

Kurashina, Hiro and Aki Sinoto. *Archaeological Reconnaissance of the Proposed Shopping Center at Lahaina, Maui, Hawaiʻi, TMK: (2) 4-5-02:009.* Honolulu, HI: Department of Anthropology, Bernice P. Bishop Museum, 1984. [SHPD ID: 2019LI80648; UH Call Number: DU629.L3 K87 1984]

Kuʻia

Andricci, Nicole and Michael F. Dega. *Archaeological Assessment of a 15.7 Acre Section of Undeveloped Land and a Proposed Road Extension, Kuʻia Ahupuaʻa, Lahaina District, Island of Maui, Hawaiʻi [TMK (2) 4-6-018:003 por.].* Honolulu, HI: Scientific Consultant Services, Inc., 2015.

Cordle, Shayna, Cathleen A. Dagher, and Michael F. Dega. *An Archaeological Monitoring Report for Work on County Roadway (WTP T2008/0014) For the Lahaina Store Water Meter Replacement Project, Lahaina, Kuʻia Ahupuaʻa, Lahaina District, Island of Maui, Hawaiʻi [TMK: (2) 4-6-09:007],* 2009. Honolulu, HI: Scientific Consultant Services, Inc. [SHPD ID: 2019LI81563]

Dega, Michael F. *An Archaeological Monitoring plan for Construction Work at Honokōwai, Māhinahina Ahupuaʻa, Kāʻanapali District, Maui Island, Hawaiʻi.* Honolulu, HI: Scientific Consultant Services, Inc., 2000. [SHPD ID: 2019LI81247]

Dega, Michael F. *Archaeological Monitoring Plan for Limited Construction Work in Lahaina, Kuʻia Ahupuaʻa, Lahaina District, Island of Maui, Hawaiʻi.* Honolulu, HI: Scientific Consultant Services, Inc., 2003. [SHPD ID: 2019LI80641]

Dega, Michael F. and Mary Sullivan. *Archaeological Monitoring Plan for Construction at the Lahaina Store, Lahaina, Kuʻia Ahupuaʻa, Lahaina District, Island of Maui, Hawaiʻi [TMK: (2) 4-6-09:007 & 062].* Honolulu, HI: Scientific Consultant Services, Inc., 2002. [SHPD ID: 2019LI81578]

Desilets, Michael and Patrick OʻDay. *Preservation Plan for Proposed Fenceline Corridor for the West Maui Forest Reserve, Kuʻia, Mākila, Pāhoa, Halakaʻa, Polaiki, Launiupoko, and Olowalu Ahupuaʻa, Lahaina District, Maui Island, Hawaiʻi.* Kailua, HI: Garcia & Associates, 2016. [SHPD ID: 2019LI81528]

Jensen, Peter M. *Archaeological Inventory Survey Honoapiʻilani Highway Realignment Project Lahaina Bypass Section—Modified Corridor Alignment, Lands of Honokōwai, Hanakaʻōʻō, Wahikuli, Panaʻewa, Kuʻia, Halakaʻa, Pūehuehu Nui, Pāhoa, Polanui, and Launiupoko, Lahaina District, Island of Maui.* Hilo, HI: Paul H. Rosendahl, Ph.D., Inc., 1991. [SHPD ID: 2019LI81242]

Medrano, Stephanie and Michael F. Dega. *An Archaeological Assessment for a 1.02-Acre Project Area in Lahaina, Kuʻia Ahupuaʻa, Lahaina District, Island of Maui, Hawaiʻi [TMK: (2) 4-6-009:036, 038, & 044].* Honolulu, HI: Scientific Consultant Services, Inc., 2013. [SHPD ID: 2019LI81581]

Monahan, Christopher M., Lauren Morawski, and Michael F. Dega. *Archaeological Monitoring Plan for Pool Installation at TMK (2) 4-5-04:037 Lahilahi Street, Kuʻia Ahupuaʻa, Lahaina District, Island of Maui.* Honolulu, HI: Scientific Consultant Services, Inc., 2003. [No location available]

OʻDay, Patrick and David Byerly. *Archaeological Inventory Survey of Proposed Fenceline Corridor for the West Maui Forest Reserve, Kuʻia, Mākila, Pāhoa, Halakaʻa, Polaiki, Launiupoko, and Olowalu Ahupuaʻa, Lahaina District, Maui Island, Hawaiʻi.* Kailua, HI: Garcia & Associates, 2015. [SHPD ID: 2019LI81533]

Rosendahl, Paul H. *Archaeological Treatment Plan for No Adverse Effect, Lahaina Bypass Highway Project, Lands of Honokōwai, Hanakaʻōʻō, Wahikuli, Panaʻewa, Kuʻia, Halakaʻa, Pūehuehu Nui, Pāhoa, Polanui, and Launiupoko, Lahaina District, Island of Maui.* Hilo, HI: Paul H. Rosendahl, Ph.D., Inc., 1994. [SHPD ID: 2019LI81439]

Rotunno-Hazuka, Lisa J. and Jeffrey Pantaleo. *Archaeological Monitoring Plan for Pool Installation at TMK (2) 4-5-04:037 Lahilahi Street, Kuʻia Ahupuaʻa, Lahaina District, Island of Maui.* Wailuku, HI: Archaeological Services Hawaii, LLC, 2002. [SHPD ID: 2019LI80627]

Yucha, Josephine M. and Hallett H. Hammatt. *Archaeological Monitoring Plan for the Lahaina Intermediate School Campus Fire Alarm Replacement Project, Panaʻewa and Kuʻia Ahupuaʻa, Lahaina District, Maui Island TMK (2) 4-6-18:013 por.* Wailuku, HI: Cultural Surveys Hawaiʻi, Inc., 2019. [No location available]

Lahaina

Ahlo, Hamilton M. and Maurice E. Morgenstein. *Archaeological Test Excavations Near the Mouth of Kahoma Stream, Lahaina, Maui.* Honolulu, HI: Hawaiʻi Marine Research, 1979.

Andricci, Nicole and Michael F. Dega. *An Archaeological Assessment for the Lahaina Square Redevelopment Project, Lahaina, Waineʻe Ahupuaʻa, District of Lahaina, Island of Maui, Hawaiʻi.* Honolulu, HI: Scientific Consultant Services, Inc., 2017. [SHPD ID: 2019LI80016]

Cleghorn, Paul L. *A Progress Report upon Completion of Fieldwork at the Seamen's Hospital, Lahaina, Maui (Phase 1).* Honolulu, HI: Department of Anthropology, Bernice P. Bishop Museum, 1975. [UH Call Number: DU629.L3 C54 1975]

Cleghorn, Paul L. *Phase 1 Archaeological Research at the Seamen's Hospital (Site D5-10), Lahaina, Maui.* Honolulu, HI: Department of Anthropology, Bernice P. Bishop Museum, 1975. [UH Call Number: DU629.L3 C544 1975]

Community Planning, Inc. *Lahaina Historical Restoration and Preservation.* Community Planning Inc., 1961. [UH Call Number: DU629.L3 M3]

Connolly, Robert D. III. *Phase I Archaeological Survey of Kahoma Stream Flood-Control-Project Area, Lahaina, Maui.* Honolulu, HI: Department of Anthropology, Bernice P. Bishop Museum, 1974.

Davis, Bertell D. *Preliminary Report, Mala Wharf Burials, Phase 1, Mala, Lahaina, Maui Island.* Lāwaʻi, HI: Archaeological Research Center Hawaiʻi, 1977. [No location available]

Dega, Michael F. *An Archaeological Monitoring Plan for the Ulupono Center Project, Lahaina, Panaʻewa Ahupuaʻa, Lahaina District, Hawaiʻi, TMK (2) 4-5-10:054.* Honolulu, HI: Scientific Consultant Services Inc., 2017. [SHPD ID: 2019LI80597]

Duensing, Dawn E. and Michael W. Foley. *Lahaina Design Guidelines, Lahaina Town, Maui, Hawaiʻi,* 2003. [SHPD ID: 2019LI81377]

Fredericksen, Walter M. and Demaris L. Fredericksen. *Archaeological Data Recovery Report on the Plantation Inn Site, Lahaina, Maui, Hawaiʻi.* Pukalani,

HI: Xamanek Researches, 1990. [SHPD ID: 2019LI81589; UH Call Number: DU629.L3 F738 1990a]

Fredericksen, Walter M. and Demaris L. Fredericksen. *Report on the Archaeological Excavation of the "Brick Palace" of King Kamehameha I at Lahaina, Maui, Hawai'i,* 1965. [SHPD ID: 2019LI81384; UH Call Number: DU629.L3 F74]

Fredericksen, Walter M., Demaris L. Fredericksen, and Erik M. Fredericksen. *An Archaeological Inventory Survey of the Plantation Inn Site, Lahaina, Maui, Hawai'i.* Pukalani, HI: Xamanek Researches, 1989. [SHPD ID: 2019LI81588]

Hammatt, Hallett H. *Archaeological Investigation and Monitoring, Mala Wharf Boat-Launch Ramp Area, Lahaina, Maui Island.* Lāwa'i, HI: Archaeological Research Center Hawai'i, Inc., 1978. [SHPD ID: 2019LI81387; UH Call Number: GN486 .H35]

Hart, Christopher. *Final Report of the Preparation for Exhibit of King Kamehameha I's "Brick Palace" at Lahaina, Maui, Hawai'i.* Maui Historic Commission, 1970.

Hommon, Robert J. *An Archaeological Reconnaissance Survey of an Area Near Waine'e Village, West Maui.* Hawai'i: Science Management, Inc., 1982. [SHPD ID: 2019LI81389; UH Call Number: DU629.W346 H66 1982]

Hommon, Robert J. *Report on a Walk Through Survey of the Kahoma Stream Flood Control Project Area.* Honolulu, HI: Department of Anthropology, Bernice P. Bishop Museum, 1973.

Joerger, Pauline King and Michael W. Kaschko. *A Cultural Historical Overview of the Kahoma Stream Flood Control Project, Lahaina, Maui and Ma'alaea Small Boat Harbor Project, Ma'alaea, Maui.* Honolulu, HI: Hawai'i Marine Research, Inc., 1979. [SHPD ID: 2019LI80298; UH Call Number: DU629.L3 J63]

John Carl Warnecke and Associates. *Lahaina Small Boat Harbor Study.* San Francisco, CA: John Carl Warnecke and Associates, Architects and Planning Consultants, 1965. [SHPD ID: 2019LI81397]

Kurashina, Hiro and Aki Sinoto. *Archaeological Reconnaissance of the Proposed Shopping Center at Lahaina, Maui, Hawai'i, TMK: (2) 4-5-02:009.* Honolulu, HI: Department of Anthropology, Bernice P. Bishop Museum, 1984. [SHPD ID: 2019LI80648; UH Call Number: DU629.L3 K87 1984]

Lash, Erik and Michael F. Dega. *An Archaeological Monitoring Plan for the Proposed Lahaina Harbor Complete Streets Project on Approximately 3.11 Acres (1.26 Hectares) in Lahaina, Paunau Ahupua'a, Lahaina District, Island of Maui, Hawai'i [TMK (2) 4-6-001:001, 004, 007, 009, 010, 012, and Adjacent*

Roadways]. Honolulu, HI: Scientific Consultant Services, Inc., 2017. [SHPD ID: 2019LI81388]

Rotunno-Hazuka, Lisa J. and Jeffrey Pantaleo. *Archaeological Monitoring Plan for the Construction of a Swimming Pool and Associated Utilities at the Allan Residence, Lahaina Ahupuaʻa, Lahaina District, Island of Maui*. Wailuku, HI: Archaeological Services Hawaiʻi, LLC, 2004. [SHPD ID: 2019LI80623]

Rotunno-Hazuka, Lisa J., Mia Watson, and Jeffrey Pantaleo. *Archaeological Monitoring Plan for the Repair and Installation of Underground Conduit at Front & Wharf Street, Lahaina and Waineʻe Ahupuaʻa, Lahaina District, Island of Maui*. Wailuku, HI: Archaeological Services Hawaii, LLC, 2008. [SHPD ID: 2019LI81385]

Sinoto, Aki. *An Archaeological Reconnaissance of the Mala Wharf Boat Launch Ramp Area, Lahaina, Maui*. Honolulu, HI: Department of Anthropology, Bernice P. Bishop Museum, 1975. [SHPD ID: 2019LI80624; UH Call Number: DU629.M353 S56 1975]

LAUNIUPOKO

Dega, Michael F. *A Preservation Plan for Multiple Archaeological Sites on Portions of a 570.3 Acre Property in the Launiupoko (Large Lot, Phase V) Subdivision No. 2, Launiupoko Ahupuaʻa, Lahaina District (Formerly Kāʻanapali), Island of Maui [TMK (2) 4-7-01:02]*. Honolulu, HI: Scientific Consultant Services, Inc., 2006. [SHPD ID: 2019LI81606]

Dega, Michael F. *Archaeological Inventory Survey of the Punakea Loop Corridor in Launiupoko and Polanui Ahupuaʻa, Lahaina District (formerly Kāʻanapali), island of Maui, Hawaiʻi [TMK: (2) 4-8-01:002 por. & 4-7-01:029 por.]*. Honolulu, HI: Scientific Consultant Services, Inc., 2008. [SHPD ID: 2019LI81597]

Dega, Michael F. *Archaeological Monitoring Plan for the Installation of a Septic System, Maui County Parks, Launiupoko Ahupuaʻa, Lahaina District, Maui Island, Hawaiʻi [TMK: (2) 4-7-01:17]*. Honolulu, HI: Scientific Consultant Services, Inc., 2005. [SHPD ID: 2019LI81619]

Desilets, Michael and Patrick OʻDay. *Preservation Plan for Proposed Fenceline Corridor for the West Maui Forest Reserve, Kuʻia, Mākila, Pāhoa, Halakaʻa, Polaiki, Launiupoko, and Olowalu Ahupuaʻa, Lahaina District, Maui Island, Hawaiʻi*. Kailua, HI: Garcia & Associates, 2016. [SHPD ID: 2019LI81528]

Graves, Donna and Susan Goodfellow. *Archaeological Inventory Survey, Launiupoko Golf Course, Land of Launiupoko, Lahaina District, Island of Maui*.

Hilo, HI: Paul H. Rosendahl, Ph.D., Inc., 1991. [SHPD ID: 2019LI81595, 2019LI81610]

Haun, Alan E. *Archaeological Assessment, Lands of Polanui, Polaiki, and Launiupoko, Lahaina District, Island of Maui.* Kailua-Kona, HI: Haun and Associates, 2002. [SHPD ID: 2019LI81608]

Haun, Alan E. and Dave Henry with Maria E. K. Orr. *Archaeological Inventory Survey Portion of TMK 4-7-01:002, Land of Launiupoko, Lahaina District, Island of Maui.* Kailua-Kona, HI: Haun and Associates, 2001. [SHPD ID: 2019LI81599]

Haun, Alan E. and Dave Henry. *Archaeological Inventory Survey, Proposed 124-Acre Mākila Subdivision, Lands of Launiupoko, Polanui and Pūehuehu Nui, Lahaina District, Island of Maui (TMK: 4-7-01: por. 1 and TMK 4-7-04: Por. 4).* Kailua-Kona, HI: Haun and Associates, 2001. [SHPD ID: 2019LI81623]

Launiupoko Associates, LLC. *Archaeological Preservation Plan, Mahanalua Nui Subdivision.* Launiupoko Associates, 1998. [SHPD ID: 2019LI81602]

Morawski, Lauren, Adam Johnson, Tomasi Patolo, and Michael F. Dega. *An Archaeological Inventory Survey of 520 Acres in the Launiupoko (Large Lot) Subdivision No. 1, Launiupoko Ahupuaʻa, Lahaina District (formerly Kāʻanapali), Island of Maui, Hawaiʻi [TMK (2) 4-7-01:002 por.].* Honolulu, HI: Scientific Consultant Services, Inc., 2008. [SHPD ID: 2019LI81603]

OʻDay, Patrick and David Byerly. *Archaeological Inventory Survey of Proposed Fenceline Corridor for the West Maui Forest Reserve, Kuʻia, Mākila, Pāhoa, Halakaʻa, Polaiki, Launiupoko, and Olowalu Ahupuaʻa, Lahaina District, Maui Island, Hawaiʻi.* Kailua, HI: Garcia & Associates, 2015. [SHPD ID: 2019LI81533]

Paraso, C. Kanani and Michael F. Dega. *An Archaeological Assessment of three parcels at the Hyatt Regency Maui Resort, Kāʻanapali, Hanakaʻōʻō Ahupuaʻa, Lahaina District, Maui Island, Hawaiʻi [TMK (2) 4-4-013:004, 005, 008];* Honolulu, HI: Scientific Consultant Services, Inc., 2006. [SHPD ID: 2019LI80041]

Rosendahl, Paul H. *Archaeological Treatment Plan for No Adverse Effect, Lahaina Bypass Highway Project, Lands of Honokōwai, Hanakaʻōʻō, Wahikuli, Panaʻewa, Kuʻia, Halakaʻa, Pūehuehu Nui, Pāhoa, Polanui, and Launiupoko, Lahaina District, Island of Maui.* Hilo, HI: Paul H. Rosendahl, Ph.D., Inc., 1994. [SHPD ID: 2019LI81439]

Rosendahl, Paul H. *Archaeological Treatment Plan for No Adverse Effect, Lahaina Bypass Highway Project, Lands of Honokōwai, Hanakaʻōʻō, Wahikuli, Panaʻewa, Kuʻia, Halakaʻa, Pūehuehu Nui, Pāhoa, Polanui, and Launiupoko, Lahaina*

District, Island of Maui. Hilo, HI: Paul H. Rosendahl, Ph.D., Inc., 1994. [SHPD ID: 2019LI81439]

Rotunno-Hazuka, Lisa J. *Archaeological Assessment for the Proposed Well Site in Launiupoko, Lahaina, Maui TMK 4-7-02:001 Lot B.* Wailuku, HI: Archaeological Services Hawaii, LLC, 1997. [SHPD ID: 2019LI81617]

Shefcheck, Donna M. and Michael F. Dega. *An Archaeological Inventory Survey of 122.84 Acres in the Launiupoko (Large Lot) Subdivision 6 Launiupoko and Polanui Ahupuaʻa, Lahaina District, Maui, Hawaiʻi [TMK (2) 4-7-01:029 por.].* Honolulu, HI: Scientific Consultant Services, Inc., 2008. [SHPD ID: 2019LI81593]

Shefcheck, Donna M. and Michael F. Dega. *An Archaeological Inventory Survey of 123.31 Acres in the Launiupoko (Large Lot) Subdivision 6 Launiupoko and Polanui Ahupuaʻa, Lahaina District (formerly Kāʻanapali) Island of Maui, Hawaiʻi TMK (2) 4-8-01:002 por.).* Honolulu, HI: Scientific Consultant Services, Inc., 2007. [SHPD ID: 2019LI81596]

Shefcheck, Donna M. and Michael F. Dega. *Site Report for a Previously Unrecorded Heiau in Launiupoko Ahupuaʻa, Lahaina District, Island of Maui, Hawaiʻi.* Honolulu, HI: Scientific Consultant Services, Inc., 2006. [SHPD ID: 2019LI81592]

MĀHINAHINA

Andricci, Nicole and Michael F. Dega. *AAAAA Rent-A-Space Extension Project Honokōwai, Māhinahina 4 Ahupuaʻa Lahaina (Kāʻanapali) District, Maui Island Hawaii [TMK (2) 4-4-01:026].* Honolulu, HI: Scientific Consultant Services, Inc., 2015.

Buffum, Amy and Michael F. Dega. *An Archaeological Monitoring Report for Construction work at Honokōwai, Māhinahina Ahupuaʻa, Kāʻanapali District, Maui Island, Hawaii.* Honolulu, HI: Scientific Consultant Services, Inc., 2002.

Chaffee, D. and C. Monahan. *A Monitoring Plan for 3.054 Acres of Partially Developed Land in Honokōwai, Māhinahina 4 Ahupuaʻa, Lahaina District, Maui Island, Hawaiʻi.* Honolulu, HI: Scientific Consultant Services, Inc., 2005.

Chun, Allison and Michael F. Dega. *Addendum Archaeological Assessment Report on 0.13 Acres of Partially Developed land in Honokōwai, Māhinahina 4 Ahupuaʻa, Maui Island, Hawaiʻi.* Honolulu, HI: Scientific Consultant Services, Inc., 2005. [SHPD ID: 2019LI81043]

Dagher, Cathleen A. and Michael F. Dega. *Archaeological Field Inspection Results and Recommendations for the Proposed Maui Police Department Communications*

Facility at Lahainaluna Water Treatment Site, Panaʻewa Ahupuaʻa, Lahaina District, Maui Island, Hawaiʻi [TMK: (2) 4-6-18:012 por.]. Honolulu, HI: Scientific Consultant Services, Inc., 2016. [SHPD ID: 2019LI81527]

Dagher, Cathleen A. and Michael F. Dega. *Archaeological Field Inspection Results and Recommendations for the Proposed Maui Police Department Communications Facility at Māhinahina Water Treatment Plant, Māhinahina Ahupuaʻa, Lahaina District, Maui Island, Hawaiʻi.* Honolulu, HI: Scientific Consultant Services, Inc., 2016. [SHPD ID: 2019LI81036]

Dagher, Cathleen A. and Michael F. Dega. *Archaeological Inventory Survey for the Proposed West Maui Water Source Development Project Māhinahina Well (State Well No. 6-5638-004) (West Maui Well No. 1) and the Kahana Well (State Well No. 6-5738-002) (West Maui Well No. 2), Honokōwai, Māhinahina, and Māhinahina 1, 2, 3 Ahupuaʻa, Lahaina (Kāʻanapali) District, Island of Maui, Hawaiʻi [TMK: (2) 4-3-01:017, (2) 4-3-01:084; (2) 4-4-02:014, 015, and 018; and (2) 4-4-004:009, 011, 017, and 019].* Honolulu, HI: Scientific Consultant Services, Inc., 2022. [SHPD ID: 2022LI00356]

Dega, Michael F. *An Archaeological Monitoring plan for Construction Work at Honokōwai, Māhinahina Ahupuaʻa, Kāʻanapali District, Maui Island, Hawaiʻi.* Honolulu, HI: Scientific Consultant Services, Inc., 2000. [SHPD ID: 2019LI81247]

Hommon, Robert J. and Hamilton M. Ahlo, Jr. *An Archaeological Reconnaissance Survey of the Site of a Proposed Airstrip at Māhinahina, West Maui.* Science Management, Inc., 1982. [SHPD ID: 2019LI81050; UH Call Number: DU629.M345 H66 1982]

McGerty, Leann and Robert L. Spear. *An Inventory Survey of a 3.3 Acre Parcel in Māhinahina 4 Ahupuaʻa, Lahaina District, Island of Maui, Hawaiʻi [TMK (2) 4-3-06:003],* 1996. [SHPD ID: 2019LI81305]

Monahan, Christopher M. *An Archaeological Assessment Report on 3.054 Acres of Partially Developed Land in Honokōwai, Māhinahina 4 Ahupuaʻa, Lahaina District, Maui Island, Hawaiʻi [TMK (2) 4-3-06:002 and 069].* Honolulu, HI: Scientific Consultant Services, Inc., 2003. [SHPD ID: 2019LI81314, 2019LI81304]

Mulrooney et al. *Archaeological Inventory Survey Report for the Kahana Solar Project in Ahupuaʻa of Kahana and Māhinahina 1–3, Moku of Kāʻanapali (Lahaina Modern Tax District), Island of Maui [TMK: (2) 4-3-01:017 por.; (2) 4-3-01:082 por.; (2) 4-3-01:084 por.].* Kailua, HI: Pacific Legacy, Inc., 2022

Olson, Larry G. *Appendix II—A Geoarchaeological Report of Site 225, Māhinahina Gulch, Maui, Hawaiʻi.* Lāwaʻi, HI: Archaeological Research Center Hawaiʻi, 1977. [No location available]

Pantaleo, Jeffrey and Paul Titchenal. *An Archaeological Inventory Survey Report for the Pulelehua Community Project TMK (2) 4-3-01:031 Por. Māhinahina 1, 2, 3, Māhinahina 4, and Kahana Ahupuaʻa, Lahaina and Kāʻanapali Districts, Island of Maui.* Wailuku, HI: Archaeological Services Hawaii, LLC, 2004. [SHPD ID: 2019LI81072]

Sinoto, Aki. *Field Examination of Six Sites in the Honolua Watershed, Maui.* Honolulu, HI: Department of Anthropology, Bernice P. Bishop Museum, 1975. [SHPD ID: 2019LI81435; UH Call Number: DU629.H69 S56 1975]

Tulchin, Jon and Hallett H. Hammatt. *Archaeological Assessment of a 0.2-Acre Parcel and Waterline, Māhinahina 4 Ahupuaʻa, Lahaina District, Island of Maui.* Wailuku, HI: Cultural Surveys Hawaiʻi, Inc., 2003. [SHPD ID: 2019LI81315]

Mailepai

Conte, Patty J. *Archaeological Assessment Report for TMK (2) 4-3-03:043 Mailepai Ahupuaʻa, Lahaina District, Island of Maui.* Makawao, HI: CRM Solutions Hawaiʻi, Inc., 2005. [SHPD ID: 2019LI81298]

Conte, Patty J. *Archaeological Monitoring Report for Off-Site Construction (Mailepai Hui Land Lots 51-C-4-A, B & C) Lahaina District, Mailepai Ahupuaʻa, Island of Maui.* Makawao, HI: CRM Solutions Hawaiʻi, Inc., 2007. [SHPD ID: 2019LI81324]

Fredericksen, Demaris L., Walter M. Fredericksen, and Erik M. Fredericksen. *Archaeological Inventory Survey of a 9.976 Acre Parcel in the Kahana/Mailepai/Akeloa Lands, Lahaina District, Maui, Hawaiʻi.* Pukalani, HI: Xamanek Researches, 1990. [SHPD ID: 2019LI81060]

Fredericksen, Erik M. *An Archaeological Monitoring Plan for a parcel of land in Napili, Mailepai Ahupuaʻa, Lahaina District, Napili, Maui, TMK: (2) 4-3-15:014.* Pukalani, HI: Xamanek Researches, 2004. [SHPD ID: 2019LI81293]

Fredericksen, Erik M. and Demaris L. Fredericksen. *Additional Archaeological Inventory Survey Level Work for Site 50-50-03-4797, Lower Honoapiʻilani Road Improvements Project Corridor; Alaeloa, Mailepai and Kahana Ahupuaʻa, Lahaina District, Maui Island [TMK (2) 4-3-15].* Pukalani, HI: Xamanek Researches, 2001. [SHPD ID: 2021LI00221]

Fredericksen, Erik M. and Jennifer J. Frey. *An Archaeological Inventory Survey of a portion of land in Mailepai Ahupua'a, Lahaina District, Maui Island.* Pukalani, HI: Xamanek Researches, 2008. [SHPD ID: 2019LI81302]

Mākila

Chaffee, David B. and Michael F. Dega. *An Archaeological Monitoring Plan for the Maui Countywide Wastewater Pump Station Renovations, Phase II Project at Multiple Locations, Hanaka'ō'ō Ahupua'a and Mākila Ahupua'a, Lahaina District, Maui Island, Hawai'i [TMK: (2) 4-4-013:003, por. and 4-6-028:054].* Honolulu, HI: Scientific Consultant Services, Inc., 2014.

Desilets, Michael and Patrick O'Day. *Preservation Plan for Proposed Fenceline Corridor for the West Maui Forest Reserve, Ku'ia, Mākila, Pāhoa, Halaka'a, Polaiki, Launiupoko, and Olowalu Ahupua'a, Lahaina District, Maui Island, Hawai'i.* Kailua, HI: Garcia & Associates, 2016. [SHPD ID: 2019LI81528]

Fredericksen, Erik M. *Archaeological Monitoring Plan for Sewer Lateral Installation Project at 460 Alio Street, Land of Nalehu, Mākila Ahupua'a, Lahaina District, Maui [TMK (2) 4-6-06:031].* Pukalani, HI: Xamanek Researches, 2003. [SHPD ID: 2019LI81270]

O'Day, Patrick and David Byerly. *Archaeological Inventory Survey of Proposed Fenceline Corridor for the West Maui Forest Reserve, Ku'ia, Mākila, Pāhoa, Halaka'a, Polaiki, Launiupoko, and Olowalu Ahupua'a, Lahaina District, Maui Island, Hawai'i.* Kailua, HI: Garcia & Associates, 2015. [SHPD ID: 2019LI81533]

Pickett, Jenny L. and Michael F. Dega. *An Archaeological Assessment for 16.8 Acres in Lahaina, Mākila Ahupua'a, Lahaina District, Maui Island, Hawai'i [TMK (2) 4-5-10:005 & 006 por.].* Honolulu, HI: Scientific Consultant Services, Inc., 2005. [SHPD ID: 2019LI80600]

Moali'i

Conte, Patty J. *Archaeological Monitoring Plan for On and Off-Site Construction Related to the Proposed Kent Property Demo/Reconstruction, TMK (2) 4-5-12:010 Moali'i Ahupua'a, Lahaina District, Island of Maui.* Makawao, HI: CRM Solutions Hawai'i, Inc., 2007. [SHPD ID: 2019LI81346]

Dega, Michael F. and David B. Chaffee. *An Archaeological Monitoring Plan for a Private Residence Demolition in Lahaina, Moali'i Ahupua'a, Lahaina District, Maui Island, Hawai'i [TMK (2) 4-6-02:003].* Honolulu, HI: Scientific Consultant Services, Inc., 2006. [SHPD ID: 2019LI81394]

Dega, Michael F. and David B. Chaffee. *Archaeological Monitoring Plan for Construction at the Lahaina Shores, Moaliʻi Ahupuaʻa, Lahaina District, Maui Island, Hawaiʻi.* Honolulu, HI: Scientific Consultant Services, Inc., 2004. [SHPD ID: 2019LI81373]

Donham, Theresa K. *Archaeological Monitoring Plan for Construction of a Pool & Spa at the Hurlock Property, Moaliʻi, Lahaina District, Maui, TMK: (2) 4-5-13:004.* Kīhei, HI: Akahele Archaeology, 2003. [SHPD ID: 2019LI81351]

Fredericksen, Erik M. *An Archaeological Monitoring Plan for the Emerald Plaza II Project, Land of Moaliʻi, Lahaina District, Island of Maui, TMK: (2) 4-5-10:052.* Pukalani, HI: Xamanek Researches, 2019. [No location available]

Fredericksen, Erik M. *Archaeological Inventory Survey for the Proposed Lahaina Cannery Fuel Station Project, Land of Moaliʻi, Lahaina District, Island of Maui [TMK: (2) 4-5-11: 004 Por.].* Pukalani, HI: Xamanek Researches, 2023. [SHPD ID: 2023LI00137]

Fredericksen, Erik M. *Archaeological Monitoring Plan for a Water Lateral and Sewer Lateral Installation Project for a Parcel of Land in Lahaina, Moaliʻi Ahupuaʻa, Lahaina District, Maui.* Pukalani, HI: Xamanek Researches, 2003. [SHPD ID: 2019LI81270]

Fredericksen, Erik M. *Archaeological Monitoring Report for a Portion of Land in Moaliʻi Ahupuaʻa, Lahaina District, Maui.* Pukalani, HI: Xamanek Researches, 2004. [SHPD ID: 2019LI81269]

Fredericksen, Erik M. and J. J. Frey. *Burial Site Component of an Archaeological Data Recovery Plan for Inadvertently Discovered Human Skeletal Remains, Site 50-50-03-08973, Located in Previously Imported Sand Fill During Utilities Installation for the Lahaina Cannery Fuel Station Project, Ahupuaʻa of Moaliʻi, Lahaina District, Island of Maui [TMK: (2) 4-5-11:004 por.].* Pukalani, HI: Xamanek Researches, 2023. [SHPD ID: 2023LI00074]

Haun, A. E. *Subsurface Archaeological Reconnaissance Survey, Lahaina Cannery Makai and Mauka Parcels, Land of Moaliʻi, Lahaina District, Island of Maui,* 1988. [SHPD ID: 2019LI80612]

Monahan, Christopher M. *An Archaeological Assessment Report on 17.746 Acres of Land (Lahaina Business Park, Phase II) on an Undeveloped Lot in Lahaina, Moaliʻi Ahupuaʻa, Lahaina District, Maui Island, Hawaiʻi [TMK: (2) 4-5-10:007].* Honolulu, HI: Scientific Consultant Services, Inc., 2003. [SHPD ID: 2019LI80604]

Rotunno-Hazuka, Lisa J. and Jeffrey Pantaleo. *Archaeological Monitoring Plan for All Improvements at the McFarland Residence TMK: (2) 4-5-13:003, Moaliʻi*

Ahupuaʻa Lahaina District, Island of Maui. Wailuku, HI: Archaeological Services Hawaii, LLC, 2006. [SHPD ID: 2019LI81352]

Nāpili

Chong Jin and Michael F. Dega. *Archaeological Monitoring Report for the Kapalua Sinkhole Remediation and Native Plant Restoration Project, Nāpili 2–3 Ahupuaʻa, Lahaina District, Island of Maui [TMK: (2) 4-2-04:025 and (2) 4-2-04:059].* Honolulu, HI: Scientific Consultant Services, Inc., 2021. [SHPD ID: 2022LI00634]

Cordle, Shayna and Michael F. Dega. *An Archaeological Monitoring Plan for 1.835 Acres in Napili, Napili 2–3 Ahupuaʻa, Lahaina District, Maui Island, Hawaiʻi.* Honolulu, HI: Scientific Consultant Services, Inc., 2008. ID: 2019LI81066]

Dagher, Cathleen A. and Michael F. Dega. *An Archaeological Monitoring Plan for the Napili Culvert Replacement Project, Nāpili 4 and 5 Ahupuaʻa, Lahaina (Kāʻanapali) District, Island of Maui, Hawaiʻi.* Honolulu, HI: Scientific Consultant Services, Inc., 2015. [SHPD ID: 2019LI81056]

Dagher, Cathleen A. and Michael F. Dega. *An Archaeological Monitoring Plan for the Proposed Kapalua Coastal Trail Corridor Located in Kapalua and Honokōhau and Nāpili 2&3 Ahupuaʻa Lahaina District, Island of Maui, Hawaiʻi [TMK: (2) 4-2-Various].* Honolulu, HI: Scientific Consultant Services, Inc., 2007. [SHPD ID: 2019LI81421]

Dagher, Cathleen A. and Michael F. Dega. *An Archaeological Monitoring Plan for the Proposed Kapalua Coastal Trail Located in the Areas of Nāpili, Kapalua, Honokahua, and Honolua, Ahupuaʻa of Nāpili 2 & 3, Honokahua, and Honolua, Lahaina district, Island of Maui, Hawaiʻi.* Honolulu, HI: Scientific Consultant Services, Inc., 2008. [SHPD ID: 2019LI81410]

Dega, Michael F. and David B. Chaffee. *Archaeological Monitoring Plan for Construction Work on Approximately 25.3 Acres in Kapalua, Napili 2-3 Ahupuaʻa, Lahaina District, Maui Island, Hawaiʻi.* Honolulu, HI: Scientific Consultant Services, Inc., 2004. [SHPD ID: 2019LI81041]

Devereux, Thomas K., William H. Folk, and Hallett H. Hammatt. *Archaeological Survey of the Lands Comprising Project District 2 at Kapalua, Honokahua, and Nāpili 2 & 3 Ahupuaʻa Lahaina District of Maui.* Wailuku, HI: Cultural Surveys Hawaiʻi, Inc., 2001. [SHPD ID: 2019LI81007]

Dockall, John E. and Hallett H. Hammatt. *An Archaeological Inventory Survey for a Proposed Town Center and Residential Village, Nāpili Ahupuaʻa, Lahaina*

District. Wailuku, HI: Cultural Surveys Hawaiʻi, Inc., 2005. [SHPD ID: 2019LI81011]

Fredericksen, Demaris L. and Erik M. Fredericksen. *An Archaeological Inventory Survey of a portion of land in Nāpili 2-3 Ahupuaʻa, Lahaina District, Island of Maui [TMK: (2) 4-2-07: Parcels 007 and 008].* Pukalani, HI: Xamanek Researches, 2003. [SHPD ID: 2019LI81044]

Fredericksen, Erik M. *An Archaeological Monitoring Plan for a parcel of land in Napili, Mailepai Ahupuaʻa, Lahaina District, Napili, Maui, TMK: (2) 4-3-15:014.* Pukalani, HI: Xamanek Researches, 2004. [SHPD ID: 2019LI81293]

Fredericksen, Erik M. *Archaeological Monitoring Plan for Lot 29 (Site 29) Honokahua and Napili 2-3 Ahupuaʻa, Lahaina District, Maui, Hawaiʻi.* Pukalani, HI: Xamanek Researches, 1999. [SHPD ID: 2019LI81028]

Fredericksen, Erik M. *Archaeological Monitoring Report for the Coconut Grove Development (Site 29), Honokahua and Napili 2-3 Ahupuaʻa Lahiana District, Island of Maui.* Pukalani, HI: Xamanek Researches, 2001. [SHPD ID: 2019LI17106]

Fredericksen, Erik M. and Demaris L. Fredericksen. *Archaeological Inventory Survey of 475 Acres in Kapalua District 2 Project Area, Located in Napili and Honokahua Ahupuaʻa, Lahaina District, Maui Island, TMK: (2) 4-2-01: por. 1.* Pukalani, HI: Xamanek Researches, 2002. [SHPD ID: 2021LI00311]

Fredericksen, Erik M., Demaris L. Fredericksen, and Walter M. Fredericksen. *An Archaeological Inventory Survey of a 12.2 Acre Parcel. Honokahua and Napili 2-3 Ahupuaʻa, Lahaina District Maui Island.* Pukalani, HI: Xamanek Researches, 1994. [SHPD ID: 2019LI81030]

Fredericksen, Erik M., Walter M. Fredericksen, and Demaris L. Fredericksen. *Additional Archaeological Inventory Survey Subsurface testing at Kapalua Bay Hotel [TMK (2) 4-2-04:26], Honokahua and Napili 2-3 Ahupuaʻa, Lahaina District, Maui Island.* Pukalani, HI: Xamanek Researches, 1996. [SHPD ID: 2019LI81024]

Hammatt, Hallett H. and Rodney Chiogioji. *Archaeological Monitoring Plan for a ½-Acre parcel in Napili 2-3 Ahupuaʻa, Lahaina District, Island of Maui.* Wailuku, HI: Cultural Surveys Hawaiʻi, Inc., 2002. [SHPD ID: 2019LI81063]

Kaschko, Michael W. *Archaeological Walk-Through Survey of Specified Areas in the Wailuku Flood Prevention Project and the Honolua Watershed, Maui.* Honolulu, HI: Department of Anthropology, Bernice P. Bishop Museum, 1974. [SHPD ID: 2019LI81443]

Kennedy, Joseph. *Archaeological Inventory Survey of TMK (2) 4-3-02:068 & 069, Located at Napili, Island of Maui.* Hale'iwa, HI: Archaeological Consultants of Hawaii, 1990. [SHPD ID: 2019LI81061]

Kennedy, Joseph. *Archaeological Walk Through Reconnaissance of (2)4-3-01:001 Napili Fire Station, TMK (2) 4-3-01:001 (por.),* 1989. [SHPD ID: 2019LI81054]

Kirch, Patrick V. *Archaeological Excavations at Site D13-1, Hawea Point, Maui, Hawaiian Islands.* Honolulu, HI: Department of Anthropology, Bernice P. Bishop Museum, 1973. [SHPD ID: 2019LI81021; UH Call Number: DU629. H393 K57 1973]

Lee-Greig, Tanya L. and Hallett H. Hammatt. *Preservation Plan for Thirty-Three Historic Properties Located in and Adjacent to the Kapalua Mauka Project Area, Honokahua, Nāpili 2 & 3, and Nāpili 4-5 Ahupua'a, Lahaina District, Maui Island.* Wailuku, HI: Cultural Surveys Hawai'i, Inc., 2005. [SHPD ID: 2019LI80997]

McGerty, Leann and Robert L. Spear. *A Cultural Impact Assessment for a portion of the Mauian Hotel Property, Nāpili Ahupua'a, Lahaina District, Maui Island, Hawai'i.* Honolulu, HI: Scientific Consultant Services, Inc., 2007. [SHPD ID: 2019LI81065]

Monahan, Christopher M. *An Archaeological Inventory Survey Report on Three Contiguous Parcels Measuring Approximately 25.3 Acres in Kapalua, Napili 2-3 Ahupua'a, Lahaina District, Maui Island, Hawai'i.* Honolulu, HI: Scientific Consultant Services, Inc., 2005. [SHPD ID: 2019LI81018]

O'Claray, Jenny. *Additional Field Work for Drainage 11 Kapalua Plantation Estates Project Area, Lands of Honokahua, Honolua, Napili 2-2 Lahaina District, Island of Maui.* Hilo, HI: Paul H. Rosendahl, Ph.D., Inc., 1991. [SHPD ID: 2019LI81415]

O'Hare, Constance, Thomas K. Devereux, William H. Folk, and Hallett H. Hammatt. *Preservation Plan for Specific Sites in the Land Comprising Project District 2 at Kapalua, Honokahua and Nāpili 2 & 3 Ahupua'a Lahaina District of Maui.* Wailuku, HI: Cultural Surveys Hawai'i, Inc., 2003. [SHPD ID: 2019LI81002]

Rosendahl, Paul H. *Additional Inventory Survey for Drainage Easement 11 Kapalua Plantation Estates Project Area, Lands of Honokahua, Honolua, and Napili 2-3, Lahaina District, Island of Maui.* Hilo, HI: Paul H. Rosendahl, Ph.D., Inc., 1991. [SHPD ID: 2019LI80996]

Rosendahl, Paul H. *Archaeological Reconnaissance Survey, The Cottages Project Area Kapalua Development Site 2-A, Lands of Honokahua and Napili 2 & 3,*

Lahaina District, Island of Maui. Hilo, HI: Paul H. Rosendahl, Ph.D., Inc., 1988. [SHPD ID: 2019LI81009]

Rosendahl, Paul H. *Subsurface Reconnaissance Testing, Kapalua Place Project Area, Kapalua Development Site 2-A, Lands of Honokahua and Napili 2 & 3, Lahaina District, Island of Maui.* Hilo, HI: Paul H. Rosendahl, Ph.D., Inc., 1988. [SHPD ID: 2019LI81000]

Rotunno-Hazuka, Lisa J. and Jeffrey Pantaleo. *Archaeological Monitoring Plan for the Renovation and Revitalization of the Napili Kai Resort, Napili Ahupuaʻa, Lahaina District, Island of Maui.* Wailuku, HI: Archaeological Services Hawaii, LLC, 2005. [SHPD ID: 2019LI81067]

Sinoto, Aki. *Field Examination of Six Sites in the Honolua Watershed, Maui.* Honolulu, HI: Department of Anthropology, Bernice P. Bishop Museum, 1975. [SHPD ID: 2019LI81435; UH Call Number: DU629.H69 S56 1975]

Tome, Guerin and Michael F. Dega. *An Archaeological Inventory Survey for the Proposed Kapalua Coastal Trail Located in the Areas of Kapalua and Honokāhau, Honokahua and Nāpili 2 & 3.* Honolulu, HI: Scientific Consultant Services, Inc., 2007. [SHPD ID: 2019LI81433]

Tome, Guerin and Michael F. Dega. *An Archaeological Monitoring Plan for the Proposed Kapalua Coastal Trail Located in the areas of Nāpili, Kapalua, Honoka-hua, and Honolua, Ahupuaʻa of Nāpili 2&3, Honokahua, and Honolua, Lahaina District, Island of Maui, Hawaiʻi.* Honolulu, HI: Scientific Consultant Services, Inc., 2008. [SHPD ID: 2019LI81410]

Olowalu

Bassford, B. A. and Michael F. Dega. *Burial Site Component of an Archaeological Data Recovery and Preservation Plan for Site 50-50-08-8284 at Camp Olowalu in Olowalu, Olowalu Ahupuaʻa, Lahaina District, Maui Island, Hawaiʻi [TMK (2) 4-8-03:084 por.].* Honolulu, HI: Scientific Consultant Services, Inc., 2015. [No location available]

Dagher, Cathleen A. and Michael F. Dega. *An Archaeological Monitoring Plan for Olowalu Lot 24, Olowalu Ahupuaʻa, Lahaina District, Island of Maui, Hawaiʻi [TMK: (2) 4-8-03:107].* Honolulu, HI: Scientific Consultant Services, Inc., 2019. [SHPD ID: 2019LI05336]

Dagher, Cathleen A. and Michael F. Dega. *An Archaeological Monitoring Plan for the Poseley Residence, Olowalu Ahupuaʻa, Lahaina District, Island of Maui,*

Hawaiʻi [TMK: (2) 4-8-03:047 and portions of 001 and 084 (Easement G)]. Honolulu, HI: Scientific Consultant Services, Inc., 2015. [SHPD ID: 2019LI81660]

Desilets, Michael and Patrick OʻDay. *Preservation Plan for Proposed Fenceline Corridor for the West Maui Forest Reserve, Kuʻia, Mākila, Pāhoa, Halakaʻa, Polaiki, Launiupoko, and Olowalu Ahupuaʻa, Lahaina District, Maui Island, Hawaiʻi.* Kailua, HI: Garcia & Associates, 2016. [SHPD ID: 2019LI81528]

Fredericksen, Demaris L. and Erik M. Fredericksen. *Archaeological Inventory Survey of Makai Portion (Phase 1) of Olowalu Development Parcel, Olowalu Ahupuaʻa, Lahaina District, Maui Island [TMK: (2) 4-8-03: por. 05].* Pukalani, HI: Xamanek Researches, 2000. [SHPD ID: 2019LI81638]

Fredericksen, Erik M. *Archaeological Monitoring Plan on a 1.3 Acre of Land on the Olowalu Makai Project Area, Olowalu Ahupuaʻa, Lahaina District, Maui [TMK: (2) 4-9-03:044].* Pukalani, HI: Xamanek Researches, 2001. [SHPD ID: 2019LI81635]

Fredericksen, Erik M. *Archaeological Monitoring Report for a 1.3 Acre of Land on the Olowalu Makai Project Area, Olowalu Ahupuaʻa, Lahaina District, Maui (TMK: 2-4-8-03:44).* Pukalani, HI: Xamanek Researches, 2003. [SHPD ID: 2019LI81637]

Lee and Michael F. Dega. *An Archaeological Assessment for a New Wastewater System at the Olowalu Plantation Manager's House in Olowalu, Olowalu Ahupuaʻa, Lahaina District, Island of Maui, Hawaiʻi [TMK: (2) 4-8-03:005 por.].* Honolulu, HI: Scientific Consultant Services, Inc., 2021. [SHPD ID: 2021LI00436]

McGerty, Leann and Robert L. Spear. *A Cultural Impact Assessment of Approximately 0.8 Acres of Land in Olowalu Ahupuaʻa, Wailuku District, Maui, Hawaiʻi [TMK (2) 4-9-003:45A].* Honolulu, HI: Scientific Consultant Services, Inc., 2006. [SHPD ID: 2019LI81636]

OʻDay, Patrick and David Byerly. *Archaeological Inventory Survey of Proposed Fenceline Corridor for the West Maui Forest Reserve, Kuʻia, Mākila, Pāhoa, Halakaʻa, Polaiki, Launiupoko, and Olowalu Ahupuaʻa, Lahaina District, Maui Island, Hawaiʻi.* Kailua, HI: Garcia & Associates, 2015. [SHPD ID: 2019LI81533]

Olowalu Elua Associates, LLC. *Archaeological Mitigation and Preservation Plan, Makai Portion (Phase 1), Olowalu Ahupuaʻa, Lahaina District, Maui Island.* Olowalu, HI: Olowalu Elua Associates, LLC, 2001.

Olowalu Elua Associates, LLC. *Archaeological Preservation Plan, Mauka Portion (Phase 2), Olowalu Ahupuaʻa, Lahaina District, Maui Island.* Olowalu, HI: Olowalu Elua Associates, LLC, 2002. [SHPD ID: 2019LI00099]

Olowalu Elua Associates, LLC. *Monitoring Plan for Sites 50-50-08-4820 and 50-50-08-4821; Olowalu Ahupuaʻa, Lahaina District; Island of Maui [TMK (2) 4-8-003: portion of 10].* Olowalu, HI: Olowalu Elua Associates, LLC, 2002. [No location available]

Riford, Mary F. and Paul L. Cleghorn. *Documentary Assessment of Archaeological Potential of Ten Prospective Power Plant Sites on Maui.* Honolulu, HI: Public Archaeology Section, Bernice P. Bishop Museum, 1989. [SHPD ID: 2022LI00168]

Stankov, Pavel and Michael F. Dega. *Archaeological Monitoring Plan for the Renovations and Landscaping at the Stakelbeck Property at Olowalu Ahupuaʻa, Lahaina District, Island of Maui, Hawaiʻi [TMK (2) 4-8-03:002 por.].* Honolulu, HI: Scientific Consultant Services, Inc., 2021. [SHPD ID: 2021LI00103]

Wiley, Tiffany E. and Michael F. Dega. *Addendum to an Archaeological Monitoring Plan for the Poseley Residence, Olowalu Ahupuaʻa, Lahaina District, Island of Maui, Hawaiʻi [TMK (2) 4-8-003:047, and portions of 001 and 084 (Easement G)].* Honolulu, HI: Scientific Consultant Services, Inc., 2017. [No location available]

Paeohi

Lee-Greig, Tanya, Robert Hill, and Hallett H. Hammatt. *An Archaeological Inventory Survey Report for the Lahaina Bypass Modified Alignment from Kahoma Stream to the Keawe Street Extension, Kelawea, Paeohi, and Wahikuli Ahupuaʻa, Lahaina District, Maui Island TMK (2) 4-5-021, 010, 015, and 031: Multiple Parcels.* Wailuku, HI: Cultural Surveys Hawaiʻi, Inc., 2008. [SHPD ID: 2019LI81368]

Lee-Greig, Tanya L. and Hallett H. Hammatt. *Archaeological Inventory Survey Plan for Honoapiʻilani Highway Realignment Phase IA, Future Keawe Street Extension to Lahainaluna Road: Ikena Avenue Alignment with Modified Extension Kelawea, Paeohi, and Wahikuli Ahupuaʻa, Lahaina District, Maui Island TMK (2) 4-5-021, 010, 015, and 031: Multiple Parcels.* Wailuku, HI: Cultural Surveys Hawaiʻi, Inc., 2008. [SHPD ID: 2019LI81341]

Lee-Greig, Tanya L. and Hallett H. Hammatt. *Archaeological Monitoring Plan for the Lahaina Bypass Modified Alignment from Kahoma Stream to the Keawe Street Extension, Kelawea, Paeohi, and Wahikuli Ahupuaʻa, Lahaina District,*

Maui Island. Wailuku, HI: Cultural Surveys Hawaiʻi, Inc., 2009. [SHPD ID: 2019LI81369]

Lee-Greig, Tanya L., Robert Hill, and Hallett H. Hammatt. *An Archaeological Survey Report for the Realignment of a Section of the Honoapiʻilani Highway, Phase IA, Kelawea, Paeohi, and Wahikuli Ahupuaʻa, Lahaina District, Maui Island TMK (2) 4-5-021, 010, 015, and 031: Multiple Parcels.* Wailuku, HI: Cultural Surveys Hawaiʻi, Inc., 2008. [SHPD ID: 2019LI81361]

Madeus, Jonas K., Tanya Lee-Greig, and Hallett H. Hammatt. *An Archaeological Monitoring Report for the Lahaina Bypass Modified Alignment from the Lahainaluna Road Intersection to the Keawe Street Extension Kelawea, Paeohi, and Wahikuli Ahupuaʻa, Lahaina District, Maui Island TMK (2) 4-5-021, 010, 015, and 031: Multiple Parcels.* Wailuku, HI: Cultural Surveys Hawaiʻi, Inc., 2010. [SHPD ID: 2019LI81338]

Pāhoa

Chong Jin and Michael F. Dega. *Archaeological Assessment for the Launiupoko Water System Line Extension to Waineʻe Project, Pūehuehu Nui and Pāhoa Ahupuaʻa, Lahaina District, Island of Maui, Hawaiʻi [TMK: (2) 4-6-013: portion of 022; 4-7-002: portion of 004; 4-7-003: portion of 031].* Honolulu, HI: Scientific Consultant Services, Inc., 2022. [SHPD ID: 2022LI00556]

Desilets, Michael and Patrick OʻDay. *Preservation Plan for Proposed Fenceline Corridor for the West Maui Forest Reserve, Kuʻia, Mākila, Pāhoa, Halakaʻa, Polaiki, Launiupoko, and Olowalu Ahupuaʻa, Lahaina District, Maui Island, Hawaiʻi.* Kailua, HI: Garcia & Associates, 2016. [SHPD ID: 2019LI81528]

Fredericksen, Erik M. and Demaris L. Fredericksen. *An Archaeological Inventory Survey of the Lahaina Watershed Flood Control Project Area, Lands of Polanui, Paha, Pueuehunui, Lahaina District, Maui Island (TMK: 4-6-13:016, 18, 26; TMK 4-7-01, 02).* Pukalani, HI: Xamanek Researches, 2003. [SHPD ID: 2019LI81442]

Haun, Alan E. *Archaeological Assessment TMK (2) 4-7-02:005 Land of Pāhoa, Lahaina District, Island of Maui.* Kailua-Kona, HI: Haun and Associates, 2001. [SHPD ID: 2019LI81616]

Haun, Alan E. *Archaeological Inventory Survey Kauaʻula Development Parcel, Lands of Pūehuehu Iki, Pāhoa, and Pola Nui, Lahaina District, Island of Maui.* Kailua-Kona, HI: Haun and Associates, 1999. [No location available]

Haun, Alan E. and Jack D. Henry. *Archaeological Site Preservation Plan Kauʻaula Development Parcel, Lands of Pūehuehu Iki, Pāhoa, and Polanui Ahupuaʻa,*

Lahaina District, Island of Maui [TMK (2) 4-7-02:04, 05, & 07, (2) 4-7-03:por. 01]. Kailua-Kona, HI: Haun and Associates, 2003. [SHPD ID: 2019LI81618]

Haun, Alan E. and Jack D. Henry. *Archaeological Site Preservation Plan, Kauaʻula Development Parcel, Lands of Pūehuehu Iki, Pāhoa, and Polo Nui, Lahaina District, Island of Maui [TMK: (2) 4-7-03:001].* Kailua-Kona, HI: Haun and Associates, 2000. [SHPD ID: 2019LI81613]

Jensen, Peter M. *Archaeological Inventory Survey Honoapiʻilani Highway Realignment Project Lahaina Bypass Section—Modified Corridor Alignment, Lands of Honokōwai, Hanakaʻōʻō, Wahikuli, Panaʻewa, Kuʻia, Halakaʻa, Pūehuehu Nui, Pāhoa, Polanui, and Launiupoko, Lahaina District, Island of Maui.* Hilo, HI: Paul H. Rosendahl, Ph.D., Inc., 1991. [SHPD ID: 2019LI81242]

Jensen, Peter M. *Letter Report: Additional Field Survey Lahaina Bypass Section, Modified Corridor Alignment, Honoapiʻilani Highway Realignment Project, Lands of Pāhoa and Polanui, Lahaina District, Island of Maui [TMK: (2) 4-7-01, 02].* Hilo, HI: Paul H. Rosendahl, Ph.D., Inc., 1992. [SHPD ID: 2019LI81609]

McCurdy, Todd D. and Hallett H. Hammatt. *Addendum Report for Archaeological Inventory Survey Documentation of Inadvertent Finds Identified during the Honoapiʻilani Highway Realignment (Lahaina Bypass) Phase 1B-1, Paunau Ahupuaʻa to Polanui Ahupuaʻa, Lahaina District, Maui Island TMK (2) 4-6-014:001, 002: (2) 4-6-018:002, 003; (2) 4-8-001:002 and (2) 4-8-003:001.* Wailuku, HI: Cultural Surveys Hawaiʻi, Inc., 2010. [SHPD ID: 2019LI81537]

McCurdy, Todd D. and Hallett H. Hammatt. *An Archaeological Monitoring Plan for the Honoapiʻilani Highway Realignment (Lahaina Bypass), Phase 1B-1, Paunau Ahupuaʻa to Polanui Ahupuaʻa, Lahaina District, Maui Island TMK: (2) 4-6-014:001-002, 4-6-018:002-003, 4-7-001:002 and 4-7-003:001.* Wailuku, HI: Cultural Surveys Hawaiʻi, Inc., 2010. [SHPD ID: 2019LI81539]

McCurdy, Todd D. and Hallett H. Hammatt. *Archaeological Inventory Survey Documentation of Inadvertent Finds Identified during the Honoapiʻilani Highway Realignment (Lahaina Bypass) Phase 1B-1, Paunau Ahupuaʻa to Polanui Ahupuaʻa, Lahaina District, Maui Island TMK: (2) 4-6-014:001, 002; (2) 4-6-018:002, 003; (2) 4-8-001:002 and (2) 4-7-003:001.* Wailuku, HI: Cultural Surveys Hawaiʻi, Inc., 2009. [SHPD ID: 2019LI81536]

McCurdy, Todd D. and Hallett H. Hammatt. *Archaeological Literature Review and Field Inspection for Honoapiʻilani Highway Realignment (Lahaina Bypass), Phase 1B-1, Paunau Ahupuaʻa to Polanui Ahupuaʻa, Lahaina District, Maui Island TMK (2) 4-6-014:001-002, 4-6-018:002-003, 4-8-001:002 and 4-7-003:001.* Wailuku, HI: Cultural Surveys Hawaiʻi, Inc., 2008. [SHPD ID: 2019LI81538]

O'Day, Patrick and David Byerly. *Archaeological Inventory Survey of Proposed Fenceline Corridor for the West Maui Forest Reserve, Kuʻia, Mākila, Pāhoa, Halakaʻa, Polaiki, Launiupoko, and Olowalu Ahupuaʻa, Lahaina District, Maui Island, Hawaiʻi.* Kailua, HI: Garcia & Associates, 2015. [SHPD ID: 2019LI81533]

Pantaleo, Jeffrey. *Archaeological Monitoring Plan Phase 2 of the Proposed Lahaina Watershed Flood Control Project, Polanui and Pāhoa Ahupuaʻa, Lahaina District, Maui Island [TMK (2) 4-8-001:por. 02; 4-7-02:por. 4, 5, 7],* 1991. [No location available]

Rosendahl, Paul H. *Archaeological Treatment Plan for No Adverse Effect, Lahaina Bypass Highway Project, Lands of Honokōwai, Hanakaʻōʻō, Wahikuli, Panaʻewa, Kuʻia, Halakaʻa, Pūehuehu Nui, Pāhoa, Polanui, and Launiupoko, Lahaina District, Island of Maui.* Hilo, HI: Paul H. Rosendahl, Ph.D., Inc., 1994. [SHPD ID: 2019LI81439]

PAKALA

Lee-Greig, Tanya, Constance OʻHare, Hallett H. Hammatt, Robert R. Hill, and Colleen Dagan. *Archaeological Data Recovery and Additional Testing at Land Commission Award 310: Pikaneleʻs Kuleana at Pakala, Pakala Ahupuaʻa, Lahaina District, Maui Island.* Wailuku, HI: Cultural Surveys Hawaiʻi, Inc., 2010. [SHPD ID: 2019LI81573]

Major, Maurice and P. Christiaan Klieger. *Historical Background and Archaeological Testing at Pikaneleʻs Kuleana in Lahaina, Maui: An Inventory Survey Report of LCA 310.3 (Royal Patent 1729.2, TMK (2) 4-6-07:013).* Honolulu, HI: Department of Anthropology, Bernice P. Bishop Museum, 1995. [SHPD ID: 2019LI81546; UH Call Number: DU629.L3 M36 1996]

PANAʻEWA

Chaffee, David B. and Michael F. Dega. *An Archaeological Monitoring Plan for Approximately 12,365 Foot sq. Property Located on Waineʻe Street in Lahaina, Ahupuaʻa of Panaʻewa, Lahaina District, Maui Island, Hawaiʻi [TMK (2) 4-6-09:024].* Honolulu, HI: Scientific Consultant Services, Inc., 2005. [SHPD ID: 2019LI81580]

Collins, Sara L., Dennis Gosser, and Stephan D. Clark. *Archaeological Assessment of a Single Developed Parcel [TMK (2) 4-6-10:006] Lahaina, Island of Maui.* Honolulu, HI: Pacific Consulting Services, Inc., 2006. [No location available]

Conte, Patty J. *Archaeological Monitoring Plan for On and Off-Site Construction Within and Related to TMK (2) 4-5-13:006 Lahaina District, Pana'ewa Ahupua'a, Island of Maui.* Makawao, HI: CRM Solutions Hawai'i, Inc., 2006. [SHPD ID: 2019LI81349]

Conte, Patty J. *Archaeological Monitoring Report Within and Related to a Parcel on Front Street, Pana'ewa Ahupua'a, Lahaina District, Maui Island, TMK (2) 4-5-13:006.* Makawao, HI: CRM Solutions Hawai'i, Inc., 2007. [No location available]

Cordle, Shayna, Jennifer Hunt, and Michael F. Dega. *An Archaeological Monitoring Report for a 12,365 Ft Sq. Property, Waine'e St., Lahaina, Pana'ewa Ahupua'a, Lahaina District, Island of Maui, Hawai'i [TMK (2) 4-6-09:244].* Honolulu, HI: Scientific Consultant Services, Inc., 2007. [SHPD ID: 2019LI81566]

Dagher, Cathleen A. and Michael F. Dega. *Archaeological Field Inspection Results and Recommendations for the Proposed Maui Police Department Communications Facility at Lahainaluna Water Treatment Site, Pana'ewa Ahupua'a, Lahaina District, Maui Island, Hawai'i [TMK: (2) 4-6-18:012 por.].* Honolulu, HI: Scientific Consultant Services, Inc., 2016. [SHPD ID: 2019LI81527]

Dega, Michael F. *An Archaeological Monitoring Plan for the Ulupono Center Project, Lahaina, Pana'ewa Ahupua'a, Lahaina District, Hawai'i, TMK (2) 4-5-10:054.* Honolulu, HI: Scientific Consultant Services Inc., 2017. [SHPD ID: 2019LI80597]

Dega, Michael F. *Archaeological Monitoring Plan for the Front Street Waterline Replacement Project, Pana'ewa Ahupua'a, Lahaina District, Island of Maui, Hawai'i [TMK (2) 4-5-04, 05, and 08].* Honolulu, HI: Scientific Consultant Services, Inc., 2002. [SHPD ID: 2019LI80631]

Fox, Robert M. *Site Survey & Inventory, Hale Pa'i o Lahainaluna.* Honolulu, HI: AIA, 1977. [SHPD ID: 2019LI81590]

Fredericksen, Erik M. *Archaeological Monitoring Plan for the Proposed Plantation Inn Improvements Project (GPC 2002/43), Pana'ewa Ahupua'a, Lahaina District, Maui [TMK: (2) 4-6-009: 036, 037 and 044].* Pukalani, HI: Xamanek Researches, 2002. [SHPD ID: 2019LI81579]

Fredericksen, Erik M. *Archaeological Monitoring Report for the Proposed Plantation Inn Improvements Project (GPC2002/43) Pana'ewa Ahupua'a, Lahaina District, Maui, TMK: (2) 4-6-09:036, 037, and 044.* Pukalani, HI: Xamanek Researches, 2003. [SHPD ID: 2019LI81574]

Fredericksen, Walter M. and Demaris L. Fredericksen. *Archaeological Data Recovery Report on the Plantation Inn Site, Lahaina, Maui, Hawaiʻi.* Pukalani, HI: Xamanek Researches, 1990. [SHPD ID: 2019LI81589; UH Call Number: DU629.L3 F738 1990a]

Fredericksen, Walter M. and Demaris L. Fredericksen. *Archaeological Data Recovery Report on the Plantation Inn Site, Lahaina, Maui, Hawaiʻi.* Pukalani, HI: Xamanek Researches, 1993. [SHPD ID: 2019LI81589]

Fredericksen, Walter M. and Demaris L. Fredericksen. *Report on the Archaeological Excavation Conducted at Hale Paʻi Site, 1981-1982.* Pukalani, HI: Xamanek Researches, 1988. [SHPD ID: 2019LI81532]

Hammatt, Hallett H. *An Archaeological Field Inspection of the Lahaina Bypass Highway, Phase 1A, Keawe Street Extension to Lahainaluna Road, and Current Condition of SIHP Number -2484.* Wailuku, HI: Cultural Surveys Hawaiʻi, Inc., 2007. [SHPD ID: 2019LI81366]

Hill, Robert, Tanya Lee-Greig, and Hallett H. Hammatt. *An Archaeological Inventory Survey Report and Mitigation Plan for the Hawaiʻi State Department of Education Cesspool Conversion Project at the Lahainaluna High School, Panaʻewa Ahupuaʻa, Lahaina District, Maui Island, TMK (2) 4-6-18:005, 007, 012.* Wailuku, HI: Cultural Surveys Hawaiʻi, Inc., 2008. [No location available]

Jensen, Peter M. *Archaeological Inventory Survey Honoapiʻilani Highway Realignment Project Lahaina Bypass Section—Modified Corridor Alignment, Lands of Honokōwai, Hanakaʻōʻō, Wahikuli, Panaʻewa, Kuʻia, Halakaʻa, Pūehuehu Nui, Pāhoa, Polanui, and Launiupoko, Lahaina District, Island of Maui.* Hilo, HI: Paul H. Rosendahl, Ph.D., Inc., 1991. [SHPD ID: 2019LI81242]

Knecht, Daniel P. and Timothy M. Rieth. *Archaeological Monitoring Plan for the Lahainaluna High School New Classroom Building Project, Panaʻewa Ahupuaʻa, Lahaina District, Maui.* Honolulu, HI: International Archaeology, LLC. [No location available]

Lee-Greig, Tanya L. and Hallett H. Hammatt. *Addendum to An Archaeological Treatment Plan for no Adverse Effect the Honoapiʻilani Highway Realignment— Lahaina Bypass Section, Phase 1A, Keawe Street Extension to Lahainaluna Road, Panaʻewa Ahupuaʻa, Lahaina District, Maui Island, TMK (2) 4-5-031: 999 por., (2) 4-5-015:010 por., and (2) 4-5-021:022 por.* Wailuku, HI: Cultural Surveys Hawaiʻi, Inc., 2007. [SHPD ID: 2019LI81365, 2019LI81340]

Lee-Greig, Tanya L. and Hallett H. Hammatt. *Archaeological Monitoring Plan for the Puʻunēnē School and Lahainaluna High School Hawaiʻi Inter-Island DOE*

Cesspool Project, Island of Maui TMK (2) 4-6-018 and (2) 3-8-006. Wailuku, HI: Cultural Surveys Hawaiʻi, Inc., 2007. [SHPD ID: 2019LI81526]

Rechtman, Robert B. *Archaeological Monitoring Plan Associated with the Demolition of the Pioneer Mill, TMK (2) 4-5-09:007, Panaʻewa Ahupuaʻa, Lahaina District, Island of Maui.* Rechtman Consulting, LLC, 2005. [SHPD ID: 2019LI80603]

Rechtman, Robert B. *Archaeological Monitoring Report Associated with the Demolition of the Pioneer Mill, Panaʻewa Ahupuaʻa, Lahaina District, Island of Maui.* Rechtman Consulting, LLC, 2006. [SHPD ID: 2019LI80602]

Rosendahl, Paul H. *Archaeological Treatment Plan for No Adverse Effect, Lahaina Bypass Highway Project, Lands of Honokōwai, Hanakaʻōʻō, Wahikuli, Panaʻewa, Kuʻia, Halakaʻa, Pūehuehu Nui, Pāhoa, Polanui, and Launiupoko, Lahaina District, Island of Maui.* Hilo, HI: Paul H. Rosendahl, Ph.D., Inc., 1994. [SHPD ID: 2019LI81439]

Rotunno-Hazuka, Lisa J. and Jeffrey Pantaleo. *Archaeological Monitoring Plan for a Waterline Installation at TMK: (2) 4-5-01:045 Old Lahaina Center, Papalua Street, Panaʻewa Ahupuaʻa, Lahaina District, Island of Maui.* Wailuku, HI: Archaeological Services Hawaii, LLC, 2002. [SHPD ID: 2019LI80638]

Rotunno-Hazuka, Lisa J. and Jeffrey Pantaleo. *Archaeological Monitoring Plan for the Renovations to the Lahaina-Kaiser Clinic, Panaʻewa Ahupuaʻa, Lahaina District, Island of Maui.* Wailuku, HI: Archaeological Services Hawaii, LLC, 2003. [SHPD ID: 2019LI80608]

Willman, Michael R., Tanya Lee-Greig, and Hallett H. Hammatt. *Addendum to Archaeological Monitoring Plan for the Puʻunēnē School and Lahainaluna High School Hawaiʻi Inter-Island DOE Cesspool Project, Island of Maui TMK (2) 4-6-18 and (2) 3-8-06.* Wailuku, HI: Cultural Surveys Hawaiʻi, Inc., 2008. [SHPD ID: 2019LI81524]

Yucha, Josephine M. and Hallett H. Hammatt. *Archaeological Monitoring Plan for the Lahaina Intermediate School Campus Fire Alarm Replacement Project, Panaʻewa and Kuʻia Ahupuaʻa, Lahaina District, Maui Island TMK (2) 4-6-18:013 por.* Wailuku, HI: Cultural Surveys Hawaiʻi, Inc., 2019. [No location available]

Paunau

Aki Sinoto Consulting. *Archaeological Monitoring During the Renovation of the Lahaina Center Parking Structure, Lahaina, Maui.* Honolulu, HI: Aki Sinoto Consulting, 1995.

Aki Sinoto Consulting. *Archaeological Monitoring Plan for Utility Trenching at the Lahaina Shopping Center, Paunau, Lahaina, Maui.* Honolulu, HI: Aki Sinoto Consulting, 1996.

Calis, Irene. *Archaeological Monitoring Report: Parking Lot Drainage System Installation, Panaʻewa Ahupuaʻa, Lahaina District, Island of Maui, Hawaiʻi.* Honolulu, HI: Scientific Consultant Services, Inc., 2002. [SHPD ID: 2019LI80642]

Chapman, Phillips, Brandt and Associates. *Lahaina Banyan Courtyard Preliminary Development and Restoration Plans,* 1972. [SHPD ID: 2019LI81398]

Chong Jin, Garcia Alondra, and Michael F. Dega. *Archaeological Monitoring Plan for 7,804 sq. ft. Parcel at 432 Ilikahi Street, Paunau Ahupuaʻa, Lahaina District, Island of Maui, Hawaiʻi [TMK: (2) 4-6-06:056 por.].* Honolulu, HI: Scientific Consultant Services, Inc., 2021. [SHPD ID: 2021LI00125]

Cliver, Blaine E., *Architectural Restorationalist. Architecturally speaking… The Baldwin House,* Lahaina, Maui, 1966. [SHPD ID: 2019LI81038]

Dagher, Cathleen A. and Michael F. Dega. *A Preservation Plan for the "Brick Palace" (A Component of State Site 50-50-03-3001) Within the Proposed Lahaina Harbor Complete Streets Project Area, Lahaina, Paunau Ahupuaʻa, Lahaina District, Island of Maui, Hawaiʻi [TMK (2) 4-6-01:004].* Honolulu, HI: Scientific Consultant Services, Inc., 2017. [SHPD ID: 2019LI81386]

Dagher, Cathleen A. and Michael F. Dega. *Archaeological Monitoring Plan for 790 Front Street Waterline (WTP T2017-00280) Lahaina, Paunau Ahupuaʻa, Lahaina District, Island of Maui, Hawaiʻi [TMK: (2) 4-6-09:999].* Honolulu, HI: Scientific Consultant Services, Inc., 2020. [SHPD ID: 2022LI00633]

Donham, Theresa K. *Archaeological Monitoring Plan for American Disabilities Act Improvements at the Lahaina Public Library, Paunau, Lahaina District, Maui, TMK: (2) 4-6-01:007 & 010.* Kīhei, HI: Akahele Archaeology, 2004. [SHPD ID: 2019LI81381]

Donham, Theresa K. *Archaeological Monitoring Report for American Disabilities Act Improvements at the Lahaina Public Library, Paunau, Lahaina District, Maui, TMK: (2) 4-6-01:007 & 010.* Kīhei, HI: Akahele Archaeology, 2005. [SHPD ID: 2019LI81403]

Folk, William. *Letter to Noel Kennett Re: End of Fieldwork of Archaeological Monitoring at Mala Wharf for an Electrical Line.* Wailuku, HI: Cultural Surveys Hawaiʻi, Inc., 1993. [SHPD ID: 2019LI80619]

Fredericksen, Erik M. *An Archaeological Monitoring Plan for the Dickenson Street Power Pole Replacement Project, Paunau Ahupua'a, Lahaina District, Island of Maui.* Pukalani, HI: Xamanek Researches, 2004. [SHPD ID: 2019LI81570]

Fredericksen, Erik M. *Archaeological Monitoring Plan for Improvements at 815 Front Street, Paunau Ahupua'a, Lahaina District, Maui.* Pukalani, HI: Xamanek Researches, 2001. [SHPD ID: 2019LI80644]

Fredericksen, Erik M. *Archaeological Monitoring Plan for the Sabia Building Development and Improvement Project at 816A Front Street, Paunau Ahupua'a, Lahaina District, Maui.* Pukalani, HI: Xamanek Researches, 2000. [SHPD ID: 2019LI80617]

Fredericksen, Erik M. *Archaeological Monitoring Report on the Pioneer Inn Swimming Pool Construction Project.* Pukalani, HI: Xamanek Researches, 1997. [SHPD ID: 2019LI81383]

Fredericksen, Erik M. and Demaris L. Fredericksen. *Archaeological Inventory Survey of The Lower Honoapi'ilani Road Improvements Project Corridor.* Pukalani, HI: Xamanek Researches, 1999. [SHPD ID: 2021LI00220]

Fredericksen, Walter M. *Archaeological Monitoring Report for the Remodeling Project of the Lahaina Yacht Club, 835 Front Street, Paunau Ahupua'a, Lahaina District, Island of Maui.* Pukalani, HI: Xamanek Researches, 2002. [SHPD ID: 2019LI80645]

Fredericksen, Walter M. and Demaris L. Fredericksen. *An Archaeological Inventory Survey on a Parcel of Land Located in the Ahupua'a of Paunau, Lahaina District, Island of Maui TMK (2) 4-6-09:012.* Pukalani, HI: Xamanek Researches, 1993. [SHPD ID: 2022LI00237]

Fredericksen, Walter M. Jr. and Demaris L. Fredericksen. *Report on the Excavation of the Outbuildings Adjacent to the Baldwin House, Undertaken for the Lahaina Restoration Foundation, Lahaina, Maui, Hawai'i.* Pukalani, HI: Xamanek Researches, 1978. [SHPD ID: 2019LI81568]

Fredericksen, Walter M., Demaris Fredericksen, and Erik M. Fredericksen. *Report on the Archaeological Inventory Survey at Historic Site #15, Lahaina Maui, Hawai'i.* Pukalani, HI: Xamanek Researches, 1988. [SHPD ID: 2019LI81406]

Fredericksen, Walter M., Demaris L. Fredericksen, and Erik M. Fredericksen. *An Archaeological Inventory Survey of a Parcel of Land Adjacent to Malu-Ulu-o-Lele Park, Lahaina, Maui, Hawai'i.* Pukalani, HI: Xamanek Researches, 1989. [SHPD ID: 2019LI81548]

Frost, Lockwood H. *A Report and Recommendations on the Restoration and Preservation of Hale Aloha, Lahaina, Maui*, 1973. [No location available]

Hammatt, Hallett H. *Lahaina (Front Street) Archaeological Test Excavations, TMK 4-5-3:012, Island of Maui*. Wailuku, HI: Cultural Surveys Hawaiʻi, Inc., 2003. [SHPD ID: 2019LI80649]

Hammatt, Hallett H. and David W. Shideler. *Draft Proposal for an Archaeological Mitigation Plan at the Lahaina Courthouse, Lahaina, Lahaina District, Maui Island, Hawaiʻi*. Wailuku, HI: Cultural Surveys Hawaiʻi, Inc., 1999. [SHPD ID: 2019LI81400]

Hammatt, Hallett H. and David W. Shideler. *Written Findings of Archaeological Monitoring at the Lahaina Courthouse, Lahaina, Lahaina District, Maui Island, Hawaiʻi*. Wailuku, HI: Cultural Surveys Hawaiʻi, Inc., 1998. [SHPD ID: 2019LI81401]

Havel, BreAnna and Michael F. Dega. *Archaeological Monitoring Plan for the Maui Islander Project, Lahaina, Paunau Ahupuaʻa District, Maui Island, Hawaiʻi [TMK: 4-6-011:008]*. Honolulu, HI: Scientific Consultant Services, Inc., 2005. [SHPD ID: 2019LI81582]

Jensen, Peter M. *Archaeological Inventory Survey Lahaina Bypass Highway New Connector Roads Project Area, Ahupuaʻa of Hanakaʻōʻō and Paunau, Lahaina District, Island of Maui*. Hilo, HI: Paul H. Rosendahl, Ph.D., Inc., 1994. [SHPD ID: 2019LI81611]

Johnston-OʻNeill, Emily and Michael F. Dega. *Archaeological Monitoring Plan for the Exterior Staircase Addition to the Convent Building at the Sacred Hearts Roman Catholic Property at 712 Waineʻe Street, Paunau Ahupuaʻa, Lahaina District, Island of Maui TMK: (2) 4-6-10:001 (por.)*. Honolulu, HI: Scientific Consultant Services, Inc., 2007. [SHPD ID: 2019LI81541]

Kennedy, Joseph. *Archaeological Report Concerning Subsurface Testing at TMK: (2) 4-6-08:012, Lahaina Maui*. Haleʻiwa, HI: Archaeological Consultants of Hawaii, 1989. [SHPD ID: 2019LI81544]

Klieger, Paul Christiaan and Lonnie Somer. *Emergency Mitigation at Maluʻulu o Lele Park, Lahaina, Maui, Hawaiʻi, Site of Mokuʻula, Residence of King Kamehameha III (Site 50-50-03-2967; TMK (2) 4-6-7 Parcel 002: BPBM 50-MA-D5-12)*. Honolulu, HI: Department of Anthropology, Bernice P. Bishop Museum, 1989. [SHPD ID: 2019LI81550]

Lash, Erik and Michael F. Dega. *An Archaeological Monitoring Plan for the Proposed Lahaina Harbor Complete Streets Project on Approximately 3.11 Acres (1.26*

Hectares) in Lahaina, Paunau Ahupuaʻa, Lahaina District, Island of Maui, Hawaiʻi [TMK (2) 4-6-001:001, 004, 007, 009, 010, 012, and Adjacent Roadways]. Honolulu, HI: Scientific Consultant Services, Inc., 2017. [SHPD ID: 2019LI81388]

Lee-Greig, Tanya L. *Archaeological Monitoring Plan for the Traffic Signal Improvements at Pāpalaua Street/Waineʻe Street Intersection, Federal Aid Project No. STP-3020 (001) Aki and Uhao Ahupuaʻa (Paunau Modern Ahupuaʻa), Lahaina Moku and Modern Tax District, Mokupuni of Maui [TMK: (2) 4-5-002:999 ROW, 4-5-006:999 ROW, 4-5-006:004, and 4-5-006:015].* Honolulu, HI: Aina Archaeology, 2023. [SHPD ID: 2023LI00149].

Liston, Jolie. *Archaeological Monitoring of Trenching Activities at Taco Bell, Lahaina, Maui.* Honolulu, HI: International Archaeological Research Institute, Inc., 1999. [SHPD ID: 2019LI80605]

McCurdy, Todd D. and Hallett H. Hammatt. *Addendum Report for Archaeological Inventory Survey Documentation of Inadvertent Finds Identified during the Honoapiʻilani Highway Realignment (Lahaina Bypass) Phase 1B-1, Paunau Ahupuaʻa to Polanui Ahupuaʻa, Lahaina District, Maui Island TMK (2) 4-6-014:001, 002: (2) 4-6-018:002, 003; (2) 4-8-001:002 and (2) 4-8-003:001.* Wailuku, HI: Cultural Surveys Hawaiʻi, Inc., 2010. [SHPD ID: 2019LI81537]

McCurdy, Todd D. and Hallett H. Hammatt. *An Archaeological Monitoring Plan for the Honoapiʻilani Highway Realignment (Lahaina Bypass), Phase 1B-1, Paunau Ahupuaʻa to Polanui Ahupuaʻa, Lahaina District, Maui Island TMK: (2) 4-6-014:001-002, 4-6-018:002-003, 4-7-001:002 and 4-7-003:001.* Wailuku, HI: Cultural Surveys Hawaiʻi, Inc., 2010. [SHPD ID: 2019LI81539]

McCurdy, Todd D. and Hallett H. Hammatt. *Archaeological Inventory Survey Documentation of Inadvertent Finds Identified during the Honoapiʻilani Highway Realignment (Lahaina Bypass) Phase 1B-1, Paunau Ahupuaʻa to Polanui Ahupuaʻa, Lahaina District, Maui Island TMK: (2) 4-6-014:001, 002; (2) 4-6-018:002, 003; (2) 4-8-001:002 and (2) 4-7-003:001.* Wailuku, HI: Cultural Surveys Hawaiʻi, Inc., 2009. [SHPD ID: 2019LI81536]

McCurdy, Todd D. and Hallett H. Hammatt. *Archaeological Literature Review and Field Inspection for Honoapiʻilani Highway Realignment (Lahaina Bypass), Phase 1B-1, Paunau Ahupuaʻa to Polanui Ahupuaʻa, Lahaina District, Maui Island TMK (2) 4-6-014:001-002, 4-6-018:002-003, 4-8-001:002 and 4-7-003:001.* Wailuku, HI: Cultural Surveys Hawaiʻi, Inc., 2008. [SHPD ID: 2019LI81538]

Mooney, Kimberly M. and Paul L. Cleghorn. *Archaeological Monitoring Report for the Lahaina Small Boat Harbor Comfort Station Improvements, Lahaina, Maui.* Kailua, HI: Pacific Legacy, Inc., 2007. [SHPD ID: 2019LI81379]

Munekiyo, Michael T. *Redevelopment of ABC Store at 726 Front Street, Application for Historic District Approval.* Wailuku, HI: Michael T. Munekiyo Consulting, Inc., 1993. [SHPD ID: 2019LI81540]

Oceanit. *Final Sampling Analysis Plan: Field Sampling and Quality Assurance Plans for the Mokuhinia Pond Site Investigation, Lahaina, Maui, Hawaiʻi.* Honolulu, HI: Oceanit, 2009. [SHPD ID: 2019LI81553]

Peterson, Charles E. *Notes on the Lahaina Court and Custom House, Lahaina, Maui, Hawaiʻi, Built 1859,* 1966. [SHPD ID: 2019LI81376]

Pyle, Dorothy. "The Intriguing Seamen's Hospital." *The Hawaiian Journal of History,* vol. 8, 1974, pp. 121–135. [UH Call Number: DU620 .H44]

Rosendahl, Paul H. *Archaeological Monitoring Plan, Mala Village Subdivision, Land of Puʻunoa, Lahaina District, Island of Maui [TMK: (2) 4-5-04:008, 009, 059, 060, 061, 062].* Hilo, HI: Paul H. Rosendahl, Ph.D., Inc., 2002. [SHPD ID: 2019LI80615]

Rotunno-Hazuka, Lisa J. and Jeffrey Pantaleo. *Archaeological Monitoring Plan For the Construction of an Accessory Dwelling at the Meston Residence at TMK (2) 4-6-07:030 Paunau Ahupuaʻa, Lahaina District, Island of Maui.* Wailuku, HI: Archaeological Services Hawaii, LLC, 2004. [SHPD ID: 2019LI81551]

Rotunno-Hazuka, Lisa J. and Jeffrey Pantaleo. *Final Archaeological Monitoring Plan for Demolition and New Construction along Front Street, Paunau Ahupuaʻa, Lahaina District, Kula Moku, Island of Maui.* Wailuku, HI: Archaeological Services Hawaii, LLC, 2018. [SHPD ID: 2019LI80633]

Shefcheck, Donna M. and Michael F. Dega. *An Archaeological Monitoring Report for the Maui Islander Project, Lahaina, Paunau Ahupuaʻa, Lahaina District, Maui Island, Hawaiʻi [TMK: (2) 4-6-011:008].* Honolulu, HI: Scientific Consultant Services, Inc., 2008. [SHPD ID: 2019LI81576]

Sinoto, Aki and Jeffrey Pantaleo. *Archaeological Inventory Survey of the Proposed Site for the New Lahaina Kingdom Hall Puunoa, Paunau Ahupuaʻa, Lahaina District, Maui Island TMK (2) 4-4-04:042 & 044).* Wailuku, HI: Archaeological Services Hawaii, LLC, 2003. [SHPD ID: 2019LI80616]

Spencer Mason Architects. *Historic Site Survey for Lahainaluna Road and Waineʻe Street Widening Projects.* Honolulu, HI: Spencer Mason Architects, 1988. [SHPD ID: 2019LI81432]

Spencer Mason Architects. *Historic Structures Report: Old Lahaina Courthouse.* Honolulu, HI: Spencer Mason Architects, 1996. [SHPD ID: 2019LI81378]

Windley, Larry. *Recommended Action Plan for the Preservation/Restoration of the Hale Paʻahao Prison Site, Lahaina.* Lahaina, HI: Lahaina Restoration Foundation, 1967. [SHPD ID: 2019LI81257]

Yeomans, Sarah K. *Archaeological Monitoring Plan Parking Lot Drainage System Installation, Panaʻewa Ahupuaʻa, Lahaina District, Island of Maui, Hawaiʻi.* Honolulu, HI: Scientific Consultant Services, Inc., 2019. [SHPD ID: 2019LI80640]

POLAIKI

Desilets, Michael and Patrick OʻDay. *Preservation Plan for Proposed Fenceline Corridor for the West Maui Forest Reserve, Kuʻia, Mākila, Pāhoa, Halakaʻa, Polaiki, Launiupoko, and Olowalu Ahupuaʻa, Lahaina District, Maui Island, Hawaiʻi.* Kailua, HI: Garcia & Associates, 2016. [SHPD ID: 2019LI81528]

Haun, Alan E. *Archaeological Assessment, Lands of Polanui, Polaiki, and Launiupoko, Lahaina District, Island of Maui.* Kailua-Kona, HI: Haun and Associates, 2002. [SHPD ID: 2019LI81608]

OʻDay, Patrick and David Byerly. *Archaeological Inventory Survey of Proposed Fenceline Corridor for the West Maui Forest Reserve, Kuʻia, Mākila, Pāhoa, Halakaʻa, Polaiki, Launiupoko, and Olowalu Ahupuaʻa, Lahaina District, Maui Island, Hawaiʻi.* Kailua, HI: Garcia & Associates, 2015. [SHPD ID: 2019LI81533]

POLANUI

Dega, Michael F. *Archaeological Inventory Survey of the Punakea Loop Corridor in Launiupoko and Polanui Ahupuaʻa, Lahaina District (formerly Kāʻanapali), island of Maui, Hawaiʻi [TMK: (2) 4-8-01:002 por. & 4-7-01:029 por.].* Honolulu, HI: Scientific Consultant Services, Inc., 2008. [SHPD ID: 2019LI81597]

Donham, Theresa K. *Field Inspection of a Proposed Culvert Location, USDA-SCS Lahaina Watershed Project, Pola Nui, Lahaina District, Maui [TMK: (2) 4-7-01:018].* Wailuku, HI: State Historic Preservation Division, Maui Section, 1991. [SHPD ID: 2019LI81607]

Fredericksen, Erik M. and Demaris L. Fredericksen. *An Archaeological Inventory Survey of the Lahaina Watershed Flood Control Project Area, Lands of Polanui, Paha, Pueuehunui, Lahaina District, Maui Island (TMK: 4-6-13:016, 18, 26; TMK 4-7-01, 02).* Pukalani, HI: Xamanek Researches, 2003. [SHPD ID: 2019LI81442]

Gallo and Michael F. Dega. *Archaeological Assessment for a New Farm Dwelling for Mākila Ranches, Lot 4, Polanui Ahupuaʻa, Lahaina District, Island of Maui, Hawaiʻi [TMK: (2) 4-7-14:004 por.].* Honolulu, HI: Scientific Consultant Services, Inc., 2021. [SHPD ID: 2022LI00382]

Haun, Alan E. *Archaeological Assessment, Lands of Polanui, Polaiki, and Launiupoko, Lahaina District, Island of Maui.* Kailua-Kona, HI: Haun and Associates, 2002. [SHPD ID: 2019LI81608]

Haun, Alan E. *Archaeological Inventory Survey Kauaʻula Development Parcel, Lands of Pūehuehu Iki, Pāhoa, and Pola Nui, Lahaina District, Island of Maui.* Kailua-Kona, HI: Haun and Associates, 1999. [No location available]

Haun, Alan E. and Dave Henry. *Archaeological Inventory Survey, Proposed 124-Acre Mākila Subdivision, Lands of Launiupoko, Polanui and Pūehuehu Nui, Lahaina District, Island of Maui (TMK: 4-7-01: por. 1 and TMK 4-7-04: Por. 4).* Kailua-Kona, HI: Haun and Associates, 2001. [SHPD ID: 2019LI81623]

Haun, Alan E. and Jack D. Henry. *Archaeological Site Preservation Plan Kauʻaula Development Parcel, Lands of Pūehuehu Iki, Pāhoa, and Polanui Ahupuaʻa, Lahaina District, Island of Maui [TMK (2) 4-7-02:04, 05, & 07, (2) 4-7-03:por. 01].* Kailua-Kona, HI: Haun and Associates, 2003. [SHPD ID: 2019LI81618]

Jensen, Peter M. *Archaeological Inventory Survey Honoapiʻilani Highway Realignment Project Lahaina Bypass Section—Modified Corridor Alignment, Lands of Honokōwai, Hanakaʻōʻō, Wahikuli, Panaʻewa, Kuʻia, Halakaʻa, Pūehuehu Nui, Pāhoa, Polanui, and Launiupoko, Lahaina District, Island of Maui.* Hilo, HI: Paul H. Rosendahl, Ph.D., Inc., 1991. [SHPD ID: 2019LI81242]

Jensen, Peter M. *Letter Report: Additional Field Survey Lahaina Bypass Section, Modified Corridor Alignment, Honoapiʻilani Highway Realignment Project, Lands of Pāhoa and Polanui, Lahaina District, Island of Maui [TMK: (2) 4-7-01, 02].* Hilo, HI: Paul H. Rosendahl, Ph.D., Inc., 1992. [SHPD ID: 2019LI81609]

Kawachi, Carol. *Archaeological Monitoring Plan for Phase 1 of the Proposed Lahaina Watershed Flood Control Project Including Conservation District Use Application MA-3204 Board Permit, Polanui Ahupuaʻa, Lahaina District, Maui, Island TMK: (2) 4-8-01: por. 002, 018, 2005.* [SHPD ID: 2019LI81601]

McCurdy, Todd D. and Hallett H. Hammatt. *Addendum Report for Archaeological Inventory Survey Documentation of Inadvertent Finds Identified during the Honoapiʻilani Highway Realignment (Lahaina Bypass) Phase 1B-1, Paunau Ahupuaʻa to Polanui Ahupuaʻa, Lahaina District, Maui Island TMK (2) 4-6-014:001, 002: (2) 4-6-018:002, 003; (2) 4-8-001:002 and (2) 4-8-003:001.* Wailuku, HI: Cultural Surveys Hawaiʻi, Inc., 2010. [SHPD ID: 2019LI81537]

McCurdy, Todd D. and Hallett H. Hammatt. *An Archaeological Monitoring Plan for the Honoapiʻilani Highway Realignment (Lahaina Bypass), Phase 1B-1, Paunau Ahupuaʻa to Polanui Ahupuaʻa, Lahaina District, Maui Island TMK: (2) 4-6-014:001-002, 4-6-018:002-003, 4-7-001:002 and 4-7-003:001.* Wailuku, HI: Cultural Surveys Hawaiʻi, Inc., 2010. [SHPD ID: 2019LI81539]

McCurdy, Todd D. and Hallett H. Hammatt. *Archaeological Inventory Survey Documentation of Inadvertent Finds Identified during the Honoapiʻilani Highway Realignment (Lahaina Bypass) Phase 1B-1, Paunau Ahupuaʻa to Polanui Ahupuaʻa, Lahaina District, Maui Island TMK: (2) 4-6-014:001, 002; (2) 4-6-018:002, 003; (2) 4-8-001:002 and (2) 4-7-003:001.* Wailuku, HI: Cultural Surveys Hawaiʻi, Inc., 2009. [SHPD ID: 2019LI81536]

McCurdy, Todd D. and Hallett H. Hammatt. *Archaeological Literature Review and Field Inspection for Honoapiʻilani Highway Realignment (Lahaina Bypass), Phase 1B-1, Paunau Ahupuaʻa to Polanui Ahupuaʻa, Lahaina District, Maui Island TMK (2) 4-6-014:001-002, 4-6-018:002-003, 4-8-001:002 and 4-7-003:001.* Wailuku, HI: Cultural Surveys Hawaiʻi, Inc., 2008. [SHPD ID: 2019LI81538]

Pantaleo, Jeffrey. *Archaeological Monitoring Plan Phase 2 of the Proposed Lahaina Watershed Flood Control Project, Polanui and Pāhoa Ahupuaʻa, Lahaina District, Maui Island [TMK (2) 4-8-001:por. 02; 4-7-02:por. 4, 5, 7],* 1991. [No location available]

Paraso, C. Kanani and Michael F. Dega. *An Archaeological Inventory Survey of 633 Acres in the Launiupoko (Large Lot) Subdivision Nos. 3, 4, and 7, Launiupoko and Polanui Ahupuaʻa, Lahaina District (formerly Kāʻanapali), Island of Maui, Hawaiʻi [TMK (2) 4-8-01:2 por.].* Honolulu, HI: Scientific Consultant Services, Inc., 2006. [SHPD ID: 2019LI81600]

Rosendahl, Paul H. *Archaeological Treatment Plan for No Adverse Effect, Lahaina Bypass Highway Project, Lands of Honokōwai, Hanakaʻōʻō, Wahikuli, Panaʻewa, Kuʻia, Halakaʻa, Pūehuehu Nui, Pāhoa, Polanui, and Launiupoko, Lahaina District, Island of Maui.* Hilo, HI: Paul H. Rosendahl, Ph.D., Inc., 1994. [SHPD ID: 2019LI81439]

Shefcheck, Donna M. and Michael F. Dega. *An Archaeological Inventory Survey of 123.31 Acres in the Launiupoko (Large Lot) Subdivision 6 Launiupoko and Polanui Ahupuaʻa, Lahaina District (formerly Kāʻanapali) Island of Maui, Hawaiʻi TMK (2) 4-8-01:002 por.).* Honolulu, HI: Scientific Consultant Services, Inc., 2007. [SHPD ID: 2019LI81596]

Puako

Fredericksen, Demaris L. and Erik M. Fredericksen. *Archaeological Inventory Survey (Phase 1) in the ʻIli of Pakala, Puako Ahupuaʻa, Lahaina District, Maui Island [TMK: (2) 4-6-07:007].* Pukalani, HI: Xamanek Researches, 1999. [SHPD ID: 2019LI81547]

Fredericksen, Erik M. *An Archaeological Monitoring Plan for an Inventory Survey Concurrent with Construction Activities on a Parcel of Land in Puako Ahupuaʻa, Lahaina District, Lahaina, Maui [TMK: (2) 4-6-08:48 and 53].* Pukalani, HI: Xamanek Researches, 2003. [SHPD ID: 2019LI81569]

Fredericksen, Erik M. *An Archaeological Monitoring Report for a Parcel of Land in Puako Ahupuaʻa, Lahaina District, Maui [TMK: (2) 4-6-008:022].* Pukalani, HI: Xamanek Researches, 2005. [SHPD ID: 2019LI81565]

Fredericksen, Erik M. *Archaeological Assessment Report for a Portion of Land in Puako Ahupuaʻa, Lahaina District, Lahaina, Maui [TMK: (2) 4-6-08:053].* Pukalani, HI: Xamanek Researches, 2004. [SHPD ID: 2019LI81545]

Fredericksen, Erik M. *Archaeological Monitoring Plan for a Parcel of Land in the ʻIli of Pakala, Puako Ahupuaʻa, Lahaina District, Island of Maui [TMK: (2) 4-6-07:003].* Pukalani, HI: Xamanek Researches, 1998. [SHPD ID: 2019LI81549]

Fredericksen, Erik M. *Archaeological Monitoring Plan for the King Kamehameha III Elementary School Building B, Building D, and PT 201 Restroom Renovation Project, Puako Ahupuaʻa, Lahaina District, Maui [TMK: (2) 4-6-02:013 & 014].* Pukalani, HI: Xamanek Researches, 2001. [SHPD ID: 2019LI81392]

Fredericksen, Erik M. *Archaeological Monitoring Plan for the Wharf Street Accessibility Improvements at Lahaina Harbor—Electrical Underground Work Project, Puako Ahupuaʻa, Lahaina District, Maui [TMK: (2) 4-6-01 and 4-6-01: Portion of Parcel 1].* Pukalani, HI: Xamanek Researches, 2002. [SHPD ID: 2019LI81402]

Fredericksen, Erik M. and Demaris Fredericksen. *Archaeological Inventory Survey Report for Portion of Land in Puako Ahupuaʻa, Lahaina District, Lahaina, Maui, [TMK: (2) 4-6-08:53 and 48].* Pukalani, HI: Xamanek Researches, 2002. [SHPD ID: 2019LI81571]

Fredericksen, Erik M. and Demaris L. Fredericksen. *An Archaeological Inventory Survey of the Lahaina Watershed Flood Control Project Area, Lands of Polanui, Paha, Pueuehunui, Lahaina District, Maui Island (TMK: 4-6-13:016, 18, 26; TMK 4-7-01, 02).* Pukalani, HI: Xamanek Researches, 2003. [SHPD ID: 2019LI81442]

Fredericksen, Erik M. and Jennifer J. Frey. *An Archaeological Monitoring Report for the King Kamehameha III Elementary School Parking Lot Improvements Project, Puako Ahupuaʻa, Lahaina District [TMK: (2) 4-6-002:13].* Pukalani, HI: Xamanek Researches, 2008. [SHPD ID: 2019LI81374]

Frey, Jennifer J. and Erik M. Fredericksen. *An Archaeological Monitoring Report for the King Kamehameha III Elementary School Campus Exterior Awning and Gutter Project, DOE Job No. P01090-06, Puako Ahupuaʻa, Lahaina District [TMK (2) 4-6-02:013, and (2) 4-6-02:014].* Pukalani, HI: Xamanek Researches, 2009. [SHPD ID: 2019LI81561]

Haun, Alan E. and Dave Henry. *Archaeological Inventory Survey, TMK 4-6-7:010 ʻIli of Pakala, Land of Puako District, Island of Maui.* Kailua-Kona, HI: Haun and Associates, 2001. [SHPD ID: 2019LI81555]

PŪEHUEHU IKI

Haun, Alan E. *Archaeological Site Documentation, Site 5401, Lands of Polanui and Pāhoa, Lahaina District, Island of Maui (TMK: 4-8-01:002, 4-7-01:001).* Kailua-Kona, HI: Haun and Associates, 2004. [SHPD ID: 2019LI81622]

Haun, Alan E. and Jack D. Henry. *Archaeological Site Preservation Plan Kauʻaula Development Parcel, Lands of Pūehuehu Iki, Pāhoa, and Polanui Ahupuaʻa, Lahaina District, Island of Maui [TMK (2) 4-7-02:04, 05, & 07, (2) 4-7-03:por. 01].* Kailua-Kona, HI: Haun and Associates, 2003. [SHPD ID: 2019LI81618]

Haun, Alan E. and Jack D. Henry. *Archaeological Site Preservation Plan, Kauaʻula Development Parcel, Lands of Pūehuehu Iki, Pāhoa, and Polo Nui, Lahaina District, Island of Maui [TMK: (2) 4-7-03:001].* Kailua-Kona, HI: Haun and Associates, 2000. [SHPD ID: 2019LI81613]

Pantaleo, Jeffrey. *Archaeological Inventory Report of a 1.65-Acre Parcel of Land Pūehuehue Iki Ahupuaʻa, Lahaina District, Island of Maui TMK (2) 4-7-04:001.* Wailuku, HI: Archaeological Services Hawaii, LLC, 2006. [SHPD ID: 2019LI81615]

Rotunno-Hazuka, Lisa J. and Jeffrey Pantaleo, M.A. *Archaeological Preservation and Monitoring Plan for Site 50-50-03-4096 Feature 1 Located on a Residential Lot, TMK (2) 4-7-01:001 Pūehuehue Iki Ahupuaʻa, Lahaina District: Island of Maui.* Wailuku, HI: Archaeological Services Hawaii, LLC, 2006. [SHPD ID: 2019LI81591]

Pūehuehu Nui

Chong Jin and Michael F. Dega. *Archaeological Assessment for the Launiupoko Water System Line Extension to Waineʻe Project, Pūehuehu Nui and Pāhoa Ahupuaʻa, Lahaina District, Island of Maui, Hawaiʻi [TMK: (2) 4-6-013: portion of 022; 4-7-002: portion of 004; 4-7-003: portion of 031].* Honolulu, HI: Scientific Consultant Services, Inc., 2022. [SHPD ID: 2022LI00556]

Fredericksen, Erik M. and Demaris L. Fredericksen. *An Archaeological Inventory Survey of the Lahaina Watershed Flood Control Project Area, Lands of Polanui, Paha, Pueuehunui, Lahaina District, Maui Island (TMK: 4-6-13:016, 18, 26; TMK 4-7-01, 02.* Pukalani, HI: Xamanek Researches, 2003. [SHPD ID: 2019LI81442]

Haun, Alan E. and Dave Henry. *Archaeological Inventory Survey, Proposed 124-Acre Mākila Subdivision, Lands of Launiupoko, Polanui and Pūehuehu Nui, Lahaina District, Island of Maui (TMK: 4-7-01: por. 1 and TMK 4-7-04: Por. 4).* Kailua-Kona, HI: Haun and Associates, 2001. [SHPD ID: 2019LI81623]

Jensen, Peter M. *Archaeological Inventory Survey Honoapiʻilani Highway Realignment Project Lahaina Bypass Section—Modified Corridor Alignment, Lands of Honokōwai, Hanakaʻōʻō, Wahikuli, Panaʻewa, Kuʻia, Halakaʻa, Pūehuehu Nui, Pāhoa, Polanui, and Launiupoko, Lahaina District, Island of Maui.* Hilo, HI: Paul H. Rosendahl, Ph.D., Inc., 1991. [SHPD ID: 2019LI81242]

McCurdy, Todd D. and Hallett H. Hammatt. *Addendum Report for Archaeological Inventory Survey Documentation of Inadvertent Finds Identified during the Honoapiʻilani Highway Realignment (Lahaina Bypass) Phase 1B-1, Paunau Ahupuaʻa to Polanui Ahupuaʻa, Lahaina District, Maui Island TMK (2) 4-6-014:001, 002: (2) 4-6-018:002, 003; (2) 4-8-001:002 and (2) 4-8-003:001.* Wailuku, HI: Cultural Surveys Hawaiʻi, Inc., 2010. [SHPD ID: 2019LI81537]

McCurdy, Todd D. and Hallett H. Hammatt. *An Archaeological Monitoring Plan for the Honoapiʻilani Highway Realignment (Lahaina Bypass), Phase 1B-1, Paunau Ahupuaʻa to Polanui Ahupuaʻa, Lahaina District, Maui Island TMK: (2) 4-6-014:001-002, 4-6-018:002-003, 4-7-001:002 and 4-7-003:001.* Wailuku, HI: Cultural Surveys Hawaiʻi, Inc., 2010. [SHPD ID: 2019LI81539]

McCurdy, Todd D. and Hallett H. Hammatt. *Archaeological Inventory Survey Documentation of Inadvertent Finds Identified during the Honoapiʻilani Highway Realignment (Lahaina Bypass) Phase 1B-1, Paunau Ahupuaʻa to Polanui Ahupuaʻa, Lahaina District, Maui Island TMK: (2) 4-6-014:001, 002; (2) 4-6-018:002, 003; (2) 4-8-001:002 and (2) 4-7-003:001.* Wailuku, HI: Cultural Surveys Hawaiʻi, Inc., 2009. [SHPD ID: 2019LI81536]

McCurdy, Todd D. and Hallett H. Hammatt. *Archaeological Literature Review and Field Inspection for Honoapiʻilani Highway Realignment (Lahaina Bypass), Phase 1B-1, Paunau Ahupuaʻa to Polanui Ahupuaʻa, Lahaina District, Maui Island TMK (2) 4-6-014:001-002, 4-6-018:002-003, 4-8-001:002 and 4-7-003:001.* Wailuku, HI: Cultural Surveys Hawaiʻi, Inc., 2008. [SHPD ID: 2019LI81538]

Rosendahl, Paul H. *Archaeological Treatment Plan for No Adverse Effect, Lahaina Bypass Highway Project, Lands of Honokōwai, Hanakaʻōʻō, Wahikuli, Panaʻewa, Kuʻia, Halakaʻa, Pūehuehu Nui, Pāhoa, Polanui, and Launiupoko, Lahaina District, Island of Maui.* Hilo, HI: Paul H. Rosendahl, Ph.D., Inc., 1994. [SHPD ID: 2019LI81439]

Puʻuiki

Kurashina, Hiro and Aki Sinoto. *Archaeological Reconnaissance of the Proposed Shopping Center at Lahaina, Maui, Hawaiʻi, TMK: (2) 4-5-02:009.* Honolulu, HI: Department of Anthropology, Bernice P. Bishop Museum, 1984. [SHPD ID: 2019LI80648; UH Call Number: DU629.L3 K87 1984]

Shefcheck, Donna M. and Michael F. Dega. *An Archaeological Monitoring Plan for the Puunoa Subdivision No. 2, Lahaina, Puʻuiki Ahupuaʻa, Lahaina District, Island of Maui, Hawaiʻi.* Honolulu, HI: Scientific Consultant Services, Inc., 2008. [SHPD ID: 2019LI80647]

Puʻunoa

Conte, Patty J. *Archaeological Monitoring Plan for On and Off-Site Construction Related to Pending and Future Improvements, Puunoa Ahupuaʻa, Lahaina District, Island of Maui.* Makawao, HI: CRM Solutions Hawaiʻi, Inc., 2008. [SHPD ID: 2019LI80599]

Fredericksen, Erik M. *An Archaeological Monitoring Plan for the Kaahanui Place Electrical Improvements Project, Land of Puunoa, Lahaina District, Maui Island [TMK: (2) 4-5-04 por.].* Pukalani, HI: Xamanek Researches, 2009. [No location available]

Rotunno-Hazuka, Lisa J. and Jeffrey Pantaleo. *Archaeological Monitoring Plan for the Demolition of an Existing Single Family Residence & Pool Cover and Construction of a New Single Family Residence at TMK: (2) 4-5-04:048 Puʻunoa Ahupuaʻa, Lahaina District, Island of Maui.* Wailuku, HI: Archaeological Services Hawaii, LLC, 2004. [SHPD ID: 2019LI80625]

Rotunno-Hazuka, Lisa J. and Jeffrey Pantaleo. *Archaeological Monitoring Plan for the Demolition of an Existing Single Family Residence and Construction of a new Single Family Residence at TMK (2) 4-5-04:004, Puʻunoa Ahupuaʻa, Lahaina District, Island of Maui.* Wailuku, HI: Archaeological Services Hawaii, LLC, 2004. [SHPD ID: 2019LI80621]

Rotunno-Hazuka, Lisa J. and Jeffrey Pantaleo. *Final Archaeological Monitoring Report for All Ground Disturbing Activities Associated with the Development of a Residential Structure Located at TMK (2) 4-05-04:048 Puʻunoa Ahupuaʻa, Lahaina District, Island of Maui.* Wailuku, HI: Archaeological Services Hawaii, LLC, 2008. [SHPD ID: 2019LI80614]

Rotunno-Hazuka, Lisa J. and Jeffrey Pantaleo. *Final Archaeological Monitoring Report for All Ground Disturbing Activities Associated with the Development of a Residential Structure Located at TMK (2) 4-5-04:004, Puʻunoa Ahupuaʻa, Lahaina District, Island of Maui.* Wailuku, HI: Archaeological Services Hawaii, LLC, 2008. [SHPD ID: 2019LI80622]

Ukumehame

Chaffee, David B. and Michael F. Dega. *An Archaeological Monitoring Plan for Subdivision Construction of a 450-Acre Parcel of Land, Ahupuaʻa of Ukumehame, Lahaina District, Island of Maui, Hawaiʻi [TMK (2) 4-8-02:09].* Honolulu, HI: Scientific Consultant Services, Inc., 2003.

Clark, Matthew R. and Robert B. Rechtman. *An Archaeological Inventory Survey of 333 Acres for the Proposed Expansion of the Kaheawa Wind Farm (TMK: 2-4-8:001: por. 001).* Rechtman Consulting, LLC, 2008. [SHPD ID: 2019LI81628]

Dagher, Cathleen A. *Request for Information Pertaining to the Ukumehame Subdivision and the Impacts to Preserved Site 50-50-08-4438 Ukumehame Ahupuaʻa, Lahaina District, Island of Maui,* 2009. [SHPD ID: 2019LI81644]

Dagher, Cathleen A. and Michael F. Dega. *Revised Preservation Plan for Site 50-50-08-4438, Ukumehame Ahupuaʻa, Lahaina District, Island of Maui, Hawaiʻi [TMK (2) 4-8-002:066; formerly (2) 4-9-002:009 por.].* Honolulu, HI: Scientific Consultant Services, Inc., 2010. [SHPD ID: 2019LI81625]

Dega, Michael F. *An Addendum Archaeological Inventory Survey in Ukumehame Ahupuaʻa, Lahaina District, Island of Maui, Hawaiʻi [TMK (2) 4-9-02:008 por.].* Honolulu, HI: Scientific Consultant Services, Inc., 2006. [SHPD ID: 2019LI81645]

Devereux, Thomas K., Ian A. Masterson, Melody Heidel, Victoria Creed, Leilani Pyle, and Hallett H. Hammatt. *Archaeological Inventory Survey and Subsurface Testing of a 440 Acre Parcel, Ahupuaʻa of Ukumehame, Lahaina District, Island of Maui.* Wailuku, HI: Cultural Surveys Hawaiʻi, Inc., 1999. [SHPD ID: 2019LI81639]

Hammatt, Hallett H. *Archaeological Preservation Plan for 10 Sites Within for 440 Acre Parcel, Ahupuaʻa of Ukumehame, Lahaina District, Island of Maui.* Wailuku, HI: Cultural Surveys Hawaiʻi, Inc., 2000. [SHPD ID: 2019LI81626]

Hammatt, Hallett H. *Restoration Plan for Pole 69 (Original Location) at Ukumehame Gulch, Maʻalaea to Lahaina Third 69 KV Transmission Line.* Wailuku, HI: Cultural Surveys Hawaiʻi, Inc., 1996. [SHPD ID: 2019LI81632]

Magnuson, Carol M. *Supplemental Archaeological Survey of Turbine Pad Alignments, Kaheawa Pastures, Upland Ukumehame Ahupuaʻa, Maui.* Honolulu, HI: International Archaeological Research Institute, Inc., 2003. [SHPD ID: 2019LI81630]

Masterson, Ian and Hallett H. Hammatt. *Report on the Completed Reconstruction of Walls at Hikiʻi Heiau Ukumehame Ahupuaʻa, Island of Maui.* Wailuku, HI: Cultural Surveys Hawaiʻi, Inc., 1999. [SHPD ID: 2019LI81631]

Neller, Earl. *An Archaeological Reconnaissance Along the Coast at Ukumehame, Maui,* 1982. [SHPD ID: 2019LI81640; UH Call Number: DU629.U38 N45 1982]

Rechtman, Robert B. and Ashton K. Dircks Ah Sam. *An Archaeological Inventory Survey for the Kaheawa Wind Power (KWP) Phase 2 Project Area [TMK (2) 3-6-001:por. 14 & (2) 4-8-01: Por. 001].* Rechtman Consulting, LLC, 2009. [SHPD ID: 2019LI80301]

Riford, Mary F. and Paul L. Cleghorn. *Documentary Assessment of Archaeological Potential of Ten Prospective Power Plant Sites on Maui.* Honolulu, HI: Public Archaeology Section, Bernice P. Bishop Museum, 1989. [SHPD ID: 2022LI00168]

Shefcheck, Donna M. and Michael F. Dega. *A Preservation Plan for Site 50-50-08-5968 and Site 50-50-08-5969 in Ukumehame Ahupuaʻa, Lahaina District, Island of Maui, Hawaiʻi [TMK: (2) 4-8-02:008 por.].* Honolulu, HI: Scientific Consultant Services, Inc., 2006. [SHPD ID: 2019LI81643]

Sinoto, Aki. *An Archaeological Assessment of the Native Plant Conservatory Project, Ukumehame Firing Range, Ukumehame, Lahaina, Maui TMK (2) 4-8-2:047.* Honolulu, HI: Aki Sinoto Consulting, 1997. [SHPD ID: 2019LI81624]

Tomonari-Tuggle, M. J. *An Archaeological Reconnaissance Survey for 27 Wind Turbines in the Ukumehame Uplands, Island of Maui.* Honolulu, HI: International Archaeological Research Institute, Inc., 2003. [SHPD ID: 2019LI81627]

Tomonari-Tuggle, M. J. and Coral Rasmussen. *Preservation Plan for Site 50-50-09-5232, An Upland Heiau in Ukumehame Ahupua'a, Island of Maui TMK 4-8-01:1.* Honolulu, HI: International Archaeological Research Institute, Inc., 2005. [SHPD ID: 2019LI81629]

WAHIKULI

Conte, Patty J. *Archaeological Monitoring Plan for Construction Within TMK (2) 4-5-14:013 Por. 8A, Lahaina District, Wahikuli Ahupua'a, Island of Maui.* Makawao, HI: CRM Solutions Hawai'i, Inc., 2005. [SHPD ID: 2019LI81348]

Conte, Patty J. *Archaeological Monitoring Plan for On and Off-Site Construction Related to the Proposed Amano Demo/Reconstruction, TMK (2) 4-5-12:008 Wahikuli Ahupua'a, Lahaina District, Island of Maui.* Makawao, HI: CRM Solutions Hawai'i, Inc., 2005. [SHPD ID: 2019LI81347]

Conte, Patty J. *Archaeological Monitoring Plan for On and Off-Site Construction Within and Related to TMK (2) 4-5-14:073 Lahaina District, Wahikuli Ahupua'a, Island of Maui.* Makawao, HI: CRM Solutions Hawai'i, Inc., 2006. [SHPD ID: 2019LI81354]

Conte, Patty J. *Archaeological Monitoring Report for Construction, Lahaina District, Wahikuli Ahupua'a, Island of Maui.* Makawao, HI: CRM Solutions Hawai'i, Inc., 2005. [SHPD ID: 2019LI81345]

Conte, Patty J. *Archaeological Monitoring Report for On and Off-Site Construction Within and Related to TMK (2) 4-5-14:073 Lahaina District, Wahikuli Ahupua'a, Island of Maui.* Makawao, HI: CRM Solutions Hawai'i, Inc., 2007. [SHPD ID: 2019LI81356]

Fredericksen, Demaris L. and Erik M. Fredericksen. *An Archaeological Inventory Survey of the Proposed Sandwich Isles Communications, Inc. Fiber Optics Landing Location near the Lahaina Post Office, Wahikuli Ahupua'a, Lahaina District, Island of Maui (TMK: 4-5-21:015).* Pukalani, HI: Xamanek Researches, 2003. [SHPD ID: 2019LI81336]

Goodwin, Conrad and Spencer Leinewebber. *Archaeological Inventory Survey Report, Pioneer Mil Company, Ltd. Sugar Enterprise Lands, Site No. 50-50-03-4420, Villages of Leiali'i Project, Lahaina, Maui Hawai'i.* Honolulu, HI: International Archaeological Research Institute, Inc., 1997. [SHPD ID: 2019LI81363]

Haun, Alan E. and Dave Henry. *Final Archaeological Monitoring Plan, TMK (2) 4-5-13:016, Wahikuli Ahupuaʻa, Lahaina District, Island of Maui*. Kailua-Kona, HI: Haun and Associates, 2014. [SHPD ID: 2019LI81350]

Jensen, Peter M. *Archaeological Inventory Survey Honoapiʻilani Highway Realignment Project Lahaina Bypass Section—Modified Corridor Alignment, Lands of Honokōwai, Hanakaʻōʻō, Wahikuli, Panaʻewa, Kuʻia, Halakaʻa, Pūehuehu Nui, Pāhoa, Polanui, and Launiupoko, Lahaina District, Island of Maui*. Hilo, HI: Paul H. Rosendahl, Ph.D., Inc., 1991. [SHPD ID: 2019LI81242]

Jensen, Peter M. *Archaeological Inventory Survey Lahaina Master Planned Project Site: Land of Wahikuli, Lahaina District, Island of Maui*. Hilo, HI: Paul H. Rosendahl, Ph.D., Inc., 1989. [SHPD ID: 2019LI80636]

Kehajit, Chonnikarn and Michael F. Dega. *Archaeological Monitoring Plan for 1191 Front Street Replacement of an Existing Water Supply Project, Lahaina, Wahikuli Ahupuaʻa, Lahaina District, Island of Maui, Hawaiʻi*. Honolulu, HI: Scientific Consultant Services, Inc., 2018. [SHPD ID: 2022LI00191]

Lee-Greig, Tanya, Robert Hill, and Hallett H. Hammatt. *An Archaeological Inventory Survey Report for the Lahaina Bypass Modified Alignment from Kahoma Stream to the Keawe Street Extension, Kelawea, Paeohi, and Wahikuli Ahupuaʻa, Lahaina District, Maui Island TMK (2) 4-5-021, 010, 015, and 031: Multiple Parcels*. Wailuku, HI: Cultural Surveys Hawaiʻi, Inc., 2008. [SHPD ID: 2019LI81368]

Lee-Greig, Tanya L. and Hallett H. Hammatt. *Archaeological Inventory Survey Plan for Honoapiʻilani Highway Realignment Phase IA, Future Keawe Street Extension to Lahainaluna Road: Ikena Avenue Alignment with Modified Extension Kelawea, Paeohi, and Wahikuli Ahupuaʻa, Lahaina District, Maui Island TMK (2) 4-5-021, 010, 015, and 031: Multiple Parcels*. Wailuku, HI: Cultural Surveys Hawaiʻi, Inc., 2008. [SHPD ID: 2019LI81341]

Lee-Greig, Tanya L. and Hallett H. Hammatt. *Archaeological Monitoring Plan for the Lahaina Bypass Modified Alignment from Kahoma Stream to the Keawe Street Extension, Kelawea, Paeohi, and Wahikuli Ahupuaʻa, Lahaina District, Maui Island*. Wailuku, HI: Cultural Surveys Hawaiʻi, Inc., 2009. [SHPD ID: 2019LI81369]

Lee-Greig, Tanya L., Robert Hill, and Hallett H. Hammatt. *An Archaeological Survey Report for the Realignment of a Section of the Honoapiʻilani Highway, Phase IA, Kelawea, Paeohi, and Wahikuli Ahupuaʻa, Lahaina District, Maui Island TMK (2) 4-5-021, 010, 015, and 031: Multiple Parcels*. Wailuku, HI: Cultural Surveys Hawaiʻi, Inc., 2008. [SHPD ID: 2019LI81361]

Madeus, Jonas K. et al. *Archaeological Inventory Survey for the Villages of Leiali ʻi, Phase 1-B Subdivision and Related Improvements Project, Wahikuli Ahupuaʻa,*

Lahaina District, Maui Island, TMKs: (2) 4-5-021:010 por., 014 por., 020, and 021 por.; (2) 4-5-36:109, 110, and 112; and Honoapiʻilani Highway Right-of-Way. Wailuku, HI: Cultural Surveys Hawaiʻi, Inc., 2022. [SHPD ID: 2022LI00589]

Madeus, Jonas K., Tanya Lee-Greig, and Hallett H. Hammatt. *An Archaeological Monitoring Report for the Lahaina Bypass Modified Alignment from the Lahainaluna Road Intersection to the Keawe Street Extension Kelawea, Paeohi, and Wahikuli Ahupuaʻa, Lahaina District, Maui Island TMK (2) 4-5-021, 010, 015, and 031: Multiple Parcels.* Wailuku, HI: Cultural Surveys Hawaiʻi, Inc., 2010. [SHPD ID: 2019LI81338]

Perzinski, David and Michael F. Dega. *Archaeological Monitoring Report for Lahaina No. 3 Force Main Replacement Project Wahikuli and Hanakaʻōʻō Ahupuaʻa, Lahaina District, Island of Maui, Hawaiʻi [TMK (2) 4-4-013].* Honolulu, HI: Scientific Consultant Services, Inc., 2014. [SHPD ID: 2019LI80661]

Rosendahl, Paul H. *Archaeological Treatment Plan for No Adverse Effect, Lahaina Bypass Highway Project, Lands of Honokōwai, Hanakaʻōʻō, Wahikuli, Panaʻewa, Kuʻia, Halakaʻa, Pūehuehu Nui, Pāhoa, Polanui, and Launiupoko, Lahaina District, Island of Maui.* Hilo, HI: Paul H. Rosendahl, Ph.D., Inc., 1994. [SHPD ID: 2019LI81439]

Smith, Helen Wong. *Historical Documentary Research in Archaeological Inventory Survey, Lahaina Master Planned Project Site, Land of Wahikuli, Lahaina District, Island of Maui.* Hilo, HI: Paul H. Rosendahl, Ph.D., Inc., 1989. [No location available]

Wasson, Eugene C. IV and Michael F. Dega. *An Archaeological Monitoring Report for the Lahaina No. 4. Force Main Replacement Project, in Lahaina, Wahikuli Ahupuaʻa, Lahaina District, Island of Maui, Hawaiʻi.* Honolulu, HI: Scientific Consultant Services, Inc., 2016. [SHPD ID: 2019LI80628]

Yucha, Josephine M. and Hallett H. Hammatt. *Archaeological Monitoring Plan for the Villages of Leialiʻi, Village 1-B Subdivision and Related Improvements Project, Wahikuli Ahupuaʻa, Lahaina District, Maui Island, TMKs: (2) 4-5-021:010 por., 014 por., 015 por., 020, and 021 por.; (2) 4-5-36:109, 110, and 112; and Honoapiʻilani Highway Right-of-Way.* Wailuku, HI: Cultural Surveys Hawaiʻi, Inc., 2022. [SHPD ID: 2023LI00106]

WAINEʻE

Ah Sam, Jessica A., Solomon H. Kailihiwa III, and Paul L. Cleghorn. *Archaeological Inventory Study and Cultural Impact Assessment for the Comfort Station*

Replacement During the Lahaina Pier Improvement Project, Lahaina, Maui [TMK (2) 4-6-01:001]. Kailua, HI: Pacific Legacy, Inc., 2004.

Andricci, Nicole and Michael F. Dega. *An Archaeological Assessment for the Lahaina Square Redevelopment Project, Lahaina, Waineʻe Ahupuaʻa, District of Lahaina, Island of Maui, Hawaiʻi*. Honolulu, HI: Scientific Consultant Services, Inc., 2017. [SHPD ID: 2019LI80016]

Andricci, Nicole and Michael F. Dega. *An Archaeological Monitoring Plan for a Residential Parcel 33 at 572 Waineʻe Street, Waineʻe Ahupuaʻa, Lahaina District, Maui Island, Hawaiʻi [TMK (2) 4-6-12:033]*. Honolulu, HI: Scientific Consultant Services, Inc., 2016.

Collins, Sara L. *Archaeological Monitoring Plan for Ground-Altering Activities During the Grading and Excavations for Construction Associated with the Mokuʻula/Mokuhinia Ecosystem Restoration Project, Phase I, Lahaina, Island of Maui*. Honolulu, HI: Pacific Consulting Services, Inc., 2007. [SHPD ID: 2019LI01493]

Fredericksen, Erik M. *An Archaeological Monitoring Plan for a Detector Check Upgrade Project for the Lahaina Square Shopping Center, Waineʻe Ahupuaʻa, Lahaina District, Maui*. Pukalani, HI: Xamanek Researches, 2008. [SHPD ID: 2019LI80611]

Fredericksen, Erik M. *An Archaeological Monitoring Plan for the West Side Resource Center in Lahaina, Waineʻe Ahupuaʻa, Lahaina District, Maui Island [TMK: 4-6-15: por. of 1 and 4-6-18: por. of 2)*. Pukalani, HI: Xamanek Researches, 2002. [SHPD ID: 2019LI81534]

Fredericksen, Erik M. *An Archaeological Monitoring Report for the West Side Resource Center in Lahaina, Waineʻe Ahupuaʻa, Lahaina District, Maui Island [TMK: (2) 4-6-15: por. of 1 and TMK: (2) 4-6-18: por. of 2]*. Pukalani, HI: Xamanek Researches, 2004. [SHPD ID: 2019LI81535]

Guerriero, Diane and Jeffrey *Pantaleo. Archaeological Inventory Survey Report of a 0.361 Acre Coastal Parcel, Waineʻe Ahupuaʻa, Lahaina District, Island of Maui*. Wailuku, HI: Archaeological Services Hawaii, LLC, 2005. [SHPD ID: 2019LI81560]

Heidel, Melody, William H. Folk, and Hallett H. Hammatt. *An Archaeological Inventory Survey for Waiola Church, Ahupuaʻa of Waineʻe, Lahaina District, Island of Maui*. Wailuku, HI: Cultural Surveys Hawaiʻi, Inc., 1994. [SHPD ID: 2019LI81552]

Kirkendall, Melissa, Kimberly M. Mooney, Elizabeth L. Kahahane, and Paul L. Cleghorn. *Archaeological Monitoring Plan for the Lahaina Pier Improvement Project, Waine'e Ahupua'a, Lahaina District, Island of Maui [TMK: (2) 4-6-01:001].* Kailua, HI: Pacific Legacy, Inc., 2010. [No location available]

Lee-Greig, Tanya L. and Hallett H. Hammatt. *Archaeological Inventory Survey Plan for the Proposed Mokuhinia Ecosystem Restoration Project Waiokama and Lower Waine'e Ahupua'a, Lahaina District, Maui Island.* Wailuku, HI: Cultural Surveys Hawai'i, Inc., 2014. [SHPD ID: 2019LI81554]

Mooney, Kimberly M., Paul L. Cleghorn, and Elizabeth L. Kahahane. *Archaeological Inventory Survey for the Lahaina Pier Improvement Project Waine'e Ahupua'a, Lahaina District, Island of Maui.* Kailua, HI: Pacific Legacy, Inc., 2008. [SHPD ID: 2019LI81382]

Perzinski, David and Michael F. Dega. *An Archaeological Inventory Survey of Three Contiguous Parcels of Land Totaling 0.417 Acres in Waine'e Ahupua'a, Lahaina District, Maui Island, Hawai'i.* Honolulu, HI: Scientific Consultant Services, Inc., 2011. [SHPD ID: 2019LI81543]

Rotunno-Hazuka, Lisa J., Mia Watson, and Jeffrey Pantaleo. *Archaeological Monitoring Plan for the Repair and Installation of Underground Conduit at Front & Wharf Street, Lahaina and Waine'e Ahupua'a, Lahaina District, Island of Maui.* Wailuku, HI: Archaeological Services Hawaii, LLC, 2008. [SHPD ID: 2019LI81385]

WAINE'E

Fredericksen, Erik M. and Demaris L. Fredericksen. *An Archaeological Inventory Survey of the Lahaina Watershed Flood Control Project Area, Lands of Polanui, Paha, Pueuehunui, Lahaina District, Maui Island (TMK: 4-6-13:016, 18, 26; TMK 4-7-01, 02).* Pukalani, HI: Xamanek Researches, 2003. [SHPD ID: 2019LI81442]

WAIOKAMA

Collins, Sara L. *Archaeological Monitoring Plan for Ground-Altering Activities During the Grading and Excavations for Construction Associated with the Moku'ula/Mokuhinia Ecosystem Restoration Project, Phase I, Lahaina, Island of Maui.* Honolulu, HI: Pacific Consulting Services, Inc., 2007. [SHPD ID: 2019LI01493]

Folio, Katie M. and Hallett H. Hammatt. *An Archaeological Monitoring Plan for Proposed Improvements at the Feast of Lele, Waiokama Ahupua'a, Lahaina*

District, Island of Maui TMK: (2) 4-6-002:007 (por.). Wailuku, HI: Cultural Surveys Hawaiʻi, Inc., 2014. [SHPD ID: 2019LI81372]

Lee-Greig, Tanya L. and Hallett H. Hammatt. *Archaeological Inventory Survey Plan for the Proposed Mokuhinia Ecosystem Restoration Project Waiokama and Lower Waineʻe Ahupuaʻa, Lahaina District, Maui Island.* Wailuku, HI: Cultural Surveys Hawaiʻi, Inc., 2014. [SHPD ID: 2019LI81554]

Madeus, Jonas K., Josephine M. Yucha, and Hallett H. Hammatt. *Archaeological Monitoring Report for Improvements at Feast of Lele, Waiokama Ahupuaʻa, Lahaina District, Maui Island, TMK (2) 4-6-002:007 (por.).* Wailuku, HI: Cultural Surveys Hawaiʻi, Inc., 2018. [No location available]

Not Designated

Barrera, William Jr. *Honoapiʻilani Highway, Maui: Archaeological Reconnaissance.* Honolulu, HI: Chiniago, Inc., 1988.

Barrera, William Jr. *North Beach, Maui: Archaeological Reconnaissance.* Honolulu, HI: Chiniago, Inc., 1986. [SHPD ID: 2019LI81288]

Burgett, Berdena and Robert L. Spear. *An Archaeological Inventory Survey of an 8.8 Acre Parcel in the Land of Kainehi, Lahaina District, Paunau Ahupuaʻa, Island of Maui.* Honolulu, HI: Aki Sinoto Consulting, 1994.

Chapman, P. S. and P. V. Kirch. *Archaeological Excavations at Seven Sites, Southeast Maui, Hawaiian Islands.* Honolulu, HI: Department of Anthropology, Bernice P. Bishop Museum, 1979. [UH Call Number: DU624.A1 B47 no.79-1]

Fredericksen, Erik M. and Demaris L. Fredericksen. *Archaeological Inventory Survey of the Lower Honoapiʻilani Road Improvements Project Corridor (TMK 4-3-03; 4-3-05; 4-3-10; 4-3-15) Lahaina District, Maui Island.* Pukalani, HI: Xamanek Researches, 1999. [SHPD ID: 2021LI00220]

Fredericksen, Walter M., Demaris L. Fredericksen, and Erik M. Fredericksen. *Archaeological Data Recovery Report on the AUS Site, Lahaina, Maui, Hawaiʻi.* Pukalani, HI: Xamanek Researches, 1989. [SHPD ID: 2019LI81562]

Fredericksen, Walter M., Demaris L. Fredericksen, and Erik M. Fredericksen. *The AUS Site: H. S. #50-03-1797 A Preliminary Archaeological Inventory Survey Report.* Pukalani, HI: Xamanek Researches, 1989. [No location available]

Hunt, Jennifer, Lauren Morawski, and Michael F. Dega. *An Archaeological Monitoring Report for the Installation of New Sewer Lines and Force Mains and the Replacement of Waterlines for the County of Maui at Shaw, Front, and Dick-*

enson Streets and Honoapiʻilani Highway in Lahaina AND The Installation of Underground Electrical Lines, Panels, and Meters at Armory Park/Kamehameha Iki Park on Front Street in Lahaina for Maui Parks and Recreation Division, Various Ahupuaʻa, Lahaina District, Island of Maui, Hawaiʻi [TMK (2) 4-6002:003, 005, 006, 007, 010, 012, 015, 016, and 027]. Honolulu, HI: Scientific Consultant Services, Inc., 2011. [SHPD ID: 2019LI81393]

Jensen, Peter A. and Jenny O'Claray. *Supplemental Archaeological Survey, Lahaina Master Planned Project Offsite Sewer, Water Improvements, and Cane Haul Road.* Hilo, HI: Paul H. Rosendahl, Ph.D., Inc., 1991. [SHPD ID: 2019LI81419]

Kirch, Patrick V. *Archaeological Survey of the Honolua Development Area, Maui.* Honolulu, HI: Department of Anthropology, Bernice P. Bishop Museum, 1973. [SHPD ID: 2019LI81019; UH Call Number: DU629.K374 K57 1973]

Major, Maurice, P. Christiaan Klieger, and Susan A. Lebo. *Historical Background and Archaeological Testing at Pikanele's Kuleana in Lahaina, Maui: An Inventory Survey Report of LCA 310.3 (Royal Patent 1729.2, TMK (2) 4-6-07:013.* Honolulu, HI: Department of Anthropology, Bernice P. Bishop Museum, 1996. [SHPD ID: 2019LI81546]

Mason Architects, Inc. *Reconnaissance Level Survey, Honokōwai Reservoir for the West Maui Recycled Water and Kāʻanapali Resort R-1 Water Distribution Expansion Project. TMK (2) 4-4-02:019.* Honolulu, HI: Mason Architects, Inc., 2022. [SHPD ID: 2023LI00017]

Masterson, Ian and Hallett H. Hammatt. *An Addendum Report for the New Alignment Section between Points 14D, 15, and 16 along the Proposed Maʻalaea-Lahaina Third 69 kV Transmission Line, Maui.* Wailuku, HI: Cultural Surveys Hawaiʻi, Inc., 1995. [SHPD ID: 2019LI81633]

Pantaleo, Jeffrey. *Archaeological Survey of the Proposed Lahainaluna Reservoir and Treatment Facility, Lahaina, Maui.* Honolulu, HI: Public Archaeology Section, Applied Research Group, Bernice P. Bishop Museum, 1991. [SHPD ID: 2019LI81530]

Perzinski, David. *Archaeological Field Inspection for the West Maui Recycled Water Expansion Project, Phase 2 County Job No. WW12-13, Lahaina, Maui, Hawaiʻi.* Honolulu, HI: Scientific Consultant Services, Inc., 2013. [No location available]

Pietrusewsky, Michael and Michele T. Douglas. *An Analysis of Additional Historic Human Skeletal Remains from the Kahoma Stream Flood Control Project, 1989, Lahaina, Maui.* Honolulu, HI: University of Hawaiʻi at Mānoa, 1990. [SHPD ID: DU629.L3 P54 1990]

Pietrusewsky, Michael, Michele T. Douglas, and Rona Ikehara. *An Osteological Study of Human Remains from the Kahoma Stream Flood Control Project, Lahaina, Maui.* Honolulu, HI: University of Hawaiʻi at Mānoa, 1989. [UH Call Number: DU629.K76 P54 1989]

Sinoto, Aki. *Proposed Kai Ala Subdivision, Kāʻanapali, Maui.* Honolulu, HI: Bernice P. Bishop Museum, 1990. [SHPD ID: 2019LI81265]

Sinoto, Aki and Jeffrey Pantaleo. *Archaeological Inventory Survey of TMK (2) 4-4-01:002, 11, and 12 (Revised Final 9-92).* Honolulu, HI: Aki Sinoto Consulting, 1991. [No location available]

Spencer Mason Architects. *Various Historic Site Survey for Lahainaluna Road and Waineʻe Street Widening Projects.* Honolulu, HI: Spencer Mason Architects, 1988. [SHPD ID: 2019LI81432]

Tomonari-Tuggle, M. J. and H. D. Tuggle. *Archaeological Survey of Two Demonstration Trails of the Hawaiʻi Statewide Trail and Access System.* Honolulu, HI: International Archaeological Research Institute, Inc., 1991. [SHPD ID: 2019LI79001; UH Call Number: DU628.M3 T66 1991]

Tourtellotte, Perry A. *Archaeological Inspection Report for Rainbow Ranch,* 1988. [SHPD ID: 2019LI81059]

Walton, Beth. *A Preliminary Report on an Archaeological Survey of the Portion of Piilani Highway from Stake 195+00 to Stake 250+00,* 1972. [SHPD ID: 2019LI79374]

Watanabe, Farley. *Archaeological Site Investigation Kahoma Stream Flood Control Project TMK (2) 4-5-15:008.* Honolulu, HI: Army Corps of Engineers, 1987. [SHPD ID: 2019LI81342]

PUBLICATIONS BY TAX MAP KEYS

Documents without TMKs indicated are at the end of the list. Partial TMKs occur above more complete TMKs.

(2) 2-4-08:001

Clark, Matthew R. and Robert B. Rechtman. *An Archaeological Inventory Survey of 333 Acres for the Proposed Expansion of the Kaheawa Wind Farm (TMK: 2-4-8:001: por. 001)*. Rechtman Consulting, LLC, 2008. [SHPD ID: 2019LI81628]

(2) 3-1-01:003

Major, Maurice. *Ridgetops and Gulch Bottoms: An Archaeological Inventory Survey of Waiōlaʻi and Waiokila Catchments, Kahakuloa, West Maui, Hawaiʻi. TMK (2) 3-1-01:003*. Honolulu, HI: Department of Anthropology, Bernice P. Bishop Museum, 1996. [SHPD ID: 2019LI80145]

(2) 3-6-01:014

Rechtman, Robert B. and Ashton K. Dircks Ah Sam. *An Archaeological Inventory Survey for the Kaheawa Wind Power (KWP) Phase 2 Project Area [TMK (2) 3-6-001: por. 14 & (2) 4-8-01: por. 001]*. Rechtman Consulting, LLC, 2009. [SHPD ID: 2019LI80301]

(2) 3-8-06:

Lee-Greig, Tanya L. and Hallett H. Hammatt. *Archaeological Monitoring Plan for the Puʻunēnē School and Lahainaluna High School Hawaiʻi Inter-Island DOE Cesspool Project, Island of Maui TMK (2) 4-6-018 and (2) 3-8-006*. Wailuku, HI: Cultural Surveys Hawaiʻi, Inc., 2007. [SHPD ID: 2019LI81526]

Willman, Michael R., Tanya Lee-Greig, and Hallett H. Hammatt. *Addendum to Archaeological Monitoring Plan for the Puʻunēnē School and Lahainaluna High School Hawaiʻi Inter-Island DOE Cesspool Project, Island of Maui TMK (2) 4-6-18 and (2) 3-8-06.* Wailuku, HI: Cultural Surveys Hawaiʻi, Inc., 2008. [SHPD ID: 2019LI81524]

(2) 4-1-01:005

Tome, Guerin, Irene Calis, and Michael F. Dega. *An Archaeological Inventory Survey in Honolua, Honolua Ahupuaʻa, Lahaina District, Island of Maui, Hawaiʻi [TMK: (2) 4-1-01:005].* Honolulu, HI: Scientific Consultant Services, Inc., 2002. [SHPD ID: 2019LI81423]

(2) 4-1-01:018

Conte, Patty J. *Archaeological Inventory Survey of the Stoops Property TMK (2) 4-1-01:018, Honolua Ahupuaʻa, Kāʻanapali District, Maui, Hawaiʻi.* Makawao, HI: CRM Solutions Hawaiʻi, Inc., 2006. [SHPD ID: 2019LI81424]

Conte, Patty J. *Archaeological Monitoring Plan for On and Off-Site Construction Within and Related to TMK (2) 4-1-01:018, Honolua Ahupuaʻa, Kāʻanapali District, Maui, Hawaiʻi.* Makawao, HI: CRM Solutions Hawaiʻi, Inc., 2006. [SHPD ID: 2019LI81424]

Conte, Patty J. *Archaeological Preservation Plan for the Portion of Site #50-50-01-1756 Within TMK (2) 4-1-01:018 Honolua Ahupuaʻa, Kāʻanapali District, Maui, Hawaiʻi.* Makawao, HI: CRM Solutions Hawaiʻi, Inc., 2007. [SHPD ID: 2019LI81428]

(2) 4-2-

Dagher, Cathleen A. and Michael F. Dega. *An Archaeological Monitoring Plan for the Proposed Kapalua Coastal Trail Corridor Located in Kapalua and Honokōhau and Nāpili 2&3 Ahupuaʻa Lahaina District, Island of Maui, Hawaiʻi [TMK: (2) 4-2-Various].* Honolulu, HI: Scientific Consultant Services, Inc., 2007. [SHPD ID: 2019LI81421]

(2) 4-2-01

Fredericksen, Erik M. and Demaris L. Fredericksen. *Archaeological Inventory Survey of 475 Acres in Kapalua District 2 Project Area, Located in Napili and*

Honokahua Ahupuaʻa, Lahaina District, Maui Island, TMK: (2) 4-2-01: por. 1.
Pukalani, HI: Xamanek Researches, 2002. [SHPD ID: 2021LI00311]

(2) 4-2-01:004

Guerriero, Diane A., Charvet-Pond, and S. Goodfellow. *Archaeological Monitoring and Data Recovery, Kapalua Ritz-Carlton Hotel Site, Land of Honokahua, Lahaina District, Island of Maui [TMK: (2) 4-2-01:004, 005, por. 012, 013, por. 018, 034].* Hilo, HI: Paul H. Rosendahl, Ph.D., Inc., 1993. [No location available]

(2) 4-2-01:005

Guerriero, Diane A., Charvet-Pond, and S. Goodfellow. *Archaeological Monitoring and Data Recovery, Kapalua Ritz-Carlton Hotel Site, Land of Honokahua, Lahaina District, Island of Maui [TMK: (2) 4-2-01:004, 005, por. 012, 013, por. 018, 034].* Hilo, HI: Paul H. Rosendahl, Ph.D., Inc., 1993. [No location available]

(2) 4-2-01:012

Guerriero, Diane A., Charvet-Pond, and S. Goodfellow. *Archaeological Monitoring and Data Recovery, Kapalua Ritz-Carlton Hotel Site, Land of Honokahua, Lahaina District, Island of Maui [TMK: (2) 4-2-01:004, 005, por. 012, 013, por. 018, 034].* Hilo, HI: Paul H. Rosendahl, Ph.D., Inc., 1993. [No location available]

(2) 4-2-01:013

Guerriero, Diane A., Charvet-Pond, and S. Goodfellow. *Archaeological Monitoring and Data Recovery, Kapalua Ritz-Carlton Hotel Site, Land of Honokahua, Lahaina District, Island of Maui [TMK: (2) 4-2-01:004, 005, por. 012, 013, por. 018, 034].* Hilo, HI: Paul H. Rosendahl, Ph.D., Inc., 1993. [No location available]

(2) 4-2-01:018

Guerriero, Diane A., Charvet-Pond, and S. Goodfellow. *Archaeological Monitoring and Data Recovery, Kapalua Ritz-Carlton Hotel Site, Land of Honokahua, Lahaina District, Island of Maui [TMK: (2) 4-2-01:004, 005, por. 012, 013, por. 018, 034].* Hilo, HI: Paul H. Rosendahl, Ph.D., Inc., 1993. [No location available]

(2) 4-2-01:034

Guerriero, Diane A., Charvet-Pond, and S. Goodfellow. *Archaeological Monitoring and Data Recovery, Kapalua Ritz-Carlton Hotel Site, Land of Honokahua, Lahaina District, Island of Maui [TMK: (2) 4-2-01:004, 005, por. 012, 013, por. 018, 034].* Hilo, HI: Paul H. Rosendahl, Ph.D., Inc., 1993. [No location available]

(2) 4-2-04:021

Fredericksen, Erik M. *Archaeological Monitoring Report for the Verizon Hawaii, Inc. Equipment Installation project at TMK: (2) 4-2-04:021 Ritz-Carlton, Kapalua, Honokahua Ahupua'a, Lahaina District, Maui, Hawai'i.* Pukalani, HI: Xamanek Researches, 2001. [SHPD ID: 2019LI81014, 2019LI81029]

(2) 4-2-04:024

Fredericksen, Demaris L. and Erik M. Fredericksen. *Archaeological Inventory Survey of a 24-Acre Parcel, Kapalua Lot 19, Located in Napili 2-3 Ahupua'a, Lahaina District, Maui Island [TMK: (2) 4-2-04: por. 024].* Pukalani, HI: Xamanek Researches, 2000. [SHPD ID: 2019LI81025]

Fredericksen, Erik M. *A Preliminary Report Summarizing Results of Field Research for an Archaeological Inventory Survey to Satisfy Requirements of SHPD at [TMK: (2) 4-2-04:por. 024] located in Honokahua Ahupua'a, Lahaina District, Island of Maui, Hawai'i.* Pukalani, HI: Xamanek Researches, 2003.

Fredericksen, Erik M. and Demaris L. Fredericksen. *Archaeological Inventory Survey for the Proposed Golf Academy Project Kapalua, Maui, Hawai'i, TMK 4-2-04: por. 24.* Pukalani, HI: Xamanek Researches, 1998. [SHPD ID: 2019LI81012]

Webb, Erika L. *Inventory Survey of Honolua Plantation Shop Buildings Located at the Kapalua Central Resort, TMK (2) 4-2-4:024.* Honolulu, HI: Mason Architects, Inc., 2005. [SHPD ID: 2019LI81047]

(2) 4-2-04:025

Chong Jin and Michael F. Dega. *Archaeological Monitoring Report for the Kapalua Sinkhole Remediation and Native Plant Restoration Project, Nāpili 2-3 Ahupua'a, Lahaina District, Island of Maui [TMK: (2) 4-2-04:025 and (2) 4-2-04:059].* Honolulu, HI: Scientific Consultant Services, Inc., 2021. [SHPD ID: 2022LI00634]

(2) 4-2-04:026

Fredericksen, Erik M., Walter M. Fredericksen, and Demaris L. Fredericksen. *Additional Archaeological Inventory Survey Subsurface testing at Kapalua Bay Hotel [TMK (2) 4-2-04:26], Honokahua and Napili 2-3 Ahupuaʻa, Lahaina District, Maui Island.* Pukalani, HI: Xamanek Researches, 1996. [SHPD ID: 2019LI81024]

(2) 4-2-04:048

Dagher, Cathleen A. and Michael F. Dega. *An Archaeological Monitoring Plan for the Napili No. 5 & 6 WWPS Force Main Replacement Honokahua Ahupuaʻa, Lahaina (Kāʻanapali) District, Island of Maui, Hawaiʻi [TMK (2) 4-2-04: portion of 48 (Lot 3-A-1 of Kapalua Makai Subdivision No. 4) and TMK (2) 4-2-04: portion of 59 (Lot A-1-A-2 of Kapalua Development (Large-Lot) Subdivision).* Honolulu, HI: Scientific Consultant Services, Inc., 2015. [SHPD ID: 2019LI81016]

(2) 4-2-04:059

Chong Jin and Michael F. Dega. *Archaeological Monitoring Report for the Kapalua Sinkhole Remediation and Native Plant Restoration Project, Nāpili 2-3 Ahupuaʻa, Lahaina District, Island of Maui [TMK: (2) 4-2-04:025 and (2) 4-2-04:059].* Honolulu, HI: Scientific Consultant Services, Inc., 2021. [SHPD ID: 2022LI00634]

Dagher, Cathleen A. and Michael F. Dega. *An Archaeological Monitoring Plan for the Napili No. 5 & 6 WWPS Force Main Replacement Honokahua Ahupuaʻa, Lahaina (Kāʻanapali) District, Island of Maui, Hawaiʻi [TMK (2) 4-2-04: portion of 48 (Lot 3-A-1 of Kapalua Makai Subdivision No. 4) and TMK (2) 4-2-04: portion of 59 (Lot A-1-A-2 of Kapalua Development (Large-Lot) Subdivision).* Honolulu, HI: Scientific Consultant Services, Inc., 2015. [SHPD ID: 2019LI81016]

(2) 4-2-05:999

Dagher, Cathleen A. and Michael F. Dega. *An Archaeological Monitoring Plan for the Nāpili No. 3 WWPS Force Main Replacement, Lower Honoapiʻilani Road Right-of-Way, Kahana Ahupuaʻa, Lahaina (Kāʻanapali) District Island of Maui, Hawaiʻi. [TMK (2) 4-2-05:999 and 4-3-10:999].* Honolulu, HI: Scientific Consultant Services, Inc., 2020. [SHPD ID: 2021LI00158]

(2) 4-2-07:007

Fredericksen, Demaris L. and Erik M. Fredericksen. *An Archaeological Inventory Survey of a portion of land in Nāpili 2-3 Ahupuaʻa, Lahaina District, Island of Maui [TMK: (2) 4-2-07: Parcels 007 and 008].* Pukalani, HI: Xamanek Researches, 2003. [SHPD ID: 2019LI81044]

(2) 4-2-07:008

Fredericksen, Demaris L. and Erik M. Fredericksen. *An Archaeological Inventory Survey of a portion of land in Nāpili 2-3 Ahupuaʻa, Lahaina District, Island of Maui [TMK: (2) 4-2-07: Parcels 007 and 008].* Pukalani, HI: Xamanek Researches, 2003. [SHPD ID: 2019LI81044]

(2) 4-3-01:001

Fredericksen, Erik M. *An Archaeological Assessment for the Proposed Maui Preparatory Academy, Alaeloa Ahupuaʻa, Lahaina District, Island of Maui [TMK (2) 4-3-01: 01 por.].* Pukalani, HI: Xamanek Researches, 2004. [SHPD ID: 2019LI81053]

Kennedy, Joseph. *Archaeological Walk Through Reconnaissance of (2)4-3-01:001 Napili Fire Station, TMK (2) 4-3-01:001 (por.),* 1989. [SHPD ID: 2019LI81054]

(2) 4-3-01:017

Dagher, Cathleen A. and Michael F. Dega. *Archaeological Inventory Survey for the Proposed West Maui Water Source Development Project Māhinahina Well (State Well No. 6-5638-004) (West Maui Well No. 1) and the Kahana Well (State Well No. 6-5738-002) (West Maui Well No. 2), Honokōwai, Māhinahina, and Māhinahina 1, 2, 3 Ahupuaʻa, Lahaina (Kāʻanapali) District, Island of Maui, Hawaiʻi [TMK: (2) 4-3-01:017, (2) 4-3-01:084; (2) 4-4-02:014, 015, and 018; and (2) 4-4-004:009, 011, 017, and 019].* Honolulu, HI: Scientific Consultant Services, Inc., 2022. [SHPD ID: 2022LI00356]

Mulrooney et al. *Archaeological Inventory Survey Report for the Kahana Solar Project in Ahupuaʻa of Kahana and Māhinahina 1-3, Moku of Kāʻanapali (Lahaina Modern Tax District), Island of Maui [TMK: (2) 4-3-01:017 por.; (2) 4-3-01:082 por.; (2) 4-3-01:084 por.].* Kailua, HI: Pacific Legacy, Inc., 2020

(2) 4-3-01:031

Kennedy, Joseph. *Archaeological Inventory Survey and Subsurface Testing Report for TMK: (2) 4-3-01:031, Located at Kahana Ahupuaʻa, Island of Maui,* Revised May 1992, 1992. [SHPD ID: 2019LI81051]

Kennedy, Joseph. *Archaeological Inventory Survey Report for TMK (2) 4-3-01:31, located at Kahana, Island of Maui.* Haleʻiwa, HI: Archaeological Consultants of Hawaii, 1991. [SHPD ID: 2019LI81069]

Kennedy, Joseph. *Archaeological Inventory Survey Report for TMK: (2) 4-3-01:031; Located at Kahana, Island of Maui.* 1990. [SHPD ID: 2019LI81054]

Kennedy, Joseph and Tim Denham. *Archaeological Inventory Survey and Subsurface Testing Report for TMK(2) 4-3-01:031, located at Kahana Ahupuaʻa, Maui.* Haleʻiwa, HI: Archaeological Consultants of Hawaii, 1992.

Pantaleo, Jeffrey and Paul Titchenal. *An Archaeological Inventory Survey Report for the Pulelehua Community Project TMK (2) 4-3-01:031 Por. Māhinahina 1, 2, 3, Māhinahina 4, and Kahana Ahupuaʻa, Lahaina and Kāʻanapali Districts, Island of Maui.* Wailuku, HI: Archaeological Services Hawaii, LLC, 2004. [SHPD ID: 2019LI81072]

(2) 4-3-01:082

Mulrooney et al. *Archaeological Inventory Survey Report for the Kahana Solar Project in Ahupuaʻa of Kahana and Māhinahina 1-3, Moku of Kāʻanapali (Lahaina Modern Tax District), Island of Maui [TMK: (2) 4-3-01:017 por.; (2) 4-3-01:082 por.; (2) 4-3-01:084 por.].* Kailua, HI: Pacific Legacy, Inc., 2021

(2) 4-3-01:084

Dagher, Cathleen A. and Michael F. Dega. *Archaeological Inventory Survey for the Proposed West Maui Water Source Development Project Māhinahina Well (State Well No. 6-5638-004) (West Maui Well No. 1) and the Kahana Well (State Well No. 6-5738-002) (West Maui Well No. 2), Honokōwai, Māhinahina, and Māhinahina 1, 2, 3 Ahupuaʻa, Lahaina (Kāʻanapali) District, Island of Maui, Hawaiʻi [TMK: (2) 4-3-01:017, (2) 4-3-01:084; (2) 4-4-02:014, 015, and 018; and (2) 4-4-004:009, 011, 017, and 019].* Honolulu, HI: Scientific Consultant Services, Inc., 2022. [SHPD ID: 2022LI00356]

Mulrooney et al. *Archaeological Inventory Survey Report for the Kahana Solar Project in Ahupuaʻa of Kahana and Māhinahina 1-3, Moku of Kāʻanapali (Lahaina*

Modern Tax District), Island of Maui [TMK: (2) 4-3-01:017 por.; (2) 4-3-01:082 por.; (2) 4-3-01:084 por.]. Kailua, HI: Pacific Legacy, Inc., 2022

(2) 4-3-02:021

Folio, Katie M. and Hallett H. Hammatt. *Archaeological Monitoring Report for the Special Use Permit Application for the Napili Point I (SMX 2015/0465) and Napili Point II (SMX 2015/0472) Project, Honokeana Ahupuaʻa, Lahaina District, Island of Maui, Napili Point I TMK: (2) 4-3-002:021 (por.), Napili Point II.* Wailuku, HI: Cultural Surveys Hawaiʻi, Inc., 2016. [SHPD ID: 2019LI81068]

(2) 4-3-02:068

Kennedy, Joseph. *Archaeological Inventory Survey of TMK (2) 4-3-02:068 & 069, Located at Napili, Island of Maui.* Haleʻiwa, HI: Archaeological Consultants of Hawaii, 1990. [SHPD ID: 2019LI81061]

(2) 4-3-02:069

Kennedy, Joseph. *Archaeological Inventory Survey of TMK (2) 4-3-02:068 & 069, Located at Napili, Island of Maui.* Haleʻiwa, HI: Archaeological Consultants of Hawaii, 1990. [SHPD ID: 2019LI81061]

(2) 4-3-03:

Fredericksen, Erik M. and Demaris L. Fredericksen. *Archaeological Inventory Survey of the Lower Honoapiʻilani Road Improvements Project Corridor (TMK 4-3-03; 4-3-05; 4-3-10; 4-3-15) Lahaina District, Maui Island.* Pukalani, HI: Xamanek Researches, 1999. [SHPD ID: 2021LI00220]

(2) 4-3-03:043

Conte, Patty J. *Archaeological Assessment Report for TMK (2) 4-3-03:043 Mailepai Ahupuaʻa, Lahaina District, Island of Maui.* Makawao, HI: CRM Solutions Hawaiʻi, Inc., 2005. [SHPD ID: 2019LI81298]

Conte, Patty J. *Archaeological Monitoring Report for Off-Site Construction (Mailepai Hui Land Lots 51-C-4-A, B & C) Lahaina District, Mailepai Ahupuaʻa, Island of Maui.* Makawao, HI: CRM Solutions Hawaiʻi, Inc., 2007. [SHPD ID: 2019LI81324]

(2) 4-3-03:108

Kennedy, Joseph. *Archaeological Inventory Survey and Subsurface Testing Report for a Property Located at TMK: 4-3-03:108 and 110, ʻAlaeloa Ahupuaʻa, Lahaina District, on the Island of Maui,* 1992. [SHPD ID: 2022LI00219]

(2) 4-3-03:110

Kennedy, Joseph. *Archaeological Inventory Survey and Subsurface Testing Report for a Property Located at TMK: 4-3-03:108 and 110, ʻAlaeloa Ahupuaʻa, Lahaina District, on the Island of Maui,* 1992. [SHPD ID: 2022LI00219]

(2) 4-3-05:

Fredericksen, Erik M. and Demaris L. Fredericksen. *Archaeological Inventory Survey of the Lower Honoapiʻilani Road Improvements Project Corridor (TMK 4-3-03; 4-3-05; 4-3-10; 4-3-15) Lahaina District, Maui Island.* Pukalani, HI: Xamanek Researches, 1999. [SHPD ID: 2021LI00220]

(2) 4-3-05:016

Moore, James R. and Joseph Kennedy. *An Archaeological Inventory Survey with Subsurface Testing Report for Portions of the Proposed Kahana Ridge Subdivision Located at TMK: (2) 4-3-05:016 & 018, in Kahana Ahupuaʻa, Lahaina District, Island of Maui.* Haleʻiwa, HI: Archaeological Consultants of Hawaii, 1994. [SHPD ID: 2019LI81329]

(2) 4-3-05:018

Moore, James R. and Joseph Kennedy. *An Archaeological Inventory Survey with Subsurface Testing Report for Portions of the Proposed Kahana Ridge Subdivision Located at TMK: (2) 4-3-05:016 & 018, in Kahana Ahupuaʻa, Lahaina District, Island of Maui.* Haleʻiwa, HI: Archaeological Consultants of Hawaii, 1994. [SHPD ID: 2019LI81329]

(2) 4-3-06:002

Monahan, Christopher M. *An Archaeological Assessment Report on 3.054 Acres of Partially Developed Land in Honokōwai, Māhinahina 4 Ahupuaʻa, Lahaina*

District, Maui Island, Hawai'i [TMK (2) 4-3-06:002 and 069]. Honolulu, HI: Scientific Consultant Services, Inc., 2003. [SHPD ID: 2019LI81314, 2019LI81304]

(2) 4-3-06:003

McGerty, Leann and Robert L. Spear. *An Inventory Survey of a 3.3 Acre Parcel in Māhinahina 4 Ahupua'a, Lahaina District, Island of Maui, Hawai'i [TMK (2) 4-3-06:003]*, 1996. [SHPD ID: 2019LI81305]

(2) 4-3-06:069

Monahan, Christopher M. *An Archaeological Assessment Report on 3.054 Acres of Partially Developed Land in Honokōwai, Māhinahina 4 Ahupua'a, Lahaina District, Maui Island, Hawai'i [TMK (2) 4-3-06:002 and 069]*. Honolulu, HI: Scientific Consultant Services, Inc., 2003. [SHPD ID: 2019LI81314, 2019LI81304]

(2) 4-3-10:

Fredericksen, Erik M. and Demaris L. Fredericksen. *Archaeological Inventory Survey of the Lower Honoapi'ilani Road Improvements Project Corridor (TMK 4-3-03; 4-3-05; 4-3-10; 4-3-15) Lahaina District, Maui Island*. Pukalani, HI: Xamanek Researches, 1999. [SHPD ID: 2021LI00220]

(2) 4-3-10:004

Frey, Jennifer J., Josephine M. Yucha, and Hallett H. Hammatt. *Archaeological Monitoring Report for the Valley Isle Resort Renovation Project, Kahana Ahupua'a, Lahaina District, Maui Island, TMK: (2) 4-3-10:004*. Wailuku, HI: Cultural Surveys Hawai'i, Inc., 2021. [SHPD ID: 2022LI00135]

Yucha, Josephine M. and Hallett H. Hammatt. *Archaeological Monitoring Plan for the Valley Isle Resort Renovation Project, Kahana Ahupua'a, Lahaina District, Maui Island, TMK: (2) 4-3-10:004*. Wailuku, HI: Cultural Surveys Hawai'i, Inc., 2020. [SHPD ID: 2021LI00211]

(2) 4-3-10:009

Madeus, Jonas K. and Hallett H. Hammatt. *An Archaeological Monitoring Plan for the Proposed Hololani Resort Condominiums Shoreline Protection Project in*

Kahananui Ahupuaʻa, Lahaina District, Maui Island TMK: (2) 4-3-010:009 por. Wailuku, HI: Cultural Surveys Hawaiʻi, Inc., 2014. [SHPD ID: 2019LI81312]

(2) 4-3-10:999

Dagher, Cathleen A. and Michael F. Dega. *An Archaeological Monitoring Plan for the Nāpili No. 3 WWPS Force Main Replacement, Lower Honoapiʻilani Road Right-of-Way, Kahana Ahupuaʻa, Lahaina (Kāʻanapali) District Island of Maui, Hawaiʻi. [TMK (2) 4-2-05:999 and 4-3-10:999].* Honolulu, HI: Scientific Consultant Services, Inc., 2020. [SHPD ID: 2021LI00158]

(2) 4-3-15

Fredericksen, Erik M. and Demaris L. Fredericksen. *Additional Archaeological Inventory Survey Level Work for Site 50-50-03-4797, Lower Honoapiʻilani Road Improvements Project Corridor; Alaeloa, Mailepai and Kahana Ahupuaʻa, Lahaina District, Maui Island [TMK (2) 4-3-15].* Pukalani, HI: Xamanek Researches, 2001. [SHPD ID: 2021LI00221]

(2) 4-3-15:

Fredericksen, Erik M. and Demaris L. Fredericksen. *Archaeological Inventory Survey of the Lower Honoapiʻilani Road Improvements Project Corridor (TMK 4-3-03; 4-3-05; 4-3-10; 4-3-15) Lahaina District, Maui Island.* Pukalani, HI: Xamanek Researches, 1999. [SHPD ID: 2021LI00220]

(2) 4-3-15:014

Fredericksen, Erik M. *An Archaeological Monitoring Plan for a parcel of land in Napili, Mailepai Ahupuaʻa, Lahaina District, Napili, Maui, TMK: (2) 4-3-15:014.* Pukalani, HI: Xamanek Researches, 2004. [SHPD ID: 2019LI81293]

(2) 4-3-15:069

Pestana, Elizabeth and Michael F. Dega. *Archaeological Inventory Survey of a 5.18 Acre Parcel in Kahana, Kahana Ahupuaʻa, Kāʻanapali District, Island of Maui, Hawaiʻi [TMK: (2)-4-3-15:069].* Honolulu, HI: Scientific Consultant Services, Inc., 2018. [SHPD ID: 2019LI81301]

(2) 4-4-01:002

Sinoto, Aki and Jeffrey Pantaleo. *Archaeological Inventory Survey of TMK (2) 4-4-01:002, 11, and 12 (Revised Final 9-92).* Honolulu, HI: Aki Sinoto Consulting, 1991. [No location available]

(2) 4-4-01:011

Sinoto, Aki and Jeffrey Pantaleo. *Archaeological Inventory Survey of TMK (2) 4-4-01:002, 11, and 12 (Revised Final 9-92).* Honolulu, HI: Aki Sinoto Consulting, 1991. [No location available]

(2) 4-4-01:012

Sinoto, Aki and Jeffrey Pantaleo. *Archaeological Inventory Survey of TMK (2) 4-4-01:002, 11, and 12 (Revised Final 9-92).* Honolulu, HI: Aki Sinoto Consulting, 1991. [No location available]

(2) 4-4-01:026

Andricci, Nicole and Michael F. Dega. *AAAAA Rent-A-Space Extension Project Honokōwai, Māhinahina 4 Ahupuaʻa Lahaina (Kāʻanapali) District, Maui Island Hawaii [TMK (2) 4-4-01:026].* Honolulu, HI: Scientific Consultant Services, Inc., 2015.

(2) 4-4-01:046

Dega, Michael F. *An Archaeological Monitoring Plan for Improvements at Honokōwai Beach Park for the County of Maui, Department of Parks and Recreation, Honokōwai Ahupuaʻa, Lahaina District, Island of Maui, Hawaiʻi [TMK (2) 4-4-01:046 por. & 047 por].* Honolulu, HI: Scientific Consultant Services, Inc., 2015. [SHPD ID: 2019LI81042]

(2) 4-4-01:047

Dega, Michael F. *An Archaeological Monitoring Plan for Improvements at Honokōwai Beach Park for the County of Maui, Department of Parks and Recreation, Honokōwai Ahupuaʻa, Lahaina District, Island of Maui, Hawaiʻi [TMK (2) 4-4-01:046 por. & 047 por].* Honolulu, HI: Scientific Consultant Services, Inc., 2015. [SHPD ID: 2019LI81042]

(2) 4-4-01:097

Fredericksen, Erik M. and Jennifer L. Frey. *An Archaeological Monitoring Report for the Kā'anapali Shores Roadway Improvements Project, Honokōwai Ahupua'a, Lahaina District, Maui [TMK: (2) 4-4-001:097, and TMK: (2) 4-4-001 (Right of Way)]*. Pukalani, HI: Xamanek Researches, 2008. [SHPD ID: 2019LI81243]

(2) 4-4-01:106

Havel, BreAnna and Michael F. Dega. *An Archaeological Assessment Report on 0.11 Acres of a Partially Developed Land in Honokōwai Ahupua'a, Lahaina District, Maui Island, Hawai'i [TMK 4-4-01:106]*. Honolulu, HI: Scientific Consultant Services, Inc., 2005. [SHPD ID: 2019LI81285]

(2) 4-4-01:RIGHT OF WAY

Fredericksen, Erik M. and Jennifer L. Frey. *An Archaeological Monitoring Report for the Kā'anapali Shores Roadway Improvements Project, Honokōwai Ahupua'a, Lahaina District, Maui [TMK: (2) 4-4-001:097, and TMK: (2) 4-4-001 (Right of Way)]*. Pukalani, HI: Xamanek Researches, 2008. [SHPD ID: 2019LI81243]

(2) 4-4-02:002

Yates and Hallett H. Hammatt. *Archaeological Monitoring Plan for the Kā'anapali 2020 Master Plan, Kā'anapali Coffee Farms Subdivision Phase II Project, Hanaka'ō'ō and Honokōwai Ahupua'a, Lahaina District, Maui Island, TMK (2) 4-4-02:002*. Wailuku, HI: Cultural Surveys Hawai'i, Inc., 2020. [SHPD ID: 2021LI00326, 2022LI00365]

Yucha, Josephine M. and Hallett H. Hammatt. *Archaeological Monitoring Plan for the Pu'ukoli'i Village Mauka Project, Hanaka'ō'ō Ahupua'a, Lahaina District, Maui Island, TMKs: (2) 4-4-02:002, 048, and 053 por., (2) 4-4-06:070, 086 and 087 por., and (2) 4-4-15:034 through 072. 24:026 (por.)*. Wailuku, HI: Cultural Surveys Hawai'i, Inc., 2023. [SHPD ID: 2023LI00111]

Yucha, Josephine M. et al. *Archaeological Inventory Survey for the Pu'ukoli'i Village Mauka Project, Hanaka'ō'ō Ahupua'a, Lahaina District, Maui Island, TMKs: (2) 4-4-02:002, 048, and 053 por., (2) 4-4-06:070, 086 and 087 por., and (2) 4-4-15:034 through 072*. Wailuku, HI: Cultural Surveys Hawai'i, Inc., 2022. [SHPD ID: 2023LI00110]

(2) 4-4-02:003

Fredericksen, Erik M. *An Archaeological Assessment Survey of a c. 5 Acre Portion of Land for the Proposed Temporary Off-Site Parking Project, Hanaka'ō'ō/Honokōwai Ahupua'a, Lahaina District, Maui Island [TMK: (2) 4-4-002: 003].* Pukalani, HI: Xamanek Researches, 2007. [No location available]

McGerty, Leann and Robert L. Spear. *A Cultural Impact Assessment of Wastewater Pump Station No. 1 in Honokōwai Ahupua'a, Kā'anapali, Lahaina District, Maui Island, Hawai'i [TMK: (2) 4-4-02:003, (2) 4-4-02:029].* Honolulu, HI: Scientific Consultant Services, Inc., 2010. [SHPD ID: 2019LI81254]

Ogg, Randy and Michael F. Dega. *An Archaeological Assessment of Lahaina Wastewater Pump Station No. 1 Improvements, Honokōwai Ahupua'a, Lahaina District, Maui Island, Hawai'i [TMK: (2) 4-4-02:003 & (2) 4-4-02:029].* Honolulu, HI: Scientific Consultant Services, Inc., 2007. [SHPD ID: 2019LI81279]

(2) 4-4-02:014

Dagher, Cathleen A. and Michael F. Dega. *Archaeological Inventory Survey for the Proposed West Maui Water Source Development Project Māhinahina Well (State Well No. 6-5638-004) (West Maui Well No. 1) and the Kahana Well (State Well No. 6-5738-002) (West Maui Well No. 2), Honokōwai, Māhinahina, and Māhinahina 1, 2, 3 Ahupua'a, Lahaina (Kā'anapali) District, Island of Maui, Hawai'i [TMK: (2) 4-3-01:017, (2) 4-3-01:084; (2) 4-4-02:014, 015, and 018; and (2) 4-4-004:009, 011, 017, and 019].* Honolulu, HI: Scientific Consultant Services, Inc., 2022. [SHPD ID: 2022LI00356]

(2) 4-4-02:015

Dagher, Cathleen A. and Michael F. Dega. *Archaeological Inventory Survey for the Proposed West Maui Water Source Development Project Māhinahina Well (State Well No. 6-5638-004) (West Maui Well No. 1) and the Kahana Well (State Well No. 6-5738-002) (West Maui Well No. 2), Honokōwai, Māhinahina, and Māhinahina 1, 2, 3 Ahupua'a, Lahaina (Kā'anapali) District, Island of Maui, Hawai'i [TMK: (2) 4-3-01:017, (2) 4-3-01:084; (2) 4-4-02:014, 015, and 018; and (2) 4-4-004:009, 011, 017, and 019].* Honolulu, HI: Scientific Consultant Services, Inc., 2022. [SHPD ID: 2022LI00356]

(2) 4-4-02:018

Chaffee, David B. and Michael F. Dega. *An Archaeological Monitoring Plan for the West Maui Recycled Water Expansion Project (Phase 2), Honokōwai Ahupuaʻa, Lahaina District, Maui Island, Hawaiʻi [TMK (2) 4-4-002:018 por]*. Honolulu, HI: Scientific Consultant Services, Inc., 2013.

Dagher, Cathleen A. and Michael F. Dega. *Archaeological Inventory Survey for the Proposed West Maui Water Source Development Project Māhinahina Well (State Well No. 6-5638-004) (West Maui Well No. 1) and the Kahana Well (State Well No. 6-5738-002) (West Maui Well No. 2), Honokōwai, Māhinahina, and Māhinahina 1, 2, 3 Ahupuaʻa, Lahaina (Kāʻanapali) District, Island of Maui, Hawaiʻi [TMK: (2) 4-3-01:017, (2) 4-3-01:084; (2) 4-4-02:014, 015, and 018; and (2) 4-4-004:009, 011, 017, and 019]*. Honolulu, HI: Scientific Consultant Services, Inc., 2022. [SHPD ID: 2022LI00356]

(2) 4-4-02:019

Mason Architects, Inc. *Reconnaissance Level Survey, Honokōwai Reservoir for the West Maui Recycled Water and Kāʻanapali Resort R-1 Water Distribution Expansion Project. TMK (2) 4-4-02:019*. Honolulu, HI: Mason Architects, Inc., 2022. [SHPD ID: 2023LI00017]

(2) 4-4-02:029

Lyman, Kepa and Michael F. Dega. *Addendum—Archaeological Monitoring Plan for Lahaina Wastewater Pump Station No. 1 Improvements Honokōwai Ahupuaʻa, Lahaina District, Maui Island, Hawaiʻi [TMK (2) 4-4-002:33 and portions of 29 & 39]*. Honolulu, HI: Scientific Consultant Services, Inc., 2018. [No location available]

McGerty, Leann and Robert L. Spear. *A Cultural Impact Assessment of Wastewater Pump Station No. 1 in Honokōwai Ahupuaʻa, Kāʻanapali, Lahaina District, Maui Island, Hawaiʻi [TMK: (2) 4-4-02:003, (2) 4-4-02:029]*. Honolulu, HI: Scientific Consultant Services, Inc., 2010. [SHPD ID: 2019LI81254]

Ogg, Randy and Michael F. Dega. *An Archaeological Assessment of Lahaina Wastewater Pump Station No. 1 Improvements, Honokōwai Ahupuaʻa, Lahaina District, Maui Island, Hawaiʻi [TMK: (2) 4-4-02:003 & (2) 4-4-02:029]*. Honolulu, HI: Scientific Consultant Services, Inc., 2007. [SHPD ID: 2019LI81279]

Shefcheck, Donna M. and Michael F. Dega. *An Archaeological Monitoring Plan for Lahaina Wastewater Pump Station No. 1 Improvements, Honokōwai Ahupuaʻa, Lahaina District Maui Island, Hawaiʻi [TMK (2) 4-4-02:033 and portions of 29 and 39].* Honolulu, HI: Scientific Consultant Services, Inc., 2008. [SHPD ID: 2019LI81253]

(2) 4-4-02:029

Six, Janet L. *A Final Archaeological Assessment Report for Maui County Work on County Roadway (WTP T20160044) and grading and grubbing (GT20160132) Proposed Sunset Terrace Lot Beautification Project, Honokōwai Ahupuaʻa, Lahaina District Maui Island, TMK (2) 4-4-02:029 and 034 (por.).* Pāhoa, HI: Sixth Sense Archaeological Consultants, LLC, 2018. [SHPD ID: 2019LI81282]

(2) 4-4-02:030

Dega, Michael F. *An Archaeological Monitoring Plan for the West Maui Recycled Water Expansion Project (Phase 2), Honokōwai Ahupuaʻa, Lahaina District, Maui Island, Hawaiʻi.* Honolulu, HI: Scientific Consultant Services, Inc., 2015. [SHPD ID: 2019LI81246]

(2) 4-4-02:033

Lyman, Kepa and Michael F. Dega. *Addendum—Archaeological Monitoring Plan for Lahaina Wastewater Pump Station No. 1 Improvements Honokōwai Ahupuaʻa, Lahaina District, Maui Island, Hawaiʻi [TMK (2) 4-4-002:33 and portions of 29 & 39].* Honolulu, HI: Scientific Consultant Services, Inc., 2018. [No location available]

Shefcheck, Donna M. and Michael F. Dega. *An Archaeological Monitoring Plan for Lahaina Wastewater Pump Station No. 1 Improvements, Honokōwai Ahupuaʻa, Lahaina District Maui Island, Hawaiʻi [TMK (2) 4-4-02:033 and portions of 29 and 39].* Honolulu, HI: Scientific Consultant Services, Inc., 2008. [SHPD ID: 2019LI81253]

(2) 4-4-02:034

Six, Janet L. *A Final Archaeological Assessment Report for Maui County Work on County Roadway (WTP T20160044) and grading and grubbing (GT20160132) Proposed Sunset Terrace Lot Beautification Project, Honokōwai Ahupuaʻa, Lahaina*

District Maui Island, TMK (2) 4-4-02:029 and 034 (por.). Pāhoa, HI: Sixth Sense Archaeological Consultants, LLC, 2018. [SHPD ID: 2019LI81282]

(2) 4-4-02:039

Dega, Michael F. *An Archaeological Monitoring Plan for the West Maui Recycled Water Expansion Project (Phase 2), Honokōwai Ahupuaʻa, Lahaina District, Maui Island, Hawaiʻi*. Honolulu, HI: Scientific Consultant Services, Inc., 2015. [SHPD ID: 2019LI81246]

Lyman, Kepa and Michael F. Dega. *Addendum—Archaeological Monitoring Plan for Lahaina Wastewater Pump Station No. 1 Improvements Honokōwai Ahupuaʻa, Lahaina District, Maui Island, Hawaiʻi [TMK (2) 4-4-002:33 and portions of 29 & 39]*. Honolulu, HI: Scientific Consultant Services, Inc., 2018. [No location available]

Shefcheck, Donna M. and Michael F. Dega. *An Archaeological Monitoring Plan for Lahaina Wastewater Pump Station No. 1 Improvements, Honokōwai Ahupuaʻa, Lahaina District Maui Island, Hawaiʻi [TMK (2) 4-4-02:033 and portions of 29 and 39]*. Honolulu, HI: Scientific Consultant Services, Inc., 2008. [SHPD ID: 2019LI81253]

(2) 4-4-02:040

Dega, Michael F. *An Archaeological Monitoring Plan for the West Maui Recycled Water Expansion Project (Phase 2), Honokōwai Ahupuaʻa, Lahaina District, Maui Island, Hawaiʻi*. Honolulu, HI: Scientific Consultant Services, Inc., 2015. [SHPD ID: 2019LI81246]

(2) 4-4-02:048

Yucha, Josephine M. and Hallett H. Hammatt. *Archaeological Monitoring Plan for the Puʻukoliʻi Village Mauka Project, Hanakaʻōʻō Ahupuaʻa, Lahaina District, Maui Island, TMKs: (2) 4-4-02:002, 048, and 053 por., (2) 4-4-06:070, 086 and 087 por., and (2) 4-4-15:034 through 072. 24:026 (por.)*. Wailuku, HI: Cultural Surveys Hawaiʻi, Inc., 2023. [SHPD ID: 2023LI00111]

Yucha, Josephine M. et al. *Archaeological Inventory Survey for the Puʻukoliʻi Village Mauka Project, Hanakaʻōʻō Ahupuaʻa, Lahaina District, Maui Island, TMKs: (2) 4-4-02:002, 048, and 053 por., (2) 4-4-06:070, 086 and 087 por., and (2) 4-4-15:034 through 072*. Wailuku, HI: Cultural Surveys Hawaiʻi, Inc., 2022. [SHPD ID: 2023LI00110]

(2) 4-4-02:049

Dega, Michael F. *An Archaeological Monitoring Plan for the West Maui Recycled Water Expansion Project (Phase 2), Honokōwai Ahupuaʻa, Lahaina District, Maui Island, Hawaiʻi.* Honolulu, HI: Scientific Consultant Services, Inc., 2015. [SHPD ID: 2019LI81246]

(2) 4-4-02:052

Wong, Charmaine and Michael F. Dega. *An Archaeological Assessment for the West Maui Hospital and Medical Center, Hanakaʻōʻō Ahupuaʻa, Lahaina (Kāʻanapali) district, Maui Island, Hawaiʻi [TMK: (2) 4-4-02:052].* Honolulu, HI: Scientific Consultant Services, Inc., 2014. [SHPD ID: 2019LI81245]

Wong, Charmaine and Michael F. Dega. *An Archaeological Assessment for the West Maui Hospital and Medical Center, Hanakaʻōʻō Ahupuaʻa, Lahaina (Kāʻanapali) District, Maui Island, Hawaiʻi, TMK: (2) 4-4-02:052.* Honolulu, HI: Scientific Consultant Services, Inc., 2008. [No location available]

(2) 4-4-02:053

Yucha, Josephine M. and Hallett H. Hammatt. *Archaeological Monitoring Plan for the Puʻukoliʻi Village Mauka Project, Hanakaʻōʻō Ahupuaʻa, Lahaina District, Maui Island, TMKs: (2) 4-4-02:002, 048, and 053 por., (2) 4-4-06:070, 086 and 087 por., and (2) 4-4-15:034 through 072. 24:026 (por.).* Wailuku, HI: Cultural Surveys Hawaiʻi, Inc., 2023. [SHPD ID: 2023LI00111]

Yucha, Josephine M. et al. *Archaeological Inventory Survey for the Puʻukoliʻi Village Mauka Project, Hanakaʻōʻō Ahupuaʻa, Lahaina District, Maui Island, TMKs: (2) 4-4-02:002, 048, and 053 por., (2) 4-4-06:070, 086 and 087 por., and (2) 4-4-15:034 through 072.* Wailuku, HI: Cultural Surveys Hawaiʻi, Inc., 2022. [SHPD ID: 2023LI00110]

(2) 4-4-04:003

Rogers, Scott. *An Archaeological Monitoring Plan for the Kāʻanapali—Hyatt Force Main Replacements, Kāʻanapali Resort Complex, Hanakaʻōʻō, Honokōwai Ahupuaʻa, Lahaina District, Island of Maui.* Pukalani, HI: Xamanek Researches, 2007. [SHPD ID: 2019LI80682]

(2) 4-4-04:004

Rogers, Scott. *An Archaeological Monitoring Plan for the Kāʻanapali—Hyatt Force Main Replacements, Kāʻanapali Resort Complex, Hanakaʻōʻō, Honokōwai Ahupuaʻa, Lahaina District, Island of Maui.* Pukalani, HI: Xamanek Researches, 2007. [SHPD ID: 2019LI80682]

(2) 4-4-04:005

Rogers, Scott. *An Archaeological Monitoring Plan for the Kāʻanapali—Hyatt Force Main Replacements, Kāʻanapali Resort Complex, Hanakaʻōʻō, Honokōwai Ahupuaʻa, Lahaina District, Island of Maui.* Pukalani, HI: Xamanek Researches, 2007. [SHPD ID: 2019LI80682]

(2) 4-4-04:013

Rogers, Scott. *An Archaeological Monitoring Plan for the Kāʻanapali—Hyatt Force Main Replacements, Kāʻanapali Resort Complex, Hanakaʻōʻō, Honokōwai Ahupuaʻa, Lahaina District, Island of Maui.* Pukalani, HI: Xamanek Researches, 2007. [SHPD ID: 2019LI80682]

(2) 4-4-04:042

Sinoto, Aki and Jeffrey Pantaleo. *Archaeological Inventory Survey of the Proposed Site for the New Lahaina Kingdom Hall Puunoa, Paunau Ahupuaʻa, Lahaina District, Maui Island TMK (2) 4-4-04:042 & 044).* Wailuku, HI: Archaeological Services Hawaii, LLC, 2003. [SHPD ID: 2019LI80616]

(2) 4-4-04:044

Sinoto, Aki and Jeffrey Pantaleo. *Archaeological Inventory Survey of the Proposed Site for the New Lahaina Kingdom Hall Puunoa, Paunau Ahupuaʻa, Lahaina District, Maui Island TMK (2) 4-4-04:042 & 044).* Wailuku, HI: Archaeological Services Hawaii, LLC, 2003. [SHPD ID: 2019LI80616]

(2) 4-4-06:015

Sinoto, Aki. *Proposed Kai Ala Subdivision, Kāʻanapali, Maui.* Honolulu, HI: Bernice P. Bishop Museum, 1990. [SHPD ID: 2019LI81265]

(2) 4-4-06:031

Hammatt, Hallett H. *Archaeological Reconnaissance at the Proposed Hyatt Regency Site, Hanakaʻōʻō, Kāʻanapali, Maui Island, Tax Map Key; 4-4-06:31 Lot 60, ARCH 14-129.* Lāwaʻi, HI: Archaeological Research Center Hawaiʻi, 1978. [SHPD ID: 2019LI81264; UH Call Number: GN486 .H35]

(2) 4-4-06:033

Keau, Charles. *Archaeological Reconnaissance (Surface Survey) for Hanakaʻōʻō (Hahakea) Beach Park. Includes cover letter: An Archaeological Reconnaissance of Hahakea Beach Park, Hanakaʻōʻō, Maui. TMK: 4-4-06:33 by Earl Neller.* State Historic Preservation Office, March 1982. [SHPD ID: 2019LI81272; UH Call Number: DU629.H364 K43 1981]

(2) 4-4-06:056

McGerty, Leann and Robert L. Spear. *A Cultural Impact Assessment on a Piece of Property Located in Kāʻanapali, Hanakaʻōʻō Ahupuaʻa, Lahaina District, Maui Island, Hawaiʻi [TMK: (2) 4-4-06:056].* Honolulu, HI: Scientific Consultant Services, Inc., 2003. [SHPD ID: 2019LI81266]

Morawski, Lauren and Michael F. Dega. *Archaeological Inventory Survey of a 7.65 Acre Property at Lot 10-H Ahupuaʻa of Hanakaʻōʻō, Lahaina District, Island of Maui, Hawaiʻi [TMK: (2) 4-4-06:056].* Honolulu, HI: Scientific Consultant Services, Inc., 2003. [SHPD ID: 2019LI81273]

(2) 4-4-06:070

Yucha, Josephine M. and Hallett H. Hammatt. *Archaeological Monitoring Plan for the Puʻukoliʻi Village Mauka Project, Hanakaʻōʻō Ahupuaʻa, Lahaina District, Maui Island, TMKs: (2) 4-4-02:002, 048, and 053 por., (2) 4-4-06:070, 086 and 087 por., and (2) 4-4-15:034 through 072. 24:026 (por.).* Wailuku, HI: Cultural Surveys Hawaiʻi, Inc., 2023. [SHPD ID: 2023LI00111]

Yucha, Josephine M. and Hallett H. Hammatt. *Archaeological Monitoring Plan for the Puʻukoliʻi Village Mauka Project, Hanakaʻōʻō Ahupuaʻa, Lahaina District, Maui Island, TMKs: (2) 4-4-02:002, 048, and 053 por., (2) 4-4-06:070, 086 and 087 por., and (2) 4-4-15:034 through 072. 24:026 (por.).* Wailuku, HI: Cultural Surveys Hawaiʻi, Inc., 2023. [SHPD ID: 2023LI00111]

Yucha, Josephine M. et al. *Archaeological Inventory Survey for the Puʻukoliʻi Village Mauka Project, Hanakaʻōʻō Ahupuaʻa, Lahaina District, Maui Island, TMKs: (2) 4-4-02:002, 048, and 053 por., (2) 4-4-06:070, 086 and 087 por., and (2) 4-4-15:034 through 072.* Wailuku, HI: Cultural Surveys Hawaiʻi, Inc., 2022. [SHPD ID: 2023LI00110]

(2) 4-4-06:086

Yucha, Josephine M. and Hallett H. Hammatt. *Archaeological Monitoring Plan for the Puʻukoliʻi Village Mauka Project, Hanakaʻōʻō Ahupuaʻa, Lahaina District, Maui Island, TMKs: (2) 4-4-02:002, 048, and 053 por., (2) 4-4-06:070, 086 and 087 por., and (2) 4-4-15:034 through 072. 24:026 (por.).* Wailuku, HI: Cultural Surveys Hawaiʻi, Inc., 2023. [SHPD ID: 2023LI00111]

Yucha, Josephine M. et al. *Archaeological Inventory Survey for the Puʻukoliʻi Village Mauka Project, Hanakaʻōʻō Ahupuaʻa, Lahaina District, Maui Island, TMKs: (2) 4-4-02:002, 048, and 053 por., (2) 4-4-06:070, 086 and 087 por., and (2) 4-4-15:034 through 072.* Wailuku, HI: Cultural Surveys Hawaiʻi, Inc., 2022. [SHPD ID: 2023LI00110]

(2) 4-4-06:087

Yucha, Josephine M. and Hallett H. Hammatt. *Archaeological Monitoring Plan for the Puʻukoliʻi Village Mauka Project, Hanakaʻōʻō Ahupuaʻa, Lahaina District, Maui Island, TMKs: (2) 4-4-02:002, 048, and 053 por., (2) 4-4-06:070, 086 and 087 por., and (2) 4-4-15:034 through 072. 24:026 (por.).* Wailuku, HI: Cultural Surveys Hawaiʻi, Inc., 2023. [SHPD ID: 2023LI00111]

Yucha, Josephine M. et al. *Archaeological Inventory Survey for the Puʻukoliʻi Village Mauka Project, Hanakaʻōʻō Ahupuaʻa, Lahaina District, Maui Island, TMKs: (2) 4-4-02:002, 048, and 053 por., (2) 4-4-06:070, 086 and 087 por., and (2) 4-4-15:034 through 072.* Wailuku, HI: Cultural Surveys Hawaiʻi, Inc., 2022. [SHPD ID: 2023LI00110]

(2) 4-4-06:999

Lee-Greig, Tanya L. and Hallett H. Hammatt. *Archaeological Monitoring Plan for the Honoapiʻilani Highway Safety Improvements at Kāʻanapali Parkway and Halelo Street Hanakaʻōʻō Ahupuaʻa, Lahaina District, Maui Island [TMK (2) 4-4-006:999 por; 4-4-009:036 por.).* Wailuku, HI: Cultural Surveys Hawaiʻi, Inc., 2014. [SHPD ID: 2019LI81271]

(2) 4-4-08:001

Pacheco, Robert. *A Cultural Impact Assessment for the Proposed Kāʻanapali Beach Restoration Project, Hanakaʻōʻō Ahupuaʻa, Lahaina District, Island of Maui, Hawaiʻi TMK (2) 4-4-008:001, 002, 003, 004, 005, 019, 022; 4-4-013:001, 002, 006, 007, 008.* Honolulu, HI: International Archaeology, LLC, 2006. [SHPD ID: 2019LI80681]

Pacheco, Robert. *An Archaeological Literature Review for the Proposed Kāʻanapali Beach Restoration Project, Hanakaʻōʻō Ahupuaʻa, Lahaina District, Island of Maui, Hawaiʻi TMK (2) 4-4-008:001, 002, 003, 004, 005, 019, 022; 4-4-013:001, 002, 006, 007, 008.* Honolulu, HI: International Archaeology, LLC, 2015. [SHPD ID: 2019LI81260]

(2) 4-4-08:002

Pacheco, Robert. *A Cultural Impact Assessment for the Proposed Kāʻanapali Beach Restoration Project, Hanakaʻōʻō Ahupuaʻa, Lahaina District, Island of Maui, Hawaiʻi TMK (2) 4-4-008:001, 002, 003, 004, 005, 019, 022; 4-4-013:001, 002, 006, 007, 008.* Honolulu, HI: International Archaeology, LLC, 2006. [SHPD ID: 2019LI80681]

Pacheco, Robert. *An Archaeological Literature Review for the Proposed Kāʻanapali Beach Restoration Project, Hanakaʻōʻō Ahupuaʻa, Lahaina District, Island of Maui, Hawaiʻi TMK (2) 4-4-008:001, 002, 003, 004, 005, 019, 022; 4-4-013:001, 002, 006, 007, 008.* Honolulu, HI: International Archaeology, LLC, 2015. [SHPD ID: 2019LI81260]

(2) 4-4-08:003

Dagher, Cathleen A. and Michael F. Dega. *An Archaeological Assessment of the Kāʻanapali Beach Hotel Beach Front Restaurant/Canoe Hale, Hanakaʻōʻō Ahupuaʻa, Lahaina District, Island of Maui, Hawaiʻi [TMK: (2) 4-4-08:003].* Honolulu, HI: Scientific Consultant Services, Inc., 2014. [SHPD ID: 2019LI81259]

Dega, Michael F. *An Archaeological Inventory Survey Plan for Kāʻanapali Beach Hotel Beach Front Restaurant/Canoe Hale, Hanakaʻōʻō Ahupuaʻa, Lahaina District, Island of Maui, Hawaiʻi [TMK: (2) 4-4-008:003 por.].* Honolulu, HI: Scientific Consultant Services, Inc., 2013. [SHPD ID: 2019LI80674]

Pacheco, Robert. *A Cultural Impact Assessment for the Proposed Kāʻanapali Beach Restoration Project, Hanakaʻōʻō Ahupuaʻa, Lahaina District, Island of Maui,*

Hawai'i TMK (2) 4-4-008:001, 002, 003, 004, 005, 019, 022; 4-4-013:001, 002, 006, 007, 008. Honolulu, HI: International Archaeology, LLC, 2006. [SHPD ID: 2019LI80681]

Pacheco, Robert. *An Archaeological Literature Review for the Proposed Kā'anapali Beach Restoration Project, Hanaka'ō'ō Ahupua'a, Lahaina District, Island of Maui, Hawai'i TMK (2) 4-4-008:001, 002, 003, 004, 005, 019, 022; 4-4-013:001, 002, 006, 007, 008.* Honolulu, HI: International Archaeology, LLC, 2015. [SHPD ID: 2019LI81260]

(2) 4-4-08:004

Pacheco, Robert. *A Cultural Impact Assessment for the Proposed Kā'anapali Beach Restoration Project, Hanaka'ō'ō Ahupua'a, Lahaina District, Island of Maui, Hawai'i TMK (2) 4-4-008:001, 002, 003, 004, 005, 019, 022; 4-4-013:001, 002, 006, 007, 008.* Honolulu, HI: International Archaeology, LLC, 2006. [SHPD ID: 2019LI80681]

Pacheco, Robert. *An Archaeological Literature Review for the Proposed Kā'anapali Beach Restoration Project, Hanaka'ō'ō Ahupua'a, Lahaina District, Island of Maui, Hawai'i TMK (2) 4-4-008:001, 002, 003, 004, 005, 019, 022; 4-4-013:001, 002, 006, 007, 008.* Honolulu, HI: International Archaeology, LLC, 2015. [SHPD ID: 2019LI81260]

(2) 4-4-08:005

Fredericksen, Demaris L. *Monitoring Report for the Sheraton-Maui Redevelopment Project Hanaka'ō'ō Ahupua'a, Lahaina District, Maui Island [TMK: (2) 4-4-08:005].* Pukalani, HI: Xamanek Researches, 1998. [SHPD ID: 2019LI81263]

Pacheco, Robert. *A Cultural Impact Assessment for the Proposed Kā'anapali Beach Restoration Project, Hanaka'ō'ō Ahupua'a, Lahaina District, Island of Maui, Hawai'i TMK (2) 4-4-008:001, 002, 003, 004, 005, 019, 022; 4-4-013:001, 002, 006, 007, 008.* Honolulu, HI: International Archaeology, LLC, 2006. [SHPD ID: 2019LI80681]

Pacheco, Robert. *An Archaeological Literature Review for the Proposed Kā'anapali Beach Restoration Project, Hanaka'ō'ō Ahupua'a, Lahaina District, Island of Maui, Hawai'i TMK (2) 4-4-008:001, 002, 003, 004, 005, 019, 022; 4-4-013:001, 002, 006, 007, 008.* Honolulu, HI: International Archaeology, LLC, 2015. [SHPD ID: 2019LI81260]

Yucha, Josephine M. and Hallett H. Hammatt. *Archaeological Monitoring Plan for the Sheraton Maui Resort & Spa Sewer Improvements Project, Hanaka'ō'ō Ahupua'a, Lahaina District, Maui Island, TMKs: (2) 4-4-08:005 and 011 (pors).* Wailuku, HI: Cultural Surveys Hawai'i, Inc., 2018. [SHPD ID: 2019LI80670]

Yucha, Josephine M. and Hallett H. Hammatt. *Archaeological Monitoring Report for the Sheraton Maui Sewer Improvements Project, Hanaka'ō'ō Ahupua'a, Lahaina District, Maui Island, TMKs: (2) 4-4-008:005 and 011 (pors.).* Wailuku, HI: Cultural Surveys Hawai'i, Inc., 2018. [SHPD ID: 2019LI81258]

(2) 4-4-08:007

Rotunno-Hazuka, Lisa J. and Jeffrey Pantaleo. *Archaeological Monitoring Plan for All Improvements Related to the Redevelopment of the Royal Lahaina Resort, Hanaka'ō'ō Ahupua'a; Lahaina District, Island of Maui, TMK:4-4-08:007& 013.* Wailuku, HI: Archaeological Services Hawaii, LLC, 2007. [SHPD ID: 2019LI80677]

(2) 4-4-08:010

Rogers, Scott. *An Archaeological Monitoring Plan for the Kā'anapali—Hyatt Force Main Replacements, Kā'anapali Resort Complex, Hanaka'ō'ō, Honokōwai Ahupua'a, Lahaina District, Island of Maui.* Pukalani, HI: Xamanek Researches, 2007. [SHPD ID: 2019LI80682]

(2) 4-4-08:011

Yucha, Josephine M. and Hallett H. Hammatt. *Archaeological Monitoring Plan for the Sheraton Maui Resort & Spa Sewer Improvements Project, Hanaka'ō'ō Ahupua'a, Lahaina District, Maui Island, TMKs: (2) 4-4-08:005 and 011 (pors).* Wailuku, HI: Cultural Surveys Hawai'i, Inc., 2018. [SHPD ID: 2019LI80670]

Yucha, Josephine M. and Hallett H. Hammatt. *Archaeological Monitoring Report for the Sheraton Maui Sewer Improvements Project, Hanaka'ō'ō Ahupua'a, Lahaina District, Maui Island, TMKs: (2) 4-4-008:005 and 011 (pors.).* Wailuku, HI: Cultural Surveys Hawai'i, Inc., 2018. [SHPD ID: 2019LI81258]

(2) 4-4-08:013

Rotunno-Hazuka, Lisa J. and Jeffrey Pantaleo. *Archaeological Monitoring Plan for All Improvements Related to the Redevelopment of the Royal Lahaina Resort,*

*Hanaka'ō'ō Ahupua'a; Lahaina District, Island of Maui, TMK:4-4-08:007&
013.* Wailuku, HI: Archaeological Services Hawaii, LLC, 2007. [SHPD ID:
2019LI80677]

(2) 4-4-08:016

Bulgrin, Lon E. and Robert B. Rechtman. *An Archaeological Assessment Survey
of TMK (2) 4-4-08:016 Hanaka'ō'ō Ahupua'a, Lahaina District, Island of Maui.*
Rechtman Consulting, LLC, 2005.

Rechtman, Robert B. *Archaeological Monitoring Plan for the Subdivision and
Development for the Subdivision and Development of TMK: (2) 4-4-08:016.* Rechtman Consulting, LLC, 2006. [SHPD ID: 2019LI80679]

(2) 4-4-08:016

Rogers, Scott. *An Archaeological Monitoring Plan for the Kā'anapali—Hyatt
Force Main Replacements, Kā'anapali Resort Complex, Hanaka'ō'ō, Honokōwai
Ahupua'a, Lahaina District, Island of Maui.* Pukalani, HI: Xamanek Researches,
2007. [SHPD ID: 2019LI80682]

(2) 4-4-08:019

Frey, Jennifer J., Josephine M. Yucha, and Hallett H. Hammatt. *Archaeological Monitoring Report for the Westin Maui Resort & Spa Master Plan Improvements Project, Parking Garage, Lobby, and Porte Cochere Driveway, Hanaka'ō'ō
Ahupua'a, Lahaina District, Island of Maui, TMK (2) 4-4-008:019.* Wailuku, HI:
Cultural Surveys Hawai'i, Inc., 2019. [SHPD ID: 2019LI80683]

Lee-Greig, Tanya L. and Hallett H. Hammatt. *Archaeological Assessment for
the Proposed Westin Maui Resort & Spa Master Plan Improvements, Hanaka'ō'ō
Ahupua'a, Lahaina District, Island of Maui, TMK (2) 4-4-008:019.* Wailuku, HI:
Cultural Surveys Hawai'i, Inc., 2014. [SHPD ID: 2019LI80684]

Pacheco, Robert. *A Cultural Impact Assessment for the Proposed Kā'anapali Beach
Restoration Project, Hanaka'ō'ō Ahupua'a, Lahaina District, Island of Maui,
Hawai'i TMK (2) 4-4-008:001, 002, 003, 004, 005, 019, 022; 4-4-013:001, 002, 006,
007, 008.* Honolulu, HI: International Archaeology, LLC, 2006. [SHPD ID:
2019LI80681]

Pacheco, Robert. *An Archaeological Literature Review for the Proposed Kā'anapali Beach Restoration Project, Hanaka'ō'ō Ahupua'a, Lahaina District, Island of*

Maui, Hawaiʻi TMK (2) 4-4-008:001, 002, 003, 004, 005, 019, 022; 4-4-013:001, 002, 006, 007, 008. Honolulu, HI: International Archaeology, LLC, 2015. [SHPD ID: 2019LI81260]

Yucha, Josephine M., Jennifer Frey, and Hallett H. Hammatt. *Burial Site Component of an Archaeological Data Recovery Plan for SIHP # 50-50-03-8842 at the Westin Maui Resort & Spa Improvements Project, Phase III, Hanakaʻōʻō Ahupuaʻa, Lahaina District, Maui, TMK: (2) 4-4-08:019.* Wailuku, HI: Cultural Surveys Hawaiʻi, Inc., 2021. [SHPD ID: 2021LI00104]

Yucha, Trevor M. and Hallett H. Hammatt. *Archaeological Monitoring Plan for the Westin Maui Resort & Spa Master Plan Improvements, Hanakaʻōʻō Ahupuaʻa, Lahaina District, Island of Maui, TMK (2) 4-4-08:019.* Wailuku, HI: Cultural Surveys Hawaiʻi, Inc., 2018. [SHPD ID: 2019LI80683]

(2) 4-4-08:022

Pacheco, Robert. *A Cultural Impact Assessment for the Proposed Kāʻanapali Beach Restoration Project, Hanakaʻōʻō Ahupuaʻa, Lahaina District, Island of Maui, Hawaiʻi TMK (2) 4-4-008:001, 002, 003, 004, 005, 019, 022; 4-4-013:001, 002, 006, 007, 008.* Honolulu, HI: International Archaeology, LLC, 2006. [SHPD ID: 2019LI80681]

Pacheco, Robert. *An Archaeological Literature Review for the Proposed Kāʻanapali Beach Restoration Project, Hanakaʻōʻō Ahupuaʻa, Lahaina District, Island of Maui, Hawaiʻi TMK (2) 4-4-008:001, 002, 003, 004, 005, 019, 022; 4-4-013:001, 002, 006, 007, 008.* Honolulu, HI: International Archaeology, LLC, 2015. [SHPD ID: 2019LI81260]

(2) 4-4-08:023

Rogers, Scott. *An Archaeological Monitoring Plan for the Kāʻanapali—Hyatt Force Main Replacements, Kāʻanapali Resort Complex, Hanakaʻōʻō, Honokōwai Ahupuaʻa, Lahaina District, Island of Maui.* Pukalani, HI: Xamanek Researches, 2007. [SHPD ID: 2019LI80682]

(2) 4-4-09:036

Lee-Greig, Tanya L. and Hallett H. Hammatt. *Archaeological Monitoring Plan for the Honoapiʻilani Highway Safety Improvements at Kāʻanapali Parkway and Halelo Street Hanakaʻōʻō Ahupuaʻa, Lahaina District, Maui Island [TMK (2)*

4-4-006:999 por; 4-4-009:036 por.). Wailuku, HI: Cultural Surveys Hawaiʻi, Inc., 2014. [SHPD ID: 2019LI81271]

(2) 4-4-13:

Perzinski, David and Michael F. Dega. *Archaeological Monitoring Report for Lahaina No. 3 Force Main Replacement Project Wahikuli and Hanakaʻōʻō Ahupuaʻa, Lahaina District, Island of Maui, Hawaiʻi [TMK (2) 4-4-013].* Honolulu, HI: Scientific Consultant Services, Inc., 2014. [SHPD ID: 2019LI80661]

(2) 4-4-13:001

Cordle, Shayna and Michael F. Dega. *An Archaeological Monitoring Report on Approximately 0.448-Acres for the Maui Marriott Vacation Club, Hanakaʻōʻō Ahupuaʻa, Lahaina District, Island of Maui, Hawaiʻi [TMK (2) 4-4-13:001].* Honolulu, HI: Scientific Consultant Services, Inc., 2007. [SHPD ID: 2019LI80029]

Dega, Michael F. *Archaeological Monitoring Plan for the Maui Marriott Vacation Club, in the Ahupuaʻa of Hanakaʻōʻō, Lahaina District, Island of Maui, Hawaiʻi [TMK: (2) 4-4-13:001].* Honolulu, HI: Scientific Consultant Services, Inc., 2005. [SHPD ID: 2019LI80663]

Pacheco, Robert. *A Cultural Impact Assessment for the Proposed Kāʻanapali Beach Restoration Project, Hanakaʻōʻō Ahupuaʻa, Lahaina District, Island of Maui, Hawaiʻi TMK (2) 4-4-008:001, 002, 003, 004, 005, 019, 022; 4-4-013:001, 002, 006, 007, 008.* Honolulu, HI: International Archaeology, LLC, 2006. [SHPD ID: 2019LI80681]

Pacheco, Robert. *An Archaeological Literature Review for the Proposed Kāʻanapali Beach Restoration Project, Hanakaʻōʻō Ahupuaʻa, Lahaina District, Island of Maui, Hawaiʻi TMK (2) 4-4-008:001, 002, 003, 004, 005, 019, 022; 4-4-013:001, 002, 006, 007, 008.* Honolulu, HI: International Archaeology, LLC, 2015. [SHPD ID: 2019LI81260]

(2) 4-4-13:002

Pacheco, Robert. *A Cultural Impact Assessment for the Proposed Kāʻanapali Beach Restoration Project, Hanakaʻōʻō Ahupuaʻa, Lahaina District, Island of Maui, Hawaiʻi TMK (2) 4-4-008:001, 002, 003, 004, 005, 019, 022; 4-4-013:001, 002, 006, 007, 008.* Honolulu, HI: International Archaeology, LLC, 2006. [SHPD ID: 2019LI80681]

Pacheco, Robert. *An Archaeological Literature Review for the Proposed Kāʻanapali Beach Restoration Project, Hanakaʻōʻō Ahupuaʻa, Lahaina District, Island of*

Maui, Hawai'i TMK (2) 4-4-008:001, 002, 003, 004, 005, 019, 022; 4-4-013:001, 002, 006, 007, 008. Honolulu, HI: International Archaeology, LLC, 2015. [SHPD ID: 2019LI81260]

(2) 4-4-13:003

Chaffee, David B. and Michael F. Dega. *An Archaeological Monitoring Plan for the Maui Countywide Wastewater Pump Station Renovations, Phase II Project at Multiple Locations, Hanaka'ō'ō Ahupua'a and Mākila Ahupua'a, Lahaina District, Maui Island, Hawai'i [TMK: (2) 4-4-013:003, por. and 4-6-028:054].* Honolulu, HI: Scientific Consultant Services, Inc., 2014.

(2) 4-4-13:004

Chaffee, David B. and Michael F. Dega. *An Archaeological Monitoring Plan Covering Three Parcels at the Hyatt Regency Maui Resort Kā'anapali, Hanaka'ō'ō Ahupua'a, Lahaina District, Maui Island, Hawai'i [TMK (2) 4-4-13:005, 008, 004].* Honolulu, HI: Scientific Consultant Services, Inc., 2014.

Paraso, C. Kanani and Michael F. Dega. *An Archaeological Assessment of three parcels at the Hyatt Regency Maui Resort, Kā'anapali, Hanaka'ō'ō Ahupua'a, Lahaina District, Maui Island, Hawai'i [TMK (2) 4-4-013:004, 005, 008];* Honolulu, HI: Scientific Consultant Services, Inc., 2006. [SHPD ID: 2019LI80041]

(2) 4-4-13:005

Chaffee, David B. and Michael F. Dega. *An Archaeological Monitoring Plan Covering Three Parcels at the Hyatt Regency Maui Resort Kā'anapali, Hanaka'ō'ō Ahupua'a, Lahaina District, Maui Island, Hawai'i [TMK (2) 4-4-13:005, 008, 004].* Honolulu, HI: Scientific Consultant Services, Inc., 2014.

Paraso, C. Kanani and Michael F. Dega. *An Archaeological Assessment of three parcels at the Hyatt Regency Maui Resort, Kā'anapali, Hanaka'ō'ō Ahupua'a, Lahaina District, Maui Island, Hawai'i [TMK (2) 4-4-013:004, 005, 008];* Honolulu, HI: Scientific Consultant Services, Inc., 2006. [SHPD ID: 2019LI80041]

(2) 4-4-13:006

Pacheco, Robert. *A Cultural Impact Assessment for the Proposed Kā'anapali Beach Restoration Project, Hanaka'ō'ō Ahupua'a, Lahaina District, Island of Maui,*

Hawaiʻi TMK (2) 4-4-008:001, 002, 003, 004, 005, 019, 022; 4-4-013:001, 002, 006, 007, 008. Honolulu, HI: International Archaeology, LLC, 2006. [SHPD ID: 2019LI80681]

Pacheco, Robert. *An Archaeological Literature Review for the Proposed Kāʻanapali Beach Restoration Project, Hanakaʻōʻō Ahupuaʻa, Lahaina District, Island of Maui, Hawaiʻi TMK (2) 4-4-008:001, 002, 003, 004, 005, 019, 022; 4-4-013:001, 002, 006, 007, 008.* Honolulu, HI: International Archaeology, LLC, 2015. [SHPD ID: 2019LI81260]

(2) 4-4-13:007

Pacheco, Robert. *A Cultural Impact Assessment for the Proposed Kāʻanapali Beach Restoration Project, Hanakaʻōʻō Ahupuaʻa, Lahaina District, Island of Maui, Hawaiʻi TMK (2) 4-4-008:001, 002, 003, 004, 005, 019, 022; 4-4-013:001, 002, 006, 007, 008.* Honolulu, HI: International Archaeology, LLC, 2006. [SHPD ID: 2019LI80681]

Pacheco, Robert. *An Archaeological Literature Review for the Proposed Kāʻanapali Beach Restoration Project, Hanakaʻōʻō Ahupuaʻa, Lahaina District, Island of Maui, Hawaiʻi TMK (2) 4-4-008:001, 002, 003, 004, 005, 019, 022; 4-4-013:001, 002, 006, 007, 008.* Honolulu, HI: International Archaeology, LLC, 2015. [SHPD ID: 2019LI81260]

(2) 4-4-13:008

Chaffee, David B. and Michael F. Dega. *An Archaeological Monitoring Plan Covering Three Parcels at the Hyatt Regency Maui Resort Kāʻanapali, Hanakaʻōʻō Ahupuaʻa, Lahaina District, Maui Island, Hawaiʻi [TMK (2) 4-4-13:005, 008, 004].* Honolulu, HI: Scientific Consultant Services, Inc., 2014.

Pacheco, Robert. *A Cultural Impact Assessment for the Proposed Kāʻanapali Beach Restoration Project, Hanakaʻōʻō Ahupuaʻa, Lahaina District, Island of Maui, Hawaiʻi TMK (2) 4-4-008:001, 002, 003, 004, 005, 019, 022; 4-4-013:001, 002, 006, 007, 008.* Honolulu, HI: International Archaeology, LLC, 2006. [SHPD ID: 2019LI80681]

Pacheco, Robert. *An Archaeological Literature Review for the Proposed Kāʻanapali Beach Restoration Project, Hanakaʻōʻō Ahupuaʻa, Lahaina District, Island of Maui, Hawaiʻi TMK (2) 4-4-008:001, 002, 003, 004, 005, 019, 022; 4-4-013:001, 002, 006, 007, 008.* Honolulu, HI: International Archaeology, LLC, 2015. [SHPD ID: 2019LI81260]

Paraso, C. Kanani and Michael F. Dega. *An Archaeological Assessment of three parcels at the Hyatt Regency Maui Resort, Kāʻanapali, Hanakaʻōʻō Ahupuaʻa, Lahaina District, Maui Island, Hawaiʻi [TMK (2) 4-4-013:004, 005, 008];* Honolulu, HI: Scientific Consultant Services, Inc., 2006. [SHPD ID: 2019LI80041]

(2) 4-4-14:003

Hill, Robert R., Tanya Lee-Greig, and Hallett H. Hammatt. *Archaeological Monitoring Report for Shoreline Improvements at Lot 1, North Kāʻanapali, Honokōwai Ahupuaʻa, Lahaina District, Maui Island TMK: (2) 4-4-014:003 (por.).* Wailuku, HI: Cultural Surveys Hawaiʻi, Inc., 2008. [SHPD ID: 2019LI80657]

Willman, Michael R., Robert R. Hill, Tanya L. Lee-Greig, and Hallett H. Hammatt. *Archaeological Monitoring Report for Sand Replenishment at Lots 1, 2, and 3, North Kāʻanapali, Honokōwai Ahupuaʻa, Lahaina District, Island of Maui [TMK (2) 4-4-014: 03, 04, 05 (por.)].* Wailuku, HI: Cultural Surveys Hawaiʻi, Inc., 2009. [SHPD ID: 2019LI80656]

(2) 4-4-14:004

Hill, Robert R., Joseph Arnold, and Hallett H. Hammatt. *Archaeological Monitoring Report for a Dust Barrier Relocation at North Kāʻanapali, Honokōwai Ahupuaʻa, Lahaina District, Island of Maui. TMK (2) 4-4-014:004 (por.)* Wailuku, HI: Cultural Surveys Hawaiʻi, Inc., 2006. [SHPD ID: 2019LI80658]

Willman, Michael R., Robert R. Hill, Tanya L. Lee-Greig, and Hallett H. Hammatt. *Archaeological Monitoring Report for Sand Replenishment at Lots 1, 2, and 3, North Kāʻanapali, Honokōwai Ahupuaʻa, Lahaina District, Island of Maui [TMK (2) 4-4-014: 03, 04, 05 (por.)].* Wailuku, HI: Cultural Surveys Hawaiʻi, Inc., 2009. [SHPD ID: 2019LI80656]

(2) 4-4-14:005

Hill, Robert R., Tanya L. Lee-Greig, and Hallett H. Hammatt. *Preservation Plan for a Fishing Koʻa, SIHP 50-50-03-6275, North Kāʻanapali, Lot 3, Honokōwai Ahupuaʻa, Maui Island [TMK (2) 4-4-014:005 por.].* Wailuku, HI: Cultural Surveys Hawaiʻi, Inc., 2008. [SHPD ID: 2019LI80654]

Hill, Robert R., Tanya L. Lee-Greig, and Hallett H. Hammatt. *Archaeological Monitoring Report for Dust Barrier Construction at Lot 3, North Kāʻanapali, Honokōwai Ahupuaʻa, Lahaina District, Island of Maui [TMK (2) 4-4-*

014:005 (por.)]. Wailuku, HI: Cultural Surveys Hawai'i, Inc., 2008. [SHPD ID: 2019LI80655]

Willman, Michael R., Robert R. Hill, Tanya L. Lee-Greig, and Hallett H. Hammatt. *Archaeological Monitoring Report for Sand Replenishment at Lots 1, 2, and 3, North Kā'anapali, Honokōwai Ahupua'a, Lahaina District, Island of Maui [TMK (2) 4-4-014: 03, 04, 05 (por.)]*. Wailuku, HI: Cultural Surveys Hawai'i, Inc., 2009. [SHPD ID: 2019LI80656]

(2) 4-4-14:005

Hill, Robert R., Joseph Arnold, and Hallett H. Hammatt. *Archaeological Monitoring Report for Shoreline Improvements at Lot 3, North Kā'anapali, Honokōwai Ahupua'a, Lahaina District, Maui Island [TMK (2) 4-4-014:005 (por.)]*. Wailuku, HI: Cultural Surveys Hawai'i, Inc., 2008. [SHPD ID: 2019LI80653]

(2) 4-4-15:

Yucha, Josephine M. and Hallett H. Hammatt. *Archaeological Monitoring Plan for the Pu'ukoli'i Village Mauka Project, Hanaka'ō'ō Ahupua'a, Lahaina District, Maui Island, TMKs: (2) 4-4-02:002, 048, and 053 por., (2) 4-4-06:070, 086 and 087 por., and (2) 4-4-15:034 through 072. 24:026 (por.)*. Wailuku, HI: Cultural Surveys Hawai'i, Inc., 2023. [SHPD ID: 2023LI00111]

Yucha, Josephine M. et al. *Archaeological Inventory Survey for the Pu'ukoli'i Village Mauka Project, Hanaka'ō'ō Ahupua'a, Lahaina District, Maui Island, TMKs: (2) 4-4-02:002, 048, and 053 por., (2) 4-4-06:070, 086 and 087 por., and (2) 4-4-15:034 through 072*. Wailuku, HI: Cultural Surveys Hawai'i, Inc., 2022. [SHPD ID: 2023LI00110]

(2) 4-5-01:045

Rotunno-Hazuka, Lisa J. and Jeffrey Pantaleo. *Archaeological Monitoring Plan for a Waterline Installation at TMK: (2) 4-5-01:045 Old Lahaina Center, Papalua Street, Pana'ewa Ahupua'a, Lahaina District, Island of Maui*. Wailuku, HI: Archaeological Services Hawaii, LLC, 2002. [SHPD ID: 2019LI80638]

(2) 4-5-02:009

Kurashina, Hiro and Aki Sinoto. *Archaeological Reconnaissance of the Proposed Shopping Center at Lahaina, Maui, Hawai'i, TMK: (2) 4-5-02:009*. Honolulu,

HI: Department of Anthropology, Bernice P. Bishop Museum, 1984. [SHPD ID: 2019LI80648; UH Call Number: DU629.L3 K87 1984]

Rotunno-Hazuka, Lisa J. and Jeffrey Pantaleo. *Archaeological Monitoring Plan for the Installation of a Grease Interceptor at TMK: (2) 4-5-02:009 Kelawea Ahupuaʻa, Lahaina District, Island of Maui.* Wailuku, HI: Archaeological Services Hawaii, LLC, 2007. [SHPD ID: 2019LI80646]

(2) 4-5-02:999

Lee-Greig, Tanya L. *Archaeological Monitoring Plan for the Traffic Signal Improvements at Pāpalaua Street/Waineʻe Street Intersection, Federal Aid Project No. STP-3020 (001) Aki and Uhao Ahupuaʻa (Paunau Modern Ahupuaʻa), Lahaina Moku and Modern Tax District, Mokupuni of Maui [TMK: (2) 4-5-002:999 ROW, 4-5-006:999 ROW, 4-5-006:004, and 4-5-006:015].* Honolulu, HI: Aina Archaeology, 2023. [SHPD ID: 2023LI00149].

(2) 4-5-04:

Dega, Michael F. *Archaeological Monitoring Plan for the Front Street Waterline Replacement Project, Panaʻewa Ahupuaʻa, Lahaina District, Island of Maui, Hawaiʻi [TMK (2) 4-5-04, 05, and 08].* Honolulu, HI: Scientific Consultant Services, Inc., 2002. [SHPD ID: 2019LI80631]

Fredericksen, Erik M. *An Archaeological Monitoring Plan for the Kaahanui Place Electrical Improvements Project, Land of Puunoa, Lahaina District, Maui Island [TMK: (2) 4-5-04 por.].* Pukalani, HI: Xamanek Researches, 2009. [No location available]

(2) 4-5-04:004

Rotunno-Hazuka, Lisa J. and Jeffrey Pantaleo. *Archaeological Monitoring Plan for the Demolition of an Existing Single Family Residence and Construction of a new Single Family Residence at TMK (2) 4-5-04:004, Puʻunoa Ahupuaʻa, Lahaina District, Island of Maui.* Wailuku, HI: Archaeological Services Hawaii, LLC, 2004. [SHPD ID: 2019LI80621]

Rotunno-Hazuka, Lisa J. and Jeffrey Pantaleo. *Final Archaeological Monitoring Report for All Ground Disturbing Activities Associated with the Development of a Residential Structure Located at TMK (2) 4-5-04:004, Puʻunoa Ahupuaʻa, Lahaina District, Island of Maui.* Wailuku, HI: Archaeological Services Hawaii, LLC, 2008. [SHPD ID: 2019LI80622]

(2) 4-5-04:008

Conte, Patty J. *Archaeological Monitoring Plan for On and Off-Site Construction Related to Pending and Future Improvements, Puunoa Ahupuaʻa, Lahaina District, Island of Maui*. Makawao, HI: CRM Solutions Hawaiʻi, Inc., 2008. [SHPD ID: 2019LI80599]

Rosendahl, Paul H. *Archaeological Monitoring Plan, Mala Village Subdivision, Land of Puʻunoa, Lahaina District, Island of Maui [TMK: (2) 4-5-04:008, 009, 059, 060, 061, 062]*. Hilo, HI: Paul H. Rosendahl, Ph.D., Inc., 2002. [SHPD ID: 2019LI80615]

(2) 4-5-04:009

Rosendahl, Paul H. *Archaeological Monitoring Plan, Mala Village Subdivision, Land of Puʻunoa, Lahaina District, Island of Maui [TMK: (2) 4-5-04:008, 009, 059, 060, 061, 062]*. Hilo, HI: Paul H. Rosendahl, Ph.D., Inc., 2002. [SHPD ID: 2019LI80615]

(2) 4-5-04:010

Kehajit, Chonnikarn and Michael F. Dega. *Archaeological Monitoring Plan for 1191 Front Street Replacement of an Existing Water Supply Project, Lahaina, Wahikuli Ahupuaʻa, Lahaina District, Island of Maui, Hawaiʻi*. Honolulu, HI: Scientific Consultant Services, Inc., 2018. [SHPD ID: 2022LI00191]

(2) 4-5-04:037

Rotunno-Hazuka, Lisa J. and Jeffrey Pantaleo. *Archaeological Monitoring Plan for Pool Installation at TMK (2) 4-5-04:037 Lahilahi Street, Kuʻia Ahupuaʻa, Lahaina District, Island of Maui*. Wailuku, HI: Archaeological Services Hawaii, LLC, 2002. [SHPD ID: 2019LI80627]

(2) 4-5-04:048

Rotunno-Hazuka, Lisa J. and Jeffrey Pantaleo. *Archaeological Monitoring Plan for the Demolition of an Existing Single Family Residence & Pool Cover and Construction of a New Single Family Residence at TMK: (2) 4-5-04:048 Puʻunoa Ahupuaʻa, Lahaina District, Island of Maui*. Wailuku, HI: Archaeological Services Hawaii, LLC, 2004. [SHPD ID: 2019LI80625]

Rotunno-Hazuka, Lisa J. and Jeffrey Pantaleo. *Final Archaeological Monitoring Report for All Ground Disturbing Activities Associated with the Development of a Residential Structure Located at TMK (2) 4-05-04:048 Puʻunoa Ahupuaʻa, Lahaina District, Island of Maui.* Wailuku, HI: Archaeological Services Hawaii, LLC, 2008. [SHPD ID: 2019LI80614]

(2) 4-5-04:059

Rosendahl, Paul H. *Archaeological Monitoring Plan, Mala Village Subdivision, Land of Puʻunoa, Lahaina District, Island of Maui [TMK: (2) 4-5-04:008, 009, 059, 060, 061, 062].* Hilo, HI: Paul H. Rosendahl, Ph.D., Inc., 2002. [SHPD ID: 2019LI80615]

(2) 4-5-04:060

Rosendahl, Paul H. *Archaeological Monitoring Plan, Mala Village Subdivision, Land of Puʻunoa, Lahaina District, Island of Maui [TMK: (2) 4-5-04:008, 009, 059, 060, 061, 062].* Hilo, HI: Paul H. Rosendahl, Ph.D., Inc., 2002. [SHPD ID: 2019LI80615]

(2) 4-5-04:061

Rosendahl, Paul H. *Archaeological Monitoring Plan, Mala Village Subdivision, Land of Puʻunoa, Lahaina District, Island of Maui [TMK: (2) 4-5-04:008, 009, 059, 060, 061, 062].* Hilo, HI: Paul H. Rosendahl, Ph.D., Inc., 2002. [SHPD ID: 2019LI80615]

(2) 4-5-04:062

Rosendahl, Paul H. *Archaeological Monitoring Plan, Mala Village Subdivision, Land of Puʻunoa, Lahaina District, Island of Maui [TMK: (2) 4-5-04:008, 009, 059, 060, 061, 062].* Hilo, HI: Paul H. Rosendahl, Ph.D., Inc., 2002. [SHPD ID: 2019LI80615]

(2) 4-5-05:

Dega, Michael F. *Archaeological Monitoring Plan for the Front Street Waterline Replacement Project, Panaʻewa Ahupuaʻa, Lahaina District, Island of Maui, Hawaiʻi [TMK (2) 4-5-04, 05, and 08].* Honolulu, HI: Scientific Consultant Services, Inc., 2002. [SHPD ID: 2019LI80631]

(2) 4-5-06:004

Lee-Greig, Tanya L. *Archaeological Monitoring Plan for the Traffic Signal Improvements at Pāpalaua Street/Waineʻe Street Intersection, Federal Aid Project No. STP-3020 (001) Aki and Uhao Ahupuaʻa (Paunau Modern Ahupuaʻa), Lahaina Moku and Modern Tax District, Mokupuni of Maui [TMK: (2) 4-5-002:999 ROW, 4-5-006:999 ROW, 4-5-006:004, and 4-5-006:015].* Honolulu, HI: Aina Archaeology, 2023. [SHPD ID: 2023LI00149].

(2) 4-5-06:015

Lee-Greig, Tanya L. *Archaeological Monitoring Plan for the Traffic Signal Improvements at Pāpalaua Street/Waineʻe Street Intersection, Federal Aid Project No. STP-3020 (001) Aki and Uhao Ahupuaʻa (Paunau Modern Ahupuaʻa), Lahaina Moku and Modern Tax District, Mokupuni of Maui [TMK: (2) 4-5-002:999 ROW, 4-5-006:999 ROW, 4-5-006:004, and 4-5-006:015].* Honolulu, HI: Aina Archaeology, 2023. [SHPD ID: 2023LI00149].

(2) 4-5-07:004

Guerriero, Diane, Lisa J. Rotunno-Hazuka, and Jeffrey Pantaleo. *Archaeological Assessment Report of a 0.428 Acre Parcel of Land at TMK 4-5-07:004 Kuholilea Ahupuaʻa, Lahaina District, Island of Maui.* Wailuku, HI: Archaeological Services Hawaii, LLC, 2005. [SHPD ID: 2019LI80606]

Rotunno-Hazuka, Lisa J. and Jeffrey Pantaleo. *Archaeological Monitoring Plan for All Ground Disturbing Activities Associated with the Construction of the Waineʻe Self Storage Facility located at TMK: (2) 4-5-07:004 Kuholilea Ahupuaʻa, Lahaina District, Island of Maui.* Wailuku, HI: Archaeological Services Hawaii, LLC, 2006. [SHPD ID: 2019LI80607]

(2) 4-5-07:034

Athens, J. Stephen. *Archaeological Monitoring Plan, Trenching at Taco Bell, Lahaina, Kāʻanapali Ahupuaʻa, Lahaina District, Maui [TMK (2) 4-5-07:034].* Honolulu, HI: International Archaeological Research Institute, Inc., 1999.

Rotunno-Hazuka, Lisa J., Mia Watson, and Jeffrey Pantaleo. *Archaeological Monitoring Plan for the Improvements to a Commercial Restaurant Facility at TMK: (2) 4-5-07:034, Kāʻanapali Ahupuaʻa, Lahaina District, Island of Maui.* Wailuku, HI: Archaeological Services Hawaii, LLC, 2010. [SHPD ID: 2019LI80610]

(2) 4-5-08:

Dega, Michael F. *Archaeological Monitoring Plan for the Front Street Waterline Replacement Project, Pana'ewa Ahupua'a, Lahaina District, Island of Maui, Hawai'i [TMK (2) 4-5-04, 05, and 08].* Honolulu, HI: Scientific Consultant Services, Inc., 2002. [SHPD ID: 2019LI80631]

(2) 4-5-09:007

Rechtman, Robert B. *Archaeological Monitoring Plan Associated with the Demolition of the Pioneer Mill, TMK (2) 4-5-09:007, Pana'ewa Ahupua'a, Lahaina District, Island of Maui.* Rechtman Consulting, LLC, 2005. [SHPD ID: 2019LI80603]

(2) 4-5-10:

Lee-Greig, Tanya, Robert Hill, and Hallett H. Hammatt. *An Archaeological Inventory Survey Report for the Lahaina Bypass Modified Alignment from Kahoma Stream to the Keawe Street Extension, Kelawea, Paeohi, and Wahikuli Ahupua'a, Lahaina District, Maui Island TMK (2) 4-5-021, 010, 015, and 031: Multiple Parcels.* Wailuku, HI: Cultural Surveys Hawai'i, Inc., 2008. [SHPD ID: 2019LI81368]

Lee-Greig, Tanya L. and Hallett H. Hammatt. *Archaeological Inventory Survey Plan for Honoapi'ilani Highway Realignment Phase IA, Future Keawe Street Extension to Lahainaluna Road: Ikena Avenue Alignment with Modified Extension Kelawea, Paeohi, and Wahikuli Ahupua'a, Lahaina District, Maui Island TMK (2) 4-5-021, 010, 015, and 031: Multiple Parcels.* Wailuku, HI: Cultural Surveys Hawai'i, Inc., 2008. [SHPD ID: 2019LI81341]

Lee-Greig, Tanya L., Robert Hill, and Hallett H. Hammatt. *An Archaeological Survey Report for the Realignment of a Section of the Honoapi'ilani Highway, Phase IA, Kelawea, Paeohi, and Wahikuli Ahupua'a, Lahaina District, Maui Island TMK (2) 4-5-021, 010, 015, and 031: Multiple Parcels.* Wailuku, HI: Cultural Surveys Hawai'i, Inc., 2008. [SHPD ID: 2019LI81361]

Madeus, Jonas K., Tanya Lee-Greig, and Hallett H. Hammatt. *An Archaeological Monitoring Report for the Lahaina Bypass Modified Alignment from the Lahainaluna Road Intersection to the Keawe Street Extension Kelawea, Paeohi, and Wahikuli Ahupua'a, Lahaina District, Maui Island TMK (2) 4-5-021, 010, 015, and 031: Multiple Parcels.* Wailuku, HI: Cultural Surveys Hawai'i, Inc., 2010. [SHPD ID: 2019LI81338]

(2) 4-5-10:005

Pickett, Jenny L. and Michael F. Dega. *An Archaeological Assessment for 16.8 Acres in Lahaina, Mākila Ahupuaʻa, Lahaina District, Maui Island, Hawaiʻi [TMK (2) 4-5-10:005 & 006 por.].* Honolulu, HI: Scientific Consultant Services, Inc., 2005. [SHPD ID: 2019LI80600]

(2) 4-5-10:006

Pickett, Jenny L. and Michael F. Dega. *An Archaeological Assessment for 16.8 Acres in Lahaina, Mākila Ahupuaʻa, Lahaina District, Maui Island, Hawaiʻi [TMK (2) 4-5-10:005 & 006 por.].* Honolulu, HI: Scientific Consultant Services, Inc., 2005. [SHPD ID: 2019LI80600]

(2) 4-5-10:007

Monahan, Christopher M. *An Archaeological Assessment Report on 17.746 Acres of Land (Lahaina Business Park, Phase II) on an Undeveloped Lot in Lahaina, Moaliʻi Ahupuaʻa, Lahaina District, Maui Island, Hawaiʻi [TMK: (2) 4-5-10:007].* Honolulu, HI: Scientific Consultant Services, Inc., 2003. [SHPD ID: 2019LI80604]

(2) 4-5-10:052

Fredericksen, Erik M. *An Archaeological Monitoring Plan for the Emerald Plaza II Project, Land of Moaliʻi, Lahaina District, Island of Maui, TMK: (2) 4-5-10:052.* Pukalani, HI: Xamanek Researches, 2019. [No location available]

(2) 4-5-10:054

Dega, Michael F. *An Archaeological Monitoring Plan for the Ulupono Center Project, Lahaina, Panaʻewa Ahupuaʻa, Lahaina District, Hawaiʻi, TMK (2) 4-5-10:054.* Honolulu, HI: Scientific Consultant Services Inc., 2017. [SHPD ID: 2019LI80597]

(2) 4-5-11: 004

Fredericksen, Erik M. *Archaeological Inventory Survey for the Proposed Lahaina Cannery Fuel Station Project, Land of Moaliʻi, Lahaina District, Island of Maui*

[TMK: (2) 4-5-11: 004 Por.]. Pukalani, HI: Xamanek Researches, 2023. [SHPD ID: 2023LI00137]

(2) 4-5-11:004

Fredericksen, Erik M. and J. J. Frey. *Burial Site Component of an Archaeological Data Recovery Plan for Inadvertently Discovered Human Skeletal Remains, Site 50-50-03-08973, Located in Previously Imported Sand Fill During Utilities Installation for the Lahaina Cannery Fuel Station Project, Ahupuaʻa of Moaliʻi, Lahaina District, Island of Maui [TMK: (2) 4-5-11:004 por.]*. Pukalani, HI: Xamanek Researches, 2023. [SHPD ID: 2023LI00074]

(2) 4-5-12:008

Conte, Patty J. *Archaeological Monitoring Plan for On and Off-Site Construction Related to the Proposed Amano Demo/Reconstruction, TMK (2) 4-5-12:008 Wahikuli Ahupuaʻa, Lahaina District, Island of Maui*. Makawao, HI: CRM Solutions Hawaiʻi, Inc., 2005. [SHPD ID: 2019LI81347]

(2) 4-5-12:009

Conte, Patty J. *Archaeological Monitoring Report for Construction, Lahaina District, Wahikuli Ahupuaʻa, Island of Maui*. Makawao, HI: CRM Solutions Hawaiʻi, Inc., 2005. [SHPD ID: 2019LI81345]

(2) 4-5-12:010

Conte, Patty J. *Archaeological Monitoring Plan for On and Off-Site Construction Related to the Proposed Kent Property Demo/Reconstruction, TMK (2) 4-5-12:010 Moaliʻi Ahupuaʻa, Lahaina District, Island of Maui*. Makawao, HI: CRM Solutions Hawaiʻi, Inc., 2007. [SHPD ID: 2019LI81346]

(2) 4-5-13:003

Rotunno-Hazuka, Lisa J. and Jeffrey Pantaleo. *Archaeological Monitoring Plan for All Improvements at the McFarland Residence TMK: (2) 4-5-13:003, Moaliʻi Ahupuaʻa Lahaina District, Island of Maui*. Wailuku, HI: Archaeological Services Hawaii, LLC, 2006. [SHPD ID: 2019LI81352]

(2) 4-5-13:004

Donham, Theresa K. *Archaeological Monitoring Plan for Construction of a Pool & Spa at the Hurlock Property, Moaliʻi, Lahaina District, Maui, TMK: (2) 4-5-13:004.* Kīhei, HI: Akahele Archaeology, 2003. [SHPD ID: 2019LI81351]

(2) 4-5-13:006

Conte, Patty J. *Archaeological Monitoring Plan for On and Off-Site Construction Within and Related to TMK (2) 4-5-13:006 Lahaina District, Panaʻewa Ahupuaʻa, Island of Maui.* Makawao, HI: CRM Solutions Hawaiʻi, Inc., 2006. [SHPD ID: 2019LI81349]

Conte, Patty J. *Archaeological Monitoring Report Within and Related to a Parcel on Front Street, Panaʻewa Ahupuaʻa, Lahaina District, Maui Island, TMK (2) 4-5-13:006.* Makawao, HI: CRM Solutions Hawaiʻi, Inc., 2007. [No location available]

(2) 4-5-13:016

Haun, Alan E. and Dave Henry. *Final Archaeological Monitoring Plan, TMK (2) 4-5-13:016, Wahikuli Ahupuaʻa, Lahaina District, Island of Maui.* Kailua-Kona, HI: Haun and Associates, 2014. [SHPD ID: 2019LI81350]

(2) 4-5-14:013

Conte, Patty J. *Archaeological Monitoring Plan for Construction Within TMK (2) 4-5-14:013 Por. 8A, Lahaina District, Wahikuli Ahupuaʻa, Island of Maui.* Makawao, HI: CRM Solutions Hawaiʻi, Inc., 2005. [SHPD ID: 2019LI81348]

(2) 4-5-14:032

Fredericksen, Erik M. *An Archaeological Monitoring Plan for a Portion of Land in Alaeloa Ahupuaʻa, Lahaina District, Maui TMK: (2) 4-5-014:032.* Pukalani, HI: Xamanek Researches, 2005. [SHPD ID: 2019LI81355]

(2) 4-5-14:073

Conte, Patty J. *Archaeological Monitoring plan for On and Off-Site Construction Within and Related to TMK (2) 4-5-14:073 Lahaina District, Wahikuli Ahupuaʻa,*

Island of Maui. Makawao, HI: CRM Solutions Hawai'i, Inc., 2006. [SHPD ID: 2019LI81354]

Conte, Patty J. *Archaeological Monitoring Report for On and Off-Site Construction Within and Related to TMK (2) 4-5-14:073 Lahaina District, Wahikuli Ahupua'a, Island of Maui.* Makawao, HI: CRM Solutions Hawai'i, Inc., 2007. [SHPD ID: 2019LI81356]

(2) 4-5-15:

Lee-Greig, Tanya, Robert Hill, and Hallett H. Hammatt. *An Archaeological Inventory Survey Report for the Lahaina Bypass Modified Alignment from Kahoma Stream to the Keawe Street Extension, Kelawea, Paeohi, and Wahikuli Ahupua'a, Lahaina District, Maui Island TMK (2) 4-5-021, 010, 015, and 031: Multiple Parcels.* Wailuku, HI: Cultural Surveys Hawai'i, Inc., 2008. [SHPD ID: 2019LI81368]

Lee-Greig, Tanya L. and Hallett H. Hammatt. *Archaeological Inventory Survey Plan for Honoapi'ilani Highway Realignment Phase IA, Future Keawe Street Extension to Lahainaluna Road: Ikena Avenue Alignment with Modified Extension Kelawea, Paeohi, and Wahikuli Ahupua'a, Lahaina District, Maui Island TMK (2) 4-5-021, 010, 015, and 031: Multiple Parcels.* Wailuku, HI: Cultural Surveys Hawai'i, Inc., 2008. [SHPD ID: 2019LI81341]

Lee-Greig, Tanya L., Robert Hill, and Hallett H. Hammatt. *An Archaeological Survey Report for the Realignment of a Section of the Honoapi'ilani Highway, Phase IA, Kelawea, Paeohi, and Wahikuli Ahupua'a, Lahaina District, Maui Island TMK (2) 4-5-021, 010, 015, and 031: Multiple Parcels.* Wailuku, HI: Cultural Surveys Hawai'i, Inc., 2008. [SHPD ID: 2019LI81361]

Madeus, Jonas K., Tanya Lee-Greig, and Hallett H. Hammatt. *An Archaeological Monitoring Report for the Lahaina Bypass Modified Alignment from the Lahainaluna Road Intersection to the Keawe Street Extension Kelawea, Paeohi, and Wahikuli Ahupua'a, Lahaina District, Maui Island TMK (2) 4-5-021, 010, 015, and 031: Multiple Parcels.* Wailuku, HI: Cultural Surveys Hawai'i, Inc., 2010. [SHPD ID: 2019LI81338]

(2) 4-5-15:008

Watanabe, Farley. *Archaeological Site Investigation Kahoma Stream Flood Control Project TMK (2) 4-5-15:008.* Honolulu, HI: Army Corps of Engineers, 1987. [SHPD ID: 2019LI81342]

(2) 4-5-15:010

Lee-Greig, Tanya L. and Hallett H. Hammatt. *Addendum to An Archaeological Treatment Plan for no Adverse Effect the Honoapiʻilani Highway Realignment—Lahaina Bypass Section, Phase 1A, Keawe Street Extension to Lahainaluna Road, Panaʻewa Ahupuaʻa, Lahaina District, Maui Island, TMK (2) 4-5-031: 999 por., (2) 4-5-015:010 por., and (2) 4-5-021:022 por.* Wailuku, HI: Cultural Surveys Hawaiʻi, Inc., 2007. [SHPD ID: 2019LI81365, 2019LI81340]

(2) 4-5-21:

Lee-Greig, Tanya, Robert Hill, and Hallett H. Hammatt. *An Archaeological Inventory Survey Report for the Lahaina Bypass Modified Alignment from Kahoma Stream to the Keawe Street Extension, Kelawea, Paeohi, and Wahikuli Ahupuaʻa, Lahaina District, Maui Island TMK (2) 4-5-021, 010, 015, and 031: Multiple Parcels.* Wailuku, HI: Cultural Surveys Hawaiʻi, Inc., 2008. [SHPD ID: 2019LI81368]

Lee-Greig, Tanya L. and Hallett H. Hammatt. *Archaeological Inventory Survey Plan for Honoapiʻilani Highway Realignment Phase 1A, Future Keawe Street Extension to Lahainaluna Road: Ikena Avenue Alignment with Modified Extension Kelawea, Paeohi, and Wahikuli Ahupuaʻa, Lahaina District, Maui Island TMK (2) 4-5-021, 010, 015, and 031: Multiple Parcels.* Wailuku, HI: Cultural Surveys Hawaiʻi, Inc., 2008. [SHPD ID: 2019LI81341]

Lee-Greig, Tanya L., Robert Hill, and Hallett H. Hammatt. *An Archaeological Survey Report for the Realignment of a Section of the Honoapiʻilani Highway, Phase IA, Kelawea, Paeohi, and Wahikuli Ahupuaʻa, Lahaina District, Maui Island TMK (2) 4-5-021, 010, 015, and 031: Multiple Parcels.* Wailuku, HI: Cultural Surveys Hawaiʻi, Inc., 2008. [SHPD ID: 2019LI81361]

Madeus, Jonas K., Tanya Lee-Greig, and Hallett H. Hammatt. *An Archaeological Monitoring Report for the Lahaina Bypass Modified Alignment from the Lahainaluna Road Intersection to the Keawe Street Extension Kelawea, Paeohi, and Wahikuli Ahupuaʻa, Lahaina District, Maui Island TMK (2) 4-5-021, 010, 015, and 031: Multiple Parcels.* Wailuku, HI: Cultural Surveys Hawaiʻi, Inc., 2010. [SHPD ID: 2019LI81338]

(2) 4-5-21:010

Madeus, Jonas K. et al. *Archaeological Inventory Survey for the Villages of Leialiʻi, Phase 1-B Subdivision and Related Improvements Project, Wahikuli Ahupuaʻa, Lahaina District, Maui Island, TMKs: (2) 4-5-021:010 por., 014 por., 020, and*

021 por.; (2) 4-5-36:109, 110, and 112; and Honoapiʻilani Highway Right-of-Way. Wailuku, HI: Cultural Surveys Hawaiʻi, Inc., 2022. [SHPD ID: 2022LI00589]

Yucha, Josephine M. and Hallett H. Hammatt. *Archaeological Monitoring Plan for the Villages of Leialiʻi, Village 1-B Subdivision and Related Improvements Project, Wahikuli Ahupuaʻa, Lahaina District, Maui Island, TMKs: (2) 4-5-021:010 por., 014 por., 015 por., 020, and 021 por.; (2) 4-5-36:109, 110, and 112; and Honoapiʻilani Highway Right-of-Way.* Wailuku, HI: Cultural Surveys Hawaiʻi, Inc., 2022. [SHPD ID: 2023LI00106]

(2) 4-5-21:014

Yucha, Josephine M. and Hallett H. Hammatt. *Archaeological Monitoring Plan for the Villages of Leialiʻi, Village 1-B Subdivision and Related Improvements Project, Wahikuli Ahupuaʻa, Lahaina District, Maui Island, TMKs: (2) 4-5-021:010 por., 014 por., 015 por., 020, and 021 por.; (2) 4-5-36:109, 110, and 112; and Honoapiʻilani Highway Right-of-Way.* Wailuku, HI: Cultural Surveys Hawaiʻi, Inc., 2022. [SHPD ID: 2023LI00106]

(2) 4-5-21:015

Fredericksen, Demaris L. and Erik M. Fredericksen. *An Archaeological Inventory Survey of the Proposed Sandwich Isles Communications, Inc. Fiber Optics Landing Location near the Lahaina Post Office, Wahikuli Ahupuaʻa, Lahaina District, Island of Maui (TMK: 4-5-21:015).* Pukalani, HI: Xamanek Researches, 2003. [SHPD ID: 2019LI81336]

Yucha, Josephine M. and Hallett H. Hammatt. *Archaeological Monitoring Plan for the Villages of Leialiʻi, Village 1-B Subdivision and Related Improvements Project, Wahikuli Ahupuaʻa, Lahaina District, Maui Island, TMKs: (2) 4-5-021:010 por., 014 por., 015 por., 020, and 021 por.; (2) 4-5-36:109, 110, and 112; and Honoapiʻilani Highway Right-of-Way.* Wailuku, HI: Cultural Surveys Hawaiʻi, Inc., 2022. [SHPD ID: 2023LI00106]

(2) 4-5-21:020

Madeus, Jonas K. et al. *Archaeological Inventory Survey for the Villages of Leialiʻi, Phase 1-B Subdivision and Related Improvements Project, Wahikuli Ahupuaʻa, Lahaina District, Maui Island, TMKs: (2) 4-5-021:010 por., 014 por., 020, and 021 por.; (2) 4-5-36:109, 110, and 112; and Honoapiʻilani Highway Right-of-Way.* Wailuku, HI: Cultural Surveys Hawaiʻi, Inc., 2022. [SHPD ID: 2022LI00589]

Yucha, Josephine M. and Hallett H. Hammatt. *Archaeological Monitoring Plan for the Villages of Leiali'i, Village 1-B Subdivision and Related Improvements Project, Wahikuli Ahupua'a, Lahaina District, Maui Island, TMKs: (2) 4-5-021:010 por., 014 por., 015 por., 020, and 021 por.; (2) 4-5-36:109, 110, and 112; and Honoapi'ilani Highway Right-of-Way.* Wailuku, HI: Cultural Surveys Hawai'i, Inc., 2022. [SHPD ID: 2023LI00106]

(2) 4-5-21:021

Madeus, Jonas K. et al. *Archaeological Inventory Survey for the Villages of Leiali'i, Phase 1-B Subdivision and Related Improvements Project, Wahikuli Ahupua'a, Lahaina District, Maui Island, TMKs: (2) 4-5-021:010 por., 014 por., 020, and 021 por.; (2) 4-5-36:109, 110, and 112; and Honoapi'ilani Highway Right-of-Way.* Wailuku, HI: Cultural Surveys Hawai'i, Inc., 2022. [SHPD ID: 2022LI00589]

Yucha, Josephine M. and Hallett H. Hammatt. *Archaeological Monitoring Plan for the Villages of Leiali'i, Village 1-B Subdivision and Related Improvements Project, Wahikuli Ahupua'a, Lahaina District, Maui Island, TMKs: (2) 4-5-021:010 por., 014 por., 015 por., 020, and 021 por.; (2) 4-5-36:109, 110, and 112; and Honoapi'ilani Highway Right-of-Way.* Wailuku, HI: Cultural Surveys Hawai'i, Inc., 2022. [SHPD ID: 2023LI00106]

(2) 4-5-21:022

Lee-Greig, Tanya L. and Hallett H. Hammatt. *Addendum to An Archaeological Treatment Plan for no Adverse Effect the Honoapi'ilani Highway Realignment— Lahaina Bypass Section, Phase 1A, Keawe Street Extension to Lahainaluna Road, Pana'ewa Ahupua'a, Lahaina District, Maui Island, TMK (2) 4-5-031: 999 por., (2) 4-5-015:010 por., and (2) 4-5-021:022 por.* Wailuku, HI: Cultural Surveys Hawai'i, Inc., 2007. [SHPD ID: 2019LI81365, 2019LI81340]

(2) 4-5-31:

Lee-Greig, Tanya, Robert Hill, and Hallett H. Hammatt. *An Archaeological Inventory Survey Report for the Lahaina Bypass Modified Alignment from Kahoma Stream to the Keawe Street Extension, Kelawea, Paeohi, and Wahikuli Ahupua'a, Lahaina District, Maui Island TMK (2) 4-5-021, 010, 015, and 031: Multiple Parcels.* Wailuku, HI: Cultural Surveys Hawai'i, Inc., 2008. [SHPD ID: 2019LI81368]

Lee-Greig, Tanya L. and Hallett H. Hammatt. *Archaeological Inventory Survey Plan for Honoapi'ilani Highway Realignment Phase 1A, Future Keawe Street*

Extension to Lahainaluna Road: Ikena Avenue Alignment with Modified Extension Kelawea, Paeohi, and Wahikuli Ahupuaʻa, Lahaina District, Maui Island TMK (2) 4-5-021, 010, 015, and 031: Multiple Parcels. Wailuku, HI: Cultural Surveys Hawaiʻi, Inc., 2008. [SHPD ID: 2019LI81341]

Lee-Greig, Tanya L., Robert Hill, and Hallett H. Hammatt. *An Archaeological Survey Report for the Realignment of a Section of the Honoapiʻilani Highway, Phase IA, Kelawea, Paeohi, and Wahikuli Ahupuaʻa, Lahaina District, Maui Island TMK (2) 4-5-021, 010, 015, and 031: Multiple Parcels.* Wailuku, HI: Cultural Surveys Hawaiʻi, Inc., 2008. [SHPD ID: 2019LI81361]

Madeus, Jonas K., Tanya Lee-Greig, and Hallett H. Hammatt. *An Archaeological Monitoring Report for the Lahaina Bypass Modified Alignment from the Lahainaluna Road Intersection to the Keawe Street Extension Kelawea, Paeohi, and Wahikuli Ahupuaʻa, Lahaina District, Maui Island TMK (2) 4-5-021, 010, 015, and 031: Multiple Parcels.* Wailuku, HI: Cultural Surveys Hawaiʻi, Inc., 2010. [SHPD ID: 2019LI81338]

(2) 4-5-31:999

Lee-Greig, Tanya L. and Hallett H. Hammatt. *Addendum to An Archaeological Treatment Plan for no Adverse Effect the Honoapiʻilani Highway Realignment—Lahaina Bypass Section, Phase IA, Keawe Street Exrtension to Lahainaluna Road, Panaʻewa Ahupuaʻa, Lahaina District, Maui Island, TMK (2) 4-5-031: 999 por., (2) 4-5-015:010 por., and (2) 4-5-021:022 por.* Wailuku, HI: Cultural Surveys Hawaiʻi, Inc., 2007. [SHPD ID: 2019LI81365, 2019LI81340]

(2) 4-5-36:109

Madeus, Jonas K. et al. *Archaeological Inventory Survey for the Villages of Leialiʻi, Phase 1-B Subdivision and Related Improvements Project, Wahikuli Ahupuaʻa, Lahaina District, Maui Island, TMKs: (2) 4-5-021:010 por., 014 por., 020, and 021 por.; (2) 4-5-36:109, 110, and 112; and Honoapiʻilani Highway Right-of-Way.* Wailuku, HI: Cultural Surveys Hawaiʻi, Inc., 2022. [SHPD ID: 2022LI00589]

Yucha, Josephine M. and Hallett H. Hammatt. *Archaeological Monitoring Plan for the Villages of Leialiʻi, Village 1-B Subdivision and Related Improvements Project, Wahikuli Ahupuaʻa, Lahaina District, Maui Island, TMKs: (2) 4-5-021:010 por., 014 por., 015 por., 020, and 021 por.; (2) 4-5-36:109, 110, and 112; and Honoapiʻilani Highway Right-of-Way.* Wailuku, HI: Cultural Surveys Hawaiʻi, Inc., 2022. [SHPD ID: 2023LI00106]

(2) 4-5-36:110

Madeus, Jonas K. et al. *Archaeological Inventory Survey for the Villages of Leiali'i, Phase 1-B Subdivision and Related Improvements Project, Wahikuli Ahupua'a, Lahaina District, Maui Island, TMKs: (2) 4-5-021:010 por., 014 por., 020, and 021 por.; (2) 4-5-36:109, 110, and 112; and Honoapi'ilani Highway Right-of-Way.* Wailuku, HI: Cultural Surveys Hawai'i, Inc., 2022. [SHPD ID: 2022LI00589]

Yucha, Josephine M. and Hallett H. Hammatt. *Archaeological Monitoring Plan for the Villages of Leiali'i, Village 1-B Subdivision and Related Improvements Project, Wahikuli Ahupua'a, Lahaina District, Maui Island, TMKs: (2) 4-5-021:010 por., 014 por., 015 por., 020, and 021 por.; (2) 4-5-36:109, 110, and 112; and Honoapi'ilani Highway Right-of-Way.* Wailuku, HI: Cultural Surveys Hawai'i, Inc., 2022. [SHPD ID: 2023LI00106]

(2) 4-5-36:112

Madeus, Jonas K. et al. *Archaeological Inventory Survey for the Villages of Leiali'i, Phase 1-B Subdivision and Related Improvements Project, Wahikuli Ahupua'a, Lahaina District, Maui Island, TMKs: (2) 4-5-021:010 por., 014 por., 020, and 021 por.; (2) 4-5-36:109, 110, and 112; and Honoapi'ilani Highway Right-of-Way.* Wailuku, HI: Cultural Surveys Hawai'i, Inc., 2022. [SHPD ID: 2022LI00589]

Yucha, Josephine M. and Hallett H. Hammatt. *Archaeological Monitoring Plan for the Villages of Leiali'i, Village 1-B Subdivision and Related Improvements Project, Wahikuli Ahupua'a, Lahaina District, Maui Island, TMKs: (2) 4-5-021:010 por., 014 por., 015 por., 020, and 021 por.; (2) 4-5-36:109, 110, and 112; and Honoapi'ilani Highway Right-of-Way.* Wailuku, HI: Cultural Surveys Hawai'i, Inc., 2022. [SHPD ID: 2023LI00106]

(2) 4-6-01-001

Fredericksen, Erik M. *Archaeological Monitoring Plan for the Wharf Street Accessibility Improvements at Lahaina Harbor—Electrical Underground Work Project, Puako Ahupua'a, Lahaina District, Maui [TMK: (2) 4-6-01 and 4-6-01: Portion of Parcel 1].* Pukalani, HI: Xamanek Researches, 2002. [SHPD ID: 2019LI81402]

(2) 4-6-01:001

Ah Sam, Jessica A., Solomon H. Kailihiwa III, and Paul L. Cleghorn. *Archaeological Inventory Study and Cultural Impact Assessment for the Comfort Station*

Replacement During the Lahaina Pier Improvement Project, Lahaina, Maui [TMK (2) 4-6-01:001]. Kailua, HI: Pacific Legacy, Inc., 2004.

Kirkendall, Melissa, Kimberly M. Mooney, Elizabeth L. Kahahane, and Paul L. Cleghorn. *Archaeological Monitoring Plan for the Lahaina Pier Improvement Project, Waineʻe Ahupuaʻa, Lahaina District, Island of Maui [TMK: (2) 4-6-01:001].* Kailua, HI: Pacific Legacy, Inc., 2010. [No location available]

Lash, Erik and Michael F. Dega. *An Archaeological Monitoring Plan for the Proposed Lahaina Harbor Complete Streets Project on Approximately 3.11 Acres (1.26 Hectares) in Lahaina, Paunau Ahupuaʻa, Lahaina District, Island of Maui, Hawaiʻi [TMK (2) 4-6-001:001, 004, 007, 009, 010, 012, and Adjacent Roadways].* Honolulu, HI: Scientific Consultant Services, Inc., 2017. [SHPD ID: 2019LI81388]

(2) 4-6-01:004

Dagher, Cathleen A. and Michael F. Dega. *A Preservation Plan for the "Brick Palace" (A Component of State Site 50-50-03-3001) Within the Proposed Lahaina Harbor Complete Streets Project Area, Lahaina, Paunau Ahupuaʻa, Lahaina District, Island of Maui, Hawaiʻi [TMK (2) 4-6-01:004].* Honolulu, HI: Scientific Consultant Services, Inc., 2017. [SHPD ID: 2019LI81386]

Lash, Erik and Michael F. Dega. *An Archaeological Monitoring Plan for the Proposed Lahaina Harbor Complete Streets Project on Approximately 3.11 Acres (1.26 Hectares) in Lahaina, Paunau Ahupuaʻa, Lahaina District, Island of Maui, Hawaiʻi [TMK (2) 4-6-001:001, 004, 007, 009, 010, 012, and Adjacent Roadways].* Honolulu, HI: Scientific Consultant Services, Inc., 2017. [SHPD ID: 2019LI81388]

(2) 4-6-01:007

Donham, Theresa K. *Archaeological Monitoring Plan for American Disabilities Act Improvements at the Lahaina Public Library, Paunau, Lahaina District, Maui, TMK: (2) 4-6-01:007 & 010.* Kīhei, HI: Akahele Archaeology, 2004. [SHPD ID: 2019LI81381]

Donham, Theresa K. *Archaeological Monitoring Report for American Disabilities Act Improvements at the Lahaina Public Library, Paunau, Lahaina District, Maui, TMK: (2) 4-6-01:007 & 010.* Kīhei, HI: Akahele Archaeology, 2005. [SHPD ID: 2019LI81403]

Lash, Erik and Michael F. Dega. *An Archaeological Monitoring Plan for the Proposed Lahaina Harbor Complete Streets Project on Approximately 3.11 Acres (1.26 Hectares) in Lahaina, Paunau Ahupua'a, Lahaina District, Island of Maui, Hawai'i [TMK (2) 4-6-001:001, 004, 007, 009, 010, 012, and Adjacent Roadways].* Honolulu, HI: Scientific Consultant Services, Inc., 2017. [SHPD ID: 2019LI81388]

(2) 4-6-01:009

Lash, Erik and Michael F. Dega. *An Archaeological Monitoring Plan for the Proposed Lahaina Harbor Complete Streets Project on Approximately 3.11 Acres (1.26 Hectares) in Lahaina, Paunau Ahupua'a, Lahaina District, Island of Maui, Hawai'i [TMK (2) 4-6-001:001, 004, 007, 009, 010, 012, and Adjacent Roadways].* Honolulu, HI: Scientific Consultant Services, Inc., 2017. [SHPD ID: 2019LI81388]

(2) 4-6-01:010

Donham, Theresa K. *Archaeological Monitoring Plan for American Disabilities Act Improvements at the Lahaina Public Library, Paunau, Lahaina District, Maui, TMK: (2) 4-6-01:007 & 010.* Kīhei, HI: Akahele Archaeology, 2004. [SHPD ID: 2019LI81381]

Donham, Theresa K. *Archaeological Monitoring Report for American Disabilities Act Improvements at the Lahaina Public Library, Paunau, Lahaina District, Maui, TMK: (2) 4-6-01:007 & 010.* Kīhei, HI: Akahele Archaeology, 2005. [SHPD ID: 2019LI81403]

Lash, Erik and Michael F. Dega. *An Archaeological Monitoring Plan for the Proposed Lahaina Harbor Complete Streets Project on Approximately 3.11 Acres (1.26 Hectares) in Lahaina, Paunau Ahupua'a, Lahaina District, Island of Maui, Hawai'i [TMK (2) 4-6-001:001, 004, 007, 009, 010, 012, and Adjacent Roadways].* Honolulu, HI: Scientific Consultant Services, Inc., 2017. [SHPD ID: 2019LI81388]

(2) 4-6-01:012

Lash, Erik and Michael F. Dega. *An Archaeological Monitoring Plan for the Proposed Lahaina Harbor Complete Streets Project on Approximately 3.11 Acres (1.26 Hectares) in Lahaina, Paunau Ahupua'a, Lahaina District, Island of Maui, Hawai'i [TMK (2) 4-6-001:001, 004, 007, 009, 010, 012, and Adjacent Roadways].* Honolulu, HI: Scientific Consultant Services, Inc., 2017. [SHPD ID: 2019LI81388]

(2) 4-6-02:003

Dega, Michael F. and David B. Chaffee. *An Archaeological Monitoring Plan for a Private Residence Demolition in Lahaina, Moaliʻi Ahupuaʻa, Lahaina District, Maui Island, Hawaiʻi [TMK (2) 4-6-02:003].* Honolulu, HI: Scientific Consultant Services, Inc., 2006. [SHPD ID: 2019LI81394]

Hunt, Jennifer, Lauren Morawski, and Michael F. Dega. *An Archaeological Monitoring Report for the Installation of New Sewer Lines and Force Mains and the Replacement of Waterlines for the County of Maui at Shaw, Front, and Dickenson Streets and Honoapiʻilani Highway in Lahaina AND The Installation of Underground Electrical Lines, Panels, and Meters at Armory Park/Kamehameha Iki Park on Front Street in Lahaina for Maui Parks and Recreation Division, Various Ahupuaʻa, Lahaina District, Island of Maui, Hawaiʻi [TMK (2) 4-6002:003, 005, 006, 007, 010, 012, 015, 016, and 027].* Honolulu, HI: Scientific Consultant Services, Inc., 2011. [SHPD ID: 2019LI81393]

(2) 4-6-02:005

Hunt, Jennifer, Lauren Morawski, and Michael F. Dega. *An Archaeological Monitoring Report for the Installation of New Sewer Lines and Force Mains and the Replacement of Waterlines for the County of Maui at Shaw, Front, and Dickenson Streets and Honoapiʻilani Highway in Lahaina AND The Installation of Underground Electrical Lines, Panels, and Meters at Armory Park/Kamehameha Iki Park on Front Street in Lahaina for Maui Parks and Recreation Division, Various Ahupuaʻa, Lahaina District, Island of Maui, Hawaiʻi [TMK (2) 4-6002:003, 005, 006, 007, 010, 012, 015, 016, and 027].* Honolulu, HI: Scientific Consultant Services, Inc., 2011. [SHPD ID: 2019LI81393]

(2) 4-6-02:006

Hunt, Jennifer, Lauren Morawski, and Michael F. Dega. *An Archaeological Monitoring Report for the Installation of New Sewer Lines and Force Mains and the Replacement of Waterlines for the County of Maui at Shaw, Front, and Dickenson Streets and Honoapiʻilani Highway in Lahaina AND The Installation of Underground Electrical Lines, Panels, and Meters at Armory Park/Kamehameha Iki Park on Front Street in Lahaina for Maui Parks and Recreation Division, Various Ahupuaʻa, Lahaina District, Island of Maui, Hawaiʻi [TMK (2) 4-6002:003, 005, 006, 007, 010, 012, 015, 016, and 027].* Honolulu, HI: Scientific Consultant Services, Inc., 2011. [SHPD ID: 2019LI81393]

(2) 4-6-02:007

Folio, Katie M. and Hallett H. Hammatt. *An Archaeological Monitoring Plan for Proposed Improvements at the Feast of Lele, Waiokama Ahupuaʻa, Lahaina District, Island of Maui TMK: (2) 4-6-002:007 (por.).* Wailuku, HI: Cultural Surveys Hawaiʻi, Inc., 2014. [SHPD ID: 2019LI81372]

Hunt, Jennifer, Lauren Morawski, and Michael F. Dega. *An Archaeological Monitoring Report for the Installation of New Sewer Lines and Force Mains and the Replacement of Waterlines for the County of Maui at Shaw, Front, and Dickenson Streets and Honoapiʻilani Highway in Lahaina AND The Installation of Underground Electrical Lines, Panels, and Meters at Armory Park/Kamehameha Iki Park on Front Street in Lahaina for Maui Parks and Recreation Division, Various Ahupuaʻa, Lahaina District, Island of Maui, Hawaiʻi [TMK (2) 4-6002:003, 005, 006, 007, 010, 012, 015, 016, and 027].* Honolulu, HI: Scientific Consultant Services, Inc., 2011. [SHPD ID: 2019LI81393]

Madeus, Jonas K., Josephine M. Yucha, and Hallett H. Hammatt. *Archaeological Monitoring Report for Improvements at Feast of Lele, Waiokama Ahupuaʻa, Lahaina District, Maui Island, TMK (2) 4-6-002:007 (por.).* Wailuku, HI: Cultural Surveys Hawaiʻi, Inc., 2018. [No location available]

(2) 4-6-02:010

Hunt, Jennifer, Lauren Morawski, and Michael F. Dega. *An Archaeological Monitoring Report for the Installation of New Sewer Lines and Force Mains and the Replacement of Waterlines for the County of Maui at Shaw, Front, and Dickenson Streets and Honoapiʻilani Highway in Lahaina AND The Installation of Underground Electrical Lines, Panels, and Meters at Armory Park/Kamehameha Iki Park on Front Street in Lahaina for Maui Parks and Recreation Division, Various Ahupuaʻa, Lahaina District, Island of Maui, Hawaiʻi [TMK (2) 4-6002:003, 005, 006, 007, 010, 012, 015, 016, and 027].* Honolulu, HI: Scientific Consultant Services, Inc., 2011. [SHPD ID: 2019LI81393]

(2) 4-6-02:012

Hunt, Jennifer, Lauren Morawski, and Michael F. Dega. *An Archaeological Monitoring Report for the Installation of New Sewer Lines and Force Mains and the Replacement of Waterlines for the County of Maui at Shaw, Front, and Dickenson Streets and Honoapiʻilani Highway in Lahaina AND The Installation of Underground Electrical Lines, Panels, and Meters at Armory Park/Kamehameha Iki*

Park on Front Street in Lahaina for Maui Parks and Recreation Division, Various Ahupuaʻa, Lahaina District, Island of Maui, Hawaiʻi [TMK (2) 4-6002:003, 005, 006, 007, 010, 012, 015, 016, and 027]. Honolulu, HI: Scientific Consultant Services, Inc., 2011. [SHPD ID: 2019LI81393]

(2) 4-6-02:013

Fredericksen, Erik M. *Archaeological Monitoring Plan for the King Kamehameha III Elementary School Building B, Building D, and PT 201 Restroom Renovation Project, Puako Ahupuaʻa, Lahaina District, Maui [TMK: (2) 4-6-02:013 & 014].* Pukalani, HI: Xamanek Researches, 2001. [SHPD ID: 2019LI81392]

Fredericksen, Erik M. and Jennifer J. Frey. *An Archaeological Monitoring Report for the King Kamehameha III Elementary School Parking Lot Improvements Project, Puako Ahupuaʻa, Lahaina District TMK (2) 4-6-002:13.* Pukalani, HI: Xamanek Researches, 2008. [SHPD ID: 2019LI81374]

Frey, Jennifer J. and Erik M. Fredericksen. *An Archaeological Monitoring Report for the King Kamehameha III Elementary School Campus Exterior Awning and Gutter Project, DOE Job No. P01090-06, Puako Ahupuaʻa, Lahaina District [TMK (2) 4-6-02:013, and (2) 4-6-02:014].* Pukalani, HI: Xamanek Researches, 2009. [SHPD ID: 2019LI81561]

(2) 4-6-02:014

Fredericksen, Erik M. *Archaeological Monitoring Plan for the King Kamehameha III Elementary School Building B, Building D, and PT 201 Restroom Renovation Project, Puako Ahupuaʻa, Lahaina District, Maui [TMK: (2) 4-6-02:013 & 014].* Pukalani, HI: Xamanek Researches, 2001. [SHPD ID: 2019LI81392]

Frey, Jennifer J. and Erik M. Fredericksen. *An Archaeological Monitoring Report for the King Kamehameha III Elementary School Campus Exterior Awning and Gutter Project, DOE Job No. P01090-06, Puako Ahupuaʻa, Lahaina District [TMK (2) 4-6-02:013, and (2) 4-6-02:014].* Pukalani, HI: Xamanek Researches, 2009. [SHPD ID: 2019LI81561]

(2) 4-6-02:015

Hunt, Jennifer, Lauren Morawski, and Michael F. Dega. *An Archaeological Monitoring Report for the Installation of New Sewer Lines and Force Mains and the Replacement of Waterlines for the County of Maui at Shaw, Front, and Dickenson Streets and Honoapiʻilani Highway in Lahaina AND The Installation of*

Underground Electrical Lines, Panels, and Meters at Armory Park/Kamehameha Iki Park on Front Street in Lahaina for Maui Parks and Recreation Division, Various Ahupua'a, Lahaina District, Island of Maui, Hawai'i [TMK (2) 4-6002:003, 005, 006, 007, 010, 012, 015, 016, and 027]. Honolulu, HI: Scientific Consultant Services, Inc., 2011. [SHPD ID: 2019LI81393]

(2) 4-6-02:016

Hunt, Jennifer, Lauren Morawski, and Michael F. Dega. *An Archaeological Monitoring Report for the Installation of New Sewer Lines and Force Mains and the Replacement of Waterlines for the County of Maui at Shaw, Front, and Dickenson Streets and Honoapi'ilani Highway in Lahaina AND The Installation of Underground Electrical Lines, Panels, and Meters at Armory Park/Kamehameha Iki Park on Front Street in Lahaina for Maui Parks and Recreation Division, Various Ahupua'a, Lahaina District, Island of Maui, Hawai'i [TMK (2) 4-6002:003, 005, 006, 007, 010, 012, 015, 016, and 027].* Honolulu, HI: Scientific Consultant Services, Inc., 2011. [SHPD ID: 2019LI81393]

(2) 4-6-02:027

Hunt, Jennifer, Lauren Morawski, and Michael F. Dega. *An Archaeological Monitoring Report for the Installation of New Sewer Lines and Force Mains and the Replacement of Waterlines for the County of Maui at Shaw, Front, and Dickenson Streets and Honoapi'ilani Highway in Lahaina AND The Installation of Underground Electrical Lines, Panels, and Meters at Armory Park/Kamehameha Iki Park on Front Street in Lahaina for Maui Parks and Recreation Division, Various Ahupua'a, Lahaina District, Island of Maui, Hawai'i [TMK (2) 4-6002:003, 005, 006, 007, 010, 012, 015, 016, and 027].* Honolulu, HI: Scientific Consultant Services, Inc., 2011. [SHPD ID: 2019LI81393]

(2) 4-6-05:014

Donham, Theresa K. *Archaeological Monitoring Plan for the Remodeling of a Dwelling at the Phleger Property, Halaka'a, Lahaina District, Maui TMK: (2) 4-6-05:014.* Kīhei, HI: Akahele Archaeology, 2004. [SHPD ID: 2019LI81558]

(2) 4-6-06:005

Rotunno-Hazuka, Lisa J. and Jeffrey Pantaleo. *Archaeological Monitoring Plan for All Improvements Related to the Proposed Construction of an Ohana and Garage at the Stiebinger Residence, Kauʻaula Ahupuaʻa, Lahaina District, Island of Maui TMK (2) 4-6-06:005.* Wailuku, HI: Archaeological Services Hawaii, LLC, 2005. [SHPD ID: 2019LI81405]

(2) 4-6-06:031

Fredericksen, Erik M. *Archaeological Monitoring Plan for Sewer Lateral Installation Project at 460 Alio Street, Land of Nalehu, Mākila Ahupuaʻa, Lahaina District, Maui [TMK (2) 4-6-06:031].* Pukalani, HI: Xamanek Researches, 2003. [SHPD ID: 2019LI81270]

(2) 4-6-06:056

Chong Jin, Garcia Alondra, and Michael F. Dega. *Archaeological Monitoring Plan for 7,804 sq. ft. Parcel at 432 Ilikahi Street, Paunau Ahupuaʻa, Lahaina District, Island of Maui, Hawaiʻi [TMK: (2) 4-6-06:056 por.].* Honolulu, HI: Scientific Consultant Services, Inc., 2021. [SHPD ID: 2021LI00125]

(2) 4-6-07:002

Klieger, Paul Christiaan and Lonnie Somer. *Emergency Mitigation at Maluʻulu o Lele Park, Lahaina, Maui, Hawaiʻi, Site of Mokuʻula, Residence of King Kamehameha III (Site 50-50-03-2967; TMK (2) 4-6-7 Parcel 002: BPBM 50-MA-D5-12).* Honolulu, HI: Department of Anthropology, Bernice P. Bishop Museum, 1989. [SHPD ID: 2019LI81550]

(2) 4-6-07:003

Fredericksen, Erik M. *Archaeological Monitoring Plan for a Parcel of Land in the ʻIli of Pakala, Puako Ahupuaʻa, Lahaina District, Island of Maui [TMK: (2) 4-6-07:003].* Pukalani, HI: Xamanek Researches, 1998. [SHPD ID: 2019LI81549]

(2) 4-6-07:007

Fredericksen, Demaris L. and Erik M. Fredericksen. *Archaeological Inventory Survey (Phase 1) in the ʻIli of Pakala, Puako Ahupuaʻa, Lahaina District, Maui Island [TMK: (2) 4-6-07:007].* Pukalani, HI: Xamanek Researches, 1999. [SHPD ID: 2019LI81547]

(2) 4-6-07:010

Haun, Alan E. and Dave Henry. *Archaeological Inventory Survey, TMK 4-6-7:010 'Ili of Pakala, Land of Puako District, Island of Maui.* Kailua-Kona, HI: Haun and Associates, 2001. [SHPD ID: 2019LI81555]

(2) 4-6-07:013

Major, Maurice and P. Christiaan Klieger. *Historical Background and Archaeological Testing at Pikanele's Kuleana in Lahaina, Maui: An Inventory Survey Report of LCA 310.3 (Royal Patent 1729.2, TMK (2) 4-6-07:013).* Honolulu, HI: Department of Anthropology, Bernice P. Bishop Museum, 1995. [SHPD ID: 2019LI81546; UH Call Number: DU629.L3 M36 1996]

Major, Maurice, P. Christiaan Klieger, and Susan A. Lebo. *Historical Background and Archaeological Testing at Pikanele's Kuleana in Lahaina, Maui: An Inventory Survey Report of LCA 310.3 (Royal Patent 1729.2, TMK (2) 4-6-07:013.* Honolulu, HI: Department of Anthropology, Bernice P. Bishop Museum, 1996. [SHPD ID: 2019LI81546]

(2) 4-6-07:030

Rotunno-Hazuka, Lisa J. and Jeffrey Pantaleo. *Archaeological Monitoring Plan For the Construction of an Accessory Dwelling at the Meston Residence at TMK (2) 4-6-07:030 Paunau Ahupua'a, Lahaina District, Island of Maui.* Wailuku, HI: Archaeological Services Hawaii, LLC, 2004. [SHPD ID: 2019LI81551]

(2) 4-6-08:012

Kennedy, Joseph. *Archaeological Report Concerning Subsurface Testing at TMK: (2) 4-6-08:012, Lahaina Maui.* Hale'iwa, HI: Archaeological Consultants of Hawaii, 1989. [SHPD ID: 2019LI81544]

(2) 4-6-08:022

Fredericksen, Erik M. *An Archaeological Monitoring Report for a Parcel of Land in Puako Ahupua'a, Lahaina District, Maui [TMK: (2) 4-6-008:022].* Pukalani, HI: Xamanek Researches, 2005. [SHPD ID: 2019LI81565]

(2) 4-6-08:048

Fredericksen, Erik M. *An Archaeological Monitoring Plan for an Inventory Survey Concurrent with Construction Activities on a Parcel of Land in Puako Ahupua'a, Lahaina District, Lahaina, Maui [TMK: (2) 4-6-08:48 and 53]*. Pukalani, HI: Xamanek Researches, 2003. [SHPD ID: 2019LI81569]

Fredericksen, Erik M. and Demaris Fredericksen. *Archaeological Inventory Survey Report for Portion of Land in Puako Ahupua'a, Lahaina District, Lahaina, Maui, [TMK: (2) 4-6-08:53 and 48]*. Pukalani, HI: Xamanek Researches, 2002. [SHPD ID: 2019LI81571]

(2) 4-6-08:053

Fredericksen, Erik M. *An Archaeological Monitoring Plan for an Inventory Survey Concurrent with Construction Activities on a Parcel of Land in Puako Ahupua'a, Lahaina District, Lahaina, Maui [TMK: (2) 4-6-08:48 and 53]*. Pukalani, HI: Xamanek Researches, 2003. [SHPD ID: 2019LI81569]

Fredericksen, Erik M. *Archaeological Assessment Report for a Portion of Land in Puako Ahupua'a, Lahaina District, Lahaina, Maui [TMK: (2) 4-6-08:053]*. Pukalani, HI: Xamanek Researches, 2004. [SHPD ID: 2019LI81545]

Fredericksen, Erik M. and Demaris Fredericksen. *Archaeological Inventory Survey Report for Portion of Land in Puako Ahupua'a, Lahaina District, Lahaina, Maui, [TMK: (2) 4-6-08:53 and 48]*. Pukalani, HI: Xamanek Researches, 2002. [SHPD ID: 2019LI81571]

(2) 4-6-09:

Fredericksen, Erik M. *Archaeological Monitoring Plan for the Proposed Plantation Inn Improvements Project (GPC 2002/43), Pana'ewa Ahupua'a, Lahaina District, Maui [TMK: (2) 4-6-009: 036, 037 and 044]*. Pukalani, HI: Xamanek Researches, 2002. [SHPD ID: 2019LI81579]

(2) 4-6-09:007

Cordle, Shayna, Cathleen A. Dagher, and Michael F. Dega. *An Archaeological Monitoring Report for Work on County Roadway (WTP T2008/0014) For the Lahaina Store Water Meter Replacement Project, Lahaina, Ku'ia Ahupua'a,*

Lahaina District, Island of Maui, Hawai'i [TMK: (2) 4-6-09:007]. Honolulu, HI: Scientific Consultant Services, Inc., 2009. [SHPD ID: 2019LI81563]

Dega, Michael F. and Mary Sullivan. *Archaeological Monitoring Plan for Construction at the Lahaina Store, Lahaina, Ku'ia Ahupua'a, Lahaina District, Island of Maui, Hawai'i [TMK: (2) 4-6-09:007 & 062].* Honolulu, HI: Scientific Consultant Services, Inc., 2002. [SHPD ID: 2019LI81578]

(2) 4-6-09:012

Fredericksen, Walter M. and Demaris L. Fredericksen. *An Archaeological Inventory Survey on a Parcel of Land Located in the Ahupua'a of Paunau, Lahaina District, Island of Maui TMK (2) 4-6-09:012.* Pukalani, HI: Xamanek Researches, 1993. [SHPD ID: 2022LI00237]

(2) 4-6-09:024

Chaffee, David B. and Michael F. Dega. *An Archaeological Monitoring Plan for Approximately 12,365 Foot sq. Property Located on Waine'e Street in Lahaina, Ahupua'a of Pana'ewa, Lahaina District, Maui Island, Hawai'i [TMK (2) 4-6-09:024].* Honolulu, HI: Scientific Consultant Services, Inc., 2005. [SHPD ID: 2019LI81580]

(2) 4-6-09:036

Fredericksen, Erik M. *Archaeological Monitoring Report for the Proposed Plantation Inn Improvements Project (GPC2002/43) Pana'ewa Ahupua'a, Lahaina District, Maui, TMK: (2) 4-6-09:036, 037, and 044.* Pukalani, HI: Xamanek Researches, 2003. [SHPD ID: 2019LI81574]

Medrano, Stephanie and Michael F. Dega. *An Archaeological Assessment for a 1.02-Acre Project Area in Lahaina, Ku'ia Ahupua'a, Lahaina District, Island of Maui, Hawai'i [TMK: (2) 4-6-009:036, 038, & 044].* Honolulu, HI: Scientific Consultant Services, Inc., 2013. [SHPD ID: 2019LI81581]

(2) 4-6-09:037

Fredericksen, Erik M. *Archaeological Monitoring Report for the Proposed Plantation Inn Improvements Project (GPC2002/43) Pana'ewa Ahupua'a, Lahaina*

District, Maui, TMK: (2) 4-6-09:036, 037, and 044. Pukalani, HI: Xamanek Researches, 2003. [SHPD ID: 2019LI81574]

(2) 4-6-09:038

Medrano, Stephanie and Michael F. Dega. *An Archaeological Assessment for a 1.02-Acre Project Area in Lahaina, Kuʻia Ahupuaʻa, Lahaina District, Island of Maui, Hawaiʻi [TMK: (2) 4-6-009:036, 038, & 044].* Honolulu, HI: Scientific Consultant Services, Inc., 2013. [SHPD ID: 2019LI81581]

(2) 4-6-09:044

Fredericksen, Erik M. *Archaeological Monitoring Report for the Proposed Plantation Inn Improvements Project (GPC2002/43) Panaʻewa Ahupuaʻa, Lahaina District, Maui, TMK: (2) 4-6-09:036, 037, and 044.* Pukalani, HI: Xamanek Researches, 2003. [SHPD ID: 2019LI81574]

Medrano, Stephanie and Michael F. Dega. *An Archaeological Assessment for a 1.02-Acre Project Area in Lahaina, Kuʻia Ahupuaʻa, Lahaina District, Island of Maui, Hawaiʻi [TMK: (2) 4-6-009:036, 038, & 044].* Honolulu, HI: Scientific Consultant Services, Inc., 2013. [SHPD ID: 2019LI81581]

(2) 4-6-09:062

Dega, Michael F. and Mary Sullivan. *Archaeological Monitoring Plan for Construction at the Lahaina Store, Lahaina, Kuʻia Ahupuaʻa, Lahaina District, Island of Maui, Hawaiʻi [TMK: (2) 4-6-09:007 & 062].* Honolulu, HI: Scientific Consultant Services, Inc., 2002. [SHPD ID: 2019LI81578]

(2) 4-6-09:244

Cordle, Shayna, Jennifer Hunt, and Michael F. Dega. *An Archaeological Monitoring Report for a 12,365 Ft Sq. Property, Waineʻe St., Lahaina, Panaʻewa Ahupuaʻa, Lahaina District, Island of Maui, Hawaiʻi [TMK (2) 4-6-09:244].* Honolulu, HI: Scientific Consultant Services, Inc., 2007. [SHPD ID: 2019LI81566]

(2) 4-6-09:999

Dagher, Cathleen A. and Michael F. Dega. *Archaeological Monitoring Plan for 790 Front Street Waterline (WTP T2017-00280) Lahaina, Paunau Ahupuaʻa,*

Lahaina District, Island of Maui, Hawai'i [TMK: (2) 4-6-09:999]. Honolulu, HI: Scientific Consultant Services, Inc., 2020. [SHPD ID: 2022LI00633]

(2) 4-6-10:001

Johnston-O'Neill, Emily and Michael F. Dega. *Archaeological Monitoring Plan for the Exterior Staircase Addition to the Convent Building at the Sacred Hearts Roman Catholic Property at 712 Waine'e Street, Paunau Ahupua'a, Lahaina District, Island of Maui TMK: (2) 4-6-10:001 (por.)*. Honolulu, HI: Scientific Consultant Services, Inc., 2007. [SHPD ID: 2019LI81541]

(2) 4-6-10:006

Collins, Sara L., Dennis Gosser, and Stephan D. Clark. *Archaeological Assessment of a Single Developed Parcel [TMK (2) 4-6-10:006] Lahaina, Island of Maui*. Honolulu, HI: Pacific Consulting Services, Inc., 2006. [No location available]

(2) 4-6-11:008

Havel, BreAnna and Michael F. Dega. *Archaeological Monitoring Plan for the Maui Islander Project, Lahaina, Paunau Ahupua'a District, Maui Island, Hawai'i [TMK: 4-6-011:008]*. Honolulu, HI: Scientific Consultant Services, Inc., 2005. [SHPD ID: 2019LI81582]

Shefcheck, Donna M. and Michael F. Dega. *An Archaeological Monitoring Report for the Maui Islander Project, Lahaina, Paunau Ahupua'a, Lahaina District, Maui Island, Hawai'i [TMK: (2) 4-6-011:008]*. Honolulu, HI: Scientific Consultant Services, Inc., 2008. [SHPD ID: 2019LI81576]

(2) 4-6-12:033

Andricci, Nicole and Michael F. Dega. *An Archaeological Monitoring Plan for a Residential Parcel 33 at 572 Waine'e Street, Waine'e Ahupua'a, Lahaina District, Maui Island, Hawai'i [TMK (2) 4-6-12:033]*. Honolulu, HI: Scientific Consultant Services, Inc., 2016.

(2) 4-6-13:016

Fredericksen, Erik M. and Demaris L. Fredericksen. *An Archaeological Inventory Survey of the Lahaina Watershed Flood Control Project Area, Lands of Polanui,*

Paha, Pueuehunui, Lahaina District, Maui Island (TMK: 4-6-13:016, 18, 26; TMK 4-7-01, 02. Pukalani, HI: Xamanek Researches, 2003. [SHPD ID: 2019LI81442]

(2) 4-6-13:018

Fredericksen, Erik M. and Demaris L. Fredericksen. *An Archaeological Inventory Survey of the Lahaina Watershed Flood Control Project Area, Lands of Polanui, Paha, Pueuehunui, Lahaina District, Maui Island (TMK: 4-6-13:016, 18, 26; TMK 4-7-01, 02.* Pukalani, HI: Xamanek Researches, 2003. [SHPD ID: 2019LI81442]

(2) 4-6-13:022

Chong Jin and Michael F. Dega. *Archaeological Assessment for the Launiu-poko Water System Line Extension to Waineʻe Project, Pūehuehu Nui and Pāhoa Ahupuaʻa, Lahaina District, Island of Maui, Hawaiʻi [TMK: (2) 4-6-013: portion of 022; 4-7-002: portion of 004; 4-7-003: portion of 031].* Honolulu, HI: Scientific Consultant Services, Inc., 2022. [SHPD ID: 2022LI00556]

(2) 4-6-13:026

Fredericksen, Erik M. and Demaris L. Fredericksen. *An Archaeological Inventory Survey of the Lahaina Watershed Flood Control Project Area, Lands of Polanui, Paha, Pueuehunui, Lahaina District, Maui Island (TMK: 4-6-13:016, 18, 26; TMK 4-7-01, 02.* Pukalani, HI: Xamanek Researches, 2003. [SHPD ID: 2019LI81442]

(2) 4-6-14:001

McCurdy, Todd D. and Hallett H. Hammatt. *Addendum Report for Archaeo-logical Inventory Survey Documentation of Inadvertent Finds Identified during the Honoapiʻilani Highway Realignment (Lahaina Bypass) Phase 1B-1, Paunau Ahupuaʻa to Polanui Ahupuaʻa, Lahaina District, Maui Island TMK (2) 4-6-014:001, 002: (2) 4-6-018:002, 003; (2) 4-8-001:002 and (2) 4-8-003:001.* Wailuku, HI: Cultural Surveys Hawaiʻi, Inc., 2010. [SHPD ID: 2019LI81537]

McCurdy, Todd D. and Hallett H. Hammatt. *An Archaeological Monitoring Plan for the Honoapiʻilani Highway Realignment (Lahaina Bypass), Phase 1B-1, Paunau Ahupuaʻa to Polanui Ahupuaʻa, Lahaina District, Maui Island TMK: (2) 4-6-014:001-002, 4-6-018:002-003, 4-7-001:002 and 4-7-003:001.* Wailuku, HI: Cultural Surveys Hawaiʻi, Inc., 2010. [SHPD ID: 2019LI81539]

McCurdy, Todd D. and Hallett H. Hammatt. *Archaeological Inventory Survey Documentation of Inadvertent Finds Identified during the Honoapiʻilani Highway Realignment (Lahaina Bypass) Phase 1B-1, Paunau Ahupuaʻa to Polanui Ahupuaʻa, Lahaina District, Maui Island TMK: (2) 4-6-014:001, 002; (2) 4-6-018:002, 003; (2) 4-8-001:002 and (2) 4-7-003:001.* Wailuku, HI: Cultural Surveys Hawaiʻi, Inc., 2009. [SHPD ID: 2019LI81536]

McCurdy, Todd D. and Hallett H. Hammatt. *Archaeological Literature Review and Field Inspection for Honoapiʻilani Highway Realignment (Lahaina Bypass), Phase 1B-1, Paunau Ahupuaʻa to Polanui Ahupuaʻa, Lahaina District, Maui Island TMK (2) 4-6-014:001-002, 4-6-018:002-003, 4-8-001:002 and 4-7-003:001.* Wailuku, HI: Cultural Surveys Hawaiʻi, Inc., 2008. [SHPD ID: 2019LI81538]

(2) 4-6-14:002

McCurdy, Todd D. and Hallett H. Hammatt. *Addendum Report for Archaeological Inventory Survey Documentation of Inadvertent Finds Identified during the Honoapiʻilani Highway Realignment (Lahaina Bypass) Phase 1B-1, Paunau Ahupuaʻa to Polanui Ahupuaʻa, Lahaina District, Maui Island TMK (2) 4-6-014:001, 002: (2) 4-6-018:002, 003; (2) 4-8-001:002 and (2) 4-8-003:001.* Wailuku, HI: Cultural Surveys Hawaiʻi, Inc., 2010. [SHPD ID: 2019LI81537]

McCurdy, Todd D. and Hallett H. Hammatt. *An Archaeological Monitoring Plan for the Honoapiʻilani Highway Realignment (Lahaina Bypass), Phase 1B-1, Paunau Ahupuaʻa to Polanui Ahupuaʻa, Lahaina District, Maui Island TMK: (2) 4-6-014:001-002, 4-6-018:002-003, 4-7-001:002 and 4-7-003:001.* Wailuku, HI: Cultural Surveys Hawaiʻi, Inc., 2010. [SHPD ID: 2019LI81539]

McCurdy, Todd D. and Hallett H. Hammatt. *Archaeological Inventory Survey Documentation of Inadvertent Finds Identified during the Honoapiʻilani Highway Realignment (Lahaina Bypass) Phase 1B-1, Paunau Ahupuaʻa to Polanui Ahupuaʻa, Lahaina District, Maui Island TMK: (2) 4-6-014:001, 002; (2) 4-6-018:002, 003; (2) 4-8-001:002 and (2) 4-7-003:001.* Wailuku, HI: Cultural Surveys Hawaiʻi, Inc., 2009. [SHPD ID: 2019LI81536]

McCurdy, Todd D. and Hallett H. Hammatt. *Archaeological Literature Review and Field Inspection for Honoapiʻilani Highway Realignment (Lahaina Bypass), Phase 1B-1, Paunau Ahupuaʻa to Polanui Ahupuaʻa, Lahaina District, Maui Island TMK (2) 4-6-014:001-002, 4-6-018:002-003, 4-8-001:002 and 4-7-003:001.* Wailuku, HI: Cultural Surveys Hawaiʻi, Inc., 2008. [SHPD ID: 2019LI81538]

(2) 4-6-15:001

Fredericksen, Erik M. *An Archaeological Monitoring Plan for the West Side Resource Center in Lahaina, Waineʻe Ahupuaʻa, Lahaina District, Maui Island [TMK: 4-6-15: por. of 1 and 4-6-18: por. of 2).* Pukalani, HI: Xamanek Researches, 2002. [SHPD ID: 2019LI81534]

Fredericksen, Erik M. *An Archaeological Monitoring Report for the West Side Resource Center in Lahaina, Waineʻe Ahupuaʻa, Lahaina District, Maui Island [TMK: (2) 4-6-15: por. of 1 and TMK: (2) 4-6-18: por. of 2].* Pukalani, HI: Xamanek Researches, 2004. [SHPD ID: 2019LI81535]

(2) 4-6-18:

Willman, Michael R., Tanya Lee-Greig, and Hallett H. Hammatt. *Addendum to Archaeological Monitoring Plan for the Puʻunēnē School and Lahainaluna High School Hawaiʻi Inter-Island DOE Cesspool Project, Island of Maui TMK (2) 4-6-18 and (2) 3-8-06.* Wailuku, HI: Cultural Surveys Hawaiʻi, Inc., 2008. [SHPD ID: 2019LI81524]

(2) 4-6-18:

Lee-Greig, Tanya L. and Hallett H. Hammatt. *Archaeological Monitoring Plan for the Puʻunēnē School and Lahainaluna High School Hawaiʻi Inter-Island DOE Cesspool Project, Island of Maui TMK (2) 4-6-018 and (2) 3-8-006.* Wailuku, HI: Cultural Surveys Hawaiʻi, Inc., 2007. [SHPD ID: 2019LI81526]

(2) 4-6-18:002

Fredericksen, Erik M. *An Archaeological Monitoring Plan for the West Side Resource Center in Lahaina, Waineʻe Ahupuaʻa, Lahaina District, Maui Island [TMK: 4-6-15: por. of 1 and 4-6-18: por. of 2).* Pukalani, HI: Xamanek Researches, 2002. [SHPD ID: 2019LI81534]

Fredericksen, Erik M. *An Archaeological Monitoring Report for the West Side Resource Center in Lahaina, Waineʻe Ahupuaʻa, Lahaina District, Maui Island [TMK: (2) 4-6-15: por. of 1 and TMK: (2) 4-6-18: por. of 2].* Pukalani, HI: Xamanek Researches, 2004. [SHPD ID: 2019LI81535]

McCurdy, Todd D. and Hallett H. Hammatt. *Addendum Report for Archaeological Inventory Survey Documentation of Inadvertent Finds Identified during the Honoapiʻilani Highway Realignment (Lahaina Bypass) Phase 1B-1, Paunau*

Ahupuaʻa to Polanui Ahupuaʻa, Lahaina District, Maui Island TMK (2) 4-6-014:001, 002: (2) 4-6-018:002, 003; (2) 4-8-001:002 and (2) 4-8-003:001. Wailuku, HI: Cultural Surveys Hawaiʻi, Inc., 2010. [SHPD ID: 2019LI81537]

McCurdy, Todd D. and Hallett H. Hammatt. *An Archaeological Monitoring Plan for the Honoapiʻilani Highway Realignment (Lahaina Bypass), Phase 1B-1, Paunau Ahupuaʻa to Polanui Ahupuaʻa, Lahaina District, Maui Island TMK: (2) 4-6-014:001-002, 4-6-018:002-003, 4-7-001:002 and 4-7-003:001.* Wailuku, HI: Cultural Surveys Hawaiʻi, Inc., 2010. [SHPD ID: 2019LI81539]

McCurdy, Todd D. and Hallett H. Hammatt. *Archaeological Inventory Survey Documentation of Inadvertent Finds Identified during the Honoapiʻilani Highway Realignment (Lahaina Bypass) Phase 1B-1, Paunau Ahupuaʻa to Polanui Ahupuaʻa, Lahaina District, Maui Island TMK: (2) 4-6-014:001, 002; (2) 4-6-018:002, 003; (2) 4-8-001:002 and (2) 4-7-003:001.* Wailuku, HI: Cultural Surveys Hawaiʻi, Inc., 2009. [SHPD ID: 2019LI81536]

McCurdy, Todd D. and Hallett H. Hammatt. *Archaeological Literature Review and Field Inspection for Honoapiʻilani Highway Realignment (Lahaina Bypass), Phase 1B-1, Paunau Ahupuaʻa to Polanui Ahupuaʻa, Lahaina District, Maui Island TMK (2) 4-6-014:001-002, 4-6-018:002-003, 4-8-001:002 and 4-7-003:001.* Wailuku, HI: Cultural Surveys Hawaiʻi, Inc., 2008. [SHPD ID: 2019LI81538]

(2) 4-6-18:003

Andricci, Nicole and Michael F. Dega. *Archaeological Assessment of a 15.7 Acre Section of Undeveloped Land and a Proposed Road Extension, Kuʻia Ahupuaʻa, Lahaina District, Island of Maui, Hawaiʻi [TMK (2) 4-6-018:003 por.].* Honolulu, HI: Scientific Consultant Services, Inc., 2015.

McCurdy, Todd D. and Hallett H. Hammatt. *Addendum Report for Archaeological Inventory Survey Documentation of Inadvertent Finds Identified during the Honoapiʻilani Highway Realignment (Lahaina Bypass) Phase 1B-1, Paunau Ahupuaʻa to Polanui Ahupuaʻa, Lahaina District, Maui Island TMK (2) 4-6-014:001, 002: (2) 4-6-018:002, 003; (2) 4-8-001:002 and (2) 4-8-003:001.* Wailuku, HI: Cultural Surveys Hawaiʻi, Inc., 2010. [SHPD ID: 2019LI81537]

McCurdy, Todd D. and Hallett H. Hammatt. *An Archaeological Monitoring Plan for the Honoapiʻilani Highway Realignment (Lahaina Bypass), Phase 1B-1, Paunau Ahupuaʻa to Polanui Ahupuaʻa, Lahaina District, Maui Island TMK: (2) 4-6-014:001-002, 4-6-018:002-003, 4-7-001:002 and 4-7-003:001.* Wailuku, HI: Cultural Surveys Hawaiʻi, Inc., 2010. [SHPD ID: 2019LI81539]

McCurdy, Todd D. and Hallett H. Hammatt. *Archaeological Inventory Survey Documentation of Inadvertent Finds Identified during the Honoapi'ilani Highway Realignment (Lahaina Bypass) Phase 1B-1, Paunau Ahupua'a to Polanui Ahupua'a, Lahaina District, Maui Island TMK: (2) 4-6-014:001, 002; (2) 4-6-018:002, 003; (2) 4-8-001:002 and (2) 4-7-003:001.* Wailuku, HI: Cultural Surveys Hawai'i, Inc., 2009. [SHPD ID: 2019LI81536]

McCurdy, Todd D. and Hallett H. Hammatt. *Archaeological Literature Review and Field Inspection for Honoapi'ilani Highway Realignment (Lahaina Bypass), Phase 1B-1, Paunau Ahupua'a to Polanui Ahupua'a, Lahaina District, Maui Island TMK (2) 4-6-014:001-002, 4-6-018:002-003, 4-8-001:002 and 4-7-003:001.* Wailuku, HI: Cultural Surveys Hawai'i, Inc., 2008. [SHPD ID: 2019LI81538]

(2) 4-6-18:005

Hill, Robert, Tanya Lee-Greig, and Hallett H. Hammatt. *An Archaeological Inventory Survey Report and Mitigation Plan for the Hawai'i State Department of Education Cesspool Conversion Project at the Lahainaluna High School, Pana'ewa Ahupua'a, Lahaina District, Maui Island, TMK (2) 4-6-18:005, 007, 012.* Wailuku, HI: Cultural Surveys Hawai'i, Inc., 2008. [No location available]

(2) 4-6-18:007

Hill, Robert, Tanya Lee-Greig, and Hallett H. Hammatt. *An Archaeological Inventory Survey Report and Mitigation Plan for the Hawai'i State Department of Education Cesspool Conversion Project at the Lahainaluna High School, Pana'ewa Ahupua'a, Lahaina District, Maui Island, TMK (2) 4-6-18:005, 007, 012.* Wailuku, HI: Cultural Surveys Hawai'i, Inc., 2008. [No location available]

(2) 4-6-18:012

Dagher, Cathleen A. and Michael F. Dega. *Archaeological Field Inspection Results and Recommendations for the Proposed Maui Police Department Communications Facility at Lahainaluna Water Treatment Site, Pana'ewa Ahupua'a, Lahaina District, Maui Island, Hawai'i [TMK: (2) 4-6-18:012 por.].* Honolulu, HI: Scientific Consultant Services, Inc., 2016. [SHPD ID: 2019LI81527]

Hill, Robert, Tanya Lee-Greig, and Hallett H. Hammatt. *An Archaeological Inventory Survey Report and Mitigation Plan for the Hawai'i State Department of Education Cesspool Conversion Project at the Lahainaluna High School, Pana'ewa*

Ahupua'a, Lahaina District, Maui Island, TMK (2) 4-6-18:005, 007, 012. Wailuku, HI: Cultural Surveys Hawai'i, Inc., 2008. [No location available]

(2) 4-6-18:013

Yucha, Josephine M. and Hallett H. Hammatt. *Archaeological Monitoring Plan for the Lahaina Intermediate School Campus Fire Alarm Replacement Project, Pana'ewa and Ku'ia Ahupua'a, Lahaina District, Maui Island TMK (2) 4-6-18:013 por.* Wailuku, HI: Cultural Surveys Hawai'i, Inc., 2019. [No location available]

(2) 4-6-28:054

Chaffee, David B. and Michael F. Dega. *An Archaeological Monitoring Plan for the Maui Countywide Wastewater Pump Station Renovations, Phase II Project at Multiple Locations, Hanaka'ō'ō Ahupua'a and Mākila Ahupua'a, Lahaina District, Maui Island, Hawai'i [TMK: (2) 4-4-013:003, por. and 4-6-028:054].* Honolulu, HI: Scientific Consultant Services, Inc., 2014.

(2) 4-6-3:005

Spear, Robert L. *Field Inspection of a Sea Wall on the Brayton Property, 303 Front Street, Aholo/Kau'aula Ahupua'a, Lahaina District, Island of Maui, Hawai'i TMK: 4-6-3-05 (Seaward).* Honolulu, HI: Scientific Consultant Services, Inc., 2007. [SHPD ID: 2019LI81559]

(2) 4-6-36:

Fredericksen, Erik M. *Archaeological Monitoring Plan for the Proposed Plantation Inn Improvements Project (GPC 2002/43), Pana'ewa Ahupua'a, Lahaina District, Maui [TMK: (2) 4-6-009: 036, 037 and 044].* Pukalani, HI: Xamanek Researches, 2002. [SHPD ID: 2019LI81579]

(2) 4-6-37:

Fredericksen, Erik M. *Archaeological Monitoring Plan for the Proposed Plantation Inn Improvements Project (GPC 2002/43), Pana'ewa Ahupua'a, Lahaina District, Maui [TMK: (2) 4-6-009: 036, 037 and 044].* Pukalani, HI: Xamanek Researches, 2002. [SHPD ID: 2019LI81579]

(2) 4-6-44:

Fredericksen, Erik M. *Archaeological Monitoring Plan for the Proposed Plantation Inn Improvements Project (GPC 2002/43), Pana'ewa Ahupua'a, Lahaina District, Maui [TMK: (2) 4-6-009: 036, 037 and 044].* Pukalani, HI: Xamanek Researches, 2002. [SHPD ID: 2019LI81579]

(2) 4-7-01:

Jensen, Peter M. *Letter Report: Additional Field Survey Lahaina Bypass Section, Modified Corridor Alignment, Honoapi'ilani Highway Realignment Project, Lands of Pāhoa and Polanui, Lahaina District, Island of Maui [TMK: (2) 4-7-01, 02].* Hilo, HI: Paul H. Rosendahl, Ph.D., Inc., 1992. [SHPD ID: 2019LI81609]

(2) 4-7-01:001

Fredericksen, Erik M. and Demaris L. Fredericksen. *An Archaeological Inventory Survey of the Lahaina Watershed Flood Control Project Area, Lands of Polanui, Paha, Pueuehunui, Lahaina District, Maui Island (TMK: 4-6-13:016, 18, 26; TMK 4-7-01, 02.* Pukalani, HI: Xamanek Researches, 2003. [SHPD ID: 2019LI81442]

Haun, Alan E. *Archaeological Site Documentation, Site 5401, Lands of Polanui and Pāhoa, Lahaina District, Island of Maui (TMK: 4-8-01:002, 4-7-01:001).* Kailua-Kona, HI: Haun and Associates, 2004. [SHPD ID: 2019LI81622]

Haun, Alan E. and Dave Henry. *Archaeological Inventory Survey, Proposed 124-Acre Mākila Subdivision, Lands of Launiupoko, Polanui and Pūehuehu Nui, Lahaina District, Island of Maui (TMK: 4-7-01: por. 1 and TMK 4-7-04: Por. 4).* Kailua-Kona, HI: Haun and Associates, 2001. [SHPD ID: 2019LI81623]

Rotunno-Hazuka, Lisa J. and Jeffrey Pantaleo, M.A. *Archaeological Preservation and Monitoring Plan for Site 50-50-03-4096 Feature 1 Located on a Residential Lot, TMK (2) 4-7-01:001 Pūehuehue Iki Ahupua'a, Lahaina District: Island of Maui.* Wailuku, HI: Archaeological Services Hawaii, LLC, 2006. [SHPD ID: 2019LI81591]

(2) 4-7-01:002

Dega, Michael F. *A Preservation Plan for Multiple Archaeological Sites on Portions of a 570.3 Acre Property in the Launiupoko (Large Lot, Phase V) Subdivision No. 2, Launiupoko Ahupua'a, Lahaina District (Formerly Kā'anapali), Island of*

Maui [TMK (2) 4-7-01:02]. Honolulu, HI: Scientific Consultant Services, Inc., 2006. [SHPD ID: 2019LI81606]

Fredericksen, Erik M. and Demaris L. Fredericksen. *An Archaeological Inventory Survey of the Lahaina Watershed Flood Control Project Area, Lands of Polanui, Paha, Pueuehunui, Lahaina District, Maui Island (TMK: 4-6-13:016, 18, 26; TMK 4-7-01, 02)*. Pukalani, HI: Xamanek Researches, 2003. [SHPD ID: 2019LI81442]

Haun, Alan E. and Dave Henry with Maria E. K. Orr. *Archaeological Inventory Survey Portion of TMK 4-7-01:002, Land of Launiupoko, Lahaina District, Island of Maui*. Kailua-Kona, HI: Haun and Associates, 2001. [SHPD ID: 2019LI81599]

Morawski, Lauren, Adam Johnson, Tomasi Patolo, and Michael F. Dega. *An Archaeological Inventory Survey of 520 Acres in the Launiupoko (Large Lot) Subdivision No. 1, Launiupoko Ahupuaʻa, Lahaina District (formerly Kāʻanapali), Island of Maui, Hawaiʻi [TMK (2) 4-7-01:002 por.]*. Honolulu, HI: Scientific Consultant Services, Inc., 2008. [SHPD ID: 2019LI81603]

(2) 4-7-01:002

McCurdy, Todd D. and Hallett H. Hammatt. *An Archaeological Monitoring Plan for the Honoapiʻilani Highway Realignment (Lahaina Bypass), Phase 1B-1, Paunau Ahupuaʻa to Polanui Ahupuaʻa, Lahaina District, Maui Island TMK: (2) 4-6-014:001-002, 4-6-018:002-003, 4-7-001:002 and 4-7-003:001*. Wailuku, HI: Cultural Surveys Hawaiʻi, Inc., 2010. [SHPD ID: 2019LI81539]

(2) 4-7-01:017

Dega, Michael F. *Archaeological Monitoring Plan for the Installation of a Septic System, Maui County Parks, Launiupoko Ahupuaʻa, Lahaina District, Maui Island, Hawaiʻi [TMK: (2) 4-7-01:17]*. Honolulu, HI: Scientific Consultant Services, Inc., 2005. [SHPD ID: 2019LI81619]

(2) 4-7-01:018

Donham, Theresa K. *Field Inspection of a Proposed Culvert Location, USDA-SCS Lahaina Watershed Project, Pola Nui, Lahaina District, Maui [TMK: (2) 4-7-01:018]*. Wailuku, HI: State Historic Preservation Division, Maui Section, 1991. [SHPD ID: 2019LI81607]

(2) 4-7-01:029

Dega, Michael F. *Archaeological Inventory Survey of the Punakea Loop Corridor in Launiupoko and Polanui Ahupuaʻa, Lahaina District (formerly Kāʻanapali), island of Maui, Hawaiʻi [TMK: (2) 4-8-01:002 por. & 4-7-01:029 por.].* Honolulu, HI: Scientific Consultant Services, Inc., 2008. [SHPD ID: 2019LI81597]

Shefcheck, Donna M. and Michael F. Dega. *An Archaeological Inventory Survey of 122.84 Acres in the Launiupoko (Large Lot) Subdivision 6 Launiupoko and Polanui Ahupuaʻa, Lahaina District, Maui, Hawaiʻi [TMK (2) 4-7-01:029 por.].* Honolulu, HI: Scientific Consultant Services, Inc., 2008. [SHPD ID: 2019LI81593]

(2) 4-7-02:

Jensen, Peter M. *Letter Report: Additional Field Survey Lahaina Bypass Section, Modified Corridor Alignment, Honoapiʻilani Highway Realignment Project, Lands of Pāhoa and Polanui, Lahaina District, Island of Maui [TMK: (2) 4-7-01, 02].* Hilo, HI: Paul H. Rosendahl, Ph.D., Inc., 1992. [SHPD ID: 2019LI81609]

(2) 4-7-02:001

Rotunno-Hazuka, Lisa J. *Archaeological Assessment for the Proposed Well Site in Launiupoko, Lahaina, Maui TMK 4-7-02:001 Lot B.* Wailuku, HI: Archaeological Services Hawaii, LLC, 1997. [SHPD ID: 2019LI81617]

(2) 4-7-02:004

Chong Jin and Michael F. Dega. *Archaeological Assessment for the Launiupoko Water System Line Extension to Waineʻe Project, Pūehuehu Nui and Pāhoa Ahupuaʻa, Lahaina District, Island of Maui, Hawaiʻi [TMK: (2) 4-6-013: portion of 022; 4-7-002: portion of 004; 4-7-003: portion of 031].* Honolulu, HI: Scientific Consultant Services, Inc., 2022. [SHPD ID: 2022LI00556]

Pantaleo, Jeffrey. *Archaeological Monitoring Plan Phase 2 of the Proposed Lahaina Watershed Flood Control Project, Polanui and Pāhoa Ahupuaʻa, Lahaina District, Maui Island [TMK (2) 4-8-001:por. 02; 4-7-02:por. 4, 5, 7],* 1991. [No location available]

(2) 4-7-02:005

Haun, Alan E. *Archaeological Assessment TMK (2) 4-7-02:005 Land of Pāhoa, Lahaina District, Island of Maui.* Kailua-Kona, HI: Haun and Associates, 2001. [SHPD ID: 2019LI81616]

Pantaleo, Jeffrey. *Archaeological Monitoring Plan Phase 2 of the Proposed Lahaina Watershed Flood Control Project, Polanui and Pāhoa Ahupua'a, Lahaina District, Maui Island [TMK (2) 4-8-001:por. 02; 4-7-02:por. 4, 5, 7],* 1991. [No location available]

(2) 4-7-02:007

Pantaleo, Jeffrey. *Archaeological Monitoring Plan Phase 2 of the Proposed Lahaina Watershed Flood Control Project, Polanui and Pāhoa Ahupua'a, Lahaina District, Maui Island [TMK (2) 4-8-001:por. 02; 4-7-02:por. 4, 5, 7],* 1991. [No location available]

(2) 4-7-03:001

Haun, Alan E. and Jack D. Henry. *Archaeological Site Preservation Plan Kau'aula Development Parcel, Lands of Pūehuehu Iki, Pāhoa, and Polanui Ahupua'a, Lahaina District, Island of Maui [TMK (2) 4-7-02:04, 05, & 07, (2) 4-7-03:por. 01].* Kailua-Kona, HI: Haun and Associates, 2003. [SHPD ID: 2019LI81618]

Haun, Alan E. and Jack D. Henry. *Archaeological Site Preservation Plan, Kaua'ula Development Parcel, Lands of Pūehuehu Iki, Pāhoa, and Polo Nui, Lahaina District, Island of Maui [TMK: (2) 4-7-03:001].* Kailua-Kona, HI: Haun and Associates, 2000. [SHPD ID: 2019LI81613]

McCurdy, Todd D. and Hallett H. Hammatt. *An Archaeological Monitoring Plan for the Honoapi'ilani Highway Realignment (Lahaina Bypass), Phase 1B-1, Paunau Ahupua'a to Polanui Ahupua'a, Lahaina District, Maui Island TMK: (2) 4-6-014:001-002, 4-6-018:002-003, 4-7-001:002 and 4-7-003:001.* Wailuku, HI: Cultural Surveys Hawai'i, Inc., 2010. [SHPD ID: 2019LI81539]

McCurdy, Todd D. and Hallett H. Hammatt. *Archaeological Inventory Survey Documentation of Inadvertent Finds Identified during the Honoapi'ilani Highway Realignment (Lahaina Bypass) Phase 1B-1, Paunau Ahupua'a to Polanui Ahupua'a, Lahaina District, Maui Island TMK: (2) 4-6-014:001, 002; (2) 4-6-018:002, 003; (2) 4-8-001:002 and (2) 4-7-003:001.* Wailuku, HI: Cultural Surveys Hawai'i, Inc., 2009. [SHPD ID: 2019LI81536]

McCurdy, Todd D. and Hallett H. Hammatt. *Archaeological Literature Review and Field Inspection for Honoapi'ilani Highway Realignment (Lahaina Bypass), Phase 1B-1, Paunau Ahupua'a to Polanui Ahupua'a, Lahaina District, Maui Island TMK (2) 4-6-014:001-002, 4-6-018:002-003, 4-8-001:002 and 4-7-003:001.* Wailuku, HI: Cultural Surveys Hawai'i, Inc., 2008. [SHPD ID: 2019LI81538]

(2) 4-7-03:031

Chong Jin and Michael F. Dega. *Archaeological Assessment for the Launiu-poko Water System Line Extension to Waine'e Project, Pūehuehu Nui and Pāhoa Ahupua'a, Lahaina District, Island of Maui, Hawai'i [TMK: (2) 4-6-013: portion of 022; 4-7-002: portion of 004; 4-7-003: portion of 031].* Honolulu, HI: Scientific Consultant Services, Inc., 2022. [SHPD ID: 2022LI00556]

(2) 4-7-04:001

Pantaleo, Jeffrey. *Archaeological Inventory Report of a 1.65-Acre Parcel of Land Pūehu-ehue Iki Ahupua'a, Lahaina District, Island of Maui TMK (2) 4-7-04:001.* Wailuku, HI: Archaeological Services Hawaii, LLC, 2006. [SHPD ID: 2019LI81615]

(2) 4-7-04:004

Haun, Alan E. and Dave Henry. *Archaeological Inventory Survey, Proposed 124-Acre Mākila Subdivision, Lands of Launiupoko, Polanui and Pūehuehu Nui, Lahaina District, Island of Maui (TMK: 4-7-01: por. 1 and TMK 4-7-04: Por. 4).* Kailua-Kona, HI: Haun and Associates, 2001. [SHPD ID: 2019LI81623]

(2) 4-7-14:004

Gallo and Michael F. Dega. *Archaeological Assessment for a New Farm Dwelling for Mākila Ranches, Lot 4, Polanui Ahupua'a, Lahaina District, Island of Maui, Hawai'i [TMK: (2) 4-7-14:004 por.].* Honolulu, HI: Scientific Consultant Ser-vices, Inc., 2021. [SHPD ID: 2022LI00382]

(2) 4-7:02:004

Haun, Alan E. and Jack D. Henry. *Archaeological Site Preservation Plan Kau'aula Development Parcel, Lands of Pūehuehu Iki, Pāhoa, and Polanui Ahupua'a, Lahaina District, Island of Maui [TMK (2) 4-7-02:04, 05, & 07, (2) 4-7-03:por. 01].* Kailua-Kona, HI: Haun and Associates, 2003. [SHPD ID: 2019LI81618]

(2) 4-7:02:005

Haun, Alan E. and Jack D. Henry. *Archaeological Site Preservation Plan Kau'aula Development Parcel, Lands of Pūehuehu Iki, Pāhoa, and Polanui Ahupua'a, Lahaina District, Island of Maui [TMK (2) 4-7-02:04, 05, & 07, (2) 4-7-03:por. 01]*. Kailua-Kona, HI: Haun and Associates, 2003. [SHPD ID: 2019LI81618]

(2) 4-7:02:007

Haun, Alan E. and Jack D. Henry. *Archaeological Site Preservation Plan Kau'aula Development Parcel, Lands of Pūehuehu Iki, Pāhoa, and Polanui Ahupua'a, Lahaina District, Island of Maui [TMK (2) 4-7-02:04, 05, & 07, (2) 4-7-03:por. 01]*. Kailua-Kona, HI: Haun and Associates, 2003. [SHPD ID: 2019LI81618]

(2) 4-8-01:

Pantaleo, Jeffrey. *Archaeological Monitoring Plan Phase 2 of the Proposed Lahaina Watershed Flood Control Project, Polanui and Pāhoa Ahupua'a, Lahaina District, Maui Island [TMK (2) 4-8-001:por. 02; 4-7-02:por. 4, 5, 7]*, 1991. [No location available]

(2) 4-8-01:001

Rechtman, Robert B. and Ashton K. Dircks Ah Sam. *An Archaeological Inventory Survey for the Kaheawa Wind Power (KWP) Phase 2 Project Area [TMK (2) 3-6-001:por. 14 & (2) 4-8-01: Por. 001]*. Rechtman Consulting, LLC, 2009. [SHPD ID: 2019LI80301]

Tomonari-Tuggle, M. J. and Coral Rasmussen. *Preservation Plan for Site 50-50-09-5232, An Upland Heiau in Ukumehame Ahupua'a, Island of Maui TMK 4-8-01:1*. Honolulu, HI: International Archaeological Research Institute, Inc., 2005. [SHPD ID: 2019LI81629]

(2) 4-8-01:002

Dega, Michael F. *Archaeological Inventory Survey of the Punakea Loop Corridor in Launiupoko and Polanui Ahupua'a, Lahaina District (formerly Kā'anapali), island of Maui, Hawai'i [TMK: (2) 4-8-01:002 por. & 4-7-01:029 por.]*. Honolulu, HI: Scientific Consultant Services, Inc., 2008. [SHPD ID: 2019LI81597]

Haun, Alan E. *Archaeological Site Documentation, Site 5401, Lands of Polanui and Pāhoa, Lahaina District, Island of Maui (TMK: 4-8-01:002, 4-7-01:001).* Kailua-Kona, HI: Haun and Associates, 2004. [SHPD ID: 2019LI81622]

Kawachi, Carol. *Archaeological Monitoring Plan for Phase 1 of the Proposed Lahaina Watershed Flood Control Project Including Conservation District Use Application MA-3204 Board Permit, Polanui Ahupua'a, Lahaina District, Maui, Island TMK: (2) 4-8-01: por. 002, 018, 2005.* [SHPD ID: 2019LI81601]

McCurdy, Todd D. and Hallett H. Hammatt. *Archaeological Literature Review and Field Inspection for Honoapi'ilani Highway Realignment (Lahaina Bypass), Phase 1B-1, Paunau Ahupua'a to Polanui Ahupua'a, Lahaina District, Maui Island TMK (2) 4-6-014:001-002, 4-6-018:002-003, 4-8-001:002 and 4-7-003:001.* Wailuku, HI: Cultural Surveys Hawai'i, Inc., 2008. [SHPD ID: 2019LI81538]

Paraso, C. Kanani and Michael F. Dega. *An Archaeological Inventory Survey of 633 Acres in the Launiupoko (Large Lot) Subdivision Nos. 3, 4, and 7, Launiupoko and Polanui Ahupua'a, Lahaina District (formerly Kā'anapali), Island of Maui, Hawai'i [TMK (2) 4-8-01:2 por.].* Honolulu, HI: Scientific Consultant Services, Inc., 2006. [SHPD ID: 2019LI81600]

Shefcheck, Donna M. and Michael F. Dega. *An Archaeological Inventory Survey of 123.31 Acres in the Launiupoko (Large Lot) Subdivision 6 Launiupoko and Polanui Ahupua'a, Lahaina District (formerly Kā'anapali) Island of Maui, Hawai'i TMK (2) 4-8-01:002 por.).* Honolulu, HI: Scientific Consultant Services, Inc., 2007. [SHPD ID: 2019LI81596]

(2) 4-8-01:002

McCurdy, Todd D. and Hallett H. Hammatt. *Addendum Report for Archaeological Inventory Survey Documentation of Inadvertent Finds Identified during the Honoapi'ilani Highway Realignment (Lahaina Bypass) Phase 1B-1, Paunau Ahupua'a to Polanui Ahupua'a, Lahaina District, Maui Island TMK (2) 4-6-014:001, 002: (2) 4-6-018:002, 003; (2) 4-8-001:002 and (2) 4-8-003:001.* Wailuku, HI: Cultural Surveys Hawai'i, Inc., 2010. [SHPD ID: 2019LI81537]

McCurdy, Todd D. and Hallett H. Hammatt. *Archaeological Inventory Survey Documentation of Inadvertent Finds Identified during the Honoapi'ilani Highway Realignment (Lahaina Bypass) Phase 1B-1, Paunau Ahupua'a to Polanui Ahupua'a, Lahaina District, Maui Island TMK: (2) 4-6-014:001, 002; (2) 4-6-018:002, 003; (2) 4-8-001:002 and (2) 4-7-003:001.* Wailuku, HI: Cultural Surveys Hawai'i, Inc., 2009. [SHPD ID: 2019LI81536]

(2) 4-8-01:018

Kawachi, Carol. *Archaeological Monitoring Plan for Phase 1 of the Proposed Lahaina Watershed Flood Control Project Including Conservation District Use Application MA-3204 Board Permit, Polanui Ahupuaʻa, Lahaina District, Maui, Island TMK: (2) 4-8-01: por. 002, 018, 2005.* [SHPD ID: 2019LI81601]

(2) 4-8-02:

Pantaleo, Jeffrey. *Archaeological Monitoring Plan Phase 2 of the Proposed Lahaina Watershed Flood Control Project, Polanui and Pāhoa Ahupuaʻa, Lahaina District, Maui Island [TMK (2) 4-8-001:por. 02; 4-7-02:por. 4, 5, 7],* 1991. [No location available]

(2) 4-8-02:008

Shefcheck, Donna M. and Michael F. Dega. *A Preservation Plan for Site 50-50-08-5968 and Site 50-50-08-5969 in Ukumehame Ahupuaʻa, Lahaina District, Island of Maui, Hawaiʻi [TMK: (2) 4-8-02:008 por.].* Honolulu, HI: Scientific Consultant Services, Inc., 2006. [SHPD ID: 2019LI81643]

(2) 4-8-02:009

Chaffee, David B. and Michael F. Dega. *An Archaeological Monitoring Plan for Subdivision Construction of a 450-Acre Parcel of Land, Ahupuaʻa of Ukumehame, Lahaina District, Island of Maui, Hawaiʻi [TMK (2) 4-8-02:09].* Honolulu, HI: Scientific Consultant Services, Inc., 2003.

(2) 4-8-02:047

Sinoto, Aki. *An Archaeological Assessment of the Native Plant Conservatory Project, Ukumehame Firing Range, Ukumehame, Lahaina, Maui TMK (2) 4-8-2:047.* Honolulu, HI: Aki Sinoto Consulting, 1997. [SHPD ID: 2019LI81624]

(2) 4-8-02:066

Dagher, Cathleen A. and Michael F. Dega. *Revised Preservation Plan for Site 50-50-08-4438, Ukumehame Ahupuaʻa, Lahaina District, Island of Maui, Hawaiʻi [TMK (2) 4-8-002:066; formerly (2) 4-9-002:009 por.].* Honolulu, HI: Scientific Consultant Services, Inc., 2010. [SHPD ID: 2019LI81625]

(2) 4-8-03:

Fredericksen, Demaris L. and Erik M. Fredericksen. *Archaeological Inventory Survey of Makai Portion (Phase 1) of Olowalu Development Parcel, Olowalu Ahupua'a, Lahaina District, Maui Island [TMK: (2) 4-8-03: por. 05].* Pukalani, HI: Xamanek Researches, 2000. [SHPD ID: 2019LI81638]

Olowalu Elua Associates, LLC. *Monitoring Plan for Sites 50-50-08-4820 and 50-50-08-4821; Olowalu Ahupua'a, Lahaina District; Island of Maui [TMK (2) 4-8-003: portion of 10].* Olowalu, HI: Olowalu Elua Associates, LLC, 2002. [No location available]

(2) 4-8-03:001

McCurdy, Todd D. and Hallett H. Hammatt. *Addendum Report for Archaeological Inventory Survey Documentation of Inadvertent Finds Identified during the Honoapi'ilani Highway Realignment (Lahaina Bypass) Phase 1B-1, Paunau Ahupua'a to Polanui Ahupua'a, Lahaina District, Maui Island TMK (2) 4-6-014:001, 002: (2) 4-6-018:002, 003; (2) 4-8-001:002 and (2) 4-8-003:001.* Wailuku, HI: Cultural Surveys Hawai'i, Inc., 2010. [SHPD ID: 2019LI81537]

(2) 4-8-03:002

Stankov, Pavel and Michael F. Dega. *Archaeological Monitoring Plan for the Renovations and Landscaping at the Stakelbeck Property at Olowalu Ahupua'a, Lahaina District, Island of Maui, Hawai'i [TMK (2) 4-8-03:002 por.].* Honolulu, HI: Scientific Consultant Services, Inc., 2021. [SHPD ID: 2021LI00103]

(2) 4-8-03:005

Lee and Michael F. Dega. *An Archaeological Assessment for a New Wastewater System at the Olowalu Plantation Manager's House in Olowalu, Olowalu Ahupua'a, Lahaina District, Island of Maui, Hawai'i [TMK: (2) 4-8-03:005 por.].* Honolulu, HI: Scientific Consultant Services, Inc., 2021. [SHPD ID: 2021LI00436]

(2) 4-8-03:044

Fredericksen, Erik M. *Archaeological Monitoring Report for a 1.3 Acre of Land on the Olowalu Makai Project Area, Olowalu Ahupua'a, Lahaina District, Maui*

(TMK 2-4-8-03:44). Pukalani, HI: Xamanek Researches, 2003. [SHPD ID: 2019LI81637]

Hammatt, Hallett H. *Lahaina (Front Street) Archaeological Test Excavations, TMK 4-5-3:012, Island of Maui*. Wailuku, HI: Cultural Surveys Hawai'i, Inc., 2003. [SHPD ID: 2019LI80649]

(2) 4-8-03:047

Dagher, Cathleen A. and Michael F. Dega. *An Archaeological Monitoring Plan for the Poseley Residence, Olowalu Ahupua'a, Lahaina District, Island of Maui, Hawai'i [TMK: (2) 4-8-03:047 and portions of 001 and 084 (Easement G)]*. Honolulu, HI: Scientific Consultant Services, Inc., 2015. [SHPD ID: 2019LI81660]

Wiley, Tiffany E. and Michael F. Dega. *Addendum to an Archaeological Monitoring Plan for the Poseley Residence, Olowalu Ahupua'a, Lahaina District, Island of Maui, Hawai'i [TMK (2) 4-8-003:047, and portions of 001 and 084 (Easement G)]*. Honolulu, HI: Scientific Consultant Services, Inc., 2017. [No location available]

(2) 4-8-03:084

Bassford, B. A. and Michael F. Dega. *Burial Site Component of an Archaeological Data Recovery and Preservation Plan for Site 50-50-08-8284 at Camp Olowalu in Olowalu, Olowalu Ahupua'a, Lahaina District, Maui Island, Hawai'i [TMK (2) 4-8-03:084 por.]*. Honolulu, HI: Scientific Consultant Services, Inc., 2015. [No location available]

(2) 4-8-03:107

Dagher, Cathleen A. and Michael F. Dega. *An Archaeological Monitoring Plan for Olowalu Lot 24, Olowalu Ahupua'a, Lahaina District, Island of Maui, Hawai'i [TMK: (2) 4-8-03:107]*. Honolulu, HI: Scientific Consultant Services, Inc., 2019. [SHPD ID: 2019LI05336]

(2) 4-8-05:

Fredericksen, Demaris L. and Erik M. Fredericksen. *Archaeological Inventory Survey of Makai Portion (Phase 1) of Olowalu Development Parcel, Olowalu Ahupua'a, Lahaina District, Maui Island [TMK: (2) 4-8-03: por. 05]*. Pukalani, HI: Xamanek Researches, 2000. [SHPD ID: 2019LI81638]

(2) 4-8-10:

Olowalu Elua Associates, LLC. *Monitoring Plan for Sites 50-50-08-4820 and 50-50-08-4821; Olowalu Ahupua'a, Lahaina District; Island of Maui [TMK (2) 4-8-003: portion of 10].* Olowalu, HI: Olowalu Elua Associates, LLC, 2002. [No location available]

(2) 4-9-02:008

Dega, Michael F. *An Addendum Archaeological Inventory Survey in Ukumehame Ahupua'a, Lahaina District, Island of Maui, Hawai'i [TMK (2) 4-9-02:008 por.].* Honolulu, HI: Scientific Consultant Services, Inc., 2006. [SHPD ID: 2019LI81645]

(2) 4-9-02:009 (FORMER TMK)

Dagher, Cathleen A. and Michael F. Dega. *Revised Preservation Plan for Site 50-50-08-4438, Ukumehame Ahupua'a, Lahaina District, Island of Maui, Hawai'i [TMK (2) 4-8-002:066; formerly (2) 4-9-002:009 por.].* Honolulu, HI: Scientific Consultant Services, Inc., 2010. [SHPD ID: 2019LI81625]

(2) 4-9-03:044

Fredericksen, Erik M. *Archaeological Monitoring Plan on a 1.3 Acre of Land on the Olowalu Makai Project Area, Olowalu Ahupua'a, Lahaina District, Maui [TMK: (2) 4-9-03:044).* Pukalani, HI: Xamanek Researches, 2001. [SHPD ID: 2019LI81635]

(2) 4-9-03:45A

McGerty, Leann and Robert L. Spear. *A Cultural Impact Assessment of Approximately 0.8 Acres of Land in Olowalu Ahupua'a, Wailuku District, Maui, Hawai'i [TMK (2) 4-9-003:45A].* Honolulu, HI: Scientific Consultant Services, Inc., 2006. [SHPD ID: 2019LI81636]

NO TMK INDICATED

Ahlo, Hamilton M. and Maurice E. Morgenstein. *Archaeological Test Excavations Near the Mouth of Kahoma Stream, Lahaina, Maui.* Honolulu, HI: Hawai'i Marine Research, 1979.

Aki Sinoto Consulting. *Archaeological Monitoring During the Renovation of the Lahaina Center Parking Structure, Lahaina, Maui.* Honolulu, HI: Aki Sinoto Consulting, 1995.

Aki Sinoto Consulting. *Archaeological Monitoring Plan for Utility Trenching at the Lahaina Shopping Center, Paunau, Lahaina, Maui.* Honolulu, HI: Aki Sinoto Consulting, 1996.

Andricci, Nicole and Michael F. Dega. *An Archaeological Assessment for the Lahaina Square Redevelopment Project, Lahaina, Wainéʻe Ahupuaʻa, District of Lahaina, Island of Maui, Hawaiʻi.* Honolulu, HI: Scientific Consultant Services, Inc., 2017. [SHPD ID: 2019LI80016]

Athens, J. Stephen. *Archaeological Reconnaissance at Honokahua Well B, Lahaina District, West Maui,* 1985.

Barrera, William Jr. *Honoapiʻilani Highway, Maui: Archaeological Reconnaissance.* Honolulu, HI: Chiniago, Inc., 1988.

Barrera, William Jr. *North Beach, Maui: Archaeological Reconnaissance.* Honolulu, HI: Chiniago, Inc., 1986. [SHPD ID: 2019LI81288]

Buffum, Amy and Michael F. Dega. *An Archaeological Monitoring Report for Construction work at Honokōwai, Māhinahina Ahupuaʻa, Kāʻanapali District, Maui Island, Hawaii.* Honolulu, HI: Scientific Consultant Services, Inc., 2002.

Burgett, Berdena and Robert L. Spear. *An Archaeological Inventory Survey of an 8.8 Acre Parcel in the Land of Kainehi, Lahaina District, Paunau Ahupuaʻa, Island of Maui.* Honolulu, HI: Aki Sinoto Consulting, 1994.

Calis, Irene. *Archaeological Monitoring Report: Parking Lot Drainage System Installation, Panaʻewa Ahupuaʻa, Lahaina District, Island of Maui, Hawaiʻi.* Honolulu, HI: Scientific Consultant Services, Inc., 2002. [SHPD ID: 2019LI80642]

Chaffee, D. and C. Monahan. *A Monitoring Plan for 3.054 Acres of Partially Developed Land in Honokōwai, Māhinahina 4 Ahupuaʻa, Lahaina District, Maui Island, Hawaiʻi.* Honolulu, HI: Scientific Consultant Services, Inc., 2005.

Chaffee, David B. and Michael F. Dega. *An Archaeological Monitoring Plan for Kāʻanapali Beach Hotel Beach Front, Restaurant/Canoe Hale, Hanakaʻōʻō Ahupuaʻa, Lahaina District, Island of Maui, Hawaiʻi.* Honolulu, HI: Scientific Consultant Services, Inc., 2014.

Chaffee, David B. and Robert L. Spear. *An Archaeological Monitoring Plan for Construction Activities on a 13,237 Square Foot Parcel in ʻAlaeloa Ahupuaʻa,*

Lahaina District, Maui Island, Hawaii. Honolulu, HI: Scientific Consultant Services, Inc., 2001.

Chapman, P. S. and P. V. Kirch. *Archaeological Excavations at Seven Sites, Southeast Maui, Hawaiian Islands.* Honolulu, HI: Department of Anthropology, Bernice P. Bishop Museum, 1979. [UH Call Number: DU624.A1 B47 no.79-1]

Chapman, Phillips, Brandt and Associates. *Lahaina Banyan Courtyard Preliminary Development and Restoration Plans,* 1972. [SHPD ID: 2019LI81398]

Ching, Francis K. W. *Archaeological Assessment of the Property on Which the Proposed Marriott Kāʻanapali Hotel is to be Built, Kāʻanapali, Maui Island.* Lāwaʻi, HI: Archaeological Research Center Hawaiʻi, 1979. [SHPD ID: 2019LI81267]

Chun, Allison and Michael F. Dega. *Addendum Archaeological Assessment Report on 0.13 Acres of Partially Developed land in Honokōwai, Māhinahina 4 Ahupuaʻa, Maui Island, Hawaiʻi.* Honolulu, HI: Scientific Consultant Services, Inc., 2005. [SHPD ID: 2019LI81043]

Cleghorn, Paul L. *A Progress Report upon Completion of Fieldwork at the Seamen's Hospital, Lahaina, Maui (Phase 1).* Honolulu, HI: Department of Anthropology, Bernice P. Bishop Museum, 1975. [UH Call Number: DU629.L3 C54 1975]

Cleghorn, Paul L. *Phase 1 Archaeological Research at the Seamen's Hospital (Site D5-10), Lahaina, Maui.* Honolulu, HI: Department of Anthropology, Bernice P. Bishop Museum, 1975. [UH Call Number: DU629.L3 C544 1975]

Cliver, Blaine E., *Architectural Restorationalist. Architecturally speaking... The Baldwin House,* Lahaina, Maui, 1966. [SHPD ID: 2019LI81038]

Collins, Sara L. *Archaeological Monitoring Plan for Ground-Altering Activities During the Grading and Excavations for Construction Associated with the Mokuʻula/Mokuhinia Ecosystem Restoration Project, Phase I, Lahaina, Island of Maui.* Honolulu, HI: Pacific Consulting Services, Inc., 2007. [SHPD ID: 2019LI01493]

Community Planning, Inc. *Lahaina Historical Restoration and Preservation.* Community Planning Inc., 1961. [UH Call Number: DU629.L3 M3]

Connolly, Robert D. III. *Phase I Archaeological Survey of Kahoma Stream Flood-Control-Project Area, Lahaina, Maui.* Honolulu, HI: Department of Anthropology, Bernice P. Bishop Museum, 1974.

Conte, Patty J. *Assessment of a Lot for Proposed Residential Construction, Kahana Ahupuaʻa, Lahaina District, Maui, Hawaiʻi.* Makawao, HI: CRM Solutions Hawaiʻi, Inc., 2004. [SHPD ID: 2019LI81300]

Cordle, Shayna and Michael F. Dega. *An Archaeological Monitoring Plan for 1.835 Acres in Napili, Napili 2-3 Ahupuaʻa, Lahaina District, Maui Island, Hawaiʻi.* Honolulu, HI: Scientific Consultant Services, Inc., 2008. ID: 2019LI81066]

Dagan, Colleen P. M. and Hallett H. Hammatt. *Archaeological Preservation Plan for SIHP 50-50-01-5672C and 50-50-01-5673H.* Wailuku, HI: Cultural Surveys Hawaiʻi, Inc., 2008. [SHPD ID: 2019LI81026]

Dagher, Cathleen A. *Request for Information Pertaining to the Ukumehame Subdivision and the Impacts to Preserved Site 50-50-08-4438 Ukumehame Ahupuaʻa, Lahaina District, Island of Maui,* 2009. [SHPD ID: 2019LI81644]

Dagher, Cathleen A. and Michael F. Dega. *A Preservation Plan for Multiple Archaeological Sites Located in the Kapalua Coastal Trail Corridor in the areas of Nāpili, Kapalua, Honokahua, and Honolua, Ahupuaʻa of Nāpili 2 & 3, Honokahua, and Honolua, Lahaina District, Island of Maui, Hawaiʻi.* Honolulu, HI: Scientific Consultant Services, Inc., 2008. [SHPD ID: 2019LI79694]

Dagher, Cathleen A. and Michael F. Dega. *An Archaeological Monitoring Plan for the Napili Culvert Replacement Project, Nāpili 4 and 5 Ahupuaʻa, Lahaina (Kāʻanapali) District, Island of Maui, Hawaiʻi.* Honolulu, HI: Scientific Consultant Services, Inc., 2015. [SHPD ID: 2019LI81056]

Dagher, Cathleen A. and Michael F. Dega. *An Archaeological Monitoring Plan for the Nāpili No. 4 WWPS Force Main Replacement, Lower Honoapiʻilani Road Right-of-Way, Honokeana and ʻAlaeloa Ahupuaʻa, Lahaina, (Kāʻanapali) District, Island of Maui, Hawaiʻi.* Honolulu, HI: Scientific Consultant Services, Inc., 2020. [SHPD ID: 2021LI00158]

Dagher, Cathleen A. and Michael F. Dega. *An Archaeological Monitoring Plan for the Proposed Kapalua Coastal Trail Located in the Areas of Nāpili, Kapalua, Honokahua, and Honolua, Ahupuaʻa of Nāpili 2 & 3, Honokahua, and Honolua, Lahaina district, Island of Maui, Hawaiʻi.* Honolulu, HI: Scientific Consultant Services, Inc., 2008. [SHPD ID: 2019LI81410]

Dagher, Cathleen A. and Michael F. Dega. *Archaeological Field Inspection Results and Recommendations for the Proposed Maui Police Department Communications Facility at Māhinahina Water Treatment Plant, Māhinahina Ahupuaʻa, Lahaina District, Maui Island, Hawaiʻi.* Honolulu, HI: Scientific Consultant Services, Inc., 2016. [SHPD ID: 2019LI81036]

Dagher, Cathleen A. and Michael F. Dega. *Archaeological Monitoring Plan for the Maui Sands Sea Wall Repair Project, Moʻomuku ʻili, Honokōwai Ahupuaʻa, Lahaina (Kāʻanapali) District, Island of Maui, Hawaiʻi.* Honolulu, HI: Scientific Consultant Services, Inc., 2018. [No location available]

Davis, Bertell D. *Archaeological Surface Survey, Honokōwai Gulch, Kāʻanapali, Maui Island.* Lāwaʻi, HI: Archaeological Research Center Hawaiʻi, 1977. [SHPD ID: 2019LI81277]

Davis, Bertell D. *Preliminary Report, Mala Wharf Burials, Phase 1, Mala, Lahaina, Maui Island.* Lāwaʻi, HI: Archaeological Research Center Hawaiʻi, 1977. [No location available]

Dega, Michael F. *An Archaeological Monitoring plan for Construction Work at Honokōwai, Māhinahina Ahupuaʻa, Kāʻanapali District, Maui Island, Hawaiʻi.* Honolulu, HI: Scientific Consultant Services, Inc., 2000. [SHPD ID: 2019LI81247]

Dega, Michael F. *An Archaeological Monitoring Plan for Improvements at D. T. Fleming Beach Park for the County of Maui, Department of Parks and Recreation, Honokahua Ahupuaʻa [sic], Lahaina District, Island of Maui, Hawaiʻi.* Honolulu, HI: Scientific Consultant Services, Inc., 2015. [SHPD ID: 2019LI81042]

Dega, Michael F. *Archaeological Inventory Survey of a 3-Acre Parcel in Kahana-Kai, Kahana Ahupuaʻa, Kāʻanapali District, Island of Maui, Hawaiʻi.* Honolulu, HI: Scientific Consultant Services, Inc., 2001. [SHPD ID: 2019LI81327]

Dega, Michael F. *Archaeological Monitoring Plan for Limited Construction Work in Lahaina, Kuʻia Ahupuaʻa, Lahaina District, Island of Maui, Hawaiʻi.* Honolulu, HI: Scientific Consultant Services, Inc., 2003. [SHPD ID: 2019LI80641]

Dega, Michael F. and David B. Chaffee. *Archaeological Monitoring Plan for Construction at the Lahaina Shores, Moaliʻi Ahupuaʻa, Lahaina District, Maui Island, Hawaiʻi.* Honolulu, HI: Scientific Consultant Services, Inc., 2004. [SHPD ID: 2019LI81373]

Dega, Michael F. and David B. Chaffee. *Archaeological Monitoring Plan for Construction Work on Approximately 25.3 Acres in Kapalua, Napili 2-3 Ahupuaʻa, Lahaina District, Maui Island, Hawaiʻi.* Honolulu, HI: Scientific Consultant Services, Inc., 2004. [SHPD ID: 2019LI81041]

Desilets, Michael and Patrick OʻDay. *Preservation Plan for Proposed Fenceline Corridor for the West Maui Forest Reserve, Kuʻia, Mākila, Pāhoa, Halakaʻa, Polaiki, Launiupoko, and Olowalu Ahupuaʻa, Lahaina District, Maui Island, Hawaiʻi.* Kailua, HI: Garcia & Associates, 2016. [SHPD ID: 2019LI81528]

Devereux, Thomas K., Ian A. Masterson, Melody Heidel, Victoria Creed, Leilani Pyle, and Hallett H. Hammatt. *Archaeological Inventory Survey and Subsurface Testing of a 440 Acre Parcel, Ahupuaʻa of Ukumehame, Lahaina Dis-*

trict, Island of Maui. Wailuku, HI: Cultural Surveys Hawai'i, Inc., 1999. [SHPD ID: 2019LI81639]

Devereux, Thomas K., William H. Folk, and Hallett H. Hammatt. *Archaeological Survey of the Lands Comprising Project District 2 at Kapalua, Honokahua, and Nāpili 2 & 3 Ahupua'a Lahaina District of Maui.* Wailuku, HI: Cultural Surveys Hawai'i, Inc., 2001. [SHPD ID: 2019LI81007]

Dobyns, Susan and Jane Allen-Wheeler. *Archaeological Monitoring at the Site of the Kā'anapali Ali'i Condominium, Island of Maui.* Honolulu, HI: Department of Anthropology, Bernice P. Bishop Museum, 1982. [SHPD ID: 2019LI80673]

Dockall, John E. and Hallett H. Hammatt. *An Archaeological Inventory Survey for a Proposed Town Center and Residential Village, Nāpili Ahupua'a, Lahaina District.* Wailuku, HI: Cultural Surveys Hawai'i, Inc., 2005. [SHPD ID: 2019LI81011]

Dockall, John E., Tanya L. Lee-Greig, and Hallett H. Hammatt. *An Archaeological Assessment of a Proposed Road Corridor for Maui Preparatory Academy, Alaeloa Ahupua'a, Lahaina District, Maui Island.* Wailuku, HI: Cultural Surveys Hawai'i, Inc., 2005. [SHPD ID: 2019LI81052]

Donham, Theresa K. *Addendum Report: Additional Subsurface Testing of Area III, Subsurface Archaeological Testing, Revised Ritz-Carlton Kapalua Hotel Project Site, Areas I, II, and III, Land of Honokahua, Lahaina District, Island of Maui.* Hilo, HI: Paul H. Rosendahl, Ph.D., Inc., 1989. [SHPD ID: 2019LI81414]

Donham, Theresa K. *Archaeological Survey Test Excavations Kapalua Hotel Development Site 2-H, Kapalua Bay Resort, Land of Honokahua, Lahaina, Island of Maui.* Hilo, HI: Paul H. Rosendahl, Ph.D., Inc., 1986. [2019LI80998]

Donham, Theresa K. *Interim Report: Kapalua Mitigation Program Data Recovery Excavations at the Honokahua Burial Site, Land of Honokahua, Lahaina District, Island of Maui.* Hilo, HI: Paul H. Rosendahl, Ph.D., Inc., 1989. [SHPD ID: 2019LI81417]

Duensing, Dawn E. and Michael W. Foley. *Lahaina Design Guidelines, Lahaina Town, Maui, Hawai'i,* 2003. [SHPD ID: 2019LI81377]

Ferguson, Lee, Arne Carlson, and Berdena Burgett. *Subsurface Archaeological Testing, Revised Ritz-Carlton Kapalua Hotel Project Site, Areas I, II and III.* Hilo, HI: Paul H. Rosendahl, Ph.D., Inc., 1989. [SHPD ID: 2019LI81006]

Folio, Katie M. and Hallett H. Hammatt. *Archaeological Monitoring Plan for the Special Use Permit Application for the Napili Point 1 AOAO (SMX 2015/0465) and Napili Point II (SMX 2015/0472) Project, Honokeana Ahupua'a, Lahaina*

District, Island of Maui, Napili Point I. Wailuku, HI: Cultural Surveys Hawai'i, Inc., 2016. [SHPD ID: 2019LI81068]

Folk, William. *Letter to Noel Kennett Re: End of Fieldwork of Archaeological Monitoring at Mala Wharf for an Electrical Line*. Wailuku, HI: Cultural Surveys Hawai'i, Inc., 1993. [SHPD ID: 2019LI80619]

Fox, Robert M. *Site Survey & Inventory, Hale Pa'i o Lahainaluna*. Honolulu, HI: AIA, 1977. [SHPD ID: 2019LI81590]

Fredericksen et al. *An Archaeological Inventory Survey of a 9.976 Acre parcel in the Kahana/Mailepai/Alaeloa District, Lahaina District, Maui, Hawai'i*. Pukalani, HI: Xamanek Researches, 1990. [SHPD ID: 2019LI81060]

Fredericksen, Demaris. *Monitoring Report for the Sheraton-Maui Redevelopment Project, Hanaka'ō'ō Ahupua'a, Lahaina District, Maui Island*. Pukalani, HI: Xamanek Researches, 1998. [SHPD ID: 2019LI81263]

Fredericksen, Demaris L. and Erik M. Fredericksen. *Archaeological Inventory Survey for Kahana-Kai Subdivision, Kahana Ahupua'a, Lahaina [Kā'anapali] District, Maui Island*. Pukalani, HI: Xamanek Researches, 1995. [SHPD ID: 2019LI81330]

Fredericksen, Demaris L. and Walter M. Fredericksen. *Archaeological Monitoring Plan for the Sheraton-Maui Redevelopment Project, Ahupua'a of Hanaka'ō'ō, Lahaina District, Maui Island*. Pukalani, HI: Xamanek Researches, 1995. [SHPD ID: 2019LI80672]

Fredericksen, Demaris L., Walter M. Fredericksen, and Erik M. Fredericksen. *Archaeological Inventory Survey of a 9.976 Acre Parcel in the Kahana/Mailepai/Akeloa Lands, Lahaina District, Maui, Hawai'i*. Pukalani, HI: Xamanek Researches, 1990. [SHPD ID: 2019LI81060]

Fredericksen, Erik M. *A Preservation Plan for the Sites Contained within Kā'anapali Coffee Estates Subdivision (aka Pioneer Farms Subdivision 1) Project Area, Hanaka'ō'ō Ahupua'a, Lahaina District, Island of Maui*. Pukalani, HI: Xamanek Researches, 2005. [SHPD ID: 2019LI81274]

Fredericksen, Erik M. *An Archaeological Monitoring Plan for a Detector Check Upgrade Project for the Lahaina Square Shopping Center, Waine'e Ahupua'a, Lahaina District, Maui*. Pukalani, HI: Xamanek Researches, 2008. [SHPD ID: 2019LI80611]

Fredericksen, Erik M. *An Archaeological Monitoring Plan for the Dickenson Street Power Pole Replacement Project, Paunau Ahupua'a, Lahaina District, Island of Maui*. Pukalani, HI: Xamanek Researches, 2004. [SHPD ID: 2019LI81570]

Fredericksen, Erik M. *An Archaeological Monitoring Plan for the Proposed Kāʻanapali Loop Road Project, Hanakaʻōʻō Ahupuaʻa, Lahaina District, Island of Maui.* Pukalani, HI: Xamanek Researches, 2004. [SHPD ID: 2019LI81268]

Fredericksen, Erik M. *An Archaeological Monitoring Plan for the Proposed Lower Honoapiʻilani Highway Improvements Phase IV Project (Hoʻohui Road to Napilihau Street) in Kahana, Mailepai, and Alaeloa Ahupuaʻa, Napili, Lahaina District, Maui [F. A. P. No. STP 3080 (8)].* Pukalani, HI: Xamanek Researches, 2005. [SHPD ID: 2019LI81299]

Fredericksen, Erik M. *An Archaeological Monitoring Report for Offsite Parking for the Lot 3 Temporary Parking Project, Kāʻanapali, Hanakaʻōʻō Ahupuaʻa Lahaina District, Island of Maui.* Pukalani, HI: Xamanek Researches, 2006. [SHPD ID: 2019LI80660]

Fredericksen, Erik M. *Archaeological Monitoring Plan for a Water Lateral and Sewer Lateral Installation Project for a Parcel of Land in Lahaina, Moaliʻi Ahupuaʻa, Lahaina District, Maui.* Pukalani, HI: Xamanek Researches, 2003. [SHPD ID: 2019LI81270]

Fredericksen, Erik M. *Archaeological Monitoring Plan for Improvements at 815 Front Street, Paunau Ahupuaʻa, Lahaina District, Maui.* Pukalani, HI: Xamanek Researches, 2001. [SHPD ID: 2019LI80644]

Fredericksen, Erik M. *Archaeological Monitoring Plan for Lot 29 (Site 29) Honokahua and Napili 2-3 Ahupuaʻa, Lahaina District, Maui, Hawaiʻi.* Pukalani, HI: Xamanek Researches, 1999. [SHPD ID: 2019LI81028]

Fredericksen, Erik M. *Archaeological Monitoring Plan for the Sabia Building Development and Improvement Project at 816A Front Street, Paunau Ahupuaʻa, Lahaina District, Maui.* Pukalani, HI: Xamanek Researches, 2000. [SHPD ID: 2019LI80617]

Fredericksen, Erik M. *Archaeological Monitoring Report for a Portion of Land in Moaliʻi Ahupuaʻa, Lahaina District, Maui.* Pukalani, HI: Xamanek Researches, 2004. [SHPD ID: 2019LI81269]

Fredericksen, Erik M. *Archaeological Monitoring Report for the Coconut Grove Development (Site 29), Honokahua and Napili 2-3 Ahupuaʻa Lahiana District, Island of Maui.* Pukalani, HI: Xamanek Researches, 2001. [SHPD ID: 2019LI17106]

Fredericksen, Erik M. *Archaeological Monitoring Report on the Pioneer Inn Swimming Pool Construction Project.* Pukalani, HI: Xamanek Researches, 1997. [SHPD ID: 2019LI81383]

Fredericksen, Erik M. *Archaeological Reconnaissance Report for the County of Maui Honokōhau Water System Improvements Project, Lahaina District, Maui Island.* Pukalani, HI: Xamanek Researches, 1998. [SHPD ID: 2019LI80994]

Fredericksen, Erik M. *Preservation Plan for Possible Burial Features Contained Within Sites 50-50-01-5139, 5142, 5157 and 5158 Located on the Kapalua Mauka Project area, Honokahua and Napili 2 & 3 Ahupuaʻa, Lahaina District, Island of Maui.* Pukalani, HI: Xamanek Researches, 2003. [SHPD ID: 2019LI81407]

Fredericksen, Erik M. and Demaris Fredericksen. *Archaeological Inventory Survey for the Proposed Honokōhau Water System Improvement Project, Honokōhau Ahupuaʻa, Kāʻanapali District, Maui Island. DRAFT.* Pukalani, HI: Xamanek Researches, 1999. [SHPD ID: 2019LI80995]

Fredericksen, Erik M. and Demaris L. Fredericksen. *An Archaeological Inventory Survey (Phase 2) of a New Alignment for the Honokōhau Waterline Project, Honokōhau, Ahupuaʻa, Kāʻanapali District, Island of Maui.* Pukalani, HI: Xamanek Researches, 2002. [SHPD ID: 2019LI81426]

Fredericksen, Erik M. and Demaris L. Fredericksen. *An Archaeological Inventory Survey of Honoapiʻilani Highway Corridor from Alaelae Point to Honolua Bay, Honolua and Honokahua Ahupuaʻa, Lahaina District, Maui Island.* Pukalani, HI: Xamanek Researches, 2000. [SHPD ID: 2019LI81045]

Fredericksen, Erik M. and Demaris L. Fredericksen. *Archaeological Inventory Survey of The Lower Honoapiʻilani Road Improvements Project Corridor.* Pukalani, HI: Xamanek Researches, 1999. [SHPD ID: 2021LI00220]

Fredericksen, Erik M. and J. J. Frey. *An Archaeological Monitoring Report for the Kāʻanapali Shores Roadway Improvements Project, Honokōwai Ahupuaʻa, Lahaina District, Maui.* Pukalani, HI: Xamanek Researches, 2008. [SHPD ID: 2019LI81243]

Fredericksen, Erik M. and Jennifer J. Frey. *An Archaeological Inventory Survey of a portion of land in Mailepai Ahupuaʻa, Lahaina District, Maui Island.* Pukalani, HI: Xamanek Researches, 2008. [SHPD ID: 2019LI81302]

Fredericksen, Erik M., Demaris Fredericksen, and W. M. Fredericksen. *An Archaeological Inventory Survey at Honokōwai Beach Park, Honokōwai Ahupuaʻa, Lahaina District, Maui Island.* Pukalani, HI: Xamanek Researches, 1994. [No location available]

Fredericksen, Erik M., Demaris L. Fredericksen, and Walter M. Fredericksen. *An Archaeological Inventory Survey of a 12.2 Acre Parcel. Honokahua and Napili*

2-3 Ahupuaʻa, Lahaina District Maui Island. Pukalani, HI: Xamanek Researches, 1994. [SHPD ID: 2019LI81030]

Fredericksen, Walter M. *An Historic and Traditional Land Use Study Utilizing Oral History Interviews for Assessing Cultural Impacts, for the Kapalua Project 2 and Expanded Project 2, Kapalua, Maui, Hawaiʻi.* Pukalani, HI: Xamanek Researches, 2001. [No location available]

Fredericksen, Walter M. *Archaeological Monitoring Report for the Remodeling Project of the Lahaina Yacht Club, 835 Front Street, Paunau Ahupuaʻa, Lahaina District, Island of Maui.* Pukalani, HI: Xamanek Researches, 2002. [SHPD ID: 2019LI80645]

Fredericksen, Walter M. and Demaris Fredericksen. *Archaeological Monitoring Report for The Kai Ala Subdivision, Ahupuaʻa of Hanakaoʻo, Lahaina District, Island of Maui.* Pukalani, HI: Xamanek Researches, 1996. [SHPD ID: 2019LI81251]

Fredericksen, Walter M. and Demaris L. Fredericksen. *Archaeological Data Recovery Report on the Plantation Inn Site, Lahaina, Maui, Hawaiʻi.* Pukalani, HI: Xamanek Researches, 1990. [SHPD ID: 2019LI81589; UH Call Number: DU629.L3 F738 1990a]

Fredericksen, Walter M. and Demaris L. Fredericksen. *Archaeological Data Recovery Report on the Plantation Inn Site, Lahaina, Maui, Hawaiʻi.* Pukalani, HI: Xamanek Researches, 1993. [SHPD ID: 2019LI81589]

Fredericksen, Walter M. and Demaris L. Fredericksen. *Report on the Archaeological Excavation Conducted at Hale Paʻi Site, 1981-1982.* Pukalani, HI: Xamanek Researches, 1988. [SHPD ID: 2019LI81532]

Fredericksen, Walter M. and Demaris L. Fredericksen. *Report on the Archaeological Excavation of the "Brick Palace" of King Kamehameha I at Lahaina, Maui, Hawaiʻi, 1965.* [SHPD ID: 2019LI81384; UH Call Number: DU629.L3 F74]

Fredericksen, Walter M. Jr. and Demaris L. Fredericksen. *Report on the Excavation of the Outbuildings Adjacent to the Baldwin House, Undertaken for the Lahaina Restoration Foundation, Lahaina, Maui, Hawaiʻi.* Pukalani, HI: Xamanek Researches, 1978. [SHPD ID: 2019LI81568]

Fredericksen, Walter M., Demaris Fredericksen, and Erik M. Fredericksen. *Report on the Archaeological Inventory Survey at Historic Site #15, Lahaina Maui, Hawaiʻi.* Pukalani, HI: Xamanek Researches, 1988. [SHPD ID: 2019LI81406]

Fredericksen, Walter M., Demaris L. Fredericksen, and Erik M. Fredericksen. *An Archaeological Inventory Survey of a Parcel of Land Adjacent to Malu-Ulu-o-Lele*

Park, Lahaina, Maui, Hawaiʻi. Pukalani, HI: Xamanek Researches, 1989. [SHPD ID: 2019LI81548]

Fredericksen, Walter M., Demaris L. Fredericksen, and Erik M. Fredericksen. *An Archaeological Inventory Survey of the Plantation Inn Site, Lahaina, Maui, Hawaiʻi.* Pukalani, HI: Xamanek Researches, 1989. [SHPD ID: 2019LI81588]

Fredericksen, Walter M., Demaris L. Fredericksen, and Erik M. Fredericksen. *Archaeological Data Recovery Report on the AUS Site, Lahaina, Maui, Hawaiʻi.* Pukalani, HI: Xamanek Researches, 1989. [SHPD ID: 2019LI81562]

Fredericksen, Walter M., Demaris L. Fredericksen, and Erik M. Fredericksen. *The AUS Site: H. S. #50-03-1797 A Preliminary Archaeological Inventory Survey Report.* Pukalani, HI: Xamanek Researches, 1989. [No location available]

Frey, Jennifer J., Ryan Luskin, Angela L. Yates, and Hallett H. Hammatt. *Archaeological Monitoring Report for the Hololani Resort Condominiums Shoreline Protection Project, Kahana Ahupuaʻa, Lahaina District, Maui Island.* Wailuku, HI: Cultural Surveys Hawaiʻi, Inc., 2019. [SHPD ID: 2019LI81312]

Frost, Lockwood H. *A Report and Recommendations on the Restoration and Preservation of Hale Aloha, Lahaina, Maui,* 1973. [No location available]

Goodwin, Conrad and Spencer Leinewebber. *Archaeological Inventory Survey Report, Pioneer Mil Company, Ltd. Sugar Enterprise Lands, Site No. 50-50-03-4420, Villages of Leialiʻi Project, Lahaina, Maui Hawaiʻi.* Honolulu, HI: International Archaeological Research Institute, Inc., 1997. [SHPD ID: 2019LI81363]

Graves, Donna and Susan Goodfellow. *Archaeological Inventory Survey, Launiupoko Golf Course, Land of Launiupoko, Lahaina District, Island of Maui.* Hilo, HI: Paul H. Rosendahl, Ph.D., Inc., 1991. [SHPD ID: 2019LI81595, 2019LI81610]

Griffin, Bion P. and George W. Lovelace, eds. *Survey and Salvage—Honoapiʻilani Highway: The Archaeology of Kāʻanapali from Honokōwai to ʻAlaeloa Ahupuaʻa.* Lāwaʻi, HI: Archaeological Research Center Hawaiʻi, Inc., 1977. [UH Call Number: DU628.M3 A7 1977]

Guerriero, Diane and Jeffrey *Pantaleo. Archaeological Inventory Survey Report of a 0.361 Acre Coastal Parcel, Waineʻe Ahupuaʻa, Lahaina District, Island of Maui.* Wailuku, HI: Archaeological Services Hawaii, LLC, 2005. [SHPD ID: 2019LI81560]

Guerriero, Diane, Lisa Rotunno-Hazuka, and Jeffrey Pantaleo. *Archaeological Assessment for the Royal Lahaina Resort Redevelopment Hanakaʻōʻō Ahupuaʻa,*

Lahaina District, Island of Maui. Wailuku, HI: Archaeological Services Hawaii, LLC, 2005. [SHPD ID: 2019LI81261]

Hammatt, Hallett H. *An Archaeological Field Inspection of the Lahaina Bypass Highway, Phase 1A, Keawe Street Extension to Lahainaluna Road, and Current Condition of SIHP Number -2484.* Wailuku, HI: Cultural Surveys Hawai'i, Inc., 2007. [SHPD ID: 2019LI81366]

Hammatt, Hallett H. *Archaeological Investigation and Monitoring, Mala Wharf Boat-Launch Ramp Area, Lahaina, Maui Island.* Lāwa'i, HI: Archaeological Research Center Hawai'i, Inc., 1978. [SHPD ID: 2019LI81387; UH Call Number: GN486 .H35]

Hammatt, Hallett H. *Archaeological Preservation Plan for 10 Sites Within for 440 Acre Parcel, Ahupua'a of Ukumehame, Lahaina District, Island of Maui.* Wailuku, HI: Cultural Surveys Hawai'i, Inc., 2000. [SHPD ID: 2019LI81626]

Hammatt, Hallett H. *Restoration Plan for Pole 69 (Original Location) at Ukumehame Gulch, Ma'alaea to Lahaina Third 69 KV Transmission Line.* Wailuku, HI: Cultural Surveys Hawai'i, Inc., 1996. [SHPD ID: 2019LI81632]

Hammatt, Hallett H. and David W. Shideler. *Draft Proposal for an Archaeological Mitigation Plan at the Lahaina Courthouse, Lahaina, Lahaina District, Maui Island, Hawai'i.* Wailuku, HI: Cultural Surveys Hawai'i, Inc., 1999. [SHPD ID: 2019LI81400]

Hammatt, Hallett H. and David W. Shideler. *Preservation Plan for Four Sites (50-50-01-5234, A Water Exploration Tunnel; -5235, A Petroglyph; -5425, A Historic Trail, and -5426, A Pre-Contact Habitation Site) Located Within a 400-Acre Parcel at Honolua Ahupua'a.* Wailuku, HI: Cultural Surveys Hawai'i, Inc., 2003. [SHPD ID: 2019LI81003]

Hammatt, Hallett H. and David W. Shideler. *Written Findings of Archaeological Monitoring at the Lahaina Courthouse, Lahaina, Lahaina District, Maui Island, Hawai'i.* Wailuku, HI: Cultural Surveys Hawai'i, Inc., 1998. [SHPD ID: 2019LI81401]

Hammatt, Hallett H. and Rodney Chiogioji. *Archaeological Monitoring Plan for a ½-Acre parcel in Napili 2-3 Ahupua'a, Lahaina District, Island of Maui.* Wailuku, HI: Cultural Surveys Hawai'i, Inc., 2002. [SHPD ID: 2019LI81063]

Hammatt, Hallett H., David W. Shideler, and Tony Bush. *Archaeological Inventory Survey of an Approximately 400-Acre Parcel at Honolua Ahupua'a Lahaina District of Maui.* Wailuku, HI: Cultural Surveys Hawai'i, Inc., 2003. [SHPD ID: 2019LI80993]

Hart, Christopher. *Final Report of the Preparation for Exhibit of King Kame-hameha I's "Brick Palace" at Lahaina, Maui, Hawai'i.* Maui Historic Commission, 1970.

Haun, A. E. *Subsurface Archaeological Reconnaissance Survey, Lahaina Cannery Makai and Mauka Parcels, Land of Moali'i, Lahaina District, Island of Maui,* 1988. [SHPD ID: 2019LI80612]

Haun, Alan E. *Archaeological Assessment, Lands of Polanui, Polaiki, and Launiu-poko, Lahaina District, Island of Maui.* Kailua-Kona, HI: Haun and Associates, 2002. [SHPD ID: 2019LI81608]

Haun, Alan E. *Archaeological Inventory Survey Kaua'ula Development Parcel, Lands of Pūehuehu Iki, Pāhoa, and Pola Nui, Lahaina District, Island of Maui.* Kailua-Kona, HI: Haun and Associates, 1999. [No location available]

Haun, Alan E. and Jack D. Henry. *Archaeological Data Recovery Plan Sites 4141 and 4143, Land of Honolua, Lahaina District, Island of Maui,* 2002. [SHPD ID: 2019LI81010]

Havel, BreAnna and Michael F. Dega. *An Archaeological Assessment Report on 0.11 Acres of Partially Developed Land in Honokōwai Ahupua'a, Lahaina District, Maui Island, Hawai'i.* Honolulu, HI: Scientific Consultant Services, Inc., 2005. [SHPD ID: 2019LI81285]

Heidel, Melody, William H. Folk, and Hallett H. Hammatt. *An Archaeological Inventory Survey for Waiola Church, Ahupua'a of Waine'e, Lahaina District, Island of Maui.* Wailuku, HI: Cultural Surveys Hawai'i, Inc., 1994. [SHPD ID: 2019LI81552]

Hill, Robert R., Thomas K. Devereux, and Hallett H. Hammatt. *An Archaeological Assessment of a 9.650 Acre Parcel, 'Alaeloa Ahupua'a, Lahaina District, Maui Island, for the West Maui Village Project.* Wailuku, HI: Cultural Surveys Hawai'i, Inc., 2006. [SHPD ID: 2019LI81037]

Hoerman, Rachel and Michael F. Dega. *An Archaeological Monitoring Plan for the Pavilion Restaurant Renovation at the Hyatt Regency Maui Resort and Spa, Kā'anapali, Hanaka'ō'ō Ahupua'a, Lahaina District, Maui Island, Hawai'i.* Honolulu, HI: Scientific Consultant Services, Inc., 2007. [SHPD ID: 2019LI80666, 2019LI80665]

Hommon, Robert J. *An Archaeological Reconnaissance Survey of an Area Near Waine'e Village, West Maui.* Hawai'i: Science Management, Inc., 1982. [SHPD ID: 2019LI81389; UH Call Number: DU629.W346 H66 1982]

Hommon, Robert J. *An Archaeological Reconnaissance Survey of the North Beach Mauka and South Beach Beach Mauka Areas, Hanaka'ō'ō, West Maui.* Hawai'i: Science Management, Inc., 1982. [No location available]

Hommon, Robert J. *Report on a Walk Through Survey of the Kahoma Stream Flood Control Project Area.* Honolulu, HI: Department of Anthropology, Bernice P. Bishop Museum, 1973.

Hommon, Robert J. and Hamilton M. Ahlo, Jr. *An Archaeological Reconnaissance Survey of the Site of a Proposed Airstrip at Māhinahina, West Maui.* Science Management, Inc., 1982. [SHPD ID: 2019LI81050; UH Call Number: DU629. M345 H66 1982]

Jensen, Peter A. and Jenny O'Claray. *Supplemental Archaeological Survey, Lahaina Master Planned Project Offsite Sewer, Water Improvements, and Cane Haul Road.* Hilo, HI: Paul H. Rosendahl, Ph.D., Inc., 1991. [SHPD ID: 2019LI81419]

Jensen, Peter M. *Archaeological Inventory Survey Honoapi'ilani Highway Realignment Project Lahaina Bypass Section—Modified Corridor Alignment, Lands of Honokōwai, Hanaka'ō'ō, Wahikuli, Pana'ewa, Ku'ia, Halaka'a, Pūehuehu Nui, Pāhoa, Polanui, and Launiupoko, Lahaina District, Island of Maui.* Hilo, HI: Paul H. Rosendahl, Ph.D., Inc., 1991. [SHPD ID: 2019LI81242]

Jensen, Peter M. *Archaeological Inventory Survey Lahaina Bypass Highway New Connector Roads Project Area, Ahupua'a of Hanaka'ō'ō and Paunau, Lahaina District, Island of Maui.* Hilo, HI: Paul H. Rosendahl, Ph.D., Inc., 1994. [SHPD ID: 2019LI81611]

Jensen, Peter M. *Archaeological Inventory Survey Lahaina Master Planned Project Site: Land of Wahikuli, Lahaina District, Island of Maui.* Hilo, HI: Paul H. Rosendahl, Ph.D., Inc., 1989. [SHPD ID: 2019LI80636]

Jensen, Peter M. *Archaeological Inventory Survey South Beach Mauka Development Site, Ahupua'a of Hanaka'ō'ō, Lahaina District, Island of Maui.* Hilo, HI: Paul H. Rosendahl, Ph.D., Inc., 1990. [SHPD ID: 2019LI81262; UH Call Number: DU628.M3 J46 1990]

Jensen, Peter M. and G. Mehalchick. *Archaeological Inventory Survey North Beach Mauka (Kā'anapali) Site, Ahupua'a of Hanaka'ō'ō, Lahaina District, Island of Maui.* Hilo, HI: Paul H. Rosendahl, Ph.D., Inc., 1993. [UH Call Number: DU628.M3 J46 1989]

Jensen, Peter M. and Gemma Mahalchick. *Archaeological Inventory Survey, The Pu'ukoli'i Village Project Area, Ahupua'a of Hanaka'ō'ō, Lahaina District, Island of Maui.* Hilo, HI: Paul H. Rosendahl, Ph.D., Inc., 1992. [SHPD ID: 2019LI81252]

Joerger, Pauline King and Michael W. Kaschko. *A Cultural Historical Overview of the Kahoma Stream Flood Control Project, Lahaina, Maui and Maʻalaea Small Boat Harbor Project, Maʻalaea, Maui.* Honolulu, HI: Hawaiʻi Marine Research, Inc., 1979. [SHPD ID: 2019LI80298; UH Call Number: DU629.L3 J63]

John Carl Warnecke and Associates. *Lahaina Small Boat Harbor Study.* San Francisco, CA: John Carl Warnecke and Associates, Architects and Planning Consultants, 1965. [SHPD ID: 2019LI81397]

Kaschko, Michael W. *Archaeological Survey of the Honolua Development Area, Maui.* Department of Anthropology, Honolulu, HI: Bernice P. Bishop Museum, 1973. [SHPD ID: 2019LI81019]

Kaschko, Michael W. *Archaeological Walk-Through Survey of Specified Areas in the Wailuku Flood Prevention Project and the Honolua Watershed, Maui.* Honolulu, HI: Department of Anthropology, Bernice P. Bishop Museum, 1974. [SHPD ID: 2019LI81443]

Kehajit, Chonnikarn and Michael F. Dega. *Archaeological Assessment for shoreline mitigation at the Hyatt Regency Maui Resort, Hanakaʻōʻō Ahupuaʻa, Lahaina District, Island of Maui, Hawaiʻi.* Honolulu, HI: Scientific Consultant Services, Inc., 2018. [No location available]

Kennedy, Joseph. *Archaeological Inventory Survey of Kahana, Maui.* Haleʻiwa, HI: Archaeological Consultants of Hawaii, 1985. [No location available]

Kennedy, Joseph. *Archaeological Investigations at Kahana, Maui,* 1986. [No location available]

Kennedy, Joseph. *Archaeological Walk Through Examination of Quarry Site located Mauka of Honoapiʻilani Highway near Lipoa Point, Honolua, Maui.* Haleʻiwa, HI: Archaeological Consultants of Hawaii, 1988. [SHPD ID: 2019LI81425]

Kennedy, Joseph. *Field Inspection: Stone Building at Kahana,* Maui, 1986. [SHPD ID: 2019LI81332]

Kennedy, Joseph. *Hawea Point Residential Project: Archaeological Review, Survey, and Assessments.* Haleʻiwa, HI: Archaeological Consultants of Hawaii, 1990. [SHPD ID: 2019LI81416]

Kirch, Patrick V. *Archaeological Excavations at Site D13-1, Hawea Point, Maui, Hawaiian Islands.* Honolulu, HI: Department of Anthropology, Bernice P. Bishop Museum, 1973. [SHPD ID: 2019LI81021; UH Call Number: DU629. H393 K57 1973]

Kirch, Patrick V. *Archaeological Survey of the Honolua Development Area, Maui.* Honolulu, HI: Department of Anthropology, Bernice P. Bishop Museum, 1973. [SHPD ID: 2019LI81019; UH Call Number: DU629.K374 K57 1973]

Klieger, Paul Christiaan and Susan A. Lebo. *Archaeological Inventory Survey of Waiōlaʻi and Waiokila Catchments, Kahakuloa, West Maui, Hawaiʻi.* Honolulu, HI: Department of Anthropology, Bernice P. Bishop Museum, 1995. [No location available]

Knecht, Daniel P. and Timothy M. Rieth. *Archaeological Monitoring Plan for the Lahainaluna High School New Classroom Building Project, Panaʻewa Ahupuaʻa, Lahaina District, Maui.* Honolulu, HI: International Archaeology, LLC. [No location available]

Komori, Eric K. *Archaeological Investigations at Kahana Gulch, Lahaina District, Maui.* Honolulu, HI: Department of Anthropology, Bernice P. Bishop Museum, 1983. [SHPD ID: 2019LI81070; UH Call Number: DU629.K343 K66 1983]

Ladd, Edmund J. *Archaeological Survey Report,* 1980. [No location available]

Launiupoko Associates, LLC. *Archaeological Preservation Plan, Mahanalua Nui Subdivision.* Launiupoko Associates, 1998. [SHPD ID: 2019LI81602]

Lee-Greig, Tanya, Constance OʻHare, Hallett H. Hammatt, Robert R. Hill, and Colleen Dagan. *Archaeological Data Recovery and Additional Testing at Land Commission Award 310: Pikaneleʻs Kuleana at Pakala, Pakala Ahupuaʻa, Lahaina District, Maui Island.* Wailuku, HI: Cultural Surveys Hawaiʻi, Inc., 2010. [SHPD ID: 2019LI81573]

Lee-Greig, Tanya L. and Hallett H. Hammatt. *An Archaeological Inventory Level Documentation for an Inadvertent Historic Property Discovery Identified During Pre-Construction Walk Through for the Lahaina Bypass Phase IA, Project: State Inventory of Historic properties 50-50-03-6277 (Lee-Greig et al. 2008).* Wailuku, HI: Cultural Surveys Hawaiʻi, Inc., 2009. [No location available]

Lee-Greig, Tanya L. and Hallett H. Hammatt. *An Archaeological Monitoring Plan for Whalers Village Renovation and Expansion Project, Hanakaʻōʻō Ahupuaʻa, Lahaina District, Maui Island.* Wailuku, HI: Cultural Surveys Hawaiʻi, Inc., 2014. [SHPD ID: 2019LI80675]

Lee-Greig, Tanya L. and Hallett H. Hammatt. *Archaeological Inventory Survey Plan for the Proposed Mokuhinia Ecosystem Restoration Project Waiokama and Lower Waineʻe Ahupuaʻa, Lahaina District, Maui Island.* Wailuku, HI: Cultural Surveys Hawaiʻi, Inc., 2014. [SHPD ID: 2019LI81554]

Lee-Greig, Tanya L. and Hallett H. Hammatt. *Archaeological Monitoring Plan for the Lahaina Bypass Modified Alignment from Kahoma Stream to the Keawe Street Extension, Kelawea, Paeohi, and Wahikuli Ahupua'a, Lahaina District, Maui Island.* Wailuku, HI: Cultural Surveys Hawai'i, Inc., 2009. [SHPD ID: 2019LI81369]

Lee-Greig, Tanya L. and Hallett H. Hammatt. *Preservation Plan for Thirty-Three Historic Properties Located in and Adjacent to the Kapalua Mauka Project Area, Honokahua, Nāpili 2 & 3, and Nāpili 4-5 Ahupua'a, Lahaina District, Maui Island.* Wailuku, HI: Cultural Surveys Hawai'i, Inc., 2005. [SHPD ID: 2019LI80997]

Liston, Jolie. *Archaeological Monitoring of Trenching Activities at Taco Bell, Lahaina, Maui.* Honolulu, HI: International Archaeological Research Institute, Inc., 1999. [SHPD ID: 2019LI80605]

Lum, Francis. *Amendment to Testing at Kahana Desilting Basin, Holoua [Honolua?] Watershed, Lahaina District, Maui, Hawai'i, Francis Lum, Soil Conservation Service.* Soil Conservation Service, 1983. [SHPD ID: 2019LI81058]

Lyman, Kepa and Michael F. *Dega. Archaeological Monitoring Plan for the Hanaka'ō'ō Beach Park Parking Improvements, Hanaka'ō'ō Ahupua'a, Lahaina (Kā'anapali) District, Island of Maui.* Honolulu, HI: Scientific Consultant Services, Inc., 2020. [SHPD ID: 2021LI00062]

Madeus, Jonas K., Tanya L. Lee-Greig, and Hallett H. Hammatt. *Archaeological Assessment of an 80-Acre Parcel in Kapalua, Honolua Ahupua'a, Lahaina District, Maui Island.* Wailuku, HI: Cultural Surveys Hawai'i, Inc., 2005. [SHPD ID: 2019LI80999]

Magnuson, Carol M. *Supplemental Archaeological Survey of Turbine Pad Alignments, Kaheawa Pastures, Upland Ukumehame Ahupua'a, Maui.* Honolulu, HI: International Archaeological Research Institute, Inc., 2003. [SHPD ID: 2019LI81630]

Masterson, Ian and Hallett H. Hammatt. *An Addendum Report for the New Alignment Section between Points 14D, 15, and 16 along the Proposed Ma'alaea-Lahaina Third 69 kV Transmission Line, Maui.* Wailuku, HI: Cultural Surveys Hawai'i, Inc., 1995. [SHPD ID: 2019LI81633]

Masterson, Ian and Hallett H. Hammatt. *Report on the Completed Reconstruction of Walls at Hiki'i Heiau Ukumehame Ahupua'a, Island of Maui.* Wailuku, HI: Cultural Surveys Hawai'i, Inc., 1999. [SHPD ID: 2019LI81631]

McGerty, Leann and Robert L. Spear. *A Cultural Impact Assessment for a portion of the Mauian Hotel Property, Nāpili Ahupua'a, Lahaina District, Maui Island,*

Hawaiʻi. Honolulu, HI: Scientific Consultant Services, Inc., 2007. [SHPD ID: 2019LI81065]

McGerty, Leann and Robert L. Spear. *A Cultural Impact Assessment for Maui Marriott Ocean Club, Situated in the Ahupuaʻa of Hanakaʻōʻō, Lahaina District, Island of Maui, Hawaiʻi*. Honolulu, HI: Scientific Consultant Services, Inc., 2002. [SHPD ID: 2019LI80664]

McGerty, Leann and Robert L. Spear. *An Archaeological Inventory Survey at the Maui Marriott Ocean Club, in the Ahupuaʻa of Hanakaʻōʻō, Lahaina District, Island of Maui, Hawaiʻi*. Honolulu, HI: Scientific Consultant Services, Inc., 2002. [SHPD ID: 2019LI80107]

McGerty, Leann and Robert L. Spear. *Cultural Impact Assessment on Two Parcels Incorporating the Royal Lahaina Hotel in Kāʻanapali, Hanakaʻōʻō Ahupuaʻa, Lahaina District, Maui Island, Hawaiʻi*. Honolulu, HI: Scientific Consultant Services, Inc., 2005. [SHPD ID: 2019LI80678]

McGerty, Leanne and Robert L. Spear. *Cultural Impact Assessment of a Parcel of Land in Lahaina Town, Alio Ahupuaʻa, Lahaina District, Maui Island, Hawaiʻi*. Honolulu, HI: Scientific Consultant Services, Inc., 2007. [SHPD ID: 2019LI81360]

Medeiros, Colleen and Hallett H. Hammatt. *Archaeological Monitoring Report for the Kāʻanapali North Beach Development Area, Lot 3, Site Excavation, Honokōwai Ahupuaʻa, Lahaina District, Maui Island*. Wailuku, HI: Cultural Surveys Hawaiʻi, Inc., 2017. [SHPD ID: 2019LI80652]

Monahan, Christopher M. *An Archaeological Inventory Survey Report on Three Contiguous Parcels Measuring Approximately 25.3 Acres in Kapalua, Napili 2-3 Ahupuaʻa, Lahaina District, Maui Island, Hawaiʻi*. Honolulu, HI: Scientific Consultant Services, Inc., 2005. [SHPD ID: 2019LI81018]

Monahan, Christopher M., Lauren Morawski, and Michael F. Dega. *Archaeological Monitoring Plan for Pool Installation at TMK (2) 4-5-04:037 Lahilahi Street, Kuʻia Ahupuaʻa, Lahaina District, Island of Maui*. Honolulu, HI: Scientific Consultant Services, Inc., 2003. [No location available]

Mooney, Kimberly M. and Paul L. Cleghorn. *Archaeological Monitoring Report for the Lahaina Small Boat Harbor Comfort Station Improvements, Lahaina, Maui*. Kailua, HI: Pacific Legacy, Inc., 2007. [SHPD ID: 2019LI81379]

Mooney, Kimberly M., Paul L. Cleghorn, and Elizabeth L. Kahahane. *Archaeological Inventory Survey for the Lahaina Pier Improvement Project Waineʻe*

Ahupuaʻa, Lahaina District, Island of Maui. Kailua, HI: Pacific Legacy, Inc., 2008. [SHPD ID: 2019LI81382]

Moore, Kenneth R. *Archaeological Survey of Honolua Valley, Maui.* Honolulu, HI: Department of Anthropology, Bernice P. Bishop Museum, 1974. [SHPD ID: 2019LI81436; UH Call Number: DU629.H69 M66 1974]

Morawski, Lauren and Michael F. Dega. *Archaeological Inventory Survey Report of an Approximate 10-Acre Parcel in Kapalua in the Ahupuaʻa of Honokahua, Lahaina District (Formerly Kāʻanapali), Island of Maui, Hawaiʻi.* Honolulu, HI: Scientific Consultant Services, Inc., 2004. [SHPD ID: 2019LI81017]

Munekiyo & Hiraga, Inc. *Historic Resources Inventory Submittal, Makaʻoiʻoi Demolition.* Wailuku, HI: Munekiyo & Hiraga, Inc., 2003. [SHPD ID: 2019LI81049]

Munekiyo & Hiraga, Inc. *Makaʻoiʻoi (Honolua Plantation Managers Residence, Pineapple Hill Restaurant), Historical Report.* Wailuku, HI: Munekiyo & Hiraga, Inc., 2003. [SHPD ID: 2019LI81022]

Munekiyo, Michael T. *Redevelopment of ABC Store at 726 Front Street, Application for Historic District Approval.* Wailuku, HI: Michael T. Munekiyo Consulting, Inc., 1993. [SHPD ID: 2019LI81540]

Nagata, Ralston H. *CDUA-MA-5/12/82-1407, Land Clearing and Planting of Commercially Valuable Tree Species at Kahakuloa, Wailuku, Maui. Memorandum to: Roger Evans, Planning Office from DLNR, Division of State Parks,* 1983. [No location available]

Nagata, Ralston H. and Martha Yent. *CDUA: MA-1436, Taro Planting at Kahakuloa Valley, Wailuku, Maui. Memorandum to Mr. Roger Evans, Planning Office from DLNR, Division of State Parks,* 1982. [UH Call Number: DU629. K344 N34 1982]

Neller, Earl. *An Archaeological Reconnaissance Along the Coast at Ukumehame, Maui,* 1982. [SHPD ID: 2019LI81640; UH Call Number: DU629.U38 N45 1982]

Neller, Earl. *An Archaeological Reconnaissance of Hahakea Beach Park, Hanakaʻōʻō, Maui.* Honolulu, HI: State of Hawaiʻi Preservation Office, 1982. [SHPD ID: 2019LI81272; UH Call Number: DU629.H364 N45 1982]

OʻClaray, Jenny. *Additional Field Work for Drainage 11 Kapalua Plantation Estates Project Area, Lands of Honokahua, Honolua, Napili 2-2 Lahaina District, Island of Maui.* Hilo, HI: Paul H. Rosendahl, Ph.D., Inc., 1991. [SHPD ID: 2019LI81415]

O'Day, Patrick and David Byerly. *Archaeological Inventory Survey of Proposed Fenceline Corridor for the West Maui Forest Reserve, Kuʻia, Mākila, Pāhoa, Halakaʻa, Polaiki, Launiupoko, and Olowalu Ahupuaʻa, Lahaina District, Maui Island, Hawaiʻi.* Kailua, HI: Garcia & Associates, 2015. [SHPD ID: 2019LI81533]

O'Hare, Constance, Thomas K. Devereux, William H. Folk, and Hallett H. Hammatt. *Preservation Plan for Specific Sites in the Land Comprising Project District 2 at Kapalua, Honokahua and Nāpili 2 & 3 Ahupuaʻa Lahaina District of Maui.* Wailuku, HI: Cultural Surveys Hawaiʻi, Inc., 2003. [SHPD ID: 2019LI81002]

Oceanit. *Final Sampling Analysis Plan: Field Sampling and Quality Assurance Plans for the Mokuhinia Pond Site Investigation, Lahaina, Maui, Hawaiʻi.* Honolulu, HI: Oceanit, 2009. [SHPD ID: 2019LI81553]

Olowalu Elua Associates, LLC. *Archaeological Mitigation and Preservation Plan, Makai Portion (Phase 1), Olowalu Ahupuaʻa, Lahaina District, Maui Island.* Olowalu, HI: Olowalu Elua Associates, LLC, 2001.

Olowalu Elua Associates, LLC. *Archaeological Preservation Plan, Mauka Portion (Phase 2), Olowalu Ahupuaʻa, Lahaina District, Maui Island.* Olowalu, HI: Olowalu Elua Associates, LLC, 2002. [SHPD ID: 2019LI00099]

Olson, Larry G. *Appendix II—A Geoarchaeological Report of Site 225, Māhinahina Gulch, Maui, Hawaiʻi.* Lāwaʻi, HI: Archaeological Research Center Hawaiʻi, 1977. [No location available]

Pantaleo, Jeffrey. *Archaeological Survey of the Proposed Lahainaluna Reservoir and Treatment Facility, Lahaina, Maui.* Honolulu, HI: Public Archaeology Section, Applied Research Group, Bernice P. Bishop Museum, 1991. [SHPD ID: 2019LI81530]

Perzinski, David. *Archaeological Field Inspection for the West Maui Recycled Water Expansion Project, Phase 2 County Job No. WW12-13, Lahaina, Maui, Hawaiʻi.* Honolulu, HI: Scientific Consultant Services, Inc., 2013. [No location available]

Perzinski, David and Michael F. Dega. *An Archaeological Assessment of a Seawall/ Revetment Structure in Honokōwai.* Honolulu, HI: Scientific Consultant Services, Inc., 2013. [SHPD ID: 2019LI81283]

Perzinski, David and Michael F. Dega. *An Archaeological Inventory Survey of Three Contiguous Parcels of Land Totaling 0.417 Acres in Waineʻe Ahupuaʻa, Lahaina District, Maui Island, Hawaiʻi.* Honolulu, HI: Scientific Consultant Services, Inc., 2011. [SHPD ID: 2019LI81543]

Perzinski, David and Michael F. Dega. *An Archaeological Inventory Survey Report for a Bridge Replacement in Honolua, Honolua Ahupuaʻa, Lahaina District, Maui Island.* Honolulu, HI: Scientific Consultant Services, Inc., 2010. [SHPD ID: 2019LI81430]

Perzinski, David and Michael F. Dega. *An Archaeological Monitoring Report for the Installation of Subsurface Utilities in Nāpili, Kapalua, Honokahua Ahupuaʻa, Lahaina District, Island of Maui, Hawaiʻi.* Honolulu, HI: Scientific Consultant Services, Inc., 2015. [SHPD ID: 2019LI81034]

Perzinski, David and Michael F. Dega. *An Archaeological Monitoring Report of the Construction at the Maui Marriott Vacation Club, Hanakaʻōʻō Ahupuaʻa, Lahaina District, Island of Maui, Hawaiʻi.* Honolulu, HI: Scientific Consultant Services, Inc., 2009. [No location available]

Perzinski, David and Michael F. Dega. *Archaeological Assessment for the West Maui Well No. 2 Exploratory, DWS Job No. 11-06, Kahana Ahupuaʻa, Lahaina (Kāʻanapali) District, Maui, Hawaiʻi.* Honolulu, HI: Scientific Consultant Services, Inc., 2014. [SHPD ID: 2019LI81057]

Peterson, Charles E. *Notes on the Lahaina Court and Custom House, Lahaina, Maui, Hawaiʻi, Built 1859,* 1966. [SHPD ID: 2019LI81376]

Pickett, Jenny L. and Michael F. Dega. *An Archaeological Inventory Survey of 583 Acres at Lipoa Point, Honolua Ahupuaʻa, Lahaina (Formerly Kāʻanapali) District, Maui Island, Hawaiʻi.* Honolulu, HI: Scientific Consultant Services, Inc., 2006. [SHPD ID: 2019LI81431]

Pietrusewsky, Michael and Michele T. Douglas. *An Analysis of Additional Historic Human Skeletal Remains from the Kahoma Stream Flood Control Project, 1989, Lahaina, Maui.* Honolulu, HI: University of Hawaiʻi at Mānoa, 1990. [SHPD ID: DU629.L3 P54 1990]

Pietrusewsky, Michael, Michele T. Douglas, and Rona Ikehara. *An Osteological Study of Human Remains from the Kahoma Stream Flood Control Project, Lahaina, Maui.* Honolulu, HI: University of Hawaiʻi at Mānoa, 1989. [UH Call Number: DU629.K76 P54 1989]

Pietrusewsky, Michael, Michele T. Douglas, Patricia A. Kalima, and Rona M. Ikehara. *Human Skeletal and Dental Remains from the Honokahua Burial Site, Land of Honokahua, Lahaina District, Island of Maui, Hawaiʻi.* Hilo, HI: Paul H. Rosendahl, Ph.D., Inc., 1991. [Call Number, DU629.H67 H86 1991a]

Pyle, Dorothy. "The Intriguing Seamen's Hospital." *The Hawaiian Journal of History,* vol. 8, 1974, pp. 121–135. [UH Call Number: DU620 .H44]

Rechtman, Robert B. *Archaeological Monitoring Report Associated with the Demolition of the Pioneer Mill, Pana'ewa Ahupua'a, Lahaina District, Island of Maui.* Rechtman Consulting, LLC, 2006. [SHPD ID: 2019LI80602]

Riford, Mary F. and Paul L. Cleghorn. *Documentary Assessment of Archaeological Potential of Ten Prospective Power Plant Sites on Maui.* Honolulu, HI: Public Archaeology Section, Bernice P. Bishop Museum, 1989. [SHPD ID: 2022LI00168]

Rogers, Donnell J. and Paul H. Rosendahl. *Archaeological Survey and Recording Iliilikea and Maiu Heiau on the North Coast of Maui, Land of Honokōhau, Lahaina District, Island of Maui.* Hilo, HI: Paul H. Rosendahl, Ph.D., Inc., 1992. [SHPD ID: 2019LI81440]

Rosendahl, Margaret L. K. *Archaeological Field Inspection, Sheraton Maui Master Plan Project Area, Lands of Honokōwai and Hanaka'ō'ō, Lahaina District, Island of Maui.* Hilo, HI: Paul H. Rosendahl, Ph.D., Inc., 1986. [No location available]

Rosendahl, Margaret L. K. *Subsurface Archaeological Reconnaissance Survey, North Beach Development Site, Ahupua'a of Hanaka'ō'ō, Lahaina Eistrict, Island of Maui.* Hilo, HI: Paul H. Rosendahl, Ph.D., Inc., 1987. [SHPD ID: 2019LI81244]

Rosendahl, Paul H. *A Plan for Archaeological Monitoring of Shoreline Construction, Kā'anapali North Beach Development Site, Ahupua'a of Hanaka'ō'ō, Lahaina District, Island of Maui.* Hilo, HI: Paul H. Rosendahl, Ph.D., Inc., 1987. [SHPD ID: 2019LI80659]

Rosendahl, Paul H. *Additional Inventory Survey for Drainage Easement 11 Kapalua Plantation Estates Project Area, Lands of Honokahua, Honolua, and Napili 2-3, Lahaina District, Island of Maui.* Hilo, HI: Paul H. Rosendahl, Ph.D., Inc., 1991. [SHPD ID: 2019LI80996]

Rosendahl, Paul H. *Archaeological Field Inspection Hawea Point Residence Site; Hawea Point, Lands of Napili 2 & 3 Lahaina District, Island of Maui.* Hilo, HI: Paul H. Rosendahl, Ph.D., Inc., 1988. [SHPD ID: 2019LI81001]

Rosendahl, Paul H. *Archaeological Reconnaissance Survey, The Cottages Project Area Kapalua Development Site 2-A, Lands of Honokahua and Napili 2 & 3, Lahaina District, Island of Maui.* Hilo, HI: Paul H. Rosendahl, Ph.D., Inc., 1988. [SHPD ID: 2019LI81009]

Rosendahl, Paul H. *Archaeological Treatment Plan for No Adverse Effect, Lahaina Bypass Highway Project, Lands of Honokōwai, Hanaka'ō'ō, Wahikuli, Pana'ewa, Ku'ia, Halaka'a, Pūehuehu Nui, Pāhoa, Polanui, and Launiupoko, Lahaina*

District, Island of Maui. Hilo, HI: Paul H. Rosendahl, Ph.D., Inc., 1994. [SHPD ID: 2019LI81439]

Rosendahl, Paul H. *Phase I Monitoring Plan: Archaeological Mitigation Program, Ritz-Carlton Hotel Project Site, Land of Honokahua, Lahaina District, Island of Maui. PHRI Memo 857-070390*. Hilo, HI: Paul H. Rosendahl, Ph.D., Inc., 1990. [No location available]

Rosendahl, Paul H. *PHRI Status Reports on Honokahua*. Hilo, HI: Paul H. Rosendahl, Ph.D., Inc., 1987. [SHPD ID: 2019LI81004]

Rosendahl, Paul H. *Subsurface Reconnaissance Testing, Kapalua Place Project Area, Kapalua Development Site 2-A, Lands of Honokahua and Napili 2 & 3, Lahaina District, Island of Maui*. Hilo, HI: Paul H. Rosendahl, Ph.D., Inc., 1988. [SHPD ID: 2019LI81000]

Rotunno-Hazuka, Lisa J. and Jeffrey Pantaleo. *Archaeological Monitoring Plan for the Construction of a Swimming Pool and Associated Utilities at the Allan Residence, Lahaina Ahupua'a, Lahaina District, Island of Maui*. Wailuku, HI: Archaeological Services Hawai'i, LLC, 2004. [SHPD ID: 2019LI80623]

Rotunno-Hazuka, Lisa J. and Jeffrey Pantaleo. *Archaeological Monitoring Plan for the Renovation and Revitalization of the Napili Kai Resort, Napili Ahupua'a, Lahaina District, Island of Maui*. Wailuku, HI: Archaeological Services Hawaii, LLC, 2005. [SHPD ID: 2019LI81067]

Rotunno-Hazuka, Lisa J. and Jeffrey Pantaleo. *Archaeological Monitoring Plan for the Renovations to the Lahaina-Kaiser Clinic, Pana'ewa Ahupua'a, Lahaina District, Island of Maui*. Wailuku, HI: Archaeological Services Hawaii, LLC, 2003. [SHPD ID: 2019LI80608]

Rotunno-Hazuka, Lisa J. and Jeffrey Pantaleo. *Final Archaeological Monitoring Plan for Demolition and New Construction along Front Street, Paunau Ahupua'a, Lahaina District, Kula Moku, Island of Maui*. Wailuku, HI: Archaeological Services Hawaii, LLC, 2018. [SHPD ID: 2019LI80633]

Rotunno-Hazuka, Lisa J. and Jeffrey Pantaleo. *Final Archaeological Monitoring Plan for the Installation of a New Water Service and Relocated Power Pole Along Kalena Street Kelawea Ahupua'a, Lahaina District, Island of Maui*. Wailuku, HI: Archaeological Services Hawaii, LLC, 2015. [No location available]

Rotunno-Hazuka, Lisa J., Mia Watson, and Jeffrey Pantaleo. *Archaeological Monitoring Plan for the Repair and Installation of Underground Conduit at Front & Wharf Street, Lahaina and Waine'e Ahupua'a, Lahaina District, Island of Maui.* Wailuku, HI: Archaeological Services Hawaii, LLC, 2008. [SHPD ID: 2019LI81385]

Scientific Consultant Services, Inc. *An Archaeological Inventory Survey for Six Proposed Solar Voltaic Cell Sites Located in the Ahupuaʻa of Honokahua, Honokeana, and Honokōwai, Lahaina (Kāʻanapali) District, Island of Maui, Hawaiʻi.* Honolulu, HI: Scientific Consultant Services, Inc., 2012. [SHPD ID: 2019LI81005]

Sea Engineering, Inc. *Final Environmental Assessment for Permanent Shore Protection of the Hololani Resort Condominiums Kahananui, Lahaina, Maui.* Honolulu, HI: Sea Engineering, Inc., 2013. [No location available]

Shefcheck, Donna M. and Michael F. Dega. *An Archaeological Monitoring Plan for the Puunoa Subdivision No. 2, Lahaina, Puʻuiki Ahupuaʻa, Lahaina District, Island of Maui, Hawaiʻi.* Honolulu, HI: Scientific Consultant Services, Inc., 2008. [SHPD ID: 2019LI80647]

Shefcheck, Donna M. and Michael F. Dega. *Site Report for a Previously Unrecorded Heiau in Launiupoko Ahupuaʻa, Lahaina District, Island of Maui, Hawaiʻi.* Honolulu, HI: Scientific Consultant Services, Inc., 2006. [SHPD ID: 2019LI81592]

Silva, C. L. *Appendix A: Preliminary Historical Documentary Research, in Archaeological Survey Test Excavations, Kapalua Hotel Development Site 2-H, Kapalua Bay Resort, Land of Honokahua, Lahaina District, Island of Maui. PHRI Report 224-052286,* 1986. [No location available]

Sinoto, Aki. *An Archaeological Reconnaissance of the Mala Wharf Boat Launch Ramp Area, Lahaina, Maui.* Honolulu, HI: Department of Anthropology, Bernice P. Bishop Museum, 1975. [SHPD ID: 2019LI80624; UH Call Number: DU629.M353 S56 1975]

Sinoto, Aki. *Field Examination of Six Sites in the Honolua Watershed, Maui.* Honolulu, HI: Department of Anthropology, Bernice P. Bishop Museum, 1975. [SHPD ID: 2019LI81435; UH Call Number: DU629.H69 S56 1975]

Six, Janet L. *Archaeological Monitoring Plan for Deck and Bar Repairs for: Leilani's on the Beach, Whalers Village Shopping Center, Building J 2435 Kāʻanapali Parkway, Hanakaʻōʻō Ahupuaʻa, Lahaina District, Maui Island.* Pāhoa, HI: Sixth Sense Archaeological Consultants, LLC, 2011. [SHPD ID: 2019LI80676]

Six, Janet L. *Final Archaeological Monitoring Plan for Maui County Work on County Roadway (WTP T20160044) and Grading and Grubbing (GT2016132) Proposed Sunset Terrace Lot Beautification Project Honokōwai Ahupuaʻa, Lahaina*

Project Honokōwai Ahupuaʻa, Lahaina District, Maui Island, Hawaiʻi. Pāhoa, HI: Sixth Sense Archaeological Consultants, LLC, 2018. [SHPD ID: 2019LI81282]

Six, Janet L. *Final Archaeological Monitoring Plan for Special Management Area Application (SMX2017/0098) for the Proposed Kahana Beach Resort DCDA Upgrade, Kahana Ahupuaʻa, Lahaina District, Island of Maui.* Pāhoa, HI: Sixth Sense Archaeological Consultants, LLC, 2018. [SHPD ID: 2019LI81303]

Six, Janet L. *Final Archaeological Monitoring Plan for Work on County Roadway Permit Application (WTP T2017-0055) Installation Communication Utilities, West Maui Village, Kohi & Napilihau St., Napili, ʻAlaeloa Ahupuaʻa, Kāʻanapali District, Island of Maui.* Pāhoa, HI: Sixth Sense Archaeological Consultants, LLC, 2018. [SHPD ID: 2019LI81317]

Smith, Helen Wong. *Historical Documentary Research in Archaeological Inventory Survey, Lahaina Master Planned Project Site, Land of Wahikuli, Lahaina District, Island of Maui.* Hilo, HI: Paul H. Rosendahl, Ph.D., Inc., 1989. [No location available]

Spencer Mason Architects. *Historic Site Survey for Lahainaluna Road and Waineʻe Street Widening Projects.* Honolulu, HI: Spencer Mason Architects, 1988. [SHPD ID: 2019LI81432]

Spencer Mason Architects. *Historic Structures Report: Old Lahaina Courthouse.* Honolulu, HI: Spencer Mason Architects, 1996. [SHPD ID: 2019LI81378]

Spencer Mason Architects. *Various Historic Site Survey for Lahainaluna Road and Waineʻe Street Widening Projects.* Honolulu, HI: Spencer Mason Architects, 1988. [SHPD ID: 2019LI81432]

Spriggs, Matthew. *Trip Report: Makaluapuna Point, Honokahua, Lahaina District, Maui,* 1989. [SHPD ID: 2019LI81413; UH Call Number: DU629.M356 S67 1989]

Tome, Guerin and Michael F. Dega. *An Archaeological Inventory Survey for the Proposed Kapalua Coastal Trail Located in the Areas of Kapalua and Honokāhau, Honokahua and Nāpili 2 & 3.* Honolulu, HI: Scientific Consultant Services, Inc., 2007. [SHPD ID: 2019LI81433]

Tome, Guerin and Michael F. Dega. *An Archaeological Monitoring Plan for the Proposed Kapalua Coastal Trail Located in the areas of Nāpili, Kapalua, Honokahua, and Honolua, Ahupuaʻa of Nāpili 2&3, Honokahua, and Honolua, Lahaina District, Island of Maui, Hawaiʻi.* Honolulu, HI: Scientific Consultant Services, Inc., 2008. [SHPD ID: 2019LI81410]

Tomonari-Tuggle, M. J. *An Archaeological Reconnaissance Survey for 27 Wind Turbines in the Ukumehame Uplands, Island of Maui.* Honolulu, HI: International Archaeological Research Institute, Inc., 2003. [SHPD ID: 2019LI81627]

Tomonari-Tuggle, M. J. and H. D. Tuggle. *Archaeological Survey of Two Demonstration Trails of the Hawai'i Statewide Trail and Access System.* Honolulu, HI: International Archaeological Research Institute, Inc., 1991. [SHPD ID: 2019LI79001; UH Call Number: DU628.M3 T66 1991]

Tourtellotte, Perry A. *Archaeological Inspection Report for Rainbow Ranch,* 1988. [SHPD ID: 2019LI81059]

Tulchin, Jon and Hallett H. Hammatt. *Archaeological Assessment of a 0.2-Acre Parcel and Waterline, Māhinahina 4 Ahupua'a, Lahaina District, Island of Maui.* Wailuku, HI: Cultural Surveys Hawai'i, Inc., 2003. [SHPD ID: 2019LI81315]

Walker, Alan T. and Paul H. Rosendahl. *Testing of Cultural Remains Associated with the Kahana Desilting Basin, Honolua Watershed, Land of Kahana, Lahaina District, County of Maui, Hawai'i.* Hilo, HI: Paul H. Rosendahl, Ph.D., Inc., 1985. [SHPD ID: 2019LI81071; UH Call Number: DU629.K343 W35 1985]

Walton, Beth. *A Preliminary Report on an Archaeological Survey of the Portion of Piilani Highway from Stake 195+00 to Stake 250+00,* 1972. [SHPD ID: 2019LI79374]

Wasson, Eugene C. IV and Michael F. Dega. *An Archaeological Monitoring Report for the Lahaina No. 4. Force Main Replacement Project, in Lahaina, Wahikuli Ahupua'a, Lahaina District, Island of Maui, Hawai'i.* Honolulu, HI: Scientific Consultant Services, Inc., 2016. [SHPD ID: 2019LI80628]

Weisler, M. *Field Inspection of Hanaka'ō'ō Construction Site, Maui.* Honolulu, HI: Department of Anthropology, Bernice P. Bishop Museum, 1983. [No location available]

Windley, Larry. *Recommended Action Plan for the Preservation/Restoration of the Hale Pa'ahao Prison Site, Lahaina.* Lahaina, HI: Lahaina Restoration Foundation, 1967. [SHPD ID: 2019LI81257]

Yeomans, Sarah K. *Archaeological Monitoring Plan Parking Lot Drainage System Installation, Pana'ewa Ahupua'a, Lahaina District, Island of Maui, Hawai'i.* Honolulu, HI: Scientific Consultant Services, Inc., 2019. [SHPD ID: 2019LI80640]

References
Works Cited in the Archaeological Reports

Abbott, Isabella. *La'au Hawai'i: Traditional Hawaiian Uses of Plants*. Honolulu: Bishop Museum Press, 1992.

Adler, Jacob. *Claus Spreckels, The Sugar King in Hawai'i*. Honolulu: Mutual Publishing, 1966.

Advisory Council on Historic Preservation (ACHP). *Guidelines for Consideration of Traditional Cultural Values in Historic Preservation Review (Draft Report)*. Washington, D.C.: Advisory Council on Historic Preservation, 1985.

Alexander, Mary Charlotte. *Dr. Baldwin of Lahaina*. Berkeley, California: Stanford University Press, 1953.

Alexander, W. D. "A Brief History of Land Titles in the Hawaiian Kingdom." In *Hawaiian Almanac and Annual for 1891: A Hand Book of Information on Interesting Matters Relating to the Hawaiian Islands,* T. G. Thrum, ed. Vol. 17, pp. 105–124. Honolulu: Press Publishing Company Print, 1890.

——— (surveyor). *Maui* [map]. 1885. Land Survey, Department of Accounting and General Services, Honolulu, Hawai'i.

———, Surveyor General. *Town of Lahaina*. 1884. 1:2400. State of Hawai'i Survey Office, Department of Accounting and General Services, Honolulu, Hawai'i.

Alexander, W. D., C. J. Lyons, M. D. Monsarrat, F. S. Dodge, S. E. Bishop, E. D. Baldwin, and W. R. Lawrence (surveyors). *Maui, Hawaiian Islands, Registered Map 1268*. 1885. 1:90,000. Hawaiian Government Survey. On file at Library of Congress Geography and Map Division, Washington, D.C.

Alexander, William DeWitt. "A Brief History of Hawaiian Land Titles in the Hawaiian Kingdom." In *The Hawaiian Almanac and Annual for 1891,* T. G. Thrum, ed. Honolulu: Press Publishing Company, 1890.

———. *A Brief History of the Hawaiian People*. New York: American Book Co., 1899.

———. "Early Industrial Teaching of Hawaiians." In *Hawaiian Almanac and Annual for 1895: A Hand Book of Information on Interesting Matters Relating to the Hawaiian Islands,* T. G. Thrum, ed., pp. 91–100. Honolulu: Press Publishing Company Print, 1895.

American Board of Commissioners for Foreign Missions. *The Missionary Herald Containing the Proceeding at Large of the American Board of Commissioners for*

Foreign Missions with a General View of Other Benevolent Operations for the year 1827. Boston: 1827.

Anderson, Rufus. *Forty-Ninth Report of the American Board of Commissioners for Foreign Missions, September 7–10.* Boston: Press of T. R. Marvin & Son, 1858.

Andrews, Lorrin. *A Dictionary of the Hawaiian Language to which is Appended an English-Hawaiian Vocabulary and Chronological Table of Remarkable Events.* Honolulu: Henry M. Whitney, 1865.

Apgar, Sally. "Charges filed in eBay skull case: Federal prosecutors say a California man put the item up for bid." *Honolulu Star-Bulletin,* 9 September 2004. http://archives.starbulletin.com/2004/09/09/news/story5.html

Apple, R. A. *Hawaiian Archaeology: Trails.* Bishop Museum Special Publication 53. Honolulu: Bishop Museum Press, 1965.

Apple, Russell A. *Lahaina (Historic District) National Historical Landmark—1974 Updated.* Honolulu: National Park Service, Hawaii Group, 1974.

Apple, Russell A. and Willian Kenji Kikuchi. *Ancient Hawaiian Shore Zone Fishponds: An Evaluation of Survivors for Historical Preservation.* Honolulu: Office of the State Director, National Park Service, 1975.

Arago, Jaques Etinne. *Narrative of a Voyage Around the World.* London: Academy of Sciences, 1823.

Architectural Style Book for Lahaina County of Maui Historic Commission. 1969. State Historic Preservation Division [SHPD]—Kapolei, No Call Number, Maui (2), Zone 4, Section 3, Plat 015–018 Kaanapali.

Armstrong, R. Warwick, ed. *Atlas of Hawaii.* Honolulu: University of Hawai'i Press, 1983.

Ashdown, Inez. "Come Travel the Old Trails of Maui." *Maui Surf,* 13 November 1968.

———. *History of Honolua Ranch.* On file at State Historic Preservation Division—Kapolei, 1972.

———. "Salute to Kaanapali." *Maui News* (Wailuku, HI), 23 January 1963, pp. 18–19.

———. *Story of Lahaina.* Dallas, TX: Taylor Publishing Company, 1947.

Ashdown, Inez MacPhee. *Ke Alaloa o Maui.* Wailuku, HI: Kama'aina Historians, Inc., Ace Printing, 1970.

———. *Stories of Old Lahaina.* Dallas, TX: privately printed, 1970.

———. "The Legend of Kahekili at Ka'anapali." *Maui News* (Wailuku, HI), 23 August 1963.

Athens, Stephen J. "Hawaiian Native Lowland Vegetation in Prehistory." In *Historical Ecology in the Pacific Islands: Prehistoric Environmental and Landscape Change,* P. V. Kirch and T. L. Hunt, eds., pp. 248–270. New Haven, CT: Yale University Press, 1997.

Bagot, F., ed. *McKenney's Hawaiian Dictionary.* California: L. M. McKenney & Co., 1884.

Baldwin, Dwight. Letter: Dwight Baldwin to Amos Cooke. On file at Hawaiian Mission Children's Society Library and Archives.

———. "Recent Intelligence: The Sandwich Islands." *The Missionary Herald,* vol. XXXV, no. 35, 1839.

Baldwin, Dwight David (surveyor) and Erdman Dwight Baldwin (mapper). *Map of Kauaula Valley, Lahaina, Maui.* No. 316H, 2 chains equal 1 inch. Land Survey, Department of Accounting and General Services, Honolulu, Hawai'i, 1892.

Barkhausen, Louis. "Manager's Report." In *Report of the Pioneer Company Limited, for the Year Ending December 31, 1902.* Honolulu: Bulletin Publishing Company, 1903.

———. "Manager's Report." In *Report of the Pioneer Mill Company, Limited, for the Year Ending December 21, 1904.* Honolulu: Bulletin Publishing Company, 1905.

Barrere, Dorothy. *Waile'a: Waters of Pleasure for the Children of Kama.* Honolulu: Department of Anthropology, Bernice P. Bishop Museum, 1975.

Bartholomew, Gail (compiler and editor). *Index to the Maui News—1900 to 1932.* Wailuku, HI: Maui Historical Society, 1985.

Bartholomew, Gail and Bren Bailey. *Maui Remembers, A Local History.* Honolulu: Mutual Publishing, 1994.

Beckwith, Martha W. *Hawaiian Mythology.* Honolulu: University of Hawai'i Press, 1970.

Bellwood, P. *The Polynesians: Prehistory of an Island People.* London: Thams and Hudson, Ltd., 1978.

Belt Collins & Associates. *Design Study for Front Street Improvement Plan, Lahainā Historic District: Past and Present.* Honolulu: Belt Collins and Associates, 1992.

Belt Collins Hawai'i Ltd. *Final Lahaina Town Drainage Master Plan.* Wailuku, HI: Department of Public Works and Environmental Management, County of Maui, 2005.

Bingham, Hiram. *A Residence of Twenty-One Years in the Sandwich Islands.* Hartford, CT, 1847.

Brigham, William T. "Stone Implements and Stone Work of the Ancient Hawaiians." In *Memoirs of the B. P. Bishop Museum,* vol. I., no. 4. Honolulu: Bishop Museum Press, 1902.

Brown, J. F. *Map of Maui Island, Registered Map 1408.* Land Survey, Department of Accounting and General Services, Honolulu, Hawai'i, 1886.

Bureau of Conveyances (Honolulu, Hawai'i). Miscellaneous Libers of Record.

Carter, Laura. "Protohistoric Material Correlates in Hawaiian Archaeology A.D. 1778–1820." Master's thesis, Department of Anthropology, University of Hawai'i at Mānoa, 1990.

Char, Winona P. *Botanical Survey Ma'alaea—Lahaina Third 69 KV Transmission Line Project.* Honolulu: Char and Associates, Botanical Consultants, 1993.

Cheever, Henry T. *Life in the Sandwich Islands.* New York: A. S. Barnes and Company, 1851.

Chinen, Jon. *Original Land Titles of Hawaii.* 1961.

Chinen, Jon J. *The Great Māhele: Hawaiian Land Division of 1848.* Honolulu: University of Hawai'i Press, 1961.

Chris Hart and Partners, Inc. *General Plan 2030, Maui Island Plan, Maui Island History: Lessons from the Past—A Guide to the Future.* Wailuku, HI: Chris Hart and Partners, Inc., 2006.

"Civil Works Projects." U.S. Army Corps of Engineers, Honolulu District. https://www.poh.usace.army.mil/Missions/Civil-Works/Civil-Works-Projects/ accessed 2023.

Clark, Ephraim Weston. "Recent Intelligence: The Sandwich Islands." *The Missionary Herald,* vol. XXXV, 1839.

Clark, John. *The Beaches of Maui County.* Honolulu: University of Hawai'i Press, 1980.

Coan, Titus. *Life in Hawaii: An Autobiographic Sketch of Mission Life and Labors, 1835– 1881.* New York: Anson D. F. Randolph & Company, 1882.

Cobb, John N. "Commercial Fisheries of the Hawaiian Islands." In *U.S. Fisheries Commission Report for 1901,.* Washington, D.C., 1901.

Code of Federal Regulations (CFR). *Part 60 National Register of Historic Places.* Washington, D.C.: U.S. Department of the Interior, National Park Service.

Conde, Daniel T. *Report of the American Board of Commissioners for Foreign Missions, Sept. 11–14 1855.* Boston: Marvin & Son, 1855.

Conde, J. C. *Sugar Trains Pictorial.* Felton, Calif.: Glenwood Publishers, 1975.

Conde, Jesse C. and Gerald M. Best. *Sugar Trains: Narrow Gauge Rails of Hawaii.* Felton, CA: Glenwood Publishers, 1973.

Cook, James. *The Journals of Captain Cook on his Voyages of Discovery,* vol. 3. J. C. Beaglehole, ed. Cambridge: Cambridge University Press (for Hakluyt Society), 1967.

Cooper, George and Gavan Daws. *Land and Power in Hawaii.* Honolulu: Benchmark Books, 1985.

Cordy, R. *Exalted Sits the Chief: The Ancient History of Hawai'i Island.* Honolulu: Mutual Publishing, Inc., 2001.

Cordy, Ross. *A Study of Prehistoric Change: The Development of Complex Societies in the Hawaiian Islands.* New York: Academic Press, 1981.

———. *Cultural Resources Study: Archaeological Reconnaissance and Literature Search, Kihei Flood Control Project, Kihei, Maui.* Honolulu: U.S. Army Corps of Engineers, 1977.

Cox, David W. *The Archaeology of Kula, Maui from Pūlehu Nui Ahupua'a to Kama'ole Ahupua'a: Surface Survey, Pi'ilani Highway.* Lāwa'i, HI: Archaeological Research Center Hawai'i, Inc., 1976.

Cuddihy, L. W. and C. P. Stone. *Alteration of Native Hawaiian Vegetation: Effects of Humans, Their Activities, and Introduction.* Honolulu: University of Hawai'i Cooperative National Park Resources Studies Unit, 1990.

Cummings, G. "Historic Lahaina." *Maui News* (Wailuku, HI), 24 November 1926.

Daws, Gavin. *Shoal of Time: A History of the Hawaiian Islands.* Honolulu: University of Hawai'i Press, 1968.

Day, A. Grove. *History Makers of Hawaii.* Honolulu: Mutual Publishing, 1984.

Dean, Arthur L. *Alexander & Baldwin, Ltd. and the Predecessor Partnerships.* Honolulu: Alexander & Baldwin Ltd. and Advertiser Publishing Company, 1950.

Degener, Otto. *Flora Hawaiiensis: The New Illustrated Flora of the Hawaiian Islands,* Books 1–4. privately printed, 1946.

DHM and Bishop Museum Public Archaeology Section. *Hawaiian Fishpond Study Islands of Hawai'i, Maui, Lāna'i, and Kaua'i.* Honolulu: DHM, Inc., 1990.

Dodge, F. S. *Map of Maui, Hawaiian Islands.* Hawaiian Government Survey (1880). On file at the Office of the Surveyor, Department of Accounting and General Services, Honolulu, Hawai'i.

Dorrance, William H. and Francis Swanzy Morgan. *Sugar Islands: The 165-Year Story of Sugar in Hawai'i.* Honolulu: Mutual Publishing, Inc., 2000.

Dunn, J. M. *Detail of Puunoa 3, Kainehe and Moanui Between Front Street and the Sea, Lahaina Maui,* 1925. 1:50. Field Book No. 1103, page 14. Registered Map No. 2727. On file at State of Hawai'i Survey Office, Department of Accounting and General Services.

Duperrey, Louis Isidore. *Plan de la rade Rahein sur l'île Mowi (Iles Sandwich),* 1826. 1:15,300. In *Hawaii in 1819: A Narrative Account,* Louis Claude de Saulses de Freycinet. Ella L. Wiswell, trans. Marion Kelly, ed. Honolulu: Bishop Museum Press, 1978.

Earl, T. K. "Prehistoric Irrigation in the Hawaiian Islands: An Evaluation of Evolutionary Significance." *Archaeology and Physical Anthropology in Oceania* Vol. 15 (1980): 1–28.

Elliott, Rex R. *Hawaiian Battles of Long Ago.* Honolulu: Hawaiian Service, 1971.

Elliot, Rex R. and Stephen C. Gould. *Hawaiian Battles of Long Ago. A little of Hawai'i's Past.* Honolulu: Hawaiian Service, 1988.

Ellis, William. *Journal of William Ellis, Narrative of a Tour of Hawaii, or Owhyee....* Honolulu: Advertiser Publishing Co., 1963.

———. *Polynesian Researches: Hawaii.* Rutland, Vermont: Charles E. Tuttle Co., 1969.

Emerson, John S. "Letters from Mr. Emerson: Kaanapali—The Church—Popery." *The Missionary Herald, containing the Proceedings of the American Board of Commissioners for Foreign Missions, with a View of other Benevolent Questions,* Vol. XLIII (1847): 99–100.

Emerson, Nathaniel B. *Unwritten Literature of Hawaii: The Sacred Songs of the Hula.* Bureau of American Ethnology Bulletin 38, Smithsonian Institution, Washington, D.C. Rutland, VT: Charles E. Tuttle, 1965.

Emory, Kenneth P. "An Archaeological Survey of Haleakala." *Bernice P. Bishop Museum Occasional Papers* Vol. 7, No. 11 (1921): 237–59.

Emory, Kenneth P. and Robert J. Hommon. *Endangered Hawaiian Archaeological Sites within Maui County: A Bishop Museum Report to the County of Maui.* Department of Anthropology, Bernice P. Bishop Museum: Honolulu, 1972.

Eversole, Dolan. "Large-Scale Beach Change: Kaanapali, Hawai'i." Master's thesis, Department of Geology and Geophysics, University of Hawai'i at Mānoa, 2002.

Fischer, John. "The Westin Maui Resort & Spa." *Go Hawaii.* http://gohawaii.about.com /od/mauilodging/ss/westin-maui-resort-and-spa_2.html last accessed April 2013.

Fitzpatrick, G. L. *The Early Mapping of Hawaii.* Honolulu: Edition Limited, 1986.

Fleming, Martha. *Old Trails of Maui.* Syracuse, NY: Gaylord Brothers Press, 1933.

Foote, D. E., E. Hill, S. Nakamura, and F. Stephens. *Soil Survey of the Islands of Oahu, Maui, Molokai, and Lanai, State of Hawaii.* Washington, D.C.: U.S. Department of Agriculture Soil Conservation Service, 1972.

Forbes, A. O. "Legend of Maui—Snaring of the Sun." In *The Hawaiian Almanac and Annual for 1881.* Thomas G. Thrum, ed. Honolulu: Thos. G. Thrum, 1881.

Fornander, Abraham. *An Account of the Polynesian Race: Its Origins and Migrations.* Rutland, VT: Charles E. Tuttle & Co., 1969.

———. *Hawaiian Antiquities and Folklore.* 6 vols. Honolulu: Bishop Museum Press, 1916–1919.

Freycinet, Louis Claude de Saulses de. *Hawai'i in 1819: A Narrative Account by Louis Claude de Saulses de Freycinet.* M. Kelly, ed. E. L. Wiswell, trans. Pacific Anthropological Records 26. Honolulu: Department of Anthropology, Bernice P. Bishop Museum, 1978.

Frost, Rossie Moodie. *Hale Pai: Printing and Engraving at Lahainaluna, 1834–1982* (1982).

Giambelluca, T. W., Q. Chen, A. G. Frazier, J. P. Price, Y. L. Chen, P. S. Chu, J. K. Eischeid, and D. M. Delparte. "Online Rainfall Atlas of Hawai'i." *Bulletin of the American Meteorological Society* 94 (2013): 313–316. http://rainfall.geography.hawaii.edu/.

Giambelluca, Thomas W., X. SHuai, M. L. Barnes, R. J. Alliss, R. J. Longman, T. Miura, Q. Chen, A. G. Frazier, R. G. Mudd, L. Cuo and A. D. Businger. *Evapotranspiration of Hawai'i. Final Report Submitted to the U.S. Army Corps of Engineers—Honolulu District, and the Commission on Water Resource Management, State of Hawai'i.* Honolulu: University of Hawai'i at Mānoa, 2014. http://climate.geography.hawaii.edu/

Gilman, Gorham. "Lahaina in the Early Days." In *Hawaiian Almanac and Annual for 1907: The Reference Book of Information and Statistics Relating to the Territory of Hawaii, of Value to Merchants, Tourists, and Others.* Thomas G. Thrum, ed. Honolulu: Thomas G. Thrum, 1906.

Gilmore, Abner Blanks. *The Gilmore Hawaii Sugar Manual.* New Orleans: Abner Blanks Gilmore, 1931.

Hale Pa'i o Lahainaluna. *Hale Pa'i, the Printing House at Lahaina, Maui, Hawai'i.* 2008.

Hamilton, Peter Freeland. *The Man Who Loved Lahaina—George Freeland.* San Mateo, CA: Peter F. Hamilton Co., 2001.

Handy, E. S. and E. G. Handy. *Native Planters of Old Hawaii: Their Life, Lore, and Environment.* Bishop Museum Bulletin No. 233. Honolulu: Bishop Museum Press, 1972.

Handy, E. S. Craighill. *The Hawaiian Planter: His Plants, Methods, and Areas of Cultivation.* Vol. 1. Bishop Museum Publication 161. Honolulu: Bishop Museum Press, 1940.

"Harvesting Contracts." *The Hawaiian Planters' Record* (Honolulu, HI), Vol. IV (1911).

Haulewahine, H. G. "Make i Aloha ia." *Ka Nupepa Kuokoa* (Honolulu, HI), 1 May 1875.

Hawai'i Administrative Rules. *Title 13, Department of Land and Natural Resources, Subtitle 13, State Historic Preservation Division Rules,* 2002. www.hawaii.gov/dlnr/hpd/draftrules2.htm

Hawai'i Commission of Public Lands. *Index of All Grants and Patent Land Sales.* Honolulu: Paradise of the Pacific Print, 1916.

Hawai'i State Archives. *Foreign Register of Kuleana Claims Recorded by the Board of Commissioners to Quiet Land Titles in the Hawaiian Islands.* N.d.

———. *Foreign Testimony Recorded by the Board of Commissioners to Quiet Land TItles in the Hawaiian Islands.* N.d.

Hawai'i State Archives, Interior Department, Land files, letter from E. Duvauchelle to William Webster, 16 July 1858.

Hawai'i State Archives, Interior Department, Land files, Letter from Wm. Enos and Joseph Sylva to John O. Dominis, 16 May 1865.

Hawai'i State Archives, Interior Department, Land, J. F. Brown, Record of Crown Lands, 1886.

Hawai'i State Archives, Interior Department, Pikanele to Minister of the Interior, 1850.

Hawai'i State Archives, Interior Department, Land, J. F. Brown, Record of Crown Lands, 1886.

Hawai'i State Archives, Interior Department, Land files, Report of P. Nahaolelua of Receipts from Crown Lands on Maui, 3 January 1872.

Hawai'i State Archives, Last Will of Kaheiheimalie, 1842.

Hawai'i State Archives, Second Circuit Court Probate 4862, 1951.

Hawai'i State Office of Environmental Quality Control. *Guidelines for Assessing Cultural Impacts.* Adopted by the Environmental Council, November 1997.

Hawaiian Sugar Planters' Association Plantation Archives, University of Hawai'i at Mānoa Library Hawaiian Collection, Honolulu.

Hawaiian Sugar Planters' Association. *Story of Sugar in Hawaii.* Honolulu: Hawaiian Sugar Planters' Association, 1926.

Henshaw, J. and L. G. James. "The Lessons of History, Making a Case for a National Forest in Hawai'i." *Forest History Today,* Spring/Fall 2011.

Hiroa, Te Rangi [Peter Buck]. *Arts and Crafts of Hawaii.* Honolulu: Bishop Museum Press, 1957.

"Homes for Hawaiian Dedicated at Leiali'i." *The Honolulu Advertiser* (Honolulu, HI), 14 April 2007.

Hommon, R. J. and R. Connelly. *Statewide Inventory of Historic Places for the Island of Maui.* 1973.

Hono-ko-hau Study Commission. *The Spirit of Ka-Loko Hono-Ko-Hau.* Washington, D.C.: U.S. Department of the Interior, National Park Service, 1974.

Hosmer, R. S. *Report of the Division of Forestry for the Year Ending December 1908.* Honolulu: Board of Agriculture and Forestry, Division of Forestry, Territory of Hawai'i, 1908.

'Ī'ī, John Papa. *Fragments of Hawaiian History.* Honolulu: Bishop Museum Press, 1973.

Iaukea, Sydney L. *Keka'a: The Making and Saving of North Beach West Maui.* Lahaina, HI: North Beach–West Maui Benefit Fund, Inc., 2014.

"Introduction to the HAS [Bernice P. Bishop Museum's Department of Anthropology Hawaiian Archaeology Survey]," Bishop Museum. http://data.bishopmuseum .org/has2/index.php?b=i : accessed 2023.

Jackson, Frances. "Point of Lahaina." *Hawaii Historical Review* Vol. 1:7, 1 April 1964.

James, Van. *Ancient Sites of Maui, Moloka'i and Lāna'i: Archaeological Places of Interest in the Hawaiian Islands.* Honolulu: Mutual Publishing, 2001.

Joerger, Pauline and Michael Kaschko. *A Cultural History Overview of the Kahoma Stream Flood Control Project, Lahiana Maui, and Maalaea Small Boat Harbor Project.* Honolulu: Hawaii Marine Research, Inc., 1979.

Judd, Lawrence M. *Annual Report of the Governor of Hawaii to the Secretary of the Interior for Fiscal Year Ended June 30, 1929.* Washington, D.C.: United States Government Printing Office, 1929.

Juvik, Sonia P. and James O. Suvik. *Atlas of Hawai'i.* 3rd ed. Honolulu: University of Hawai'i Press, 1998.

Ka'ai, M. *Honokohau Ahupuaa, Maui: An example of Rural Hawaiian Settlement and Land Use.* On file at State Historic Preservation Division—Kapolei.

Kahā'ulelio, Daniel. *Ka 'Oihana Lawai'a, Hawaiian Fishing Traditions.* M. P. Nogelmeier, ed. M. K. Pukui, trans. Honolulu: Bishop Museum Press, 2006.

Kalakaua, King David. *The Legends and Myths of Hawaii.* New York: Charles L. Webster and Co., 1888.

Kalama, Simona P. *Na Mokupuni o Hawaii Nei.* Lahaina, HI: Kulanui Lahainaluna, 1837. On file at the Hale Pa'i, Lāhaināluna H.S.

Kamakau, Samuel M. *Ka Po'e Kahiko: The People of Old.* Honolulu: Bishop Museum Press, 1964.

———. *Ruling Chiefs of Hawaii.* Honolulu: Kamehameha Schools Press, 1961.

———. *Tales and Traditions of People of Old.* Honolulu: Bishop Museum Press, 1991.

Kamakau, Samuel Māniakalani. *The Works of the People of Old.* Mary Kawena Pukui, trans. Honolulu: Bishop Museum Press, 1976.

Kamehameha III. *Buke Kakau Paa, no ka mahele aina i Hooholoia iwaena o Kamehameha III a me Na Lii a me Na Konohiki ana.* Honolulu: Hale Ali'i, 1858.

Kame'eleihiwa, Lilikalā. "Land and the Promise of Capitalism." Ph.D. dissertation, University of Hawai'i at Mānoa, 1986.

———. *Native Land and Foreign Desires; Pehea Lā e Pono Ai?* Honolulu: Bishop Museum Press, 1992.

Kauhi, George K. (drawn by). *Map of the Kalo Lands and School Premises Lahainaluna Seminary Surveyed by the Class of 1882.* 5 rods to an inch. Government Survey Registration No. 952.

Kay, E. A. *Hawaiian Marine Shells, Reef and Shore Fauna of Hawaii, Section 4: Mollusca.* Bernice P. Bishop Museum Special Publication 64 (4). Honolulu: Bishop Museum Press, 1979.

Kelly, Marion. "A Gunboat Diplomacy, Sandalwood Lust and National Debt." In *Ka Wai Ola,* Vol. 15:4 (April 1998).

———. *Nā Māla o Kona: Gardens of Kona.* Honolulu: Bishop Museum Press, 1983.

Kent, Noel. *Hawaii: Islands Under the Influence.* Honolulu: University of Hawai'i Press, 1983.

Kikuchi, William Kenji. "Hawaiian Aquacultural System." Ph.D. thesis, University of Arizona, 1973.

Kingdom of Hawai'i. "An Act Relating to the Lands of His Majesty the King and of the Government." In *A Supplement to the State Laws of His Majesty, Kamehameha III., King of the Hawaiian Islands, Containing the Acts and Resolutions Passed by the Houses of Nobles and Representatives. During the Twenty-Third Year of His Reign and the Sixth Year of His Public Recognition, A.D. 1848.* 22–43. Honolulu: Government Press, 1848.

————. *Buke Kakau Paa no ka mahele aina i hooholoia iwaena o Kamehameha III ame Na Lii a me Na Konohiki Ana.* Honolulu: Hale Aliʻi, 1848.

Kirch, P. V. "Archaeological Excavations at Palauea, Southeast Maui, Hawaiian Islands." *Archaeology and Physical Anthropology in Oceania,* vol. IV (1), 1971, pp. 62–86.

————. *Feathered Gods and Fishhooks: An Introduction to Hawaiian Archaeology and Prehistory.* Honolulu: University of Hawaiʻi Press, 1985.

————. *Kuaʻāina Kahiko: Life and Land in Ancient Kahikinui, Maui.* Honolulu: University of Hawaiʻi Press, 2014.

————. "Monumental Architecture and Power in Polynesian Chiefdoms: A Comparison of Tonga and Hawaii." *World Archaeology* vol. 22, no. 2, 1990.

————. "The Chronology of Early Hawaiian Settlement." *Archaeology and Physical Anthropology in Oceania,* vol. 9, 1974, pp. 110–119.

Kirch, Patrick. *The Evolution of Polynesian Chiefdoms.* New York: Cambridge University Press, 1984.

Kirch, Patrick V. "Valley Agricultural Systems in Prehistoric Hawaii: An Archaeological Consideration." *Asian Perspectives,* vol. 20, no. 2, 1980, pp. 246–280.

Kirch, Patrick V. and Marshall Sahlins. *Anahulu: The Anthropology of History in the Kingdom of Hawaii.* 2 vols. Chicago: University of Chicago Press, 1991.

Klieger, P. C. *Mokuʻula: Maui's Sacred Island.* Honolulu: Bishop Museum Press, 1999.

Klieger, P. Christaan, ed. *Na Maka o Halawa: A History of Halawa Ahupuaʻa, Oʻahu.* Honolulu: Bishop Museum Press, 1995.

Kolb, Michael. "Social Power, Chiefly Authority, and Ceremonial Architecture, in an Island Polity, Maui, Hawaii." Ph.D. dissertation, University of California at Los Angeles, 1991.

Kubota, Gary. "Alleged Hawaiian skull taken off eBay: A native group protests the auction of the Maui Artifact." *Honolulu Star-Bulletin* (Honolulu, HI), 6 February 2004. http://archives.starbulletin.com/2004/02/06/news/story3.html

————. "Maui Mill's Preservation in Limbo." *Honolulu Star-Bulletin* (Honolulu, HI), 2004.

————. "Wainee Tenants Cherish Old Lifestyle." *Honolulu Star-Bullletin* (Honolulu, HI), 19 April 1999.

Kupau, Summer. *Exploring Historic Lahaina.* Honolulu: Watermark Publishing, 2001.

Kuykendall, R. and A. Grove Day. *Hawaii: A History from Polynesian Kingdom to American Statehood.* Englewood Cliffs, NJ: Prentice-Hall, Inc., 1976.

Kuykendall, Ralph S. *The Hawaiian Kingdom.* 3 vols. Honolulu: University of Hawaiʻi Press, 1938 (Vol. 1).

Kyselka, Will and Ray Lanterman. *Maui, How It Came to Be.* Honolulu: The University Press, 1980.

Larrison, G. K. *Water Resources of Hawaii.* Washington, D.C.: U.S. Geological Survey, Department of the Interior, U.S. Government Printing Office, 1913.

Lass, Barbara. *Hawaiian Adze Production and Distribution for the Development of Chiefdoms.* Monograph 37, Institute of Archaeology. Los Angeles: University of California, Los Angeles, 1994.

Lebo, Susan A. *Native Hawaiian and Euro-American Culture Change in Early Honolulu.* Honolulu: Department of Archaeology, Bernice P. Bishop Museum, 1997.

Lecker, George Theodore. "Lahainaluna 1831–1877: A Study of the History of Hawaii's Pioneer Educational Institution and Its Socio-Economic Influence at Home and Abroad." Master's. thesis, University of Hawai'i, June 1936.

Lucas, Paul F. Nahoa. *A Dictionary of Hawaiian Legal Land-terms.* Honolulu: University of Hawai'i Press, 1995.

Lutz, M. E., surveyor. *Hawaii Territory Survey: Wahikuli Lahaina Maui.* 1913. 1:1000. On file at State of Hawai'i Survey Office, Department of Accounting and General Services, Honolulu.

Lyons, C. J. "Land Matters in Hawaii." *The Islander,* vol. 1, 1875.

MacDonald, Gordon, A., A. T. Abbott and Frank L. Peterson. *Volcanoes in the Sea.* Honolulu: University of Hawai'i Press, 1983.

Maipinepine, John (drawn by). *Map of the Kalo Lands and School Premises Lahainaluna Seminary, Surveyed by the Class of 1882.* 10 rods to an inch. On file at the Hale Pa'i, Lāhaināluna H.S.

Major, Maurice. "The Cultural Construction of Culture Reconstruction: An Ethnography for Contract Archaeologists in Hawai'i." Master's thesis, Department of Anthropology, University of Hawai'i at Mānoa, 1995.

Malo, Davida. *Hawaiian Antiquities.* Nathaniel B. Emerson, trans. B. P. Bishop Museum Special Publication 2. Honolulu: Bishop Museum Press, 1903.

Maly, Kepa. "Historical Documentary Research, Appendix A." In *Archaeological Subsurface Inventory Survey, Sheraton—Maui Redevelopment Project, Land of Hanaka'o'o, Lahaina District Island of Maui* by Graves.

Maly, Kepā and Onaona Maly. *He Wahi Mo'olelo no Kaua'ula a me Kekahi 'Aina o Lāhainā i Maui, A Collection of Traditions and Historical Accounts of Kaua'ula and Other Lands, Lāhainā, Maui.* 2 vols. Honolulu: Kumu Pono Associates, 2007.

Martin, Kenneth R. *Maui During the Whaling Boom: The Travels of Captain Gilbert Pendelton, Jr.* Honolulu: Hawaiian Historical Society, 1979.

Maui Department of Public Works. *Government Swamp Lands Lahaina T.H.* [map]. 1916. Lahaina, HI: Maui Department of Public Works. On file at the Hale Pa'i, Lāhaināluna H.S.

Maui Historical Society, Inez Ashdown papers, 11, Inez Ashdown's personal notes, n.d.

Maui Historical Society, Inez Ashdown papers, "Sacred Stones of Ka-pae-mahu," n.d.

Maui Historical Society, *Lahaina Historical Guide.* Rutland, VT: Charles E. Tuttle Company, 1971.

Maui News, Industrial Edition. *Maui News* (Wailuku, HI), 1926.

Maunupau, Thomas K. *A Visit to Kaupo, Maui.* Honolulu: Bishop Museum Press, 1988.

McCandless, James Sutton. *A Brief History of the McCandless Brothers and Their Part in the Development of Artesian Water in the Hawaiian Islands, 1880–1936.* Honolulu: Advertiser Publishing Co., 1936.

McGregor, Davianna Pōmaika'i. "'Āina Ho'opulapula: Hawaiian Homesteading." *Hawaiian Journal of History,* vol. 24, 1990.

McKinzie, Edith Kawelohea. *Hawaiian Genealogies: Extracted from Hawaiian Language Newspapers.* 2 vols. Honolulu: University of Hawai'i Press, 1986.

Menzies, Archibald. *Hawai'i Nei 128 Years Ago.* W. F. Wilson, ed. Honolulu: The New Freedom Press, 1920.

Moffat, Riley M. and Gary L. Fitzpatrick. *Surveying the Mahele: Mapping the Hawaiian Land Revolution.* Honolulu: Palapala'āina Editions Limited, 1995.

Morison, Samuel E. "Boston Traders in the Hawaiian Islands, 1789–1823." Massachusetts Historical Society, eds. *Proceedings* vol. LIV, October 1920–June 1921, pp. 9–47.

Moses, Manu. "The Legend of Ke-ao-melemele [Ka Nupepa Kuokoa]." In *Hawaiian Ethographic Notes* vol. 2, p. 875, Bishop Museum, Honolulu.

Munekiyo & Hiraga, Inc. *Historic District Application for the Proposed Lahaina Harbor Complete Streets Project (TMK (2) 4-6-001:001, 004, 007, 009, 010, and 012).* Wailuku, HI: Munekiyo & Hiraga, Inc., 2014.

———. *Historic District Application for the Proposed Lahaina Harbor Complete Streets Project (TMK (2) 4-6-001:001, 004, 007, 009, 010, and 012).* Wailuku, HI: Munekiyo & Hiraga, Inc., 2014.

———. *Kaanapali 2020: Environmental Impact Statement Preparation Notice.* Wailuku, HI: Munekiyo & Hiraga, Inc., 2002.

Munsell Color. *Munsell Soil Color Charts.* Baltimore, MD: McBeth Division of Kollmorgen Instruments Corporation, 1990.

Nakuina, Emma Metcalf. *Hawaii, Its People, Their Legends.* Honolulu: Hawaii Promotion Committee, 1904.

Neal, Marie C. *In Gardens of Hawaii.* Honolulu: Bishop Museum Press, 1965.

Nicholson, Capt. H. Whalley. *From Sword to Share; or a Fortune in Five Years at Hawaii.* London: W. H. Allen & Co., 1881.

Nickerson, Roy. *Lahaina: Royal Capital of Hawaii.* Honolulu: Hawaiian Service, 1978.

Nishimoto, Warren S., Michi-Kodama-Nishimoto, Holly Yamada, Cynthia A. Oshiro, and Maria E. Ka'imipono Orr. *Pioneer Mill Company: A Maui Sugar Plantation Legacy.* Honolulu: Center for Oral History Social Science Research Institute, University of Hawai'i at Mānoa, 2003.

Oliver, D. *The Pacific Islands.* Honolulu: University of Hawai'i Press, 1961.

Olowalu Town. "West Maui Sugar Association and Olowalu Plantation 1864–1881." Digital document. http://olowalu.net/index.cfm?fuseaction=ig.page&PageID=127

Orr, Maria. *Ka'anapali 2020 Cultural Impact Assment, Ahupua'a of Honokawai, Hanako'o, Kahua, Wahikuli, Districts of Ka'anapali & Lahaina, Maui.* 2002.

Pearson, R. J. "The Archaeology of Hana: Preliminary Survey of Waianapanapa State Park." *Hawaii State Archaeological Journal,* vol. 70, no. 2, 1970.

"Pioneer in Name and Fact Also." *The Maui News* (Wailuku, HI), 4 December 1926.

Pioneer Mill Company Ltd. *Annual Report of the Pioneer Mill Company Limited for the Year Ending December 31, 1944.* Published 1945.

———. *Cane Fields.* 1918. 1:500. Lahaina, HI: Pioneer Mill Co., Ltd.

———. *Pioneer Mill Company Limited Annual Report for 1945.* Published 1946.

———. *Pioneer Mill Company Limited Annual Report for 1950.* Published 1951.

"Pioneer Mill Company History [in the Finding Aid]." Hawaiian Sugar Planters' Association Plantation Archives, University of Hawai'i at Mānoa Library Hawaiian Collection, Honolulu.

"Pioneer Mill District." 1974. Hawai'i Register of Historic Places Site Form 50–50–03–1208, Dep't. of Land and Natural Resources, Division of State Parks.

Pogue, John F. *Moolelo Hawaii.* Rev. Ed. Honolulu: Hale Paipalapala Aupuni, 1978.

Portlock, N. *A Voyage Round the World… in 1784–1788.* London: Stockdale, 1789.

Pratt, Linda W. and Samuel M. Gon, III. "Terrestrial Ecosystems." In *Atlas of Hawai'i,* 3rd ed., S. P. Juvik and J. O Juvik, eds., pp. 121–129.

Pukui, Mary Kawena. *'Ōlelo No'eau.* Honolulu: Bishop Museum Press, 1983.

Pukui, Mary Kawena and S. H. Elbert. *Hawaiian Dictionary.* Honolulu: University of Hawai'i Press, 1986.

Pukui, Mary Kawena, S. H. Elbert and E. T. Mookini. *Place Names of Hawaii.* Honolulu: University of Hawai'i Press, 1974.

Quayle, Buck. "12-Story Maui Surf Hotel to Open Monday." *The Lahaina Sun* (Lahaina, HI), 1971. http://www.maui-lahaina-sun.com/maui-surf-hotel.html.

Resource Mapping Hawai'i. *Hawai'i Orthos: Hawai'i Schools.* Kea'au, Hawai'i: Resource Mapping Hawai'i, 2017.

Richards, William. "Recent Intelligence, October 1830." *The Missionary Herald,* vol. XXVII, 1831.

———. "Recent Intelligence from the Sandwich Islands." *The Missionary Herald,* vol. XX, 1826.

———. "Situation of the Missionaries at Lahinah, August 30, 1823 Mission at the Sandwich Islands Letters from the Missionaries." *The Missionary Herald,* vol. XX, 1824, pp. 110–112. American Board of Commissioners for Foreign Missions, eds.

Richards, William and Jonathan Smith Green. "Extracts from a Letter of Messrs. Richards and Green, Dated at Lahaina, Oct. 2, 1830." *The Missionary Herald,* vol. XXVII, 1831, pp. 180–184.

Ritz, Mary Kaye. "Lahaina Memories." *The Honolulu Advertiser,* 10 October 2007.

Rolph, George M. *Something About Sugar: Its History, Growth, Manufacture, and Distribution.* San Francisco: John J. Newbegin Publisher, 1917.

Sanborn Map of Lahaina. 1:600. New York: Sanborn Map Company, 1914.

Schilt, Rose. *Subsistence and Conflict in Kona, Hawai'i.* Report 84–1. Honolulu: Department of Anthropology, Bernice P. Bishop Museum, 1984.

Schmitt, Robert C. *Historical Statistics of Hawaii.* Honolulu: University Press of Hawai'i, 1977.

———. *The Missionary Censuses of Hawaii.* Pacific Anthropological Records No. 20, Dept. of Anthropology, Bernice Pauahi Bishop Museum. Honolulu: Bernice Pauahi Bishop Museum Press, 1973.

School of Ocean and Earth Science Technology [SOEST], University of Hawai'i at Mānoa. *Maui Ortho-rectified Historical Shoreline Mosaics: Kaanapali* [maps]. Honolulu: SOEST, University of Hawai'i at Mānoa, 1949, 1963, 1975, 1987.

State Historic Preservation Division [SHPD]. 1994/6 Title 13, Sub-Title 13, Chapter 279 Rules Governing Standards for Archaeological Monitoring Studies and Reports (Draft). Honolulu: SHPD, 1994/1996.

Simpich, F. *Dynasty in the Pacific.* New York: McGraw-Hill Book Co., 1974.

Sinclair, Marjorie J. P. *Nahienaena: Sacred Daughter of Hawaii.* Honolulu: University of Hawai'i Press, 1976.

Smith, Jared G. "Pupils at Lahaina Aid Plantation Hand-Workers Tilling Amazing Hillside Rock Heaps, Writer Finds New Farming No White Collar Menace on Maui, Smith Declares." *Maui News* (Wailuku, HI), 17 August 1932.

Speakman, Cummins E. *Mowee: An Informal History.* San Rafael, CA: Pueo Press, 1981.

Spriggs, M. T. and P. L. Tanaka. *Na Mea 'Imi i ka Wa Kahiko: An Annotated Bibliography of Hawaiian Archaeology.* Honolulu: Social Science Research Institute, University of Hawai'i at Mānoa, 1988.

State of Hawaii, State Historic Preservation Division. *County of Maui Historic Preservation Review of the Special Management Area and Shoreline Setback Variance, Kai Ala Subdivision (I.D. No. 94/SM1–021, 94/SSV-006) Hanakao'o, Lahaina District, Island of Maui, Hawaii.* 1994.

Stearns, Harold T. and Gordon A. MacDonald. *Geology and Ground-Water Resources of the Island of Maui, Hawaii (Including Haleakala Section, Hawaii National Park).* Honolulu: Territory of Hawaii, Division of Hydrography in cooperation with the Geological Survey, United States Dep't. of the Interior, 1942.

Sterling, Elspeth P. *Sites of Maui.* Honolulu: Bishop Museum Press, 1998.

Stewart, Charles S. *Journal of a Residence in the Sandwich Islands During the Years 1823, 1824, and 1825.* London: H. Fisher, Son, and Jackson, 1828.

Stokes, John F. G. "Dune Sepulture, Battle Mortality and Kamehameha's Alleged Defeat on Kauai." *Forty-Fifth Annual Report of the Hawaiian Historical Society.* Honolulu: Hawaiian Historical Society, 1937.

Stubbs, A. M. *Cultivation of Sugar Cane in Two Parts. Part First Sugar Cane: A Treatise on Its History, Botany, and Agriculture.* Savannah, GA: The Morning News Print, 1900.

Summers, Catherine C. *Hawaiian Archaeology. Hawaiian Fishponds.* Bernice P. Bishop Museum Special Publication 52. Honolulu: B. P. Bishop Museum, 1964.

Tagami, Takahiro, Yoshitomo Nishimitsu, and David R. Sherrod. "Rejuvenated-stage after 0.6-m.y. quiescence at West Maui Volcano, Hawaii: New evidence from K-Ar ages and chemistry of Lahaina Volcanics." *Journal of Volcanology and Geothermal Research,* vol. 120, nos. 3–4, pp. 207–214.

Takaki, Ronald. *Pau Hana: Plantation Life and Labor in Hawaii, 1835–1920.* Honolulu: Univesrity of Hawai'i Press, 1983.

Taliaferro, T. *Rainfall of the Hawaiian Islands.* Honolulu: Hawaii Water Authority, 1959.

Taylor, A. P. "Lahaina: The Versailles of Old Hawaii." *Thirty-Seventh Annual Report of the Hawaiian Historical Society.* Honolulu: Hawaiian Historical Society, 1928.

Territory of Hawai'i. *Island and County of Maui, Lahaina District, Mala Quadrangle (map).* 1923. On file at the University of Hawai'i, Map G 4382.M3.

———. *Private Wharves and Landings in Hawaii, Report of the Commission Appointed to Investigate Private Wharves and Landings Throughout the Territory of Hawaii, in Conformity with Joint Resolution No. 2 of the Legislative Session of 1909.* Honolulu: Hawaiian Gazette Company, 1910.

Thompson, Lynn H. "Nomination Form for National Register of Historic Places." 1970. On file at State Historic Preservation Division—Kapolei.

Thrum, T. "Heiau and Heiau Sites throughout the Hawaiian Islands." In *Hawaiian Almanac and Annual for 1909,* pp. 36–48. Honolulu: Thos G. Thrum, 1909.

———. "Maui's Heiaus and Heiau Sites Revisited." *Hawaiian Almanac and Annual for 1917,* pp. 52–62. Honolulu: Thos. G. Thrum, 1917.

Thrum, Thomas. "Heiaus and Heiau Sites Throughout the Hawaiian Islands." In *Hawaiian Almanac and Annual for 1909.* Honolulu: Thos. G. Thrum, 1909.

———. "Notes on the History of Coffee in the Hawaiian Islands." In *Hawaiian Almanac and Annual for 1876.* Honolulu: Thomas G. Thrum, 1875.

Thrum, Thomas G. "Hawaii A Republic." In *Thrum's Hawaiian Almanac and Annual for 1895.* Honolulu: Thomas G. Thrum, 1894.

———. "Hawaiian Sugar Crops 1906–1912." In *Hawaiian Almanac and Annual for 1913.* Honolulu: Thos. G. Thrum, 1912.

———. "The Hinas of Hawaiian Folk-lore; more evidence of old temples, articles." In *Thrum's Hawaiian Almanac and Annual for 1921.* Honolulu: Thos G. Thrum, 1920.

———. "Sugar Crops of the Hawaiian Plantations, 1891–1900." In *Hawaiian Almanac and Annual for 1901.* Honolulu: Thos. G. Thrum, 1901.

———. "Sugar Production, Table." In *Thrum's Hawaiian Almanac and Annual for 1902.* Honolulu: Hawaiian Gazette Co., 1901.

Thurston, Lorrin. "Intelligence from the Sandwich Islands." *The Missionary Herald,* vol. 50, 1822.

Tinker, Spencer. *Fishes of Hawaii. A Handbook of the Marine Fishes of Hawaii and the Central Pacific Ocean.* Honolulu: Hawaiian Service, Inc., 1991.

Tinker, Spencer W. *Fish Ponds of the Hawaiian Island.* Ms. 1939.

Titcomb, M. *Native Use of Marine Invertebrates of Old Hawaii.* Honolulu: University of Hawai'i Press, 1978.

Titcomb, Margaret. *Native Use of Fish in Hawaii.* Honolulu: University Press of Hawai'i, 1972.

Twain, Mark. *Sandwich Islands Letters.* 1866.

U.S. Department of Agriculture. *Aerial Photograph.* Washington, D.C.: U.S. Department of Agriculture, 1965.

U.S. Department of Agriculture Soil Survey Staff. *Soil Survey Manual.* Washington, D.C.: U.S. Government Printing Office, 1951.

———. *Supplement Replacing Soil Survey Manual.* Washington, D.C.: U.S. Government Printing Office, 1962.

U.S. Department of Agriculture, Natural Resources Conservation Service. *Soil Survey Geographical Database (SSURGO).* https://www.nrcs.usda.gov/resources/data -and-reports/soil-survey-geographic-database-ssurgo

U.S. Geological Survey. *Aerial Orthophotosquad, Honolua Quadrangle.* U.S. Geological Survey, 1978.

———. *Aerial Photograph.* Honolulu: MAGIS, University of Hawai'i at Mānoa, 1950.

———. *Annual Report for the Year Ending June 30, 1883, Hawaiian Volcanoes, Chapter*

XII, Maui. Washington, D.C.: U.S. Department of the Interior, Government Printing Office, 1883.

———. *Lahaina Quadrangle, Hawaii*. Reston: Department of the Interior, USGS, 1933.

———. *Lahaina Quadrangle, Maui, Hawaiian Islands*. U.S. Geological Survey, 1983.

———. *Napili Quadrangle, Maui, Hawaiian Islands*. U.S. Geological Survey, 1983.

———. *Napili Quadrangle, Hawai'i*. Reston: U.S. Department of the Interior, USGS, 1997.

U.S. Department of Commerce. *Coast Pilot Notes on Hawaiian Islands*. 2nd ed. Washington, D.C.: Government Printing Office, 1919.

U.S. Department of the Interior. *Reports of the Department of the Interior for the Fiscal Year Ended June 30, 1918 [Vol. II: Indian Affairs Territories]*. Washington, D.C.: Government Printing Office.

Van Dyke, Jon M. *Who Owns the Crown Lands of Hawai'i*. Honolulu: University of Hawai'i Press, 2008.

Vancouver, George. *A Voyage of Discovery to the North Pacific Ocean and Round the World Performed in the Years 1790–1795*. London: John Stockdale, 1792.

———. *A Voyage of Discovery to the North Pacific and Round the World*. London: Robinson, 1984.

Vandercook, John W. *King Cane: The Story of Sugar in Hawaii*. New York: Harper and Brothers Publishers, 1939.

Waal, Arthur. *Lahaina in 1897*. Collection of Maui Historical Society/the Bailey House Museum Archives.

Wadsworth, H. A. "A Historical Summary of Irrigation in Hawaii." In *The Hawaii Sugar Manual*, A. B. Gilmore, ed., 1932.

Wagner, Warren L., Derral A. Herbst, S. H. Sohmer. *Manual of the Flowering Plants of Hawaii*. Honolulu: Bishop Museum Press, 1990.

"Wailuku Sugar Company Centennial, 1862–1962." Wailuku Sugar Company, ed. Wailuku, HI, 1962.

Walker, Winslow. *Archaeological Survey of the Island of Maui*. Honolulu, 1931.

Wall, Walter E. *Honokowai, Kaanapali, Maui*. 1:200. 1912.

Weizheimer, Ludwig. "Drought at West Maui." Honolulu, 1914.

———. "Manager's Report." *Report of the Pioneer Company Limited, for the Year Ending December 31, 1910*. Honolulu: Bulletin Publishing Company, 1911.

Westervelt, William D. *Legends of Ma-ui—A Demi-God of Polynesia and of His Mother Hina*. Honolulu: Hawaiian Gazette Co., 1910.

Whistler, W. Arthur. *Wayside Plants of the Islands: A Guide to the Lowland Flora of the Pacific Islands including Hawai'i, Samoa, Tonga, Tahiti, Fiji, Guam, and Belau*. Hong Kong: Everbest Printing Company, Ltd., 1995.

Wilcox, Carol. *Sugar Water: Hawaii's Plantation Ditches*. Honolulu: University of Hawai'i Press, 1995.

Wilkes, C. *Narrative of the United States Exploring Expedition*. Philadelphia: Lea and Blanchard, 1845.

Wright, George F. and T. Y. Awana. *Cane Fields, Lahaina, Maui, Pioneer Mill Co. Ltd.*, 1 inch = 500 ft. 1918.

Wyban, Carol. *Master Plan for Ualapuʻe Ahupuaʻa: Blending Tradition and Technology.* Honolulu: State of Hawaiʻi Department of Business, Economic Development, and Tourism, 1990.

Wyban, Carol. *Tide and Current: Fishponds of Hawaiʻi.* Honolulu: University of Hawaiʻi Press, 1992.

Yap, Brittany. "Our Schools—Lahainaluna High School 175—and still going strong." *The Honolulu Advertiser* (Honolulu, HI), 17 August 2006.

Young, Charles C. "Waiola Church Dedicated," *Honolulu Star-Bulletin* (Honolulu, HI), 16 May 1953.

Zambucka, Kristin. *Kalakaua: Hawaii's Last King.* Honolulu: Mana, 1983.

About the Contributors

AMI MĀLIE MULLIGAN is currently a PhD candidate in the Department of History at the University of Hawai'i at Mānoa and a professional genealogist. Her genealogical research led her to pursue a graduate degree in history with a focus on marriage and kinship, particularly in Hawai'i, during the nineteenth century.

BRIAN RICHARDSON is a public services librarian at the University of Hawai'i, Hamilton Library, where he focuses on expanding the library's online educational resources and serving as the liaison to the College of Education. He won the Board of Regents Excellence in Teaching award at WCC in 2006. Brian's fields of research include website design in higher education and eighteenth- and nineteenth-century European exploration in the Pacific. He has written a book on the voyages of Captain Cook entitled *Longitude and Empire: How Captain Cook's Voyages Changed the World* and also edited the journal of James Macrae, the botanist on HMS *Blonde* who visited Hawai'i in 1825.